FOURTH EDITION

TEN STEPS
to
ADVANCING
COLLEGE
READING SKILLS

John Langan

ATLANTIC CAPE COMMUNITY COLLEGE

Books in the Townsend Press Reading Series:

Groundwork for College Reading with Phonics
Groundwork for College Reading
Ten Steps to Building College Reading Skills
Ten Steps to Improving College Reading Skills
Ten Steps to Advancing College Reading Skills
Ten Steps to Advanced Reading

Books in the Townsend Press Vocabulary Series:

Vocabulary Basics
Groundwork for a Better Vocabulary
Building Vocabulary Skills
Building Vocabulary Skills, Short Version
Improving Vocabulary Skills
Improving Vocabulary Skills, Short Version
Advancing Vocabulary Skills
Advancing Vocabulary Skills, Short Version
Advanced Word Power

Supplements Available for Most Books:

Instructor's Edition
Instructor's Manual and Test Bank
Online Exercises

Copyright © 2004 by Townsend Press, Inc.
Printed in the United States of America
9 8 7 6

ISBN-13: 978-1-59194-023-4
ISBN-10: 1-59194-023-0

Send book orders and requests for desk copies or supplements to:

Townsend Press Book Center
439 Kelley Drive
West Berlin, New Jersey 08091

For even faster service, contact us in any of the following ways:

By telephone: **1-800-772-6410**
By fax: **1-800-225-8894**
By e-mail: cs@townsendpress.com
Through our website: **www.townsendpress.com**

Contents

Preface:
To the Instructor

We all know that many students entering college today do not have the reading skills needed to do effective work in their courses. A related problem, apparent even in class discussions, is that students often lack the skills required to think in a clear and logical way.

The purpose of *Ten Steps to Advancing College Reading Skills, Fourth Edition*, is to develop effective reading and clear thinking. To do so, **Part I** presents a sequence of ten reading skills that are widely recognized as essential for basic and advanced comprehension. The first six skills concern the more literal levels of comprehension:

- Understanding vocabulary in context
- Recognizing main ideas
- Identifying supporting details
- Recognizing implied main ideas and the central point
- Understanding relationships that involve addition and time
- Understanding relationships that involve illustration, comparison and/or contrast, and cause and effect

The remaining skills cover the more advanced, critical levels of comprehension:

- Distinguishing between facts and opinions
- Making inferences
- Identifying an author's purpose and tone
- Evaluating arguments

In every chapter in Part I, the key aspects of a skill are explained and illustrated clearly and simply. Explanations are accompanied by a series of practices, and each chapter ends with four review tests. The last review test consists of a reading selection so that students can apply the skill just learned to real-world reading materials, including newspaper and magazine articles and textbook selections. Together, the ten chapters provide students with the skills needed for both basic and more advanced reading comprehension.

Following each chapter in Part I are **at least six mastery tests for the skill in question.** The tests progress in difficulty, giving students the additional practice and challenge they may need for the solid learning of each skill. While designed for quick grading, the tests also require students to think carefully before answering each question.

Part II is made up of ten additional readings that will improve both reading and thinking skills. Each reading is followed by *Basic Skill Questions* and *Advanced Skill Questions* so that students can practice all ten skills presented in Part I. In addition, an *Outlining, Mapping, or Summarizing* activity after each reading helps students think carefully about the basic content and organization of a selection. *Discussion Questions* then afford instructors a final opportunity to engage students in a variety of reading and thinking skills and thus deepen their understanding of a selection.

Part III serves a variety of purposes. Fifteen combined-skills passages and tests review the skills in Part I and help students prepare for the standardized reading test that is often a requirement at the end of a semester. A section on summarizing and outlining offers additional instruction and practice in these important techniques. Part III also presents a series of five short textbook selections that instructors can use to give students practice in taking notes. Next, there is a section on logical fallacies that can be covered depending on student needs and course requirements. In addition, a section on bias offers instruction in a skill that some (but probably not all) instructors will have time to address. Finally, there are writing assignments for all twenty readings in the text. When time permits, asking students to write about a selection will help reinforce the reading and thinking skills they have practiced in the book.

Important Features of the Book

- **Focus on the basics.** The book is designed to explain in a clear, step-by-step way the essential elements of each skill. Many examples are provided to ensure that students understand each point. In general, the focus is on teaching the skills—not just on explaining or testing them.

- **Frequent practice and feedback.** Because abundant practice and careful feedback are essential to learning, this book includes numerous activities. Students can get immediate feedback on the practice exercises in Part I by turning to the limited answer key at the back of the book. The answers to the review and mastery tests in Part I, the reading questions in Part II, and the combined-skills tests in Part III are in the *Instructor's Manual*.

The limited answer key increases the active role that students take in their own learning. They are likely to use the answer key in an honest and positive way if they know they will be tested on the many activities and selections for which answers are not provided. (Answers not in the book can be easily copied from the *Instructor's Edition* or the *Instructor's Manual* and passed out at the teacher's discretion.)

- **High interest level.** Dull and unvaried readings and exercises work against learning. Students need to experience genuine interest and enjoyment in what they read. Teachers as well should be able to take pleasure in the selections, for their own good feeling can carry over favorably into class work. The readings in the book, then, have been chosen not only for the appropriateness of their reading level but also for their compelling content. They should engage teachers and students alike.

- **Ease of use.** The logical sequence in each chapter—from explanation to example to practice to review test to mastery test—helps make the skills easy to teach. The book's organization into distinct parts also makes for ease of use. Within a single class, for instance, teachers can work on a new skill in Part I, review other skills with one or more mastery tests, and provide variety by having students read one of the selections in Part II. The limited answer key at the back of the text also makes for versatility: the teacher can assign some chapters for self-teaching. Finally, the mastery tests—each on its own tear-out page—and the combined-skills tests make it a simple matter for teachers to test and evaluate student progress.

- **Integration of skills.** Students do more than learn the skills individually in Part I. They also learn to apply the skills together through the reading selections in Parts I and II as well as the combined-skills tests in Part III. They become effective readers and thinkers through repeated practice in applying a combination of skills.

- **Online exercises.** As they complete each of the ten chapters, students are invited to go online to the Townsend Press website to work on two additional practice exercises for each skill—exercises that reinforce the skill taught in the chapter.

- **Thinking activities.** Thinking activities—in the form of outlining, mapping, and summarizing—are a distinctive feature of the book. While educators agree that such organizational abilities are important, these skills are all too seldom taught. From a practical standpoint, it is almost impossible for a teacher to respond in detail to entire collections of class outlines or summaries. This book then, presents activities that truly involve students in outlining, mapping, and summarizing—in other words, that truly make students *think*—and yet enable a teacher to give immediate feedback. Again, it is through continued practice *and* feedback on challenging material that a student becomes a more effective reader and thinker.

- **Supplementary materials.** The three helpful supplements listed below are available at no charge to instructors who have adopted the text. To obtain a copy of either print supplement, instructors who have adopted the book may e-mail Customer Service at **cs@townsendpress.com**. Alternatively, instructors may call our toll-free number, 1-800-772-6410; fax us toll-free at 1-800-225-8894; or write to us at the address shown on the copyright page.

  1 An *Instructor's Edition*—chances are that you are holding it in your hand—is identical to the student book except that it also provides hints for teachers (see the front of the book), answers to all the practices and tests, and comments on selected items.

  2 A combined *Instructor's Manual and Test Bank* includes suggestions for teaching the course, a model syllabus, and readability levels for the text and the reading selections. The test bank contains four additional mastery tests for each of the ten skills and four additional combined-skills tests—all on letter-sized sheets so they can be copied easily for use with students.

  3 *Online exercises,* available at the Online Learning Center area of **www.townsendpress.com**, also accompany the book. These exercises consist of two additional tests for each of the ten skills chapters in the book. The program includes a number of user- and instructor-friendly features: brief explanations of answers, a sound option, frequent mention of the user's first name, a running score at the bottom of the screen, and a record-keeping score file.

- **One of a sequence of books.** There are six books in the Townsend Press reading series. The first two books in the series, *Groundwork for College Reading with Phonics* and *Groundwork for College Reading,* are suitable for ESL students and basic adult learners. The third book, *Ten Steps to Building College Reading Skills,* is often the choice for a first college reading course. The fourth book, *Ten Steps to Improving College Reading Skills,* is an intermediate text appropriate for the core developmental reading course offered at most colleges. *Ten Steps to Advancing College Reading Skills* is a higher developmental text than the *Improving* book. It can be used as the core book for an advanced reading class, as a sequel to *Ten Steps to Improving College Reading Skills,* or as a second-semester alternative to it. Finally, *Ten Steps to Advanced Reading* is the most advanced text in the series. It can be used as the core book for a more advanced class or as a sequel (or a second-semester alternative) to either *Improving* or *Advancing.*

  A companion set of vocabulary books, listed on the copyright page, has been designed to go with the *Ten Steps* books. Recommended to accompany this book is *Advancing Vocabulary Skills* (300 words and word parts) or *Advancing Vocabulary Skills, Short Version* (200 words).

  Together, the books and all their supplements form a sequence that should be ideal for any college reading program.

To summarize, *Ten Steps to Advancing College Reading Skills, Fourth Edition*, provides ten key reading skills to help developmental college students become independent readers and thinkers. Through an appealing collection of readings and a carefully designed series of activities and tests, students receive extensive guided practice in the skills. The result is an integrated approach to learning that will, by the end of the course, produce better readers and stronger thinkers.

Changes in the Fourth Edition

Teacher suggestions and class use of the text have led to a number of major changes in the book:

- **Online exercises for each of the ten chapters in the book.** These are signaled at the end of each chapter with the following icon: 💻. Students can go to the Townsend Press website (**www.townsendpress.com**) to do two additional practice exercises for each skill. Each exercise consists of ten items, and as students answer the items, they are provided with both a running score and explanations of each answer. The exercises, in other words, teach as well as offer practice, and they should serve as an excellent supplement to the activities and tests in each chapter of the book.

- **New teaching features within the chapters.** Three new features—Study Hints and Tips, "Check Your Understanding" exercises, and Chapter Reviews—make the book even easier to use. In addition, a new format for practice and test questions makes them even simpler to grade. If you were happy before with the notably clear format of the book, you'll be even more pleased with the Fourth Edition.

- **A completely revised chapter on main ideas.** No skill is more important to good comprehension, so a great deal of time and class testing went into developing a fresh approach to teaching main ideas. The result is a chapter that, in an exceptionally clear, step-by-step way, shows students three specific ways to locate main ideas. This central skill will now be even more accessible to students.

- **Answers and annotations in a separate color.** Annotations are now included for almost all of the answer options (both correct and incorrect) that are part of the practices and tests. The many comments have been carefully checked for their clarity and usefulness. In addition, comments and answers are now set off in a separate dark red color for ease of use and instant reference by instructors.

- **New section on figurative language.** Students learn to infer the meanings of similes and metaphors that are so often a part of literary writing.

- **New introductory chapter.** A short added chapter presents some quick study tips every student should know.

- **Greater visual appeal.** Additional photographs and cartoons in this edition create visual appeal and also help teach key skills. Boxes, rules, and screens set off patterns of organization, chapter reviews, and important points. The book is more visually friendly without becoming visually cluttered.

- **Many new models and practice materials and four new readings.** For example, the popular combined-skills tests in the previous edition have been expanded now to fifteen passages. One new high-interest reading deals with the problem of anger in everyday life; a second reading reminds us that the way we think about ourselves can strongly influence our behavior; a third selection describes a dramatic argument between a husband and wife that teaches an important lesson about self-esteem; a fourth reading presents the photographs and story of a heroic woman who overcomes childhood adversities to become a champion for reading literacy in her community.

Acknowledgments

I am grateful for the many helpful suggestions provided by the following reviewers: Eva Griffin, Dundalk Community College; Patricia Hale, Kilgore College; Jacquelin Hanselman, Copper Mountain Community College; Jennifer Hurd, Harding University; Elizabeth Ligon, Florida Memorial College; Margaret Ann Maricle, Cuesta College; Hilda McRaney, Hinds Community College; Judith Schurger, Miami-Dade Community College; Daniel Strumas, Indian River Community College; Karen Waska, Cuesta College; Rosalie Wolf, City College of San Francisco; and Cheryl Ziehl, Cuesta College. For this new edition, instructive reviews were provided by Chandler Clifton, Edmonds Community College; Joanne Ernst, Manatee Community College; Dianne F. Kostelny, Okaloosa-Walton Community College; Diane Schellack, Burlington County College; and Phyllis West, El Camino College. And I particularly appreciate the invaluable comments and suggestions made by Iris Hill, a reading instructor at Wake Technical Community College. Her insights led to changes in both the content and the format of the Fourth Edition and were pivotal to the new approach taken in the chapter on main ideas.

At Townsend Press, I thank Bill Blauvelt, Beth Johnson, Paul Langan, Carole Mohr, and Virginia Villalon for the help they provided along the way. And I owe special thanks to editor extraordinaire Janet Goldstein. Because of her superb design and editing skills, the book enjoys an even more clear and "user-friendly" format than the previous edition. Her talents have also made possible the creation of the *Instructor's Edition*, complete with answers and marginal comments, that accompanies the book. It is always a special pleasure to work with people who aspire toward excellence. With help from my colleagues in the teaching profession and at Townsend Press, I have been able to create a much better book than I could have managed on my own.

John Langan

INTRODUCTION

1

How to Become a Better Reader and Thinker

The chances are that you are not as good a reader as you should be to do well in college. If so, it's not surprising. You live in a culture where people watch an average of *over seven hours of television every day!!!* All that passive viewing does not allow much time for reading. Reading is a skill that must be actively practiced. The simple fact is that people who do not read very often are not likely to be strong readers.

- How much TV do you guess you watch on an average day? _____

Another reason besides TV for not reading much is that you may have a lot of responsibilities. You may be going to school and working at the same time, and you may have a lot of family duties as well. Given a hectic schedule, you're not going to have much time to read. When you have free time, you're exhausted, and it's easier to turn on the TV than to open up a book.

- Do you do any regular reading (for example, a daily newspaper, weekly magazines, occasional novels)? _____

- When are you most likely to do your reading? _____

A third reason for not reading is that school may have caused you to associate reading with worksheets and drills and book reports and test scores. Experts agree that many schools have not done a good job of helping students discover the pleasures and rewards of reading. If reading was an unpleasant experience in school, you may have concluded that reading in general is not for you.

• Do you think that school made you dislike reading, rather than enjoy it?

_____

Here are three final questions to ask yourself:

• Do you feel that perhaps you don't need a reading course, since you "already know how to read"? _____

• If you had a choice, would you be taking a reading course? (It's okay to be honest.) _____

• Do you think that a bit of speed reading may be all you need? _____

Chances are that you don't need to read _faster_ as much as you need to read _smarter._ And it's a safe bet that if you don't read much, you can benefit enormously from the reading course in which you are using this book.

One goal of the book is to help you become a better reader. You will learn and practice ten key reading comprehension skills. As a result, you'll be better able to read and understand the many materials in your other college courses. The skills in this book have direct and practical value: they can help you perform better and more quickly—giving you an edge for success—in all of your college work.

The book is also concerned with helping you become a stronger thinker, a person able not just to understand what is read but to analyze and evaluate it as well. In fact, reading and thinking are closely related skills, and practice in thoughtful reading will also strengthen your ability to think clearly and logically. To find out just how the book will help you achieve these goals, read the next several pages and do the brief activities as well. The activities are easily completed and will give you a quick, helpful overview of the book.

HOW THE BOOK IS ORGANIZED

The book is organized into four main parts:

Introduction (pages 1–11)

In addition to this chapter, which will give you a good sense of the book, there is one other part to the introduction. "Some Quick Study Tips" presents four hints that can make you a better student. If I had time to say just four things to incoming college students based on my thirty years of teaching experience, these are the things I would say.

Turn to page 10 and then write, in the space on the next page, the second of these tips:

_____

_____

Part I: Ten Steps to Advancing College Reading Skills (pages 13–420)

To help you become a more effective reader and thinker, this book presents a series of ten key reading skills. They are listed in the table of contents on pages v and vi. Turn to those pages to fill in the skills missing below:

1 Vocabulary in Context

2 _____

3 Supporting Details

4 Implied Main Ideas and the Central Point

5 _____

6 Relationships II

7 Fact and Opinion

8 _____

9 Purpose and Tone

10 Argument

Each chapter is developed in the same way.

    First of all, clear explanations and examples help you *understand* each skill. Practices then give you the "hands-on" experience needed to *learn* the skill.

- How many practices are there for the second chapter, "Main Ideas" (pages 49–92)? _____

    Closing each chapter are four review tests. The first review test provides a check of the information presented in the chapter.

- On which page is the first review test for "Main Ideas"? _____

The second and third review tests consist of activities that help you practice the skill learned in the chapter.

- On which pages are Review Tests 2 and 3 for "Main Ideas"? _____

The fourth review test consists of a story, essay, or textbook selection that both gets you reading and gives you practice in the skill learned in the chapter as well as skills learned in previous chapters.

- What is the title of the reading selection in the "Main Ideas" chapter?

_____

Following each chapter are six mastery tests which gradually increase in difficulty.

- On what pages are the mastery tests for the "Main Ideas" chapter? _____

The tests are on tear-out pages and so can be easily removed and handed in to your instructor. So that you can track your progress, there is a score box at the top of each test. Your score can also be entered into the "Reading Performance Chart" on the inside back cover of the book.

Part II: Ten Reading Selections (pages 421–532)

The ten reading selections that make up Part II are followed by activities that give you practice in all of the skills studied in Part I. Each reading begins in the same way. Look, for example, at "The Professor Is a Dropout," which starts on page 423. What are the headings of the two sections that come before the reading itself?

- _____
- _____

Note that the vocabulary words in "Words to Watch" are followed by the numbers of the paragraphs in which the words appear. Look at the first page of "The Professor Is a Dropout" and explain how each vocabulary word is marked in the reading itself.

- _____

Activities Following Each Reading Selection

After each selection, there are four kinds of activities to improve the reading and thinking skills you learned in Part I of the book.

1 The first activity consists of **basic skill questions**—questions involving vocabulary in context, main ideas (including implied main ideas and the central point), supporting details, and relationships.

- Look at the basic skill questions for "The Professor Is a Dropout" on pages 431–433. Note that the questions are labeled so you know what skill you are practicing in each case. How many questions deal with understanding vocabulary in context? _____

2 The second activity is made up of **advanced skill questions**—ones involving fact and opinion, inferences, purpose and tone, and argument.

- Look at the advanced skill questions on pages 433–435. How many questions deal with making inferences? _____

3 The third activity involves **outlining**, **mapping**, or **summarizing**. Each of these activities will sharpen your ability to get to the heart of a piece and to think logically and clearly about what you read.

- What kind of activity is provided for "The Professor Is a Dropout" on page 435?_____

- What kind of activity is provided for the reading titled "Taming the Anger Monster" on page 445? _____

Note that a **map**, or diagram, is a highly visual way of organizing material. Like an outline, it shows at a glance the main parts of a selection.

4 The fourth activity consists of **discussion questions**. These questions provide a chance for you to deepen your understanding of each selection.

- How many discussion questions are there for "The Professor Is a Dropout" (page 436)—and indeed for every other reading? _____

Part III: For Further Study (pages 533–639)

This part of the book contains additional materials that can help improve your reading.

1 The first section, "Combined-Skills Tests," on pages 535–566, is made up of short passages that give you practice in all ten of the skills in the book.

- How many such tests are there in all? _____

2 The second section, "More About Summarizing and Outlining," on pages 567–591, provides additional information and activities that your instructor may choose to cover, depending on the needs of the class.

- How many practices are in this section? _____

3 The third section, "Five Additional Readings," presents a series of short textbook selections that your instructor may assign for note-taking practice.

- What is the topic of the first selection (pages 592–593)? _____

_____

4 The fourth section, "More About Argument: Errors in Reasoning," explains a number of logical fallacies.

- How many fallacies are treated on pages 603–611? _____

5 The fifth section, "Bias," on pages 615–624, describes how to recognize a speaker's or writer's point of view.

  • What is another name for biased language? _____

6 The sixth section, "Writing Assignments," on pages 625–639, presents writing assignments for all twenty of the reading selections in the book. Reading and writing are closely connected skills, and writing practice will improve your ability to read closely and to think carefully.

  • How many assignments are offered for each reading? _____

HELPFUL FEATURES OF THE BOOK

1 The book centers on *what you really need to know* to become a better reader and thinker. It presents ten key comprehension skills and explains the most important points about each one.

2 The book gives you *lots of practice.* We seldom learn a skill only by hearing or reading about it; we make it part of us by repeated practice. There are, then, numerous activities in the text. They are not "busywork" but carefully designed materials that should help you truly learn each skill.

Notice that after you learn each skill in Part I, you progress to review tests and mastery tests that enable you to apply the skill. And as you move from one skill to the next, the reading selections help you practice and reinforce the skills already learned.

3 The selections throughout the book are *lively and appealing.* Dull and unvaried readings work against learning, so subjects have been carefully chosen for their high interest level. Almost all of the selections here are good examples of how what we read can capture our attention. For instance, begin "The Professor Is a Dropout," which is about the dramatic steps one woman took to educate herself and her children—and try to stop reading. Or look at the textbook selection on pages 499–503, which identifies and discusses the warning signs that mark different types of bad managers. Or read the textbook selection "The Life of the Urban Working Class," which, despite its unexciting title, is full of fascinating—and frightening—details about the lives of workers in the nineteenth century.

4 The readings include *twelve selections from college textbooks.* Therefore, you will be practicing on materials very much like those in your other courses. Doing so will increase your chances of transferring what you learn in your reading class to your other college courses.

HOW TO USE THE BOOK

1 A good way to proceed is to read and review the explanations and examples in a given chapter in Part I until you feel you understand the ideas presented. Then carefully work through the practices. As you finish each one, check your answers with the "Limited Answer Key" that starts on page 645.

For your own sake, *don't just copy in the answers without trying to do the practices!* The only way to learn a skill is to practice it first and then use the answer key to give yourself feedback. Also, take whatever time is needed to figure out just why you got some answers wrong. By using the answer key to help teach yourself the skills, you will prepare yourself for the review and mastery tests at the end of each chapter as well as the other reading tests in the book. Your instructor can supply you with answers to those tests.

If you have trouble catching on to a particular skill, stick with it. In time, you will learn each of the ten skills.

2 Read the selections first with the intent of simply enjoying them. There will be time afterward for rereading each selection and using it to develop your comprehension skills.

3 Keep track of your progress. Fill in the charts at the end of each chapter in Part I and each reading in Part II. And in the "Reading Performance Chart" on the inside back cover, enter your scores for all of the review and mastery tests as well as the reading selections. These scores can give you a good view of your overall performance as you work through the book.

In summary, *Ten Steps to Advancing College Reading Skills* has been designed to interest and benefit you as much as possible. Its format is straightforward, its explanations are clear, its readings are appealing, and its many practices will help you learn through doing. *It is a book that has been created to reward effort*, and if you provide that effort, you will make yourself a better reader and a stronger thinker. I wish you success.

John Langan

2

Some Quick Study Tips

While it's not my purpose in this book to teach study skills, I do want to give you four quick hints that can make you a better student. The hints are based on my thirty years of experience working with first-year college students and teaching reading and study skills.

TIP *Tip 1* The most important steps you can take to succeed in school are to go to every class and take a lot of notes. If you don't go to class, or you go but just sit there without taking notes, chances are you're heading for a heap of trouble.

TIP *Tip 2* Let me ask you a question: Which is more important—learning how to read a textbook or learning how to read your professor? Write your answer here:

_____

You may be surprised at the answer: What is far more important is learning how to read your professor—to understand what he or she expects you to learn in the course and to know for tests.

I remember becoming a good student in college only after I learned the truth of this statement. And I have interviewed hundreds of today's students who have said the same thing. Let me quote just one of them:

> *You absolutely have to be in class. Then you learn how to read the teacher and to know what he or she is going to want on tests. You could read an entire textbook, but that wouldn't be as good as being in class and writing down a teacher's understanding of ideas.*

TIP *Tip 3* Many teachers base their tests mainly on the ideas they present in class. But when you have to learn a textbook chapter, do the following.

First, read the first and last few paragraphs of the chapter; they may give you a good overview of what the chapter is about.

Second, as you read the chapter, look for and mark off definitions of key terms and examples of those definitions.

Third, as you read the chapter, number any lists of items; if there are series of points and you number them *1, 2, 3,* and so on, it will be easier to understand and remember them.

Fourth, after you've read the chapter, take notes on the most important material and test yourself on those notes until you can say them to yourself without looking at them.

TIP *Tip 4* Here's another question: Are you an organized person? Do you get out of bed on time, do you get to places on time, do you keep up with school work, do you allow time to study for tests and write papers?

If you are *not* an organized person, you're going to have trouble in school. Here are three steps to take to control your time:

First, pay close attention to the course outline, or *syllabus,* your instructors will probably pass out at the start of a semester. Chances are that syllabus will give you the dates of exams and tell you when papers or reports are due.

Second, move all those dates onto a *large monthly calendar*—a calendar that has a good-sized block of white space for each date. Hang the calendar in a place where you'll be sure to see it every day—perhaps above your desk or on a bedroom wall.

Third, buy a small notebook and write down every day a *"to do" list* of things that need to get done that day. Decide which items are most important and focus on them first. (If you have classes that day, going to those classes will be "A" priority items.) Carry your list with you during the day, referring to it every so often and checking off items as you complete them.

Questions

1. Of the four hints listed above, which is the most important one for you? Why?

2. Which hint is the second most important for you, and why?

3. You may not realize just how quickly new information can be forgotten. For example, how much class material do you think most people forget in just two weeks? Check (✓) the answer you think is correct.

   _____ 20 percent is forgotten within two weeks

   _____ 40 percent is forgotten within two weeks

   _____ 60 percent is forgotten within two weeks

   _____ 80 percent is forgotten within two weeks

   The truth is that within two weeks most people forget almost 80 percent of what they have heard! Given that fact, what should you be sure to do in all your classes?

Part I

TEN STEPS TO ADVANCING COLLEGE READING SKILLS

1

Vocabulary in Context

If you were asked to define the words *raucous, ubiquitous,* and *advocate,* you might have some difficulty. On the other hand, if you saw these words in sentences, chances are you could come up with fairly accurate definitions. For example, see if you can define the words in *italics* in the three sentences below. In the space provided, write the letter of the meaning you think is correct in each case.

Do not use a dictionary for this work. Instead, in each sentence, try the word you think is the answer. For example, put *boring* or *noisy* or *dangerous* into the sentence in place of *raucous* to see which one makes the best sense.

_____ The homecoming celebration was *raucous,* with people wildly shouting and cheering, blowing whistles, and pounding on drums.

Raucous (rô′kəs) means

A. boring.   B. noisy.   C. dangerous.

_____ Cell phones have become *ubiquitous*; you can see—and hear—them every-where.

Ubiquitous (yōo-bĭk′wĭ-təs) means

A. unaffordable.   B. complicated.   C. widespread.

_____ Those who *advocate* capital punishment often argue that it prevents crime, but those who oppose it say it has no such effect.

Advocate (ăd′və-kāt′) means

A. support.   B. disregard.   C. resist.

In each sentence above, the *context*—the words surrounding the unfamiliar word—provides clues to the word's meaning. You may have guessed from the context that *raucous* means "noisy," that *ubiquitous* means "widespread," and that *advocate* means "support."

Using context clues to understand the meaning of unfamiliar words will help you in several ways:

• It will save you time when reading. You will not have to stop to look up words in the dictionary. (Of course, you won't *always* be able to understand a word from its context, so you should always have a dictionary nearby as you read.)

• After you figure out the meaning of a particular word more than once through its context, it may become a part of your working vocabulary. You will therefore add to your vocabulary simply by reading thoughtfully.

• You will get a good sense of how a word is actually used, including any shades of meaning it might have.

TYPES OF CONTEXT CLUES

There are four common types of context clues:

1 Examples

2 Synonyms

3 Antonyms

4 General Sense of the Sentence or Passage

In the following sections, you will read about and practice using each type. The practices will sharpen your skills in recognizing and using context clues. They will also help you add new words to your vocabulary.

Remember *not* to use a dictionary for these practices. Their purpose is to help you develop the skill of figuring out what words mean without using a dictionary. Pronunciations are provided in parentheses for the words, and a brief guide to pronunciation is on pages 643–644.

1 Examples

If you are given **examples** that relate to an unknown word, you can often figure out its meaning. For instance, note the examples in the sentence "The home-coming celebration was *raucous*, with people wildly shouting and cheering, blowing whistles, and pounding on drums." The examples—people wildly shouting and cheering, blowing whistles, and pounding on drums—help you figure out that the word *raucous* means "noisy."

Now read the items that follow. An *italicized* word in each sentence is followed by examples that serve as context clues for that word. These examples, which are in **boldfaced** type, will help you figure out the meaning of each word. On the answer line, write the letter of each meaning you think is correct.

Note that examples are often introduced with signal words and phrases like *for example, for instance, including,* and *such as.*

_____ 1. As they moved westward, early pioneers faced many *adversities*, such as **scarce food, extreme weather,** and **loneliness**.

 Adversities (ăd-vûr′sĭ-tēz) means

 A. criminals.   B. decisions.   C. hardships.

 Hint: For this and all the exercises in this chapter, actually insert into the sentence the word you think is the answer. For example, substitute *criminals* or *decisions* or *hardships* in the sentence in place of *adversities* to see which one fits.

_____ 2. The neighborhood is so *affluent* that most residents have **Olympic-sized swimming pools, tennis courts,** and **luxury cars**.

 Affluent (ăf′lōō-ənt) means

 A. wealthy.   B. crowded.   C. far away.

_____ 3. Each of my coworkers has a strange *idiosyncrasy*. For instance, our receptionist **wears only pink**. The mail clerk **always speaks in a whisper**. And my office mate **lives on peanuts and apples**.

 Idiosyncrasy (ĭd′ē-ō-sĭng′krə-sē) means

 A. hidden thought.   B. unusual goal.   C. unusual personal trait.

In the first sentence, the examples of what the pioneers faced show that *adversities* means "hardships." In the second sentence, the examples—pools, tennis courts, and luxury cars—show that *affluent* means "wealthy." Finally, the examples in the third sentence indicate that an *idiosyncrasy* is an "unusual personal trait."

➤ Practice 1: Examples

In each of the sentences below, underline the examples of the italicized word. Then write the letter of the meaning of that term on the answer line. Note that the last five sentences have been taken from college textbooks.

_____ 1. The mayor introduced various *stringent* financial measures, including cutting the police force in half and reducing the pay of all city employees.

 Stringent (strĭn′jənt) means

 A. minor.   B. severe.   C. expensive.

_____ 2. There was obvious *animosity* between Carmen and Jack—for example, they glared at each other and refused to stay in the same room together.

 Animosity (ăn′ə-mŏs′ĭ-tē) means

 A. space.   B. nothing.   C. ill will.

_____ 3. The police officer was trying to deal with two *distraught* people at once—a trembling mugging victim and a crying lost child.

Distraught (dĭ-strôt′) means
A. very troubled.   B. unhealthy.   C. reasonable.

_____ 4. The prices in the gourmet shop were *exorbitant:* for instance, twelve dollars for a pound of butter, eight dollars for a small loaf of multigrain bread, twenty-five dollars for a pound of prime steak.

Exorbitant (ĭg-zôr′bĭ-tənt) means
A. too high.   B. reasonable.   C. bargain-basement.

_____ 5. Circus performers generally dress in *ostentatious* costumes, with plenty of sequins, feathers, and gold trim to dazzle the eye.

Ostentatious (ŏs′tĕn-tā′shəs) means
A. inexpensive.   B. showy.   C. athletic.

_____ 6. Unused muscles will begin to *atrophy;* thus a broken leg is noticeably thinner when the cast is removed, and a patient bedridden for too long will lack the lower-body strength needed to stand up.

Atrophy (ăt′rə-fē) means
A. develop.   B. be replaced.   C. waste away.

_____ 7. *Indigenous* life forms—the cactus and the camel in the desert, the polar bear and the seal in the Arctic, and so on—are suited to their environments in very specific ways.

Indigenous (ĭn-dĭj′ə-nəs) means
A. recent.   B. extinct.   C. native.

_____ 8. The nonphysical portion of culture includes three *components:* 1) knowledge and beliefs, 2) rules of behavior and values, and 3) signs and language.

Components (kəm-pō′nənts) means
A. questions.   B. parts.   C. reasons.

_____ 9. *Turbulent* periods in nineteenth-century Europe included the Napoleonic wars, the revolutions of 1848, the Crimean War in the 1850s, and the Franco-Prussian War of 1870.

Turbulent (tûr′byə-lənt) means
A. violently disturbed.   B. forgotten.   C. financially well off.

_____ 10. In earlier centuries, people looked with fear upon a number of *innocuous* practices, such as eating tomatoes, taking a bath, and letting a baby kick its legs.

Innocuous (ĭ-nŏk′yoo-əs) means
A. dangerous.   B. harmless.   C. superstitious.

2 Synonyms

Context clues are often found in the form of **synonyms**: one or more words that mean the same or almost the same as the unknown word. In the sentence on page 15, "Cell phones have become *ubiquitous*; you see—and hear—them everywhere," the synonym "everywhere" tells you the meaning of *ubiquitous*. A synonym may appear anywhere in a sentence as a restatement of the meaning of the unknown word.

Each of the following items includes a word or phrase that is a synonym of the italicized word. Underline the synonym for each italicized word.

1. In the sentence "I actually love the sport of bowling," not only is the word "actually" unnecessary, but the words "the sport of" are also *superfluous* (sŏo-pûr′flōo-əs): All the sentence has to say is "I love bowling."

2. That five-year-old girl must have *innate* (ĭ-nāt′) musical talent; playing piano so well at her age requires an inborn gift.

3. Gaining a *mentor* (mĕn′tôr′) is helpful when you are beginning a new job. A wise and trusted adviser can greatly assist your career.

You should have underlined "unnecessary" as a synonym for *superfluous,* "inborn" as a synonym for *innate,* and "wise and trusted adviser" as a synonym for *mentor.* (Remember, by the way, that you can turn to your dictionary whenever you want to learn to pronounce an unfamiliar word.)

> ## Practice 2: Synonyms

Each item below includes a word that is a synonym of the italicized word. Write the synonym of the italicized word in the space provided. Note that the last five sentences have been taken from college textbooks.

_____ 1. I swore not to reveal Anita's secret, but then I did *divulge* (dĭ-vŭlj′) it to my brother.
    Hint: What must the speaker have done to Anita's secret?

_____ 2. My boss has an *abrasive* (ə-brā′sĭv) personality. It's so irritating that he has trouble keeping friends.

_____ 3. When I saw the doctor's *somber* (sŏm′bər) expression, I feared that serious news awaited me.

_____ 4. The rescue team had *explicit* (ĭk-splĭs′ĭt) directions to the site of the helicopter crash in the mountains. Without such clear directions, they might never have found the place.

_____ 5. "This is a *poignant* (poin′yənt) book, as it is filled with touching stories of the author's days in a small Southern town," wrote the reviewer.

_____ 6. Some consider terrorism the most *heinous* (hā′nəs) crime; others consider treason, torture, or crimes against children the worst evils.

_____ 7. *Charlatans* (shär′lə-tənz) often get rich when medical science is not yet able to treat a disease effectively. Patients desperate for a cure will try anything, and so they fall into the hands of quacks.

_____ 8. Children aged three to six become more *dexterous* (dĕk′stər-əs) as a result of small-muscle development and increased eye-hand coordination. They are increasingly skillful, for instance, at drawing, using a spoon and cup, and dressing themselves.

_____ 9. Many people believe that lava is the main material *extruded* (ĭk-strood′əd) from a volcano. However, huge quantities of broken rock, fine ash, and dust are also cast out by volcanic explosions.

_____ 10. Researchers have learned a *disconcerting* (dĭs′kən-sûrt′ĭng) fact: eyewitnesses often identify innocent people as being guilty. Scientists have also discovered the equally disturbing fact that there is no relationship between how confident witnesses are and how correct they are.

3 Antonyms

Antonyms—words and phrases that mean the opposite of a word—are also useful as context clues. Antonyms are sometimes signaled by words and phrases such as *however, but, yet, on the other hand,* and *in contrast.* In the sentence on page 15, "Those who *advocate* capital punishment often argue that it prevents crime, but those who oppose it say it has no such effect," the antonym "oppose" helps you figure out the meaning of *advocate.*

In each of the following sentences, underline the word or phrase that means the *opposite* of the italicized word. Then, on the answer line, write the letter of the meaning of the italicized word.

_____ 1. The teacher would have achieved better results if she had been as quick to *commend* students for their successes as she was to criticize them for their failures.

Commend (kə-mĕnd′) means
A. blame.   B. grade.   C. praise.

_____ 2. A memo that is brief and to the point is more likely to be read than one that is *verbose* and rambling.

Verbose (vər-bōs′) means
A. argumentative.   B. wordy.   C. short.

_____ 3. Most of my friends' mothers seemed ordinary; mine, however, did such *bizarre* things as spraying green paint on the dead tree in front of our house.

Bizarre (bĭ-zär′) means
A. odd.   B. easy.   C. dangerous.

In the first sentence, the opposite of *commend* is "criticize"; thus *commend* means "praise." In the second sentence, *verbose* is the opposite of "brief," so *verbose* means "wordy." Last, *bizarre* is the opposite of "ordinary"; thus *bizarre* means "odd."

➤ Practice 3: Antonyms

Each item below includes a word or phrase that is an antonym of the italicized word. Underline the word or phrase that is an antonym of the italicized word in each case. Then, on the answer line, write the letter of the meaning of the italicized word. Note that the last five items have been taken from college textbooks.

_____ 1. My piano teacher's criticism was always *profuse,* but her praise was scarce.

Hint: If the piano teacher's praise was scarce, what must her criticism have been?

Profuse (prə-fyo͞os′) means
A. loud.   B. well-founded.   C. plentiful.

_____ 2. It was hard to know what the speaker was really feeling—was his enthusiasm *feigned* or genuine?

Feigned (fānd) means
A. secret.   B. faked.   C. formal.

_____ 3. Those who agreed with the mayor's tax proposal were in the majority, but there were also some outspoken *dissidents.*

Dissidents (dĭs′ĭ-dənts) means
A. those in the majority.   B. supporters.   C. people who disagree.

_____ 4. Roberto's mother was *lenient* when he took money from her dresser drawer, but when he stole candy from a drugstore, her punishment was harsh.

Lenient (lē′nē-ənt) means
A. not strict in punishing.   B. tough.   C. complimentary.

_____ 5. My sister thinks it's *futile* to try to talk my parents into exercising, but I feel it could be useful to show them statistics that tell how beneficial exercise is.

Futile (fyoot′l) means
A. unlikely.   B. useless.   C. sentimental.

_____ 6. A *sedentary* lifestyle is a risk to health. Physically active people have a much better chance of avoiding heart disease and premature death.

Sedentary (sĕd′n-tĕr′ē) means
A. free of stress.   B. inactive.   C. unusual.

_____ 7. The Judeo-Christian religions believe in an *omnipotent* deity, but that is not true of all religions. Some, both ancient and modern, believe in a god or gods whose power is limited.

Omnipotent (ŏm-nĭp′ə-tənt) means
A. helpful.   B. invisible.   C. all-powerful.

_____ 8. In the United States, there is no *stigma* attached to divorce. Divorce has gained approval as a solution to marital unhappiness.

Stigma (stĭg′mə) means
A. honor.   B. shame.   C. cost.

_____ 9. The social and environmental influences on aging suggest that if the aging process can be sped up, it can also be *impeded.*

Impeded (ĭm-pēd′ĭd) means
A. recognized.   B. slowed down.   C. healthy.

_____ 10. The United States has a varied population; it is multicultural, multi-racial, and multiethnic. In contrast, Japan's population is *homogeneous*—practically all of its people are ethnic Japanese.

Homogeneous (hō′mə-jē′nē-əs) means
A. Asian.   B. large.   C. uniform.

4 General Sense of the Sentence or Passage

Sometimes it takes a bit more detective work to puzzle out the meaning of an unfamiliar word. In such cases, you must draw conclusions based on the information given. Asking yourself questions about the passage may help you make a fairly accurate guess about the meaning of the unfamiliar word.

Each of the sentences below is followed by a question. Think about the answer to each question; then write the letter of the answer you think is the correct meaning of the italicized word.

_____ 1. One argument against capital punishment is that if an innocent person is executed, the mistake cannot be *rectified.*

(What cannot be done about a mistake as final as an execution?)

Rectified (rĕk′tə-fīd) means
A. remembered.   B. predicted.   C. corrected.

_____ 2. It took two days for volunteers to *extricate* the little girl from the bottom of the well.

(How would volunteers try to help the trapped girl?)

Extricate (ĕk′strĭ-kāt′) means
A. free.   B. delay.   C. remember.

_____ 3. Sonya and Liz thought they'd stay good friends forever. But after graduation, their lives *diverged:* Sonya got married, and Liz moved away.

(What relationship did their lives have after graduation?)

Diverged (dĭ-vûrjd′) means
A. came together.   B. improved.   C. went in different directions.

The first sentence provides enough evidence for you to guess that *rectified* means "corrected." *Extricate* in the second sentence means "free." And *diverged* means "went in different directions." (You may not hit on the exact dictionary definition of a word by using context clues, but you will often be accurate enough to make good sense of what you are reading.)

➤ *Practice 4: General Sense of the Sentence or Passage*

Try to answer the question in parentheses that follows each item below. Then, using the logic of each answer, write the letter of the meaning you think is correct. Note that the last five sentences have been taken from college textbooks.

_____ 1. My three-year-old often fights for her *autonomy* by saying, "I can do it myself."

(What is being sought with the statement "I can do it myself"?)

Autonomy (ô-tŏn′ə-mē) means
A. sister.   B. independence.   C. toys.

_____ 2. After lying *dormant* in their burrows every winter, the chipmunks come out again in the spring, looking lively but a bit thin.

(How would you describe animals that have been lying in their burrows all winter?)

Dormant (dôr′mənt) means
A. sick.   B. busy.   C. inactive.

_____ 3. People who suffer from migraine headaches are frequently advised to avoid things that can *precipitate* an attack, such as red wine, chocolate, and some cheeses.

(What do red wine, chocolate, and some cheeses do to a migraine headache?)

Precipitate (prĭ-sĭp′ĭ-tāt′) means
A. trigger.   B. prevent.   C. follow.

_____ 4. Emily's signature, *embellished* with loops and swirls, was easy to recognize.

(What do loops and swirls do to the signature?)

Embellished (ĕm-bĕl′ĭsht) means
A. hidden.   B. decorated.   C. made plain.

_____ 5. Hector thought his mother's suggestion to use peanut butter to remove the gum from his hair was *ludicrous*—but it worked!

(What is a likely first opinion of Hector's mother's suggestion?)

Ludicrous (lo͞o′dĭ-krəs) means
A. practical.   B. delicious.   C. ridiculous.

_____ 6. Research shows that almost any unpleasant event, such as frustration, foul odors, and high room temperature, can *provoke* aggression.

(What can unpleasant events do to aggression?)

Provoke (prə-vōk′) means

A. imitate.   B. bring about.   C. eliminate.

_____ 7. Social psychologists agree that attitudes and actions can have a *reciprocal* relationship: Although attitudes may influence actions, actions can also influence attitudes.

(What type of relationship is described?)

Reciprocal (rĭ-sĭp′rə-kəl) means

A. two-way.   B. disconnected.   C. peaceful.

_____ 8. Forgetting has benefits. The mind's ability to *eradicate* unnecessary information keeps the memory from becoming overloaded.

(What would the mind do to unnecessary information to keep the memory from being overloaded?)

Eradicate (ĭ-răd′ĭ-kāt′) means

A. erase.   B. hold on to.   C. change.

_____ 9. To test a new drug, subjects in the experimental group are given the drug while subjects in the control group are given a *placebo* that looks identical.

(What type of substance might the scientists use to show the effects of the real drug?)

Placebo (plə-sē′bō) means

A. surgery.   B. dangerous chemical.   C. harmless pretend drug.

_____ 10. Because of a natural barrier between the blood and brain, many substances cannot leave the blood and *permeate* the brain tissues.

(What does the barrier stop substances from doing?)

Permeate (pûr′mē-āt′) means

A. resemble.   B. spread through.   C. disappear from.

An Important Point about Textbook Definitions

You don't always have to use context clues or the dictionary to find definitions. Very often, textbook authors provide definitions of important terms. They usually follow a definition with one or more examples to ensure that you understand the word being defined. Here is a short textbook passage that includes definitions and examples:

> [1]In all societies there is some **vertical mobility**—moving up or down the status ladder. [2]The upward movement is called *upward mobility* and the downward movement, *downward mobility*. [3]The promotion of a teacher to the position of principal is an example of upward mobility, and demotion from principal to teacher is downward mobility.

Textbook authors, then, often do more than provide context clues: they set off their definitions in *italic* or **boldface** type, as above. When they take the time to define and illustrate a word, you should assume that the material is important enough to learn.

More about textbook definitions and examples appears on pages 217–218 in the "Relationships II" chapter.

CHAPTER REVIEW

In this chapter, you learned the following:

- To save time when reading, you should try to figure out the meanings of unfamiliar words. You can do so by looking at their *context*—the words surrounding them.

- There are four kinds of context clues: **examples** (marked by words like *for example, for instance, including,* and *such as*); **synonyms** (words that mean the same as unknown words); **antonyms** (words that mean the opposite of unknown words); and **general sense of the sentence** (clues in the sentence or surrounding sentences about what words might mean).

- Textbook authors typically set off important words in *italic* or **boldface** and define those words for you, often providing examples as well.

The next chapter—Chapter 2—will introduce you to the most important of all comprehension skills, finding the main idea.

On the Web: If you are using this book in class, you can visit our website for additional practice in understanding vocabulary in context. Go to **www.townsendpress.com** and click on "Online Exercises."

➤ Review Test 1

To review what you've learned in this chapter, answer the following questions by filling in the blank or writing the letter of the correct answer.

1. By using _____ to understand the meaning of unfamiliar words, you can save time when reading and help make words part of your working vocabulary.

____ 2. In the sentence below, which type of context clue is used for the italicized word?

   A. example   B. synonym   C. antonym

   Over thirty years ago, it was found that high-school boys *aspired* (ə-spīrd') to be star athletes and girls wished to be popular; neither wanted to be brilliant students.

____ 3. In the sentence below, which type of context clue is used for the italicized word?

   A. example   B. synonym   C. antonym

   In happy couples, each partner both brings and seeks *assets* (ăs'ĕts'); men typically offer status and seek attractiveness; women more often do the reverse.

____ 4. In the sentence below, which type of context clue is used for the italicized word?

   A. example   B. synonym   C. antonym

   Many students are simply *passive* (păs'ĭv) during lectures, but it is more productive to be active, taking notes and asking yourself questions about what is being said.

5. When textbook authors introduce a new word, they often set it off in *italic* or **boldface** type. They also define the word and often follow it

   with _____ that help make the meaning of the word clear.

➤ Review Test 2

A. Using context clues for help, write, in the space provided, the letter of the best meaning for each italicized word.

_____ 1. Imagine my *chagrin* (shə-grĭn′) when I looked in the mirror right after giving a report in front of class—and discovered that on my shirt was some of the blueberry pie I had eaten for lunch.

   A. embarrassment   C. pleasure
   B. encouragement   D. hatred

_____ 2. There were many things about the library that made it *conducive* (kən-doo′sĭv) to study, including good lighting, quiet, and nearby reference books.

   A. harmful   C. unattractive
   B. cold   D. helpful

_____ 3. Because of residential segregation, schools in urban areas are often *predominantly* (prĭ-dŏm′ə-nənt-lē) black while those in the suburbs are mostly white.

   A. in small part   C. hopefully
   B. reasonably   D. mainly

_____ 4. After the funeral, the widow's friends were very *solicitous* (sə-lĭs′ĭ-təs)— they came to see her each day and took turns calling every evening to be sure she was all right.

   A. bold   C. annoyed
   B. concerned   D. careless

_____ 5. When several members of the president's staff were charged with various crimes, the public's confidence in the government *eroded* (ĭ-rōd′ĭd). Once public trust wears down, it is difficult to rebuild.

   A. deteriorated   C. grew
   B. healed   D. repeated

B. Using context clues for help, write the definition for each italicized word. Then write the letter of the definition in the space provided. Choose from the definitions in the box below. Each definition will be used once.

A. sociable	B. by chance	C. insulting
D. continuous	E. lack of essentials	

_____ 6. *Deprivation* in early life—poor food, inadequate health care, insufficient education—may be hard to overcome later on.

Deprivation (dĕp′rə-vā′shən) means: _____

_____ 7. Little Amanda hid shyly behind her mother when she met new people, yet her twin brother Adam was very *gregarious.*

Gregarious (grĭ-gâr′ē-əs) means: _____

_____ 8. During the argument, the angry woman called her husband such *derogatory* names as "idiot" and "fool."

Derogatory (dĭ-rŏg′ə-tôr′ē) means: _____

_____ 9. The noise in the nursery school classroom was *incessant;* the crying, laughing, and yelling never stopped for a second.

Incessant (ĭn-sĕs′ənt) means: _____

_____10. No one knows how humans acquired the concept of cooking food, but their first experience of cooking was probably *fortuitous;* very likely, some meat fell into a fire by accident.

Fortuitous (fôr-tōō′ĭ-təs) means: _____

➤ Review Test 3

A. Use context clues to figure out the meaning of the italicized word in each of the following sentences, and write your definition in the space provided.

1. If you express yourself clearly the first time you say something, you should not have to *reiterate* it a second time.

Reiterate (rē-ĭt′ə-rāt′) means: _____

2. The physician could only *conjecture* about the cause of the bad bruise on the unconscious man's head.

Conjecture (kən-jĕk′chər) means: _____

3. Freshman are often *naive* about college at first, but by their second semester they are usually quite sophisticated in the ways of their new school.

Naive (nä-ēv′) means: _____

4. The lawyer tried to confuse the jury by bringing in many facts that weren't *pertinent* to the case.

    Pertinent (pûr′tn-ənt) means: _____

5. When the economy is troubled and weak, the president of the country takes the blame; however, when the economy is *robust*, the president gets the credit.

    Robust (rō-bŭst′) means: _____

B. Use context clues to figure out the meanings of the italicized words in the following textbook passages. Write your definitions in the spaces provided.

> [1]Divorce, death, and demands on family members' time can isolate senior citizens, producing deep loneliness which then *adversely* affects their health. [2]Increasingly, doctors are recommending that lonely older Americans acquire pets to help halt their slide into despair, which is *debilitating* physically as well as mentally. [3]Dogs, cats, parakeets, and other sociable pets can provide seniors with companionship. [4]And caring for their dependent pets makes senior citizens feel appreciated and needed—an important factor in preventing *despondency*. [5]Both pets and their owners win in this relationship.

6. *Adversely* (ăd-vûrs′lē) means: _____

7. *Debilitating* (dĭ-bĭl′ĭ-tāt′ĭng) means: _____

8. *Despondency* (dĭ-spŏn′dən-sē) means: _____

> [1]One writer, using a *pseudonym* instead of his real name, mailed a typewritten copy of Jerzy Kosinski's novel *Steps* to twenty-eight major publishers and literary agencies. [2]All rejected it, including Random House, which had published the book ten years before and watched it win the National Book Award and sell more than 400,000 copies. [3]The novel came closest to being accepted by Houghton Mifflin, publisher of three other Kosinski novels. [4]"Several of us read your untitled novel here with admiration for writing and style. [5]Jerzy Kosinski comes to mind as a point of comparison. . . . [6]The drawback to the manuscript, as it stands, is that it doesn't add up to a satisfactory whole." [7]This example is not unusual. [8]Editors' *assessments* of manuscripts can reveal surprising errors and unreliability.

9. *Pseudonym* (sōōd′n-ĭm′) means: _____

10. *Assessments* (ə-sĕs′mənts) means: _____

➤ *Review Test 4*

Here is a chance to apply the skill of understanding vocabulary in context to a full-length selection. In the following article, Robert Mayer suggests a way to eliminate the rule of the television set over family life. After reading the selection, answer the vocabulary questions that follow.

Words to Watch

Below are some words in the reading that do not have strong context support. Each word is followed by the number of the paragraph in which it appears and its meaning there. These words are indicated in the article by a small circle (°).

slack (2): loose
byword (5): an accepted truth
byproduct (7): side effect
pompous (14): given an exaggerated importance
drivel (14): nonsense

THE QUIET HOUR

Robert Mayer

1   What would you consider an ideal family evening? Call me a romantic, but that question calls up in my mind pictures of parents and children lingering around the dinner table to cozily discuss the day's events; munching popcorn from a common bowl as they engage in the friendly competition of a board game; or perhaps strolling through their neighborhood on an early summer evening, stopping to chat with friends in their yards.

2   Let me tell you what "an ideal family evening" does not conjure up for me: the image of a silent group of people—the intimate word "family" seems hardly to apply—bathed in the faint blue light of a television screen that barely illuminates their glazed eyes and slack° jaws.

3   Yet we all know that such a scenario is the typical one. I would like to suggest a different scenario. I propose that for sixty minutes each evening, right after the early-evening news, all television broadcasting in the United States be prohibited by law. Let us pause for a moment while the howls of protest subside.

4   Now let us take a serious, reasonable look at what the results might be if such a proposal were adopted.

New Explorations

5   Without the distraction of the tube, families might sit around together after dinner and actually talk to one another. It is a byword° in current psychology that many of our emotional problems—everything, in fact, from the generation gap to the soaring divorce rate to some forms of mental illness—are caused at least in part by failure to communicate.

We do not tell each other what is bothering us. Resentments build. The result is an emotional explosion of one kind or another. By using the quiet family hour to discuss our problems, we might get to know each other better, and to like each other better.

6   On evenings when such talk is unnecessary, families could rediscover more active pastimes. Freed from the chain of the tube, forced to find their own diversions, they might take a ride together to watch the sunset. Or they might take a walk together (remember feet?) and explore the neighborhood with fresh, innocent eyes.

Pros and Cons

7   With time to kill and no TV to slay it for them, children and adults alike might rediscover reading. There is more entertainment and intellectual nourishment in a decent book than in a month of typical TV programming. Educators report that the generations that grew up under television can barely write an English sentence, even at the college level. Writing is often learned from reading. A more literate new generation could be a major byproduct° of the quiet hour.

8   A different form of reading might also be dug up from the past: reading aloud. Few pastimes bring a family closer together than gathering around and listening to Mother or Father read a good story.

9   It has been fifty years since my mother read to me, a chapter a night, from *Tom Sawyer*. After five decades, the whitewashing of the fence, Tom and Becky in the cave, Tom at his own funeral remain more vivid in my mind than any show I have ever seen on TV.

10   When the quiet hour ends, the networks might even be forced to come up with better shows in order to lure us back from our newly discovered diversions.

11   Now let us look at the other side of the proposal. What are the negatives?

12   At a time when "big government" is becoming a major political bugaboo, a television-free hour created by law would be attacked as further intrusion by the government on people's lives. But that would not be the case. Television stations already must be federally licensed. A simple regulation making TV licenses invalid for sixty minutes each evening would hardly be a major violation of individual freedom.

13   It will be argued that every television set ever made has an "off" knob; that any family that wants to sit down and talk, or go for a drive, or listen to music, or read a book need only switch off the set, without interfering with the freedom of others to watch. That is a strong, valid argument— in theory. But in practice, it doesn't hold up. Many years of saturation television have shown us the hypnotic lure of the tube. Television viewing tends to expand to fill the available time. What's more, what is this "freedom to watch" of which we would be deprived? It is the freedom to watch three or four quiz or reality shows, mediocre sitcoms, and made-for-TV movies. That's all. In practice, the quiet hour would not limit our freedom; it would expand it. It would revitalize a whole range of activities that have wasted away in the consuming glare of the tube.

A Radical Notion?

14   Economically, the quiet hour would produce screams of outrage from the networks, which would lose an hour or so of prime-time advertising revenues; and from the sponsors, who would have that much less opportunity to peddle us deodorants and hemorrhoid preparations while we are trying to digest our dinners. But given the vast sums the networks waste on such pompous° drivel° as almost any of the TV "mini-series," I'm sure they could make do. The real question is, how long are we going to keep passively selling our own and our children's souls to keep Madison Avenue on Easy Street?

At first glance, the notion of a TV-   15
less hour seems radical. What will parents do without the electronic baby sitter? How will we spend the quiet? But it is not radical at all. It has been only about fifty years since television came to dominate American free time. Those of us 60 and older can remember television-free childhoods, spent partly with radio—which at least involved the listener's imagination—but also with reading, learning, talking, playing games, inventing new diversions, creating fantasylands.

It wasn't that difficult. Honest.   16
The truth is, we had a ball.   17

Vocabulary Questions

Use context clues to help you decide on the best definition for each italicized word. Then, on the answer line, write the letter of each of your choices.

_____ 1. In the excerpt below, the word *lingering* (lĭng′gər-ĭng) means
    A. rushing.
    B. leaving.
    C. staying.
    D. arguing.

    ". . . an ideal family evening . . . calls up in my mind pictures of parents and children lingering around the dinner table to cozily discuss the day's events. . . ." (Paragraph 1)

_____ 2. In the excerpt below, the words *conjure up* (kŏn′jər ŭp) mean
    A. provide help.
    B. question.
    C. bring to mind.
    D. discover.

    ". . . an ideal family evening . . . calls up in my mind pictures of parents and children lingering around the dinner table. . . . Let me tell you what 'an ideal family evening' does not conjure up for me: the image of a silent group of people . . . bathed in the faint blue light of a television screen. . . ." (Paragraphs 1–2)

_____ 3. In the excerpt below, the word *scenario* (sǐ-nâr'ē-ō') means
   A. imagined scene.
   B. television show.
   C. light.
   D. achievement.

   ". . . a silent group of people . . . bathed in the faint blue light of a television screen that barely illuminates their glazed eyes and slack jaws . . . such a scenario is the typical one." (Paragraphs 2–3)

_____ 4. In the excerpt below, the word *subside* (səb-sīd') means
   A. investigate.
   B. persuade.
   C. inform.
   D. quiet down.

   "I propose that for sixty minutes each evening . . . all television broadcasting in the United States be prohibited by law. Let us pause for a moment while the howls of protest subside." (Paragraph 3)

_____ 5. In the sentence below, the word *distraction* (dǐ-strǎk'shən) means
   A. great cost.
   B. drawing away of attention.
   C. common principle.
   D. great disappointment.

   "Without the distraction of the tube, families might sit around together after dinner and actually talk to one another." (Paragraph 5)

_____ 6. In the excerpt below, the word *diversions* (dǐ-vûr'zhənz) means
   A. facts.
   B. stories.
   C. pastimes.
   D. friends.

   " . . . forced to find their own diversions, they might take a ride together to watch the sunset. Or they might take a walk together (remember feet?) and explore the neighborhood. . . ." (Paragraph 6)

_____ 7. In the sentence below, the word *slay* (slā) means
   A. build up.
   B. forget.
   C. rediscover.
   D. kill.

   "With time to kill and no TV to slay it for them, children and adults alike might rediscover reading." (Paragraph 7)

_____ 8. In the excerpt below, the word *literate* (lĭt′ər-ĭt) means
   A. able to read and write.
   B. active outdoors.
   C. having a close family.
   D. being understanding of others.

> ". . . children and adults alike might rediscover reading. . . . Writing is often learned from reading. A more literate new generation could be a major byproduct of the quiet hour." (Paragraph 7)

_____ 9. In the excerpt below, the word *revitalize* (rē-vīt′l-īz′) means
   A. bury.
   B. bring new life to.
   C. cleverly invent.
   D. follow.

> ". . . the quiet hour . . . would revitalize a whole range of activities that have wasted away in the consuming glare of the tube." (Paragraph 13)

_____ 10. In the excerpt below, the word *radical* (răd′ĭ-kəl) means

   A. secure.
   B. extreme.
   C. useful.
   D. old-fashioned.

> "At first glance, the notion of a TV-less hour seems radical. What will parents do without the electronic baby sitter? . . . But it is not radical at all. It has been only about fifty years since television came to dominate American free time." (Paragraph 15)

Discussion Questions

1. What were family evenings like in your home as you grew up? Were they more like the images in paragraph 1 of the reading or more like the scenario in paragraph 2?

2. How many hours a day do you watch TV now? How might cutting down by an hour or so affect what you do each week? For instance, would you exercise, read, or study more?

3. Authors often strengthen their argument by raising possible objections to it and then showing the weaknesses of those objections. What objections does Mayer raise to his own point, and how does he show their weaknesses? (See paragraphs 12–15.) Do you agree or disagree with his analysis of each point?

4. Mayer writes, "With time to kill and no TV to slay it for them, children and adults alike might discover reading." He suggests one way for children to enjoy books—by having them read aloud. In what other ways might parents help their children enjoy reading?

Note: Writing assignments for this selection appear on page 627.

Note: Writing assignments for this selection appear on page 627.

Check Your Performance	VOCABULARY IN CONTEXT		
Activity	*Number Right*	*Points*	*Score*
Review Test 1 (5 items)	_____	× 2 =	_____
Review Test 2 (10 items)	_____	× 3 =	_____
Review Test 3 (10 items)	_____	× 3 =	_____
Review Test 4 (10 items)	_____	× 3 =	_____
	TOTAL SCORE	=	_____%

Enter your total score into the **Reading Performance Chart: Review Tests** on the inside back cover.

VOCABULARY IN CONTEXT: Mastery Test 1

A. For each item below, underline the **examples** that suggest the meaning of the italicized word. Then, on the answer line, write the letter of the meaning of that word.

_____ 1. We all have our *foibles* (foi′bəlz). Lily, for instance, eats with her mouth open; Earl cracks his knuckles; and Jenelle calls everyone "honey."
    A. emotional disturbances   C. hobbies
    B. minor faults   D. good points

_____ 2. The company president has an *austere* (ô-stîr′) office: it is furnished with just an ordinary metal desk, an armless chair, and a file cabinet.
    A. very plain   C. luxurious
    B. unclean   D. large and roomy

_____ 3. If you have a taste for the *macabre* (mə-kä′brə), visit the Chamber of Horrors, an exhibit at Madame Tussaud's Wax Museum in London that features ax murderers, poisoners, and stranglers.
    A. gruesome   C. historic
    B. artistic   D. unknown

B. Each item below includes a word or words that are a **synonym** of the italicized word. Write the synonym of the italicized word in the space provided.

_____ 4. When Kim needed to have a tooth pulled, her boyfriend came along to *bolster* (bōl′stər) her courage. But she was the one who had to support him—he fainted dead away.

_____ 5. To *forestall* (fôr-stôl′) the need for last-minute cramming, keep up with each course throughout the term. Keeping up will also prevent "test anxiety."

(Continues on next page)

C. Each item below includes a word or words that are an **antonym** of the italicized word. Underline the antonym of each italicized word. Then, on the answer line, write the letter of the meaning of the italicized word.

_____ 6. The document that is on display at the museum is only a *facsimile* (făk-sĭm′ə-lē). The original is on loan to another museum for a few months.
    A. poor effort   C. inexpensive item
    B. copy   D. miniature

_____ 7. Automobiles *depreciate* (dĭ-prē′shē-āt′) sharply in a short time. In contrast, real estate will typically increase in value.
    A. rust   C. lose value
    B. wear out   D. drive

_____ 8. Test results sometimes show that a person who has only a *tenuous* (tĕn′yo͞o-əs) grasp of mathematics nevertheless has very strong verbal abilities.
    A. inborn   C. acquired
    B. weak   D. surprising

D. Use the **general sense of each sentence** to figure out the meaning of each italicized word. Then, on the answer line, write the letter of the meaning of the italicized word.

_____ 9. Because she enjoyed her work, the new job offer left Elena in a *quandary* (kwŏn′də-rē). She couldn't decide what to do.
    A. state of uncertainty   C. state of anger
    B. state of fear   D. state of confidence

_____ 10. There is a growing *disparity* (dĭ-spăr′ĭ-tē) between the rich and the poor in the United States. The richest 20 percent of Americans own more than 75 percent of all the nation's wealth.
    A. mistrust   C. inequality
    B. understanding   D. violence

VOCABULARY IN CONTEXT: Mastery Test 2

A. For each item below, underline the **examples** that suggest the meaning of the italicized word. Then, on the answer line, write the letter of the meaning of that word.

_____ 1. The employees had put up *facetious* (fə-sē′shəs) signs by their desks, such as "A clean desk is the sign of a sick mind," "THIMK!" and "If you don't believe the dead come back to life, you should see this place at five o'clock."
   A. useful   C. expensive
   B. humorous   D. insulting

_____ 2. Immigrants to the United States were once urged to *assimilate* (ə-sĭm′ə-lāt′)—to speak only English, to wear American clothes, to eat American food, to adopt American customs.
   A. succeed   C. leave
   B. work hard   D. blend in

_____ 3. Calls for reform may produce violent *fanaticism* (fə-năt′ĭ-sĭz′əm). For example, during the seventeenth century, some 20,000 peasants in Russia burned themselves as a way of protesting church reforms. And in 1420, a religious cult in Europe set about making a holy war to kill "the unholy" who were calling for reform.
   A. government   C. extreme and irrational enthusiasm
   B. harming oneself   D. endless fighting

B. Each item below includes a word or words that are a **synonym** of the italicized word. Write the synonym of the italicized word in the space provided.

_____ 4. When Reba lost fifty pounds, there was not just a change in her appearance. Her personality also underwent a *metamorphosis* (mĕt′ə-môr′fə-sĭs)—she became much more outgoing.

_____ 5. Some drivers *circumvented* (sûr′kəm-vĕnt′ĭd) the traffic jam at the bridge. They avoided the tie-up by taking the turnoff a mile back.

(Continues on next page)

C. Each item below includes a word or words that are an **antonym** of the italicized word. Underline the antonym of each italicized word. Then, on the answer line, write the letter of the meaning of the italicized word.

_____ 6. Most offices expect employees to wear clothing that is fairly quiet and conservative, so save your *flamboyant* (flăm-boi′ənt) clothes for when you're out with friends.

    A. flashy   C. expensive

    B. old-fashioned   D. new

_____ 7. Someone from outside the group is needed to give an *objective* (əb-jĕk′tĭv) viewpoint. Anyone from the group would be too biased.

    A. thoughtless   C. favorable

    B. open-minded   D. useful

_____ 8. Many people still believe that rubbing butter on a burn will relieve it. However, that practice can actually *exacerbate* (ĭg-zăs′ər-bāt′) the injury.

    A. soothe   C. protect

    B. worsen   D. cover

D. Use the **general sense of each sentence** to figure out the meaning of each italicized word. Then, on the answer line, write the letter of the meaning of the italicized word.

_____ 9. "You keep wandering off into thoughts that are not *germane* (jər-mān′) to your topic," the instructor wrote on my paper. "You must learn to stick to the point."

    A. grammatically correct   C. interesting

    B. damaging   D. related

_____ 10. Stephen King is known as a *prolific* (prə-lĭf′ĭk) writer, sometimes completing two long novels in a single year.

    A. secret   C. unimportant

    B. very productive   D. very frightening

VOCABULARY IN CONTEXT: Mastery Test 3

Using context clues for help, write, in the space provided, the letter of the best meaning for each italicized word.

_____ 1. President Calvin Coolidge was so *reticent* (rĕt′ĭ-sənt) that he was nicknamed "Silent Cal."
   A. powerful as a speaker   C. uncommunicative
   B. popular   D. well-known

_____ 2. The *paramount* (păr′ə-mount′) duty of the physician is to do no harm. Everything else—even healing—must take second place.
   A. successful   C. mysterious
   B. chief   D. least

_____ 3. Ideas about *decorum* (dĭ-kôr′əm) change greatly over time. In our society, for instance, until relatively recently polite people did not appear bareheaded on the street, and a man always tipped his hat to a woman.
   A. beauty   C. proper behavior
   B. physical fitness   D. style

_____ 4. The expert witness in the lawsuit chose his words with great care. He didn't want anyone to *misconstrue* (mĭs′kən-strōō′) his statements.
   A. repeat   C. accept
   B. recall   D. misinterpret

_____ 5. The fatty food was so *repugnant* (rĭ-pŭg′nənt) to Fran that she could not force herself to finish the meal.
   A. amusing   C. disgusting
   B. new   D. surprising

_____ 6. When reporters asked if he would be a mayoral candidate again, the mayor would only *equivocate* (ĭ-kwĭv′ə-kāt′), saying, "Ladies and gentlemen, I still feel that public service is a high calling."
   A. predict   C. clearly deny
   B. be purposely unclear   D. forget

(Continues on next page)

_____ 7. By forming a *coalition* (kō′ə-lǐsh′ən), the small political parties gained more power in the government than they each had separately.
- A. separation
- B. publication
- C. competition
- D. partnership

_____ 8. Some people seek *vicarious* (vī-kâr′ē-əs) experiences. For example, the "stage mother" claims success through her child, and the "peeping Tom," who is emotionally disturbed, gets sexual pleasure from spying on others.
- A. varied
- B. ordinary
- C. indirect
- D. inexpensive

_____ 9. The *noxious* (nǒk′shəs) fumes from the chemical spill made people so ill that some had to go to the hospital.
- A. permanent
- B. silent
- C. mild
- D. unhealthy

_____ 10. Many folk sayings warn against *impetuous* (ǐm-pěch′ōo-əs) actions: "Marry in haste, repent at leisure," "Look before you leap," and the traditional advice to carpenters and dressmakers, "Measure twice, cut once."
- A. mean
- B. surprise
- C. hasty
- D. forgotten

VOCABULARY IN CONTEXT: Mastery Test 4

Using context clues for help, write, in the space provided, the letter of the best meaning for each italicized word. Note that all of the sentences have been taken from college textbooks.

_____ 1. To carry out his economic programs, Roosevelt had to *contend* (kən-tĕnd′) with a Supreme Court that was deeply opposed to them.
  A. travel
  B. surrender
  C. struggle
  D. join

_____ 2. Being unable to write clearly is a *liability* (lī′ə-bĭl′ĭ-tē) in a business career, in which one must often express opinions and ideas in writing.
  A. drawback
  B. surprise
  C. necessity
  D. penalty

_____ 3. The idea that off-track betting will work in Alaska because it works in New York is a questionable *analogy* (ə-năl′ə-jē). New York and Alaska may not be alike when it comes to off-track betting.
  A. comparison
  B. purpose
  C. contrast
  D. requirement

_____ 4. To *facilitate* (fə-sĭl′ĭ-tāt′) the college admission process, many application forms have been shortened and simplified, and they can be posted on a website, sent by e-mail, or faxed.
  A. begin
  B. frustrate
  C. complicate
  D. make easier

_____ 5. There is an *optimum* (ŏp′tə-məm) way to approach each kind of exam question. For a multiple-choice item, for example, first eliminate any clearly wrong answers. For an essay question, jot down an outline first.
  A. inconvenient
  B. best
  C. annoying
  D. time-consuming

_____ 6. Studies indicate that a *predisposition* (prē′dĭs-pə-zĭsh′ən) to schizophrenia is inherited. People who are schizophrenic are more likely than others to have schizophrenic children.
  A. tendency
  B. understanding
  C. fear
  D. avoidance

(Continues on next page)

_____ 7. By giving military aid to dictatorships in Latin America, the United States has seemed to *sanction* (săngk′shən) their cruel policies.
   A. criticize   C. remember
   B. approve of   D. create

_____ 8. A *provocative* (prə-vŏk′ə-tĭv) question can be an effective way to open an essay. Students have begun essays with such interesting questions as, "What do you think your name means?" and "How long do you think it would take you to count to one billion?"
   A. funny   C. unanswerable
   B. arousing interest   D. very brief

_____ 9. Manic depression is an emotional disorder in which the patient alternates between feeling delightfully *euphoric* (yōō-fôr′ĭk) and being plunged into deep gloom.
   A. overjoyed   C. exhausted
   B. bored   D. curious

_____ 10. Although relatively few people in the United States lack food desperately, about 36,000,000 American people—approximately 14 percent of the population—live in what is officially *designated* (dĕz′ĭg-nāt′ĭd) as poverty.
   A. predicted   C. labeled
   B. designed   D. forgotten

VOCABULARY IN CONTEXT: Mastery Test 5

A. Using context clues for help, write, in the space provided, the letter of the best meaning for each italicized word. Note that all of the sentences have been taken from college textbooks.

_____ 1. Because of the decreasing supply of natural gas, researchers are now considering several methods of *converting* (kən′vûrt-ĭng) oil and coal to gas.
   A. arranging   C. leaving
   B. finding   D. changing

_____ 2. Marriages are rarely *static* (stăt′ĭk). They continually change as the partners experience and adjust to their own life tasks.
   A. successful   C. unchanging
   B. serious   D. violent

_____ 3. We now know that two centers in the brain are especially important in controlling hunger. One center *stimulates* (stĭm′yə-lāts′) eating; the other reduces the feeling of hunger.
   A. stops   C. knows
   B. finds   D. encourages

_____ 4. Those romantic cigarette ads don't exactly claim in words that smoking will make you gorgeous and sexy and give you an exciting life, but that is the *implicit* (ĭm-plĭs′ĭt) message.
   A. unfriendly   C. unbelievable
   B. unstated   D. healthy

_____ 5. Minor traffic *infractions* (ĭn-frăk′shəns), such as parking in a no-parking zone, are punished by a fine; but a major offense such as drunk driving can put you in jail.
   A. violations   C. exceptions
   B. laws   D. explanations

(Continues on next page)

B. Use context clues to figure out the meaning of the italicized word in each of the following textbook items. Then write your definition in the space provided.

6. The *prime* sources of protein are animal products, including meat, fish, eggs, milk, and cheese. In addition, some plants, such as soybeans, contain useful proteins.

   Prime (prīm) means: _____

7. An infant learns very quickly to *differentiate* his or her main caretaker from everyone else.

   Differentiate (dĭf′ə-rĕn′shē-āt′) means: _____

8. San Quentin prison, which was designed to hold 2,700 prisoners, *confines* its 3,900 inmates to their cells except for meals and showers.

   Confines (kən-fīnz′) means: _____

9. In *retrospect*, elderly and middle-aged people often conclude that they should have spent more time with their children.

   Retrospect (rĕt′rə-spĕkt′) means: _____

10. Cultural standards influence advertising. For instance, one French ad showed a man's bare arm being grasped by a woman's hand. That ad was *modified* for display in Saudi Arabia. The Saudi version clothed the man's arm in a dark suit sleeve and showed the woman's hand just brushing it.

    Modified (mŏd′ə-fīd′) means: _____

VOCABULARY IN CONTEXT: Mastery Test 6

A. Five words are **boldfaced** in the textbook passage below. Write the definition for each boldfaced word, choosing from the definitions in the box. Then write the letter of the definition in the space provided.

Be sure to read the entire passage before making your choices. Note that five definitions will be left over.

A. adjust	D. asked about	G. beginning	I. behave
B. denied	E. death	H. loaded	J. filled
C. put forth as a theory	F. said to be caused by		

¹About 65 million years ago, more than half of all plant and animal species died out. ²The dinosaurs met their **demise** then, along with large numbers of other animal and plant groups, both terrestrial and marine. ³Equally important, of course, is the fact that many species survived the disaster. ⁴Human beings are descended from these survivors. ⁵Perhaps this fact explains why an event that occurred 65 million years ago has captured the interest of so many people. ⁶The extinction of the great reptiles is generally **attributed to** this group's inability to **adapt** to some basic change in environmental conditions. ⁷What event could have triggered the sudden extinction of the dinosaurs—the most successful group of land animals ever to have lived?

⁸One modern view proposes that about 65 million years ago, a large asteroid or comet about 10 kilometers in diameter collided with the Earth. ⁹The impact of such a body would have produced an overwhelming cloud of dust. ¹⁰For many months, the dust-**laden** atmosphere would have greatly restricted the amount of sunlight that penetrated to the Earth's surface. ¹¹Without sunlight for plant growth, delicate food chains would collapse. ¹²It is further **hypothesized** that large dinosaurs would be affected more negatively by this chain of events than would smaller life forms. ¹³In addition, acid rains and global fires may have added to the environmental disaster. ¹⁴It is estimated that when the sunlight returned, more than half of the species on Earth had become extinct.

_____ 1. *Demise* (dĭ-mīz′) means: _____

_____ 2. *Attributed to* (ə-trĭb′yo͞ot-ĭd toͦo) means: _____

_____ 3. *Adapt* (ə-dăpt′) means: _____

_____ 4. *Laden* (lād′n) means: _____

_____ 5. *Hypothesized* (hī-pŏth′ĭ-sīzd′) means: _____

(Continues on next page)

B. Five words are **boldfaced** in the textbook passage below. Write the definition for each boldfaced word, choosing from the definitions in the box. Also, write the letter of the definition in the space provided.

Be sure to read the entire passage before making your choices. Note that five definitions will be left over.

A. excited	D. had a strong desire	G. great anger	I. loose
B. strict	E. ignored	H. seen	J. straight
C. unequaled	F. something very popular		

[1]Thanks to the prosperity of the 1920s, Americans had more money for leisure activities than ever before. [2]The 1920s were a decade of contrasts, and popular fiction was no exception. [3]People wanted virtuous heroes and old-time value in their fiction, but a lot of them also wanted to be **titillated**. [4]One of the major publishing trends of the 1920s was the boom in "confession magazines." [5]The rise of the city, the liberated woman, and the impact of the movie industry all relaxed the **stern** Victorian moral standards. [6]Into the vacuum came the confession magazine—borderline pornography with stories of romantic success and failure, divorce, fantasy, and adultery. [7]Writers survived the cuts of the censors by expressing their stories as moral lessons advising readers to avoid similar mistakes in their own lives.

[8]Another **rage** of the 1920s was spectator sports. [9]Because the country **yearned** for individual heroes to stand out larger than life in an increasingly impersonal, organized society, prize-fighting enjoyed a huge following, especially in the heavyweight division, where hard punchers like Jack Dempsey became national idols. [10]Team sports flourished in colleges and high schools, but even then Americans focused on individual superstars, people whose talents or personalities earned them a cult following. [11]Notre Dame emerged as a college football powerhouse in the 1920s, but it was head coach Knute Rockne and his "pep talks" on dedication and persistence which became part of the fabric of American popular culture.

[12]Baseball was even more popular than football. [13]Fans spent countless hours of calculating, memorizing, and quizzing one another on baseball statistics. [14]The sport's superstar was George Herman "Babe" Ruth, the "Sultan of Swat." [15]The public loved Ruth for his **unparalleled** skills as well as his personal weaknesses. [16]While hitting or pitching as nobody had before, Ruth was also known for his huge appetite and his capacity to drink himself into a stupor. [17]His beer belly, like his swing, was unique.

_____ 6. *Titillated* (tĭt′l-āt′ĭd) means: _____

_____ 7. *Stern* (stûrn) means: _____

_____ 8. *Rage* (rāj′) means: _____

_____ 9. *Yearned* (yûrnd) means: _____

_____ 10. *Unparalleled* (ŭn-păr′ə-lĕld′) means: _____

2

Main Ideas

WHAT IS THE MAIN IDEA?

"What's the point?" You've probably heard these words before. It's a question people ask when they want to know the main idea that someone is trying to express. The same question can guide you as you read. Recognizing the **main idea**, or point, is the most important key to good comprehension. To find it in a reading selection, ask yourself, "What's the main point the author is trying to make?" For instance, read the following paragraph, asking yourself as you do, "What is the author's point?"

> [1]Many people feel that violence on television is harmless entertainment. [2]However, we now know that TV violence does affect people in negative ways. [3]One study showed that frequent TV watchers are more fearful and suspicious of others. [4]They try to protect themselves from the outside world with extra locks on the doors, alarm systems, guard dogs, and guns. [5]In addition, that same study showed that heavy TV watchers are less upset about real-life violence than non-TV watchers. [6]It seems that the constant violence they see on TV makes them less sensitive to the real thing. [7]Another study, of a group of children, found that TV violence increases aggressive behavior. [8]Children who watched violent shows were more willing to hurt another child in games where they were given a choice between helping and hurting. [9]They were also more likely to select toy weapons over other kinds of playthings.

A good way to find an author's point, or main idea, is to look for a general statement. Then decide if that statement is supported by most of the other material in the paragraph. If it is, you have found the main idea.

On the next page are four statements from the passage. Pick out the general statement that is supported by the other material in the passage. Write the letter of that statement in the space provided. Then read the explanation that follows.

Four statements from the passage:

A. Many people feel that violence on television is harmless entertainment.

B. However, we now know that TV violence does affect people in negative ways.

C. One study showed that frequent TV watchers are more fearful and suspicious of others.

D. They try to protect themselves from the outside world with extra locks on the doors, alarm systems, guard dogs, and guns.

The general statement that expresses the main idea of the passage is _____.

Explanation:

Sentence A: The paragraph does not support the idea that TV violence is harmless, so sentence A cannot be the main idea. However, it does introduce the topic of the paragraph: TV violence.

Sentence B: The statement "TV violence does affect people in negative ways" is a general one. And the rest of the passage goes on to describe three negative ways that TV violence affects people. Sentence B, then, is the sentence that expresses the main idea of the passage.

Sentence C: This sentence is about only one study. It is not general enough to include the other studies that are also cited in the paragraph. It is the first supporting idea for the main idea.

Sentence D: This sentence provides detailed evidence for the first supporting idea, which is that frequent TV watchers are more fearful and suspicious of others. It does not cover the other material in the paragraph.

The Main Idea as an "Umbrella" Idea

Think of the main idea as an "umbrella" idea. The main idea is the author's general point; under it fits all the other material of the paragraph. That other material is made up of supporting details—specific evidence such as examples, causes, reasons, or facts. The diagram on the next page shows the relationship.

The explanations and activities on the following pages will deepen your understanding of the main idea.

Frequent TV watchers are more fearful and suspicious of others.

Heavy TV watchers are less upset about real-life violence than non-TV watchers.

TV violence increases aggressive behavior in children.

HOW DO YOU RECOGNIZE A MAIN IDEA?

As you read through a passage, you must **think as you read**. If you merely take in words, you will come to the end of the passage without understanding much of what you have read. Reading is an active process as opposed to watching television, which is passive. You must actively engage your mind, and, as you read, keep asking yourself, "What's the point?" Here are three strategies that will help you find the main idea.

1 Look for general versus specific ideas.
2 Use the topic to lead you to the main idea.
3 Use clue words to lead you to the main idea.

Each strategy is explained on the following pages.

1 Look for General versus Specific Ideas

You saw in the paragraph on TV violence that the main idea is a *general* idea supported by *specific* ideas. The following practices will improve your skill at separating general from specific ideas. Learning how to tell the difference between general and specific ideas will help you locate the main idea.

➤ *Practice 1*

Each group of words below has one general idea and three specific ideas. The general idea includes all the specific ideas. Identify each general idea with a **G** and the specific ideas with an **S**. Look first at the example.

Example

   _S_ dishonesty
   _S_ greed
   _G_ vices
   _S_ selfishness

(*Vices* is the general idea which includes three specific types of vices: dishonesty, greed, and selfishness.)

1. ____ lobster
    ____ seafood
    ____ clams
    ____ oysters

2. ____ appearance
    ____ handsome
    ____ well-dressed
    ____ shabby

3. ____ heavy traffic
    ____ bus not on time
    ____ alarm didn't go off
    ____ excuses for being late

4. ____ paper cuts
    ____ broken nails
    ____ minor problems
    ____ wrong numbers

5. ____ giggling
    ____ childish behavior
    ____ tantrums
    ____ playing peek-a-boo

6. ____ poor pay
    ____ undesirable job
    ____ mean boss
    ____ very dull work

7. ____ try to be kinder
    ____ eat healthier foods
    ____ go to bed earlier
    ____ resolutions

8. ____ take stairs instead of elevator
    ____ ride bike instead of driving
    ____ exercise opportunities
    ____ walk instead of riding bus

9. ____ skip breakfast
    ____ grab a donut mid-morning
    ____ poor eating habits
    ____ order supersize portions

10. ____ different goals
    ____ no common interests
    ____ dislike each other's friends
    ____ reasons for breaking up

➤ *Practice 2*

Write out the answers to each question on the spaces provided. For each question, the answers are specific details that illustrate the general idea, which is underlined.

1. There are probably many <u>places in the world you'd like to visit</u>. If you were offered an all-expense-paid vacation anywhere in the world, what are three specific locations you would consider?

   _____

   _____

   _____

2. If you were suddenly wealthy, you could hire other people to do <u>tasks that you dislike</u>. What are three specific chores that you'd hand over to somebody else?

   _____

   _____

   _____

3. There have been many <u>technological improvements over the last century that you would not like to do without</u>. What are three of the inventions you would most hate to give up?

   _____

   _____

   _____

4. Most of us enjoy a good movie, but we have different <u>ideas of what makes a film "good."</u> What are three specific qualities that a movie needs in order for you to really like it?

   _____

   _____

   _____

5. We all know people whom we find difficult. Think of a person that you find hard to get along with. Name <u>three specific reasons you find this person difficult</u>.

   _____

   _____

   _____

➤ *Practice 3*

In the following groups, one statement is the general point and the other statements are specific support for the point. Identify each point with a **P** and each statement of support with an **S**.

1. ___ The children often start fights at school.
   ___ The children are poorly behaved.
   ___ The kids walk into neighbors' houses uninvited.
   ___ The children use foul language.

2. ___ Some vegetables in the salad were moldy.
   ___ The chicken was hard to chew.
   ___ The rolls were rock-hard.
   ___ The meal was very unpleasant.

3. ___ The man doesn't use his turn signals.
   ___ The man drives too fast down narrow residential streets.
   ___ The man is an unsafe driver.
   ___ The man doesn't come to a complete stop at stop signs.

4. ___ This has been a difficult year for Rita's family.
   ___ In January, Rita's grandmother died.
   ___ Last summer, Rita's dad was laid off from work.
   ___ Rita's younger brother developed severe asthma in September.

5. ___ Students stay in touch with friends by e-mail.
   ___ Students often shop over the Internet.
   ___ Students do all their research online.
   ___ Students have practical uses for computers.

➤ *Practice 4*

In each of the following groups, one statement is the general point, and the other statements are specific support for the point. Identify each point with a **P** and each statement of support with an **S**.

1. ___ A. When answering the phone, some people's first words are "Who's this?"
   ___ B. Some people never bother to identify themselves when calling someone.
   ___ C. Some people have terrible telephone manners.
   ___ D. Some people hang up without even saying goodbye.

2. ___ A. High-heeled shoes can cause foot and back pain.

___ B. Some women's clothing is impractical.

___ C. Tight skirts make it difficult to move quickly.

___ D. Pantyhose are constantly getting snags and runs.

3. ___ A. The plates of food that emerge from the kitchens of pricey restaurants often look more like abstract art than supper.

___ B. The tiny portions served in many upscale restaurants wouldn't curb the hunger of a small child, let alone a large adult.

___ C. Some expensive restaurants use trendy ingredients with names that most diners can neither recognize nor pronounce.

___ D. At many expensive restaurants, dining has more to do with style than nourishment.

4. ___ A. Federal law should prohibit banks from giving credit cards to college students.

___ B. Credit-card debt is the leading cause of bankruptcy for young Americans.

___ C. Taking advantage of the fact that many parents will pay their children's credit-card debts, banks extend excessive credit to students.

___ D. When they receive their monthly credit-card bills, many students can pay only the minimum required and so have hefty interest charges on large unpaid amounts.

5. ___ A. Bats are so rarely rabid that a person has a better chance of catching rabies from a cow than from a bat.

___ B. Bats, in spite of their bad reputation, are not a danger to human beings.

___ C. Bats are afraid of humans and do their best to stay away from them.

___ D. Unlike movie vampires, bats do not bite people unless frightened or under attack.

➤ Practice 5

In each of the following groups—all based on textbook selections—one statement is the general point, and the other statements are specific support for the point. Identify each point with a **P** and each statement of support with an **S**.

1. ___ A. Disagreeing parties can accept the status quo, agreeing to just live with the situation as it stands.

___ B. When faced with a disagreement, the parties involved have several ways to proceed.

___ C. One party may use physical, social, or economic force to impose a solution on the others.

___ D. Negotiation, or reaching a mutually acceptable solution, is a means of dealing with conflict.

2. ___ A. With bribes, Prohibition-era bootleggers persuaded politicians, police, and other public officials to ignore the illegal sale of alcoholic beverages.

   ___ B. Prohibition glamorized drinking and made it fashionable for people to drink in illegal bars and break the law.

   ___ C. Prohibition encouraged the formation of organized-crime empires that illegally manufactured, transported, and sold liquor.

   ___ D. Prohibition, which banned alcoholic beverages in the United States from 1920 to 1933, resulted in much illegal activity.

3. ___ A. Our social roles—whether we're students, employees, visitors, etc.—dictate what emotions are acceptable for us to express.

   ___ B. Given the widespread habit of suppressing our emotions, many of us have trouble recognizing what we're really feeling.

   ___ C. Most of us rarely express our deepest emotions because of a number of factors.

   ___ D. We often hide our emotions rather than display them so as not to seem weak or needy to others.

4. ___ A. Our state of health significantly affects how we experience the world.

   ___ B. A variety of influences determine how people take in and interpret information.

   ___ C. Older people view the world differently than younger ones because they've had more experiences.

   ___ D. Whether we are hungry or have recently eaten will affect how we feel about the world.

5. ___ A. When doing business in Latin America or Arab countries, Americans must become accustomed to standing very close to their colleagues.

   ___ B. The Chevy Nova did very poorly in Latin American countries because "No va" means "It doesn't go" in Spanish.

   ___ C. In order to do business successfully in other countries, it is necessary to understand those countries' languages and cultures.

   ___ D. When a Japanese businessman hands you his card, it is considered very rude to put it away without studying it first.

2 Use the Topic to Lead You to the Main Idea

You already know that to find the main idea of a selection, you look first for a general statement. You then check to see if that statement is supported by most of the other material in the paragraph. If it is, you've found the main idea. Another approach that can help you find the main idea of a selection is to find its topic.

The **topic** is the general subject of a selection. It can often be expressed in one or more words. Knowing the topic can help you find a writer's main point about that topic.

Textbook authors use the title of each chapter to state the overall topic of that chapter. They also provide many topics and subtopics in boldface headings within the chapter. For example, here is the title of a chapter in a psychology textbook:

Theories of Human Development (26 pages)

And here are the subtopics:

Psychoanalytic Theories (an 8-page section)

Learning Theories (a 9-page section)

Cognitive Theories (a 9-page section)

If you were studying the above chapter, you could use the topics to help find the main ideas. (Pages 10–11 explain just how to do so, as well as other textbook study tips.)

But there are many times when you are not given topics—with standardized reading tests, for example, or with individual paragraphs in articles or textbooks. To find the topic of a selection when the topic is not given, ask this simple question:

Who or what is the selection about?

For example, look again at the beginning of the paragraph that started this chapter:

Many people feel that violence on television is harmless entertainment. However, we now know that TV violence does affect people in negative ways.

What, in a phrase, is the above paragraph about? On the line below, write what you think is the topic.

Topic: _____

You probably answered that the topic is "TV violence." As you reread the paragraph, you saw that, in fact, every sentence in it is about TV violence.

The next step after finding the topic is to decide what main point the author is making about the topic. Authors often present their main idea in a single sentence. (This sentence is also known as the **main idea sentence** or the **topic sentence**.) As we have already seen, the main point about TV violence is "we now know that TV violence does affect people in negative ways."

☑ *Check Your Understanding*

Let's look now at another paragraph. Read it and then see if you can answer the questions that follow.

> [1]Recently a family of four were found dead in their suburban home in New Jersey—victims of carbon monoxide. [2]Such cases are tragically common. [3]Carbon monoxide is deadly for many reasons. [4]To begin with, it is created in the most ordinary of ways—by the burning of wood, coal, or petroleum products. [5]Once created, this gas is impossible to detect without instruments: it is colorless, odorless, and tasteless. [6]Also, carbon monoxide mingles with and remains in the air rather than rising and being carried away by the wind. [7]Then, when people unsuspectingly breathe it in, it chokes them, taking the place of the oxygen in their blood. [8]Furthermore, it can do its lethal work in very small quantities: anyone exposed to air that is just 1 percent carbon monoxide for even a few minutes will almost certainly die.

1. What is the *topic* of the paragraph? In other words, what is the paragraph about? (It often helps as you read to look for and even circle a word, term, or idea that is repeated in the paragraph.)

   _____

2. What is the *main idea* of the paragraph? In other words, what point is the author making about the topic? (Remember that the main idea will be supported by the other material in the paragraph.)

   _____

Explanation:

As the first sentence of the paragraph suggests, the topic is "carbon monoxide." Continuing to read the paragraph, you see that, in fact, everything in it is about carbon monoxide. And the main idea is clearly that "Carbon monoxide is deadly for many reasons." This idea is a general one that sums up what the entire paragraph is about. It is an "umbrella" statement under which all the other material in the paragraph fits. The parts of the paragraph could be shown as follows:

Topic: Carbon monoxide

Main idea: Carbon monoxide is deadly for many reasons.

Supporting details:
1. Is easily created.
2. Is difficult to detect.
3. Remains in the air.
4. Chokes by taking the place of oxygen in the blood.
5. Works in small quantities.

The following practices will sharpen your sense of the difference between a topic, the point about the topic (the main idea), and supporting details.

➤ *Practice 6*

Below are groups of four items. In each case, one item is the topic, one is the main idea, and two are details that support and develop the main idea. Label each item with one of the following:

T — for the **topic** of the paragraph
MI — for the **main idea**
SD — for the **supporting details**

Note that an explanation is provided for the first group; reading it will help you do this practice.

Group 1

_____ A. One bite from a piranha's triangular-shaped teeth can sever a person's finger or toe.

_____ B. The piranha.

_____ C. The piranha—only eight to twelve inches long—is an extremely dangerous fish.

_____ D. A school of piranha can strip a four-hundred-pound hog down to a skeleton in just a few minutes.

Explanation:

All of the statements in Group 1 are about piranhas, so item B must be the topic. (Topics are easy to spot because they are short phrases, not complete sentences.) Statements A and D are specific examples of the damage that piranhas can do. Statement C, on the other hand, presents the general idea that piranhas can be extremely dangerous. It is the main idea about the topic of "the piranha," and statements A and D are supporting details that illustrate that main idea.

Group 2

_____ A. Joint custody of a divorced couple's children has become more common.

_____ B. The number of men with sole custody of children has also grown.

_____ C. Alternatives to giving the mother sole child custody have increased in recent years.

_____ D. Alternative child-custody arrangements.

Group 3

_____ A. Benjamin Franklin discovered that lightning is an electrical charge.

_____ B. In addition to being a statesman, Franklin was a scientist and an inventor.

_____ C. Benjamin Franklin's work.

_____ D. Franklin invented bifocals, the Franklin stove, and an electric storage battery.

Group 4

_____ A. Bureaucracies are divided into departments and subdivisions.

_____ B. Bureaucracies.

_____ C. Through a division of labor, individuals in bureaucracies specialize in performing one task.

_____ D. Bureaucracies have certain characteristics in common.

Group 5

_____ A. Scientists used to think of the brain as the center of an electrical communication system.

_____ B. The way scientists view the brain's role has changed greatly.

_____ C. Today it is known that "the brain is a bag of hormones," as one scientist puts it.

_____ D. How scientists think about the role of the brain.

➤ Practice 7

Following are five paragraphs. Read each paragraph and do the following:

1 Ask yourself, "What seems to be the topic of the paragraph?" (It often helps to look for and even circle a word or idea that is repeated in the paragraph.)

2 Next, ask yourself, "What point is the writer making about this topic?" This will be the main idea. It is stated in one of the sentences in the paragraph.

3 Then test what you think is the main idea by asking, "Is this statement supported by most of the other material in the paragraph?"

> *Hint:* When looking for the topic, make sure you do not pick one that is either **too broad** (covering a great deal more than is in the selection) or **too narrow** (covering only part of the selection). The topic and the main idea of a selection must include everything in that selection—no more and no less.

Paragraph 1

[1]Blood, as it circulates through the body, performs many functions. [2]It carries nutrients and oxygen to all the cells of the body. [3]It brings hormones from the hormone-secreting glands to the appropriate cells. [4]Blood also carries waste products to the organs that will dispose of them. [5]When there is an infection, blood brings white cells from the immune system to attack it. [6]Blood forms clots that help close wounds. [7]It helps regulate bodily temperature and acidity. [8]Unfortunately, blood has another function as well: when the body has developed a cancer, blood may carry malignant cells from the original tumor to new sites, causing the cancer to spread.

    1. What is the *topic* of the paragraph? In other words, what (in one or more words) is the paragraph about? _____

_____ 2. What point is the writer making about the topic? In other words, which sentence states the *main idea* of the paragraph? In the space provided, write the number of the sentence containing the main idea.

Paragraph 2

[1]The Great Wall of China is a truly remarkable creation. [2]At 4500 miles long, taller than five men, and wide enough to allow at least six horses to gallop side by side atop it, the Great Wall is so huge it can be seen from space. [3]The Wall is constructed of four-inch blocks made of compressed earth, stone, willow twigs, and the remains of laborers who died among the millions who worked on its construction. [4]The Great Wall follows mountain slopes and has inclines as great as seventy degrees. [5]The paths on the Wall are even more difficult to travel because the steps are of uneven depth, width, and height. [6]Through much of its 2500-year history, armies marched and camped on the Wall, keeping lookout for invaders and repelling trespassers who dared to pitch ladders to try to mount it. [7]Today the Great Wall is a tourist attraction that brings many visitors to China. [8]Tourists are eager to make the strenuous hike over precarious paths to take in the greatness of its size and history.

    1. What is the *topic* of the paragraph? In other words, what (in one or more words) is the paragraph about? _____

_____ 2. What point is the writer making about the topic? In other words, which sentence states the *main idea* of the paragraph? In the space provided, write the number of the sentence containing the main idea.

Paragraph 3

[1]Barbecue is a popular dish in many parts of America, but it can be a different dish depending on where you eat it. [2]When people who live west of the Mississippi serve barbecue, it's usually beef that has been cooked over an open fire. [3]East of the Mississippi, pork is more common, and it's often cooked in an iron smoking oven. [4]In some parts of the South, barbecue is typically served in a wet sauce that contains tomatoes, vinegar, and chili peppers. [5]But in other southern towns, the barbecue meat is rubbed with seasonings before cooking and then served dry, with no sauce at all. [6]In Hawaii, barbecue often refers to a whole pig that's been wrapped in leaves and cooked in a pit dug into the ground. [7]To make matters even more confusing, a barbecue dinner in the northeastern states or California might feature fish or chicken cooked on a charcoal grill.

1. What is the *topic* of the paragraph? In other words, what (in one or more words) is the paragraph about? _____

_____ 2. What point is the writer making about the topic? In other words, which sentence states the *main idea* of the paragraph? In the space provided, write the number of the sentence containing the main idea.

Paragraph 4

[1]Busing was implemented in 1971 to achieve racial balance in schools. [2]Studies indicate that it has had positive effects, such as better performance of black children on standardized tests when they attend white-majority schools. [3]However, busing has its negative effects, too. [4]For one thing, busing has contributed to whites' departure from public schools. [5]In Boston, for example, fewer than 20 percent of public school children today are white—compared with more than 50 percent when busing began there in 1974. [6]In addition, busing has fragmented neighborhoods. [7]Children do not necessarily go to the school their friends and relatives attend. [8]Another negative effect is that busing has forced children into long bus rides to and from school. [9]Black and white students both experience what has come to be called "busing fatigue."

1. What is the *topic* of the paragraph? In other words, what (in one or more words) is the paragraph about? _____

_____ 2. What point is the writer making about the topic? In other words, which sentence states the *main idea* of the paragraph? In the space provided, write the number of the sentence containing the main idea.

Paragraph 5

¹Cardiovascular disease—disease of the heart or blood vessels—is the leading cause of death in the United States, killing about 1 million people a year. ²Cardiovascular disease is actually a group of disorders. ³This group includes high blood pressure, or hypertension, which significantly increases the risk of other diseases in the group. ⁴Atherosclerosis, or coronary artery disease, is another member of the group. ⁵In this cardiovascular disorder, a fatty deposit, plaque, builds up on the walls of the arteries, restricting the flow of blood and causing strain to the heart, which must work harder to pump blood through the narrowed arteries. ⁶Sometimes an aneurysm occurs: the artery ruptures. ⁷Heart attack—technically, myocardial infarction—is also in this group. ⁸It happens when plaque builds up so much that blood flow to the heart is cut off and some heart muscle dies. ⁹Congestive heart failure, a chronic disease, is part of the group as well. ¹⁰In this disorder the heart has been weakened and can no longer pump enough blood. ¹¹Stroke, too, is a cardio-vascular disease: it occurs when blood flow to the brain is restricted or cut off.

1. What is the *topic* of the paragraph? In other words, what (in one or more words) is the paragraph about? _____

_____ 2. What point is the writer making about the topic? In other words, which sentence states the *main idea* of the paragraph? In the space provided, write the number of the sentence containing the main idea.

3 Find and Use Clue Words to Lead You to the Main Idea

Sometimes authors make it fairly easy to find their main idea. They announce it using **clue words or phrases** that are easy to recognize. One type of clue word is a **list word**, which tells you a list of items is to follow. For example, the main idea in the paragraph about TV violence was stated like this: *However, we now know that TV violence does affect people in negative ways.* The expression *negative ways* helps you zero in on your target: the main idea. You realize that the paragraph may be about specific ways that TV violence affects people. As you read on and see the series of negative effects, you know your guess about the main idea was correct.

Here are some common words that often announce a main idea. Note that all of them end in **s**—a plural that suggests the supporting details will be a list of items.

List Words

several kinds (or ways) of	several causes of	some factors in
three advantages of	five steps	among the results
various reasons for	a number of effects	a series of

When expressions like these appear in a sentence, look carefully to see if that sentence might be the main idea. Chances are a sentence with such clue words will be followed by a list of major supporting details.

☑ Check Your Understanding

Underline the list words in the following sentences.

> *Hint:* Remember that list words usually end in **s**.

Example   Emotional decisions can be divided into <u>two main types</u>.

1. At least five job trends deserve watching in today's world.

2. Pathologists identify four different stages of cancer in the body.

3. Several steps can be effective in helping people deal with prejudice.

4. Winners of presidential elections share various traits in common.

5. Giving birth to and raising a child requires a number of adjustments in the parents' lives.

Explanation:

You should have underlined the following groups of words: *five job trends; four different stages; several steps; various traits;* and *a number of adjustments.* Each of these phrases tells you that a list of details may follow.

There is another type of clue word that can alert you to the main idea. This type of clue word, called an **addition word**, is generally used right before a supporting detail. When you see this type of clue, you can assume that the detail it introduces fits under the umbrella of a main idea.

Here is a box of words that often introduce major supporting details and help you discover the main idea.

Addition Words

one	to begin with	in addition	last
first	another	next	last of all
first of all	second	moreover	finally
for one thing	also	furthermore	

☑ *Check Your Understanding*

Reread the paragraph about TV violence and underline the addition words that alert you to supporting details. Also, see if you can underline the list words that suggest the main idea.

[1]Many people feel that violence on television is harmless entertainment. [2]However, we now know that TV violence does affect people in negative ways. [3]One study showed that frequent TV watchers are more fearful and suspicious of others. [4]They try to protect themselves from the outside world with extra locks on the doors, alarm systems, guard dogs, and guns. [5]In addition, that same study showed that heavy TV watchers are less upset about real-life violence than non-TV watchers. [6]It seems that the constant violence they see on TV makes them less sensitive to the real thing. [7]Another study, of a group of children, found that TV violence increases aggressive behavior. [8]Children who watched violent shows were more willing to hurt another child in games where they were given a choice between helping and hurting. [9]They were also more likely to select toy weapons over other kinds of playthings.

Explanation:

The words that introduce each new supporting detail for the main idea are *One*, *In addition*, and *Another*. When you see these addition words, you realize the studies are all being cited in support of an idea—in this case, that TV violence affects people in negative ways.

That main idea includes the list words "negative ways," which suggest that the supporting details will be a list of negative ways TV violence affects people. In this and many paragraphs, list words and addition words often work hand in hand.

The following chapter, "Supporting Details," includes further practice in the words and phrases that alert you to the main idea and the details that support them. But what you have already learned here will help you find main ideas.

LOCATIONS OF THE MAIN IDEA

Now you know how to recognize a main idea by 1) distinguishing between the general and the specific, 2) identifying the topic of a passage, and 3) using clue words. You are ready to find the main idea no matter where it is located in a paragraph.

A main idea may appear at any point within a paragraph. Very commonly, it shows up at the beginning, as either the first or the second sentence. However, main ideas may also appear further within a paragraph or even at the very end.

Main Idea at the Beginning

Main Idea
Supporting Detail
Supporting Detail
Supporting Detail
Supporting Detail

or

Introductory Detail
Main Idea
Supporting Detail
Supporting Detail
Supporting Detail

In textbooks, it is very common for the main idea to be either the first or the second sentence. See if you can underline the main idea in the following paragraph.

> ¹People tend to cling to their first impressions, even if they are wrong. ²Suppose you mention the name of your new neighbor to a friend. ³"Oh, I know him," your friend replies. ⁴"He seems nice at first, but it's all an act." ⁵Perhaps this appraisal is off-base. ⁶The neighbor may have changed since your friend knew him, or perhaps your friend's judgment is simply unfair. ⁷Whether the judgment is accurate or not, once you accept your friend's evaluation, it will probably influence the way you respond to the neighbor. ⁸You'll look for examples of the insincerity you've heard about, and you'll probably find them. ⁹Even if this neighbor were a saint, you would be likely to interpret his behavior in ways that fit your expectations.

In this paragraph, the main idea is in the *first* sentence. All the following sentences in the paragraph provide a detailed example of how we cling to first impressions.

☑ Check Your Understanding

Now read the following paragraph and see if you can underline its main idea:

> ¹For shy people, simply attending class can be stressful. ²Several strategies, though, can lessen the trauma of attending class for shy people. ³Shy students should time their arrival to coincide with that of most other class members—about two minutes before the class is scheduled to begin. ⁴If they arrive too early, they may be seen sitting alone or, even worse, may actually be forced to talk with another early arrival. ⁵If they arrive late, all eyes will be upon them. ⁶Before heading to class, the shy student should dress in the least conspicuous manner possible—say, in the blue jeans, sweatshirt, and sneakers that 99.9 percent of their classmates wear. ⁷That

way they won't stand out from everyone else. [8]They should take a seat near the back of the room. [9]But they shouldn't sit at the very back, since instructors sometimes make a point of calling on students there.

Explanation:

In the above paragraph, the main idea is stated in the *second* sentence. The first sentence introduces the topic, shy people in class, but it is the idea in the second sentence—several strategies can lessen the trauma of attending class for shy people—that is supported in the rest of the paragraph. So keep in mind that the first sentence may simply introduce or lead into the main idea of a paragraph.

> **Hint:** Very often, a contrast word like *however, but, yet,* or *though* signals the main idea, as in the paragraph you have just read.

Main Idea in the Middle

Introductory Detail
Introductory Detail
Main Idea
Supporting Detail
Supporting Detail

The main idea at times appears in the middle of a paragraph. Here is an example of a paragraph in which the main idea is somewhere in the middle. Try to find it and underline it. Then read the explanation that follows.

[1]A television ad for a new sports car showed scenes of beautiful open country that suggested freedom and adventure. [2]The car never appeared in the ad at all. [3]An ad for a hotel chain showed a romantic couple in bed together. [4]They were obviously on vacation and having a leisurely, romantic, sexy morning. [5]As these ads suggest, advertisers often try to sell products and services by associating them with positive images rather than by providing relevant details about the product or service. [6]An ad giving the car's gas mileage, safety rating, or repair frequency would be more important to a buyer, but it might not draw the viewer's interest as much as beautiful scenery. [7]Similarly, details on the hotel's prices and service would be more informative than images of a glamorous vacation. [8]But the romantic couple gets people's attention and associates the hotel in viewers' minds with a good time.

If you thought the fifth sentence gives the main idea, you were correct. The first four sentences introduce the topic of advertisers and provide specific examples of the main idea. The fifth sentence then presents the writer's main idea, which is that advertisers often try to sell their products by associating them with appealing images rather than with relevant details. The rest of the paragraph continues to develop that idea.

Main Idea at the End

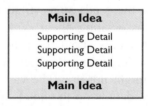

Sometimes all the sentences in a paragraph will lead up to the main idea, which is presented at the end. Here is an example of such a paragraph.

[1]Only about 1 percent of insect species are destructive to crops and property. [2]Nevertheless, this small group causes several billion dollars of damage each year in the United States alone. [3]Harmful insects include household pests, such as termites; crop and livestock pests, such as boll weevils; and hosts of disease-causing organisms, such as mosquitoes infected with parasitic protozoa. [4]Many insects, on the other hand, are beneficial to human society. [5]Some insects pollinate fruit trees, flowers, and many field crops. [6]Bees produce honey and beeswax, silkworms form cocoons from which silk is spun, and lac insects provide the raw material for commercial shellac. [7]Some kinds of insects are natural enemies of destructive insects. [8]For example, the larvae of certain wasps feed on caterpillars that destroy plants. [9]**Clearly, insects are both harmful and beneficial to human society.**

Main Idea at the Beginning and End

At times an author may choose to state the main idea near the beginning of the paragraph and then emphasize it by restating it in other words later in the paragraph. In such cases, the main idea is both at the beginning and the end. Such is the case in the following paragraph.

[1]**An important result of medical advances is an increase in the number of conditions thought to be of medical concern.** [2]In the not-too-distant past, birth and death usually occurred at home. [3]Family members and friends were there or close by. [4]Now most people are born and die in a hospital, surrounded by bright lights and expensive machines. [5]People who were addicted to alcohol or drugs were once considered sinful or lacking in willpower. [6]Now they are considered "sick." [7]Problems that used to be accepted as part of life—baldness, wrinkles, small breasts, sleeplessness—are now deemed proper matters for medical attention. [8]Some criminologists have even defined antisocial behavior as a medical problem. [9]Lawbreakers of all kinds, from the shoplifter to the mass murderer, may potentially be labeled "sick." [10]**Because of current medical knowledge, what were once thought to be problems of life or of character are now considered medical issues.**

Note that the main idea—because of medical advances, more problems are considered medical issues—is expressed in different words in the first and last sentences.

➤ *Practice 8*

The main ideas of the following paragraphs appear at different locations—the beginning, somewhere in the middle, or at the end. Identify each main idea by filling in its sentence number in the space provided.

_____ 1. [1]Many people think of thieves as clever. [2]In reality, thieves can be especially unthinking. [3]One evening, a Los Angeles woman was walking her miniature poodle when a man came up behind her, pushed her to the ground, grabbed the plastic bag she was holding, and drove away. [4]Afterward, when asked about the mugging, the woman cheerfully commented, "I only wish there had been more in the bag." [5]The woman had used the bag when she cleaned up her dog's messes. [6]In Baltimore, an even dumber burglar broke into a house while the woman who lived there was home, ransacked the place, and, having found only $11.50 in cash, demanded that the victim write him a check for $30. [7]When the woman asked to whom she should make the check payable, the thief gave his own name, in full. [8]He was arrested a few hours later. [9]But an Oklahoma thief may have been dumbest of all. [10]Charged with purse-snatching, he decided to act as his own attorney. [11]At his trial, he cross-examined the victim: "Did you get a good look at my face when I took your purse?" [12]Not surprisingly, he was convicted.

_____ 2. [1]At the beginning of the twentieth century, schools treated the sexes very differently. [2]First of all, boys and girls were prepared for different careers. [3]Boys were expected to grow up to be political figures, company presidents, and military leaders. [4]Girls, on the other hand, were expected to be good mothers and obedient wives. [5]Also, boys were encouraged to study courses in math, literature, philosophy, and science. [6]Girls' classes were focused on learning to read and learning proper manners and behaviors—so they could teach their children. [7]A final difference in the treatment of men and women by schools concerned the issue of morality. [8]Schools taught that women were morally superior to men—that they were to be examples of how the rest of society should act and behave.

_____ 3. [1]For 250 million years, reptiles—which appeared on Earth long before the first mammals—have been fighting over territory. [2]Today, human beings do battle over property as well. [3]But the reptiles' way of fighting is generally more civilized and humane than the humans'. [4]Lizards will take a few rushes at one another to test which one is stronger. [5]After a few passes, the loser rolls over on his back to signal defeat. [6]The winner allows him to leave unharmed. [7]Rattlesnakes, similarly, will duel over territory. [8]But they do it with their necks twined together so that they cannot injure each other with their fangs. [9]Humans, of course, generally fight with the intent of injuring one another. [10]The victor often seems to feel he hasn't really won until he's wounded and humiliated his opponent, if not killed him.

_____ 4. [1]If asked to describe ourselves, most of us would not answer that we are mostly water, but that's exactly what we are. [2]A 150-pound person is actually 100 pounds of water and only 50 pounds of everything else. [3]Our blood plasma is 92% water, and our brains are 75% water. [4]We use the expression "dry as a bone," but in fact our bones are not dry at all—they are about 20% water. [5]Our "inner sea" is constantly in motion, flowing through us every moment, bringing food and oxygen to our cells, carrying away wastes, lubricating our joints, cushioning our brains and regulating our temperatures. [6]If the percentage of water in our bodies drops even 1 or 2 percent, we feel thirsty. [7]A drop of 10% is usually fatal. [8]Every day, we lose about two and a half quarts of water. [9]Surprisingly, we replace less than half this lost water through drinking. [10]The rest we replenish with food which, just like us, is mostly water. [11]A tomato, for example, is over 87% water, which is released into the body when we eat it.

_____ 5. [1]Today, as many as one and a half million children are believed to be homeschooled; twenty years ago, only 12,500 students were educated at home. [2]This dramatic increase in the number of homeschooled children can be explained in part by the growth of membership in fundamentalist Christianity, whose members often choose to educate their children at home. [3]While religious motivation is the reason that most families choose homeschooling, it is not the only reason. [4]A number of reasons draw parents to homeschooling. [5]Some parents prefer to educate their children in the security of their own homes away from the dangers of guns and violence in many urban schools today. [6]Other parents believe that homeschooling provides their children a more intimate and nurturing learning environment. [7]Economics can also play a role. [8]One parent can stay home and be a home teacher, saving the high cost of childcare. [9]Finally, motivations can even be negative: sometimes racism, anti-Semitism, or some other hateful reason can cause parents to reject public schooling for homeschooling.

CHAPTER REVIEW

In this chapter, you learned the following:

- Recognizing the main idea is the most important key to good comprehension. The main idea is a general "umbrella" idea under which fits all the specific supporting material of the passage.

- Three strategies that will help you find the main idea are to 1) look for general versus specific ideas; 2) use the topic (the general subject of a selection) to lead you to the main idea; 3) use clue words to lead you to the main idea.

- The main idea often appears at the beginning of a paragraph, though it may appear elsewhere in a paragraph.

The next chapter—Chapter 3—will sharpen your understanding of the specific details that authors use to support and develop their main ideas.

On the Web: If you are using this book in class, you can visit our website for additional practice in recognizing main ideas. Go to **www.townsendpress.com** and click on "Online Exercises."

➤ **Review Test 1**

To review what you've learned in this chapter, answer the following questions by filling in the blank or writing the letter of the correct answer.

1. To become an active reader, you need to think as you read by constantly asking yourself the question, "What is the _____?"

2. One strategy that will help you find the main idea is to look for the _____—the general subject of a selection.

_____ 3. What kind of writing typically provides many topics and subtopics that will help you find main ideas?
   A. Magazines   B. Fiction books   C. Textbooks

4. *Two benefits, three reasons, four steps, five effects* are all examples of _____ that can help you find main ideas.

5. While a main idea may appear at any point within a paragraph, in textbooks it most often appears at the _____.

➤ **Review Test 2**

A. In each of the following groups, one statement is the general point, and the other statements are specific support for the point. Identify each point with a **P** and each statement of support with an **S**.

1. ____ A. Among teenage girls, gossip contributes to bonding.

   ____ B. Political gossip often is leaked to the media as a way of learning how the public is likely to react to a particular policy.

   ____ C. Gossip takes many forms and serves various purposes.

   ____ D. In the business world, gossip can provide insights unavailable through official facts and figures.

2. ___ A. The night before a fox hunt, "earth stoppers" roam the countryside filling in fox holes and other burrows to prevent a hunted fox from escaping underground.

___ B. During the hunt, the fox is pursued—sometimes for hours—by dozens of hounds followed by mounted hunters; a fox caught by hounds is torn apart.

___ C. Many fox hunters practice "blooding," a ritual in which blood from a killed fox is smeared on the cheeks of children attending their first hunt.

___ D. There are good reasons to find fox hunting bizarre and cruel.

B. Each group of statements below includes one topic, one main idea, and two supporting details. In the space provided, label each item with one of the following:

T — for the **topic** of the paragraph
MI — for the **main idea**
SD — for the **supporting details**

Group 1

_____ A. Lack of exercise leads to "older" joints and muscles.

_____ B. Signs of aging.

_____ C. Smoking and spending a great deal of time in the sun lead to wrinkling.

_____ D. Everyday habits can produce signs of aging.

Group 2

_____ A. Electronic tutors, no larger or more costly than today's calculators, will become as commonplace as the radio.

_____ B. Modern technology will change the very nature of our educational system.

_____ C. Technology's effect on education.

_____ D. Portable electronic libraries, half the size of an average book, will be able to hold all the books ever printed.

➤ Review Test 3

The main idea appears at various places in the following paragraphs. Write the number of each main idea in the space provided.

_____ 1. ¹Individuals sometimes develop amazing strengths by uniting to overcome trouble. ²At the end of World War II, for example, a group of six children who had lost their parents, their homeland, and their native language were freed from a concentration camp. ³They were so strongly attached to one another that they refused to be separated even when one became ill with a contagious disease. ⁴In the refugee hostel, they resisted being singled out for treats. ⁵At mealtimes, each made certain the other five had food before eating. ⁶Only after several months had passed and they knew their safety was assured did they show the competitiveness and need for attention normal children do.

_____ 2. ¹Among the tasks of public schools is the teaching of reading, writing, and arithmetic. ²Evidence makes clear, though, that public schools often do not succeed in teaching the basic skills. ³As many as one young adult in three is functionally illiterate—that is, unable to read at an eighth-grade level. ⁴The rate of functional illiteracy among minority youth is even higher than the national average: about 40 percent. ⁵Few seventeen-year-olds can express their thoughts effectively in writing. ⁶Even when their spelling and grammar are adequate, they use short, childlike sentences and cannot organize coherent paragraphs. ⁷And although young adults can perform basic mathematical operations, they have trouble using these operations to solve problems. ⁸Less than half can read a federal income tax table, and just 1 percent can balance a checkbook.

_____ 3. ¹On December 1, 1955, a black seamstress, Mrs. Rosa Parks, boarded the Cleveland Avenue bus in downtown Montgomery, Alabama. ²She was returning home after her regular day's work in Montgomery Fair—a leading department store. ³Tired from long hours on her feet, Mrs. Parks sat down in the first seat behind the section reserved for whites. ⁴Not long after she took her seat, the bus operator ordered her, along with three other black passengers, to move back in order to accommodate boarding white passengers. ⁵By this time every seat in the bus was taken. ⁶This meant that if Mrs. Parks followed the driver's command, she would have to stand while a white male passenger, who had just boarded the bus, would sit. [7]The other three black passengers immediately complied with the driver's request. [8]But Mrs. Parks quietly refused, and she was arrested. [9]The result was a boycott of the city's bus system by the city's black population and the beginning of the civil rights movement of the 1950s and 1960s. [10]Thanks to Rosa Parks, a bus incident in the South became a doorway to greater civil rights.

_____ 4. [1]It is generally believed that geniuses are only born, not created. [2]However, there is evidence that a special upbringing can create geniuses. [3]Take the case of Edith, who finished grammar school in four years, skipped high school, and went straight to college. [4]She graduated from college at age 15 and obtained a doctorate before she was 18. [5]Was she born a genius? [6]Not at all. [7]Her father had seen to it that her days were filled with reading, mathematics, classical music, intellectual discussions, and debates. [8]When she felt like playing, her father told her to play chess with someone like himself, who would be a challenge to her. [9]Another example is a boy named Norbert, who would eventually contribute to the development of computers. [10]He entered college at age 11 and received his Ph.D. from Harvard at 18. [11]According to his father, Norbert was basically an average child who had the advantage of superior training.

_____ 5. [1]After experiencing an extremely shocking event, some people will continue to reexperience it through dreams and recollections. [2]They may even reexperience it through a flashback—the sudden feeling that one is back in the traumatic experience. [3]They may also feel a sense of emotional "numbness," as if their bodies have shut down in order to protect them from further emotional damage. [4]They may avoid any stimuli that remind them of the traumatic event. [5]This collection of symptoms, called posttraumatic stress disorder (PTSD), afflicts people who have experienced any of various seriously damaging experiences. [6]PTSD is best known because of its association with the Vietnam War veterans. [7]But it is also often found in individuals who have been victims of violent crimes such as rape or extreme child abuse. [8]In addition, it may happen to people who have endured natural or man-made disasters, such as earthquakes and airplane crashes.

➤ *Review Test 4*

Here is a chance to apply your understanding of main ideas to a textbook passage. Read the passage below, and then answer the questions that follow on main ideas. There are also vocabulary questions to help you continue practicing the skill of understanding vocabulary in context.

Words to Watch

Below are some words in the reading that do not have strong context support. Each word is followed by the number of the paragraph in which it appears and its meaning there. These words are indicated in the article by a small circle (°).

tangible (1): concrete
afloat (7): out of difficulty
perception (7): judgment
longitudinal survey (7): a study that follows the same people over a period of time

HOW DUAL-EARNER COUPLES COPE

Diane E. Papalia and Sally Wendkos Olds

1   The growing number of marriages in which both husband and wife are gainfully employed presents both opportunities and challenges. A second income raises some families from poverty to middle-income status and makes others affluent. It makes women more independent and gives them a greater share of economic power, and it reduces the pressure on men to be providers; 47 percent of working wives contribute half or more of family income. Less tangible° benefits may include a more equal relationship between husband and wife, better health for both, greater self-esteem for the woman, and a closer relationship between a father and his children.

2   However, this way of life also creates stress. Working couples face extra demands on time and energy, conflicts between work and family, possible rivalry between spouses, and anxiety and guilt about meeting children's needs. Each role makes greater or lesser demands at different times, and partners have to decide which should take priority when. The family is most demanding, especially for women, when there are young children. Careers are especially demanding when a worker is getting established or being promoted. Both kinds of demands frequently occur in young adulthood.

3   Men and women tend to be stressed by different aspects of the work-family situation. Among 314 spouses with relatively high income and education, husbands were more likely to suffer from overload (perhaps because they had not been socialized to deal with domestic as well as occupational responsibilities). Women, on the other hand, were more likely to feel the strain of conflicting role expectations—for example, the need to be

aggressive and competitive at work but compassionate and nurturing at home.

4   Temporary withdrawal from social interaction after a busy workday helped settle men down and softened the effects of overload. "Talking things over" seemed to worsen their stress, perhaps because they were uncomfortable expressing feelings or because the outcome of such discussions might be even greater demands. For both men and women, the most successful way of coping was rethinking the way they looked at the situation.

5   Dual-income couples fall into three patterns: conventional, modern, and role sharing. In a conventional marriage, both partners consider household chores and childcare "women's work." The husband may "help," but his career comes first; he earns more than his wife and sees it as "her choice" to add outside employment to her primary domestic role. In modern couples, the wife does most of the housework, but the husband shares parenting and wants to be involved with his children. In the role-sharing pattern, characteristic of at least one-third of dual-income marriages, both husband and wife are actively involved in household and family responsibilities as well as careers. However, even among such couples, tasks tend to be gender-typed: wives buy the groceries and husbands mow the lawn.

6   Men, on average, earn more and have more powerful positions than women. But in general, the burdens of the dual-earner lifestyle fall most heavily on the woman. Women tend to work more hours—20 percent more in industrialized countries and 30 percent more in less developed countries. Women put in a longer "second shift" at home, as well. Although men's participation has been increasing, even husbands in non-traditional marriages still do only one-third of the domestic work. A Swedish study found that working women with three or more children put in one and a half times as many hours as men at home and on the job. A father is most likely to take on childcare when his work schedule is different from his wife's.

7   Women's personal activities tend to suffer more than men's, probably owing to the disproportionate time they put into domestic work, and in the long run the compromises women make to keep the dual-earner lifestyle afloat° may weaken the marriage. An unequal division of work may have contributed to the higher degree of marital distress reported by wives in a study of three hundred mostly managerial and professional dual-earner couples. On the other hand, unequal roles are not necessarily seen as inequitable; it may be a perception° of unfairness that contributes most to marital instability. A national longitudinal survey° of 3,284 women in two-income families found greater likelihood of divorce the more hours the woman worked, but only when the wife had a nontraditional view of marriage. Nontraditional wives who work full time may feel more resentment of their husbands' failure to share equally in household tasks, whereas traditional wives may be more willing to accept additional burdens.

8   What spouses perceive as fair may depend on how much money the wife's earnings contribute, whether she thinks of herself as someone who supplements her husband's income, and what meaning and importance she and her husband place on her work. Whatever the actual division of labor, couples who agree on that division and who enjoy a more harmonious, caring, involved family life are more satisfied than those who don't.

9   Family-friendly policies in the workplace can help alleviate the strains experienced by dual-earner families. A flexible work environment is one that could include part-time, flextime, and shared jobs. Supportive companies might also provide more at-home work (without loss of fringe benefits), more affordable high-quality childcare, and tax credits or other assistance to let new parents postpone returning to work. One encouraging change is the Family and Medical Leave Act, which requires businesses with fifty or more workers to offer twelve weeks of unpaid leave for the birth or adoption of a child.

Reading Comprehension Questions

Vocabulary in Context

_____ 1. In the sentence below, the word *socialized* (sō′shə-līzd′) means
   A. afraid.
   B. taught through experience.
   C. paid well.
   D. strong enough.

> "Among 314 spouses with relatively high income and education, husbands were more likely to suffer from overload (perhaps because they had not been socialized to deal with domestic as well as occupational responsibilities)." (Paragraph 3)

_____ 2. In the sentence below, the word *conventional* (kən-vĕn′shə-nəl) means
   A. convenient.
   B. happy.
   C. traditional.
   D. modern.

> "In a conventional marriage, both partners consider household chores and childcare 'women's work.'" (Paragraph 5)

_____ 3. In the excerpt below, the word *disproportionate* (dĭs′prə-pôr′shə-nĭt) means
   A. unequal in ratio.
   B. too short.
   C. equal.
   D. late.

> "Women's personal activities tend to suffer more than men's, probably owing to the disproportionate time they put into domestic work . . . " (Paragraph 7)

_____ 4. In the sentence below, the word *inequitable* (ĭn-ĕk′wĭ-tə-bəl) means
  A. fair.
  B. surprising.
  C. ideal.
  D. unequal.

  "On the other hand, unequal roles are not necessarily seen as inequitable; it may be a perception of unfairness that contributes most to marital instability." (Paragraph 7)

Main Ideas

_____ 5. The main idea of paragraphs 1 and 2 is the
  A. first sentence of paragraph 1.
  B. second sentence of paragraph 1.
  C. first sentence of paragraph 2.
  D. last sentence of paragraph 2.

_____ 6. The main idea of paragraph 3 is its
  A. first sentence.
  B. second sentence.
  C. third sentence.

_____ 7. The main idea of paragraph 5 is its
  A. first sentence.
  B. second sentence.
  C. third sentence.
  D. last sentence.

_____ 8. The main idea of paragraph 6 is its
  A. first sentence.
  B. second sentence.
  C. third sentence.
  D. fourth sentence.

_____ 9. The topic of paragraph 9 is
  A. companies that support at-home work.
  B. the strains experienced by dual-earner families.
  C. family-friendly policies in the workplace.
  D. the Family and Medical Leave Act.

_____ 10. The main idea of paragraph 9 is its
  A. first sentence.
  B. second sentence.
  C. third sentence.
  D. last sentence.

Discussion Questions

1. Discuss some of the challenges in a dual-income marriage. Draw upon your own experience if you are married, or use the example of a married couple you know.

2. Discuss some of the benefits in a dual-income marriage. Again, draw upon your own experience if you are married, or use the example of a married couple you know.

3. The author states, "Dual-income couples fall into three patterns: conventional, modern, and role sharing." What view of marriage did your family have as you grew up? How did that view affect your family's lifestyle? If you're married, which view do you and your spouse have?

4. How do you think dual-earner marriages affect children?

Note: Writing assignments for this selection appear on page 628.

Check Your Performance   **MAIN IDEAS**

Activity	Number Right	Points	Score
Review Test 1 (5 items)	_____	× 2 =	_____
Review Test 2 (16 items)	_____	× 2.5 =	_____
Review Test 3 (5 items)	_____	× 4 =	_____
Review Test 4 (10 items)	_____	× 3 =	_____
		TOTAL SCORE =	_____%

Enter your total score into the **Reading Performance Chart: Review Tests** on the inside back cover.

MAIN IDEAS: Mastery Test 1

A. In each of the following groups, one statement is the general point, and the other statements are specific support for the point. Identify each point with a **P** and each statement of support with an **S**.

1. ____ A. One mother created what she called the homework zone—the kitchen table after dinner—where she and her young children did their assignments.

   ____ B. Some adult students have taken classes at a nearby community college during their lunch hour.

   ____ C. Adult students often find creative ways to balance school, employment, and family responsibilities.

   ____ D. By listening to taped lectures in the car, working students turn travel time into learning time.

2. ____ A. By relieving tension, laughing can prevent an angry eruption.

   ____ B. Instead of allowing anger to build, a person should deal with anger-arousing situations as they arise.

   ____ C. Sometimes the best way to deal with particular people or situations that arouse anger is to avoid them as much as possible.

   ____ D. Different coping strategies can help people to curb their anger.

3. ____ A. In ancient Greece, women could not vote or hold public office.

   ____ B. The women of ancient Greece lived under very strict constraints in family and civic life.

   ____ C. A wife in ancient Greece was expected to do little else than bear and raise children and be a housekeeper.

   ____ D. After marriage a woman had no independent standing; she was her husband's responsibility.

(Continues on next page)

B. Each group of statements below includes one topic, one main idea, and two supporting details. In the space provided, label each item with one of the following:

        T — for the **topic** of the paragraph
      MI — for the **main idea**
      SD — for the **supporting details**

Group 1

_____ A. Through its life and death, a tree will serve a variety of important functions.

_____ B. Functions of a tree.

_____ C. While alive, a tree provides food, nesting sites, shade, wind protection, and concealment for wildlife.

_____ D. After a tree begins to die, stored nutrients are released, and it continues to provide protection and food for many forms of plant and animal life.

Group 2

_____ A. In later adulthood, we begin to come to terms with our own mortality.

_____ B. Stages of human development.

_____ C. Adolescence is typically a time of identity crisis.

_____ D. According to psychologists, we pass through various stages of human development throughout our lives.

MAIN IDEAS: Mastery Test 2

A. In each of the following groups—all based on textbook selections—one statement is the general point, and the other statements are specific support for the point. Identify each point with a **P** and each statement of support with an **S**.

1. ____ A. In urban areas, infant mortality is 25 percent higher than the national average.

   ____ B. Urban children face greater risks than other children.

   ____ C. Forty percent of urban children live below the poverty level.

   ____ D. Between 30 and 50 percent of urban children are inadequately immunized.

2. ____ A. Companies that lose lawsuits commonly pass the cost along to consumers.

   ____ B. To protect themselves from malpractice suits, doctors now give more patients unneeded tests, the cost of which totals hundreds of millions of dollars a year.

   ____ C. The cost of fighting a lawsuit forces some small businesses to close, even when they have successfully defended themselves.

   ____ D. The ever-growing number of lawsuits has had a number of negative consequences.

3. ____ A. The introduction of handguns in Europe in the early 1300s had a great impact on road travel.

   ____ B. The handgun allowed fourteenth-century travelers to protect themselves from highwaymen who robbed and assaulted travelers.

   ____ C. In the 1300s, most road travelers (being right-handed) kept their handguns under their left arms, leading to the common practice of keeping to the right side of the road.

   ____ D. Later in the fourteenth century, villages and towns began to hire men who could use handguns to protect travelers on sections of roadway; this practice was the forerunner of modern highway patrols.

(Continues on next page)

B. Each group of statements below includes one topic, one main idea, and two supporting details. In the space provided, label each item with one of the following:

>   **T** — for the **topic** of the paragraph
>   **MI** — for the **main idea**
>   **SD** — for the **supporting details**

Group 1

_____ A. Kinds of power.

_____ B. Force, which the Italian statesman Machiavelli called "the method of beasts," is the use of physical coercion.

_____ C. Influence, the ability to control or affect the behavior of others, is also a form of power.

_____ D. Power, the ability to control or change the behavior of others, takes different forms.

Group 2

_____ A. Adults seek out spicy or bitter foods to stimulate their smaller supply of taste buds.

_____ B. Sensitivity to flavors.

_____ C. The difference in the sensitivity to flavors between children and adults lies in the taste buds, the tiny taste receptors that line the tongue.

_____ D. Young children's tongues are loaded with taste buds and are especially sensitive; therefore, sour or spicy flavors seem too intense to them.

MAIN IDEAS: Mastery Test 3

The main idea may appear at any place within each of the five paragraphs that follow. Write the number of each main idea sentence in the space provided.

_____ 1. [1]Many ancient cultures believed that garlic had magical healing qualities, and it was used for health purposes thousands of years ago in Egypt, Greece, and India. [2]Modern scientists have found that eating garlic really does have several valuable health benefits. [3]Allicin, the same substance that gives garlic its odor, kills bacteria, viruses, and funguses. [4]Cloves of garlic also contain selenium, a nutrient that helps prevent the oxidation in cells which can lead to cancer. [5]Garlic has also been shown to lower blood pressure. [6]It can help reduce the chance of heart attack or stroke by thinning the blood, which prevents clots from forming. [7]And garlic can clear the sinuses and relieve cold symptoms; like commercial decongestants, it thins mucus so sinuses and lungs can flush themselves out more easily.

_____ 2. [1]Police officers complain that many of the criminals they arrest end up very soon on the streets to commit crimes again. [2]Judges argue that because of the technicalities of the law, they are forced to free many defendants, some of whom may be guilty as charged. [3]Government officials lament that they don't have the funds or space to build new prisons. [4]And many citizens charge that the police, the judges, or the government officials are not doing their jobs well. [5]Clearly, the way the huge problem of crime is being handled angers and frustrates many segments of our society.

_____ 3. [1]A century ago, medical practice left much to be desired. [2]In the late 1800s, surgeons still operated with bare hands, wearing the same clothes they had worn on the street. [3]Their shoes carried into the surgery room the debris of the streets and hospital corridors. [4]Spectators were often permitted to observe operations, gathering around the patient within touching distance of the incision. [5]Surgeons used surgical dressings made from pressed sawdust, a waste product from the floors of sawmills. [6]Surgical instruments were washed in soapy water, but not heat-sterilized or chemically disinfected. [7]The mortality rate following operations in many hospitals was as high as 90 percent.

(Continues on next page)

_____ 4. [1]When we speak of a "*close* friend," we usually mean an intimate friend, not a friend who is standing close by. [2]However, according to researchers who study human behavior, there are in fact four "distance zones" in human interaction. [3]Intimate distance is the closest zone, eighteen inches or less. [4]This is the zone of making love, for instance, and also of physical confrontations ("in your face!"). [5]Second is personal distance, eighteen inches to four feet, which is used for everyday conversations with friends. [6]Then there is social distance, four to seven feet, which we use for most interactions with strangers, such as buying something in a store. [7]The fourth zone is public distance, twelve feet or more. [8]A public speaker or a singer at a concert is usually at least twelve feet from the nearest audience members.

_____ 5. [1]Have you ever wondered why products come in the colors they do? [2]For instance, why is toothpaste often green or blue and shampoo often golden-yellow? [3]Manufacturers pick the colors that are associated with qualities consumers value in certain products. [4]For example, it's known that blue symbolizes purity to most people and that green is refreshing. [5]These are both desirable qualities in toothpastes. [6]Manufacturers also know that golden-yellow symbolizes richness (as in real gold or egg yolks), so they frequently choose this color for shampoos and cream rinses—products in which consumers value richness. [7]Baby products, such as body lotion, are often tinted pink because that is a color commonly associated with softness and gentleness—the very qualities consumers want for a baby's care.

MAIN IDEAS: Mastery Test 4

The main idea may appear at any place within each of the five paragraphs that follow. Write the number of each main idea sentence in the space provided.

_____ 1. [1]One writer spent nine hundred hours over the course of eight years watching the action in singles bars and learning about male-female relationships. [2]Although men may think of themselves as the aggressors, says this writer, it is really women who call the shots when a courtship is beginning. [3]He has observed that women are the ones who pick a potential mate out of the crowd. [4]They position themselves near the man they've selected and, with a glance or a smile, invite him to make contact. [5]Similarly, as conversation begins, the woman initiates each increasingly intimate stage. [6]Her continuing eye contact, moving closer, and touching the man all signal her permission for him to make further advances. [7]In most cases, the woman's signals are so subtle that the man is only subconsciously aware of them.

_____ 2. [1]In everyday advertising, one observes many obvious attempts to package and sell products and ideas (toothpaste, aspirin, presidential candidates) through clever influence tactics. [2]Many people claim that such blatant attempts at persuasion are so pitifully obvious that they are not much affected by them. [3]Nevertheless, the sales of Benson & Hedges 100s cigarettes increased sevenfold during a four-year period of heavy advertising. [4]The Mattel Toy Company increased company size twenty-four-fold after it began to advertise extensively on television. [5]Grape-Nuts, a venerable but nearly forgotten cereal, experienced a sudden 30 percent increase in sales when a well-known natural foods enthusiast began plugging this rather bland cereal. [6]And there are many other advertising success stories as well. [7]It appears that tremendous numbers of consumers are influenced by advertising, despite their claims to the contrary.

_____ 3. [1]Pedal error occurs when the driver of an automobile mistakenly presses down on the accelerator instead of the brake pedal. [2]This leads to unintended acceleration, which, in turn, can frequently result in an accident. [3]It seems as though stepping on the wrong pedal would be an unlikely occurrence. [4]However, an analysis of pedal error shows that this mistake is easier to make than you might think. [5]A driver sometimes turns his upper body a little to the left at the same moment that he moves his right foot toward the brake pedal. [6]The driver might turn his upper body to the right to look in the left side mirror or to reach for his seatbelt. [7]Or, if he is in reverse, he might look over his left shoulder to make sure

(Continues on next page)

that it is safe to back up. [8]This turning of the upper body could cause his right foot to move slightly to the right. [9]As he unconsciously moves his foot to the right, he may end up hitting the accelerator rather than the brake. [10]Instead of stopping and remaining stationary, the car in fact begins to accelerate. [11]Believing that his foot is on the brake, the driver presses his foot down harder in an effort to stop the car. [12]Obviously, this action only makes the problem worse. [13]Pedal error is more likely to occur if the driver has just gotten into the car and started it, if the driver is unfamiliar with the car, or if the driver is shorter than average.

_____ 4. [1]Criminal and civil cases, the two types of court cases, differ in significant ways. [2]Criminal cases involve the enforcement of criminal laws, that is, laws against acts such as murder and robbery. [3]The case is brought by a government—a state or the federal government—against someone who is charged with committing a crime. [4]The government, then, is the prosecutor, and the accused is the defendant. [5]The defendant will be found "guilty" or "not guilty," usually by a jury. [6]A civil case involves a legal dispute between individuals and organizations, such as businesses. [7]One party to the case, the plaintiff, has filed a complaint against the other party, the defendant. [8]Civil lawsuits arise, for example, over personal injuries (as in automobile accidents), disagreements about contracts, and—more and more often these days—medical malpractice. [9]There is no verdict of "guilty" or "not guilty" in a civil case; instead, a jury, a judge, or a panel of judges will decide in favor of the plaintiff or the defendant.

_____ 5. [1]The American author Mark Twain is famous for the humor in his writing. [2]His novels, stories, and essays have brought laughter to millions. [3]However, Twain's own life in the sixteen years leading up to his death in 1910 was marked more by sorrow than humor, as he faced several personal tragedies. [4]He had invested a significant amount of money in the development of a mechanical typesetting machine. [5]In 1894 the project failed, and his investment was lost. [6]In addition, a publishing company that he had begun ten years earlier went bankrupt. [7]So at the age of 59, this once-rich man went on a two-year worldwide lecture tour in order to earn money. [8]He took his wife with him on this tour but left his three daughters at home in Hartford, Connecticut. [9]While he was gone, his favorite daughter, Susy, died of meningitis, an inflammation of the brain and spinal cord. [10]Although his wife, Olivia, was ten years younger than he, she had a long history of health problems. [11]In 1903, Twain took his family to live in Italy in hopes that the move would help his ailing wife. [12]Olivia died there in 1904. [13]In December of 1909, just five months before Twain's own death, his daughter Jean died. [14]Only one of his three daughters outlived him.

MAIN IDEAS: Mastery Test 5

The main idea may appear at any place within each of the five paragraphs that follow. Write the number of each main idea sentence in the space provided.

_____ 1. ¹Social scientists have begun to study leaders of work groups. ²Observed in action, group leaders are seen to adopt one of three different styles of leadership. ³One type, the democratic leader, tends to emphasize participation by the individual group members as equals. ⁴Such a leader seeks the opinions of the members so that decisions are made by the group as a whole. ⁵In contrast, the authoritarian leader tends to exert direct control over the group members, procedures, and decision-making. ⁶Authoritarian leaders typically assign tasks to group members. ⁷The third type of leader, the "nonleader," exerts no control or direction at all. ⁸This style can be appropriate in a social group but tends to make a work group ineffective. ⁹As a result, when the designated head of the group is a nonleader, another member may emerge as the actual leader, trying to keep the group on course.

_____ 2. ¹When labor-management disputes are reported on news broadcasts, listeners sometimes think that mediation and arbitration are simply two interchangeable words for the same thing. ²But mediation and arbitration are very different processes, with different outcomes, though both involve the use of a neutral third party. ³In mediation, the third party (called a mediator) is brought in to assist in the negotiations so that the opponents will keep talking to each other. ⁴Mediators can only make suggestions about how to resolve a dispute; neither side is obliged to accept them. ⁵In arbitration, on the other hand, the third party—the arbitrator—is called in to settle the issue, and the arbitrator's decision is final and binding on both sides.

_____ 3. ¹Just as there are rules of the road for drivers of cars, trucks, and buses, there are "rules of the sidewalk" for pedestrians. ²The sociologist Erving Goffman points out that, for one thing, pedestrians on a sidewalk keep to their right, relative to an imaginary dividing line in the middle of the sidewalk. ³Thus people sort themselves into lanes going in opposite directions, as on a vehicular roadway. ⁴And people who are walking slowly often tend to stay closer to the buildings, while to their left, in a "passing lane," are the people who are moving more quickly. ⁵Also, like drivers, pedestrians scan the route ahead so that they can swerve around obstacles—say, a puddle or a hole in the walkway—and so that they will not collide with anyone else. ⁶If a head-on collision

(Continues on next page)

seems possible, pedestrians will make eye contact and maneuver to keep out of each other's way. [7]Goffman notes one obvious difference, though: rules of the road are often codified in laws and regulations, whereas rules of the sidewalk are informal social customs.

_____ 4. [1]The early days of World War I saw the line between patriotism and intolerance blur and disappear. [2]As war hysteria mounted, volunteerism blossomed into an orgy of "100-percent Americanism." [3]Immigrants, aliens, radicals, and pacifists came under suspicion as an urge to force conformity took hold. [4]German Americans naturally became special targets. [5]Local influenza epidemics were blamed on German spies contaminating water supplies. [6]In Iowa the governor made it a crime to speak German in public. [7]Hamburgers were renamed "Salisbury steak"; German measles, "liberty measles." [8]In April 1918 a mob outside of St. Louis seized Robert Praeger, a naturalized German American who had tried to enlist in the navy, bound him in an American flag, and lynched him. [9]After deliberating for twenty-five minutes, a jury found the leaders not guilty.

_____ 5. [1]A biological virus can attach itself to a human host cell and take charge, using the cell's functions to make the substances needed to form new virus particles, which then leave that cell and spread, repeating the process in other cells. [2]Biological viruses cause many diseases—some minor, like the common cold; but some life-threatening, like polio or AIDS. [3]Biological viruses may kill the host cell or make the cell itself malignant, or the virus may set off a dangerously violent response in the immune system. [4]Biological viruses reproduce and spread in various ways, and they may be very hard to treat because they can take forms that the immune system cannot detect. [5]Computer viruses are programs designed to attach themselves to ordinary software, take it over, and then reproduce and spread. [6]A computer virus can do its damage by attacking the startup program, at which point antivirus devices cannot yet detect it; or by attacking the operating system; or by attacking applications such as databases. [7]In any case, the virus can distort or kill computer memory. [8]A computer virus, as the name implies, is very much like a biological virus.

MAIN IDEAS: Mastery Test 6

The main idea may appear at any place within each of the five paragraphs that follow. Write the number of each main idea sentence in the space provided.

_____ 1. [1]An old saying has it that "Many hands make light the work." [2]Thus we might expect that three individuals can pull three times as much as one person and that eight can pull eight times as much. [3]Research reveals that persons individually average 130 pounds of pressure when tugging on a rope. [4]However, in groups of three, they average 351 pounds (only 2.5 times the solo rate); and in groups of eight, only 546 pounds (less than 4 times the solo rate). [5]One explanation is that faulty coordination produces group inefficiency. [6]However, when subjects are blindfolded and believe they are pulling with others, they also slacken their effort. [7]Apparently when we work in groups, we cut down on our efforts, a process termed social loafing.

_____ 2. [1]Recent research has provided techniques for significantly improving short-term and long-term memory. [2]Short-term memory can be improved by rote rehearsal and chunking. [3]Rote rehearsal involves repeatedly going over something in your head, and chunking is a method of organizing long lists into chunks of seven or fewer. [4]Long-term memory can be improved by organizing material for meaningful association. [5]The more associations you can make between new information and information already known, the more likely it is you'll remember the new information. [6]Another organizing technique is mnemonics, or the use of memory-aiding formulas. [7]An example of a mnemonic device is using the acronym HOMES as a clue to recall the names of the five Great Lakes: Huron, Ontario, Michigan, Erie, and Superior.

_____ 3. [1]We tend to think of retail sales as taking place in stores. [2]However, there are various types of *nonstore* retail operations. [3]The latest is home shopping on television channels and online at sites such as amazon.com. [4]A more traditional nonstore retail method is telemarketing. [5]Telemarketing is the sale of goods and services by telephone. [6]Anyone whose number is listed in the phone book is likely to have been called by various salespeople. [7]Mail-order is another nonstore retailing method that continues to be extremely popular. [8]Mail-order firms provide customers with a variety of goods ordered from catalogs and shipped by mail. [9]Many of the most successful mail-order firms are specialty stores, focusing on a narrow range of

(Continues on next page)

merchandise. [10]They include L.L. Bean, The Sharper Image, and Lillian Vernon, to name a few. [11]An additional widely used nonstore retail site is vending machines. [12]For certain types of products, vending machines are an important retail outlet. [13]Soda pop, coffee, candy, and sandwiches are all commonly sold this way.

_____ 4. [1]In his book *Ethics*, Aristotle expressed his moral philosophy, which was concerned with life in this world rather than as a path to otherworldly salvation. [2]Aristotle taught first in his book that the highest good consists in human self-realization, the harmonious functioning of mind and body in the practical and contemplative lives. [3]For most this means exercising reason in practical affairs. [4]Aristotle also taught that in practical affairs, good conduct is virtuous conduct and that virtue resides in aiming for the *golden mean*: for example, courage rather than rashness or cowardice, temperance rather than excessive indulgence or ascetic denial. [5]However, better even than the practical life, Aristotle stated, is the contemplative life, for such a life allows men (he meant males alone) the possibility of exercising their rational capacities to the utmost. [6]He thus believed that philosophers were the happiest of men, though he understood that even they could not engage in contemplation without interruption. [7]He advised them to intersperse their speculative activities with practical life in the real world.

_____ 5. [1]In one tribe in New Guinea, aggression is encouraged in boys from early infancy. [2]The child cannot obtain nourishment from his mother without carrying on a continuous battle with her. [3]Unless he grasps the nipple firmly and sucks vigorously, his mother will withdraw it and stop the feeding. [4]In his frantic effort to get food, the child frequently chokes—an annoyance to both himself and his mother. [5]Thus the feeding situation itself is "characterized by anger and struggle rather than by affection and reassurance" (Mead, 1939). [6]The people of another New Guinea tribe are extremely peaceful and do everything possible to discourage aggression. [7]They regard all instances of aggression as abnormal. [8]A similar tribe—the Tasaday of the Philippines—has been discovered. [9]These people are extremely friendly and gentle. [10]They possess no weapons for fighting or food-gathering; in fact, they are strict vegetarians who live off the land. [11]Evidence of this sort suggests that, rather than being basically aggressive animals, human beings are peaceful or aggressive depending upon their early childhood training.

3

Supporting Details

In Chapter 2 you worked on the most important reading skill—finding the main idea. A closely related reading skill is locating supporting details. Supporting details provide the added information that is needed for you to make sense of a main idea.

This chapter describes supporting details and presents three techniques that will help you take study notes on main ideas and their supporting details: outlining, mapping, and summarizing.

WHAT ARE SUPPORTING DETAILS?

Supporting details are reasons, examples, facts, steps, or other kinds of evidence that explain a main idea. In the paragraph below, three major details support the main idea that the penny should be phased out of our economy. As you read the paragraph, try to identify and check (✓) the three major details.

[1]"A penny saved is a penny earned," the old saying goes. [2]But there are now good reasons for our government to phase the penny out of the economy, allowing the nickel to stand as the lowest-valued coin. [3]For one thing, pennies take up more space than they are worth. [4]We can all recall a time when we needed a nickel, dime, or quarter to make an important phone call, buy a vending machine snack, or make a photocopy, and all we could come up with was a fistful of useless pennies. [5]Pennies are also a nuisance to the business community. [6]According to the National Association of Convenience Stores, 5.5 million hours and 22 million dollars are wasted by businesses on the extra time and effort it takes to handle pennies. [7]Finally, keeping pennies in circulation costs the nation as a whole. [8]The manufacturing, storage, and handling expenses involved in a penny's production and distribution add up to considerably more than the one cent it is worth.

Now see if you can complete the basic outline below that shows the three major details supporting the main idea.

Main idea: Our government should phase the penny out of the economy.

Supporting detail 1: _____

Supporting detail 2: _____

Supporting detail 3: _____

Explanation:

You should have added 1) pennies take up more space than they are worth; 2) pennies are a nuisance to the business community, and 3) pennies cost the nation as a whole. These major supporting details help you fully understand the main idea. To read effectively, then, you must learn to recognize main ideas and the details that support these ideas.

In the paragraph above, the supporting details are *reasons*. Now look at the paragraph below, in which the main idea is explained by a series of *examples*.

¹To protect their self-esteem, some people will practice suppression, which is a deliberate attempt to avoid stressful thoughts. ²For instance, Jeff wants to avoid thinking about an argument he had with his girlfriend, so he spends a lot of time with his buddies playing sports. ³An elderly woman whose husband has died keeps herself busy with chores and volunteer work. ⁴Scarlett O'Hara in the novel and movie *Gone with the Wind* is among the more famous practitioners of suppression. ⁵Remember her line "I shall think about it tomorrow"? ⁶Scarlett was suppressing her unpleasant thoughts.

☑ Check Your Understanding

Put a check (✓) by the number of separate examples given to support the main idea that suppression is a deliberate attempt to avoid stressful thoughts:

___ One example   ___ Two examples   ___ Three examples

Explanation:

There are three supporting examples of what is meant by suppression: 1) Jeff suppresses an argument with his girlfriend by playing sports; 2) an elderly widow keeps herself busy with chores and volunteer work; and 3) Scarlett O'Hara in *Gone with the Wind* suppresses unpleasant thoughts by putting them aside until "tomorrow." The supporting details give the added information we need to clearly understand the main idea.

OUTLINING

Preparing an outline of a passage often helps you understand and see clearly the relationship between a main idea and its supporting details. Outlines start with a main idea (or a heading that summarizes the main idea) followed by supporting details. There are often two levels of supporting details—major and minor. The **major details** explain and develop the main idea. In turn, the **minor details** help fill out and make clear the major details.

Below is the paragraph on TV violence that appeared in Chapter 2. Its supporting details are *factual evidence* found in two studies. Reread the paragraph, and put a check (✓) next to the each of three major supporting details.

[1]Many people feel that violence on television is harmless entertainment. [2]However, we now know that TV violence does affect people in negative ways. [3]One study showed that frequent TV watchers are more fearful and suspicious of others. [4]They try to protect themselves from the outside world with extra locks on the doors, alarm systems, guard dogs, and guns. [5]In addition, that same study showed that heavy TV watchers are less upset about real-life violence than non-TV watchers. [6]It seems that the constant violence they see on TV makes them less sensitive to the real thing. [7]Another study, of a group of children, found that TV violence increases aggressive behavior. [8]Children who watched violent shows were more willing to hurt another child in games where they were given a choice between helping and hurting. [9]They were also more likely to select toy weapons over other kinds of playthings.

☑ *Check Your Understanding*

Now see if you can fill in the missing items in the following outline of the paragraph, which shows both major and minor details.

Main idea: We now know that TV violence does affect people in negative ways.

Major detail: 1. Frequent TV watchers are more fearful and suspicious of others.

  Minor details: Protect themselves with extra locks, alarms, dogs, and guns.

Major detail: 2. _____

  _____

  Minor details: Constant violence on TV makes them less sensitive to the real thing.

Major detail: 3. _____

  Minor details: _____

  _____

Explanation:

You should have added two major supporting details: (2) Heavy TV watchers are less upset about real-life violence than non-TV watchers; (3) TV violence increases aggressive behavior in children. And to the third major supporting detail you should have added the minor detail that children watching violent shows are more likely to choose toy weapons instead of other playthings.

Notice that just as the main idea is more general than its supporting details, major details are more general than minor ones. For instance, the major detail "Frequent TV watchers are more fearful and suspicious of others" is more general than the minor details about people protecting themselves with "extra locks on the doors, alarm systems, guard dogs, and guns," which illustrate the major detail.

Outlining Tips

The following tips will help you prepare outlines:

TIP *Tip 1* **Look for words that tell you a list of details is coming.** Here are some common list words:

List Words

several kinds of	various causes	a few reasons
a number of	a series of	three factors
four steps	among the results	several advantages

For example, look again at the main ideas in two paragraphs already discussed and underline the list words:

- In fact, we now know that TV violence does affect people in negative ways.
- But there are now good reasons for our government to phase the penny out of the economy.

Here the words *negative ways* and *good reasons* each tell us that a list of major details is coming. But you will not always be given such helpful signals that a list of details will follow. For example, there are no list words in the paragraph with this main idea: "To protect their self-esteem, some people will practice suppression, which is a deliberate attempt to avoid stressful thoughts." However, you want to note such list words when they are present as they help you to understand quickly the basic organization of a passage.

Tip 2 **Look for words that signal major details.** Such words are called **addition words**, and they will be explained further on page 172. Here are some common addition words:

Addition Words

one	to begin with	also	further
first (of all)	for one thing	in addition	furthermore
second(ly)	other	next	last (of all)
third(ly)	another	moreover	final(ly)

Check Your Understanding

Now look again at the selection on TV violence on page 95:

1. The word *one* (in *One study*) signals the first major supporting detail.
2. What addition words introduce the second major supporting detail?

   _____

3. What addition word introduces the third major supporting detail?

   _____

And look again at the selection on phasing out the penny on page 93:

1. What words introduce the first major detail? _____
2. What word introduces the second major detail? _____
3. What word introduces the third major detail? _____

Explanation:

In the selection on TV violence, the second major detail is introduced by the words *In addition*, and the third major detail by the word *Another*. In the selection on phasing out the penny, the first major detail is introduced by the words *For one thing*; the second major detail by the word *also*; and the third major detail by the word *Finally*.

 Tip 3 **When making an outline, put all supporting details of equal importance at the same distance from the margin.** In the outline on TV violence on page 95, the three major supporting details all begin at the margin. Likewise, all of the minor supporting details are all indented at the same distance from the margin. You can therefore see at a glance the main idea, the major details, and the minor details.

☑ *Check Your Understanding*

Put appropriate numbers *(1, 2, 3)* and letters *(a, b)* in front of the items in the following outline.

Main idea

___ **Major detail**

   ___ Minor detail

   ___ Minor detail

___ **Major detail**

   ___ Minor detail

   ___ Minor detail

___ **Major detail**

Explanation:

You should have put a *1, 2,* and *3* in front of the major details and an *a* and *b* in front of the minor details. Note that an outline proceeds from the most general to the most specific, from main idea to major details to minor details.

The practice that follows will give you experience in finding major details, in separating major details from minor details, and in preparing outlines.

➢ *Practice 1*

Read and then outline each passage. Begin by writing in the main idea, and then fill in the supporting details. The first outline requires only major details; the second calls for you to add minor details as well.

A.   [1]In view of the overwhelming health problems among the poor, it is important to make massive efforts to prevent such problems. [2]Prevention is usually much less costly than treating these problems later on. [3]There are a few important approaches to take in working to prevent illness among the poor. [4]First of all, there should be a major focus on preventive health services to poor children and their families. [5]Such programs should include immunization schedules, along with parent education on the need for such immunization and help in getting the children to the clinics. [6]The clinics should emphasize dental care, an often neglected service. [7]They should also offer more extensive prenatal care. [8]In addition, society must fight the social conditions of poverty that breed disease. [9]We have to help more low-income people get better housing, free from the rats that bite their babies and the lead paint that poisons their toddlers. [10]We have to help them get better education and better jobs. [11]Only by ending the cycle of poverty, illiteracy, and unemployment are we going to make the promise of medical progress a reality for all our citizens.

Main idea: _____

_____

Major detail: 1. _____

Major detail: 2. _____

Major detail: 3. _____

B.   [1]A crowd is a temporary, relatively unorganized gathering of people. [2]Since a wide range of behavior is covered by the concept, sociologist Herbert Blumer distinguishes among four basic types of crowds. [3]The first, a casual crowd, is a collection of people with little in common except for participating in a common event, such as looking through a department-store window. [4]The second, a conventional crowd, is a number of people who have assembled for some specific purpose, such as attending a baseball game or concert. [5]Members of a conventional crowd typically act in accordance with established norms. [6]The third, an expressive crowd, is a group of people who have gotten together for self-stimulation and personal satisfaction, such as a religious revival or a rock festival. [7]And fourth, an acting crowd is an excited, explosive collection of people, including those who engage in rioting, looting, or other forms of aggressive behavior in which established norms carry little weight.

Main idea: According to sociologist Herbert Blumer, there are _____

_____

Major detail: 1. _____

_____

Minor detail: _____

Major detail: 2. _____

_____

Minor detail: _____

Major detail: 3. _____

_____

Minor detail: _____

Major detail: 4. _____

Minor detail: _____

> *Study Hint:* At times you will want to include minor details in your study notes; at other times, it may not be necessary to do so. If you are taking notes on one or more textbook chapters, use your judgment. It is often best to be aware of minor details but to concentrate on writing down the main ideas and major details.

MAPPING

Students sometimes find it helpful to use maps rather than outlines. **Maps,** or diagrams, are highly visual outlines in which circles, boxes, or other shapes show the relationships between main ideas and supporting details. Each major detail is connected to the main idea, often presented in title form. If minor details are included, each is connected to the major detail it explains.

☑ *Check Your Understanding*

Read the following passage and then see if you can complete the map and the questions that follow.

[1]Weber says that there are three types of authority from which governments gain their right to command. [2]One type of authority is based on tradition. [3]Kings, queens, feudal lords, and tribal chiefs do not need written rules in order to govern. [4]Their authority is based on long-standing customs and is handed down through generations from parent to child. [5]People may also submit to authority because of charisma, the exceptional personal quality of an individual. [6]Such leaders as Napoleon and Gandhi illustrate authority that derives its legitimacy from charismatic personalities. [7]The political systems of industrial states are based largely on a third type of authority: legal authority. [8]These systems derive legitimacy from a set of explicit rules and procedures that spell out the ruler's rights and duties. [9]Typically, the rules and procedures are put in writing. [10]The people grant their obedience to "the law." [11]It specifies procedures by which certain individuals hold offices of power, such as governor or president or prime minister. [12]But the authority is vested in those offices, not in the individuals who temporarily hold the offices.

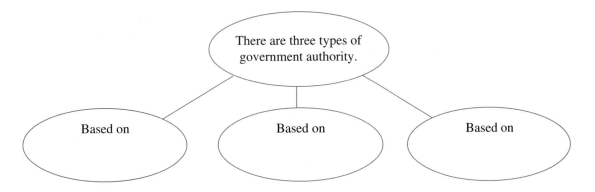

Which word or words introduce:

    1. The first major detail? _____

    2. The second major detail? _____

    3. The third major detail? _____

Explanation:

The map sets off the major details in a very visual way. You see at a glance what Weber's three types of governmental authority are based on: tradition, charisma, and law. The words that introduce the major details are *One*, *also*, and *third*.

➤ Practice 2

Read each passage, and then complete the maps that follow. The main ideas are given so that you can focus on finding the supporting details. The first passage requires only major details. The second passage calls for you to add both major and minor details.

A.   [1]A number of factors have been found to reduce the dissatisfaction often felt by industrial workers. [2]First of all, higher wages give workers a sense of accomplishment apart from the task before them. [3]Also, a shortened workweek has increased the amount of time that people can devote to recreation and leisure, thereby reducing some of the discontent stemming from the workplace. [4]For example, the average industrial worker spent sixty hours a week on the job in 1880, compared with the forty-hour workweek which began in the 1930s. [5]Moreover, numerous studies have shown that positive relationships with coworkers can make a boring job tolerable or even enjoyable. [6]Last of all, unions have given many workers an opportunity to exercise some influence in decision-making.

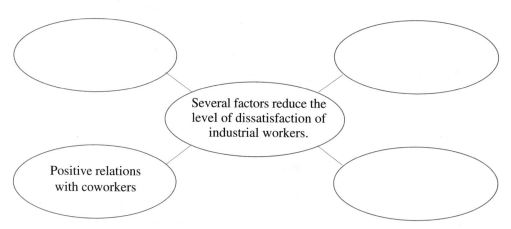

Several factors reduce the level of dissatisfaction of industrial workers.

Positive relations with coworkers

B.   [1]The life of the ocean is divided into distinct realms, each with its own group of creatures that feed upon each other in different ways. [2]There is, first of all, the tidal zone, where land and sea meet. [3]Then comes the realm of the shallow seas around the continents, which goes down to about 500 feet. [4]It is in these first two realms that the vast majority of marine life occurs. [5]Finally, the realm of the deep ocean adds two regions, the zone of light and the zone of perpetual darkness. [6]In the clear waters of the western Pacific, light could still be seen at a depth of 1,000 feet. [7]But for practical purposes the zone of light ends at about 600 feet. [8]Below that level there is too little light to support the growth of the "grass" of the sea—the tiny, single-celled green plants whose ability to form sugar and starch with the aid of sunlight makes them the base of the great food pyramid of the ocean.

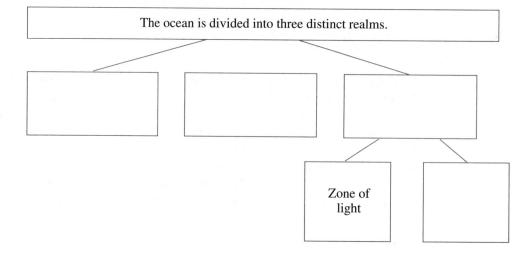

The ocean is divided into three distinct realms.

Zone of light

SUMMARIZING

A **summary** is the reduction of a large amount of information to its most important points. The length and kind of summary will depend upon one's purpose as well as the material in question. Often, a summary will consist of a main idea and its major supporting details. As a general guideline, a paragraph might be reduced to a sentence or two, an article might be reduced to a paragraph, and a textbook chapter might be reduced to about three pages of notes.

One of the most common types of summarizing occurs when you are taking study notes on textbook material. Very often you will find it helpful to summarize examples of key terms. For instance, look at the following textbook passage and the summary that follows.

[1]People under severe stress may react to their problems with **regression**, a return to childlike behavior and defenses. [2]Adults who cry when their arguments fail may expect those around them to react sympathetically, as their parents did when they were children. [3]Other adults may use temper tantrums in a similar way. [4]In both examples, people are drawing on childish behaviors to solve current problems, in the hope that someone will respond to them the way adults did when they were children. [5]Inappropriate as it may seem, such immature and manipulative behavior often works—at least for a while.

Summary:

Regression—a return to childlike behavior and defenses to solve current problems. For example, an adult whose argument fails may cry to get sympathy.

Note that a textbook definition of a key term (such as *regression*) should generally not be summarized, but should be worded in the language chosen by the author. On the other hand, it usually makes sense to summarize the supporting information. Summarizing often involves two steps:

1 *Select* one example from several that might be given. Which example you select is up to you, as long as it makes the term clear for you. In the summary above, the example about losing an argument and crying was chosen to illustrate regression. The other example, about temper tantrums, could have been chosen as well.

2 *Condense* the example if it's not already very brief. Notice that the example about the adult who cries when an argument fails has been condensed from a long sentence to a short one.

A definition of a key term followed by one condensed example is a very useful way to take notes—especially in introductory college courses, where many terms are defined and illustrated.

Study Hint: If you have a textbook chapter to learn, very often you can get what you need by doing two things: 1) writing down the definitions in the chapter and summarized examples of the definitions, and 2) writing down lists of major supporting details and any minor details that you think are important.

Summarizing a Passage

Read the selection below, taken from an introductory textbook for a college social science course. As is often the case in such introductory texts, a new term is presented and then followed by an extended example. Complete the study notes by circling the answer choice that best summarizes that example.

[1]The tendency for members to be so intent on maintaining group agreement that they overlook or put aside the flaws in their decision is called **groupthink**. [2]Once a tentative decision has been made, members withhold information or opinions that might cast doubt on that course of action. [3]They do not want to be seen as criticizing their colleagues or as "rocking the boat." [4]If outside experts raise questions about the wisdom of their decision, members unite in opposing and discrediting the new information. [5]The classic example of "groupthink" occurred during President Kennedy's administration. [6]Kennedy sought the advice of a small group of trusted advisers in deciding whether to support the Bay of Pigs invasion of Cuba in 1961. [7]Although several advisers had strong objections to the plan, not one expressed doubts. [8]As far as Kennedy knew, his advisers were unanimously in favor. [9]The invasion was a military and public relations disaster.

Study notes:

Groupthink—the tendency for members to be so intent on maintaining group agreement that they overlook or put aside the flaws in their decision.

Example—

A. During Kennedy's administration, the Bay of Pigs invasion of Cuba in 1961 was a military and public relations disaster.
B. The classic example occurred during President Kennedy's administration.
C. Kennedy went ahead with the disastrous Bay of Pigs invasion because advisers withheld their objections.

Explanation:

Useful study notes should clearly show how an example illustrates a new term. In the case of the paragraph above, the notes should include the key point that Kennedy's advisers overlooked the flaws in a decision. Only answer C includes the idea that advisers withheld their objections in order to seem unanimously in favor of the Bay of Pigs invasion, which turned out to be a disaster. Answer A tells about the results of the Bay of Pigs invasion, but says nothing about how the advisers withheld their true opinions. Answer B also makes no mention of what the advisers did. It refers to the example so generally that the event isn't even mentioned.

➤ Practice 3

Read each textbook selection below. Then complete the study notes by circling the letter of the answer that best summarizes an example of the term being defined.

A. ¹People are often motivated by the direct object of a desire, such as food or water. ²A **secondary reinforcer** is something one learns to desire through association with other, direct rewards. ³It is referred to as secondary not because it is less important, but because it is learned. ⁴A rat learns to get food by pressing a bar; then a buzzer is sounded every time the rat presses the bar and gets food. ⁵Even if the rat stops getting the food, it will continue to press the bar just to hear the buzzer. ⁶Although the buzzer by itself has no value to the rat, it has become a secondary reinforcer. ⁷For humans, money is a secondary reinforcer. ⁸Money is just paper or metal, but through its association with food, clothing, and other objects of desire, it becomes a powerful reward. ⁹Children come to value money only after they learn that it will buy such things as candy, something that has direct value to them. ¹⁰Then the money becomes a secondary reinforcer, something they have learned to want.

Study notes:

Secondary reinforcer—something one learns to desire through association with other, direct rewards

Example—

A. People are motivated by the direct objects of their desires, such as food, water, clothing, and candy.
B. Money is desired not for its own sake but because of its association with direct rewards of desire.
C. After a rat learns to get food by pressing a bar, a buzzer is sounded every time the rat presses the bar to get food.

B. ¹According to one sociologist, virtually every organization includes "higher participants" (such as the administrators) and "lower participants" (the rank and file). ²**Coercive organizations** are among the most common types of organizations. ³Prisons, concentration camps, and custodial mental hospitals are examples of coercive organizations. ⁴In each, force or the threat of force is used to achieve the organization's main goal: keeping the inmates in. ⁵The inmates obviously do not enjoy being imprisoned; they will run away if they have the chance. [6]They are alienated from the organization and do not support its goals at all. [7]Understandably, the higher participants—such as prison administrators—have to act tough toward the inmates, seeking compliance by threatening solitary confinement if they try to escape. [8]In brief, in this kind of organization, coercion, or force, is the main form of power used, and the involvement by lower participants is alienative.

Study notes:

Coercive organizations—organizations in which force or the threat of force is used to achieve the main goal: keeping in inmates, who are alienated from the organization

Example—

A. Every organization includes "higher participants" (such as administrators) and "lower participants" (rank and file).
B. In coercive organizations, force is the main form of power used, and the involvement by lower participants is alienative.
C. In a prison, inmates will run away if they can, and the administrators seek obedience by threatening solitary confinement.

➤ Practice 4

Read each textbook selection below. Then take study notes by 1) writing down the key term and its definition, 2) selecting an example that makes the definition clear, and 3) writing that example in your notes, condensing it if possible.

A. [1]A **Pyrrhic victory** is a victory won at enormous cost. [2]A good example of such a victory is provided by the person whose name the term comes from: Pyrrhus, a Greek mercenary general who invaded Italy and attacked the Romans in 281 B.C. [3]Pyrrhus defeated the Roman army sent against him, but his own army suffered terrible losses. [4]"One more such victory and I am ruined," he exclaimed. [5]The Battle of Borodino in 1812 was another classic instance of a Pyrrhic victory. [6]Napoleon's invading French army defeated a defending Russian army near Moscow and occupied the city. [7]But the French suffered so greatly from the battle and the winter that followed that the invasion turned into a disaster that cost Napoleon his throne.

Study notes:

A Pyrrhic victory—_____

Example—_____

_____

B. [1]The historic distinction between cities and rural areas is eroding in many Western societies. [2]In many cases, the rural spaces between metropolitan centers have filled with urban development, making a "strip city," or **megalopolis**. [3]The northeastern seaboard is a good illustration of such a strip city. [4]A gigantic megalopolis lies along a six-hundred-mile axis from southern New Hampshire to northern Virginia, encompassing 10 states, 117 counties, 32 cities larger than 500,000 people, and embracing nearly a fifth of the United States population. [5]Urban projections suggest that by the year 2050, if not sooner, another urbanized strip will extend from New York State through Pennsylvania, Ohio, northern Indiana, and Illinois to Green Bay, Wisconsin, and Minneapolis-St. Paul.

Study notes:

_____—_____

_____

Example—_____

_____

A Final Note

This chapter has centered on supporting details as they appear in well-organized paragraphs. But keep in mind that supporting details are part of readings of any length, including selections that may not have an easy-to-follow list of one major detail after another. Starting with the reading at the end of this chapter (page 113), you will be given practice in answering all kinds of questions about key supporting details. These questions will develop your ability to pay close, careful attention to what you are reading.

CHAPTER REVIEW

In this chapter, you learned the following:

- Major and minor details provide the added information you need to make sense of a main idea.

- List words and addition words can help you to find major and minor supporting details.

- Outlining, mapping, and summarizing are useful note-taking strategies.

- Outlines show the relationship between the main idea, major details, and minor details of a passage.

- Maps are very visual outlines.

- Writing a definition and summarizing an example is a good way to take notes on a new term.

The next chapter—Chapter 4—will show you how to find implied main ideas and central points.

On the Web: If you are using this book in class, you can visit our website for additional practice in identifying supporting details. Go to **www.townsendpress.com** and click on "Online Exercises."

➤ Review Test 1

To review what you've learned in this chapter, answer each of these questions about supporting details by filling in the blank.

1. Two key reading skills that go hand in hand are finding the main idea and identifying the major and minor _____ that support the main idea.

2. **List words**—words such as *several kinds of, four steps, three factors,* and *four reasons*—are important words to note because they alert you that a list of _____ is coming.

3. A traditional outline shows at a glance the relationship between _____ and supporting details; it is a very helpful way to take textbook study notes.

4. Another good way to take study notes is to use a _____— a highly visual outline that uses circles, boxes, and other shapes to set off main ideas and supporting details.

5. Very often textbook study notes will include definitions of key terms and summaries of _____ that make those key terms clear and understandable.

➤ Review Test 2

A. Answer the supporting-detail questions that follow the passage. Note that the main idea is boldfaced.

[1]In the United States, people moved to the suburbs for a variety of reasons. [2]**Peter H. Rossi divided the causes for moving to suburbia into two categories.** [3]One category is what Rossi called "push" factors. [4]Persons were pushed toward the suburbs by the difficulties associated with life in central cities—crime, pollution, overcrowding, and the like. [5]Rossi's second category of reasons for moving to suburbia was "pull" factors. [6]At the same time that people were trying to escape the difficulties of city life, they were pulled toward suburbia by a desire to live in smaller communities, to own their own homes and gardens, to find better schools for their children, or simply to enjoy the status linked to life in an affluent suburb.

_____ 1. In general, the major details of the paragraph are
   A. the things that pushed people to suburbia.
   B. Rossi's two categories of causes for people moving to the suburbs.
   C. the reasons people prefer to live in smaller communities and own their own homes and gardens.

_____ 2. Specifically, the major details of the paragraph are
   A. push factors and pull factors.
   B. suburbs and cities.
   C. difficulties associated with life in central cities.

3. What addition word introduces the first major detail? _____

4. *Fill in the blank:* What is one specific difficulty mentioned that pushed people away from the cities? (The answer is a minor detail.)

   _____

5. *Fill in the blank:* What is one specific attraction of the suburbs? (The answer is a minor detail.)

   _____

B. (6–9.) Map the following passage by filling in the main idea and the major supporting details.

> [1]Functional illiteracy—the inability to read and write well enough to carry out everyday activities—is a complex social problem that stems from several sources. [2]One source of the problem is our educational system. [3]Our schools are too quick to pass children from one grade to the next even when their learning is woefully deficient. [4]The community also contributes to functional illiteracy. [5]Local businesses and agencies, indifferent to education, do not work with schools toward improving children's motivation and learning. [6]Another source is the home. [7]Millions of children grow up with illiterate parents who do not give them the opportunity or encouragement to learn language skills.

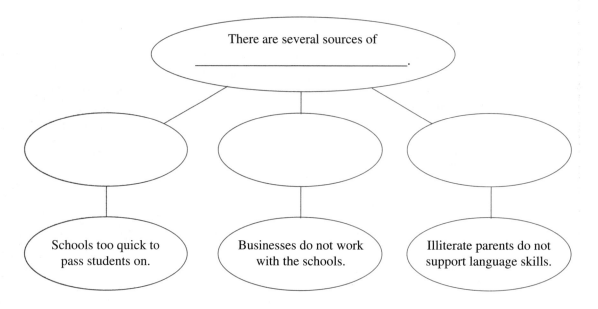

There are several sources of

_____ .

| Schools too quick to pass students on. | Businesses do not work with the schools. | Illiterate parents do not support language skills. |

10. What addition word introduces the final major detail? _____

➤ *Review Test 3*

A. (1–5.) Outline the following passage by completing the main idea and filling in the missing major and minor supporting details.

> [1]Advertisers must consider the various benefits and drawbacks of the mediums available to them. [2]A brief look at television reveals that it has some key advantages and disadvantages to advertisers. [3]The most important of television's advantages is the ability to reach a mass audience. [4]In addition, this is done with the powerful combination of sight and sound— more effective than if consumers were only to see the ad or only to hear it. [5]Also, advertisers can aim their messages at the most likely customers. [6]For example, they can purchase network time to advertise widely available products or local time for local products and services. [7]Or they can buy time on specific types of programs. [8]Thus a kitchen appliance company might advertise on cooking shows. [9]A disadvantage of TV advertising is that the large number of ads takes away from each ad's impact. [10]Also, television ads are extremely expensive. [11]Creating a TV commercial costs at least $125,000, and showing it on popular prime-time shows costs at least double that amount. [12]Finally, the wide use of video recorders means that many viewers can watch prerecorded shows and bypass the commercials.

Main idea: Television has key advantages and _____

_____

1. _____

   a. _____

   b. Powerful combination of sight and sound

   c. Ability to aim messages at most likely customers

      1) Network time for widely available products

      2) Local time for local products and services

      3) Matching of products to types of program

2. _____

   a. Weakening of ad's impact by large number of ads

   b. Great expense in creating and showing an ad

   c. _____

B. (6–9.) Map the following passage by filling in the main idea and the missing major supporting details.

> ¹There are a few differing theoretical points of view on television violence. ²Supporters of the catharsis theory contend that viewing scenes of aggression helps to purge the viewers' own aggressive feelings. ³In other words, experiencing violence indirectly may make the individual less likely to commit a violent act. ⁴In contrast, the supporters of the stimulation theory maintain that seeing scenes of violence helps to stimulate an individual to behave more violently. ⁵The last group, the supporters of the null theory, maintain that fictionalized violence has no influence on real violence.

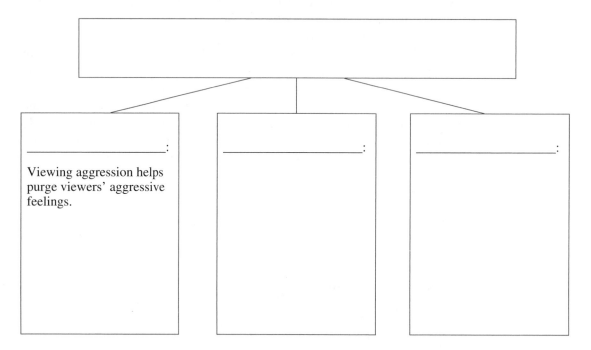

C. (10.) Read the textbook selection below. Then complete the study notes by circling the letter of the answer choice that best summarizes the example of the term being defined.

> ¹Some animals exhibit **warning coloration**, bright coloring that protects the animals by warning predators of a distasteful and often poisonous meal. ²Since poisoning your predator is little comfort if you have already been eaten, the bright colors declare: "Eat me at your own risk." ³After a single unpleasant experience, predators avoid these conspicuous prey. ⁴For instance, a toad who tries to eat a yellow and black bee and gets stung will avoid brightly colored bees in the future. ⁵A bird that eats the distasteful, colorful monarch butterfly will no longer be tempted to dine on monarchs.

Study notes:

Warning coloration—the bright coloring sometimes shared by different species that effectively warns predators of a distasteful and often poisonous meal.

Example—

A. Since poisoning your predator is little comfort if you're eaten, the bright colors warn your predator beforehand.
B. After being stung when trying to eat a bee, a toad will avoid brightly colored bees.
C. Different species of dangerous animals have similar warning coloration, such as the bee.

➤ Review Test 4

How important to an infant's basic development is the care it receives? This question is addressed in the following selection from the college textbook *Psychology*, by Mary M. Gergen and others (Harcourt Brace Jovanovich). Read the passage and then answer the supporting-detail questions that follow.

To help you continue to strengthen your work on the skills taught in previous chapters, there are also questions on vocabulary in context and main ideas.

Words to Watch

Below are some words in the reading that do not have strong context support. Each word is followed by the number of the paragraph in which it appears and its meaning there. These words are indicated in the article by a small circle (°).

innate (3): inborn
mutually (3): in a manner in which giving and receiving are equal
reinforcer (4): reward causing a positive response
reciprocated (9): returned

BABY LOVE

Mary M. Gergen et al.

1 At the base of an infant's social life is its first experience of love. During the first two years, infants normally acquire a basic sense of attachment. By **attachment**, we mean a feeling of dependence, trust, and the desire to be physically close to the major caregiver, usually the mother. Developmentalists such as Erik Erikson believe that the basic trust formed during this period provides the foundation for all other social and emotional development.

We do not know how quickly infants 2 develop attachment. Psychologists had once believed that infants in the first few weeks of life were not yet able to distinguish their mother from other people, but recent research indicates that they are able to. By six months or so, they have clearly developed attachment. One indication of this is that many infants will cry if their mothers disappear from sight. Also, children often will show fear and distress in the presence of a stranger. The presence of a caretaker will soothe them.

3   What is the basis of the infant's attachment to its mother? Some learning theorists believe that the attachment between mother and child develops because of the child's ability to cry and smile. Crying and smiling are innate° responses in infants; these responses reflect the child's need states, which the child communicates in a primitive way to parents. The child cries when in distress, and the parent relieves the distress. At this point, the child smiles (which in a sense rewards the parent's actions). The behaviors of parents and infants are *mutually° reinforcing*—the infant provides smiles and the parent provides food and care—so both parties become attached.

4   For some time psychologists thought that the nourishment provided by the parent was the principal reinforcer° for infants, but research suggests that the physical comfort provided by parents may be even more important. Harry and Margaret Harlow conducted several experiments on infant monkeys who were separated from their mothers at birth and reared with *surrogate,* or substitute, mothers. In some cases, the surrogate mother was made of wire with a wooden block for a head. This was not a very cozy mother to cuddle up to. In other cases, the surrogate mother had a soft, cuddly, terry-cloth body. In one experiment, the infant monkeys were raised in a cage with both the terry-cloth "mother" and the wire "mother." However, only the wire mother was equipped with a milk bottle, so nourishment came from the wire mother alone.

5   The Harlows and their associates observed the behavior of the infants and discovered an important tendency. The infant monkey had become attached to the terry-cloth mother, even though the wire mother provided the food. If an infant monkey was frightened (by sounds, lights, or a new object), it would seek the security of the terry-cloth mother. It would feed from the wire mother's bottle, but it spent most of its time with the cloth-covered mother. Also, when an infant monkey proceeded to investigate the cage, it would keep one foot on the terry-cloth mother and would return and cling to this surrogate mother whenever frightened. These results suggest that *contact comfort* is in many ways more important for attachment than nourishment.

6   Even though the terry-cloth mothers provided the infant monkeys with security, these monkeys did not develop into normal adults. While they were less disturbed than monkeys raised only with wire mothers, as adults they exhibited disturbed behavior. They constantly rocked, sucked on themselves, and behaved in an aggressive manner when released into a group of monkeys. This behavior lasted through their adult lives.

7   Obviously, the terry-cloth and wire mothers were not enough. Attachment to real monkeys seemed important for the young monkeys to develop into proper adults. But need the mother be present for this to occur? Harry Harlow looked at this question as well. He found that infant monkeys that were separated from their mothers and raised with other infants showed more clinging behavior and tended to be more timid as adults than normally reared monkeys. These infants showed some negative effects of being raised without a mother, but they were not so badly affected as infants who

were raised completely isolated from other monkeys.

8   Of course, you may have doubts about generalizing to humans from experiments with monkeys. This is a reasonable doubt. But we should note that apes and monkeys are our closest nonhuman relatives. Thus, we may suspect that some similarities might exist. Also, studies of children brought up in orphanages show that those who are not given the opportunity to form strong attachments to caregivers suffer from social and emotional difficulties.

9   Harlow also tested whether or not the effects of early isolation could be reversed. In one study, he placed young monkeys who had not been isolated with older monkeys that had been isolated. The younger monkeys showed a lot of clinging behavior, and very little aggressive behavior. The usual response of the younger monkeys was to cling and attach themselves to the older monkeys. Over time, the isolates reciprocated° this behavior, and after six months the isolates behaved much like the younger monkeys. The younger monkeys apparently provided nonthreatening models to the isolates.

10   Studies of young children in orphanages have shown that giving loving attention and care to formerly neglected babies improves their lives significantly. Listless, dull babies became lively, normal youngsters when they were lovingly cared for. In one study, the children who did not receive loving care became mentally retarded and remained institutionalized all of their lives, while the others who were cared for developed into normal adults living in the community. We should point out that this series of studies merely observed some orphanages; it was not an experiment. It would appear that the effects of the early experience of isolation may be correctable. Recently, a review of twenty studies on early separation of mothers from their children indicated that children do not usually suffer permanent harm from this experience. What seems to matter is that someone give loving care to the infants.

11   We have emphasized attachment to the principal caretaker, but typically by one year of age children extend their attachments to others, such as the father, grandparents, and other caretakers. Also at this time the fear of strangers, which peaks around eight months, begins to decrease, and will be reduced markedly by the time the child is eighteen months old. The attachment to others provides the foundation for future social relationships.

Reading Comprehension Questions

Vocabulary in Context

_____ 1. In the sentence below, the word *listless* (lĭst´lĭs) means
   A. well-cared for.
   B. tall.
   C. bright.
   D. inactive.

"Listless, dull babies became lively, normal youngsters when they were lovingly cared for." (Paragraph 10)

_____ 2. In the excerpt below, the word *markedly* (mär′kĭd-lē) means
A. not at all.
B. very noticeably.
C. only rarely.
D. unfortunately.

"... at this time the fear of strangers ... begins to decrease, and will be reduced markedly by the time the child is eighteen months old." (Paragraph 11)

Main Ideas

_____ 3. The main idea of paragraph 3 is expressed in the
A. first sentence of the paragraph.
B. second sentence of the paragraph.
c. third sentence of the paragraph.

_____ 4. The main idea of paragraphs 4 and 5 is expressed in the
A. last sentence of paragraph 3.
B. first sentence of paragraph 4 and the last sentence of paragraph 5.
C. second sentence of paragraph 4 and the first sentence of paragraph 5.

Supporting Details

_____ 5. The authors define *attachment* as
A. dependence, trust, and desire to be close to the major caregiver.
B. a parent's feeling for his or her child.
C. children's fear in the presence of a stranger or strangers.
D. the negative effects of early isolation.

_____ 6. Some learning theorists believe that infants and mothers form attachments to each other
A. in all situations.
B. because their behaviors reinforce one another.
C. because the mother provides smiles.
D. when the child is in distress.

_____ 7. In forming an attachment,
A. touch appears to be more important than food.
B. isolation is best.
C. monkeys prefer wire mothers over terry-cloth mothers.
D. food appears to be more important than touch.

8–10. Add the details missing in the following partial outline of the reading. Do so by filling in each blank with the letter of one of the sentences in the box below.

Details Missing from the Outline

> A. Monkey and human studies show that it's possible to overcome the negative effects of previous isolation or neglect.
> B. Studies of young children in orphanages have shown that loving attention and care can greatly improve the lives of previously neglected children.
> C. Experiments in which surrogate, nonliving mothers were provided for isolated monkeys suggest that for attachment, contact comfort is more important than nourishment.

Central point: Psychologists' experiments and studies suggest much about the development of infants and young children.

A. The Harlows' experiments with monkeys suggest important conclusions about how attachments are formed.

　　1. _____

　　2. Experiments showed that there are fewer but still some negative effects in being raised without a mother but with other infant monkeys.

B. _____

　　1. When Harlow placed previously isolated older monkeys with young normal monkeys, the isolates' behavior became much like that of the normal monkeys.

　　2. _____

　　3. A review of twenty studies on early separation of mothers and children indicates that the negative effects of such separation can be overcome with loving care.

Discussion Questions

1. Think about the babies you've known or know now. Who was the person each first formed an attachment to? In what ways could you observe that attachment?

2. What does the Harlows' experiment with a terry-cloth "mother" teach us about childcare?

3. If you were the head of an orphanage, how might you use the information in "Baby Love" to benefit the children?

4. The authors write, "You may have doubts about generalizing to humans from experiments with monkeys." Then they go on to present two reasons why they feel the experiments on monkeys raise issues important to humans. Explain these reasons. Do you think they are good reasons? Why or why not?

Note: Writing assignments for this selection appear on page 628.

Note: Writing assignments for this selection appear on page 628.

Check Your Performance	SUPPORTING DETAILS		
Activity	*Number Right*	*Points*	*Score*
Review Test 1 (5 items)	_____	× 2 =	_____
Review Test 2 (10 items)	_____	× 3 =	_____
Review Test 3 (10 items)	_____	× 3 =	_____
Review Test 4 (10 items)	_____	× 3 =	_____
		TOTAL SCORE =	_____ %

Enter your total score into the **Reading Performance Chart: Review Tests** on the inside back cover.

SUPPORTING DETAILS: Mastery Test 1

A. Answer the supporting-detail questions that follow the textbook passage.

> ¹People who have no or low self-control share common traits. ²First, they seem to have an unwillingness or inability to defer gratification. ³Given a choice between getting five dollars today or fifteen dollars if they wait sixty days, they'll take the five dollars today. ⁴They also get immediate gratification when the thrill of risk is immediate. ⁵They consider committing risky criminal acts to be exciting and thrilling. ⁶People with weak self-control get immediate gratification through behavior that is not illegal, too— smoking, drinking, gambling, and engaging in unprotected sex with strangers. ⁷Second, they lack diligence, tenacity, and persistence in a course of action. ⁸They prefer actions that are simple and easy, such as getting money without working or obtaining sex without establishing a relationship. ⁹They tend to have poor work records, high rates of absenteeism when employed, unstable marital and family relationships, and other problems caused by an unwillingness to "work" at life. ¹⁰At school, they usually learn little and quit early. ¹¹They lack all skills that require practice and training— they won't know how to fix a car or play a trumpet. ¹²Finally, people with a lack of self-control are selfish. ¹³Self-centered, indifferent, and insensitive to the suffering and needs of others, they impose loss and suffering on others. ¹⁴They wreak havoc on all in their path without a qualm.

_____ 1. The first sentence provides
    A. the main idea.
    B. a major detail.
    C. a minor detail.

_____ 2. Sentences 3 to 6 provide
    A. the main idea.
    B. major details.
    C. minor details.

_____ 3. Sentence 7 provides
    A. the main idea.
    B. a major detail.
    C. a minor detail.

_____ 4. How many major supporting details does the paragraph include?
    A. Two
    B. Three
    C. Four
    D. Five

(Continues on next page)

B. (5–10.) Complete the outline of the following textbook passage by adding the main idea and the missing major or minor details.

> [1]Why do people seem so preoccupied with money—even those who already have plenty of it? [2]There are several explanations for why money is such a priority for people besides the obvious financial concerns. [3]The first reason is that money is a traditional reward in Western culture. [4]Our society raises us with the expectation that we will receive money for work. [5]Also, we are raised with the idea of receiving money as a reward for achievements such as a strong report card, success in a competition, or even turning one year older. [6]A second explanation for the importance of money is that it is tangible. [7]Unlike a boss's praise or a job promotion, money can be held and counted. [8]It can also be seen and appreciated by others. [9]A final reason for money's appeal is that it is symbolic. [10]For many people, money is a measure of self-worth as well as a way of keeping score on how successful they are in competing with others.

Main idea: _____

_____

Major detail: **1.** _____

Minor details: a. Reward for work

                     b. _____

                     _____

Major detail: **2.** _____

Minor details: a. Can be held and counted

                     b. Can be seen and appreciated by others

Major detail: **3.** _____

Minor details: a. _____

                     b. Way of keeping score in competition with others

SUPPORTING DETAILS: Mastery Test 2

A. Answer the supporting-detail questions that follow the textbook passage.

¹All speakers have several vocal characteristics. ²Pitch refers to the highness or lowness of your voice. ³Fortunately, most people speak at a pitch that is about right for them, although a few persons talk using notes that are too high or too low for their voice. ⁴The volume or loudness of your voice is another vocal characteristic. ⁵Each person, regardless of size, can make his or her voice louder. ⁶If you have trouble talking loudly enough to be heard in a large classroom, work on increasing pressure from the abdominal area on exhalation. ⁷The rate of speech of our voice is the speed at which we talk. ⁸Although most of us utter between 140 and 180 words per minute, the optimal rate is a highly individual matter. ⁹The test of rate is whether listeners can understand what you are saying. ¹⁰The tone, the timbre, or the sound of your voice is known as its quality. ¹¹The best vocal quality is a clear, pleasant-to-listen-to voice. ¹²Problems of quality include nasality (too much resonance in the nose on vowel sounds), breathiness (too much air escaping during phonation), harshness (too much tension in the throat and chest), and hoarseness (a raspy sound to the voice).

_____ 1. In general, the major details of this paragraph are
   A. sounds.
   B. types of voices.
   C. pitches of voices.
   D. vocal characteristics.

_____ 2. Specifically, the major details of the paragraph are
   A. sound and voices.
   B. pitches that are about right, too high, and too low.
   C. pitch, volume, rate of speech, quality.
   D. tone, timbre, sound, and quality of the voice.

_____ 3. Sentence 1 provides
   A. the main idea.
   B. a major detail.
   C. a minor detail.

_____ 4. Sentence 4 provides
   A. the main idea.
   B. a major detail.
   C. a minor detail.

(Continues on next page)

_____ 5. Sentence 8 provides
    A. the main idea.
    B. a major detail.
    C. a minor detail.

6. *Fill in the blank:* One problem of voice _____ is harshness.

B. (7–10.) Complete the outline of the following textbook passage by filling in the missing supporting details.

> [1]There are two main forms of survey, and each has its own advantages. [2]One type of survey is the interview. [3]An interview can obtain a high response rate because people find it more difficult to turn down a personal request for an interview than to throw away a written questionnaire. [4]In addition, a skillful interviewer can go beyond written questions and probe for a subject's underlying feelings and reasons. [5]Questionnaires, the second main form of survey, also have two advantages. [6]They are cheaper than interviews, especially when large samples are used. [7]Moreover, since the questions are written, the researcher knows that there is a guarantee of consistency, whereas five interviewers can ask the same question in five different ways.

Main idea: There are two main forms of survey, and each has its own advantages.

1. _____

    a. _____

       _____

    b. Can go beyond written questions

2. _____

    a. _____

       _____

    b. Guarantee of consistency (since questions are written)

SUPPORTING DETAILS: Mastery Test 3

A. Answer the supporting-detail questions that follow the textbook passage.

[1]More has been written on the fall of Rome than on the death of any other civilization. [2]While scholars are still debating this issue today, most agree that a number of factors led to Rome's demise at the hands of Germanic attackers in 476 A.D. [3]First, Rome was vulnerable to outside attackers because of internal political instability. [4]The Roman constitution did not have a clear law of succession. [5]As a result, each time a ruler died, civil war would break out—killing thousands and causing great political struggle. [6]Another factor that made Rome ripe for conquest was severe economic turmoil. [7]Rome's economy relied heavily upon slave labor. [8]However, years of harsh work and poor living conditions reduced the population of Rome's slaves. [9]Fewer slaves working on farms meant that the empire had fewer goods for trade and less food for its citizens. [10]Rome was also weakened by a lack of manpower. [11]The empire's long borders required more soldiers than were available to protect it from attack. [12]In addition, the need for soldiers abroad meant that there were fewer people to keep peace and order within the empire.

_____ 1. The main idea is expressed in sentence
    A. 1.
    B. 2.
    C. 4.
    D. 12.

_____ 2. The major supporting details of this paragraph are
    A. events.
    B. effects.
    C. theories.
    D. factors.

_____ 3. The second major detail of the paragraph is introduced in sentence
    A. 2.
    B. 4.
    C. 6.
    D. 8.

_____ 4. The third major detail of the paragraph is introduced in sentence
    A. 7.
    B. 8.
    C. 9.
    D. 10.

(Continues on next page)

_____ 5. The last major detail is signaled with the addition word(s)
   A. *first.*
   B. *another.*
   C. *also.*
   D. *in addition.*

B. (6–10.) Complete the map of the following textbook passage by filling in the missing major supporting details.

> [1]A good many factors influence whether a situation is seen as too crowded. [2]Duration is one factor. [3]For instance, people typically find it easier to tolerate a brief exposure to high-density conditions such as a ride on a crowded elevator than prolonged exposure on a cross-country bus. [4]A second factor is predictability. [5]People typically find crowded settings even more stressful when they are unable to predict them. [6]A third factor has to do with frame of mind. [7]There are times when individuals welcome solitude and other times when they prefer the presence of others. [8]A fourth factor involves the environmental setting. [9]People generally report that they can tolerate crowding better in impersonal settings such as a shopping center or an airline terminal than in a home or apartment. [10]Finally, people's attitude toward a situation determines how they feel about crowding. [11]If people are fearful and antagonistic—or excited and friendly—crowding tends to intensify the feelings. [12]Crowding makes a doctor's waiting room and a subway car all the more unpleasant, whereas it makes a football game and a party all the more enjoyable. [13]And even though a crowded New York subway car turns people off, a crowded San Francisco cable car, crammed with people hanging over the sides, is defined as a "tourist attraction."

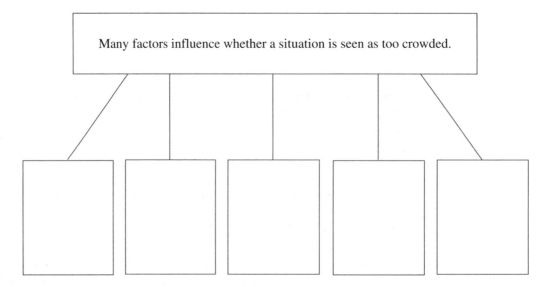

Many factors influence whether a situation is seen as too crowded.

SUPPORTING DETAILS: Mastery Test 4

A. Answer the supporting-detail questions that follow the textbook passage.

[1]The people of the Republic of Abkhasia in the southwest corner of the former Soviet Union have the distinction of living, on the average, longer than any other people on Earth. [2]In one village of twelve hundred people studied by anthropologists, for example, almost two hundred people were over the age of 81. [3]Although there is no proven explanation for the longevity of the Abkhasians, a few theoretical explanations have been advanced. [4]Perhaps the centuries of grueling warfare in Abkhasia have allowed only the most physically sturdy to survive and pass on their genes. [5]The Abkhasian diet, low in saturated fat, lacking caffeine, but high in fruits and vegetables, may be a component. [6]The regular exercise that is a part of the Abkhasian agricultural lifestyle may also help explain the villagers' long lives. [7]And researchers suggest that the Abkhasian culture, which expects all members to perform meaningful work and provides all members with a clear sense of identity, may produce in the most elderly citizens a healthful sense of being needed and valued members of their communities.

_____ 1. In general, the major details of the paragraph are
   A. problems of the Abkhasians.
   B. possible reasons for the Abkhasians' longevity.
   C. examples of the Abkhasians' lifestyle.
   D. components of the Abkhasians' diet.

_____ 2. The first major detail of the paragraph is
   A. a proven explanation.
   B. a sturdy genetic heritage.
   C. regular exercise.
   D. the Abkhasians' diet.

_____ 3. The third major detail of the paragraph is
   A. the survival of the physically sturdy.
   B. no caffeine.
   C. regular exercise.
   D. a sense of being needed and valued members of the community.

4. Fill in the blank: The addition word signaling the third major detail is

_____.

B. (5–10.) Outline the following textbook passage by filling in the main idea and the missing major and minor details.

[1]The college population in the United States today has changed significantly in recent years. [2]The most obvious difference is in the sheer numbers of students. [3]In 1970, there were about six million students in college in

(Continues on next page)

the country. [4]By the year 2000, more than fifteen million students were enrolled in college. [5]Another major difference is in attendance patterns. [6]Over the past thirty years, the number of people attending four-year residential colleges has remained steady. [7]But during the same period, the enrollment in public two-year colleges has risen by more than 400 percent. [8]The two-year schools are the choice of many students who pursue education on a part-time basis. [9]They are also chosen by students seeking career-based studies rather than a traditional liberal arts education.

[10]A third difference between today's college population and that of the recent past is in the demographic background of students. [11]The sex ratio of college students has changed in the last twenty years. [12]In 1980, 55 percent of college students were male. [13]Today female students make up about 56 percent of college students. [14]Ethnic diversity on campus has also followed these trends. [15]Today there are twice as many Latino students as there were in 1975. [16]African American students have also increased, rising from about one million in the mid-1970s to almost two million today. [17]Finally, besides having more gender and ethnic diversity, today's students are also older than previous students. [18]In 1970, older adult students accounted for just 25 percent of the college student population. [19]Today more than 40 percent of all college students are over the age of 24.

Main idea: _____

_____

1. Difference in numbers
   a. Six million college students in 1970
   b. More than fifteen million college students today

2. _____
   a. _____
   b. Enrollment in two-year schools has risen more than 400 percent.
      (1) Choice of students who attend school on a part-time basis
      (2) _____

3. _____
   a. Sex ratios
      (1) 55 percent male in 1980
      (2) 56 percent female today
   b. Ethnic diversity since the 1970s
      (1) Twice as many Latinos today as in 1975
      (2) Almost twice as many African Americans as in the mid-1970s
   c. _____
      (1) 1970—adult students accounted for 25 percent
      (2) More than 40 percent of students are over 24 today

SUPPORTING DETAILS: Mastery Test 5

A. Answer the supporting-detail questions that follow the textbook passage.

> ¹*Heuristics* (pronounced *hyoo-ris'tiks*) are rules of thumb that help us to simplify problems. ²They do not guarantee a solution, but they may bring it within reach. ³A very simple heuristic method is hill-climbing. ⁴In this process, we try to move continually closer to our final goal without ever digressing or going backward. ⁵On a multiple-choice test, for example, one useful strategy in answering each question is to eliminate the alternatives that are obviously incorrect. ⁶Even if this does not leave you with the one correct answer, you are closer to a solution. ⁷Or in trying to balance a budget, each reduction in expenses brings you closer to the goal and leaves you with a smaller deficit to deal with. ⁸Another heuristic method is the creation of subgoals. ⁹By setting subgoals, we can often break a problem into smaller, more manageable pieces, each of which is easier to solve than the problem as a whole. ¹⁰A student whose goal is to write a history paper might set subgoals by breaking down the work into a series of separate tasks: choosing a topic, doing the research, preparing an outline, writing the first draft, editing, rewriting, and so on.

_____ 1. The main idea is expressed in sentence
   A. 1.
   B. 3.
   C. 4.
   D. 8.

_____ 2. The major supporting details of this paragraph are
   A. events.
   B. reasons.
   C. methods.
   D. questions.

_____ 3. The first major detail of the paragraph is introduced in sentence
   A. 2.
   B. 3.
   C. 4.
   D. 5.

_____ 4. The second major detail of the paragraph is introduced in sentence
   A. 5.
   B. 7.
   C. 8.
   D. 10.

(Continues on next page)

5–6. Complete the following study notes that summarize the paragraph.

Heuristics—rules of thumb that help us to simplify problems

1. Hill-climbing—try to move continually closer to final goal without digressing.

    Example— _____

    _____

2. Creation of subgoals—break a problem into smaller, more manageable pieces.

    Example— _____

    _____

B. (7–10.) Complete the map of the following textbook passage by filling in the main idea and the missing major details.

> [1]Public speaking is very different from everyday conversation. [2]First of all, speeches are much more structured than a typical informal discussion. [3]A speech usually imposes strict time limitations on the speaker. [4]In addition, for most situations, speeches do not allow listeners to interrupt with questions or commentary. [5]Another difference to keep in mind when speaking to groups is that public speaking generally requires more formal language. [6]Slang, jargon, and bad grammar have little place in public speeches. [7]Audiences usually react negatively to speakers who do not elevate and polish their language when giving a public talk. [8]A third significant difference between public and private discussion is that public speaking requires a different method of delivery. [9]Unlike casual conversation, which is usually quiet, effective public speakers adjust their voices to be heard clearly throughout the audience. [10]Speaking to a group also requires the speaker to assume a more erect posture and avoid distracting mannerisms and verbal habits.

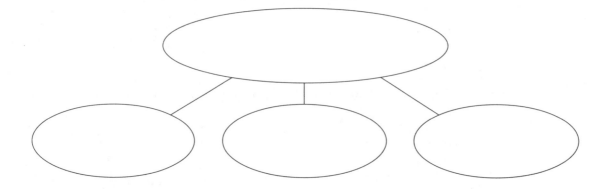

Name _____

Section _____ Date _____

SCORE: (Number correct) _____ × 10 = _____%

SUPPORTING DETAILS: Mastery Test 6

A. (1–3.) The main idea of the following textbook passage is **boldfaced**. Complete the map below by filling in the three major details, including brief explanations of each detail.

[1]In Latin, *plagiarism* means "kidnapper." [2]*To plagiarize* means to use another person's words or ideas as if they were one's own original creations. [3]Quite simply, it is theft. [4]Common thieves steal material goods that legally belong to others and then use this property as it if were rightfully theirs. [5]Plagiarists do the same with words and ideas. [6]**This theft can occur in three forms: global, patchwork, and incremental.** [7]Global plagiarism is stealing all the words and ideas from another source and passing them off as one's own. [8]This is the most blatant kind of plagiarism and is considered to be grossly unethical. [9]Patchwork plagiarism occurs when words and ideas are pilfered from several sources and then patched together. [10]In other words, instead of copying everything from one single source, the thief copies word for word from several sources. [11]In global and patchwork plagiarism, entire sections are copied verbatim. [12]A third kind of plagiarism, incremental plagiarism, occurs when small portions (choice words or phrases) are borrowed from different parts of one source without proper credit being given.

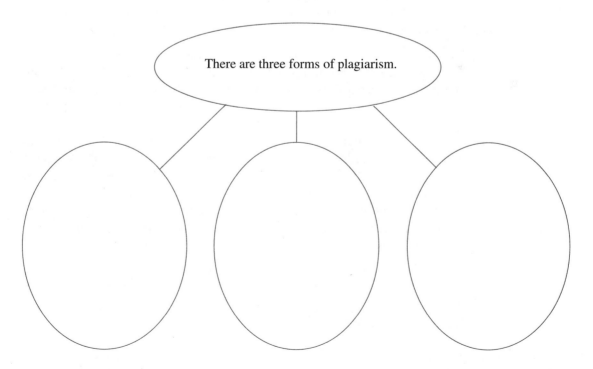

There are three forms of plagiarism.

(Continues on next page)

B. (4–6.) Outline the following textbook passage by filling in the main idea and the two major supporting details.

> [1]What causes forgetting? [2]Research has established that most forgetting occurs because of interference from other information, which can take place in two ways. [3]In proactive interference, prior information inhibits our ability to remember new information. [4]For instance, if you have a new locker combination each year, you may have difficulty remembering it because you keep recalling the old one. [5]In retroactive interference, new information inhibits our ability to remember old information. [6]Now that you finally know your new locker combination, you may find that you have forgotten the old one. [7]In both cases, we forget because competing information displaces the information we are trying to retrieve.

Main idea: _____

_____

1. _____

2. _____

C. (7–10.) Outline the following textbook passage by filling in the main idea and the major supporting details, including brief explanations of each detail.

Note: The number of answer lines given does not indicate the number of major details in the passage.

> [1]There are stages to children's play. [2]Initially, they engage in solitary play. [3]They may show a preference for being near other children and show some interest in what those others are doing, but their own individual play runs an independent course. [4]Solitary play is eventually replaced by parallel play, in which children use similar materials (such as a pail and toy shovel) and engage in similar activity (such as digging sand), typically near one another; but they hardly interact at all. [5]By age 3, most children show at least some cooperative play, a form that involves direct child-to-child interaction and requires some cooperative role-taking. [6]Examples of such role-taking can be found in the "pretend" games that children use to explore such mysteries as adult relationships (for example, games of "Mommy and Daddy") and other children's anatomy (for example, games of "doctor").

Main idea: _____

_____

_____

_____

_____

4

Implied Main Ideas and the Central Point

In Chapters 2 and 3 you learned the two basic parts of anything you read: a main idea and the supporting details that explain and develop that idea. A main idea may be clearly stated in one sentence of a paragraph.

This chapter explains and offers practice in two more advanced ways of finding a main idea:

- **Figuring out implied main ideas.** A main idea that is only suggested by supporting details but not clearly stated in one sentence is called an **implied main idea**. The reader must figure out an implied main idea by considering those supporting details.

- **Finding central points.** A selection consisting of several paragraphs or more has an overall main idea called the **central point**, or **thesis**. The paragraphs that make up the selection provide the supporting details for that central point. As with the main idea of a paragraph, the central point may be either clearly stated or implied.

IMPLIED MAIN IDEAS

Sometimes a selection lacks a sentence that directly states the main idea. In such cases, the author has simply decided to let the details of the selection suggest the main idea. You must figure out what that implied idea is by deciding upon the point all the details support. For example, read the following paragraph.

[1]Slashing their swords wildly, swordfish swim through schools of fish, trying to slice as many as possible; then they feast. [2]When hooked by fishermen, they have been known to fight nonstop for three or four hours. [3]They have pulled some fishermen to their deaths, and if they are not clubbed senseless when captured, they will slash fishermen on deck. [4]A puncture wound by a swordfish bill means a severe and nearly instantaneous infection. [5]Their sword, which is a bony extension of the upper jaw, is deadly sharp on the sides and can grow to a length of four or five feet. [6]It is a weapon backed up by five hundred pounds of sleek, muscular fish. [7]Swordfish have even been known to attack boats, driving their swords right through the hull and at times sinking them.

You can see that no sentence in the paragraph is a good "umbrella" statement that covers all of the other sentences. To decide on the main idea, we must ask the same three questions we've already used to find main ideas:

- "Who or what is this paragraph about?" That will be the topic.

- "What is the main point the author is trying to make about that topic?"

- And when we think we know the main point, we can test it by asking, "Does *all or most* of the material in the paragraph support this idea?"

In the paragraph above, all of the details are about swordfish, so that must be the topic. Which of the following statements expresses the general point that the author is trying to make about the topic? Check (✓) the answer you think is correct.

____   A. Swordfish will attack entire schools of fish.

____   B. Swordfish will fight for hours when hooked and have even pulled some fisherman to their deaths.

____   C. A swordfish bill can cause severe infections and even sink a boat.

____   D. Swordfish are aggressive, dangerous fish.

The details reveal the author's general point to be answer D: swordfish are aggressive, dangerous fish. All the other statements above are supporting details for this main idea—each tells of a way in which swordfish are aggressive and dangerous. Although the main idea is not directly stated, it is clearly implied by all the material in the paragraph.

Figuring Out Implied Main Ideas

Remember, to find implied main ideas, it often helps to decide on the topic first. Do so by asking yourself, "Who or what is the selection about?" After you find the topic, then ask yourself, "What is the author's main point about the topic?"

☑ *Check Your Understanding*

Read the following selection and try to answer the questions that follow.

¹All writers get bogged down now and then. ²Accept the fact that sooner or later writer's block will happen to you. ³When it does, one response is to try to write something—no matter how awkward or imprecise it may seem. ⁴Just jot a reminder to yourself in the margin ("Fix this," "Redo," or "Ugh!") to fine-tune the section later. ⁵Another way to deal with a writing snag is leave a blank space—a spot for the right words when they finally come to mind at a later time. ⁶Then move on to an easier section, see if you can write that, and then return to the challenging part. ⁷It may also help to reread to yourself or out loud what you've already written. ⁸Regaining a sense of the large context may be enough to overcome writer's block. ⁹You might also try talking your way through a troublesome section. ¹⁰Like most people, you probably speak more easily than you write; by speaking aloud, you tap this oral fluency and put it to work in your writing.

_____ 1. What is the topic of the above paragraph?
   A. Writer's block
   B. Writing and talking
   C. The writing process
   D. Rereading your writing

_____ 2. Which statement best expresses the unstated main idea of the paragraph?
   A. Writing is not easy.
   B. There are various ways to deal with writer's block.
   C. Talking about what you are trying to write may help you break out of a writing snag.
   D. Write easier sections of a paper first and come back later to a harder section.

Explanation:

The topic, referred to directly or indirectly in several sentences, is writer's block. The implied main idea about writer's block is that there are various ways to deal with it. Statement A, "Writing is not easy," is too broad, and statements C and D are too narrow—each referring to only one specific way to deal with writer's block.

When you think you have determined an implied main idea, test yourself by asking, "Does all or most of the material in the paragraph support this idea?" In fact, the entire paragraph is made up of practical suggestions for responding to writer's block.

➤ *Practice 1*

Read each paragraph and then answer the questions that follow. Remember to find a topic by asking "Who or what is the selection about?" and to find an implied main idea by asking "What is the author's point about the topic?"

> *Hint:* Noticing addition words (such as *first, another, also, moreover,* and *finally*) will help you identify the major supporting details that can suggest the main idea.

Paragraph 1

¹What way do you prefer to learn? ²Some people find it easier to understand what they see in print than what they hear. ³Others find it easier to understand things they hear. ⁴Some people prefer seeing a picture to reading words. ⁵Think about your own learning preferences. ⁶For example, imagine that you need to get from your home to someplace you have never been before. ⁷What would be the easiest way for you to find the place? ⁸Some people want to look at a map. ⁹Others prefer to read a list of step-by-step directions. ¹⁰Still others prefer to be *told* a list of step-by-step directions so that they can *hear* them. ¹¹Know what is best for you.

_____ 1. What is the topic of the above paragraph?
   A. Learning preferences
   B. Learning through hearing
   C. Learning through pictures
   D. Learning through print

_____ 2. Which statement best expresses the unstated main idea?
   A. Some people understand better by reading something rather than hearing it.
   B. Some people learn best by seeing a picture rather than reading words.
   C. Directions that are helpful for one person may not be helpful for another.
   D. People should be aware of and take advantage of their learning preferences.

Paragraph 2

¹According to Dale Carnegie, one way to make people feel important is to remember their names. ²Greeting people by name makes them feel liked and valued. ³So does greeting them warmly and enthusiastically. ⁴Convey delight when you see or hear from someone you know, Carnegie advises. ⁵In conversations, allow people to talk about themselves: their experiences, their views, their goals, their work, their hobbies, their relationships. ⁶Encourage

them by listening attentively, asking questions, and otherwise showing interest. [7]Also, be generous with your praise. [8]Compliment people—not falsely, but in genuine appreciation of their accomplishments and merits.

_____ 1. What is the topic of the above paragraph?
   A. Ways to greet people
   B. Ways to make people feel important
   C. The values of attentive listening
   D. The benefits of providing compliments

_____ 2. Which statement best expresses the unstated main idea?
   A. Greeting people by name makes them feel liked and valued.
   B. Compliment people in a sincere way.
   C. Dale Carnegie suggested a number of ways to make people feel important.
   D. In conversations, allow people to talk about themselves.

Paragraph 3

[1]Flextime, or flexibility of working hours, has become popular in recent years. [2]The most obvious advantage is less absenteeism. [3]When employees can choose working hours that meet their needs, they are less likely to take time off. [4]Another advantage of flextime is more efficient use of the physical plant. [5]The additional hours that a company is "open for business" could mean higher productivity and greater profits. [6]Finally, giving employees a choice of working hours permits them more control over their work environment, leading to increased job satisfaction and less turnover.

_____ 1. What is the topic of the above paragraph?
   A. Giving employees a choice
   B. Absenteeism at work
   C. Flextime
   D. The most popular employee benefits

_____ 2. Which statement best expresses the unstated main idea?
   A. Flextime leads to increased job satisfaction and higher productivity.
   B. People who can choose their working hours are less likely to take time off.
   C. Companies have found that flextime keeps employee turnover down.
   D. Companies have found that flextime has several advantages.

Paragraph 4

[1]South America contains the world's largest tropical rain forest—the Amazon. [2]It also contains a desert, the Atacama, that is one of the driest in the world. [3]It has steamy lowlands and icy high regions, including the Andes, mountains tall enough to have glaciers. [4]In just one South American country, Chile, we find a dry desert in the north and then, as we go southward, fertile green valleys, unspoiled pine forests, and then canyons carved by wild rivers. [5]In the southernmost part of Chile there are frigid mountains, and here, off the coast, there are frigid seas—this is the part of the world that is nearest to Antarctica. [6]Ecuador, a small country, nevertheless contains both tropical forests and snow-capped mountains.

_____ 1. What is the topic of the above paragraph?
   A. The geography of South America
   B. Deserts and rain forests of South America
   C. Mountains and valleys of South America
   D. Features of Chile and Ecuador

_____ 2. Which statement best expresses the unstated main idea?
   A. South America is a region of extreme geographic contrasts.
   B. Many people have an inaccurate idea of South America's geography.
   C. Of all South American countries, Chile and Ecuador are the most geographically diverse.
   D. South America is not a desirable vacation destination.

➤ Practice 2

The main idea of each of the following paragraphs is unstated, and each paragraph is followed by four sentences. In the space provided, write the letter of the sentence that best expresses each unstated main idea.

Remember to consider carefully all of the information given and to ask yourself the following two questions:

- Who or what is the selection about? In other words, what is the topic?

- What is the author's main point about that topic? In other words, what is the implied main idea?

Then test your answer by asking:

- Does *all or most* of the material in the paragraph support this idea?

Paragraph 1

[1]Cosmetic surgery is often presented as easy and painless, not like surgery at all but rather like dyeing hair or putting on nail polish. [2]This idea is reflected in casual, lighthearted terms like "tummy tuck." [3]But the risks of cosmetic surgery include an adverse reaction to the anesthesia used, excessive bleeding, and postoperative infection. [4]Also, muscles and nerves can be damaged during the surgery, and the patient may be paralyzed or may even, in rare instances, die. [5]Even if the patient recovers well, there is also the risk of an unacceptable result—that is, the patient looks worse, not better—in which case further surgery may be needed, perhaps several times. [6]Finally, even a reasonably successful outcome may be disappointing because it does not miraculously change the patient's whole life: a prettier nose, say, will not ensure fame, fortune, or romance.

_____ Which statement best expresses the unstated main idea of the paragraph?
- A. People often get cosmetic surgery in hopes of improving their romantic lives.
- B. Merely looking more attractive is not a good enough reason to get cosmetic surgery.
- C. Cosmetic surgery is much riskier than what it's often portrayed to be.
- D. Casual, lighthearted terms like "tummy tucks" should be eliminated from cosmetic surgery advertising.

Paragraph 2

[1]In some countries defeated by Nazi Germany during World War II, almost the entire Jewish population was murdered. [2]But in Denmark, the story was different. [3]After the Nazis took over Denmark in April 1940, complaints from the Danish people prevented the Germans from freely pursuing Danish Jews. [4]Then, in August 1943, the Nazis made demands that the Danes take action against the Jews. [5]Unwilling to obey, every important government official resigned. [6]When the German military commander decided to send Danish Jews to concentration camps, average citizens in Denmark began hiding Jews in their homes until they could be moved to the coast. [7]Also, the Danish church, royal family, and a variety of organizations protested the new German policy. [8]In the end, Danish fishermen succeeding in transporting about seven thousand Jews to Sweden. [9]When the Germans moved the five hundred Danish Jews they found to a concentration camp, the Danish people kept up a public outcry and sent food and clothing packages to help save their countrymen. [10]All but about one hundred Danish Jews survived the war.

_____ Which statement best expresses the unstated main idea of the paragraph?
   A. The Nazis were determined to take widespread action against the Danish Jews.
   B. Danish fishermen were the real heroes in saving their Jewish fellow citizens.
   C. Jews in other European countries could have been saved if their fellow citizens had acted as the Danes did.
   D. The Danish people, acting with their government, saved thousands of lives by refusing to cooperate with Nazi invaders.

Paragraph 3

[1]The most common means of communication for insects is chemical. [2]Pheromones are chemicals with which an insect influences the behavior of other insects in its group. [3]For example, the queen bee, on her flight from the hive, secretes a pheromone that attracts drones, whose sole function is to mate with the queen. [4]Ants secrete pheromones that mark a trail from the nest to a food source. [5]Only members of the ant's own colony recognize the trail. [6]Fireflies communicate during the mating season not with chemicals but by flashing a light. [7]The female of each species emits a special series of flashes that males of her species recognize. [8]Other insects communicate by tapping, rubbing, or stroking each other. [9]Sometimes these are part of an elaborate courtship ritual. [10]Perhaps the most complex of all forms of insect communication is the dance of the honeybee. [11]When a forager bee finds a source of nectar, she returns to the hive and does a "waggle dance." [12]The dance lets other bees know where the food is.

_____ Which statement best expresses the unstated main idea of the paragraph?
   A. Research has shown that animals do not communicate as people do.
   B. All creatures need to communicate with each other.
   C. Insects communicate through chemicals, visual signals, certain touching, and motions.
   D. Insects have ways of communicating with each other about food sources.

Paragraph 4

[1]Many Americans think of the West as being a virgin territory that was largely unpopulated prior to the coming of the pioneers. [2]However, in 1840, before large numbers of pioneers and farmers crossed the Mississippi, at least 300,000 Indians lived in the West. [3]Twenty-three Indian tribes lived on the Great Plains and hunted buffalo. [4]On the eastern Plains, Indians combined farming and hunting. [5]South and west of the Plains, in the huge arid region that is now Arizona and New Mexico, sophisticated farmers, like the Hopi

and Zuni, coexisted with nomadic hunters and gatherers, like the Apache and Navajo. ⁶In California, Indians occupied small villages during the winter but moved during the rest of the year, gathering wild plants and seeds, hunting small game, and fishing in the rivers. ⁷More than 100,000 Indians still lived in California when the area was acquired by the United States in 1848. ⁸And along the northwest Pacific Coast lived a great number of tribes that found an abundant food supply in the sea, coastal rivers, and forests.

_____ Which statement best expresses the unstated main idea of the paragraph?
- A. Indians were farmers and hunters.
- B. About a third of Western Indians lived in California.
- C. Many of Americans' popular beliefs about the West in the 1800s, including the myths about the American Indians, do not correspond with the facts of history.
- D. Contrary to popular belief, there were numerous Indian tribes living throughout the West—hunting, farming, gathering, and fishing—before the pioneers arrived.

Putting Implied Main Ideas into Your Own Words

When you read, you often have to **infer**—figure out on your own—an author's unstated main idea. The implied main idea that you come up with should cover all or most of the details in the paragraph.

See if you can find and write the topic of the paragraph below. Then write the implied main idea in your own words. Finally, read the explanation that follows.

> *Hints:* Remember that you can help yourself identify the topic and main idea if you 1) look for repeated words as you read and 2) try to mark major supporting details. Major details are often signaled by such common addition words as the following:

Addition Words

one	to begin with	also	further
first (of all)	for one thing	in addition	furthermore
second (ly)	other	next	last (of all)
third (ly)	another	moreover	final (ly)

¹Nonverbal messages are more emotionally powerful than verbal ones. ²Nonverbal behaviors tell people about our emotional state. ³When we want to convey how we feel about someone, language often fails us. ⁴Nonverbal messages are also more universal than verbal ones. ⁵Members of different linguistic groups must spend a lot of time and effort to learn each other's verbal codes, but they can communicate instantly by smiling or wrinkling

their faces in disgust. [6]Some researchers have shown a number of emotions to be expressed in the same way by members of different cultural groups. [7]Last, nonverbal messages are more continuous and natural than spoken language. [8]Because gestures and body movements flow into one another without obvious beginnings and endings, they seem to be a more natural part of our existence than words.

What is the topic of this paragraph? _____

What is the implied main idea of this paragraph? _____

_____

Explanation:

One key to the topic here is the words *nonverbal messages*, which are repeated through the paragraph. The other key to the topic is major details in the paragraph. Two of the details are signaled by addition words (*also* in "Nonverbal messages are also" and *last* in "Last, nonverbal messages are"). Here are the three major details in the paragraph:

- Nonverbal messages are more emotionally powerful than verbal ones.
- They are more universal.
- They are more continuous and natural.

What do those three major details have in common? They're all about nonverbal messages (or behaviors), so that phrase can be considered the topic. And the author's main point about that topic could be stated like this: *Nonverbal messages have several advantages over verbal ones.*

➤ Practice 3

In the spaces provided, fill in the topic of each paragraph. Then, using your own words, write the implied main ideas of the paragraphs.

> **Hints:**
>
> **1.** To find the topic, it often helps to look for repeated words in a paragraph.
>
> **2.** To identify the topic and main idea, mark major supporting details as you read. These major details are often signaled by such common addition words as the ones shown in the box on the previous page.

A.   [1]A hurricane is a relatively flat system of winds rotating around a center where the atmospheric pressure is abnormally low. [2]This system can be hundreds of miles across and usually brings heavy rains along with its powerfully strong winds. [3]As with a hurricane, air pressure at the center of a tornado is very low; but a tornado is a violently rotating column or "funnel" of air, usually reaching down from a thundercloud, and is typically only a few hundred yards across. [4]Wind speeds in a hurricane are about 75 to 150 miles per hour, but the wind speed in a tornado might be 300 miles per hour. [5]A hurricane may last for one or more days; a tornado lasts only a few minutes. [6]Locally, tornadoes are even more destructive than hurricanes.

Topic: _____

Implied main idea: _____

_____

B. [1]A broiler, which is the name for a chicken raised for its meat, typically has no contact with its mother. [2]Instead, it is incubated in a hatchery until it breaks out of its egg. [3]Then, it is immediately moved to the floor of a broiler house, crowded with twenty to sixty thousand birds. [4]Because of the limited space, the birds frequently climb over one another with their sharp claws, and they may show their stress by pecking at each other. [5]Most buildings are not equipped with adequate ventilation, so the animals suffer extreme heat and sometimes suffocation. [6]The environment is also unhealthy because the factory is only cleaned every two to three years. [7]To counteract the unsanitary conditions, factory owners give the birds regular low doses of antibiotics. [8]They also overfeed them to ensure that their breast tissue grows as fast as possible, which may damage the birds' hearts and other supporting parts, especially their legs and abdomens. [9]Sometimes chickens become too ill to stand. [10]The average broiler is slaughtered between the ages of four and ten weeks, and shortly afterward it appears on your plate.

Topic: _____

Implied main idea: _____

_____

C. [1]Body language is a form of nonverbal communication in which physical motions and gestures provide signals. [2]A good illustration is the "preening behavior" that accompanies courtship—women stroking their hair and checking their makeup and men adjusting their hair and tugging at their ties are examples. [3]Another system of nonverbal communication is paralanguage: Voice pitch, volume, pacing of speech, silent pauses, and sighs provide a rich source of information. [4]Proxemics—the way we employ personal social space—also contains nonverbal messages. [5]For instance, students who sit in the front rows of a classroom tend to be the most interested. [6]We also convey nonverbal messages through touch—stroking, hitting, holding, shaking hands, and so on. [7]Finally, we employ certain objects—clothing, makeup, perfume, etc.—to communicate our gender, rank, status, and attitude.

Topic: _____

Implied main idea: _____

_____

D.   [1]During the American Revolution, the British army far outnumbered the American colonial army, and the British frequently fought with cannons, while the Americans had none. [2]However, the British troops had to fight more than three thousand miles away from home, which meant that reinforcements, money, and supplies took months to reach the battlefront. [3]Americans fought in their own territory, which was undeveloped and unfamiliar to the British, and American troops were supported by local and French supplies stationed nearby. [4]The British forces were much more organized and disciplined than the American side, which was cobbled together from a diverse group of men, many of whom had little military experience. [5]The British wore bright red uniforms that made them easily recognized. [6]They were more likely to fight in straight lines across the battlefield, kneeling down in the open to reload their weapons. [7]American troops also used linear tactics, but they were just as likely to fight using the cover of trees and buildings. [8]Whenever the British retreated from a battle, they would do so in single file, and this allowed the colonists to sneak around the British formation to pick off more soldiers. [9]Perhaps the most important difference between the two armies, however, was that of motivation. [10]The British troops fought to control the colonists and secure wealth for the English king. [11]The Americans fought for freedom and the defense of their homeland, and every colonial soldier had a high personal stake in the war's outcome.

Topic: _____

Implied main idea: _____

_____

CENTRAL POINTS

Just as a paragraph has a main idea, so a longer selection has a **central idea**, also known as a **central point** or **thesis**. The longer selection may be an essay, an article, or even a section within a textbook chapter. The central point may be clearly stated, or it may be implied. In the practices that follow, the central points are clearly stated; but in the readings throughout this book, some are stated and some are implied.

You can find a central point in the same way that you find a main idea—by looking for a topic (which is often suggested by the title of a longer selection) and by considering the supporting material. The paragraphs within the longer reading will provide supporting details for the central point.

In the following essay, the central point is stated in one sentence. See if you can find and underline this sentence. Then write its number in the space provided.

Modifying Behavior

[1]Can people modify their own behavior? [2]The answer is yes. [3]By following a few steps recommended by experts, you can change your own behavior.

[4]The first thing to do is to decide what behavior you want to acquire—the "target" behavior. [5]What if you want to get rid of some behavior? [6]Behavior modification specialists emphasize a positive approach called "ignoring." [7]Much better results are achieved when the emphasis is on the new behavior to be acquired rather than on the behavior to be eliminated. [8]For example, instead of setting a target of being less shy, you might define the target behavior as becoming more outgoing or more sociable. [9]Other possible target behaviors are behaving more assertively, studying more, and getting along better with your roommate. [10]In each case, you have focused on the behavior that you want to acquire rather than on the behavior that you want to reduce or eliminate.

[11]The next step is to define the target behavior precisely: What exactly do you mean by "assertive" or by "sociable"? [12]One way to do this is to imagine situations in which the target behavior could be performed. [13]Then describe in writing these situations and the way in which you now respond to them. [14]For example, in the case of shyness, you might write: "When I am sitting in the lecture hall, waiting for class to begin, I don't talk to the people around me." [15]Next, write down how you would rather act in that situation: "Ask the people sitting next to me how they like the class or the professor; or ask if they have seen any particularly good movies recently."

[16]The next step is to monitor your present behavior by keeping a daily log of activities related to the target behavior in order to establish your present rate of behavior. [17]At the same time, try to figure out if your present, undesirable behavior is being reinforced in some way. [18]For example, if you find yourself unable to study, record what you do instead and try to determine how that undesirable behavior is being reinforced.

[19]The last step—which gets to the heart of self-modification—is to provide yourself with a positive reinforcer that is gained only upon specific improvements in the target behavior. [20]You may be able to use the same reinforcer that now maintains your undesirable behavior, or you may want to pick a new reinforcer. [21]Researchers use the example of a student who wanted to improve his relationship with his parents. [22]He first counted the times he said something pleasant to them and then rewarded himself for improvement by making his favorite pastime, playing pool, dependent on predetermined increases in the number of pleasant remarks he made. [23]You can also use tokens: Give yourself one token for every thirty minutes of studying and cash in those tokens for reinforcement. [24]For instance, the privilege of going to a movie might require ten tokens.

_____   is the number of the sentence that states the central point.

Explanation:

The central point is a general statement that covers all or most of the details in a reading. To find the central point of the essay above, look first at its topic. Since the title is "Modifying Behavior," and every paragraph is about that subject, we can say "modifying behavior" is the topic. Then decide on what point is being made about the topic by looking at the major details of the essay. The first major detail, presented in paragraph 1, is about the first thing to do if you want to change your behavior. Paragraphs 2, 3, and 4 present the next three steps to follow in the process of modifying your own behavior.

The central point, then, will be a general statement that covers all of the steps explained. As is often the case, the central point is stated in the first paragraph near the start of the essay. Sentence 3 in that paragraph refers generally to the goal of changing behavior and the steps that can be followed, so that is the central point.

➤ Practice 4

Read the following essay, and see if you can find the clearly stated central point that covers most of the supporting details. Then, in the space provided, write the number of the sentence that states the point.

Our Shopping Mania

¹Every day, Americans head out in droves for our country's department stores, discount centers, and shopping malls. ²It seems we all have to buy something we think we really need or we feel is an incredible bargain. ³But our motives are more complicated than that.

⁴One reason for our mania for shopping is that Americans believe in competition, even when it comes to acquiring possessions. ⁵The old sports cliché, "Winning isn't everything—it's the *only* thing" applies to our feelings about ourselves when we buy as well as when we play games. ⁶We feel like losers if we don't own the cars, appliances, clothes, and furniture our neighbors and friends own. ⁷For instance, the Browns' four-year-old car seems fine until the Smiths next door buy a brand-new model. ⁸Suddenly every paint chip and dent on the older model seems enormous. ⁹The Browns begin to wonder what their "old clunker" says about them. ¹⁰Are people pitying them for driving it? ¹¹Are they whispering that the Browns must not be doing too well? ¹²Do they think the Browns are cheap? ¹³Then the Browns will show them! ¹⁴Driven by the competitive instinct to stay ahead in the game, the Browns go out scouting the car lots. ¹⁵They "just have to" replace their car. ¹⁶Forget the fact that a few weeks ago they thought their car was OK. ¹⁷Their perception of an OK car was changed when the Smiths acquired a new one.

[18]The Browns are victims of the competitive urge. [19]That urge tells us that people's success in life is measured by how much they own. [20]So we admire those with the most material possessions: the ones who own three cars or enough shoes to fill a walk-in closet. [21]By buying a new car, the Browns are satisfying that urge. [22]The problem is that the competitive urge never stays satisfied long. [23]Next week, the Smiths may install a swimming pool.

[24]Another reason for the American addiction to consumer goods is the widespread belief that "new is better." [25]Americans visiting other countries are often amazed at the way less affluent people make do with what they have. [26]A sewing machine or bicycle will be lovingly repaired and cared for until it has served its owner for many, many years. [27]Children play with toys ingeniously fashioned from "junk" that Americans would have put in the wastebasket. [28]It never occurs to many of us that it is possible to fix a broken toaster, mend torn clothing, or make do with an outdated refrigerator. [29]We're encouraged in this attitude by manufacturers who want us to buy the newest model as soon as the old one fails in any way. [30]They even invent items that are intended to be used once and thrown away: not just paper plates and napkins, but disposable cameras and contact lenses. [31]Fix-it shops are hard to find in many towns. [32]Why should we repair the old when we can buy the new? [33]As a result, we have junkyards and dumps bursting with the still-usable items we no longer want. [34]Instead of reusing or recycling, which would make more economic sense, we throw away.

[35]Finally, our urge to buy is maintained and heightened by the media. [36]We are bombarded by television and print ads that carry seductive messages telling us that a particular product—a stereo, motorcycle, or dishwasher—is all we need to be happy. [37]Every shampoo, makeup, or cologne ad tries to convince us that a single item can transform us into the ideal self we fantasize about. [38]Not just advertisers, but the media generally do a good job of reinforcing the idea that we've got to have the newest and the best. [39]Unless a television show or movie is specifically about "poor people," the setting we see on the screen is almost always sparkling new and jam-packed with expensive furniture, appliances, and other items. [40]The unspoken message conveyed to us is "This is how people are supposed to live. [41]If your home, your car, your belongings aren't this nice, there's something wrong with you."

[42]Because of our competitive urge, our desire for what is new, and our manipulation by the media, Americans are addicted to shopping. [43]Like any addiction, it's one that can never be fully satisfied, and unless a change occurs in our cultural priorities, it will continue to eat away at us.

_____ is the number of the sentence that states the central point.

➤ *Practice 5*

Read the following selection from a history textbook. See if you can find the clearly stated central point—one sentence that covers most of the supporting details. Then, in the space provided, write the number of the sentence that states the point.

An Effect of Rising Crime in Nineteenth-Century America

¹Until the 1840s, America's cities and towns were policed by unsalaried volunteers. ²It took an increase in violence in the 1800s, resulting from various social forces as well as weak performance by volunteer law enforcers, to get people to turn to professional police.

³During the mid-1830s, a wave of rioting without parallel in earlier American history swept the nation's cities. ⁴All together there were at least 115 incidents of mob violence during the 1830s, compared with just 7 incidents in the 1810s and 21 in the 1820s. ⁵Mob violence during the 1830s had a variety of sources.

⁶A rate of urban growth faster than that in any previous decade was one major contributor to social turbulence during the 1830s. ⁷Urban populations grew by 60 percent, and the sharp upsurge in foreign immigration heightened religious and ethnic tensions. ⁸The number of immigrants entering the country jumped from just 5,000 a year at the beginning of the century to over 50,000 annually during the 1830s.

⁹Another source of violence was abolitionism, which emerged at the beginning of the decade and produced a violent reaction. ¹⁰The belief that abolitionists favored interracial marriages inflamed anti-Negro sentiment. ¹¹The mobs that attacked black homes and churches, burned white abolitionists' homes and businesses, and disrupted antislavery meetings were often led by "gentlemen of property and standing."

¹²The birth of a new two-party political system also contributed to a growing climate of violence. ¹³Mob violence frequently broke out on election days as rival Democratic and Whig gangs tried to steal ballot boxes and keep the opposition's voters from reaching local polling places.

¹⁴Traditional methods of preserving public order proved totally inadequate by the 1830s. ¹⁵The nation's cities were "policed" by a handful of unpaid, untrained, ununiformed, and unarmed sheriffs, aldermen, marshals, constables, and night watchmen. ¹⁶In New England towns, men armed with long black sticks tipped with brass patrolled streets searching for drunkards, disorderly children, and wayward servants.

¹⁷These law officers were not a particularly effective deterrent to crime. ¹⁸Night watchmen generally held other jobs during the day and sometimes slept at their posts at night. ¹⁹Sheriffs, aldermen, marshals, and constables made a living not by investigating crime or patrolling city streets but by

collecting debts, foreclosing on mortgages, and serving court orders. [20]Victims of crime had to offer a reward if they wanted these unpaid law officers to investigate a case.

[21]This early system of maintaining public order worked in earlier decades when the rates of serious crime were extremely low. [22]After 1830, however, drunken brawls, robberies, beatings, and murders all increased in number. [23]Fear of crime led city leaders to look for new ways of preserving public order.

[24]At first there was great resistance to the establishment of professional police. [25]By the mid-1840s, however, continued rising crime rates overcame opposition to trying another approach. That approach was to use professional police forces.

_____ is the number of the sentence that states the central point.

CHAPTER REVIEW

In this chapter, you learned the following:

- At times authors imply, or suggest, a main idea without stating it clearly in one sentence. In such cases, you must figure out that main idea by considering the supporting details.

- To find central points—which may be stated or implied—in longer reading selections, you must again look closely at the supporting material.

The next chapters—Chapters 5 and 6—will explain common ways that authors organize their material.

On the Web: If you are using this book in class, you can visit our website for additional practice in recognizing implied main ideas and the central point. Go to **www.townsendpress.com** and click on "Online Exercises."

➤ Review Test 1

To review what you've learned in this chapter, complete each of the following sentences.

1. At times authors _____, or suggest, a main idea without stating it clearly in one sentence.

2. To figure out an implied idea, it often helps to determine the _____ of the paragraph by asking, "Who or what is this paragraph about?"

3. After you figure out what you think is the implied main idea of a paragraph, test yourself by asking, "Does all or most of the material in the paragraph _____ this idea?"

4. Just as a paragraph has a main idea, so a longer selection has a central _____ that is supported by all or most of the material in the selection.

5. The central point of a long selection may be stated directly or it may be _____.

➤ Review Test 2

A. In the space provided, write the letter of the sentence that best expresses the implied main idea of each of the following paragraphs.

_____ 1. [1]One of the most common sleep disorders is insomnia. [2]Such things as noise, light, temperature, stress, nasal congestion, allergies, indigestion, pain, worrying, and the snoring of a sleep partner are factors that contribute to insomnia, which affects about 58 percent of American adults in any given year. [3]In narcolepsy, another sleep disorder, a person has sudden and irresistible "sleep attacks" that last about fifteen minutes. [4]Sleep paralysis sometimes accompanies narcoleptic episodes. [5]Apnea is a dangerous sleep disorder in which the air passages are obstructed, causing cessation of breathing as often as ten times an hour or more. [6]This dangerous disorder can lead to high blood pressure, heart attacks, and strokes. [7]Three other sleep disorders—sleep terrors, bed-wetting, and sleepwalking—occur during deep sleep, are more common among children, and may be related to immaturity of the nervous system.

    A. Many things contribute to insomnia.
    B. There are a number of sleep disorders.
    C. Apnea presents several dangers to a person who has it.
    D. Several sleep disorders are more common among children.

_____ 2. ¹For many working-class couples, the first baby in the family arrives just nine months after marriage. ²They hardly have time to adjust to being husband and wife before being thrust into the demanding roles of mother and father. ³The result can be financial problems, bickering, and interference from in-laws. ⁴The young husbands may not be ready to "settle down," and they resent getting less attention from their wives. ⁵In contrast, middle-class couples often postpone the birth of their first child, which gives them more time to adjust to each other. ⁶On average, their first baby arrives three years after marriage. ⁷Their greater financial resources also work in their favor, making life as parents a lot easier and the marriage more pleasant.

    A. Couples may have a good deal of difficulty in adjusting to their roles as husband and wife.
    B. Middle-class couples postpone having children for several reasons.
    C. Social class makes a significant difference in how couples adjust to the arrival of children.
    D. Financial resources are a major key to the success of a marriage.

_____ 3. ¹When there are problems between various family members, family therapy should certainly be considered. ²It should also be considered when an individual's therapy is slowed by the family, or when a family member is not adjusting well to the improvement of the person in therapy. ³Not all families, however, will benefit from such therapy. ⁴Some family members, for example, may not be willing to cooperate, and without them, meeting as a family may be fruitless. ⁵Or one family member may take so much of a session's time that therapy as a family cannot succeed. ⁶In such cases, other types of therapy may be more useful.

    A. Family therapy will work only when family members are willing to cooperate in the therapy.
    B. Family therapy may be helpful in some situations, but in some cases, other types of therapy may be more useful.
    C. Family therapy has advantages over many other types of therapy.
    D. There are various types of therapy.

B. In the space provided, write out, in your own words, the implied main idea of each paragraph.

4. ¹Birds that roost in communities keep warmer and save more energy than those that roost separately. ²Another advantage of staying in flocks is that many birds are more likely to find food and detect danger than a solitary bird—several pairs of eyes are better than one. ³In addition, birds that eat on the ground with their flock can more easily escape attack than a single bird because at least one member of the flock will

alert the others. [4]Then, when all the birds fly upward to escape together, they cause confusion, turning a predator's interest away from any one individual. [5]Several small birds may even act together to "mob" a larger intruder and drive it away.

Implied main idea: _____

_____

5. [1]During the first, or dilation, stage of the birth process, the uterus contracts and the cervix flattens and dilates to allow the fetus to pass through. [2]This labor stage can last from about two to sixteen hours, or even longer; it tends to be longer with the first child. [3]When the contractions start, they usually come at approximately fifteen- to twenty-minute intervals and are generally mild. [4]Near the end of this first stage, the contractions change, becoming more difficult, longer, and more frequent. [5]This period, lasting about an hour, is called transition and is the most difficult part of labor for many women. [6]The second stage of birth involves the actual delivery of the baby. [7]This expulsion stage is quite variable and can last anywhere from two to sixty minutes or more. [8]In the average delivery, the baby's head appears first, an event referred to as crowning. [9]The rest of the body soon follows. [10]The third stage of the birth process involves the delivery of the placenta (or afterbirth) and fetal membranes. [11]During this stage mild contractions continue for some time. [12]They help decrease the blood flow to the uterus and reduce the uterus to normal size.

Implied main idea: _____

_____

➤ Review Test 3

A. In the space provided, write the letter of the sentence that best expresses the implied main idea of each of the following paragraphs.

_____ 1. [1]Have you ever caught yourself dozing off after lunch, while trying to work or study? [2]A common reaction to the body's natural mid-day sleepiness is to consume caffeine or sugar, but these remedies will only provide temporary energy and increase fatigue later on. [3]Studies show that "power naps" of twenty to thirty minutes reduce stress, increase energy, and improve mental focus. [4]In fact, the brains of people who nap regularly are more active than those of people who don't. [5]Naps can also decrease the risk of heart disease. [6]Experts agree that you should take a nap at the same time each day, approximately eight hours after waking up in the morning, and eight hours before going to sleep at night. [7]Your nap shouldn't last longer than thirty minutes; otherwise, you will enter a deeper sleep that will make you feel groggy and listless. [8]If you suffer from a severe lack of sleep, naps will not fix your problem, but they will aid you more than artificial stimulants. [9]If you are still not convinced that naps are good for you, consider the example set by these creative people: Albert Einstein, Thomas Edison and Winston Churchill. [10]All of these men were nap enthusiasts known for their great accomplishments. [11]A coincidence? [12]Take a nap and find out!

A. Einstein, Edison, and Churchill all owed their success to their habit of taking daily naps.
B. People who don't benefit from an afternoon nap are not doing it correctly.
C. A healthy way to regain energy during the day is to take a short, well-timed afternoon nap.
D. The abuse of caffeine and sugar is a major health problem for many people.

_____ 2. [1]Filmmakers know that our attention is most likely to be drawn to the central portion of the movie screen. [2]We expect elements within the frame to be balanced, with dominant elements near the center or slightly above the center in the case of most medium shots. [3]When a director's purpose is to achieve realism, most shots will be balanced in this way since that is what he or she knows the audience expects. [4]But when a sense of drama is needed, the "norm" is usually violated. [5]Dominant figures or elements may be placed near the edge of the screen, perhaps even fading out of the picture. [6]To create a sense of dominance or power, important elements may be emphasized by placing them in the top third of the screen. [7]Also, using a low camera angle can make a figure on the screen appear more dominant or menacing, as it looks down on us or on other characters or objects. [8]The opposite effect can be achieved by placing characters in the lower portion of the frame. [9]Characters placed this way look especially vulnerable or helpless, and even more so if the rest of the screen is empty or stark in contrast to the lonely figure at the bottom of the screen.

A. Filmmakers use different areas of the screen and camera angles to communicate ideas and moods.
B. There are several steps filmmakers must take to complete a film.
C. Filmmakers use the central portion of the movie screen when presenting realistic situations.
D. Artists in all fields use tricks of the trade in their work.

B. (3.) In the space provided, write out, in your own words, the implied main idea of the following paragraph.

> [1]Many people think of the hippopotamus as a harmless, playful beast. [2]But it kills more people per year than crocodiles and poisonous snakes combined. [3]Hippos have been known to upset boats and kill the swimming passengers, using their strong jaws and sharp teeth to attack and rip their victims apart. [4]In one case, a hippo turned over a canoe carrying a safari hunter, and ripped off the man's head and shoulders. [5]These fierce animals also pose a considerable threat on land, since they feel particularly vulnerable out of water. [6]If you get between a hippo and its favorite river, or between a mother and its calf, then watch out! [7]A hippo can weigh over five thousand pounds and can run as fast as eighteen miles per hour, which makes it a difficult predator to escape. [8]People can usually avoid danger by keeping their distance from these creatures. [9]However, some hippos in Niger, Africa, recently went out of their way to make trouble. [10]Traveling in marauding hordes, these rogue animals threatened fishermen, destroyed rice fields and attacked cattle. [11]The government was forced to kill the animals before they did any more damage.

Implied main idea: _____

C. (4.) Read the following selection from a history textbook. Find the clearly stated central point that covers most of the supporting details. Then, in the space provided, write the number of the sentence that contains the central point.

The Slavery Reparations Debate

[1]African captives and their enslaved descendants made enormous economic contributions to the developing United States. [2]Slave labor sustained agriculture, built railroads, and erected many national landmarks, including the United States Capitol building in Washington, D.C. (where the slaves' owners were paid five dollars per month per slave). [3]Immediately after the war, the federal government promised the freed slaves forty acres of abandoned or confiscated Confederate land and an army mule, but that offer soon withered away, as Southerners were allowed to reclaim their farms. [4]Today the former slaves are long deceased, but many of their descendants continue to suffer from the tragic legacies of slavery—the poverty, discrimination, inferior education, and hopelessness that have reverberated down through the generations. [5]Some African American leaders have asked the United States government and corporations who profited from slavery to pay withheld wages and profits, with interest and compensation for pain and suffering, to the descendants of the slaves. [6]This renewed debate about slave reparations raises complex questions about American history, and about economic and social justice for all Americans.

[7]Advocates cite the $20,000 that Congress decided in 1988 should be paid to survivors of the Japanese internment camps in the United States during World War II, and the reparations that the German government paid to survivors of Nazi oppression. [8]They suggest that reparations could come as massive economic investment in African American communities, free college educations for African American youth, or lump-sum payments to African American citizens. [9]Critics of reparations (both black and white) reply that it is unfair to require payment from today's taxpayers, most of whose ancestors did not directly profit from slavery. [10]Today's taxpayers include African Americans, and descendants of Europeans, Asians, and Latinos who immigrated to America long after the end of slavery. [11]Corporations who benefited from slavery in the nineteenth century have new owners now. [12]Critics of reparations for slavery ask if Native Americans would be equally entitled to reparations—are reservations and existing federal programs fair compensation for their stolen lands and suffering? [13]And what about Irish and Chinese immigrants who were exploited as laborers in the nineteenth century? [14]Critics of reparations suggest that it is just too complicated for a country to try to right long-ago wrongs through payments. [15]Some argue that continued commitment to affirmative-action programs or a Congressional apology to African Americans for slavery would be more appropriate actions at this late date.

_____ is the number of the sentence that states the central point.

➤ Review Test 4

Before modern times, family life in quiet rural villages was peaceful and loving, right? Wrong! In the following richly detailed selection from the textbook *Sociology,* Seventh Edition, by Rodney Stark (Wadsworth, 1998), the common romantic image of preindustrial rural life is shown to be far from true.

To help you continue to strengthen your skills, the reading is followed by questions not only on implied ideas and central points but also on what you've learned in previous chapters.

Words to Watch

Below are some words in the reading that do not have strong context support. Each word is followed by the number of the paragraph in which it appears and its meaning there. These words are indicated in the article by a small circle (°).

dowry (1): the goods, money, or estate that a bride brings to her husband
devastating (3): overwhelming
abounded with (3): had plenty of
grudgingly (7): with reluctance
perforated (9): penetrated
radically (10): greatly

PERSONAL RELATIONSHIPS IN THE NOT-SO-GOOD OLD DAYS

Rodney Stark

Relations between Husbands and Wives

1   Only in modern times have most people married for love. In the good old days, most married for money and labor—marriage was an economic arrangement between families. How much land or wealth did the man have? How large a dowry° would the bride bring to her spouse? Emotional attachments were of no importance to parents in arranging marriages, and neither the bride nor the groom expected emotional fulfillment from marriage.

2   Shorter [a historical researcher] noted an absence of emotional expression between couples and doubted that more than a few actually felt affection. The most common sentiments seem to have been resentment and anger. Not only was wife-beating commonplace, but so was husband-beating. And when wives beat their husbands, it was the husband, not the wife, who was likely to be punished by the community. In France, a husband beaten by his wife was often made to ride backward through the village on a donkey, holding the donkey's tail. He had shamed the village by not controlling his wife properly. The same practice of punishing the husband was frequently employed when wives were sexually unfaithful.

3   The most devastating° evidence of poor husband-wife relations was the reaction to death and dying. Just as the deaths of children often caused no sorrow, the death of a spouse often prompted no regret. Some public expression of grief was expected, especially by widows, but popular culture abounded with° contrary beliefs. Shorter reported the following proverbs:

> *The two sweetest days of a fellow in life,*
> *Are the marriage and burial of his wife.*
>
> *Rich is the man whose wife is dead and horse alive.*

4   Indeed, peasants who rushed for medical help whenever a horse or cow took sick often resisted suggestions by neighbors to get a doctor for a sick wife. The loss of a cow or a horse cost money, but a wife was easily replaced by remarriage to a younger woman who could bring a new dowry. . . .

Bonds between Parents and Children

5   Besides the lack of emotional ties to infants and young children, emotional bonds between parents and older children were also weak. First, most of the children left the household at an early age. Second, when they did so, it was largely a case of "out of sight, out of mind." If a child ventured from the village, he or she was soon forgotten, not just by the neighbors but by the parents as well. All traces of those who moved away were lost. According to Shorter, a French village doctor wrote in his diary in 1710 that he had heard about one of his brothers being hanged but that he had completely lost track of the others.

6   Finally, even the children who stayed in the village did not come to love their parents. Instead, they fought constantly with their parents about inheritance rights and about when their parents would retire, and they openly awaited their parents' deaths. Shorter concluded that dislike and hatred were typical feelings experienced by children who stayed at home.

Peer Group Bonds

7   Surely people in traditional societies must have liked someone. Unfortunately for our image of traditional family life, the primary unit of society and attachment was not the family but the peer group. The family provided for reproduction, child rearing (such as it was), and economic support (often grudgingly°), but emotional attachments were primarily to persons of the same age and sex *outside* the family.

8   Wives had close attachments to other wives, and husbands to other husbands. Social life was highly segregated by sex and was based on childhood friendships and associations. For example, a group of neighborhood boys would become close friends while still very young, and these friendships remained the primary ties of these people all their lives. The same occurred among women. While this no doubt provided people with a source of intimacy and self-esteem, it hindered the formation of close emotional bonds within the family.

9   A woman would enter marriage expecting to share her feelings not with her husband but with her peers. Men reserved intimate feelings for their peers, too. In this way the weak boundaries defining the household were perforated° by primary relations beyond the family. Thus, outsiders determined much that went on within a household. Husbands and wives often acted to please their peers, not one another.

10   Of course, sometimes people loved their children, and some couples undoubtedly fell in love. But most evidence indicates life in the preindustrial household was the opposite of the popular, nostalgic image of quiet, rural villages where people happily lived and died, secure and loved, amidst their large families and lifelong friends. It was instead a nasty, spiteful, loveless life that no modern person would willingly endure. Indeed, as industrialization made other options possible, the family changed radically° because no one was willing to endure the old ways any longer.

Reading Comprehension Questions

Vocabulary in Context

_____ 1. In the excerpt below, the word *ventured* (věn′chərd) means
   A. refused to go.
   B. briefly went away.
   C. dared to go.
   D. stole money or goods.

   ". . . it was largely a case of 'out of sight, out of mind.' If a child ventured from the village, he or she was soon forgotten." (Paragraph 5)

_____ 2. In the excerpt below, the word *hindered* (hĭn′dərd) means
   A. expanded.
   B. got in the way of.
   C. learned from.
   D. helped.

> ". . . [childhood] friendships remained the primary ties of these people. . . . While this no doubt provided people with a source of intimacy and self-esteem, it hindered the formation of close emotional bonds within the family." (Paragraph 8)

Main Ideas

_____ 3. The main idea of paragraph 3 is that in preindustrial times,
   A. proverbs were colorful.
   B. many children died.
   C. poor husband-wife relations could be seen in the reaction to a spouse's death.
   D. people whose spouses died, especially widows, were expected to show some grief.

_____ 4. The main idea of paragraphs 5 and 6 is best expressed in the
   A. first sentence of paragraph 5.
   B. second sentence of paragraph 5.
   C. first sentence of paragraph 6.
   D. last sentence of paragraph 6.

_____ 5. Which sentence best expresses the main idea of paragraphs 8 and 9?
   A. Wives had close attachments to other wives.
   B. Men reserved intimate feelings for their peers.
   C. Women didn't expect to share their feelings with their husbands.
   D. Social life was segregated by sex and was reserved for peers, who thus got in the way of family life.

Supporting Details

_____ 6. Which of the following would *not* be a factor in a preindustrial marriage?
   A. How much land the groom owned
   B. How much money the groom had
   C. The bride and groom's emotional attachment
   D. The size of the bride's dowry

7. Just as the main idea of a paragraph is supported by major details, so is the central point of a longer selection. Following is an outline of the selection. Fill in the missing major detail.

Personal Relationships in the Not-So-Good Old Days

A. The ties between husbands and wives were mainly economical; the most common sentiments among them seem to have been negative ones.

B. The emotional bonds between parents and children were weak.

C. _____

_____

Implied Main Ideas

_____ 8. Which sentence best expresses the implied main idea of paragraph 2?
   A. In preindustrial times, husbands and wives did not show love to each other.
   B. In preindustrial times, husbands and wives disliked each other.
   C. There were more instances of wife-beating than of husband-beating.
   D. Bad feelings between married couples often led to wife beating and also to husband beating, for which the beaten husband was usually blamed.

_____ 9. Which sentence best expresses the implied main idea of paragraph 4?
   A. Wives were of less value to husbands than cows or horses were.
   B. Wives got sick less often than cows or horses did.
   C. Husbands whose wives died always married again.
   D. Doctors charged more to heal humans than they charged to heal animals.

Central Point

_____ 10. Which sentence best expresses the central point of the selection?
   A. People should marry for love.
   B. The main ties in preindustrial families were economic, with the primary emotional bonds being between peers.
   C. Life was difficult in preindustrial society.
   D. Social life in preindustrial society, based on childhood associations, was highly segregated by sex.

Discussion Questions

1. What is your reaction to this reading? Do its facts surprise you? Why or why not?

2. The author writes that "when wives beat their husbands, it was the husband, not the wife, who was likely to be punished. . . . He had shamed the village by not controlling his wife properly." Do you think there are still men today who feel they are supposed to "control" their wives? Explain.

3. In paragraph 7, Stark states that in the traditional family "the primary unit of society and attachment was not the family but the peer group." Does this statement apply at all to our society? At which stages or in what situations might people today feel closer to their peers than to their family members?

4. The author writes, "Only in modern times have most people married for love." Do you think love is the only thing people consider today when choosing a mate? What other factors might be important to consider when selecting a potential life partner?

Note: Writing assignments for this selection appear on page 629.

Check Your Performance	**IMPLIED MAIN IDEAS / CENTRAL POINT**		
Activity	*Number Right*	*Points*	*Score*
Review Test 1 (5 items)	_____	× 2 =	_____
Review Test 2 (5 items)	_____	× 6 =	_____
Review Test 3 (4 items)	_____	× 7.5 =	_____
Review Test 4 (10 items)	_____	× 3 =	_____
	TOTAL SCORE	=	_____%

Enter your total score into the **Reading Performance Chart: Review Tests** on the inside back cover.

IMPLIED MAIN IDEAS AND THE CENTRAL POINT: Mastery Test 1

A. In the space provided, write the letter of the sentence that best expresses the implied main idea of each of the following paragraphs.

_____ 1. [1]One form of jumping to conclusions is putting words into a speaker's mouth. [2]Because we are so sure of what others mean or are going to say, we simply don't listen to what they actually say. [3]Sometimes we don't even hear them out. [4]Instead of listening, we leap to a meaning that they may not have intended to communicate. [5]Another form of jumping to conclusions is rejecting others' ideas too early as boring or misguided. [6]We decide that others have nothing valuable or useful to say. [7]We simply tune out and hear nothing because we decide early on that we can spend our mental effort in a better way.

    A. We "tune out" in several ways.

    B. For several reasons, we might find it difficult to listen to others.

    C. There is more than one way to jump to conclusions.

    D. Communication problems are common in relationships.

_____ 2. [1]The first farm animals were sheep and goats, the most suitable species for driving in small flocks while people might still be traveling. [2]For millennia wild animals had been slaughtered on the spot, but then some bright person realized that sheep and goats could be captured and driven home, thereby saving the effort of dragging their carcasses. [3]Evidently, once the animals were alive at home, it became clear that they could be kept alive for longer periods to serve as dietary insurance policies— ready meat on the hoof. [4]In time it became clear that stocks of sheep and goats could be kept alive to reproduce so that one might have a continuous supply without hunting.

    A. Little by little, humans came to own and breed livestock.

    B. Sheep and goats were the most suitable species for traveling flocks.

    C. At first, humans slaughtered wild animals on the spot and dragged them home.

    D. Keeping livestock is easier than hunting.

_____ 3. [1]The divorce rate in the United States is estimated to be as high as 57.7 percent, and the average length of new marriages is 26 months. [2]Sixty-two percent of our citizens are obese. [3]Emotional neglect of children has increased 330 percent in the last decade. [4]One in four women has been sexually molested. [5]Suicide is on the rise. [6]One out of every six people in America will have a serious, function-impairing episode of

(Continues on next page)

depression in a lifetime. [7]Antidepressant and anxiety-reducing remedies are now a multibillion-dollar business. [8]Violence is evident everywhere, and 25 percent of us fall prey to violent crimes. [9]Teenagers commit about four thousand murders a year. [10]Half of our children have experimented with alcohol by the time they reach the eighth grade, and a fourth have experimented with drugs.

A. American society is overmedicated.
B. American society is troubled in many ways.
C. American society is marked by too much violence.
D. Children and teenagers are at risk in American society.

B. (4.) The author has stated the central point of the following textbook selection in one sentence. Find that sentence, and write its number in the space provided.

Prewriting Strategies

[1]Prewriting refers to strategies you can use to generate ideas *before* starting the first draft of a paper. [2]Prewriting techniques have various advantages. [3]They encourage imaginative exploration and therefore also help you discover what interests you most about your subject. [4]Having such a focus early in the writing process keeps you from plunging into your initial draft without first giving some thought to what you want to say. [5]Prewriting thus saves you time in the long run by keeping you on course.

[6]Prewriting can help in other ways, too. [7]When we write, we often interfere with our ability to generate material because we continually critique what we put down on paper. [8]"This makes no sense," "This is stupid," "I can't say that," and other critical thoughts pop into our minds. [9]Such negative, self-critical comments stop the flow of our thoughts and reinforce the fear that we have nothing to say and aren't very good at writing. [10]During prewriting, you deliberately ignore your internal critic. [11]Your purpose is simply to get ideas down on paper *without evaluating* their effectiveness. [12]Writing without immediately judging what you produce can be liberating. [13]Once you feel less pressure, you'll probably find that you can generate a good deal of material. [14]And that can make your confidence soar.

[15]One final advantage of prewriting: The random associations typical of prewriting tap the mind's ability to make unusual connections. [16]When you prewrite, you're like an archaeologist going on a dig. [17]On the one hand, you may not unearth anything; on the other hand, you may stumble upon one interesting find after another. [18]Prewriting helps you appreciate—right from the start—this element of surprise in the writing process.

_____   is the number of the sentence that states the central point.

IMPLIED MAIN IDEAS AND THE CENTRAL POINT: Mastery Test 2

A. In the space provided, write the letter of the sentence that best expresses the implied main idea of each of the following paragraphs.

_____ 1. [1]Feedback to workers should be timely. [2]Timely feedback is that which occurs soon after a behavior occurs—the sooner the better. [3]Although an annual performance evaluation may be important for other reasons, it is not very effective as a feedback mechanism. [4]The feedback must also be accurate. [5]To maintain motivation and performance, give positive feedback to people doing the best work and negative feedback to people doing the poorest work. [6]If people receive inappropriate feedback, the entire system looks foolish and will fail. [7]It is also discouraging to give the same feedback to everyone. [8]Not everyone can be doing the best job (or the worst, either). [9]If everyone receives the same feedback, then the feedback becomes meaningless, or worse. [10]If the better workers are receiving the same feedback as the poorer workers, the better workers may become unmotivated, and their performance may drop. [11]Why perform well if you earn the same feedback (and rewards) as those doing less well?

    A. Positive feedback is a very useful tool in managing motivation and performance.

    B. To be effective, job feedback must be timely and accurate.

    C. An annual performance evaluation is a poor feedback tool.

    D. To be timely, feedback should be given as soon as possible after what is being evaluated takes place.

_____ 2. [1]Primary relationships—with our relatives, friends, or neighbors—are very precious to us. [2]As research has shown, they are particularly helpful when we are going through stressful life events. [3]They help ease recovery from heart attacks, prevent childbirth complications, make child rearing easier, lighten the burden of household finances, and cushion the impact of job loss by providing financial assistance and employment information. [4]However, secondary relationships have their own special benefits. [5]Our close friends may not help us, for instance, get as good a job as our acquaintances can. [6]Our friends move in the same social circle as we do, but our acquaintances, to whom we have only weak ties, move in different circles. [7]As a result, we may already be aware of the job openings known to our friends, but we may not know of the many other job opportunities our acquaintances can tell us about.

    A. Primary relationships and secondary relationships each have their own special benefits.

    B. Primary and secondary relationships are necessary for our very survival.

(Continues on next page)

161

    C. Secondary relationships can be invaluable if we are looking for jobs.

    D. We would probably not be able to get through stressful life events without primary relationships.

_____ 3. ¹It is difficult to do the intense, active thinking that clear writing demands. ²(Perhaps television has made us all so passive that the active thinking necessary in both writing and reading now seems doubly hard.) ³It is frightening to sit down before a blank sheet of paper and know that an hour later, nothing on it may be worth keeping. ⁴It is frustrating to discover how much of a challenge it is to transfer thoughts and feelings from one's head onto a sheet of paper. ⁵It is upsetting to find that an apparently simple writing assignment often turns out to be complicated. ⁶But writing is not an automatic process: we will not get something for nothing, and we cannot expect something for nothing.

    A. Writing is hard work.

    B. Writing offers rich rewards.

    C. Anything worthwhile requires patience and effort.

    D. Television is making active thinking more difficult than ever.

B. (4.) The author has stated the central point of the following textbook selection in one sentence. Find that sentence, and write its number in the space provided.

Bug Protection

¹Almost all insects will flee if threatened. ²Many insects, however, have more specialized means of defense. ³Roaches and stinkbugs, for example, secrete foul-smelling chemicals that deter aggressors. ⁴Bees, wasps, and some ants have poisonous stings that can kill smaller predators and cause pain for larger ones. ⁵The larvae of some insects have hairs filled with poison. ⁶If a predator eats one of these larvae, it may suffer a toxic reaction. ⁷Insects that defend themselves by unpleasant or dangerous chemicals gain two advantages. ⁸On one hand, they often deter a predator from eating them. ⁹On the other hand, predators learn not to bother them in the first place.

¹⁰Other insects gain protection by mimicry, or similarity of appearance. ¹¹In one kind of mimicry, insects with similar defense mechanisms look alike, and predators learn to avoid them all. ¹²Bees and wasps mimic each other in this way. ¹³In another kind of mimicry, insects with no defenses of their own mimic the appearance of stinging or bad-tasting insects. ¹⁴Predators avoid the mimic as well as the insect with the unpleasant taste or sting. ¹⁵For example, syrphid flies look like bees but do not sting.

¹⁶Another kind of defense based on appearance is camouflage, or the ability to blend into surroundings. ¹⁷Many kinds of insects and animals have distinctive color markings that make them difficult to see. ¹⁸Predators have trouble locating prey that looks like its background. ¹⁹An insect is more likely to survive and produce offspring if it is camouflaged than if it is not.

_____ is the number of the sentence that states the central point.

IMPLIED MAIN IDEAS AND THE CENTRAL POINT: Mastery Test 3

A. In the space provided, write the letter of the sentence that best expresses the implied main idea of each of the following paragraphs.

_____ 1. [1]A line graph shows changes, especially changes over specific time periods. [2]It might show outdoor temperatures hour by hour, or weight loss week by week. [3]Bar graphs display and compare amounts: the higher or longer a bar, the greater the amount. [4]A bar graph might show, for instance, the number of male and female smokers in several age groups, or death rates from various causes. [5]A circle or "pie" graph shows parts of a whole. [6]Each sector of the circle—each wedge of the pie—is one part. [7]Circle graphs are often used for budgets: 50 percent for rent, 25 percent for food, and so on. [8]They're also used for polls: for instance, 45 percent "yes," 40 percent "no," and 15 percent "undecided."

A. The sectors of a circle graph look like wedges of a pie.
B. Line graphs, bar graphs, and circle graphs are used to show different kinds of information.
C. Line graphs are the most useful kind of graph.
D. We often see line graphs, bar graphs, and circle graphs in newspapers, magazines, and textbooks.

_____ 2. [1]One condition of society that lies at the roots of political conflict in America is scarcity. [2]Society has limited resources, but people have unlimited appetites, so there is never enough money in even the wealthiest countries. [3]This scarcity creates conflict over how the available resources will be distributed. [4]How will taxes be used? [5]Who will be eligible for welfare benefits? [6]How much will those eligible for benefits receive? [7]These issues best demonstrate the conflict over scarcity. [8]The other condition of society that creates political conflict is differences in values. [9]People don't see things the same way and therefore bring to politics a wide range of conflicting values—about abortion, the environment, defense spending, crime and punishment, the poor, the economy, and almost everything else imaginable.

A. Political conflict in America is rooted in two general conditions of society.
B. People view politics in differing ways.
C. Conflict in America is a natural outcome of our many differences in values.
D. Because of the scarcity of available resources, conflict is inevitable.

(Continues on next page)

163

_____ 3. [1]One factor that kept FM radio from developing as much as AM was that more people had AM receivers than FM receivers, and it was not possible to pick up FM on a standard AM radio. [2]Moreover, many of the same people who owned AM stations owned FM stations; to simplify the programming effort, they would broadcast the same show over both frequencies. [3]Third, after World War II, the Federal Communications Commission (FCC) moved FM from the place it had originally occupied on the broadcast spectrum; this made all existing FM radios useless.

A. Standard AM radios could not pick up FM.
B. Several factors held back FM radio's development.
C. Many owners of AM stations also owned FM stations.
D. By moving FM to a different broadcast spectrum, the FCC made all existing FM radios useless.

B. (4.) The author has stated the central point of the following textbook selection in one sentence. Find that sentence, and write its number in the space provided.

Peer Pressure

[1]We often hear about the dangers of peer pressure to teenagers. [2]Teens take drugs, skip school, get drunk, or have sex to impress their friends. [3]However, there is another, perhaps equally bad, effect of peer pressure. [4]Desperate to conform to their friends' values, teens may give up their interests in school, in hobbies, and even in certain people.

[5]Teens may lose or hide their interest in school in order to be like their friends. [6]They adopt a negative attitude in which school is seen as a battlefield, with teachers and other officials regarded as the enemy. [7]In private, they may enjoy certain teachers, but in front of their friends, they put on a sarcastic or hostile act. [8]In addition, teenagers may stop participating in class. [9]They may refuse to join in class discussions, even when the topic interests them. [10]They may decide it is cool to show up without the assigned homework. [11]If their peers demand it, they may interfere with others' learning by disrupting class. [12]Conforming also means not joining in after-school activities.

[13]Teenagers also give up private pleasures and hobbies to be one of the crowd. [14]Certain pastimes, such as writing poems, practicing piano, reading books, or fooling around with a chemistry set may be off-limits because the crowd laughs at them.

[15]Most sadly, teenagers sometimes give up the people they love in order to be accepted. [16]If necessary, they sacrifice the old friend who no longer dresses well enough, listens to the wrong kind of music, or refuses to drink or take drugs. [17]Potential boyfriends or girlfriends may be rejected, too, if the crowd doesn't like their looks or values. [18]Teens can even cut their families out of their lives if they are too poor, too conventional, or too different from their friends' parents.

_____ is the number of the sentence that states the central point.

IMPLIED MAIN IDEAS AND THE CENTRAL POINT: Mastery Test 4

A. In the space provided, write the letter of the sentence that best expresses the implied main idea of each of the following paragraphs.

_____ 1. [1]When a person does something that causes you discomfort or inconvenience, you may think of him or her as being a jerk, geek, airhead—or perhaps some other more colorful label. [2]Seeing a person as a "jerk" puts the person in an entirely negative light. [3]Such labeling involves overgeneralizing, perhaps on the basis of only a single event. [4]In reality, we all perform our share of "jerklike" behaviors. [5]But if we label someone else as the jerk, we see ourselves as being somewhat superior. [6]We then feel more justified in becoming angry with this person, since he or she is the essence of badness, rather than just a person who chose a behavior that we consider to be undesirable.

    A. People may use a negative label for someone who causes discomfort or inconvenience.

    B. It is unfair to label someone negatively on the basis of a single event.

    C. We tend to judge others in ways that make us feel superior.

    D. To justify our own anger or discomfort, we may use unfair labels that make us feel superior.

_____ 2. [1]In college, students experience a lot of stress around exam time. [2]Knowing that, researchers took saliva samples from healthy college students before, during, and after final exams. [3]They tested the saliva for the presence of a substance which fights infection. [4]The tests showed that the infection-fighter was at its lowest level during the exam period. [5]In addition, many of the students developed colds during final exams. [6]In a related study, older adults who were receiving flu shots were interviewed. [7]About half of those adults reported living with a high degree of stress. [8]Six months after receiving the shot, blood tests showed that the group that had reported having little stress in their lives had a far higher degree of immunity than the highly-stressed group. [9]The adults living with more stress were at much greater risk for catching flu.

    A. Flu epidemics could be eliminated if more people would learn how to deal with stress.

    B. College students who do not prepare ahead of time for exams are more likely to get sick.

    C. Older adults often have to cope with a high degree of stress.

    D. Apparently, the more stressed a person is, the lower his or her immunity to disease.

(Continues on next page)

B. (3.) Write out, in your own words, the implied main idea of the following paragraph.

[1]Our senses of sight, hearing, taste, and smell are constantly bombarded by stimuli. [2]These stimuli are stored in our sensory memory, where they remain for just a fraction of a second. [3]When we look up a phone number and remember it long enough to dial it, we are using another form of memory, our short-term memory. [4]Ideal for briefly remembering such small chunks of information, short-term memory decays quickly, which is why we would probably have to look up that same phone number again if we needed it a few hours later. [5]The third type of memory is long-term memory, where we store information that we've judged as important. [6]Our long-term memories can last a lifetime.

Implied main idea: _____

_____

C. (4.) The author has stated the central point of the following textbook passage in one sentence. Find that sentence, and write its number in the space provided.

Extracting Salt in San Francisco Bay

[1]Each year about 30 percent of the world's supply of salt is extracted from seawater. [2]At the southern end of San Francisco Bay, salt is extracted in a long process in which seawater is held in shallow ponds while the sun evaporates the water.

[3]The process begins when bay water is admitted to the first of the concentrating ponds in early summer when the discharge of the rivers entering the bay is reduced and the water in the bay is at its highest salinity. [4]Once in the ponds, the brine is moved from pond to pond as it reaches certain pre-established levels of salinity. [5]Evaporation continues until the solution is concentrated enough to crystallize virtually pure sodium chloride.

[6]During the first stages in the evaporation process, small fish thrive and are netted commercially. [7]Toward the middle of the cycle, the brine becomes too concentrated for fish to survive. [8]Instead, tiny shrimp find this environment to their liking. [9]They are harvested for sale as fish food for aquariums. [10]As the brine becomes more concentrated in the final concentrating pond, most plant and animal life begins to die.

[11]In the spring, the concentrated brine is pumped into carefully cleaned twenty- to sixty-acre crystallizers. [12]Shortly after these ponds are filled to a depth of about 0.5 meter, tiny crystals of pure salt begin to grow. [13]By fall, a twelve- to fifteen-centimeter-thick layer of salt crystals has collected on the bottom. [14]The salt is ready to harvest, five years after the seawater first entered the process.

_____ is the number of the sentence that states the central point.

IMPLIED MAIN IDEAS AND THE CENTRAL POINT: Mastery Test 5

A. In the space provided, write the letter of the sentence that best expresses the implied main idea of each of the following paragraphs.

_____ 1. [1]"Anybody can go to college if he or she really wants to. [2]I didn't have any money, but I worked nights, lifted myself up by my bootstraps, and got a college degree. [3]If I could do it, anyone can!" [4]Is that assumption necessarily true? [5]What if a person has a large family to support and is living up to or beyond the limits of his or her income? [6]What if a person hasn't had the good fortune to be born with great mental abilities? [7]The exceptions could go on and on.

[8]"I work because I need the money. [9]Wendy shouldn't be working here. [10]Her husband makes good money, so she doesn't even have to work." [11]Isn't this person assuming that what is true for one is true for all? [12]Couldn't there be other reasons for working besides the quest for money? [13]How about the need to socialize with others or the need to make a contribution? [14]Every individual's situation is different.

A. Not everybody can go to college if he or she really wants to.
B. What is true for one person or situation is never true for anyone else.
C. What is true for one person in a situation may or may not be true for someone else.
D. People are more alike than they realize.

_____ 2. [1]Criminal courts in most jurisdictions are very busy. [2]The large number of people arrested and prosecuted, the limited availability of defense attorneys to help an accused person prepare and offer a defense, and the overcrowded courts create a heavy caseload demand on everyone associated with criminal justice—prosecutors, public and private defenders, and judges. [3]The result of the crowded court calendars, court delays, and clogged caseloads is that most cases do not go to trial at all. [4]Most are "settled" through guilty pleas, pleas arranged among the prosecutor, defense attorney, the accused, and the judge. [5]Guilty pleas are induced through negotiations whereby the defendant pleads guilty to reduced charges in exchange for a lenient sentence, that is, a lighter sentence than the judge would normally give after conviction at trial. [6]This entire process is generally known as plea-bargaining, or plea negotiation.

A. Crime is a major problem in the United States.
B. In plea-bargaining, defendants plead guilty to lesser charges in exchange for a more lenient sentence.
C. Because of heavy court caseloads, most cases are settled through plea-bargaining.
D. The criminal courts are crowded because a large number of people are arrested.

(Continues on next page)

167

B. (3.) Write out, in your own words, the implied main idea of the following paragraph.

[1]For more than a quarter century, voter turnout for Presidential elections has been declining. [2]In 2000, for example, slightly under 51 percent of American adults turned out to cast their ballots. [3]Some non-voters say it's too much trouble to get to the polls during a busy workday. [4]Others claim that the voter-registration process is overly complicated. [5]Many say that they don't know enough about the issues in order to make a responsible decision between candidates. [6]Others blame regional politics, saying there's no point for a Democrat to vote in the North or for a Republican to vote in the South. [7]Still more point to a feeling of estrangement from government that began during the Vietnam War era.

Implied main idea: _____

_____

C. (4.) The author has stated the central point of the following textbook passage in one sentence. Find that sentence, and write its number in the space provided.

A Medical Mystery

[1]Medical researchers were perplexed. [2]Reports were coming in from all over the country indicating that women, who live longer than men, were twice as likely to die after coronary bypass surgery. [3]Medical records at one hospital showed that of almost 2,300 coronary bypass patients, 4.6 percent of the women died as a result of the surgery, compared with only 2.6 percent of the men.

[4]Initial explanations were based on biology. [5]Coronary bypass surgery involves taking a blood vessel from one part of the body and stitching it to a coronary artery on the surface of the heart. [6]This operation was supposedly more difficult to perform on women because of their smaller hearts and coronary arteries. [7]But researchers who tested this theory soon found that the operation was not more difficult to perform on women.

[8]As the researchers continued to probe, a surprising answer slowly unfolded. [9]The cause of the greater number of deaths of women after bypass surgery was sexual discrimination by physicians. [10]They simply did not take the chest pains of their women patients as seriously as those of their men patients. [11]Physicians were ten times more likely to give men exercise stress tests and radioactive heart scans. [12]And they sent men to surgery on the basis of abnormal stress tests but waited until women showed clear-cut symptoms of coronary heart disease before recommending surgery. [13]Being referred for surgery later in the course of the disease decreases the chances of survival.

_____ is the number of the sentence that states the central point.

IMPLIED MAIN IDEAS AND THE CENTRAL POINT: Mastery Test 6

A. In the space provided, write the letter of the sentence that best expresses the implied main idea of each of the following paragraphs.

_____ 1. ¹Every wage earner covered under the Social Security Act pays a tax; the employer also pays a tax, which is equal to that paid by the employee. ²The amount that one can expect to receive each month in old-age insurance benefits depends on one's average monthly earnings. ³Also, the size of the benefits depends on the number of years one has worked. ⁴If a person retires at 65, the monthly benefits are greater than if he or she retires at 62. ⁵These benefits are a retirement annuity. ⁶In other words, they are paid to the wage earner from the date of retirement to the time he or she dies. ⁷In addition, when a wage earner dies, Social Security provides payments to his or her spouse, to dependent parents, and to children until they are about 18 years of age (21 if they are in school). ⁸Further, payments are made to a wage earner (and dependents) if he or she is totally disabled and unable to work.

    A. Social Security pays retirement annuities, which are paid to the wage earner from the date of retirement until death.

    B. Both wage earners and employers make payments to Social Security.

    C. The government makes direct payments to various individuals and institutions.

    D. A complicated set of rules governs the funding and payment of Social Security.

_____ 2. ¹*Verbal irony,* which is often tongue-in-cheek, involves a discrepancy between the words spoken and what is actually meant. ²For example, "Here's some news that will make you sad. ³You received the highest grade in the course." ⁴If the ironic comment is designed to be hurting or insulting, it qualifies as *sarcasm.* ⁵An illustration is the comment "Congratulations! You failed the final exam." ⁶In *dramatic irony,* the discrepancy is between what the speaker says and what the author means or what the audience knows. ⁷For instance, in Shakespeare's *King Lear,* the old king gives all his wealth to two cold-blooded daughters who flatter and manipulate him with false words; he then entrusts himself to their care. ⁸He banishes the daughter who so truly loves him that she will tell him nothing but the truth. ⁹The audience watches Lear make this catastrophic misjudgment and waits for tragedy to unfold.

    A. Irony takes a few forms.

    B. Shakespeare made good use of irony.

    C. Sarcasm is a type of irony with a biting quality.

    D. Dramatic irony adds power to a work of fiction.

(Continues on next page)

B. (3.) Write out, in your own words, the implied main idea of the following paragraph.

[1]For an older person who lives alone, having a dog in the house or apartment provides companionship. [2]Physical contact with a dog can also be helpful. [3]Patting a dog has been shown to lower the blood pressure of both the human and the dog. [4]A dog owner frequently talks to the pet, and talking helps keep the owner's mind active. [5]In addition, the dog depends on the person for its survival. [6]Being needed by another living creature creates a sense of purpose in a senior citizen's life. [7]The dog must be fed and walked at regular intervals. [8]This helps the person maintain a daily routine and stay physically active in older age. [9]Dog walking also encourages the owner to have contact with other human beings.

Implied main idea: _____

C. (4.) The author has stated the central point of the following textbook selection in one sentence. Find that sentence, and write its number in the space provided.

From a Lake to a Forest

[1]Imagine a lake that has recently been carved by a glacier out of solid rock. [2]Its water is perfectly clear. [3]This lake is so new that it contains no sediment and no living organisms of any kind.

[4]This lake may remain free of life for a short time, but soon dust blows into it, and soil slides in after a heavy rain. [5]In addition, sediments are carried into the lake by the rivers that feed it. [6]Wind-borne spores of bacteria, algae, fungi, and protozoa fall into the lake. [7]These grow in the sediment that has settled there. [8]These organisms are called pioneer species because they are the first to inhabit a new community. [9]Adaptable to life in low-nutrient conditions, they thrive and eventually die, adding new nutrients, such as carbon and nitrogen, to the lake. [10]The process of adding nutrients to an ecosystem is called eutrophication.

[11]As eutrophication proceeds, the lake can support a few plants such as water lilies and quillworts. [12]These plants take root in the shallow water at the lake's edge. [13]They catch and hold soil. [14]Some animals, such as frogs and insects, find suitable habitats in the plants at the lake's edge.

[15]As the water lilies, quillworts, and insects die and decompose, their remains further eutrophicate the lake. [16]The decaying organic matter collects on the lake's edge and bottom. [17]The lake gradually becomes shallower. [18]Cattails and rushes invade the shallow water. [19]They grow tall and eventually shade out the water lilies.

[20]After a while vegetation grows throughout the lake and the lake becomes a marsh—another community that exists as the site continues to change. [21]When the marsh becomes drier, willow trees start to invade its borders, and a willow community forms. [22]Over time other communities, such as a birch forest, a pine forest, and an oak forest, replace one another on the site once occupied by the lake. [23]A climax forest, perhaps one dominated by beech trees, finally forms—after as little as five hundred years or as much as ten thousand years or more—and primary succession is complete. [24](A climax community is a relatively stable, almost permanent, community.) [25]Thus a lake may be transformed into a forest by gradually passing through a sequence of ecological communities.

_____ is the number of the sentence that states the central point.

5

Relationships I

Authors use two common methods to show relationships and make their ideas clear. The two methods—**transitions** and **patterns of organization**—are explained in turn in this chapter. The chapter also explains two common types of relationships:

- Relationships that involve **addition**
- Relationships that involve **time**

TRANSITIONS

Look at the following items and put a check (✓) by the one that is easier to read and understand:

____ You can reduce the number of colds you catch. You should wash your hands frequently during the cold season.

____ You can reduce the number of colds you catch. First of all, you should wash your hands frequently during the cold season.

You probably found the second item easier to understand. The words *first of all* make it clear that the writer plans on explaining two or more ways to reduce the number of colds. **Transitions** are words or phrases (like *first of all*) that show relationships between ideas. They are like signs on the road that guide travelers.

Two major types of transitions are words that show addition and words that show time.

Words That Show Addition

Once again, put a check (✓) beside the item that is easier to read and understand:

____ A virus cannot move or grow. It can reproduce only inside a cell of another organism.

____ A virus cannot move or grow. Furthermore, it can reproduce only inside a cell of another organism.

In the first item, we're not sure of the relationship between the two sentences. The word *furthermore* in the second item makes the relationship clear: The author is listing two altogether different qualities of a virus. *Furthermore* and words like it are known as addition words.

Addition words signal added ideas. These words tell you a writer is presenting one or more ideas that continue along the same line of thought as a previous idea. Like all transitions, addition words help writers organize their information and present it clearly to readers. Here are some common words that show addition:

Addition Words

one	to begin with	also	further
first (of all)	for one thing	in addition	furthermore
second (ly)	other	next	last (of all)
third (ly)	another	moreover	final (ly)

Examples:

The following examples contain addition words. Notice how these words introduce ideas that *add to* what has already been said.

We communicate to exchange information. We *also* communicate to develop relationships.

Tiger sharks eat fish, squid, sea turtles, seals, and smaller sharks. *In addition,* they have been known to swallow car license plates and gasoline cans.

Consumers today want much more information about food products than they did twenty or more years ago. Why? *For one thing,* they are much more aware of nutrition than they used to be.

➤ *Practice 1*

Complete each sentence with a suitable addition word from the box on the previous page. Try to use a variety of transitions.

> *Hint:* Make sure that each addition word or phrase that you choose fits smoothly into the flow of the sentence. Test each choice by reading the sentence aloud.

1. An important dental warning sign is a tooth that shows sensitivity to hot or cold. _____ sign is bleeding gums.

2. Paranoid people often believe that someone is plotting against them. They may _____ believe that everyone is talking about and staring at them.

3. A two-thousand-year-old tomb in England contained remnants of a wooden board game. _____, the tomb contained a set of surgical instruments.

4. A person in a crowd is less likely to offer help in an emergency than a person by himself. One reason is that he may be afraid of embarrassing himself by overreacting to the situation. A _____ reason is that he may assume that a better-qualified person will respond.

5. Education has a very real effect on one's earning power. A recent survey showed that high-school dropouts earned an average of $18,900 annually, while high-school graduates earned $25,900. _____, adding a college degree brought the average salary up to $45,400.

Words That Show Time

Put a check (✓) beside the item that is easier to read and understand:

____ I fill in the answers to the test questions I'm sure I know. I work on the rest of the exam.

____ First I fill in the answers to the test questions I'm sure I know. Then I work on the rest of the exam.

The words *first* and *then* in the second item clarify the relationship between the sentences. The author begins work on the rest of the exam after answering the questions that he or she is sure about. *First, then,* and words like them are time words.

These transitions indicate a time relationship. **Time words** tell us *when* something happened in relation to when something else happened. They help writers organize and make clear the order of events, stages, and steps in a process.

Here are some common words that show time:

Time Words

before	immediately	when	until
previously	next	whenever	often
first (of all)	then	while	frequently
second (ly)	following	during	eventually
third (ly)	later	as	final (ly)
now	after	soon	last (of all)

Note: Additional ways of showing time are dates ("In 1850 . . ."; "Throughout the 20th century . . ."; "By 2010 . . .") and other time references ("Within a week . . ."; "by the end of the month . . ."; "in two years . . .").

Examples:

The following examples contain time words. Notice how these words show us *when* something takes place.

> *During* the last ice age, there were huge icebergs in the ocean as far south as Mexico City.

> I cross the street *whenever* I see someone coming toward me whose name I've forgotten.

> *Before* assuming something you read on the Internet is true, remember that anyone can post information there.

Helpful Tips about Transitions

Here are two points to keep in mind about transitions.

TIP *Tip 1* Some transition words have the same meaning. For example, *also, moreover,* and *furthermore* all mean "in addition." Authors typically use a variety of transitions to avoid repetition.

TIP *Tip 2* Certain words can serve as two different types of transitions, depending on how they are used. For example, the word *first* may be used as an addition word to show that the author is beginning to list a series of ideas, as in the following:

> Plant researchers have developed promising new types of apples. *First,* the apples are disease-resistant and don't need pesticides. *Moreover,* . . . .

First may also be used to signal a time sequence, as in this sentence:

> When you feel anger building up within you, take several steps to deal with it. *First,* start to breathe slowly and deeply.

➤ *Practice 2*

Complete each sentence with a suitable time word from the box on the previous page. Try to use a variety of transitions.

> *Hint:* Make sure that each time word or phrase that you choose fits smoothly into the flow of the sentence. Test each choice by reading the sentence aloud.

1. _____ a great white shark was spotted a half-mile off shore, lifeguards made everyone get out of the water.

2. Tension headaches generally begin in the morning or early afternoon. They _____ worsen during the day.

3. _____ the summer, our dog Floyd spends most of his day sprawled on the cool tiles of the kitchen floor, panting and drooling.

4. San Francisco tailor Levi Strauss originally made jeans from canvas. It wasn't _____ the early 1860s that he started using a softer fabric imported from France, which in the United States was called denim.

5. Advances in medical technology have forced doctors to redefine when death actually occurs. _____ such advances, the definition of death had seemed fairly simple.

PATTERNS OF ORGANIZATION

You have learned that transitions show the relationships between ideas in sentences. In the same way, **patterns of organization** show the relationships between supporting details in paragraphs, essays, and chapters. It helps to recognize the common patterns in which authors arrange information. You will then be better able to understand and remember what you read.

The rest of this chapter discusses two major patterns of organization:

- The **list of items pattern**
  (Addition words are often used in this pattern of organization.)
- The **time order pattern**
  (Time words are often used in this pattern of organization.)

Noticing the transitions in a passage can often help you become aware of its pattern of organization. Transitions can also help you locate the major supporting details.

1   THE LIST OF ITEMS PATTERN

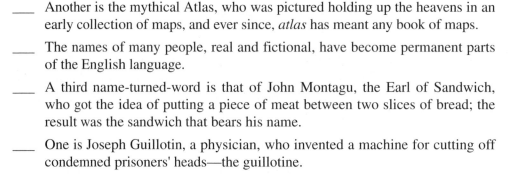

To get a sense of the list of items pattern, try to arrange the following sentences in a logical order. Put a *1* in front of the sentence that should come first, a *2* in front of the sentence that comes next, a *3* in front of the third sentence, and a *4* in front of the sentence that should come last. The result will be a short paragraph. Use the addition words as a guide.

____   Another is the mythical Atlas, who was pictured holding up the heavens in an early collection of maps, and ever since, *atlas* has meant any book of maps.

____   The names of many people, real and fictional, have become permanent parts of the English language.

____   A third name-turned-word is that of John Montagu, the Earl of Sandwich, who got the idea of putting a piece of meat between two slices of bread; the result was the sandwich that bears his name.

____   One is Joseph Guillotin, a physician, who invented a machine for cutting off condemned prisoners' heads—the guillotine.

This paragraph begins with the main idea: "The names of many people, real and fictional, have become permanent parts of the English language." The next three sentences go on to list people whose names have become parts of the language, resulting in the pattern of organization known as a *list of items*. The transitions *one, another,* and *third* each introduce one of the names being listed and indicate their order. Here is the whole paragraph in its correct order:

> [1]The names of many people, real and fictional, have become permanent parts of the English language. [2]One is Joseph Guillotin, a physician, who invented a machine for cutting off condemned prisoners' heads—the guillotine. [3]Another is the mythical Atlas, who was pictured holding up the heavens in an early collection of maps, and ever since, *atlas* has meant any book of maps. [4]A third name-turned-word is that of John Montagu, the Earl of Sandwich, who got the idea of putting a piece of meat between two slices of bread; the result was the sandwich that bears his name.

A **list of items** refers to a series of reasons, examples, or other supporting details that support an idea. The items have no time order, but are listed in whatever order the author prefers. Addition words are often used in a list of items to tell us that other supporting points are being added to a point already mentioned. Textbook authors frequently organize material into lists of items, such as a list of types of financial institutions, symptoms of iron deficiency, or reasons for alcohol abuse by college students.

☑ *Check Your Understanding*

The paragraph below is organized as a list of items. Complete the outline of the list by first filling in the missing part of the main idea. Then add to the outline the three major details listed in the paragraph.

To help you find the major details, do two things:

- Underline the addition words that introduce the major details in the list;
- Number (*1, 2, . . .*) each item in the list.

¹Self-disclosure is revealing information about oneself. ²Meaningful self-disclosure includes three important elements. ³First of all, it must be done on purpose. ⁴If you accidentally mention to a friend that you're thinking about quitting a job, that is not self-disclosure. ⁵Second, the information must be significant. ⁶Telling trivial facts, opinions, or feelings—that you like fudge, for example—hardly counts as disclosure. ⁷The third requirement is that the information being shared is private. ⁸There's nothing noteworthy about telling others that you are depressed or happy if they already know that.

Main idea: Meaningful self-disclosure includes _____

_____ .

1. _____

2. _____

3. _____

Explanation:

The main idea is that meaningful self-disclosure includes three important elements. (At times you may also express the main idea in a short heading: the heading here could be "Elements in meaningful self-disclosure.") Following are the three elements you should have added to the outline:

1. Done on purpose. (This element is signaled with the addition phrase *first of all).*

2. Significant. (This element is signaled by the addition word *second).*

3. Private. (This element is signaled by the addition word *third.)*

➤ *Practice 3*

A. The following passage uses a listing pattern. Outline the passage by filling in the main idea and the major details.

> *Hint:* Underline the addition words that introduce the items in the list and number the items.

> [1]All of us, at one time or another, have said something to someone that we regretted. [2]Researchers have discovered five general categories of "regrettable comments." [3]The most common kind of regrettable comment is the blunder. [4]Examples are forgetting someone's name or getting it wrong, or asking, "How's your mother?" and hearing the reply, "She died." [5]The next most common category is direct attack—a generalized criticism of the other person or of his or her family or friends. [6]Another type of regrettable remark is the negative group reference, which often contains racial or ethnic slurs. [7]The fourth category is direct and specific criticism such as "You never clean house" or "You shouldn't go out with that guy." [8]The final type of regrettable comment is saying too much. [9]It includes telling other people's secrets or telling hurtful things said by others.

Main idea: _____

_____

    1. _____

    2. _____

    3. _____

    4. _____

    5. _____

B. The following passage uses a listing pattern. Complete the map of the passage by filling in the main idea and the missing major and minor details.

> [1]Preventive medicine sounds ideal as a way of ensuring good health and reducing costs, but how do you actually prevent something from happening? [2]A number of practitioners and health planners have figured out ways of putting preventive medicine into practice. [3]Primary prevention consists of actions that keep a disease from occurring at all. [4]An example would be childhood vaccinations against polio, measles, and smallpox. [5]Secondary prevention involves detection before a disease comes to the attention of the physician. [6]An example would be self-examination by women for breast cancer. [7]Finally, tertiary prevention devotes itself to preventing further damage from already existing disease. [8]Keeping a diabetic on insulin and controlling pneumonia so it does not lead to death are examples of tertiary prevention.

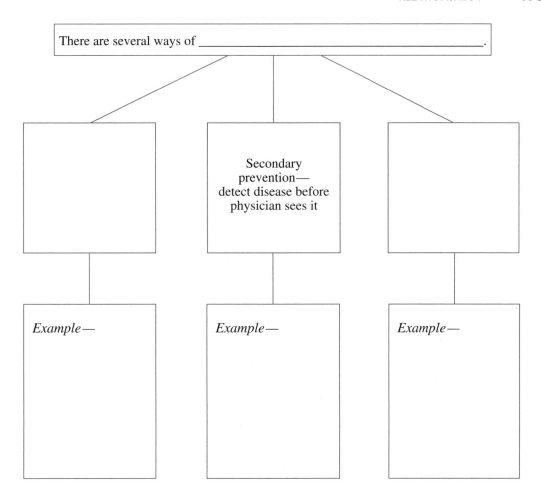

There are several ways of _____.

Secondary prevention—detect disease before physician sees it

Example—

Example—

Example—

2 THE TIME ORDER PATTERN

To get a sense of the time order pattern, try to arrange the following sentences in a logical order. Put a *1* in front of the sentence that should come first, a *2* in front of the sentence that comes next, and a *3* in front of the sentence that should come last. The result will be a short paragraph. Use the time words as a guide.

____ The water then begins to expand and rise, to be replaced by cold water from the upper regions of the pot.

____ In the convection process, water from the bottom of a heating pot begins to move faster.

____ Eventually, after this heated water gets to the top, it cools off and sinks, to be replaced by newly heated water from the bottom.

Authors usually present events and processes in the order in which they happen, resulting in a pattern of organization known as **time order**. Clues to the pattern of the above sentences are the transitions *(then, eventually,* and *after)* that show time. The sentences should read as follows:

> ¹In the convection process, water from the bottom of a heating pot begins to move faster. ²The water then begins to expand and rise, to be replaced by cold water from the upper regions of the pot. ³Eventually, after this heated water gets to the top, it cools off and sinks, to be replaced by newly heated water from the bottom.

As a student, you will see time order used frequently. Textbooks in all fields describe events and processes, such as the events leading to the outbreak of the French Revolution; the important incidents in the life of Dr. Martin Luther King, Jr.; the steps in filing a lawsuit; the process involved in digesting a meal; or the stages in recovering from the death of a loved one.

In addition to time transitions, many of which are listed on page 174, signals for the time order pattern include dates, times, and such words as *stages, series, steps,* and *process.*

The two most common kinds of time order are 1) a series of events or stages and 2) a series of steps (directions for how to do something). Each is discussed below and on the following pages.

Series of Events or Stages

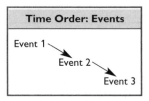

☑ *Check Your Understanding*

On the next page is a paragraph that is organized according to time order. Complete the outline of the paragraph by listing the missing stages in the order in which they happen.

To help you find the stages, do two things:

* Underline the words that introduce each stage;

* Number *(1, 2, . . .)* each stage.

[1]The study of volunteers in sleep laboratories has led researchers to believe that humans go through four different stages of sleep in a normal night's rest. [2]After falling asleep, people enter stage 1 sleep, also called "light sleep" or "REM" (rapid eye movement) sleep. [3]During this stage the sleeper's brain waves are irregular, and the person is easily awakened. [4]The next period of sleep, stage 2 sleep, is marked by bursts of fast brain-wave activity called "spindles." [5]Then, during stage 3 sleep, the spindles disappear, and brain waves become long and slow. [6]Last, the deepest level of sleep, during which the sleeper is hardest to awaken, occurs during stage 4 sleep. [7]Extremely slow brain waves known as delta waves are present during this deep-sleep phase.

Main idea: Researchers believe that humans go through four different stages of sleep in a normal night's rest.

1. _____

   _____

2. _____

   _____

3. Stage 3—spindles disappear; brain waves become long and slow.

4. _____

   _____

Explanation:

You should have added these points to the outline:

1. Stage 1—light, or REM, sleep: irregular brain waves; easily awakened.
2. Stage 2—burst of fast brain-wave activity called "spindles."
4. Stage 4—deepest level: very slow brain waves called "delta waves"; most difficult to awaken.

As emphasized by the transitions *After, next, Then,* and *Last* (and the stage numbers 1, 2, 3, and 4), the relationship between the points is one of time: The first stage happens *after* the person falls asleep. The second stage happens *next*, and so on.

➤ *Practice 4*

The following passage describes a sequence of events. Outline the paragraph by filling in the main idea and major details. Note that the major details are signaled by time words.

> *Hint:* Underline the time word or words that introduce each major detail, and number each major detail.

[1]We can think of the scientific method in terms of four stages, which are usually carried out by different scientists, sometimes many years apart. [2]The first stage is the formulation of a problem. [3]The scientist may have a theory, perhaps only a hunch, about some aspect of nature but cannot come to a definite conclusion without further study. [4]The next stage is observation and experiment, activities which are carried out with extreme care. [5]Facts about nature are the building blocks of science and the ultimate proof of its results. [6]This insistence on the importance of accurate, objective data is what sets science apart from other modes of intellectual effort. [7]The third stage is interpretation, which may lead to a general rule, or it may be a more ambitious attempt to account for what has been found in terms of how nature works. [8]The last stage is testing the interpretation, which involves making new observations or performing new experiments to see whether the interpretation correctly predicts the results. [9]If the results agree with the predictions, the scientist is clearly on the right track.

Main idea:_____.

   1. _____

   2. _____

   3. _____

   4. _____

Series of Steps (Directions)

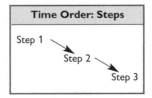

When authors give directions, they use time order. They explain step 1, then step 2, and so on through the entire series of steps that must be taken toward a specific goal.

☑ *Check Your Understanding*

Below is a paragraph that gives directions. Complete the outline of the paragraph that follows by filling in the main idea and listing the missing steps in the correct sequence. To help yourself identify each step, do two things:

- Underline the time words that introduce each item in the sequence;
- Number (*1, 2, . . .*) each step in the sequence.

   ¹If you mention the word PROM to people, they are going to think of a high-school rite of passage. ²In fact, PROM is also the name of a proven study method. ³The first step in this system is to *preview* a reading assignment. ⁴Note the title and read the first and last paragraphs; also look quickly at headings and subheads and anything in boldface or italic. ⁵Next, *read* a selection straight through while marking off important ideas such as definitions, examples, and lists of items. ⁶The third step is to *organize* the material you've read by taking study notes on it. ⁷Get all the important ideas down on paper in outline form, relating one idea to another as much as possible. ⁸Last of all, *memorize* the study notes that you will need to remember for tests. ⁹Do this by writing key words in the margins of your study outline and turning those words into questions. ¹⁰For instance, the key words "three types of rocks" can be converted into the question "What are the three types of rocks?" ¹¹Recite the answers to these and other key questions until you can answer them without referring to your notes. ¹²Not all learning involves memorization, but some of it does, so don't hesitate to commit to memory anything you might need for a test.

Main idea:_____.

   1. _____

   2. _____

   3. _____

   4. _____

Explanation:

You should have added the main idea—"PROM is a proven study method"—and the following steps to the outline:

   1. Preview a reading assignment. (The author signals this step with the time word *first.*)

   2. Read the selection straight through, marking off important ideas as you do. (This step is signaled with the time word *Next.*)

3. Organize the material you've read by taking study notes on it. (This step is signaled with the time word *third.*)

4. Memorize the study outline by turning key words into questions. (The author signals this last step with the time transition *Last of all.*)

As indicated by the transitions used, the relationship between the steps is one of time: The second step happens *after* the first, and so on.

➤ Practice 5

The following passage gives directions involving several steps that must be done in order. Complete the map below by filling in the main idea in the top box and the three missing steps. To help identify each step, you may want to underline the time words that introduce each step.

[1]When you feel overwhelmed by a heavy workload, there are several steps you can take to gain control. [2]The first is to list as quickly as possible everything that needs to get done. [3]This can mean jotting down as many ideas you can think of onto paper in ten minutes, without worrying about order or form. [4]Second, divide the tasks into three groups: what has to be done immediately, what can be done within the next week or so, and what can be postponed till a later date. [5]Next, break each task down into the exact steps you must take to get it done. [6]Then, as on a test, do the easiest ones first and go back to the hard ones later. [7]Instead of just worrying about what you ought to be doing, you'll be getting something done. [8]And you'll be surprised at how easily one step leads to another.

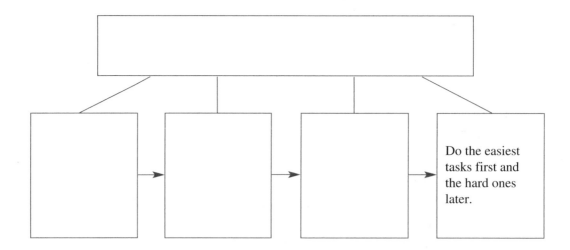

Do the easiest tasks first and the hard ones later.

A Note on Main Ideas and Patterns of Organization

A paragraph's main idea may indicate its pattern of organization. For example, here's the main idea of the paragraph you just read: "When you feel overwhelmed by a heavy workload, there are several steps you can take to gain control." The words *several steps* suggest that this paragraph will be organized according to time order. Another good example is the main idea of the earlier paragraph about self-disclosure: "Meaningful self-disclosure includes three important elements." The words *three important elements* suggest that this paragraph will be a list of three items.

Paying close attention to the main idea, then, can often give you a quick sense of a paragraph's pattern of organization. Try, for instance, to guess the pattern of the paragraph with this main idea:

> While there are thousands of Internet chat groups, they all fall into three basic categories.

The statement that Internet chat groups "fall into three basic categories" is a strong indication that the paragraph will list those categories. The main idea helps us guess that the paragraph will be a list of three items.

➤ Practice 6

Most of the main ideas below have been taken from college textbooks. In the space provided, write the letter of the pattern of organization that each main idea suggests.

_____ 1. Traditionally, efforts to prevent the abuse of drugs have been divided into three types of intervention.
A. List of items   B. Time order

_____ 2. A predictable sequence of motor development leads to a child's learning to walk.
A. List of items   B. Time order

_____ 3. In the United States there are many myths about rape.
A. List of items   B. Time order

_____ 4. Less dependence on foreign oil is only one of many benefits of energy-efficient automobiles.
A. List of items   B. Time order

_____ 5. Few products last forever; most go through a product life cycle, passing through four distinct stages in sales and earnings.
A. List of items   B. Time order

_____ 6. The American colonists that remained loyal to the British crown did so for a number of reasons.
   A. List of items   B. Time order

_____ 7. Three questions, if explored carefully, will carry us a long way to deciding what moral action to take in the very human dilemmas in which we find ourselves caught.
   A. List of items   B. Time order

_____ 8. The story of the Gold Rush begins with a carpenter noticing several bright bits of yellow mineral near a sawmill on a California ranch.
   A. List of items   B. Time order

_____ 9. Speakers should take advantage of specific, proven techniques to boost their credibility while speaking.
   A. List of items   B. Time order

_____ 10. Progressive muscle relaxation is a procedure in which each of several muscle groups in turn is systematically contracted and relaxed.
   A. List of items   B. Time order

Three Final Points

1 While many passages have just one pattern of organization, often the patterns are mixed. For example, you may find that part of a passage uses a list of items pattern, and another part of the same passage uses a time pattern.

2 Very often, passages with a time pattern also use a list of items pattern. For example, look at this time order passage:

> [1]To find a job, follow these key steps. [2]First of all, tell everyone you know that you're looking for work. [3]Most jobs are found through word-of-mouth, rather than newspaper advertisements. [4]Second, call a potential employer and ask to schedule an interview. [5]Be sure you sound friendly and enthusiastic on the phone. [6]The next step is the interview itself. [7]Dress nicely, be on time, and answer your interviewer's questions fully and politely. [8]Finally, send your interviewer a thank-you note in a day or two. [9]That doesn't guarantee you'll get the job, but it will add to the positive impression you've already made.

The passage both describes a series of steps you should follow in a time sequence, and it also lists those steps one at a time.

3 Remember that not all relationships between ideas are signaled by transitions. An author may present a list of items, for example, without using addition words. So as you read, watch for the relationships themselves, not just the transitions.

CHAPTER REVIEW

In this chapter, you learned how authors use transitions and patterns of organization to make their ideas clear. Just as transitions show relationships between ideas in sentences, patterns of organization show relationships between supporting details in paragraphs and longer pieces of writing.

You also learned two common kinds of relationships that authors use to make their ideas clear:

- **Addition relationships**

  — Authors often present a list or series of reasons, examples, or other details that support an idea. The items have no time order, but are listed in whatever order the author prefers.

  — Transition words that signal such addition relationships include *for one thing, second, also, in addition,* and *finally*.

- **Time relationships**

  — Authors usually discuss a series of events or steps in the order in which they happen, resulting in a time order.

  — Transition words that signal such time relationships include *first, next, then, after,* and *last*.

The next chapter—Chapter 6—will help you learn three other important kinds of relationships: definition-example, comparison and/or contrast, and cause-effect.

On the Web: If you are using this book in class, you can visit our website for additional practice in understanding relationships that involve addition and time. Go to **www.townsendpress.com** and click on "Online Exercises."

➤ Review Test 1

To review what you've learned in this chapter, fill in the blanks in the following items.

1. _____ are words or phrases (like *first of all* or *another* or *then* or *finally*) that show the relationship between ideas. They are like signs on the road that guide travelers.

2. Words such as for *one thing, also,* and *furthermore* are known as _____ words. They tell us the writer is presenting one or more ideas that add to the same line of thought as a previous idea.

3. Words such as *then, next,* and *after* are known as _____ words. They tell us *when* something happened in relation to when something else happened.

4. Transitions show the relationships between ideas in sentences. Patterns of organization show the relationships between _____ in a paragraph or longer passage.

5. The main idea of a paragraph may indicate its _____ _____.

➤ Review Test 2

A. Fill in each blank with one of the words in the box. Use each word once. Then write the letter of the word in the space provided.

A. after	B. another	C. also
D. before	E. last of all	

_____ 1. Many students today have very little access to books in their homes.

They _____ have no quiet, comfortable place to read, free from the televisions that are turned on loud a good deal of the time.

_____ 2. _____ the invention of television, people probably spent more of their leisure time reading.

_____ 3. One reason that singles join a health club is to get in shape. _____ reason is that it's a great place to meet people.

_____ 4. Our natural environment includes several visible forms of water: fog, clouds, dew, rain, frost, snow, sleet, and, _____, hail.

_____ 5. _____ people are fired, it is common for them to lapse into a period of mental pain and depression. Many experience a sharp sense of loss—both of the job they held and of the coworkers and friends they knew as part of the job.

B. Read the textbook paragraph below, and then answer the questions that follow.

[1]To turn a corpse into a mummy, ancient Egyptians first washed the body with water from the Nile River. [2]Next they removed all organs except the heart, which was thought to house a person's spirit. [3]Following organ removal, they rinsed the body cavity with wine, stuffed it, and covered the body with salty powder. [4]After the body dried in this powder for thirty-five to forty days, they replaced the stuffing with salty powder and linen soaked in a plant-derived glue. [5]Then they closed all incisions, covered the skin with glue, wrapped the entire body in linen, and placed a mask (of either the dead person or an Egyptian god) on the mummy's head. [6]Finally, they placed the mummy inside a coffin (decorated to resemble a person) and sealed the coffin inside a tomb, along with food and other items that they believed the dead person would need or desire in the afterlife.

_____ 6. The relationship of sentence 2 to sentence 1 is one of
  A. addition.   B. time.

7. The key transition word in sentence 4 is _____.

8. The key transition word in sentence 5 is _____.

9. The key transition word in sentence 6 is _____.

_____ 10. The paragraph is organized as a
  A. list of items.
  B. series of events or stages.

➤ *Review Test 3*

A. Fill in each blank with the appropriate transition from the box. Use each transition once.

> | A. next | B. until | C. while | D. first |
> |---------|----------|----------|----------|

> [1]I do not like to write. [2]In fact, I dislike writing so much that I have developed a series of steps for postponing the agony of doing writing assignments. [3](1)_____, I tell myself that to proceed without the proper equipment would be unwise. [4]So I go out to buy a new pen. [5]This kills at least an hour. [6](2)_____ I begin to stare at the blank page. [7]Before long, however, I realize that writing may also require thought; so I begin to think deeply about my subject. [8]Soon I feel drowsy. [9]This naturally leads to the conclusion that I need a nap because I can't throw myself into my writing (3)_____ I am at my very best. [10]After a refreshing nap, I again face the blank page. [11]It is usually at this stage that I actually write a sentence or two—disappointing ones. [12]I wisely decide that I need inspiration, perhaps from an interesting magazine or a television movie. [13]If thoughts of my writing assignment should interfere (4)_____ I am reading or watching TV, I comfort myself with the knowledge that, as any artist knows, you can't rush these things.

> _____ 5. The pattern of organization of the above selection is
>   A. list of items.   B. time order.

B. Below are the beginnings of five passages. Label each one with the letter of its pattern of organization. (You may find it helpful to underline the transition or transitions in each item.)

>   A   List of items
>   B   Time order

_____ 6. [1]There are certain steps which, taken in order, will help you remember your dreams. [2]The first step is to place a notebook and pencil beside your bed. [3]The second is to make up your mind, before going to sleep, that you will remember what you are going to dream. . . .

_____ 7. [1]Weeds may seem harmful in the garden, but they have great value in nature. [2]Some so-called weeds serve as food. [3]Pokeweed, for instance, is often eaten as greens. [4]Other weeds are sources of drugs, medicines, and dyes. [5]Also, many weed seeds make up an important part of the diet of songbirds, game birds, and other types of wildlife. . . .

_____ 8. ¹*The Glass Menagerie,* the well-known play by Tennessee Williams, opens with the narrator of the play. ²Tom introduces himself, briefly discusses the play, and explains that the other characters will be his mother, his sister, and a gentleman caller. ³Tom then walks onto the set of a dining room, takes a seat, and his mother, Amanda, begins to speak. . . .

_____ 9. ¹People considering adopting a dog or cat should ask themselves a few important questions. ²First of all, do they really want the responsibility of caring for an animal for the next ten to fifteen years? . . .

_____ 10. ¹Abraham Lincoln took an unusual path to the Presidency. ²He lost his first job and then declared bankruptcy. ³Later on, he suffered a nervous breakdown. . . .

➤ Review Test 4

Here is a chance to apply your understanding of addition and time relationships to a full-length reading. The following story tells of a child of uneducated teen parents who has become a champion of literacy in her own community. To help you continue to strengthen your skills, the reading is followed by questions not only on what you've learned in this chapter but also on what you've learned in previous chapters.

Words to Watch

Below are some words in the reading that do not have strong context support. Each word is followed by the number of the paragraph in which it appears and its meaning there. These words are indicated in the article by a small circle (°).

brawling (2): fighting
frigid (16): cold
refuge (17) : shelter
renovation (42): restoring to good condition
penalty (47): fee charged as a punishment

JULIA BURNEY: THE POWER OF A WOMAN'S DREAM

Beth Johnson

1   Julia Burney was afraid of many things as a child. Mostly, she was afraid of Fridays.

2   Fridays were the days her parents headed out to the bars. Julia would go to bed but lie awake for hours, too tense to sleep. Eventually her mother and father would return home, and then the brawling° would begin.

3   Voices would grow louder. Crashes would echo through the apartment. There would be the sound of blows and cries.

Julia keeps this photograph of herself in a ragged dress to remind herself of the poverty she grew up in. She is shown with her younger sister, and her mother and father, who were 13 and 17 when she was born.

4   "Call the police!" her mother would often scream. "He's killing me!"

5   "You call the cops and I'll beat you too!" her father would shout.

6   "Julia Mae, do something!" the younger children would shriek.

7   And eight-year-old Julia, the oldest of what were eventually twelve siblings, (two died in infancy), would try to dodge her father's fist to reach the phone. If she made it, and if the phone hadn't been disconnected, she would dial the number of the police department.

8   And then, she remembers, it was as if a miracle happened.

9   "The moment the officers appeared, everything changed. My dad would sit up, listen to them, and act right. My home would be peaceful again.

10   "So that became my dream," Julia says today. "Someday, I would do that for another child."

11   Julia would achieve her dream. But she had a lot to go through first.

12   Julia lived in Racine, Wisconsin. Her parents were hardly more than children themselves; when Julia was born, her mother was 13 and her father 17. Neither had finished junior high school. Neither could read or write well.

13   Julia's memories of her parents are bittersweet.

14   "They were hard-working people," she says. "They had plenty of common sense, what my father called 'motherwit.' He'd say, 'You might have more schooling than I do, but I have motherwit.' And he did.

15   "But they were so young when they had us, and there were so many of us," she goes on. "Imagine all those mouths to feed! I am amazed that they accomplished what they did. With all they had to cope with, I can understand why they drank. But alcohol ruined a large portion of our lives. I loved my parents, but I hated their drinking."

16   The family's poverty was crushing. The electricity was turned off so many times that Julia says today, "I grew up in the dark." During many frigid° Wisconsin winters, her family tried to warm itself with space heaters, candles, and extra layers of clothing.

17   By contrast, school was a welcome refuge° for Julia. Her first readers introduced her to Dick, Jane, and Spot, and to a lifelong love affair with books. "Reading came naturally to me," she

says. "But any encouragement to read stopped at our front door." Her parents were supportive of their children attending school. But the idea of reading for pleasure was so foreign that they did not understand it in Julia. More than that was the problem of money.

18 "To my parents, a book might as well have cost a million dollars," she explains. "If I did bring home a school book, they were afraid I'd lose it or damage it. So up it would go on top of the refrigerator, where it would be safe."

19 But Julia found a place where she could read to her heart's content. That place was her Aunt Ruby's house, where she would often go to babysit. Aunt Ruby had many books, as well as magazines like *True Stories* that Julia read to learn about "love and life and romance—stuff my parents didn't talk about."

20 Julia says today, "I learned to read at school. I learned to *love* reading at Aunt Ruby's."

21 Julia's love of reading helped her become a girl determined to prepare for a better future. She simply ignored peers who suggested she should not care about her schooling. Also, drink and drugs attracted her not at all. "You know how most kids at least try cigarettes? Not me. I have never smoked even one cigarette. Never tasted alcohol. Never used an ounce of marijuana. I looked at my parents' example and thought, 'That's what I'd become.'"

22 But Julia had her own kind of weakness. Her parents had never been ones to show affection. "To them, putting a roof over our heads and food on the table was love. But I wanted someone to *tell* me." When Julia was 17, a boy came along. He told Julia, "I love you." She soon found herself pregnant with her first child.

23 "I confused sex with love," she says today. "And eventually, I was raising four kids on my own."

24 Adjusting to motherhood was not as difficult for Julia as it might have been for another teenager. She'd been taking care of babies since she was just a small child herself. When her first child was born, Julia transferred to a school that offered night classes in order to earn her high-school diploma. She started working, usually two jobs at once, to support her children. On her eighteenth birthday, she moved out of her parents' house and into her own apartment. Despite the challenges, she maintained a loving, disciplined home for her children, who are all successful professional people today.

Julia Burney today

25   As the years went on, Julia worked as a restaurant chef and then as a teacher's assistant. In 1979, she was hired as a clerk by the Racine police department. Five years later, she fulfilled her early dream of becoming a police officer. She was especially skilled at dealing with calls to homes where fighting was going on. As she dealt with the parents and comforted the children, Julia noticed something that many other officers might have missed: If there were any books in the house at all, they were on top of the refrigerator.

26   The sight tore at her heart. She knew what the children in those homes were being denied: not only books, but the hopes and dreams that books could inspire.

27   "I knew from the time I was a little girl that reading was power," she says. "My parents were crippled by their inability to read well. You *cannot* thrive in this society without reading well. I arrest people who are unable to read their rights, and I think how hopeless life must look for them."

28   Julia herself not only enjoys reading, but her love of books has benefited her professionally. She speaks beautifully, with a large vocabulary at her command. At the police station, she was frequently complimented on her clearly-written arrest reports. "I write well because I read," she says. "If you read, you learn to write. You absorb the style, you learn good grammar, you learn to talk properly. Using language well becomes second nature."

29   Remembering all these things, a vision came to Julia. She wanted to do for these children what her Aunt Ruby had done for her. "I knew I had to get books into these children's hands. But I didn't know where the books were going to come from."

30   She adds, "But then I went on a burglary call and God gave them to me."

31   It was on a night in 1997 that Julia responded to a false alarm at a Racine warehouse. When the warehouse owner unlocked the door to let the officers in, Julia saw a beautiful sight: boxes and boxes of children's books. The books had slight imperfections, so they were going to be shredded and recycled. The warehouse owner agreed to let her have them.

32   Julia and some of her fellow officers began hauling the books around in the trunks of their squad cars. When they had any contact with children, out would come the books. They gave books away during school visits, at the police station, even during traffic stops. At Christmas, the officers hosted a book give-away. Children came to it pulling wagons and carrying bags to take their precious books home.

33   After the Christmas book give-away, the Cops 'n Kids program began to take on a life of its own. The local newspaper, the *Journal-Times*, did a story about Julia's efforts. In response, people called to ask how they could help. Some businesses held drives to collect used books. Others donated money. Individuals volunteered their time to help sort the books. Police officers loaded bags of books into their squad cars every morning. They gave them out in local parks, on patrol, and on calls. Children who had formerly been afraid of the police began chasing squad cars down the street, yelling, "Can I have a book?"

34   All this was wonderful. But it still wasn't enough for Julia. She wanted a *place* for children to come: a peaceful, comfortable center where kids could experience the joy of reading.

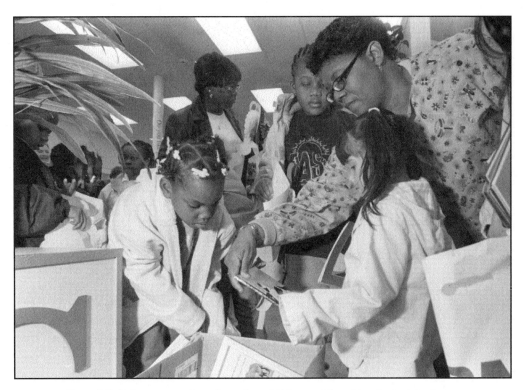

One of Julia's greatest joys is seeing children pick out books to take home.

35   She began searching for a building. Then she spotted it—a brick building, in the middle of the inner city, that had been boarded up for twenty-eight years. Faced with the irresistible force of Julia's energy, the building's owner donated it to Cops 'n Kids.

36   Meanwhile, the *Journal-Times* article had been picked up by the Associated Press and reprinted all over the world. In January of 1999, Julia received a call from a producer of NBC's *Today* show. *Today* wanted Julia to come to New York to be interviewed by the show's host, Katie Couric. The producer also wanted to send a camera crew to Racine to take pictures of officers handing books out to kids on the streets.

37   To the producer's astonishment, Julia said no. "I said, thank you very much, but I'm too busy to come to New York.

And besides, we don't pass books out on the sidewalk in the middle of the winter in Wisconsin! Do you know how cold it gets here? If you want to do this story, you ought to come here next summer when you can do it right."

38   The producer tried again. "She said, 'Julia, do you understand—this is the *Today* show? The biggest morning show in the country?'"

39   Julia said she understood. But she still wasn't coming to New York.

40   And the following July, the *Today* show came to Racine. Katie Couric interviewed Julia and did a touching episode on her efforts to bring books to her community's neediest children.

41   Julia had great faith in the Cops 'n Kids idea. But what happened next was almost too much for even her to believe.

42   Producers at the Oprah Winfrey

The warm, cozy reading center she dreamed of is now a reality.
Every morning, Julia unlocks the door of Cops 'n Kids to the children of her community.

show contacted Julia and told her she had received one of Oprah's "Use Your Life" awards. In September 2000, Julia appeared on the *Oprah* show to accept the $100,000 award and explain her dreams for the center. With the award money, she was able to buy supplies for the renovation° of the building. The Racine community came out in force to provide volunteer labor for the job. Many police officers and firefighters contributed their time. Members of the local labor unions worked for free. Businesses and churches raised funds for new windows. High school kids ripped out old drywall and painted. Gradually, the run-down building became a clean, solid home for Cops 'n Kids. There wasn't much *inside* the building but books and some mismatched furniture, but it was a start.

Then in March 2001, Julia got another call from the Oprah organization. The producers wanted her to be on the show again, they said, to update the audience on the center. Julia was picked up in a limousine and taken to Chicago, where *Oprah* is filmed. She was given a room in a hotel and then told that there would be a delay in filming the show.   43

For the next three days, Julia waited impatiently in her hotel room. She kept getting calls from the producer, saying, "We'll be filming soon—get dressed!" But when she was all ready she'd get another call, saying that another problem had come up and that she would have to wait a little while longer.   44

45   Finally the real call came—it was time to tape the show. Julia went to the studio and walked onstage with Oprah. At that point, Oprah confessed that Julia had been told a white lie—in fact, a whole string of them. She wasn't there to do an update on the program. Instead, during the past three days, an army of people had been very, very busy in Racine. Julia was then invited to look at the Cops 'n Kids Reading Center over a video monitor onstage.

46   The bare rooms of the center had been filled with beautiful sofas, easy chairs, craft tables, and office furniture. Colorful paintings hung on the walls. Thick rugs covered the floors. Artists had covered one huge wall with a bright mural. A baby grand piano stood in the auditorium. There was a complete computer lab. Even the smallest details had been taken care of, down to a basket of warm socks to cover the feet of little readers. Watching the video, Julia sobbed with joy. Many people in the audience shared her happy tears.

47   The next June, the Cops 'n Kids Reading Center officially opened for business. And today, it is as busy as it is beautiful. Racine's children, from pre-schoolers through eighth-graders, stream through its doors every day. More than 5,000 books are waiting there for the children to read and borrow. Because the books are donated to the Center, the children are not fined if they lose or damage one. "We talk about the responsibility of keeping the book safe," Julia explains. "We help the children learn to care for books, but without a penalty°."

48   But the Center is far more than a library. Retired teachers offer tutoring. Children produce works of art in a crafts room. Plays, concerts, parties, and authors' book-signings take place in the auditorium. Writing classes encourage children to get their thoughts down on paper. Student teachers from a nearby college come in to help. Doctors and nurses and dentists volunteer their time to check the kids' hearing and vision and teeth. Guest readers come in often, sometimes from local schools. "The kids love seeing their teachers and principals come into *their* neighborhood," Julia says.

49   And Julia loves to see a wide variety of people become involved with the Center and its kids. "Every time another person sits down with the children, the kids are learning *life skills*. Not just book skills. These kids are as smart and capable as any other children, but they can't aspire to be something that they've never seen."

50   She explains by giving an example. "The first guest reader we had here was Mark Hertzberg, the head photographer from the Racine newspaper. He read the book *Goodnight, Moon.* The kids could see him and talk to him and realize that yes, he's a real person, a dad and a husband who also happens to be a newspaper photographer. And now they can think, 'Hey, maybe I'd like to be a photographer' instead of 'maybe I'll be a drug dealer.' Because before, dealing drugs might have been the only 'career' they really knew about."

51   Other life skills are taught as the need comes up. When Julia realized that the older children didn't understand how a newspaper is organized, she quickly organized a class on newspaper reading, and the Racine paper began donating five copies to the Center each day. Now the older children routinely keep up with the news. Other children, members of a book club, munch on pizza as they discuss a story they've all read. And every day, volunteers sit in rocking chairs and read

stories aloud to any youngsters who want to listen. "I'm 51 years old, and it still hurts to remember that no one ever read to me," Julia says. "These children won't have to say that."

52   As Julia talks, those old memories keep surfacing: the books atop her family's refrigerator, the longing for someone to read to her. It seems that Julia can never quite forget the little girl that she once was.

53   "Every little girl that walks in here—she's me," she says today. "Every child living in a house without books—that's me too. There are none that are poorer than I was. One of my earliest goals was to own a bottle of Ivory Liquid. We washed our dishes with the same powdered detergent we washed our clothes with. When I first saw dish-washing liquid, I wanted that so bad!"

54   Because it helps her understand and reach the children around her, Julia never tries to whitewash her own difficult past. "I tell the children, 'Maybe the phone and the lights have been cut off at your house. Maybe your parents are drinking and fighting. Maybe your clothes are raggedy. Maybe your house is full of cockroaches. Maybe you and your brothers and sisters all have to sleep in one bed. That's okay. That's how Ms. Burney lived, too.' And the children say, 'Naaaw, you didn't!' So I show them a photograph I keep in my office." That photo shows Julia as a young girl, standing with her parents. The hem is hanging out of her dress, and her coat has lost all its buttons but one.

55   "They look at the picture, and I tell them, 'That's how I grew up. But what's important is that *now* I have my own house, and my own car, and a good job. Your job now is to think what *you* want when you grow up, and to go to school

and get it.'" Then she hugs them, and that night she asks God to help the children achieve their dreams.

56   If you want to see one answer to Julia Burney's prayers, look no further than 8th and Villa Streets in Racine, Wisconsin. There stands a handsome brick building, bursting with books and cozy sofas, soft chairs, quilts to snuggle up with, crayons and paints and hugs and love, and—always—children. Children by the dozen come trooping into the reading center that they call "Ms. Burney's place." They run to her with their report cards, shyly hand her thank-you notes they have created for her, and ask her to read them a story. They never leave disappointed.

57   Twenty-four hours a day, the big plate-glass window at the front of the Center is brightly lit. It has been "adopted" by the local Barnes & Noble store, and it is always colorfully decorated with a display of books to suit the season: spring, Christmas, St. Patrick's Day, Halloween, autumn. In the darkness of inner-city Racine, that window glows like a beacon, a symbol of Julia Burney's loving commitment to the children of her city.

58   In February 2001, after twenty-two years of service, Julia retired from the police force. She proudly turned her badge over to her daughter, Vanessa, who has become a Racine police officer herself. She now devotes all of her time and energy to the Cops 'n Kids Reading Center.

59   Julia tells whoever asks that she is repaying the debt she owes to her beloved aunt. "I believe in these children, because Aunt Ruby believed in me," she says. "I may not be around when these children are adults. But I know I've passed on the help I received. I'm just doing what I would want done for me."

*As the children at Cops 'n Kids read, write, and work on projects,
Julia Burney is never very far away.*

Reading Comprehension Questions

Vocabulary in Context

_____ 1. In the excerpt below, the word *thrive* (thrīv) means
   A. succeed.
   B. argue.
   C. escape.
   D. fail.

> "I knew from the time I was a little girl that reading was power," she
> says. "My parents were crippled by their inability to read well. You
> *cannot* thrive in this society without reading well." (Paragraph 27)

Central Point and Main Ideas

_____ 2. Which sentence best expresses the implied central point of the
   selection?
   A. Despite being raised by poor, uneducated parents, Julia Burney
      developed a passionate love for books that endures to this day.
   B. The Cops 'n Kids Reading Center of Racine, Wisconsin, has created
      a unique bond between the community's police and children.

    C. After learning to love reading during a difficult childhood, police officer Julia Burney founded an inner-city reading and cultural center.

    D. The Cops 'n Kids Reading Center has brought its founder, Julia Burney, national attention.

_____ 3. The implied main idea of paragraphs 4–7 is
    A. Julia's father and mother fought only when they were drunk.
    B. At a young age, Julia felt responsible for keeping peace in her home.
    C. The phone bill in Julia's parents' house was often unpaid.
    D. Julia's brothers and sisters were often beaten.

_____ 4. The main idea of paragraphs 13–15 is
    A. stated in paragraph 13.
    B. stated in the first sentence of paragraph 14.
    C. stated in the first sentence of paragraph 15.
    D. unstated.

Supporting Details

_____ 5. When Julia visited homes in her work as a police officer, she often noticed that
    A. the electricity was turned off.
    B. the houses were very cold.
    C. the children were afraid of police.
    D. there were no books in the house.

_____ 6. According to Julia, she writes well because
    A. her Aunt Ruby made her write essays.
    B. her reading has taught her to write.
    C. she learned a great deal correcting her children's homework.
    D. she took adult education courses in writing.

Transitions

_____ 7. The relationship of the third sentence below to the second sentence is one of
    A. addition.
    B. time.

    "Julia's love of reading helped her become a girl determined to prepare for a better future. She simply ignored peers who suggested she should not care about her schooling. Also, drink and drugs attracted her not at all." (Paragraph 21)

_____ 8. Which word from the following sentence indicates a time transition?
    A. But
    B. Next
    C. Almost
    D. Even

        "But what happened next was almost too much for even her to believe." (Paragraph 41)

Patterns of Organization

_____ 9. The pattern of organization in paragraphs 44–45 is one of
    A. list of items.
    B. time order.

_____ 10. The pattern of organization in paragraph 48 is one of
    A. list of items.
    B. time order.

Discussion Questions

1. Julia is passionate about the importance of reading. What is your attitude about reading? Explain. Do you read much in your everyday life? If not, what kinds of reading do you think you might like to do more of?

2. The story implies that her parents' example kept Julia from experimenting with drugs, alcohol, or tobacco. Based on your observation, what are the most important influences on children when it comes to making a similar decision? Is it their parents' example, for better or worse? The behavior of peers? Or something else?

3. Julia credits her Aunt Ruby with encouraging her to love reading. She says that through her work with the Cops 'n Kids Center, she is repaying a debt to her aunt. As a child, did you have an adult in your life who provided a special kind of support and encouragement? Explain. What effect did that adult's actions have upon you?

4. How can adults most effectively encourage children to become readers? If you eventually have children yourself or are in contact with young children, what do you think you might do to encourage them to read?

Note: Writing assignments for this selection appear on page 630.

Check Your Performance   **RELATIONSHIPS I**

Activity	Number Right	Points		Score
Review Test 1 (5 items)	_____	× 2	=	_____
Review Test 2 (10 items)	_____	× 3	=	_____
Review Test 3 (10 items)	_____	× 3	=	_____
Review Test 4 (10 items)	_____	× 3	=	_____
		TOTAL SCORE	=	_____%

Enter your total score into the **Reading Performance Chart: Review Tests** on the inside back cover.

RELATIONSHIPS I: Mastery Test 1

A. Fill in each blank with an appropriate transition from the box. Use each transition once. Then, in the spaces provided, write the letter of the transition you have chosen.

A. another	B. first of all	C. later
D. in addition	E. soon	

_____ 1. ¹Competition is often considered a good thing. ²However, psychologists see some problems with it. ³ _B First of all_ , competition may not always make the most efficient use of people's time and resources. ⁴Also, with competition, one person's success is another person's failure. ⁵Furthermore, too much competition can cause great hostility between groups.

_____ 2. ¹Two months prior to the major eruption of the Mount St. Helens volcano, a series of minor earth tremors hinted at the awakening of the mountain. ²Nine days ___later___, a small amount of ash and steam rose from the summit; sporadic eruptions followed over the next several weeks. ³Much of the mountain then erupted with a huge blast that blew out its entire north face.

_____ 3. ¹A man who pleaded guilty to illegal trading of $20 million with Swiss banks received a $30,000 fine and a suspended sentence. ²A few days later, the same judge heard ___another___ case, one in which an unemployed shipping clerk pleaded guilty to stealing a television set worth $100. ³The judge sentenced the clerk to one year in jail.

_____ 4. ¹According to the World Health Organization, malaria (also called swamp fever) kills about 2.7 million people each year. ²Most of the victims are children under 5. ³ _in addition_ , malaria infects 300 to 500 million others, mostly in Africa, but also in Southeast Asia and Central and South America. ⁴According to scientists, it may have killed one out of every two humans who ever lived.

_____ 5. ¹Suppose a fish dies and settles to the bottom of a lake. ²The bottom is covered with soft sediments—fine materials, such as sand or mud. ³The fish's body sinks into the material, and water currents sweep over the fish and gradually bury it. ⁴Other sediments then settle on top, and the soft parts of the fish ___Soon___ decay. ⁵But the bones are left buried in sediment. ⁶More and more layers of sediment pile up. ⁷Water may add minerals that act like glue. ⁸Over numerous years, the old sediments harden into rock. ⁹And inside the rock is a fossil—the bones of the fish. *(Continues on next page)*

B. (6–9.) Fill in each blank with an appropriate transition word from the box. Use each transition once.

A. second	B. for one thing	C. also
D. final		

[1]A review of the ways America deals with its garbage reveals the continuing problems that we face in getting rid of and limiting our waste. [2](6)_____, most of the 500,000 tons of waste generated each day in the United States is buried in landfills. [3]Landfills are expensive to construct, fill up rapidly, and can contaminate ground water. [4]A (7)___second___ method, incineration, is cheaper and theoretically can pay for itself by producing energy in the form of electricity or steam. [5]The initial construction expense, however, is enormous, and mechanical problems are common. [6](8)___Also___ disturbing is the potential threat incinerators pose to public health because of the dangerous toxic gases they emit during burning. [7]The (9)___final___ and most important way to deal with our garbage problem lies in recycling—a process that can reduce the amount of garbage produced in the first place. [8]It has been estimated that up to 80 percent of our garbage can be eliminated through separation and recycling. [9]To succeed, this method will have to be much more widely used than it is now.

_____ 10. The pattern of organization of the above selection is
   A. list of items.
   B. time order.

RELATIONSHIPS I: Mastery Test 2

A. Fill in each blank with an appropriate transition from the box. Use each transition once. Then, in the spaces provided, write the letter of the transition you have chosen.

A. after	B. another	C. before
D. eventually	E. also	

_____ 1. [1] _Before_ going to the doctor's office, write down all your questions. [2]Then, when you are face to face with the doctor, use this list of questions to find out everything you want to know about your condition.

_____ 2. [1]The legend of Faust tells of a scholar who is approached by the Devil. [2]The Devil successfully tempts Faust to sell his soul in exchange for power and knowledge. [3]For a while, Faust enjoys all sorts of pleasures; _eventually_, though, he dies and becomes the Devil's property for eternity.

_____ 3. [1]A chimp by the name of Sherman participated in an interesting math experiment. [2]He was given two pairs of cups containing chocolates. [3]One pair contained five candies—three in one cup and two in the other. [4]The second pair held only four candies—three in one and only one in the other. [5]Sherman chose the pair of cups with the most chocolates 90 percent of the time. [6] _another_ chimp, Lana, can match the numbers 1, 2, or 3 with a picture of the matching number of boxes 80 percent of the time.

_____ 4. [1]According to people who have survived long falls, the acceleration of gravity is heart-stoppingly fast. [2]A body accelerates roughly twenty miles an hour for every second it's in the air. [3]In just one second, it's falling twenty miles an hour. [4] _After_ two seconds, speed is up to forty miles an hour, and so on, up to a hundred and thirty miles an hour, when the body is said to reach terminal velocity.

_____ 5. [1]Some strange and disturbing events have happened around extra-high-voltage electrical lines. [2]The lines often glow a weird blue. [3] _Also_, they can cause unconnected fluorescent bulbs to light up. [4]Perhaps more scary, however, is the fact that many people near the extra-high-voltage lines have gotten unexpected shocks. [5]People living near such wires, for instance, have complained about getting shocks when touching wire fences or farm machines. [6]Some have even complained of receiving shocks from damp clotheslines and while sitting on the toilet.

(Continues on next page)

B. Read the passage and answer the question that follows.

[1]The modern police department of today is the product of hundreds of years of evolution. [2]The origins of policing can be traced back to England in the twelfth century. [3]During this time, criminals were tracked down by groups of armed citizens led by the "Shire Reeve"—"leader of the county." [4]Our modern word "sheriff" is derived from these early words. [5]Centuries later, as towns grew, law enforcement fell to the hands of bailiffs, or watchmen. [6]The bailiff's job was to alert people to theft by yelling loudly when a crime occurred. [7]Once alerted, townsfolk would track down the culprit—often beating and torturing him on the spot. [8]This system worked with limited success until the 1720s, when gin was invented. [9]Then, the availability of cheap alcohol increased crime and created the need for better law enforcement. [10]Finally, in 1829 Robert Peel created the first true police force by securing funds and hiring a thousand handpicked officers. [11]Peel's "bobbies" were given uniforms and instructed to patrol London's streets. [12]Eventually, they became the model for police departments worldwide.

_____ 6. The main pattern of organization of the passage is
   A. list of items.
   B. time order.

C. (7–10.) Fill in each blank with an appropriate transition word from the box. Use each transition once. Then answer the question that follows.

A. during	B. finally	C. then

[1]Salmon may migrate thousands of miles, but no matter how far they go, they (7)_____ return to the rivers in which they were spawned, to produce the next generation. [2]Their journey is an amazing feat. [3]One of the longest of those return journeys is in the Yukon River in Canada, where salmon travel nearly two thousand miles. [4]They travel day and night, with occasional rests in quiet pools. [5]At first, they swim at speeds of ten to twenty miles a day, but (8) _____ accelerate to as much as sixty miles a day, using their strong tails to propel them. [6](9)_____ their entire journey, they eat nothing. [7]After a month, they arrive at their birthplace, sickly and battered. [8]The female soon deposits her eggs, and the male, waiting nearby, releases his sperm. [9]Within days, both adults will die.

_____ 10. The pattern of organization of the above selection is
   A. list of items.
   B. time order.

RELATIONSHIPS I: Mastery Test 3

A. (1–5.) Arrange the scrambled sentences below into a logical paragraph by numbering them *1, 2, 3,* and *4* in an order that makes sense. Then, in the space provided, write the letter of the pattern of organization used.

Note that transitions will help you by clarifying the relationships between sentences.

_____ For one thing, alcohol consumption begins in junior high school or earlier.

_____ Experimentation with marijuana and mind-altering pills of all sorts also seems commonplace.

_____ Today's students have to confront the reality that drug use is all around them.

_____ Last, tobacco consumption is everywhere, despite the fact it is illegal for those under 18 to purchase cigarettes.

_____ 5. The pattern of organization of the above selection is
   A. list of items.
   B. time order.

B. Read the passage and answer the question that follows. You may find it helpful to underline transitions as you read.

[1]On its way to becoming the most recognized brand name on Earth, Coca-Cola has gone through lots of changes. [2]Coke was invented in 1886 by an Atlanta pharmacist named John Pemberton, who mixed it in a copper pot and sold it as a headache remedy. [3]A few years later, in 1899, a couple of businessmen bought the rights to bottle and sell the beverage. [4]Coke grew steadily in popularity, soon becoming the world's best-selling soft drink. [5]In the 1980s, Diet Coke was introduced, quickly becoming the world's best-selling diet soda. [6]This success was followed by Coca-Cola's decision to change the original Coke formula. [7]Although people had loved "new" Coke in taste tests, real-world consumers angrily rejected any change in the taste of their favorite soft drink. [8]In less than three months, the embarrassed Coca-Cola company returned to its original formula. [9]Having learned its lesson, Coca-Cola now introduces new varieties of its old favorite, such as Vanilla Coke and Diet Coke with Lemon.

_____ 6. The pattern of organization of the above selection is
   A. list of items.
   B. time order.

(Continues on next page)

C. (7–10.) Read the textbook passage below, and then answer the question and complete the outline.

> [1]Researchers have debated for many years about what causes people to commit crimes. [2]Today many theories exist, among them the popular explanation that crime is caused by the celebration of violence in our culture. [3]This approach argues that the glamorous portrayal of violence on TV and in movies encourages young people to become criminals. [4]Another theory holds that crime is the result of social and economic inequalities. [5]If class, racial, and social differences were eliminated, the theory goes, then crime would disappear. [6]A third popular explanation is that psychological reasons account for criminal actions. [7]Children who receive poor or inadequate parenting are more likely to become criminals because they have never received a solid grounding in conventional social and moral behavior. [8]Yet another theory suggests that crime is caused by biological factors. [9]According to this point of view, biology, genetics, and nutrition are all elements that can lead people to a life of crime. [10]There is no absolute evidence to disprove any of these theories, and conventional wisdom suggests that all of them may have some validity.

_____ 7. The pattern of organization of the above selection is
   A. list of items.
   B. time order.

8–10. Complete the outline of the passage.

   Main idea: _____

   _____

   Major supporting details:

   1. _____

   _____

   2. Social and economic inequalities

   3. _____

   _____

   4. Biological factors

RELATIONSHIPS I: Mastery Test 4

A. (1–4.) Arrange the scrambled sentences below into a logical paragraph by numbering them *1, 2, 3,* and *4* in an order that makes sense. Then, in the space provided, write the letter of the pattern of organization used.

Note that transitions will help you by clarifying the relationships between sentences.

_____ Last of all, let any intruding thoughts drift away as you repeat the word or phrase continually for ten to twenty minutes.

_____ Physician Herbert Benson's antidote to stress, which he calls the "relaxation response," involves a few simple steps.

_____ Next, close your eyes and concentrate on a single word or a phrase—or perhaps a favorite prayer.

_____ First of all, assume a comfortable position, breathe deeply, and relax your muscles from feet to face.

_____ 5. The pattern of organization of the above selection is
   A. list of items.
   B. series of events or stages.
   C. series of steps (directions).

B. Read the passage below and answer the question that follows.

¹Water evaporates from the seas, rivers, lakes, trees, and land surfaces, adding moisture to the atmosphere. ²When the moisture in the air cools, it condenses to form water droplets or ice crystals. ³As these droplets and crystals become larger, they fall toward the earth as precipitation—rain, snow, hail, etc. ⁴Some evaporate while falling, or they fall on tree leaves and evaporate; but some reach the ground. ⁵A portion of the water that reaches the ground evaporates. ⁶As water accumulates on the ground, some of it runs off to form rivers and lakes, with most eventually flowing back to the sea. ⁷Evaporation from all of these surfaces completes the water cycle. ⁸Water in the atmosphere is recycled every two weeks.

_____ 6. The purpose of the above selection is to
   A. list forms of water.
   B. list types of evaporation.
   C. describe stages in the water cycle.
   D. describe a series of events in the history of the Earth.

(Continues on next page)

C. (7–10.) Complete the map of the following textbook passage by filling in the missing main idea and major and minor details.

[1]Monogamy, the practice of each person marrying one other person in his or her lifetime, is just one of several types of marriage that occur throughout the world. [2]A separate but related form of marriage is serial monogamy, which allows a person to have several spouses in a lifetime, but only one at a time. [3]The practice of polygamy allows persons to have multiple spouses at the same time. [4]There are two forms of polygamy. [5]One variety is polygyny, in which one man has several wives at once. [6]The other is polyandry, in which a woman may have multiple husbands.

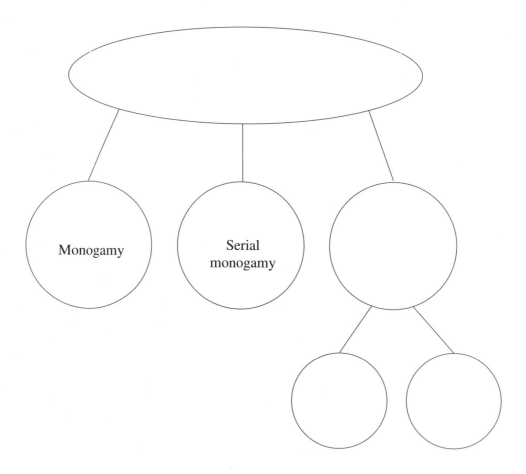

RELATIONSHIPS I: Mastery Test 5

Read each textbook passage and answer the questions or follow the directions provided.

A. [1]When a president needs to appoint someone to the Supreme Court, the first step is to find a list of good candidates. [2]Next, the president shortens the list, considering the political impact of each candidate's appointment and his or her fitness to serve. [3]Then each candidate on the short list is thoroughly investigated by the Federal Bureau of Investigation. [4]Weighing numerous political and ideological factors, as well as the chances for Senate confirmation, the president formally nominates a candidate. [5]The nominee meets informally with members of the Senate Judiciary Committee. [6]The committee then holds a formal hearing, takes a vote, and passes the nomination on to the full Senate. [7]Finally, the full Senate then approves or rejects the nomination by a simple majority vote.

_____ 1. The pattern of organization of the above selection is
   A. list of items.
   B. time order.

2. A transition that introduces one of the major details of the paragraph is

_____.

B. [1]What causes people to join groups? [2]One reason is for security, a factor that leads people to form neighborhood-watch groups. [3]Another common reason for joining a group is a desire to be with others who share one's interests and values. [4]Some people, for instance, join computer support groups to share ideas, knowledge, and software. [5]Managers may join service groups, such as Rotary Clubs, to exchange ideas with other managers. [6]Individuals may also form groups to acquire power that is difficult if not impossible to attain alone. [7]Membership in a union or employee association, for example, provides workers with influence that they lack as individual employees. [8]Goal accomplishment is a further reason people join groups. [9]Mountain climbers and astronauts generally function in groups.

_____ 3. The pattern of organization of the above selection is
   A. list of items.
   B. time order.

4. A transition that introduces one of the major details of the paragraph is

_____.

(Continues on next page)

C. ¹There are three main ways people respond to those who offend or annoy them. ²One of the most common ways people deal with negative situations is through passive behavior. ³Passive people are those who do not share their opinions, feeling, or emotions when they are upset. ⁴Instead of trying to get an offensive individual to stop hurting them, passive people will often remain silent, allowing the unfair or unkind actions to continue. ⁵Another way people address a negative situation is through aggressive behavior. ⁶Aggressive people lash out at those who have hurt them—with little regard for the situation or the feelings of those they are attacking. ⁷Aggressive behavior is judgmental, harsh, and hurtful. ⁸The final way of dealing with conflicts is through assertive behavior. ⁹Assertive people, like those who are aggressive, also actively address the cause of their problem—but they do it differently. ¹⁰Instead of yelling at the person who has offended them, assertive people will discuss what has annoyed them, and then work to find a way to fix it.

_____ 5. The pattern of organization of the above selection is
      A. list of items.
      B. time order.

    6. The transition that signals the third major detail is _____.

7–10. Complete the map of the paragraph.

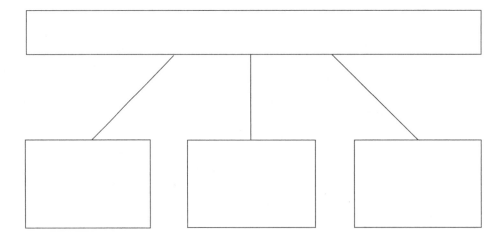

RELATIONSHIPS I: Mastery Test 6

Read each textbook passage and answer the questions or follow the directions provided.

A. ¹Consumer products are commonly divided into categories that reflect buyers' behavior. ²One category is convenience goods (such as milk and newspapers) and convenience services (such as fast-food restaurants), which are consumed rapidly and regularly. ³They are relatively inexpensive and must be purchased frequently and with little expenditure of time and effort. ⁴Another category is shopping goods (such as stereos and tires) and shopping services (such as insurance). ⁵Shopping goods and services are more expensive and are purchased less frequently than convenience goods and services. ⁶Consumers often compare brands, sometimes in different stores. ⁷The last category is specialty goods (such as wedding gowns) and specialty services (such as catering for wedding receptions). ⁸Specialty goods are extremely important and expensive purchases. ⁹Consumers usually decide on precisely what they want and will accept no substitutes. ¹⁰They will often go from store to store, sometimes spending a great deal of money and time to get a specific product.

_____ 1. The pattern of organization of the above selection is
    A. list of items.
    B. time order.

2. The second major detail is signaled with the transition _____.

_____ 3. The total number of major details is
    A. two.
    B. three.
    C. four.

B. ¹Although people move through courtship in different ways, researchers have identified a number of stages common to the process. ²First, relationships begin when two individuals feel attraction toward each other. ³In this early stage, both people show interest in each other and choose to spend time together. ⁴Then, after a period of "dating," both partners declare themselves a couple, telling their friends and relatives about the new person in their lives. ⁵Next, couples make a commitment to each other. ⁶Here, expectations become more serious, and partners agree to have an exclusive relationship with each other. ⁷Eventually, both partners begin coordinating their activities so that they function as a couple in important matters. ⁸In this stage, schedules, finances, and career plans are mutually decided. ⁹Finally, the couple makes a permanent commitment to marry or cohabitate.

(Continues on next page)

213

_____ 4. The pattern of organization of the above selection is
    A. list of items.
    B. time order.

5–7. Three of the transitions that introduce the major details of the paragraph are

_____ _____ _____.

C.   [1]Jargon—a specialized vocabulary used by a particular group, such as lawyers, teenagers, or musicians—has several benefits for group members. [2]One benefit of jargon is that it provides a way of setting insiders apart from outsiders because only the insiders know what it means. [3]Another benefit is that jargon strengthens the ties between insiders. [4]They use it to communicate only with each other, not with anyone else. [5]In addition, jargon is an important way for a group to maintain its identity and project a clear group image. [6]Last, jargon gives individual group members a sense of belonging, and so it raises their self-esteem.

_____ 8. The pattern of organization of the above selection is
    A. list of items.
    B. time order.

9–10. Complete the outline of the paragraph.

Main idea: Jargon has several benefits for group members.

1. Provides a way of setting insiders apart from outsiders

2. _____

_____

3. Maintains a group identity and projects a clear group image

4. _____

_____

6

Relationships II

In Chapter 5, you learned how authors use transitions and patterns of organization to show relationships and make their ideas clear. You also learned about two common types of relationships:

- Relationships that involve **addition**
- Relationships that involve **time**

In this chapter you will learn about three other types of relationships:

- Relationships that involve **illustration**
- Relationships that involve **comparison and contrast**
- Relationships that involve **cause and effect**

1 ILLUSTRATION

Words That Show Illustration

Put a check (✓) beside the item that is easier to understand:

____ Certain types of anxiety are very common. Most people feel anxious at the thought of speaking in front of a large group.

____ Certain types of anxiety are very common. For instance, most people feel anxious at the thought of speaking in front of a large group.

The second item is easier to follow. The words *for instance* make it clear that speaking in front of a small group is one type of common anxiety. *For instance* and other words and phrases like it are illustration words.

Illustration words indicate that an author will provide one or more *examples* to develop and clarify a given idea. Here are some common words that show illustration:

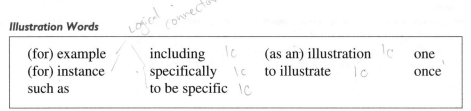

Illustration Words

(for) example	including	(as an) illustration	one
(for) instance	specifically	to illustrate	once
such as	to be specific		

Examples:

The following items contain illustration words. Notice how these words signal that one or more *examples* are coming.

Birds sing for various reasons, *such as* to proclaim territory, to signal hunger, or to attract a mate.

As obesity becomes more common in the United States, the rates for related health problems, *including* diabetes among children, have soared.

Some common beliefs about the United States are really myths. *For example*, Betsy Ross did not design the American flag.

➤ Practice 1

Complete each item with a suitable illustration word or phrase from the above box. Try to use a variety of transitions.

> **Hint:** Make sure that each word or phrase that you choose fits smoothly into the flow of the sentence. Test each choice by reading the sentence aloud.

1. Throughout history, men have chosen to marry for different reasons. In ancient Sparta, _for example_, men needed wives solely for childbearing.

2. Common courtesies, _such as_ saying *please* and *thank you,* are becoming less and less common.

3. Sometimes drivers don't seem to be paying full attention to their driving. _For instance_, this morning I saw people driving while talking on car phones, combing their hair, and glancing at newspapers.

4. Color in the workplace can serve a functional purpose. ___*To illustrate*___, different colors can be used to mark secure and unsecured areas, areas where visitors are and are not allowed, or various levels of safety and danger.

5. We have come to understand in recent years how the English language is riddled with sexism. Most blatant is the generic "he," which excludes women from whatever group is being discussed, ___*once*___ in the line "When a college student studies for an exam, he should be sure to review all his lecture notes."

Illustration words are common in all types of writing. One way they are used in textbooks is in the pattern of organization known as the definition and example pattern.

The Definition and Example Pattern

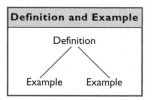

To get a sense of the definition and example pattern, try to arrange the following sentences in an order that makes sense. Put a *1* in front of the sentence that should come first, a *2* in front of the sentence that comes next, and a *3* in front of the sentence that should be last. The result will be a short paragraph. Then read the explanation that follows.

_2_ For instance, a football player recovering from an operation may want to return to his team, yet he also knows that he may limp for the rest of his life if he is injured again.

_1_ An approach-avoidance conflict is a situation in which someone is both attracted to and repelled by the same goal.

_3_ People who feel loyal to their present employer but are interested in a new and better job are another example.

This paragraph begins with a definition: "An approach-avoidance conflict is a conflict in which someone is both attracted to and repelled by the same goal." The second sentence provides an illustration of that type of conflict: "For instance, a football player recovering from an operation may want to return to his team, yet he also knows that he may limp for the rest of his life if he is injured again." The third sentence then provides a second example: "People who feel loyal to their present employer but are interested in a new and better job are another example." The second and third sentences include the illustration words *for instance* and *example*. As you can see, the **definition and example pattern of organization** includes just what its name suggests: a definition and one or more examples.

> *An Important Study Hint:* Good textbook authors want to help readers understand the important ideas and terms in a subject— whether it is psychology, sociology, business, biology, or any other field. Such authors often take time, then, to include key definitions. These ideas and terms are usually set off in *italic* or **boldface** type, and the definitions are signaled by such words as *is, are, is called, termed,* and *refers to.* Here are some definitions from a variety of textbooks:
>
> - A method for the gradual removal of fearful associations is sometimes referred to as **desensitization**.
>
> - The amount of current that actually flows in a wire is measured in a unit called the **ampere**, or **amp**.
>
> - A court's **jurisdiction** is its authority to hear cases of a particular type.
>
> - **Microwaves** are electromagnetic waves whose wavelengths range from about one meter to one millimeter.
>
> - When the press plays what is termed a **common-carrier role**, it provides a channel through which political leaders can reach the public.
>
> - Leading experts define **sales promotion** as an action-focused marketing event whose goal is a direct impact on the behavior of a firm's customers.
>
> - The most important fact in describing any atom is the number of protons in its nucleus—the **atomic number**.
>
> (**Note:** Sometimes a dash is used to signal a definition.)
>
> If an author defines a term, you can assume that it is important enough to learn. So when reading and taking notes on a textbook, always do two things:
>
> 1) Write down key definitions.
> 2) Write down a helpful example for each definition. When a definition is general and abstract, examples are often essential to help make its meaning clear.

☑ *Check Your Understanding*

The following paragraph defines a term, explains it a bit, and then gives an example of it. After reading the paragraph, see if you can answer the questions that follow.

> [1]A loss leader is a product or service that sells at a loss but generates customer interest that can lead to a later profit. [2]A classic example of a loss leader is the ice-cream counter at a Thrifty's variety store. [3]Ice-cream cones are sold for less than the cost of the stand, equipment, supplies, and labor. [4]But the ice-cream counter, strategically placed near the store entrance, helps draw customers into the store. [5]Once inside, they often buy other items as well, so the store turns an overall profit. [6]The loss-leader principle is used in many other applications. [7]For instance, television networks take a loss on special events like the Olympic Games because they believe that the viewers they attract will then "stay tuned" for their other, moneymaking shows.

What term is being defined? _____

Which sentence contains the definition? _____

In which sentence does the first example begin? _____

In what sentence does a second example appear? _____

Explanation:

The term *loss leader* is defined in the first sentence: "a product or service that sells at a loss but generates customer interest that can lead to a later profit." The first example of a loss leader is the ice-cream counter at a Thrifty's variety store; that example is first mentioned in sentence 2. A second example is taking a loss on special events like the Olympic Games; it appears in sentence 7.

➤ *Practice 2*

Each of the following passages includes a definition and one or more examples. Underline the term being defined. Then, in the spaces provided, write the number of the definition sentence and the number of the sentence where each example begins.

A.   [1]A point of purchase display is advertising or other display materials set up at retail locations to promote products as customers are making their purchase decisions. [2]Such a display may be simple, such as the end-of-aisle stacks of soda pop in a supermarket. [3]Or it may be more elaborate. [4]For example, Estée

Lauder uses "computers" to encourage consumers to buy the Clinique line. [5]Potential buyers enter facts about their skin and makeup problems into a "data bank." [6]On the basis of this information, the Clinique "computer" recommends a complete cosmetics program tailored to the woman's specific needs.

Definition _____   *Example 1* _____   *Example 2* _____

B. [1]The self-handicapping strategy is a technique for making up protective excuses ahead of time. [2]Research has shown that people use this strategy often. [3]For instance, they'll offer an excuse before they take an exam, saying, "I had to work, so I didn't get much studying done. [4]I may not do very well." [5]Or in advance of a social occasion, they might say, "I didn't get much sleep last night, so I'm probably not going to have anything interesting to say." [6]In either case, the excuse planted ahead of time takes the heat off the individual and places the blame on the circumstance.

Definition _____   *Example 1* _____   *Example 2* _____

2 COMPARISON AND CONTRAST

Words That Show Comparison

Put a check (✓) beside the item that is easier to understand:

____ The computerized scanner has streamlined the supermarket checkout line. Computerized fingerprint identification allows the police to do in seconds what once took two hours.

____ The computerized scanner has streamlined the supermarket checkout line. Similarly, computerized fingerprint identification allows the police to do in seconds what once took two hours.

The first item makes us wonder, "What has supermarket work got to do with police work?" In the second item, the transition word *similarly* makes it clear that the author is *comparing* the benefits of computerization in both types of work. *Similarly* and words like it are comparison words.

Comparison words signal similarities. Authors use a comparison transition to show that a second idea is *like* the first one in some way. Here are some common words that show comparison:

Comparison Words

(just) as	both	in like fashion	in a similar fashion
(just) like	equal(ly)	in like manner	in a similar manner
alike	resemble	similar(ly)	(in) the same way
same	likewise	similarity	(in) common

Examples:

The sentences below contain comparison words. Notice how these words show that things are *alike* in some way.

> *Both* alligators and crocodiles use nerve-packed bumps in their jaws to sense the movement of nearby prey.

> Surveys show that women who work out of the home and stay-at-home moms are *equally* concerned about their children's welfare.

> Many thousands of plant species are in danger of vanishing from the earth. *Likewise*, up to five thousand species of animals could soon be extinct.

➤ Practice 3

Complete each sentence with a suitable comparison word or phrase from the box on the previous page. Try to use a variety of transitions.

1. A swarm of locusts looks ___just like___ a massive dark cloud moving across the sky.

2. As a young boy, Raymond was often beaten by his parents. Unfortunately, he now treats his own children ___in a similar manner___.
   In the same way that

3. ___Just as___ people put their best foot forward for romance, birds show off their skills or looks during courtship.

4. My cousin, who gets around in a wheelchair, had kitchen counters built at a convenient height for him. ___Similarly___, he created a flower container garden at a height he can easily reach.

5. American films are enormously popular in almost every country. ___In the same way___, American clothing styles influence fashions around the world.

Words That Show Contrast

Put a check (✓) beside the item that is easier to understand:

____ The company pays the manager handsomely. He doesn't do much work.

_✓_ The company pays the manager handsomely even though he doesn't do much work.

The first item is puzzling: does the company pay the manager well *because* he doesn't do much work? The second item makes it clear that the company pays the manager well *even though* he doesn't do much work. *Even though* and words and phrases like it are contrast words.

Contrast words signal that an author is pointing out differences between subjects. A contrast word shows that two things *differ* in one or more ways. Contrast words also inform us that something is going to *differ from* what we might expect. Here are some common words that show contrast:

Contrast Words

but	instead (of)	even though	difference
yet	in contrast	as opposed to	different (ly)
however	on the other hand	in spite of	differ (from)
although	on the contrary	despite	unlike
nevertheless	converse (ly)	rather than	while
still	opposite		

Examples:

The sentences below contain contrast words. Notice how these words signal that one idea is *different from* another idea.

Women communicate *differently* in the workplace than men do.

Although the cost of attending college has tripled over the last twenty years, sources of financial aid have decreased.

The average person can safely tolerate ten bee stings for each pound of body weight. This means that the average adult could withstand more than a thousand stings. *However,* one sting can cause death in a person who is allergic to such stings.

➤ Practice 4

Complete each sentence with a suitable contrast word or phrase from the above box. Try to use a variety of transitions.

1. People are capable of making some adjustment to a constant noise level. ___However/Conversely___, if the noise exceeds eighty-five to ninety decibels, their productivity will decrease over the course of the workday.

2. ___Although___ Americans claim to be concerned with fitness, the typical adult can't climb a flight of steps without getting short of breath. *unlike*

3. ___In contrast to___ perennial plants, which return year after year, annuals survive for only one season.

4. Most American-born college students cannot converse in a foreign language. _____In contrast_____, it is a rare student in Europe who cannot speak at least one language besides his or her own.

5. The most effective bridge from low levels of reading ability to higher levels is pleasure reading. _____Nevertheless_____, this is exactly the kind of reading that is missing from the lives of many students.

Comparison and contrast transitions are often used in paragraphs organized in the comparison and/or contrast pattern.

The Comparison and/or Contrast Pattern

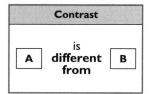

Arrange the following group of sentences into an order that makes sense. Put a *1* in front of the sentence that should come first, a *2* in front of the sentence that comes next, and a *3* in front of the sentence that should be last. The result will be a short paragraph. Then read the explanation that follows.

___ New products are often introduced with "informational" advertising, telling what the products are, why they are needed, and where they are available.

___ New products are generally advertised differently from established products.

___ Established products, on the other hand, can rely on "reminder" advertisements, which provide little hard information about the product.

Explanation:

The first sentence of this paragraph is the general one, the one with the main idea: "New products are generally advertised differently from established products." The word *differently* suggests a comparison and/or contrast pattern of organization. As the contrast phrase *on the other hand* suggests, the other two sentences, in fact, do contrast two things—two types of advertising: "New products are often introduced with 'informational' advertising, telling what the products are, why they are needed, and where they are available. Established products, on the other hand, can rely on 'reminder' advertisements, which provide little hard information about the product."

The **comparison and/or contrast pattern** shows how two things are alike or how they are different, or both. When things are compared, their similarities are pointed out; when they are contrasted, their differences are discussed (for example, the difference in advertising used for new and established products).

Authors frequently find it useful to compare and contrast. Here are three examples:

- The author of a psychology text contrasts genuine and artificial facial expressions. He explains that smiles resulting from actual joy involve the outer muscles that surround the eyes, while smiles used to hide negative emotions tend to involve the muscles around the lips and eyes that are usually linked to disgust.

- The author of a sociology text compares and contrasts the political beliefs of Catholics, Protestants, and Jews. In most policy issues, he notes, the three groups hold similar opinions. Catholics and fundamentalist Protestants oppose abortion more strongly than the other groups, while Catholics and Jews are more supportive of food programs for the poor than are most Protestants.

- The author of an economics text contrasts the philosophies of two men, Adam Smith and Karl Marx. In his book *The Wealth of Nations*, Smith argues for a free-market economy that is controlled solely by supply and demand. In the book *Das Kapital*, Marx argues that free-market economy exploits workers, and proposes an economy that the workers control.

☑ Check Your Understanding

In the following paragraph, the main idea is stated in the first sentence. As is often the case, the main idea suggests a paragraph's pattern of organization. Here the transition *different* is a hint that the paragraph may be organized in a comparison-contrast pattern. Read the paragraph and answer the questions below. Then read the explanation that follows.

> [1]The feeling of awe is mostly different from the feeling of fear. [2]In both cases, we may feel a sense of being overwhelmed, of confronting someone or something much more powerful than ourselves. [3]But awe is a positive feeling, an expansive feeling. [4]While fear makes us want to run away, awe makes us want to draw closer even as we hesitate to get too close. [5]When we are in awe, we stand open-mouthed in appreciation of something greater than ourselves rather than being anxious about it. [6]To stand at the edge of a steep cliff and look down is to experience fear. [7]We want to get out of that situation as quickly and safely as we can. [8]In contrast, to stand securely on a mountaintop and look around us is to feel awe. We could linger there forever.

1. Is this paragraph comparing, contrasting, or both? _____

2. What two things are being compared and/or contrasted? _____

_____

3. What are four of the comparison and/or contrast signal words used in the paragraph? _____

Explanation:

This paragraph is both comparing and contrasting—it discusses both a similarity and differences. The two things being compared and contrasted are (1) awe and (2) fear. One comparison transition is used—*both*. Five contrast transitions are used—*different, but, while, rather than,* and *in contrast.*

➤ Practice 5

The following passages use the pattern of comparison and/or contrast. Read each passage and answer the questions that follow.

A. ¹The difference between work and play is in the purpose of and reward for performing an activity. ²Work has a definite purpose. ³Something is being accomplished when work is performed. ⁴Some resource such as raw material or information is being changed. ⁵Play, however, need not have a purpose; sometimes people engage in play for its own sake. ⁶The rewards for work are mainly external ones. ⁷Money may be the most common external reward; others are recognition and promotion. ⁸In contrast, the rewards for play are internal ones: satisfaction, enjoyment, a sense of achievement.

Check (✓) the pattern which is used in this passage:

____ Comparison

____ Contrast

____ Comparison and contrast

What two things are being compared, contrasted, or compared *and* contrasted?

1. _____   2. _____

B. ¹The similarity in causes and characteristics of the First and Second World Wars was more than superficial. ²Both were triggered by threats to the balance of power, and both were conflicts between peoples, entire nations, rather than between governments. ³On the other hand, there were notable differences between the two conflicts. ⁴The methods of warfare in the

Second World War had little in common with those of the earlier conflict. [5]Instead of the trench warfare of the First World War, the Second had bombing and sudden air attacks on civilian populations as well as on military installations. [6]Thus, to a much greater degree than in the First World War, those at home shared with soldiers the dangers of the war. [7]Finally, this war was not greeted with the almost universal, naive enthusiasm that had marked the outbreak of the other. [8]Men and women still remembered the horrors of the First World War. [9]They entered the Second with determination, but also with a keener appreciation of the frightful devastation that war could bring than their predecessors had possessed.

Check (✓) the pattern which is used in this passage:

____ Comparison

____ Contrast

____ Comparison and contrast

What two things are being compared, contrasted, or compared *and* contrasted?

1. _____   2. _____

3   CAUSE AND EFFECT

Words That Show Cause and Effect

Put a check (✓) beside the item that is easier to understand:

____ The young woman decided to go away to school. Her boyfriend began talking about getting married.

____ The young woman decided to go away to school because her boyfriend began talking about getting married.

In the first item, we're not sure about the relationship between the two sentences. Did the young woman's boyfriend discuss marriage because she decided to go away to school? Or was it the other way around? The word *because* in the second item makes it clear that the young woman decided to go away to school *as a result* of her boyfriend's interest in marriage. *Because* and words like it are cause and effect words.

Cause and effect words signal that the author is explaining *the reason why* something happened or *the result* of something happening. Here are some common words that show cause and effect:

Cause and Effect Words

therefore	so	owing to	because (of)
thus	(as a) result	effect	reason
(as a) consequence	results in	cause	explanation
consequently	leads to	if...then	accordingly
due to	since	affect	

Examples:

The following examples contain cause and effect words. Notice how these words introduce a *reason* for something or the *results* of something.

> The first street traffic lights were created in 1920 by a Detroit policeman. He picked the colors red, yellow, and green *because* railroads used them.

> In England during the sixteenth century, the color red was thought to be helpful to the sick. *Consequently,* patients were dressed in red nightgowns.

> Don't eat an egg that has a crack in it. The *reason* is that the egg may be contaminated.

➤ Practice 6

Complete each sentence with a suitable cause and effect word or phrase from the box above. Try to use a variety of transitions.

1. The _____ many people support organic farming is that it is less destructive to the environment than farming with chemicals and pesticides.

2. Antibiotics should be taken for the full prescribed duration. Failure to do so could _____ in a relapse or in the emergence of resistant bacteria strains.

3. Human behavior is so complicated that we are not always aware of the _____s of our own actions.

4. Although reduced-fat foods may sound healthy, the fat is often replaced by carbohydrates that may _____ weight gain.

5. Information overload is all around us, coming with terrifying speed via fax, phone, and e-mail, over scores of cable channels, even at the newsstand. _____ so much information bombards us constantly, we fail to remember a great deal of it.

Cause and effect transitions often signal the cause and effect pattern of organization.

The Cause and Effect Pattern

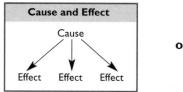 **or**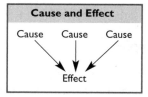

To get a sense of the cause and effect pattern, try to arrange the following sentences in an order that makes sense. Put a *1* in front of the sentence that should come first, a *2* in front of the sentence that comes next, and a *3* in front of the sentence that should be last. The result will be a short paragraph. Then read the explanation that follows.

____ As a result, federal authorities required that ships carry enough lifeboats to save everyone on board.

____ The sinking of the ship *Titanic* led to safer sea travel.

____ When the *Titanic* sank, many died because there were too few lifeboats.

As the words *led to, because,* and *as a result* suggest, this paragraph is organized in a cause and effect pattern. The paragraph begins with the general idea: "The sinking of the ship *Titanic* led to safer sea travel." Next comes the detailed explanation: "When the *Titanic* sank, many died because there were too few lifeboats. As a result, federal authorities required that ships carry enough lifeboats to save everyone on board."

Information in a **cause-effect pattern** addresses the questions "Why does a behavior or event happen?" and/or "What are the results of a behavior or event?" An author may then discuss causes, or effects, or both causes and effects.

Authors usually don't just tell what happened. They try to tell about events in a way that explains both *what* happened and *why*. A textbook section on the sinking of the ship *Titanic*, for example, would be incomplete if it did not include the cause of the disaster—going at high speed, the ship collided with an iceberg. Or if the number of people out of work in the country increases, journalists may not simply report the increase. They may also explore the reasons for and effects of that increase.

☑ *Check Your Understanding*

Read the paragraph below and see if you can answer the questions about cause and effect. Then read the explanation to see how you did.

[1]Each year, thousands of square miles of tropical rain forests are burned or cut down, causing much damage to land, animals, and humans everywhere on Earth. [2]Destroying the forests, first of all, causes the forest to become a lifeless, useless desert. [3]A second effect of the destruction is the threat to animal life. [4]Much of the variety of Earth's life consists of creatures who live in the rain forests. [5]Many species are becoming extinct, even before scientists ever find out about them. [6]The disappearance of the rain forests is a threat to human life as well as to animals. [7]As we breathe, we use up oxygen. [8]The oxygen is constantly being resupplied by plants—and the tropical rain forests provide a major share of that fresh oxygen. [9]Therefore, as we burn or hack down the rain forests, we are destroying more and more of the very oxygen supply we depend on to breathe.

1. What is the single *cause* being discussed in the paragraph?

   _____

2. What are the three *effects* discussed?

   A. _____

   B. _____

   C. _____

3. What four cause and effect transitions are used in the paragraph?

   _____

Explanation:

The paragraph begins with the main idea: "Each year, thousands of square miles of tropical rain forests are burned or cut down, causing much damage to land, animals, and humans everywhere on Earth." That point, or cause, is then supported by three effects: 1) the forests' becoming lifeless, useless deserts; 2) the threat to animals, with many species becoming extinct; and 3) the threat to human life through the loss of some of our oxygen supply. The cause and effect transitions used are *causing, causes, effect,* and *Therefore.*

➤ *Practice 7*

A. Read the paragraph below, looking for one effect and four causes (the four major supporting details of the paragraph). Then complete the diagram that follows.

> ¹There are a number of motivations for shoplifting. ²Poverty is one cause, shown both by the evidence that poor people are more likely than others to shoplift and by the fact that shoplifting becomes more common when unemployment is high. ³A second reason for shoplifting is frugal customers, ones who can afford to buy the things they need but are driven to steal them by a desire to stretch their budget. ⁴Another explanation is the sense of excitement and fun that shoplifters experience when committing the crime. ⁵Yet another cause, especially among youngsters, is the desire for social acceptance; when asked why they shoplift, many young people say, "Because my friends are doing it."

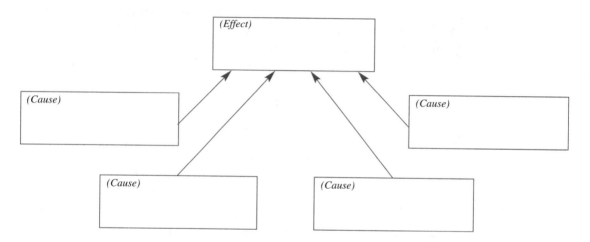

B. Read the paragraph below, looking for the one effect and the two causes. Then complete the outline that follows.

> ¹The number of humans on Earth continues to rise dramatically. ²One reason is technology. ³A hundred years ago it was not unusual to find countries with infant mortality rates over 50 percent. ⁴Today, however, infants in even the most impoverished countries have well over an 80 percent chance to live. ⁵Technological advances have also reduced the death rate by eliminating fatal diseases such as smallpox, improving crop yields, and devising new means of distributing food. ⁶Another major cause of the population explosion is the changing rates of deaths and births. ⁷In under-developed countries, people depend on their children for support and security. ⁸Parents typically have had many children to ensure that a few will survive. ⁹But the decline in death rates has now resulted in the population in

these countries growing rapidly. [10]In many affluent countries, such as Japan and the United States, the birthrate is actually declining, but because the death rate is declining even faster, their populations continue to grow.

Main idea *(the effect):* _____

_____

Major supporting details *(the causes):*

1. _____

2. _____

A Note on Main Ideas and Patterns of Organization

As mentioned in Chapter 5, a paragraph's main idea often indicates its pattern of organization. Try, for instance, to guess the pattern of the paragraph with this main idea:

Norms are the standards of behavior accepted as appropriate in a society.

This sentence defines the word *norms*. A definition suggests that the author may be using the definition and example pattern. In fact, the paragraph continues with these sentences:

For instance, in Europe, it is normal for meat to be eaten with the fork facing down in the left hand. In America, however, the fork is transferred to the right hand after the meat is cut.

Recognizing a main idea, and the pattern of organization that may be implied in a main idea, are both helpful steps in understanding the material in the paragraph.

➤ Practice 8

Most of the main ideas below have been taken from college textbooks. In the space provided, write the letter of the pattern of organization that each suggests.

_____ 1. Depressed economic times often lead to an increase in spouse abuse and divorce.
   A. Definition and   B. Comparison and/or   C. Cause and effect
      example   contrast

_____ 2. While Randy Jarvis and Octavio Ruiz live only a few miles from one another, their lives are so different that they might as well be living in separate countries.
   A. Definition and   B. Comparison and/or   C. Cause and effect
      example   contrast

_____ 3. A franchise is a business arrangement in which an individual obtains rights from a larger company to sell a well-known product or service.
    A. Definition and example
    B. Comparison and/or contrast
    C. Cause and effect

_____ 4. Because of the high cost of raising a family and of housing, two-income families have become a way of life in America.
    A. Definition and example
    B. Comparison and/or contrast
    C. Cause and effect

_____ 5. White-collar crimes refer to crimes that respectable people of high social status commit in the course of their occupations.
    A. Definition and example
    B. Comparison and/or contrast
    C. Cause and effect

_____ 6. A high-fat meal and a high-carbohydrate meal may provide the same food energy, but they affect the appetite differently.
    A. Definition and example
    B. Comparison and/or contrast
    C. Cause and effect

_____ 7. Among the reasons that people daydream are to help tolerate boredom and to discharge hostile feelings.
    A. Definition and example
    B. Comparison and/or contrast
    C. Cause and effect

_____ 8. The jobs created by small businesses differ from those created by big companies in several key respects.
    A. Definition and example
    B. Comparison and/or contrast
    C. Cause and effect

_____ 9. Monotremes are mammals that lay eggs; the duck-billed platypus, which lives only in Australia, is one of the two types of monotremes that are alive today.
    A. Definition and example
    B. Comparison and/or contrast
    C. Cause and effect

_____ 10. For a variety of reasons, fiction in the modern sense of the word began to flourish in the late seventeenth and eighteenth centuries.
    A. Definition and example
    B. Comparison and/or contrast
    C. Cause and effect

A Final Point

Keep in mind that a paragraph or passage may often be made up of more than one pattern of organization. For instance, the paragraph in this chapter explaining the term *loss leader* uses a definition and example pattern. The term is defined and examples are given; the examples are the ice-cream counter at a Thrifty's variety store and television networks taking a loss on special events such as the Olympics. But the explanations of how loss leaders work incorporate a cause-effect pattern— the loss leaders are used because of the positive effects they have.

Or consider the following passage:

[1]According to the United Nations, women in poor countries have lives very different from, and worse than, the lives of men in those countries. [2]For one thing, women have much lower literacy rates than men. [3]In South Asia, females' literacy rates are only around 50 percent of males'. [4]In addition, women lag far behind in education. [5]The females' rates for secondary education represent 72 percent of the men's rates and, for college education, only 51 percent. [6]Also, women in poor countries have fewer opportunities for paid employment. [7]There are only fifty-eight women employees for every one hundred men, and they are paid considerably less. [8]Women not gainfully employed are far from idle, however. [9]In fact, they usually work an average of twelve hours a day, while men work only eight hours.

The paragraph uses a contrast pattern: Women in poor countries are contrasted with men in the same countries. It also uses a list of items pattern, listing points of contrast between the men and women regarding literacy, education, employment, and hours of work. Pages 259–264 offer practice on passages with more than one pattern of organization.

CHAPTER REVIEW

In this chapter, you learned about three kinds of relationships that authors use to make their ideas clear:

- **Definitions and examples**
  - To help readers understand the important ideas and terms in a subject, textbook authors often take time to include key definitions (often setting them off in *italic* or **boldface**) and examples of those definitions. When reading a textbook, it is usually a good idea to mark off both definitions and examples. (Underline each definition, and put *Ex* in the margin next to each example.)

(Continues on next page)

— Transition words that signal the definition and example pattern include *for example, for instance, to illustrate,* and *such as.*

- **Comparison and/or contrast**

  — Authors often discuss how two things are alike or how they are different, or both.

  — Transition words that signal comparisons include *alike* and *similar.*

  — Transition words that signal contrasts include *but, however,* and *in contrast.*

- **Cause and effect**

  — Authors often discuss the reasons why something happens or the effects of something that has happened.

  — Transition words that signal causes include *reason* and *because.*

  — Transition words that signal effects include *therefore, consequently,* and *as a result.*

Note that pages 258–264 list and offer practice in all the transitions and patterns of organization you have studied in "Relationships I" and "Relationships II."

The next chapter—Chapter 7—will be devoted to helping you distinguish between fact and opinion in writing.

On the Web: If you are using this book in class, you can visit our website for additional practice in understanding relationships that involve examples, comparison or contrast, and cause and effect. Go to **www.townsendpress.com** and click on "Online Exercises."

➤ Review Test 1

To review what you've learned in this chapter, choose the best answer or fill in the blank for the following items.

_____ 1. Words such as *for example, for instance,* and *such as* are known as
  A. illustration words.
  B. definition words.
  C. cause-and-effect words.

_____ 2. Words such as *just as, similarly,* and *in the same way* are known as
  A. illustration words.
  B. comparison words.
  C. contrast words.

_____ 3. Words such as *however, on the other hand,* and *differs from* are known as
  A. illustration words.
  B. contrast words.
  C. cause-and-effect words.

_____ 4. Words such as *therefore, as a result,* and *reason* are known as
  A. definition words.
  B. contrast words.
  C. cause-and-effect words.

5. In textbooks, definitions of key terms are often followed by one or more _____ that help make those definitions clear.

➤ Review Test 2

A. Fill in each blank with one of the words in the box. Use each word once. Then write the letter of the word in the space provided.

A. similarly	B. because	C. despite
D. even though	E. for instance	

_____ 1. Many products are named after specific individuals. _____, the man who created the Tootsie Roll named it after his daughter, whom he had nicknamed Tootsie.

_____ 2. _____ a learning disability which made it difficult for her to learn to read, Darla worked hard and became a successful businesswoman.

_____ 3. The button factory was built near the river _____ it made buttons out of shells that were found there.

_____ 4. Some people hate driving small cars _____ the gas mileage is far superior to that of a large, luxurious "gas-guzzler."

_____ 5. In one study, men and women who merely walked for a half hour to an hour every day at a fast but comfortable pace cut their health risks by half or more. _____, a study of five hundred women between the ages of 42 and 50 found that as little as three brisk twenty-minute walks each week can lower the risk of heart disease.

B. Below are the beginnings of five passages. Label each one with the letter of its pattern of organization. (You may find it helpful to underline the transition or transitions in each item.)

     A Definition and example
     B Comparison and/or contrast
     C Cause and effect

_____ 6. [1]Preventive medicine is like changing a car's oil. [2]Just as we must change the oil regularly for a car to operate smoothly, we must have regular checkups with our doctors. . . .

_____ 7. [1]A fetus can be affected by all kinds of sensory stimulation while in the mother's womb. [2]A bright light shining on the mother's abdomen will cause the fetus to raise its hands over its eyes. [3]Loud sounds will make it cover its ears. . . .

_____ 8. [1]Jungles are areas of land that are densely overgrown with tropical trees and other vegetation. [2]In South America, for instance, the Amazon is the largest jungle. . . .

_____ 9. [1]Although American culture stresses the importance of a strong mother-child relationship, traditional Samoan families do not see the relationship as essential. [2]Rather than having just one family, many Samoan children are passed around between several foster families during childhood, with no apparent negative effect.

_____ 10. [1]We can prevent soil from being blown away by wind or from being washed away by rain simply by planting bushes and trees on the land. [2]The roots of these plants penetrate the soil; consequently, it is held in place. . . .

▶ Review Test 3

Read each paragraph and answer the questions that follow.

A. ¹Vitamins are powerful substances, as seen when people consume too little or too many. ²A deficiency of vitamin A can lead to blindness. ³A lack of the B-vitamin niacin can cause symptoms of mental illness, and an absence of the B-vitamin thiamin can eventually produce nerve, heart, and brain abnormalities. ⁴Doing without vitamin C can lead to scurvy, and failing to take in vitamin D can retard bone growth. ⁵The consequences of deficiencies are so dire, and the effects of restoring vitamins so dramatic, that people spend billions of dollars every year on vitamin pills. ⁶They are advised to remember that many vitamins hold the potential for toxicity if taken in amounts that far exceed recommended dietary allowances.

_____ 1. The main pattern of organization of the paragraph is
    A. definition and example.
    B. comparison and/or contrast.
    C. cause and effect.

2. One transition that signals the pattern of organization of this paragraph

is _____.

B. ¹Working backward is the name given to a strategy in which the search for a solution begins at the goal and works backward. ²This method is often used when we have more information about the goal than about the details of a situation and when the operations can work both forward and backward. ³Say, for instance, that we wanted to spend exactly $100 on clothing. ⁴It would be difficult to reach that goal by simply buying some items and hoping that they totaled exactly $100. ⁵A better strategy would be to purchase one item and subtract its cost from $100 in order to determine how much money is left. ⁶Then we would purchase another item, subtract its cost, and so on until we have spent $100.

_____ 3. The main pattern of organization of the paragraph is
    A. definition and example.
    B. comparison and/or contrast.
    C. cause and effect.

4. The transition that signals the pattern of organization of this paragraph

is _____.

C. ¹Young children and very elderly people represent opposite extremes of the life cycle, but their similarities are striking. ²All children are physically and mentally dependent on others. ³Likewise, many elderly people need assistance with eating and dressing. ⁴Just as a toddler cannot be left unsupervised at home, an older person suffering from dementia must be under constant watch. [5]Both are apt to fall, although the danger for an elderly person is much greater than that for a child, whose extra padding protects him or her from injury. [6]Interestingly, however, the young and old possess more proportional body fat than a normal adult. [7]Both groups are at greater risk for physical abuse, disease and illness, and all medication must be modified to fit their unique needs. [8]Because the health concerns of children and elderly can be radically different from those of adults, medical practice for these patients has developed into two special branches, pediatrics and geriatrics. [9]Socially, children and senior citizens share a common plight, usually depending on others to get them out of the house. [10]Elderly people who still work can face job discrimination, and many establishments have "no-children" policies. [11]In addition, children and the elderly often find that their opinions do not hold as much weight in society as those of adults, and they frequently have decisions made for them.

_____ 5. The main pattern of organization of the paragraph is
    A. definition and example.
    B. comparison and/or contrast.
    C. cause and effect.

    6. One transition that signals the pattern of organization of this paragraph

       is _____.

D.   [1]Doing something nice for someone can affect us in an interesting way—it can make us like that person better. [2]In experiments, doing a favor for another subject or tutoring a student usually increases liking of the person helped. [3]In 1793, Benjamin Franklin tested the idea that doing a favor has the effect of increasing liking. [4]As clerk of the Pennsylvania General Assembly, he was disturbed by opposition from another important legislator. [5]Franklin set out to win him over:

> [6]Having heard that he had in his library a certain very scarce and curious book I wrote a note to him . . . requesting he would do me the favour of lending it to me for a few days. [7]He sent it immediately and I return'd it in about a week, expressing strongly my sense of the favour. [8]When we next met in the House he spoke to me (which he had never done before), and with great civility; and he ever after manifested a readiness to serve me on all occasions, so that we became great friends and our friendship continued to his death.

_____ 7. The main pattern of organization of the paragraph is
    A. definition and example.
    B. comparison and/or contrast.
    C. cause and effect.

    8. One transition that signals the pattern of organization of this paragraph

       is _____.

E.   ¹Animals know their environment by direct experience only. ²In contrast, humans crystallize their knowledge and feelings in symbolic representations. ³Using those written symbols, they accumulate knowledge and pass it on to further generations of humans. ⁴Animals feed themselves where they find food, but humans, coordinating their efforts with the efforts of others through language, often feed themselves abundantly and with food prepared by a hundred hands and brought from great distances. ⁵Animals exercise limited control over each other. ⁶However, humans, again by employing symbols, establish laws and ethical systems.

_____ 9. The main pattern of organization of the paragraph is
    A. definition and example.
    B. comparison and/or contrast.
    C. cause and effect.

        10. One transition that signals the pattern of organization of this paragraph

            is _____.

➤ Review Test 4

Here is a chance to apply your understanding of relationships and patterns of organization to a passage from a college textbook: *Looking Out Looking In,* Tenth Edition, by Ronald B. Adler and Neil Towne (Harcourt). The reading may make you think twice the next time you hear yourself saying, "I just *knew* that would happen."

To help you continue to strengthen your skills, the reading is followed by questions not only on what you've learned in this chapter but also on what you've learned in previous chapters.

Words to Watch

Below are some words in the reading that do not have strong context support. Each word is followed by the number of the paragraph in which it appears and its meaning there. These words are indicated in the article by a small circle (°).

phenomenon (1): an observable fact or event
preconceptions (3): opinions or ideas formed about something before experiencing it
peers (5): equals; people of the same social standing
sabotage (5): undermine; damage
disposition (6): frame of mind

THE INFLUENCE OF THE SELF-FULFILLING PROPHECY

Ronald B. Adler and Neil Towne

1   The self-concept is such a powerful force on the personality that it not only determines how you see yourself in the present but also can actually influence your future behavior and that of others. Such occurrences come about through a phenomenon° called the self-fulfilling prophecy.

2   A **self-fulfilling prophecy** occurs when a person's expectations of an event make the event more likely to occur than would otherwise have been true. Self-fulfilling prophecies occur all the time, although you might never have given them that label. For example, think of some instances you may have known.

- You expected to become nervous and botch a job interview and later did so.
- You anticipated having a good (or terrible) time at a social affair and found your expectations being met.
- A teacher or boss explained a new task to you, saying that you probably wouldn't do well at first. You did not do well.
- A friend described someone you were about to meet, saying that you wouldn't like the person. The prediction turned out to be correct—you didn't like the new acquaintance.

3   In each of these cases there is a good chance that the event occurred because it was predicted to occur. You needn't have botched the interview, the party might have been boring only because you helped make it so, you might have done better on the job if your boss hadn't spoken up, and you might have liked the new acquaintance if your friend hadn't given you preconceptions°. In other words, what helped each event occur was the expectation of it.

Types of Self-Fulfilling Prophecies

4   There are two types of self-fulfilling prophecies. *Self-imposed prophecies* occur when your own expectations influence your behavior. In sports you've probably "psyched" yourself into playing either better or worse than usual, so that the only explanation for your unusual performance was your attitude. Similarly, you've probably faced an audience at one time or another with a fearful attitude and forgotten your remarks, not because you were unprepared, but because you said to yourself, "I know I'll blow it."

5   Research has demonstrated the power of self-imposed prophecies. In one study, people who considered themselves incompetent proved less likely to pursue rewarding relationships with others. Compared to their more confident peers°, they were also more likely to sabotage° existing relationships. On the other hand, students who perceived themselves as capable achieved more academically. In another study, subjects who were sensitive to social rejection tended to expect rejection, perceive it where it might not have existed, and act as if it had occurred even when it did not. Such a response strains relationships and can result in exactly what the sensitive person was trying to avoid—rejection. Research also suggests that communicators who feel anxious about giving speeches seem to create self-fulfilling prophecies about doing poorly that cause them to perform less effectively. The self-fulfilling

prophecy also operates on the job. For instance, salespeople who view themselves as being effective communicators are more successful than those who view themselves as less effective, despite the fact that there was no difference in the approach that members of each group used with customers. In other words, the apparent reason why some salespeople are successful is that they expect to succeed.

6 Self-imposed prophecies operate in many ways that affect everyday communication. You've had the experience of waking up in an irritable mood and saying to yourself, "This will be a bad day." After you made such a decision, you may have acted in ways that made it come true. If you approached a class expecting to be bored, you most probably did lose interest, owing partly to a lack of attention on your part. If you avoided the company of others because you expected they had nothing to offer, your expectations would have been confirmed—nothing exciting or new did happen to you. However, if you approached the same day with the idea that it could be a good one, this expectation probably would have been met also. Researchers have found that putting a smile on your face, even if you're not in a good mood, can lead to a more positive disposition°. Likewise, if you approach a class determined to learn something, you probably will—even if it's how not to instruct students! Approach many strangers with the idea that some of them will be good to know, and you'll most likely make some new friends. In these cases and ones like them, your attitude has a great deal to do with how you see yourself and how others will see you.

7 A second category of self-fulfilling prophecies is imposed by one person on another, so that the expectations of one person govern another's actions. The classic example was demonstrated by Robert Rosenthal and Lenore Jacobson in a study they described in their book *Pygmalion in the Classroom.* The experimenters randomly selected 20 percent of a school's population and convinced teachers that the selected students showed unusual potential for intellectual growth. Eight months later these unusual or "magic" children showed significantly greater gains in IQ than did the remaining children, who had not been singled out for the teachers' attention. The change in the teachers' expectations had led to an actual change in the performance of these randomly selected children. In other words, the children did better, not because they were any more intelligent than their classmates, but because they learned that their teachers—significant others—believed that they could.

8 To put this phenomenon in context with the self-concept, we can say that when a teacher communicates to a child the message "I think you're bright," the child accepts that evaluation and changes her self-concept to include it. Unfortunately, we can assume that the same principle holds for students whose teachers send the message, "I think you're stupid."

9 This type of self-fulfilling prophecy has been shown to be a powerful force for shaping the self-concept and thus the behavior of people in a wide range of settings outside the schools. In medicine, patients who unknowingly use placebos—substances such as injections of sterile water or doses of sugar pills that have no curative value—often respond just as favorably to treatment as those who actually received a drug. The patients believe they have taken a substance that will help them feel better, and this belief actually brings about a "cure." In psychotherapy Rosenthal and Jacobson

describe several studies suggesting that patients who believe they will benefit from treatment do so regardless of the type of treatment they receive. In the same vein, when a doctor believes that a patient will improve, the patient may do so precisely because of this expectation, whereas another person for whom the doctor has little hope often fails to recover. Apparently the patient's self-concept as sick or well—as shaped by the doctor—plays an important role in determining the actual state of health.

Reading Comprehension Questions

Vocabulary in Context

_____ 1. In the sentence below, the word *strains* (strānz) means
   A. improves.
   B. deepens.
   C. has no impact upon.
   D. injures.

   "Such a response strains relationships and can result in exactly what the sensitive person was trying to avoid—rejection." (Paragraph 5)

Central Point and Main Ideas

_____ 2. Which sentence best expresses the central point of the selection?
   A. People who expect to like other people usually have no trouble making friends.
   B. There are two types of self-fulfilling prophecy, which is what occurs when our expectations of a situation influence what happens.
   C. Self-fulfilling prophecies are what determine whether we succeed or fail in life.
   D. Children whose teachers have faith in them perform better academically than other children.

_____ 3. The main idea of paragraph 9 is stated in its
   A. first sentence.
   B. second sentence.
   C. third sentence.
   D. last sentence.

Supporting Details

_____ 4. In the experiment described in the book *Pygmalion in the Classroom,*
   A. experimenters convinced teachers that certain children were especially bright.
   B. experimenters told teachers to give extra attention to their most problematic students.
   C. children were allowed to take over their teachers' jobs.
   D. experimenters asked teachers to ignore certain students.

_____ 5. Substances known as placebos are
   A. experimental drugs not yet approved for general use.
   B. a form of antibiotic.
   C. substances without curative value that patients believe are medicine.
   D. psychiatric drugs that often increase people's self-confidence.

Transitions

_____ 6. The relationship of the second to the first sentence below is one of
   A. illustration.
   B. cause and effect.
   C. addition.
   D. comparison.

   "Researchers have found that putting a smile on your face, even if
   you're not in a good mood, can lead to a more positive disposition.
   Likewise, if you approach a class determined to learn something,
   you probably will—even if it's how not to instruct students!"
   (Paragraph 6)

_____ 7. The relationship of the second to the first sentence below is one of
   A. illustration.
   B. addition.
   C. effect.
   D. contrast.

   "The self-fulfilling prophecy also operates on the job. For instance,
   salespeople who view themselves as being effective communicators
   are more successful than those who view themselves as less effective
   . . . ." (Paragraph 5)

_____ 8. The relationship of the second to the first sentence below is one of
   A. illustration.
   B. contrast.
   C. effect.
   D. addition.

   "Compared to their more confident peers, they were also more
   likely to sabotage existing relationships. On the other hand, students
   who perceived themselves as capable achieved more academically."
   (Paragraph 5)

Patterns of Organization

_____ 9. The selection mainly
   A. defines and illustrates related terms.
   B. narrates a series of events in time order.
   C. discusses the many causes of a particular effect.
   D. lists a variety of types of prophecies.

_____ 10. Paragraph 7 uses definition-example and what other two patterns of
organization?
A. Comparison and contrast.
B. List of items and contrast.
C. Comparison and cause-effect.
D. Time order and cause and effect.

Discussion Questions

1. In general, do you accept the premise of this reading: that our expectations
   have a great deal to do with what we later experience? What evidence have
   you seen that makes you agree or disagree with the author's premise?

2. Is it better to expect good things to happen, or to expect the worst and then
   be pleasantly surprised when things go well? Explain your answer.

3. The authors write about people who are especially sensitive to rejection, and
   who seem to perceive it where it may not exist. Have you ever witnessed this
   happening? Why do you think it occurs?

4. How might parents and teachers make use of what was demonstrated by
   Pygmalion in the Classroom?

Note: Writing assignments for this selection appear on page 630.

Check Your Performance   **RELATIONSHIPS II**

Activity	Number Right	Points	Score
Review Test 1 (5 items)	_____	× 2 =	_____
Review Test 2 (10 items)	_____	× 3 =	_____
Review Test 3 (10 items)	_____	× 3 =	_____
Review Test 4 (10 items)	_____	× 3 =	_____
	TOTAL SCORE	=	_____%

Enter your total score into the **Reading Performance Chart: Review Tests** on the inside back cover.

RELATIONSHIPS II: Mastery Test 1

A. Fill in each blank with an appropriate transition from the box. Use each transition once. Then, in the spaces provided, write the letter of the transition you have chosen.

A. because	B. for example	C. in contrast
D. similar	E. therefore	

Hint: Make sure that each word or phrase that you choose fits smoothly into the flow of the sentence. Test your choices by reading each sentence to yourself.

_____ 1. ¹Most listeners don't simply absorb your message like human sponges. ²They send back messages of their own called feedback. ³_____, when you phone your friend to say you will be late, you may hear, "Oh, no you don't! ⁴I don't care what your problem is: get here on time!" ⁵That is feedback.

_____ 2. ¹The period and the semicolon are marks of punctuation that have a _____ use. ²Both can serve to mark the division between two complete thoughts.

_____ 3. ¹There are actually two types of smog: the London type and the Los Angeles type. ²The London variety is caused by the burning of fossil fuels, mainly coal with high sulfur content. ³_____, Los Angeles smog results when cool ocean air slips under a layer of warmer air and becomes trapped, along with exhaust emissions from automobiles. ⁴This type of smog occurs in valleys and other areas with poor air circulation.

_____ 4. ¹The ancient Chinese taught that it was distasteful to serve meat in large pieces that resembled the original animal. ²They also believed it rude to expect diners to struggle at the table to cut up hunks of meat. ³_____, they preferred to cut the meat into bite-size pieces in the kitchen. ⁴People then used chopsticks at the table to eat the small morsels of meat.

_____ 5. ¹As a result of millions of years of evolution, people from different racial backgrounds may have similar physical characteristics. ²American Plains Indians, Ethiopians, and northern Europeans, for example, share the trait of a high-bridged, narrow nose. ³They all lived in similar cold, dry climates or higher latitudes. ⁴A high, narrow nose is an advantage under these conditions _____ it allows the air in the nasal passage to be moisturized before entering the lungs. *(Continues on next page)*

B. Label each item with the letter of its main pattern of organization.

      A Definition and example   C Contrast
      B Comparison   D Cause and effect

_____ 6. [1]In the late nineteenth century, American psychologist William James proposed that much of human behavior was instinctive. [2]Instincts are unlearned, automatic actions that are triggered by external cues. [3]For instance, if you hear a loud noise, you will tend to look toward the source of the noise automatically, perhaps without even realizing you're doing so.

_____ 7. [1]Air pollution has disastrous effects on forests. [2]Trees dying from pollution lose their leaves or needles, allowing sunlight to reach the forest floor. [3]During this process, grass prospers in the increased light and pushes out the native plants and moss, which help to hold rainwater. [4]The soil thus loses absorbency and becomes hard, causing rain and snow to flow over the ground instead of sinking into it. [5]This in turn results in erosion of the soil.

_____ 8. [1]There's an important difference between informative speeches and persuasive speeches. [2]Informative speeches generally concentrate on explaining—telling how something works, what something means, or how to do something. [3]A speaker who gives an informative speech usually tries to give the audience information without taking sides. [4]In contrast, the speaker in a persuasive speech takes a particular position and tries to get the audience to accept and support that position. [5]In a persuasive speech, information is selected according to how well it supports the speaker's point of view, not according to how informative it is.

_____ 9. [1]The atmosphere of Earth resembles a window by letting in light at the same time that it permits us to look out to the stars, planets, and all of space. [2]The atmosphere also serves as a shield to keep out undesirable things. [3]A normal glazed window lets us keep our houses warm by keeping out cold air, and it stops unwanted or harmful elements such as dirt, insects, and animals from coming in. [4]In a similar fashion, Earth's atmospheric window keeps our planet at a comfortable temperature by holding back radiated heat, and it protects us from dangerous levels of ultraviolet light.

_____ 10. [1]Humans differ from other animals in their reactions to drugs. [2]Penicillin is one of the safest, most effective antibiotics in humans. [3]In contrast, it kills hamsters and guinea pigs. [4]Another staple of human medicine, aspirin, produces birth defects in mice and rats and poisons cats. [5]Although they tested safe in nonhuman animals, numerous drugs have been removed from the market after human patients have suffered serious harm, such as paralysis, blindness, or death.

RELATIONSHIPS II: Mastery Test 2

Read each paragraph and answer the questions that follow.

A. ¹There are significant differences in the way men and women carry out everyday interactions. ²According to researchers, men tend to see everyday encounters as competitive situations. ³Men do not want to have other people "one up" them. ⁴This fear of "losing" to others prevents men from asking for help or directions when needed. ⁵On the other hand, women go to the opposite extreme. ⁶Unlike men, women have been socialized to hold a more subordinate position in day-to-day interactions. ⁷Instead of avoiding help, women are likely to seek it out. ⁸Ironically, studies have also found that women often seek assistance even when they don't need it.

_____ 1. The main pattern of organization of the paragraph is
    A. definition and example.   C. comparison.
    B. cause and effect.   D. contrast.

    2. One transition that signals the pattern of organization of this paragraph

      is _____.

B. ¹A primary group is made up of a small number of people who relate intimately with each other over a long period. ²The members of such a group know each other personally and behave informally together. ³Examples of the primary group are families and small circles of friends. ⁴Such groups are important units within the larger social structure. ⁵In fact, in some traditional small-scale societies, the social structure is based almost totally on primary groups.

_____ 3. The main pattern of organization of the selection is
    A. definition and example.   C. comparison.
    B. cause and effect.   D. contrast.

    4. The transition that signals the pattern of organization is _____.

C. ¹Although caffeine is the world's most widely consumed drug, few of its users realize how powerful it is. ²Caffeine is a drug that acts fast. ³In less than five minutes after you've drunk a cup of coffee, caffeine is racing to every part of your body. ⁴Its effects are many, including increasing the flow of urine and stomach acid, relaxing involuntary muscles, and stepping up the intake of oxygen. ⁵In addition, caffeine heightens the pumping strength of the heart. ⁶Therefore, too much caffeine can cause an irregular heartbeat. ⁷A small dose of caffeine can improve your performance as you type or drive; however, too much caffeine will make you shaky and unsteady.

(Continues on next page)

_____ 5. The main pattern of organization of the paragraph is
   A. definition and example.   C. comparison.
   B. cause and effect.   D. contrast.

6. One transition that signals the pattern of organization of this paragraph

   is _____.

D. [1]There are interesting similarities between the Renaissance and the present time. [2]The exploration of the Americas during the Renaissance created the same kind of excitement as today's space program: [3]Columbus's voyages were like the astronauts' moon landings or the missions to Mars. [4]The discovery of gunpowder in the Renaissance revolutionized war, just as the atom bomb did at the end of World War II. [5]The invention of the printing press in the Renaissance made more information available to many more people, much as radio, television, and the Internet have done in our day.

_____ 7. The main pattern of organization of the paragraph is
   A. definition and example.   C. comparison.
   B. cause and effect.   D. contrast.

8. One transition that signals the pattern of organization of this paragraph

   is _____.

E. [1]In the next fifteen years, the population of people over the age of fifty in the United States will soar upward by 75 percent. [2]During the same period, the number of people under the age of fifty will increase by just 2 percent. [3]There are two reasons for this rapid aging of our society. [4]The first is the baby boom that began in the late 1940s. [5]With the end of World War II, men and women quickly settled into family life and, by 1965, had some 75 million babies. [6]This enormous population boom led to the youth culture of the 1960s. [7]And as the baby boomers continue to age, they will produce an "elder boom" which is expected to peak around 2025. [8]The second explanation for the aging of our society is increasing life expectancy. [9]Improvements in medicine and nutrition have resulted in people living longer than ever. [10]Newborns today can expect to live thirty years longer than those born in 1900. [11]The sharp and recent increase in the number of elderly people—here and around the world—supports the surprising fact that more than half of all the elderly people who have ever lived are alive today.

_____ 9. The main pattern of organization of the paragraph is
   A. definition and example.   C. comparison.
   B. cause and effect.   D. contrast.

10. One transition that signals the pattern of organization of this paragraph

   is _____.

RELATIONSHIPS II: Mastery Test 3

A. (1–4.) Arrange the scrambled sentences below into a logical paragraph by numbering them *1, 2, 3,* and *4* in an order that makes sense. Then, in the space provided, write the letter of the main pattern of organization used.

Note that transitions will help you by clarifying the relationships between sentences.

____ Or if you associate a certain group with a particular talent, you may be disappointed when a member of that group cannot do what you expect.

____ For instance, if you believe that a particular group is pushy, you will automatically judge someone who belongs to that group to be pushy— without waiting to see what that person is really like.

____ Stereotyping is holding a set of beliefs about the personal nature of a group of people.

____ It can greatly interfere with our making accurate judgments about others.

_____ 5. The main pattern of organization is
    A. contrast.
    B. comparison.
    C. cause and effect.
    D. definition and example.

B. Read each paragraph and answer the questions that follow.

[1]When life inflicts setbacks and tragedies on optimists, they weather those storms better than pessimists do. [2]Optimists look on the bright side. [3]After a setback, they pick up the pieces and start again. [4]On the other hand, pessimists give up and fall into depression. [5]With their ability to spring back, optimists achieve more at work and in school. [6]Optimists have better physical health and may even live longer. [7]However, even when things go well for pessimists, they are haunted by fears of catastrophe.

_____ 6. The selection mainly
    A. defines and illustrates the terms "optimist" and "pessimist."
    B. shows similarities between optimists and pessimists.
    C. shows differences between optimists and pessimists.
    D. explains the causes of optimism and pessimism.

7. One transition that signals the main pattern of organization of this

paragraph is _____.

(Continues on next page)

8. Another transition that signals the main pattern of organization of this paragraph is _____.

[1]Cults are religious movements that represent a new or different religious tradition, whereas churches and sects represent the prevailing tradition in a society. [2]From this point of view, all religions begin as cult movements. [3]Early on, today's great world faiths were most assuredly regarded as weird, crazy, foolish, and sinful; they were typically treated with hostility. [4]For example, Roman intellectuals in the first century laughed at the notion that a messiah and his tiny flock in Palestine, an obscure corner of the empire, posed a threat to the mighty pagan temples. [5]But from an obscure cult movement, Christianity arose. [6]Other established religions, including Islam and Buddhism, were once cults. [7]Today they inspire hundreds of millions of faithful followers.

_____ 9. The main pattern of organization of the paragraph is
    A. cause and effect.
    B. contrast.
    C. comparison.
    D. definition and example.

10. One transition that signals the pattern of organization of this paragraph is _____.

RELATIONSHIPS II: Mastery Test 4

A. (1–4.) Arrange the scrambled sentences below into a logical paragraph by numbering them *1, 2, 3,* and *4* in an order that makes sense. Then, in the space provided, write the letter of the main pattern of organization used.

Note that transitions will help you by clarifying the relationships between sentences.

____ Also, by the ninth grade, one child in six will have tried marijuana, and one in three will have experimented with alcohol.

____ Last, and worst of all, is the fact that the suicide rate for young people under fifteen has tripled since 1960.

____ Because of peer pressure, some children begin smoking while they are still in grade school.

____ Stresses of the modern world severely affect today's children.

_____ 5. The paragraph lists
   A. points of contrast.
   B. points of comparison.
   C. effects.
   D. examples of a defined term.

B. Read each paragraph and answer the questions that follow.

[1]People often feel that domestic cats and their larger relatives, the jungle cats, are very different. [2]In reality, however, cats at home and cats in the wild have many traits in common. [3]Both have eyes suited for night vision, and both prefer to sleep by day and move about at night. [4]Also, just as pet cats use their tails to keep their balance and to signal emotions, so do lions and other large cats. [5]In addition, both kinds of cats can leap great distances. [6]Pet cats are often found on top of bookcases or refrigerators. [7]Similarly, the puma, the champion jumper of the cat family, has been known to jump twenty feet up and forty feet ahead. [8]Finally, little cats are not the only ones that purr; the cheetah, puma, and snow leopard all purr when content.

_____ 6. The main idea is expressed in the
   A. first sentence.
   B. second sentence.
   C. third sentence.
   D. last sentence.

(Continues on next page)

_____ 7. The selection mainly
   A. defines and illustrates the term *cat*.
   B. shows similarities between domestic cats and jungle cats.
   C. contrasts domestic cats with jungle cats.
   D. explains the effects of different environments on domestic and jungle cats.

8. One transition that signals the main pattern of organization of this paragraph is _____.

[1]One of the most important—and overlooked—effects of the discovery of the New World was the introduction of new foods into Europe. [2]Potatoes, peanuts, peppers, tomatoes, and corn are just a few of the many crops that had not existed in Europe prior to Columbus's first voyage. [3]These crops, long domesticated by Native Americans, caused an enormous increase in Europe's food supply. [4]Because of the sudden availability of food, the population of Europe rapidly expanded. [5]Germany, England, and Ireland, for example, experienced vast population growth due to the potato, a plant originally from South America. [6]In the late 1500s, China also experienced a population boom largely as a result of huge crops of corn. [7]Today, the impact of these plants still influences the world. [8]About one third of the world's food crops are plants that are from the Americas and domesticated by Native Americans.

_____ 9. The main pattern of organization of the selection is
   A. definition and example.
   B. cause and effect.
   C. comparison.
   D. contrast.

10. One transition that signals the main pattern of organization of this paragraph is _____.

RELATIONSHIPS II: Mastery Test 5

A. Read the textbook paragraph below. Then answer the question and complete the outline that follows.

> ¹Instead of firing workers at times of hardship, some companies slice a few hours off everybody's workweek and pay. ²Sharing work in this manner has positive effects on workers and the company. ³Workers are less anxious about being unemployed and feel they are part of a community of people working together. ⁴In addition, quality remains high because the company retains all of its experienced workers, rather than firing them to save money. ⁵Consequently, because they are fully staffed, companies that have instituted work sharing are better equipped to meet increased demand when business recovers. ⁶Also, when times get brighter, workers are more willing to put in long hours for a company that helped them through a tough spell.

_____ 1. The main organizational patterns of the paragraph are list of items and
   A. definition and example.
   B. cause and effect.
   C. comparison.
   D. contrast.

2–5. Complete the outline of the paragraph by writing in the four major supporting details.

Main idea: Work sharing has positive effects on workers and the company.

Major supporting details:

   1. _____

   _____

   2. _____

   _____

   3. _____

   _____

   4. _____

   _____

(Continues on next page)

B. Read the textbook paragraph below. Then answer the question and complete the map that follows.

> [1]Why do people have differing needs for achievement? [2]One researcher found that the need for achievement is related to parental attitudes. [3]Parents who are high achievers themselves usually demand independence from their children. [4]The children must become self-reliant at a relatively early age. [5]As a result, the children develop a sense of confidence and find enjoyment in their own achievements. [6]On the other hand, parents who have low needs for achievement are more protective of their children. [7]They help their children perform everyday tasks, such as dressing and feeding, far more than necessary. [8]The consequence is that children are less independent and often have low achievement needs.

_____ 6. The paragraph
   A. defines and illustrates *achievement*.
   B. compares two types of parents and their effects.
   C. contrasts two types of parents and their effects.

7–10. Complete the map of the paragraph by writing in the missing supporting details.

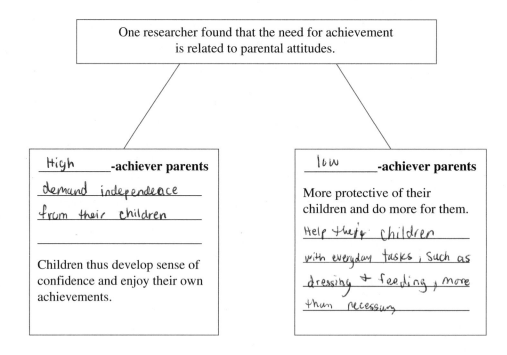

One researcher found that the need for achievement is related to parental attitudes.

High -achiever parents

demand independence from their children
_____

Children thus develop sense of confidence and enjoy their own achievements.

low -achiever parents

More protective of their children and do more for them.

Help their children with everyday tasks, such as dressing + feeding, more than necessary

RELATIONSHIPS II: Mastery Test 6

A. Read the textbook paragraph below. Then answer the question and complete the outline that follows.

> [1]Today's divorce rate is nearly 300 percent higher than it was in 1965. [2]Why the sudden increase? [3]One reason is that today there is greater social acceptance of divorce. [4]This increased tolerance has resulted from a relaxation of negative attitudes toward divorce among religious denominations. [5]Although divorce is still seen as unfortunate, it is no longer treated as a sin by most religious leaders. [6]An increase in family income has also led to the rise in divorce rates. [7]As couples acquire more wealth, they are more likely to be able to afford the cost of divorce proceedings. [8]Finally, as society provides greater opportunities for women, more and more wives are becoming less dependent on their husbands—both economically and emotionally. [9]Consequently, they are more likely to leave if their marriage seems hopeless.

_____ 1. The organizational patterns of the paragraph are list of items and
  A. definition and example.
  B. comparison and/or contrast.
  C. cause and effect.

2–5. Complete the outline of the paragraph by writing in the main idea and three major supporting details.

Main idea: _____

_____

1. _____

   _____

2. _____

   _____

3. _____

   _____

(Continues on next page)

B. (6–10.) Read the textbook passage below. Then answer the question and complete the map that follows.

> [1]Animal development usually proceeds down one of two quite different paths: indirect development or direct development. [2]In indirect development, the juvenile animal that hatches from the egg differs significantly from the adult, as a caterpillar differs from a butterfly. [3]Animals with indirect development typically produce huge numbers of eggs, and each egg has only a small amount of yolk. [4]The yolk nourishes the developing embryo during a rapid transformation into a small, sexually immature feeding stage called a larva.
>
> [5]Other animals, including such diverse groups as reptiles, birds, mammals, and land snails, show direct development, in which the newborn animal, or juvenile, is a sexually immature, miniature version of the adult. [6]These juveniles are typically much larger than larvae, and consequently need much more nourishment before emerging into the world. [7]Two ways of providing such nourishment have evolved: large eggs containing large amounts of yolk (like an ostrich's egg, which weighs several pounds) or nourishing the developing embryo within the body of the mother. [8]Either way, providing food for directly developing embryos places great demands on the mother, and relatively few offspring are produced.

_____ 6. The organizational pattern of the passage is
     A. comparison.
     B. contrast.
     C. cause and effect.

7–10. Complete the map of the passage by writing in the missing supporting details.

Animal development may be either indirect or direct.

indirect development

1. Juvenile differs greatly from the adult.

2. Nourishment is a small amount of yolk in each of a great many eggs.

3. Numerous larvae hatch.

direct development

1. _Juveniles are typically much larger than larvae & need much more Nourishment_

2. Nourishment is either
(1) large amounts of yolk or
(2) within the mother's body.

3. _providing food....._

TO THE STUDENT

The pages that follow contain three mastery tests that offer additional practice in the skills covered in Chapters 5 and 6:

- Relationships that involve **addition**
- Relationships that involve **time**
- Relationships that involve **illustration**
- Relationships that involve **comparison and/or contrast**
- Relationships that involve **cause and effect**

For ease in reference, the lists of words that show these relationships have been reprinted on the next page.

Addition Words

one	to begin with	also	further
first (of all)	for one thing	in addition	furthermore
second (ly)	other	next	last (of all)
third (ly)	another	moreover	final (ly)

Time Words

before	immediately	when	until
previously	next	whenever	often
first (of all)	then	while	frequently
second (ly)	following	during	eventually
third (ly)	later	as	final (ly)
now	after	soon	last (of all)

Illustration Words

(for) example	including	(as an) illustration	one
(for) instance	specifically	to illustrate	once
such as	to be specific		

Comparison Words

(just) as	both	in like fashion	in a similar fashion
(just) like	equal (ly)	in like manner	in a similar manner
alike	resemble	similar (ly)	(in) the same way
same	likewise	similarity	(in) common

Contrast Words

but	instead (of)	even though	difference
yet	in contrast	as opposed to	different (ly)
however	on the other hand	in spite of	differ (from)
although	on the contrary	despite	unlike
nevertheless	converse (ly)	rather than	while
still	opposite		

Cause and Effect Words

therefore	so	owing to	because (of)
thus	(as a) result	effect	reason
(as a) consequence	results in	cause	explanation
consequently	leads to	if ... then	accordingly
due to	since	affect	

RELATIONSHIPS I AND II: Mastery Test 1

A. Fill in each blank with an appropriate transition from the box. Use each transition once. Then, in the spaces provided, write the letter of the transition you have chosen.

A. finally	B. later	C. for instance
D. because	E. unlike	

_____ 1. [1]If there is one product that American business can manufacture in large amounts, it is doublespeak. [2]Doublespeak is a term applied to the use of words that are evasive, vague, or stilted for the purpose of deceiving or confusing the reader or listener. [3]_____, a company that decides to fire workers may talk of the need for "re-engineering," "restructuring," or "downsizing" its work force.

_____ 2. [1]Here are some pointers for reading without eyestrain. [2]First, whenever possible, read by natural light. [3]Second, avoid reading in a dark room with light only on your reading material. [4]Third, so that your page-turning hand doesn't cast a shadow across the text, position your reading light to your left if you are right-handed and to your right if you are left-handed. [5]_____, hold your reading material fourteen to eighteen inches from your eyes.

_____ 3. [1]On average, we sleep one-third of our life. [2]Usually, the amount that we sleep decreases with age. [3]As newborns, we sleep up to 20 hours a day. [4]At age 4 or so, we sleep about 12 hours. [5]By the time we're 10, we sleep about 10 hours. [6]_____, as adults, we sleep 7–9 hours. [7]Eventually, when we're elderly, we may sleep only 4–6 hours.

_____ 4. [1]Most animal expressions are based in falsehood. [2]Far from being "chicken," hens fiercely defend their chicks, and roosters bravely protect their flock. [3]Instead of sweating or eating "like a pig," pigs lack functional sweat glands and do not overeat. [4]In contrast to human "rats," rats loyally, tenderly, even selflessly assist companions in need. [5]And _____ a human "wolf," actual wolves are faithful to one mate.

_____ 5. [1]Sunburn is skin damage caused by the sun's ultraviolet rays. [2](Ultraviolet rays do not penetrate glass; consequently, we cannot get sunburned from sunlight shining through a closed window.) [3]When ultraviolet rays destroy skin cells, an increased amount of blood flows to the area, bringing new cells and other repair materials. [4]The red of sunburn results from this increased blood flow. [5]Sunburn hurts _____ nerve endings in the skin send pain signals in response to cell damage.

(Continues on next page)

B. Fill in each blank with an appropriate transition from the box. Use each transition once. Then, in the spaces provided, write the letter of the transition you have chosen.

A. for instance	B. on the other hand	C. lastly
D. result	E. after	

_____ 6. [1]Struggling in quicksand creates a vacuum, which causes a person to sink. [2]But the human body is more buoyant in quicksand than it is in fresh or ocean water, meaning that it is actually easier to float on quicksand than it is in a pool or the ocean. [3]_____ falling into quicksand, a person should slowly spread-eagle and allow the body to gradually come to a back-floating position. [4]By moving cautiously in this position, the quicksand victim can then maneuver back to solid ground and out of danger.

_____ 7. [1]While it's strange but true, white wine is often made from red grapes. [2]In making wine, the grapes are crushed and placed in a large tank. [3]If the skins of the grapes remain in contact with the juice during this step, red wine results. [4]_____, if the winemaker separates the skins from the juice, then white wine is made.

_____ 8. [1]The catch-and-release way of fishing doesn't really help the fish; in fact, it may _____ in their death. [2]On a hook and line, fish struggle to breathe. [3]Because of overexertion and inadequate oxygen intake, many fish are brain-damaged, paralyzed, or in shock when released—often fatally. [4]In addition, netting and handling sometimes remove portions of a fish's thin outer skin, leaving it vulnerable to potentially deadly infection.

_____ 9. [1]The term *diffusion* refers to the spread of things, ideas, beliefs, or other cultural items from one society to another. [2]Diffusion results from contact between societies. [3]Generally, the more contacts a society establishes with others, the higher its rate of cultural change. [4]The fast pace of change in the United States, _____, can be credited to the numerous diverse cultures brought here by immigrants from around the world. [5]This immigration brought to the country new ideas, beliefs, foods, and so on.

_____ 10. [1]Psychologist Abraham Maslow theorized that people are motivated by eight basic needs which must be fulfilled in turn: four "deficiency" needs and four "growth" needs. [2]The deficiency needs are, first, food, water, and sleep; second, safety and security; third, love, friendship, and a sense of belonging; and, fourth, approval and respect. [3]Prompted by their growth needs, people seek to know and understand; to enjoy beauty; to "self-actualize" (realize their creative potential); and, _____, to "transcend" (help others to realize *their* potential).

RELATIONSHIPS I AND II: Mastery Test 2

Read each selection and answer the questions that follow. Note that paragraphs D and E have **two** patterns of organization.

A. [1]An infomercial is a televised commercial message lasting approximately thirty minutes and used to sell a product by convincing viewers that they must have this product. [2]Kitchen products such as a food dehydrator and a juice extractor are successful goods shown on infomercials. [3]Other examples of products that have made it big on infomercials include a cleaning solution that promises to clean any household surface safely and inexpensively, and a similar product that claims it will shine and polish your car with next to no effort. [4]Infomercials can be very convincing, but viewers are wise to remember the Latin term *caveat emptor:* Let the buyer beware!

_____ 1. The main pattern of organization of the selection is
    A. list of items.
    B. comparison and/or contrast.
    C. definition and example.

2. One transition that signals the pattern of organization of this paragraph is

_____.

B. [1]Bats have some fascinating characteristics. [2]For one thing, they are the only mammals that truly fly. [3]Furthermore, they are the only animals that roost hanging upside down. [4]Insect-eating bats have astonishing hearing. [5]Some can hear individual insects walk or flutter their wings. [6]Most insect-eating bats use echo-location to catch insects at night: the bats emit squeaks (too high-pitched for us to hear) that bounce off insects and surrounding objects and echo back, enabling them to follow a moth's zigzag flight or distinguish, say, a mosquito from a gnat. [7]Bats are so adept at locating insects that a single bat may eat several thousand within one night.

_____ 3. The main pattern of organization of the selection is
    A. list of items.
    B. time order.
    C. comparison and/or contrast.

4. One transition that signals the pattern of organization of this paragraph is

_____.

C. [1]The flamingo obtains its food through an unusual method. [2]First, it stomps on the ground underwater, using its large webbed feet to churn up food, such as seeds, blue-green algae and crustaceans, from the muddy bottom. [3]Next, it puts its head into the water so that its beak can collect the particles. [4]Then, using its spiny tongue as a pump, it draws the food past special finger-like projections inside its beak. [5]These projections, called lamellae, act as strainers to separate the bird's meal from the water before it swallows.   *(Continues on next page)*

_____ 5. The main pattern of organization of the selection is
   A. definition and example.
   B. time order.
   C. comparison and/or contrast.

6. One transition that signals the pattern of organization of this paragraph is

_____.

D.   ¹For hundreds of years, women were not allowed to sing in church or on the stage; consequently, young boys would sing the high parts. ²Unfortunately, when the boys reached puberty, their voices would change. ³By the 1700s, some enterprising Italians came up with a solution to preserve a boy's voice. ⁴If the boy was castrated, then he could never go through puberty, and therefore his voice would never change. ⁵It was said that these singers, known as the castrati, had voices that could make the angels in heaven cry. ⁶Although the Church forbade castration, the voices of the castrati were highly prized at church services. ⁷The golden age of this cruel custom began to fade during the 1800s, mostly because it became socially acceptable for women to sing professionally.

_____ 7. The main patterns of organization of the selection are time order and
   A. list of items.
   B. comparison and/or contrast.
   C. cause and effect.

8. One transition that signals the pattern of organization you selected is

_____.

E.   ¹Because they are similar in size, density, and location (second and third planets from the sun), Venus and Earth have been called "the twin planets." ²In reality, the two planets radically differ. ³Earth has climates ranging from subfreezing to tropical. ⁴Venus, however, has only one surface temperature: 864°F, hot enough to melt lead. ⁵Nearly three-fourths of the Earth's surface is water. ⁶In contrast, Venus has no surface water. ⁷Unlike Earth, Venus has no magnetic field. ⁸Earth's clouds are composed of water droplets and ice crystals, but Venus's clouds consist mainly of sulfuric acid. ⁹Although Earth's atmosphere is primarily nitrogen (77%) and oxygen (21%), Venus's is overwhelmingly carbon dioxide (96%), with relatively small amounts of nitrogen (3.5%) and oxygen (less than 0.5%). ¹⁰Perhaps the most important difference between the two planets is this: Venus is devoid of life.

_____ 9. The main patterns of organization of the selection are list of items and
   A. cause and effect.
   B. time order.
   C. comparison and/or contrast.

10. One transition that signals the pattern of organization you selected is

_____.

RELATIONSHIPS I AND II: Mastery Test 3

Each of the following selections uses **two** patterns of organization. Read each selection and then, in the spaces provided, write the letter of the two patterns of organization.

A. ¹Dinosaurs did not become extinct—not all of them, that is. ²Most scientists who study fossils now believe that some small, predatory dinosaurs called theropods evolved into birds. ³In a number of striking ways, birds resemble their probable dinosaur ancestors. ⁴Like theropods, birds have light, hollow bones (crucial to bird flight). ⁵Theropod forelimbs could pivot similarly to bird wings. ⁶Theropods stood erect on two feet, with their ankles held above the ground. ⁷Birds stand the same way. ⁸Also, theropods had four toes on each foot: three front toes pointing forward and one rear toe pointing backward. ⁹So do many birds. ¹⁰Claws are another shared feature. ¹¹In addition, like all other dinosaurs, theropods laid eggs. ¹²Some even had feathers.

_____ 1. The main patterns of organization of the selection are
    A. definition-example and cause-effect.
    B. cause-effect and list of items.
    C. comparison and list of items.

B. ¹Your home is "private territory"—space used by an individual or group for an extended period of time. ²Your "secondary territory" is any space (such as a classroom) that you use regularly but share with others. ³Finally, "public territory" is space that is not owned by anyone, but claimed on a first-come, first-served basis. ⁴A seat in a waiting room is an example of public territory.

_____ 2. The main patterns of organization of the selection are
    A. definition-example and list of items.
    B. definition-example and cause-effect.
    C. time order and comparison.

C. ¹The aging of our population will have far-reaching implications for what life will be like in the years to come. ²For one thing, society will need to provide many support services to the frail elderly, because many of them will have out-lived their savings and will not be able to pay for their own care. ³Moreover, as the over-65 population becomes more influential at the polls and in the market-place, we're likely to see changes in governmental programs, in television programming, in new products, in housing patterns, in population shifts from state to state, and so forth. ⁴The effects of this change are virtually infinite.

_____ 3. The main patterns of organization of the selection are
    A. definition-example and time order.
    B. comparison and time order.
    C. list of items and cause-effect. *(Continues on next page)*

D.   [1]George Washington's famous crossing of the Delaware River on Christmas morning might never have happened if not for John Honeyman, an American spy working in Trenton. [2]In a clever plan he devised with Washington, Honeyman first faked being captured and interrogated by the Americans. [3]Washington then arranged for Honeyman to escape. [4]After returning to Trenton, Honeyman entertained his friends in the British military command with his tale of capture and escape. [5]He told them that he was able to escape only because the American army was weak and undisciplined, and that they wouldn't be able to attack Trenton until spring, if ever. [6]Thus, Washington caught the enemy sleeping off their Christmas Eve celebration, and the result was an important victory.

_____   4. The main patterns of organization of the selection are
   A. definition-example and cause-effect.
   B. time order and cause-effect.
   C. comparison and list of items.

E.   [1]In the book *He Says, She Says*, Lillian Glass shows that, in general, men and women communicate differently. [2]They differ in their body language, facial expressions, displayed emotions, language, and favored topics of conversation. [3]While men gesture away from their body and often sit with outstretched limbs, women gesture toward their bodies and usually sit with their arms and legs held close. [4]Men lean back when listening, but women lean forward. [5]While listening, women tend to smile and nod. [6]In contrast, men tend to frown and squint. [7]Women laugh and cry more than men. [8]On the other hand, men shout and curse more than women. [9]Less polite than women, men are more inclined to mumble and interrupt. [10]Women offer more compliments and apologies. [11]Women's speech is more formal and correct than men's, containing less slang and less faulty grammar. [12]Men especially like to joke, talk about their activities, and discuss sports. [13]Women, however, prefer to talk about their feelings and discuss relationships.

_____   5. The main patterns of organization of the selection are
   A. list of items and comparison.
   B. time order and contrast.
   C. list of items and contrast.

7

Fact and Opinion

Look at the personals ad below that appeared in a retirement community newspaper in Florida. In the spaces provided, do the following:

1. Write what you think are the **facts** in the ad.
2. Write what you think may be considered the **opinions** in the ad.

> **FOXY LADY.** Blue-haired beauty, 80s, slim 5′4″ (used to be 5′6″). Widow who has just buried fourth husband. Has original teeth and new parts including hip, knee, cornea, and valves. A groovy chick who is still the life of the party.

Facts: _____

_____

_____

_____

Opinions: _____

_____

_____

_____

On the following page, read the information on facts and opinions to see how you did.

FACT

A **fact** is information that can be proved true through objective evidence. This evidence may be physical proof or the spoken or written testimony of witnesses. The ad on the previous page includes these facts: The woman is blue-haired, in her 80s, 5′4″ tall; and a recent widow (for the fourth time) who still has her own teeth as well as some new body parts.

Following are some more facts—they can be checked for accuracy and thus proved true.

> *Fact:* My grandfather has eleven toes.
>
> (Someone can count them.)

> *Fact:* In 1841, William Henry Harrison served as president of the United States for only thirty-one days; he died of pneumonia.
>
> (We can check history records to confirm that this is true.)

> *Fact:* Tarantulas are hairy spiders capable of inflicting on humans a painful but not deadly bite.
>
> (We can check biology reports to confirm that this statement is true.)

OPINION

An **opinion** is a belief, judgment, or conclusion that cannot be objectively proved true. As a result, it is open to question. For instance, the woman in the ad says she is "foxy," a "beauty," "slim," and "a groovy chick who is still the life of the party," but we have no way of knowing for sure. These statements are opinions.

Or consider this example: Your friend might visit a new restaurant and report to you that the food was great but the service was terrible. These statements may be reasonable ones with which other people would agree, but they cannot be objectively proved. They are opinions. You might eat at the same restaurant and reach very different conclusions.

Here are some more opinions:

> *Opinion:* My grandfather's feet are ugly.
>
> (There's no way to prove this statement because two people can look at the same thing and come to different conclusions about its beauty. For instance, the speaker's grandmother may have found those feet attractive. *Ugly* is a **value word**, a word we use to express a value judgment. Value words are signals that an opinion is being expressed. By their very nature, these words represent opinions, not facts.)

> *Opinion:* Harrison should never have been elected president in the first place.
>
> (Those who voted for him would not have agreed.)

Opinion: Tarantulas are disgusting.

(Who says? Not the people who keep them as pets.)

Writing Facts and Opinions

To get a better sense of fact and opinion, take a few minutes to write three facts about yourself and then to write three of your opinions. Here, for example, are three facts about me and three of my opinions.

Three facts about me:

- Some gray hairs have begun to appear in my beard.
- Almost every day I run or lift weights.
- My father died in October 1992.

Three of my opinions:

- A bagel shop near my home makes the greatest bagels on the planet.
- The most important thing about clothes is how comfortable they are.
- Reading for pleasure is one of the joys of life.

Now write your facts and opinions in the space below.

Three facts about you:

- _____
   _____

- _____
   _____

- _____
   _____

Three of your opinions:

> **Hint:** To make sure that these are opinions, do not begin them with "I." For example, do not write, "I think capital punishment should be outlawed." Simply write, "Capital punishment should be outlawed."

- _____
   _____

- _____
   _____

- _____
   _____

Fact and Opinion in Reading

The amount of fact and opinion in a piece of writing varies, depending on the author's purpose. For example, news articles and scientific reports, which are written to inform readers, are supposed to be as factual as possible. On the other hand, the main points of editorials, political speeches, and advertisements—materials written to persuade readers—are opinions. Such writings may contain facts, but, in general, they are facts carefully selected to back up the authors' opinions.

Both facts and opinions can be valuable to readers. However, it is important to recognize the difference between the two.

☑ Check Your Understanding

To sharpen your understanding of fact and opinion, read the following statements and decide whether each is fact or opinion. Put an **F** (for "fact") or an **O** (for "opinion") beside each statement. Put **F+O** beside the **one** statement that is a mixture of fact *and* opinion. Then read the explanation that follows.

> **Hint:** Remember that opinions are signaled by value words— words such as *great* or *hard* or *beautiful* or *terrible* that express a value judgment. Take care to note such words in your reading.

_____ 1. No flower is more beautiful than a simple daisy.

_____ 2. In the U.S. presidential election of 2000, the Electoral College—not the direct vote of the people—determined who became president.

_____ 3. It is riskier for a woman to have a first child after age 40 than before.

_____ 4. It is stupid for women over 40 to get pregnant.

_____ 5. Redheads should never wear pink or purple—they look awful in those colors.

_____ 6. In Egypt, 96 percent of the land is desert.

_____ 7. There is too much violence in children's television programs.

_____ 8. Among Americans aged 10 to 24, suicide is the third-leading cause of death (after car accidents and homicides).

_____ 9. It's a fact that parents and teachers must bear the responsibility for not recognizing signs of teenage depression.

_____ 10. Each year, over 1,600 American teenagers kill themselves, and many of these deaths could be easily prevented.

Explanation:

1. This is an opinion. Many people may consider other flowers more beautiful than the daisy. The word *beautiful* is a value word.

2. This is a fact. As reported by the media and in public records, in the 2000 election Governor George Bush won the majority of electoral-college votes (271 to 266), but Vice President Al Gore won the most popular votes (50,922,335 to 50,455,156).

3. This is a fact that can be verified by checking medical statistics.

4. This is an opinion. Some people might admire the woman who has children in her 40s.

5. This is an opinion. As the value words *should* and *awful* suggest, a judgment is being expressed. Many feel that redheads look wonderful in pink and purple.

6. This is a fact, agreed upon and written down by experts who study geography.

7. As the words *too much* suggest, this is an opinion. Some people may conclude there is little harm in children's watching the existing amount of violence in children's shows.

8. All the details here are facts that can be confirmed by looking them up in public records.

9. This is an opinion. Just saying that something is a fact doesn't make it so. Studies show that there are often no warning signs of teenage depression. Even when there are signs, the extent of adult responsibility is a matter of opinion.

10. The first part of the sentence is a fact that can be confirmed by checking records on teen suicides. The second part is an opinion: *easily* is a judgment word—people may differ on how easy or difficult they consider something to be.

➤ Practice 1

Some of the statements below are facts, and some are opinions. Label facts with an **F** and opinions with an **O**. Remember that facts can be proved, but opinions give personal views.

_____ 1. Few torments are worse than itching from poison ivy.

_____ 2. A microscopic amount of poison-ivy sap is enough to cause itchy, inflamed, and blistered skin.

_____ 3. Poison-ivy sap can be harmful even when it no longer is part of a living plant—for example, when it lingers inside dead vines, on shoes, or on yard tools.

_____ 4. Our company allows each employee ten days of paid sick leave per year.

_____ 5. Too many employees misuse the sick leave policy.

_____ 6. In England, election campaigns last for six weeks.

_____ 7. The United States should also limit campaigns for presidential elections to six weeks.

_____ 8. The microwave oven is the most useful kitchen appliance ever invented.

_____ 9. Everyone who can afford a microwave oven should own one.

_____ 10. A microwave oven heats food by creating a magnetic field that causes the food's water molecules to vibrate more than two billion times per second.

➤ Practice 2: Using the Internet

If a computer with an online service is easily available to you, do the following exercises. If not, use a Sunday edition of a newspaper to do the A and B exercises.

A. Look up a recent newspaper. For example, you might go to the current issue of the national newspaper *USA Today* on the Internet by typing in **www.usatoday.com**. After recording the name and date of the paper, write down one fact and one opinion from the paper.

Name and date of the newspaper: _____

_____

One fact in the paper: _____

_____

One opinion in the paper: _____

_____

B. Look up a movie review site. For example, you might go the popular movie site **www.rottentomatoes.com**. Look up reviews of a movie that has come out recently and record the following:

Name of the movie and of the reviewer: _____

_____

One fact the reviewer includes about the movie: _____

_____

One opinion the reviewer expresses about the movie: _____

_____

C. Go to a book site. For example, you might go to the well-known Barnes & Noble book site **www.bn.com**. Look up a review of one of the following books: 1) *White Fang*; 2) *Night*; or 3) *Watership Down*. Record the following:

Name of the book and of the reviewer: _____

One fact the reviewer includes about the book: _____

_____

One opinion the reviewer expresses about the book: _____

_____

Other Points about Fact and Opinion

There are several more points to keep in mind when separating fact from opinion.

1 Statements of fact may be found to be untrue.

Suppose a new breed of tarantula was discovered whose bite was deadly to humans. The earlier "fact"—that tarantulas inflict a painful but not deadly bite—would then be an error, not a fact. It is not unusual for evidence to show that a "fact" is not really true. It was once considered to be a fact that the world was flat, for example, but that "fact" turned out to be an error.

2 Opinions may be masked as facts.

People sometimes present their opinions as facts, as shown in practice sentence 9 on page 268. Here are two more examples:

In point of fact, New York is a more pleasant city to live in than San Francisco.

The truth of the matter is that olive oil tastes much better than butter.

Despite the words to the contrary, the comments above are not statements of fact but statements of opinion.

3 Remember that value (or judgment) words often represent opinions. Here are examples of these words:

Value Words

best	great	beautiful
worst	terrible	bad
better	lovely	good
worse	disgusting	wonderful

Value words often express judgments—they are generally subjective, not objective. While factual statements report on observed reality, subjective statements evaluate or interpret reality. For example, the observation that it is raining outside is objective. The statement that the weather is bad, however, is subjective, an evaluation of reality. (Some people—for example, farmers whose crops need water—consider rain to be good weather.)

4 The words *should* and *ought to* often signal opinions. Those words introduce what people think should, or ought to, be done. Other people may disagree.

> Couples with young children should not be allowed to divorce.

> Parents who abuse their children ought to be put in jail.

5 Finally, remember that much of what we read and hear is a mixture of fact and opinion.

Recognizing facts and opinions is important because much information that sounds factual is really opinion. A used-car salesman, for example, could say, "This vehicle is an exceptional purchase." Buyers would be wise to wonder what the value word *exceptional* means to this salesman. Or an advertisement may claim that a particular automobile is "the most economical car on the road today," a statement that at first seems factual. But what is meant by *economical*? If the car offers the most miles per gallon but the worst record for expensive repairs, you might not agree that it's economical.

It is also worth noting that some opinions are more widespread than others—and may seem like facts. If 90 percent of those who see a movie think it's terrible, then many people will take it as a fact that the movie is a poor one. Nevertheless, this widespread belief is still opinion; it's possible that another generation of moviegoers will disagree with the popular opinion of the moment. Similarly, if many people believe the rumor that a particular politician has cheated on his taxes, it doesn't mean the rumor is a fact. Fair-minded people will base their own conclusion on more than widespread belief; they will want facts.

➤ Practice 3

Some of the statements below are facts, and some are opinions; in addition, **three** include fact and opinion. Label facts with an **F**, opinions with an **O**, and the three statements of fact *and* opinion with an **F+O**.

_____ 1. The easiest way to get rich quick is to play the lottery every day.

_____ 2. The odds for hitting one state's $10 million jackpot are 120 million to 1.

_____ 3. Many states that run lotteries also have unfair laws that prohibit other forms of gambling.

_____ 4. A lightning bolt, which can produce a billion volts of electricity and travel a thousand miles per second, is nature's most awe-inspiring phenomenon.

_____ 5. Lightning rarely kills someone unless it crosses the person's spinal column or heart.

_____ 6. The majority of American doctors charge their patients entirely too much.

_____ 7. In some states, malpractice insurance can cost a doctor over $125,000 a year.

_____ 8. Mark Twain, whose real name was Samuel Clemens, died in 1910.

_____ 9. Mark Twain's novel _The Prince and the Pauper_ is about a young king and a look-alike poor boy who get confused with one another.

_____ 10. _The Adventures of Huckleberry Finn,_ first published in 1884, is still the best birthday present a twelve-year-old boy could receive.

➤ Practice 4

A. Here are short descriptions taken from a restaurant guide. Some descriptions present only factual information; others contain opinions as well. Identify the **three** factual descriptions with an **F** and the **two** descriptions that include both fact _and_ opinion with an **F+O**.

_____ 1. **Pizza Hut.** 1277 Highway 80, across from People's Mall. Pizzas, salad bar, pastas. Eat in or take out.

_____ 2. **Ruby's Diner.** Baking on the premises. Friendly service. Good home-style food in large portions. Open every night until 1 a.m.

_____ 3. **Tofu Heaven.** A vegetarian menu with dairy dishes. Desserts include tofu chocolate pudding and tofu pumpkin pie. Owners recommend reservations on weekends.

_____ 4. **Dinner at Andre's.** Open only for dinner, Thursday–Sunday. Reservations required. Menu changes often, but always features fresh seafood and pasta—and sometimes fresh waiters. Expensive, but worth it.

_____ 5. **The Riverview.** Menu features soups, a number of sandwiches and salads, seafood (including Chilean sea bass), chicken, and beef and ostrich steaks. Desserts include chef Joe Wolfson's own creation, pistachio-kiwi cheesecake. The restaurant's name comes from the wall of picture windows facing the river.

B. Here are short reviews taken from a newspaper movie guide. Some reviews present only facts; others contain opinions about the movie as well. Identify the **two** factual reviews with an **F** and the **three** reviews that include both fact *and* the reviewer's opinion with an **F+O**.

_____ 6. *The Matrix Reloaded,* **2003.** Keanu Reeves, Laurence Fishburne. In this sequel to *The Matrix*, Neo, the computer hacker who has learned the true nature of reality, accepts his role as savior of mankind.

_____ 7. *Alligator,* **1980.** Robert Forster, Robin Riker. A baby alligator is flushed down the toilet and grows into a mutant monster in the New York City sewers. Intelligent, above-average scary-creature flick.

_____ 8. *Swept Away,* **2002.** Madonna, Adriano Giannini. Dreadful remake of a far superior 1974 film. A spoiled rich woman and a rough-edged sailor are stranded together on a desert island and must learn to coexist.

_____ 9. *Chicago,* **2002.** Renee Zellweger, Catherine Zeta-Jones. Musical in which two chorus girls, each accused of murder, battle for newspaper headlines and the attention of the lawyer they share. Won several Oscars, including Best Picture and Best Supporting Actress (Zeta-Jones).

_____ 10. *Patch Adams,* **1998.** Robin Williams. Based on a real life story, *Patch Adams* tells the story of an unconventional medical student who treats his patients with humor and understanding. Of all the gooey Robin Williams movies, this is the gooiest.

Facts and Opinions in Passages

People tend to accept what they read as fact, but much of what is written is actually opinion. Keeping an eye out for opinion will help you to think for yourself and to question what you read.

☑ *Check Your Understanding*

Two sentences in the following passage are facts, one is an opinion, and two combine fact and opinion. Read the passage, and identify the facts with an **F**, the opinion with an **O**, and the statements of fact *and* opinion with an **F+O**.

¹It was by accident that someone invented the air conditioner, one of the world's most important machines. ²In the summer of 1902, a Brooklyn, New York, printer was having trouble with color printing: the size of paper

on the presses was changed enough by the hot, humid air to cause distortions in printing. [3]That problem must have been the printer's worst nightmare. [4]A young engineer named Willis Haviland Carrier, trying to solve the problem, made the wonderful discovery that he could reduce the amount of humidity in the air with a machine that blew cool air. [5]Carrier's concept was later used to create the home air conditioner.

1. _____ 2. _____ 3. _____ 4. _____ 5. _____

Explanation:

Sentence 1 is a mixture of fact and opinion: The first part of sentence 1 contains a fact set down in historical records; however, the second part represents the author's opinion—many people may not consider the air conditioner one of the world's most important machines. Sentence 2 contains more facts of the historical event. Sentence 3 expresses the author's opinion about the printer's problem; maybe the printer actually found the problem to be a minor one and even an interesting one. Sentence 4 is a mixture of fact and opinion; while it is mainly factual, the word *wonderful* represents the author's opinion of the discovery. Sentence 5 is fact; it tells more of what is in the historical record.

➤ Practice 5

A. The following passage contains five sentences. Two sentences are facts, two are opinions, and one combines fact and opinion. Identify the facts with an **F**, the opinions with an **O**, and the statement of fact *and* opinion with an **F+O**.

[1]One of the greatest frauds ever committed was the radio drama *The War of the Worlds.* [2]On October 30, 1938, Orson Welles and his Mercury Theater of the Air presented the play, which is about Martians invading Earth. [3]The broadcast, which lasted less than one hour, showed that people who listen to the radio are far too gullible. [4]Terror set in among listeners who believed the play was reality, and hundreds of listeners were treated for shock and hysteria in hospital emergency rooms. [5]Orson Welles should have received a prison sentence for his abuse of the airwaves.

1. _____ 2. _____ 3. _____ 4. _____ 5. _____

B. (6–10.) The following paragraph from a newspaper editorial page contains five sentences. Two sentences are facts, two are opinions, and one combines fact and opinion. Identify the facts with an **F**, the opinions with an **O**, and the statement of fact *and* opinion with an **F+O**.

[6]The government ought to start making dollar coins again. [7]The Susan B. Anthony dollar coin introduced in 1979 was almost the same size as quarters, a situation that can undoubtedly be attributed to the bureaucratic decision-making process. [8]Because of the similarity in size, people sometimes confused the quarter and the Anthony dollar. [9]The new dollar coins should be much bigger than the Anthony coins. [10]Since coins don't need to be replaced nearly as often as paper money, coins cost the government less money to produce than paper money.

6. _____   7. _____   8. _____   9. _____   10. _____

➤ Practice 6

Here are four book reviews. Identify the two factual descriptions with an **F** and the two descriptions that include both fact *and* the reviewer's opinion with an **F+O**.

_____ 1. [1]*The Elements of Style* by William Strunk, Jr., and E. B. White has been around for decades. [2]Strunk, the original author, had it privately printed for his students at Cornell University. [3]E. B. White was one of those students. [4]In the introduction to the third edition, White writes that when he was a student in 1919, the book was required reading. [5]Thirty-eight years later, after Strunk had died, White was asked by a publisher to revise the book. [6]He did so, and the new edition was published in 1959. [7]White revised the book again, and the second edition was published in 1972. [8]A third edition came out in 1979. [9]This guidebook, recommended by writing teachers, has sold millions of copies.

_____ 2. [1]One book that should be read by anyone who is interested in writing is *The Elements of Style* by William Strunk, Jr., and E. B. White. [2]It is short (fewer than 75 pages); in fact, Strunk, its original author, always called it "the little book." [3]But packed into "the little book" are perhaps the most helpful rules and guidelines ever compiled on the art and craft of writing. [4]Written in a down-to-earth style, it follows its own advice to "avoid fancy words" and to aim for "clarity, clarity, clarity." [5]It also provides many helpful examples. [6]For instance, to show the benefit of specific, concrete language, the book contrasts two sentences: "He showed satisfaction as he took possession of his well-earned reward" and "He grinned as he pocketed the coin." [7]You may grin as you read this jewel of a book.

_____ 3. [1]Frederick Douglass, born to a slave mother and a white father he never knew, lived as a slave in Maryland until he was about 24. [2]He then escaped to the North, where he became known as an anti-slavery lecturer. [3]In his autobiography, *Narrative of the Life of Frederick Douglass* (first published in 1845), Douglass details the lives of American slaves. [4]He describes the beatings, hunger, and humiliations that were part of every slave's daily life. [5]Douglass also discusses the widespread practice of forbidding slaves to learn to read and write.

_____ 4. [1]Although *The Wind in the Willows*, by Kenneth Grahame, is nearly a century old, it has lost none of the fresh appeal that has made it a favorite with readers of all ages. [2]This charming story tells of faithful friends Mole, Rat, Badger, and Toad and their adventures in the sinister Wild Wood and along their beloved River. [3]When Toad's silly, boastful ways finally land him in jail, the friends rally to his defense in a way that is both hilarious and touching. [4]A book that is a classic in every sense of the word.

A Note on Informed Opinion

In much of what we read, the distinction between fact and opinion is not nearly as clear-cut as in the practice materials in this chapter. But the chapter has helped you to begin looking at information with the questioning eye of a critical reader.

As you question what you read, remember that you should never dismiss an opinion just because it is an opinion. Opinions are fundamental to much of our lives (democracy is the best form of government, everyone should receive basic health care, etc.). However, look for realistic, meaningful support for opinions. Solid support is often made up of facts based on direct observation, expert commentary, and research. Textbook authors, in particular, work very hard to back up their opinions with such factual support.

The textbook passage below is an example. One sentence represents an opinion. The rest of the passage is made up of facts used in support of that opinion. Somebody with an opposite view would choose very different information to support his or her opinion. Which sentence presents the author's opinion? Write its number in the space provided.

Sentence with the opinion: _____

[1]One invention stands out as producing the greatest change in the everyday lives of men and women: the personal computer. [2]It can bring people into instant communication with each other across continents. [3]Letters can be "mailed" through the Internet more quickly than through the U.S. Postal Service. [4]Information can be easily loaded onto a website which can then be accessed by people from any place in the world—for no more than the cost of a local telephone call. [5]For instance, the Internal Revenue

Service now makes all its tax forms available online. [6]Instead of having to go pick up forms, anyone with a computer and a modem can now download what he or she needs in order to file a tax return. [7]In addition, personal computers provide access to full databanks of information: entire library catalogs, for example, are now available to users in their own homes and offices.

Explanation:

Sentences 2–7 present facts about computers that either are well known or can be checked out through personal experience with a computer or in newspapers, magazines, and other publications. The first sentence, however, represents the author's opinion. The author makes the judgment that no other invention has made such a great change in people's lives as the personal computer. However, you may feel that there is another invention—for instance, electric lights, the car, the telephone, or indoor plumbing—that has changed people's lives as much as or more than the computer. What one person thinks of as "the greatest change" may not seem so to another person.

CHAPTER REVIEW

In this chapter, you learned the difference between fact and opinion:

- A **fact** is information that can be proved true through objective evidence. This evidence may be physical proof or the spoken or written testimony of witnesses.

- An **opinion** is a belief, judgment, or conclusion that cannot be objectively proved true. As a result, it is open to question.

Both facts and opinions can be valuable. However, it is important to distinguish between the two, and you should look at information with the questioning eye of a critical reader.

The next chapter—Chapter 8—will sharpen your ability to make inferences in reading.

 On the Web: If you are using this book in class, you can visit our website for additional practice in distinguishing facts from opinions. Go to **www.townsendpress.com** and click on "Online Exercises."

➤ Review Test 1

To review what you've learned in this chapter, complete each of the following sentences about facts and opinions.

_____ 1. Statements that cannot be objectively proved true are
   A. facts.   B. opinions.

_____ 2. Value or judgment words such as *best, worst, great,* and *beautiful* often represent
   A. facts.   B. opinions.

_____ 3. Textbook authors work very hard to back up their opinions with
   A. judgments.   B. beliefs.   C. facts.

_____ 4. Much of what we read is
   A. fact.   B. opinion.   C. a mixture of fact and opinion.

_____ 5. Direct observation, expert reporting, and research are all sources of
   A. facts.   B. opinions.

➤ Review Test 2

A. Two of the statements below are facts, and two are opinions. Identify facts with an **F** and opinions with an **O**.

_____ 1. The world's first "test-tube baby," conceived outside her mother's body, was born in England in 1978.

_____ 2. People unable to conceive children in the normal way should accept that fact and try to adopt children.

_____ 3. Satin feels wonderful, but it's still not as comfortable as cotton.

_____ 4. Eli Whitney never made any money on his invention, the cotton gin, because he didn't have a valid patent on it.

B. Here are short reviews taken from a newspaper movie guide. Some reviews present only facts; others contain opinions about the movie as well. Identify the factual reviews with an **F** and the reviews that include both a factual report *and* an opinion with an **F+O**.

_____ 5. *The Perfect Storm,* **2000.** George Clooney, Mark Wahlberg. An intense storm catches the crew of a commercial fishing boat off-guard. While the sailors battle the storm, their loved ones wait at home. Based on a true story.

_____ 6. ***Bruce Almighty, 2003.*** Jim Carrey, Morgan Freeman, Jennifer Aniston. Bruce, a TV newsman, is given the power of God and uses it to try to advance his career. Predictable and preachy.

_____ 7. ***Titanic, 1997.*** Leonardo DiCaprio, Kate Winslet. Academy-Award-winning story about two passengers who fall in love aboard the doomed ship *Titanic,* which sank on its maiden voyage in 1912.

_____ 8. ***The Sting, 1973.*** Paul Newman, Robert Redford. When a mutual friend is killed by the mob, a young con man and an old pro team up to get even. Newman's and Redford's chemistry and immense personal charm make this movie a perennial favorite.

C. Here are two book reviews. Identify the factual review with an **F**; identify the review that includes both facts about the book *and* the reviewer's opinion with an **F+O**.

_____ 9. [1]The author of *The Joy Luck Club* has written another novel that reveals in rich and often painful detail much about Chinese life and tradition—*The Kitchen God's Wife.* [2]Through a vivid narrative of Winnie Louie's life, the book draws a memorable picture of the repressive society that influenced that life. [3]Winnie offers her story as a gift of personal history and shared secrets to her daughter Pearl. [4]Tan has woven a colorful tapestry illustrating a compelling life and time.

_____ 10. [1]*White Fang* is the story of a wolf-dog born in the Canadian wilderness. [2]As a puppy, White Fang is captured by a Native American who partially tames him and trains him as a sled dog. [3]White Fang earns a reputation as a savage fighter, and he is eventually sold to a man who makes money forcing White Fang to engage in fights to the death. [4]When White Fang is nearly killed himself, he is rescued by Weedon Scott, a mining engineer who shows White Fang the first kindness he has known. [5]As he learns to trust and finally love Scott, White Fang's domestic dog-nature overcomes his wild wolf-nature. [6]He returns with Scott to a ranch in California, where he proves his worth by saving the lives of Scott's family.

> ## Review Test 3

A. Some of the statements below are facts, and some are opinions; in addition, **three** include both fact and opinion. Identify facts with an **F**, opinions with an **O**, and statements of fact *and* opinion with an **F+O**.

_____ 1. A hamburger doesn't taste right without at least a little salt.

_____ 2. Many canned and frozen vegetables contain salt, so people should eat only fresh vegetables.

_____ 3. Salt, which is now common, was once so rare that Roman soldiers were paid with it.

_____ 4. A growing number of public school districts require their students to wear school uniforms.

_____ 5. School uniforms promote order, conformity, and blind obedience to authority figures.

_____ 6. Although school uniforms are ugly to look at, schools that require them report better academic results.

_____ 7. Popularly called "lie detectors," polygraphs show changes in blood pressure, breathing rate, and perspiration rate—all of which tend to increase with stress.

_____ 8. No accused person is required by law to take a lie detector test, but the time has come for the law to change.

_____ 9. People who refuse to take lie detectors tests must be guilty.

_____ 10. Some states do admit the results of polygraph tests if the prosecution and defendant agree prior to the test that its results will be admissible.

B. (11–20.) Each passage below contains five sentences. Two are facts, two are opinions, and one combines fact and opinion. Identify facts with an **F**, opinions with an **O**, and the statement of fact _and_ opinion with an **F+O**.

1. [11]Depression is the most serious problem affecting young people today. [12]According to the latest research, teenagers in affluent suburbs are just as likely to be victims of depression as kids from poor rural and inner-city areas. [13]Between 1950 and 2002, suicide rates among U.S. teenagers quadrupled, sending a sad message that parents are failing their children. [14]Studies indicate that girls are twice as likely as boys to suffer from depression sometime during high school. [15]The best solution to the problem of teenage depression is for school systems to hire additional counselors to help address the needs of teens.

    11. _____   12. _____   13. _____   14. _____   15. _____

2. [16]The solution to America's obesity problem has finally been discovered. [17]A Harvard researcher named Steven Gortmaker recently published a study of sixth-, seventh- and eighth-graders who participated in a school-based program called Planet Health. [18]The study revealed that children reduced their risk of obesity by 15 percent for every hour of reduction in their TV time. [19]This discovery comes not a moment too soon, especially considering that the rate of obesity in children has climbed to 25 percent in recent years. [20]Planet Health should be implemented in all of the nation's schools as soon as possible.

    16. _____   17. _____   18. _____   19. _____   20. _____

➤ *Review Test 4*

How do you handle the conflicts in your life? Whatever your methods, you will probably recognize them in the following excerpt from the widely used textbook *Communicate!* Eighth Edition, by Rudolph F. Verderber (Wadsworth).

To help you continue to strengthen your skills, the reading is followed by questions not only on what you've learned in this chapter but also on what you've learned in previous chapters.

Words to Watch

Below are some words in the reading that do not have strong context support. Each word is followed by the number of the paragraph in which it appears and its meaning there. These words are indicated in the article by a small circle (°).

disengagement (9): becoming free of a situation
contention (14): argument
entails (15): involves
coercion (15): force
obscured (16): hidden
degenerate (18): worsen
implement (20): carry out

MANAGING CONFLICTS IN RELATIONSHIPS

Rudolph F. Verderber

1   Conflicts include clashes over facts and definitions ("Charley was the first one to talk." "No, it was Mark." or "Your mother is a battle-ax." "What do you mean, a 'battle-ax'?"); over values ("Bringing home pencils and pens from work is not stealing." "Of course it is." or "The idea that you have to be married to have sex is completely outdated." "No, it isn't."); and, perhaps the most difficult to deal with, over ego involvement ("Listen, I've been a football fan for thirty years; I ought to know what good defense is." "Well, you may be a fan, but that doesn't make you an expert.").

2   Although many people view conflict as bad (and, to be sure, conflict situations are likely to make us anxious and uneasy), it is inevitable in any significant relationship. Moreover, conflict is sometimes useful in that it forces us to make choices; to resolve honest differences; and to test the relative merits of our attitudes, behaviors, needs, and goals. Now let's consider methods of dealing with conflict.

Methods of Dealing with Conflict

3   Left to their own devices, people engage in many behaviors, both negative and positive, to cope with or manage their conflicts. The various methods of dealing with conflict can be grouped into

five major patterns: withdrawal, surrender, aggression, persuasion, and problem-solving discussion. Let's consider each of these methods in turn.

4   **Withdrawal.** One of the most common, and certainly one of the easiest, ways to deal with conflict is to withdraw. When people *withdraw,* they physically or psychologically remove themselves from the situation.

5   Physical withdrawal is, of course, easiest to identify. Suppose Eduardo and Justina get into a conversation about Eduardo's smoking. Justina says, "Eduardo, I thought you told me that whether you stopped smoking completely or not, you weren't going to smoke around the house. Now here you are lighting up!" Eduardo may withdraw physically by saying "I don't want to talk about it" and going to the basement to finish a project he was working on.

6   Psychological withdrawal may be less noticeable but is every bit as common. Using the same example, when Justina begins to talk about Eduardo's smoking in the house, Eduardo may sit quietly in his chair looking at Justina, but all the time she speaks he is thinking about the poker game he will be going to the next evening.

7   Besides being quite common, both kinds of withdrawal are basically negative. Why? Because they neither eliminate nor attempt to manage the conflict. As researchers Roloff and Cloven note, "Relational partners who avoid conflicts have more difficulty resolving disputes." In the case of the physical withdrawal, Justina may follow Eduardo to the basement, where the conflict will be resumed; if not, the conflict will undoubtedly resurface later—and will probably be intensified—

when Justina and Eduardo try to resolve another, unrelated issue. In the case of the psychological withdrawal, Justina may force Eduardo to address the smoking issue, or she may go along with Eduardo's ignoring it but harbor a resentment that may negatively affect their relationship.

8   Another reason why withdrawal is negative is that it results in what Cloven and Roloff call "mulling behavior." By *mulling* they mean thinking about or stewing over an actual or perceived problem until the participants perceive the conflict as more severe and begin engaging in blaming behavior. Thus, in many cases, not confronting the problem when it occurs only makes it more difficult to deal with in the long run.

9   Nevertheless, conflicts do occasionally go away if left alone. There appear to be two sets of circumstances in which withdrawal may work. First, when the withdrawal represents temporary disengagement° for the purpose of letting the heat of the conflict subside, it can be an effective technique for managing conflict. Consider this example: Bill and Margaret begin to argue over inviting Bill's mother for Thanksgiving dinner. During the conversation, Margaret begins to get angry about what her mother-in-law said to her recently about the way she and Bill are raising their daughter. Margaret says, "Hold it a minute; let me make a pot of coffee. We can both relax a bit, and then we'll talk about this some more." A few minutes later, having calmed down, she returns, ready to approach the conflict more objectively. Margaret's action is not true withdrawal; it's not meant as a means of avoiding confrontation. Rather, it provides a cooling-off period that will probably benefit them both.

10   The second set of circumstances in which withdrawal may work is when a conflict occurs between people who communicate infrequently. Consider Josh and Mario, who work in the same office. At two office gatherings, they have gotten into arguments about whether the company really cares about its employees. At the next office gathering, Mario avoids sitting near Josh. Again, this form of withdrawal serves as a means of avoiding conflict rather than contributing to it. In this case, Mario judges that it simply isn't that important to resolve the disagreement. It is fair to say that not every conflict needs to be resolved. Withdrawal is a negative pattern only when it is a person's major way of managing conflict.

11   **Surrender.** A second method of managing conflict is to surrender. As you might suspect, *surrender* means giving in immediately to avoid conflict. Although altering a personal position in order to accommodate another can be positive when it's done in the spirit of cooperation, using surrender as a primary coping strategy is unhealthy.

12   Some people are so upset by the prospect of conflict that they will do anything to avoid it. For instance, Juan and Mariana are discussing their vacation plans. Juan would like just the two of them to go, but Mariana has talked with two of their friends who will be vacationing the same week about going together. After Juan mentions that he'd like the two of them to go alone, Mariana says, "But I think it would be fun to go with another couple, don't you?" Juan replies, "OK, whatever you want." Even though Juan really wants the two of them to go alone, rather than describe his feelings or give reasons for his position, he gives in to avoid conflict.

13   Habitual surrender is a negative way of dealing with conflict for at least two reasons. First, decisions should be made on their merits, not to avoid conflict. If one person gives in, there is no testing of the decision—no one knows what would really be best. Second, surrender can be infuriating to the other person. When Mariana tells Juan what she thinks, she probably wants Juan to see her way as the best. But if Juan simply surrenders, Mariana might believe that Juan still dislikes her plan but is playing the martyr. And his unwillingness to present his reasons could lead to even more conflict.

14   The contention° that surrender is a negative way of dealing with conflict should be qualified to the extent that it reflects a Western cultural perspective. In some cultures, surrendering is a perfectly legitimate way of dealing with conflict. In Japanese culture, for instance, it is thought to be more humble and face-saving to surrender than to risk losing respect through conflict.

15   **Aggression.** A third method of dealing with conflict is through aggression. *Aggression* entails° the use of physical or psychological coercion° to get one's way. Through aggression, people attempt to force others to accept their ideas or wishes, thereby emerging as "victors" in conflicts.

16   Aggression seldom improves a relationship, however. Rather, aggression is an emotional reaction to conflict. Thought is short-circuited, and the person lashes out physically or verbally. People who use aggression are not concerned with the merits of an issue but only with who is bigger, who can talk louder, who can act nastier, or who can force the other to give in. With either physical or verbal aggression, conflict is escalated or obscured° but not managed.

17 **Persuasion.** A fourth method of managing conflict is by persuasion. *Persuasion* is the attempt to change either the attitude or the behavior of another person in order to seek accommodation. At times during the discussion of an issue, one party may try to persuade the other that a particular action is the right one. Suppose that at one point in their discussion about buying a car, Sheila says, "Don't we need a lot of room?" Kevin might reply, "Enough to get us into the car together, but I don't see why we need more than that." Sheila and Kevin are now approaching a conflict situation. At this point, Sheila might say, "Kevin, we are constantly complaining about the lack of room in our present car. Remember last month when you were upset because we couldn't even get our two suitcases into the trunk and we had to put one of them in the back seat? And how many times have we been embarrassed when we couldn't drive our cars with friends because the back seat is too small for even two normal-sized people?" Statements like these represent an attempt at resolving the conflict through persuasion.

18 When persuasion is open and reasonable, it can be a positive means of resolving conflict. However, persuasion can also degenerate° into manipulation, as when a person says, "You know, if you back me on this, I could see to it that you get a few more of the good accounts, and if you don't, well . . ." Although persuasive efforts may fuel a conflict, if that persuasion has a solid logical base, it is at least possible that the persuasion will resolve the conflict.

Discussion. A fifth method of dealing 19 with conflict is *problem-solving discussion*—the verbal weighing and considering of the pros and cons of the issues in conflict. Discussion is the most desirable means of dealing with conflict in a relationship because it provides for open consideration of issues and because it preserves equality. Resolving conflict through discussion is often difficult to accomplish, however, because it requires all parties involved to cooperate: the participants must be objective in their presentation of issues, honest in stating their feelings and beliefs, and open to the solution that proves to be most satisfactory and in the best interests of those involved.

Problem-solving discussion includes 20 defining and analyzing the problem, suggesting possible solutions, selecting the solution that best fits the analysis, and working to implement° the decision. In everyday situations, all five steps are not always considered completely, nor are they necessarily considered in the order given. But when two people perceive a conflict emerging, they need to be willing to step back from the conflict and proceed systematically toward a solution.

Does this process sound too 21 idealized? Or impracticable? Discussion is difficult, but when two people commit themselves to trying, chances are that they will discover that through discussion they arrive at solutions that meet both their needs and do so in a way that maintains their relationship.

Reading Comprehension Questions

Vocabulary in Context

_____ 1. In the sentence below, the word *harbor* (här′bər) means
   A. hold onto.
   B. avoid.
   C. give up.
   D. pretend.

> "Justina may force Eduardo to address the smoking issue, or she may go along with Eduardo's ignoring it but harbor a resentment that may negatively affect their relationship." (Paragraph 7)

Central Point and Main Ideas

_____ 2. Which sentence best expresses the central point of the selection?
   A. Many people have a negative view of conflict.
   B. There are five main ways, both positive and negative, with which people deal with conflict.
   C. Conflicts can force people to make choices and to test their attitudes, actions, needs, and aims.
   D. It is better not to intensify or hide conflict.

_____ 3. The main idea of paragraphs 9 and 10 can be found in the
   A. second sentence of paragraph 9.
   B. third sentence of paragraph 9.
   C. first sentence of paragraph 10.
   D. second sentence of paragraph 10.

Supporting Details

_____ 4. According to the author,
   A. withdrawal never works.
   B. whether or not surrender is generally a good way to manage conflict is related to one's cultural perspective.
   C. aggression is an attempt to change either the attitude or the behavior of another person in order to seek accommodation.
   D. discussion is the easiest and most desirable way of dealing with conflict in a relationship.

Transitions

_____ 5. The relationship between the two sentences on the next page is one of
   A. comparison.
   B. contrast.
   C. cause and effect.
   D. illustration.

"When persuasion is open and reasonable, it can be a positive means of resolving conflict. However, persuasion can also degenerate into manipulation . . . ." (Paragraph 18)

Patterns of Organization

_____ 6. Just as paragraphs are organized according to patterns, so are longer selections. The overall pattern of organization of this selection is
   A. time order.
   B. cause and effect.
   C. list of items.
   D. comparison and/or contrast.

_____ 7. The main pattern of organization of paragraphs 7 and 8 is
   A. time order.
   B. definition and example.
   C. cause and effect.
   D. contrast.

Fact and Opinion

_____ 8. The entire selection is made up of
   A. only facts.
   B. only opinions.
   C. both facts and opinions.

_____ 9. The opinion words in paragraph 4 are
   A. "certainly one of the easiest."
   B. "ways to deal with conflict."
   C. "physically or psychologically."
   D. "remove themselves."

_____ 10. The sentence below is
   A. all fact.
   B. at least partly opinion.

"Discussion is the most desirable means of dealing with conflict in a relationship because it provides for open consideration of issues and because it preserves equality." (Paragraph 19)

Discussion Questions

1. Which of Verderber's five methods of dealing with conflict do you or people you know typically use? Give examples.

2. Why do you think Verderber regards discussion as "the most desirable means of dealing with conflict in a relationship"? And why might he feel that discussion "is often difficult to accomplish"?

3. Verderber writes that conflict is sometimes useful because it forces us to make choices and test attitudes. When in your life has conflict been a good thing? What did you learn from it?

4. Suggest ways that someone you know could be encouraged to deal effectively with his or her specific conflict.

Note: Writing assignments for this selection appear on page 631.

Check Your Performance   **FACT AND OPINION**

Activity	Number Right	Points		Score
Review Test 1 (5 items)	_____	× 2	=	_____
Review Test 2 (10 items)	_____	× 3	=	_____
Review Test 3 (20 items)	_____	× 1.5	=	_____
Review Test 4 (10 items)	_____	× 3	=	_____
		TOTAL SCORE	=	_____ %

Enter your total score into the **Reading Performance Chart: Review Tests** on the inside back cover.

FACT AND OPINION: Mastery Test 1

A. Five of the statements below are facts, and five are opinions. Identify statements of fact with an **F** and statements of opinion with an **O**.

_____ 1. Scientists at MIT have developed a robot that recognizes human emotions.

_____ 2. Within thirty years, robots will completely change the way Americans live.

_____ 3. The United States government was given the right to tax its citizens in 1913, in the Sixteenth Amendment to the Constitution.

_____ 4. It is unfair for elderly people living on fixed incomes to have to pay income taxes.

_____ 5. To avoid harsh winter conditions, some animals migrate, while others build nests, hide away in caves and burrows, and enter a sleep-like state called hibernation.

_____ 6. There could be no scarier experience in life than to awaken a bear from a state of hibernation.

_____ 7. The best time of the year to visit New England is in the fall when the trees change color.

_____ 8. Leaves turn color in the fall when green chlorophyll reproduction ends and other pigments in leaves become visible.

_____ 9. To control blood pressure, people everywhere need to develop the habit of daily meditation.

_____ 10. When blood is pumped by the heart, it exerts pressure on artery walls; this is referred to as blood pressure.

(Continues on next page)

B. Here are short reviews taken from a newspaper movie guide. Some reviews provide only facts; others contain opinions about the movie as well. Identify the factual reviews with an **F**; identify reviews that also contain the reviewer's opinion with an **F+O**.

_____ 11. *Charlie's Angels: Full Throttle,* **2003**. Cameron Diaz, Drew Barrymore, Lucy Liu. Watching this plotless movie is like being pummeled for two hours with a feather duster. It leaves no scars, but you do feel the pain.

_____ 12. *Rush Hour,* **1998.** Jackie Chan, Chris Tucker. Chinese action star Chan and American comic Tucker team up as detectives working to rescue the kidnapped daughter of a Chinese official.

_____ 13. *In the Heat of the Night,* **1967.** Sidney Poitier. Oscar-winning mystery about a Philadelphia cop caught up in a murder investigation in a Mississippi town.

_____ 14. *The Hulk,* **2003.** Eric Bana, Jennifer Connelly. This comic book character is a tough one to nail to the screen. An admirable but disappointing effort.

_____ 15. *Lethal Weapon 4,* **1998.** Mel Gibson, Danny Glover. Los Angeles cops chase smugglers in a violent but witty and thoroughly entertaining sequel.

C. The passage below contains five sentences. Identify each sentence with an **F** (for fact), an **O** (for opinion), or **F+O** (for a combination of fact *and* opinion). Note that **one** sentence combines fact and opinion.

[16]The Amazon River, which empties into the Atlantic Ocean, is an awe-inspiring natural wonder. [17]It's so wide that one-fifth of all the moving fresh water on Earth flows from its mouth. [18]In addition to being the widest river in the world, it is one of the longest, being about four thousand miles long. [19]Furthermore, the Amazon covers the largest area of any river: 2,772,000 square miles. [20]Instead of being called the Amazon River, it should be called the Amazing River!

16. _____   17. _____   18. _____   19. _____   20. _____

FACT AND OPINION: Mastery Test 2

A. Five of the statements below are facts, and five are opinions. Identify statements of fact with an **F** and statements of opinion with an **O**.

_____ 1. The book most frequently stolen from public libraries is the *Guinness Book of World Records*.

_____ 2. One of the most fascinating books in the world to read is the *Guinness Book of World Records*.

_____ 3. Yellow is a color used for writing pencils, highway signs, and school buses.

_____ 4. Yellow is the most meaningful of all colors, making us all think of warmth and sunshine.

_____ 5. A golden retriever is the best pet for a young child.

_____ 6. Retrievers and other hunting dogs are bred to have mouths that won't damage the game they bring back.

_____ 7. Vacant buildings ought to be turned into apartment buildings for the homeless.

_____ 8. Today there are more than half a million homeless people living in the United States; 15 percent of them are under the age of 5.

_____ 9. A university study found that heavy drug use seriously affects a teenager's transition to adulthood.

_____ 10. The most appropriate sentence for convicted drug pushers is life imprisonment without any possibility of parole.

B. Here are five short book reviews. Identify a factual review with an **F**; identify a review that includes both facts about the book *and* the reviewer's opinion with an **F+O**.

_____ 11. ¹In *Jane Eyre*, Charlotte Brontë has created one of the most memorable of all fictional couples. ²Jane, a spirited orphan, meets Rochester, the mysterious master of Thornfield Hall, when she becomes governess to his little ward Adele. ³Jane and Rochester fall deeply in love, but a terrible secret from Rochester's past threatens their happiness. ⁴The struggles of these two fascinating characters so capture the reader's imagination that the book has become one of the favorite novels of all time.

(Continues on next page)

_____ 12. [1]*American Fried,* by the journalist Calvin Trillin, is a collection of short pieces subtitled *Adventures of a Happy Eater.* [2]Trillin investigates, among other things, spareribs in Kansas City, a crawfish festival in Louisiana, knishes in New York, and the search for the world's greatest hamburger. [3]This is the first of three books about eating, which the author calls his "tummy trilogy."

_____ 13. [1]In the mid-1960s, Jonathan Kozol went to teach in an inner-city public school in Boston. [2]His compelling book, *Death at an Early Age,* is a vivid account of his experiences there. [3]As his title suggests, Kozol argues that shabby, overcrowded, understaffed schools are destroying children, specifically African American children, by killing their minds and their spirits. [4]Anyone who cares about America's ailing public school system must read this book.

_____ 14. [1]D-Day, June 6, 1944, was the day of the Allies' successful invasion of France, considered by historians to be a decisive step in the defeat of Nazi Germany. [2]Cornelius Ryan's *The Longest Day* is an hour-by-hour reconstruction of the battle that focuses not on military history but on the individuals involved. [3]Ryan personally interviewed hundreds of people, from generals to ordinary soldiers, and wove their stories together to create this book.

_____ 15. [1]One of the most memorable books of recent years is *All Over But the Shoutin'*, a haunting memoir by the Pulitzer Prize-winning journalist Rick Bragg. [2]Now a national correspondent for the *New York Times,* Bragg tells the story of himself, a child of poor white Southerners, and his family—an alcoholic, mostly absent father, and an extraordinary mother, quietly heroic in the face of devastating poverty. [3]Bragg celebrates not just his mother but also the importance of family, and chances are his story will touch you deeply.

C. The passage below contains five sentences. Identify each sentence with an **F** (for fact), an **O** (for opinion), or **F+O** (for a combination of fact *and* opinion). Note that **one** sentence combines fact and opinion.

[16]More young adults of today's generation choose to live together before marriage than in their grandparents' generation, but they should take the time to find out the risks of cohabitation. [17]Research shows that the divorce rate for people who move in together before marriage is 46 percent higher than for married couples who don't live together first. [18]This statistic clearly refutes the belief that living together is a good way to find out if two people are "marriage material." [19]Research also shows that co-habitors experience more depression, physical violence and a lower standard of living than married couples. [20]These facts alone should discourage young people from moving in together.

16. _____   17. _____   18. _____   19. _____   20. _____

FACT AND OPINION: Mastery Test 3

A. Identify facts with an **F**, opinions with an **O**, and the **two** combinations of fact *and* opinion with an **F+O.**

_____ 1. Without the work of Susan B. Anthony, women would never have gotten the right to vote.

_____ 2. Women were granted the right to vote with the passage of the Nineteenth Amendment in 1920.

_____ 3. Not enough men or women in the United States take advantage of their right to vote.

_____ 4. Every nature-loving person should be a member of the World Wildlife Federation, an organization working on behalf of endangered species.

_____ 5. About twelve thousand years ago, the wildlife in Alaska included elephants, lions, and camels.

_____ 6. The koala, a native of Australia, gets all its nourishment from one tree, the eucalyptus; it doesn't even need to add water to its diet.

_____ 7 It's unfortunate and even shameful that the koala, hunted for both fur and food, is now an endangered species.

_____ 8. Federal income taxes first started early in the twentieth century.

_____ 9. The Internal Revenue Service has the power to seize the property of people who cheat on taxes.

_____ 10. Cheating on taxes isn't as bad as some other crimes, such as robbery.

B. Here are five short book reviews. Identify a factual review with an **F**; identify a review that includes both facts about the book *and* the reviewer's opinion with an **F+O**.

_____ 11. [1]In the dark, gritty novel *Third and Indiana*, Ofelia Santoro rides her bicycle through the inner-city streets every night to look for her fourteen-year-old son, Gabriel. [2]After working as a lookout, Gabriel has been promoted to crack dealer, but now he's in serious trouble with a vicious drug lord named Diablo. [3]A heartbreaking novel about today's urban wasteland.

(Continues on next page)

_____ 12. [1]On August 6, 1945, at 8:15 a.m. local time, the United States dropped the atom bomb on the Japanese city Hiroshima. [2]The next year, John Hersey, an American writer, published *Hiroshima,* an account of what happened on the day of the bombing and in the immediate aftermath. [3]The book focuses on six survivors: two women and four men, of whom five are Japanese and the sixth is a German priest.

_____ 13. [1]Shirley Jackson's book *Life Among the Savages* is a heartwarming, funny account of her own family—her husband, their four children, their pets. [2]Jackson also wrote "The Lottery," one of the most famous and most terrifying short stories of all time. [3]Readers who were chilled with horror by that tale will be interested to see a very different side of this versatile writer.

_____ 14. [1]The fabulous popularity of the movie *Titanic* has interested many people in reading about the legendary shipwreck. [2]One of the earliest book-length accounts of the disaster, and still one of the best, is *A Night to Remember,* by Walter Lord, written in the 1950s. [3]After more than forty years, it remains as readable and as fascinating as ever.

_____ 15. [1]In *An Anthropologist on Mars,* Oliver Sacks writes about neurological patients, who, he has said, are "travelers to unimaginable lands." [2]The first patient is a painter who became so colorblind in an accident that he now sees only black and white. [3]Included in the book are photos of his artwork before and after the accident. [4]Another subject is a physician with Tourette's syndrome, a disease characterized by various involuntary movements and words, including obscenities.

C. The passage below contains five sentences. Identify each sentence with an **F** (for fact), an **O** (for opinion), or **F+O** (for a combination of fact *and* opinion). Note that **one** sentence combines fact and opinion.

[16]Recently, three thousand California high-school students had a physics lesson at an amusement park. [17]A Valencia teacher had a truly inspired idea, using thrill rides to serve as a living physics lab. [18]As the students rode the roller coaster, for instance, they took instrument readings to try to learn how much force is needed to keep a person from flying out of the seat. [19]Ordinarily, science courses are terribly dull. [20]This teacher definitely deserves an award for thinking of such a great way to spice science up for students.

16. _____   17. _____   18. _____   19. _____   20. _____

FACT AND OPINION: Mastery Test 4

A. Identify facts with an **F**, opinions with an **O**, and the **two** combinations of fact *and* opinion with an **F+O.**

_____ 1. The American lifestyle has changed for the worse.

_____ 2. In the 1950s, middle-class American families often had one bread-winner—Dad—and a stay-at-home mom; and the family generally shared a home-cooked meal at the dinner table.

_____ 3. In the 2000s, working mothers, fast foods, divorce, stepparents, and children home alone are daily realities in millions of American households.

_____ 4. A tick, common in woods and forests throughout the United States, fastens itself to a host with its teeth, then secretes a cement-like material to reinforce its hold.

_____ 5. The world would be a better place if wasps and other biting insects were exterminated.

_____ 6. Americans in different regions of the country celebrate some of the strangest holidays in the world, such as Graveyard Cleaning and Decoration Day and Rattlesnake Roundup Day.

_____ 7. Americans should hold the Fourth of July dearer to their hearts than all other holidays.

_____ 8. Responsible employers should provide daycare for all their employees.

_____ 9. Today about eight thousand companies in the United States offer on-site daycare to their employees, up from approximately two hundred over twenty years ago.

_____ 10. Margaret Sanger is the most noteworthy figure in the history of family planning.

_____ 11. A maternity nurse, Sanger sought repeatedly to learn about contraception, but sadly outdated sexist attitudes made such information almost impossible to get.

_____ 12. Sanger persisted and succeeded in opening the world's first birth control clinic in Brooklyn in 1916.

(Continues on next page)

B. The following passage contains five sentences. Identify each sentence with an **F** (for fact), an **O** (for opinion), or **F+O** (for a combination of fact *and* opinion). Note that **one** sentence combines fact and opinion.

[13]A number of recent, well-publicized court cases have involved people accused of profiting from insider trading on stocks. [14]Insider trading involves buying or selling stocks based on information that has not been disclosed to the public. [15]One of the most outrageous such cases involved home-decorating diva Martha Stewart, who was accused of selling her shares of a company's stock based on a tip from the head of that company, a personal friend. [16]Ordinary people deeply resent the kind of "white-collar" crime which Stewart was accused of committing. [17]Insider trading by already wealthy individuals is motivated by a frightening level of greed.

13. _____   14. _____   15. _____   16. _____   17. _____

C. Read the following passage from a history textbook. Then identify each listed excerpt from the passage as either fact (**F**) or opinion (**O**).

[1]The harshest critics of "suburban values" of the 1950s were American young people. [2]Their criticism took different forms. [3]Some of it was thoughtful and inspiring, the result of the best efforts of young intellectuals. [4]At other times it was a protest that came from the gut rather than the mind. [5]Of the second type none was more widely embraced by youngsters—or more roundly attacked by adults—than rock and roll.

[6]Most of the criticism of rock and roll focused on Elvis Presley, who more than any other artist fully fused country music with rhythm and blues. [7]In his first record, he gave the rhythm-and-blues song "That's All Right Mama" a country feel and the country classic "Blue Moon Over Kentucky" a rhythm-and-blues swing. [8]It was a unique exhibition of genius. [9]In addition, Presley exuded sexuality. [10]When he appeared on the *Ed Sullivan Show*, network executives instructed cameramen to avoid shots of Elvis's lower-body physical movements.

_____ 18. Some of it was thoughtful and inspiring, the result of the best efforts of young intellectuals.

_____ 19. It was a unique exhibition of genius.

_____ 20. When he appeared on the *Ed Sullivan Show*, network executives instructed cameramen to avoid shots of Elvis's lower-body physical movements.

FACT AND OPINION: Mastery Test 5

A. Read the following textbook excerpts, and identify facts with an **F**, opinions with an **O**, and the **three** combinations of fact *and* opinion with an **F+O**.

_____ 1. The age of the average soldier serving in Vietnam was 19, compared with 26 for World War II.

_____ 2. In 1939, there were fewer than two thousand private TV sets in the entire United States.

_____ 3. Television watching, a habit linked by researchers to health problems such as obesity, should be limited for young people to just one hour per day.

_____ 4. The most important benefit of TV is that it has helped people remain in closer touch with world events.

_____ 5. Today, TVs have spread into almost every home in the country, with over 90 percent of American homeowners reporting that they own at least one television.

_____ 6. At the turn of the century, methods for coping with waste produced in cities were really quite dreadful.

_____ 7. In 1900, horses deposited some 26 million pounds of manure and 10 million gallons of urine on the streets of New York City each week.

_____ 8. During the early development of cities such as Philadelphia, herds of municipal pigs were used as street cleaning crews.

_____ 9. The increasing size of administration is the most serious problem in education today.

_____ 10. It is shameful that half of our education spending goes to administration, compared with only 20 percent in many European countries.

_____ 11. On April 4, 1968, Martin Luther King, Jr., traveled to Memphis to lead a demonstration in support of striking sanitation workers; he was assassinated that same day.

_____ 12. King produced his "Letter from Birmingham Jail," one of the most eloquent documents of the civil rights movement, while detained in a prison cell in 1963.

(Continues on next page)

B. The following passage contains five sentences. Two sentences are facts, two are opinions, and one combines fact and opinion. Identify the facts with an **F**, the opinions with an **O**, and the one statement of fact *and* opinion with an **F+O**.

> [13]Many young people expect to be parents, yet few schools offer courses in parenting. [14]Doctors aren't allowed to practice without many years of schooling, nor are pilots allowed to fly without extensive training. [15]But parents are allowed to have as many children as they wish without any formal education on parenting, a situation that we all should be concerned about. [16]Our public schools simply must incorporate education for parenting into the curriculum. [17]If they do not, America's future will be grim.

13. _____   14. _____   15. _____   16. _____   17. _____

C. Read the following textbook passage. Then identify each listed excerpt from the passage as either fact (**F**) or opinion (**O**).

> [1]It is well documented that existing automobile prototypes are far more efficient than today's cars and that some get more than eighty miles per gallon. [2]Our first strategy should be to insist that the new cars be put on the market. [3]Burning less fuel will automatically reduce pollution. . . .
>
> [4]We don't want only one type of car. [5]We need electric cars for some uses and organically fueled cars for other uses. [6]And we need to think about leasing, sharing, and co-owning vehicles, too. [7]Several apartment complexes across the country have successful car-sharing programs. [8]Participants sign up for "car time" and make their travel arrangements accordingly, thus avoiding the need for families to own second cars. [9]This works especially well when a long-distance car is used only occasionally. [10]In such a case, a "city car" (maybe electric) could meet most of a family's requirements with high efficiency.

_____ 18. Our first strategy should be to insist that these new cars be put on the market.

_____ 19. Burning less fuel will automatically reduce pollution. . . .

_____ 20. We need electric cars for some uses and organically fueled cars for other uses.

FACT AND OPINION: Mastery Test 6

A. Identify the **three** facts with an **F**, the **three** opinions with an **O**, and the **four** combinations of fact and opinion with an **F+O.**

_____ 1. Today, the world's population is doubling about every 37 years.

_____ 2. Pittsburgh today is one of the most pleasant and livable cities in North America.

_____ 3. The image of the elderly as frail and helpless is insultingly inaccurate; in fact, only 5 percent of Americans over age 65 live in nursing homes.

_____ 4. Two kinds of animals—birds and mammals—maintain a constant body temperature despite the temperature of their surroundings, and both have evolved methods to control the flow of heat into and out of their bodies.

_____ 5. Three centuries ago in France, children began to leave home to work as shepherds, servants, and apprentices at age 7 or 8, and sadly, by age 10 nearly all children had left home.

_____ 6. More than 80 percent of Americans who divorce eventually remarry.

_____ 7. It is a great deal easier to refrain from eating than to burn off the weight by exercise.

_____ 8. *Democracy in America*, a collection of observations written by French aristocrat Alexis de Tocqueville in 1835, remains one of the most insightful studies of early U.S. society.

_____ 9. The men in all too many homeless shelters receive despicable treatment.

_____ 10. Many women entered the labor force for the first time during World War II, giving them a significant, much needed experience of social and economic equality with men.

B. The following passage contains five sentences. Two sentences are facts, two are opinions, and one combines fact and opinion. Identify the facts with an **F**, the opinions with an **O**, and the one statement of fact *and* opinion with an **F+O**.

[11]One of the ocean's most fascinating creatures, the octopus, has been taught various skills by scientists testing its intelligence. [12]Octopuses have been taught, for instance, to distinguish squares from crosses and to slip and

(Continues on next page)

slide their way through simple mazes. [13]One project provided the most dramatic and interesting evidence yet for the invertebrate's intelligence. [14]In 1992, researchers taught a group of octopuses to grab a red ball instead of a white one; then another group learned the same skill simply by watching the first group. [15]The octopus may well prove to be as intelligent a creature of the sea as the dolphin.

11. _____   12. _____   13. _____   14. _____   15. _____

C. Read the following textbook passage. Then identify each listed excerpt from the passage as either a fact (**F**) or an opinion (**O**).

[1]*Uncle Tom's Cabin* was one of the most important and controversial of American novels. [2]Written by Harriet Beecher Stowe, the novel was a young woman's response to the Fugitive Slave Act. [3]Although the act was probably responsible for sending only about three hundred slaves back to the South, Stowe was outraged by it, calling it a "nightmare abomination."

[4]*Uncle Tom's Cabin* first appeared in serial form in the *National Era,* an abolitionist journal. [5]Although simplistic and overly melodramatic, the novel was also deeply affecting. [6]Indeed, sales reached 300,000 copies within a year. [7]However, not everyone welcomed Stowe's work. [8]In the South, Stowe was criticized as naive or a liar. [9]In one infamous incident, she received an anonymous parcel containing the ear of a disobedient slave. [10]When Stowe was faced with the charge that the book was deceitful, she answered with *A Key to Uncle Tom's Cabin,* which provided documentation that every incident in the novel had actually happened.

[11]In 1862, Lincoln met Harriet Beecher Stowe and reportedly said, "So you're the little woman that wrote the book that made this great war." [12]Indeed, although the copies sold can be counted, the emotional impact of Stowe's novel will never be fully known.

_____ 16. *Uncle Tom's Cabin* was one of the most important and controversial of American novels.

_____ 17. *Uncle Tom's Cabin* first appeared in serial form in the *National Era,* an abolitionist journal.

_____ 18. Written by Harriet Beecher Stowe, the novel was a young woman's response to the Fugitive Slave Act.

_____ 19. Although simplistic and overly melodramatic, the novel was also deeply affecting.

_____ 20. When Stowe was faced with the charge that the book was deceitful, she answered with *A Key to Uncle Tom's Cabin,* which provided documentation that every incident in the novel had actually happened.

8

Inferences

You have probably heard the expression "to read between the lines." When you "read between the lines," you pick up ideas that are not directly stated in what you are reading. These implied ideas are often important for a full understanding of what an author means. Discovering the ideas in writing that are not stated directly is called *making inferences,* or *drawing conclusions.*

AN INTRODUCTION TO INFERENCES

Consider first some inferences you might make in everyday life.

- After a thunderstorm, you get home to discover that your clocks are all twelve minutes slow. What might you infer?

  _____

- When you turn on the kitchen light late at night, you see something small dart quickly into the shadows. What might you infer?

  _____

- It's the last day of the school year. The desk of one teacher is covered with gifts and cards. Students from all over the school keep coming by. Some of them are crying. What might you infer?

  _____

In the first situation, you probably inferred that the electricity in your home had gone off for twelve minutes when a brief power outage occurred during the thunderstorm. In the second situation, you probably concluded that you have a mouse or some insect in the kitchen. In the last situation, you could infer that a teacher is leaving the school and students are saying goodbye. In each case, you made a reasonable guess based on the evidence presented.

You have already practiced making inferences in this book. Do you remember the following sentence from Chapter 1?

> The homecoming celebration was *raucous*, with people wildly shouting and cheering, blowing whistles, and pounding on drums.

That sentence does not tell the meaning of *raucous*, but the examples help us infer that *raucous* means *noisy*.

You also made inferences in the chapter on implied main ideas. Implied ideas are ones that are not stated directly. Instead, you must use the evidence in a selection to find them through inference.

In this chapter, you will get more practice in drawing inferences. Read the following passage, and then check (✓) the **two** inferences that are most firmly based on the information given.

> [1]Jim Johnson panicked when he came home from work to find his neighbor's pet rabbit dead and in the jaws of his German shepherd, Fido. [2]Johnson took the filthy, slightly chewed-up bunny into his house, washed it with care, and then used the blow dryer to restore its fur as best he could. [3]A short time later he secretly put the rabbit back into its outdoor cage.
>
> [4]The next day, Jim's neighbor stopped him as they were both doing yard work. [5]"Did you hear that Thumper died?"
>
> [6]"Uh, no," stammered Johnson.
>
> [7]"We went out a couple days ago and found him dead. [8]What's really weird, though, is that the day after we buried him, we went outside and discovered that someone had dug him up, given him a bath, styled his fur, and put him back into his cage!"

_____ 1. Johnson's neighbor had children who took care of the rabbit.

_____ 2. Fido had probably dug up the rabbit's grave.

_____ 3. The neighbor was convinced Johnson had dug up the rabbit.

_____ 4. Jim Johnson assumed his dog had killed the rabbit.

_____ 5. The rabbit had been very sick.

Explanation:

1. There is no mention of Johnson's children. You should not have checked this item.

2. Since the rabbit had been buried, it is logical to infer that the only way Fido could have gotten it was to dig it up. You should have checked this item.

3. The neighbor in a matter-of-fact way told Johnson the story of what happened to Thumper. This suggests he did not suspect Johnson had anything to do with it. You should not have checked this item.

4. Johnson's efforts to cover up what happened to Thumper imply that he believed his dog had killed it. You should have checked this item.

5. There is no suggestion that the rabbit had been sick before the neighbor had found it dead in its cage. You should not have checked this item.

☑ Check Your Understanding

Take a minute now to look at the following *Philadelphia Inquirer* cartoon. What do you think is the artist's point?

Put a check (✓) by the **two** inferences that are most logically based on the information suggested by the cartoon. Then read the explanations that follow.

_____ 1. The children are enjoying themselves.

_____ 2. The house was built on stilts so the children could play underneath it.

_____ 3. The children probably seldom watch real television.

_____ 4. The cartoonist wishes to emphasize how television keeps children from more active play.

_____ 5. The cartoonist means to emphasize the children's creativity in building a realistic sand sculpture.

Explanation:

1. This inference is well supported by the big smiles on the children's faces.

2. This is not a logical inference. Since the house is so close to the water, we can assume that the stilts have a more practical purpose—to keep the house above high tide.

3. This is also an illogical inference. The fact that the children have chosen to watch a fake television set rather than play on the beach suggests that watching TV is a significant part of their lives.

4. This inference is well supported by the cartoon. We can deduce that the cartoonist has purposely contrasted the passive experience of watching TV with an environment in which children are usually quite active.

5. This is not a logical inference. The sand sculpture is not a challenging one— it's basically a square box. In addition, the children's pose—sitting and watching, and not interacting—suggests passivity, not creativity.

➤ Practice 1

Put a check (✓) by the inference most logically based on the information provided. Look first at the example.

Example

Two cash registers are open at a department store. Although one line is shorter than the other, customers keep leaving the short line to stand in the long one.

____ A. The cashier at the register with the short line is unpopular.

____ B. Some problem is keeping the short line from moving.

____ C. People in the longer line are receiving discounts on their purchases.

____ D. Long lines give people more time to reconsider their purchases.

The correct answer is B. On the basis of the information we are given, we can conclude only that some problem has stalled the short line.

1. Your phone rings and a slightly bored voice on the other end, clearly reading from a script, tells you that you've won a free weekend in Bermuda.

____ A. You are the first person the caller has offered this prize today.

____ B. You are very fortunate to have won this prize.

____ C. There is probably a catch to this "free weekend" in Bermuda.

____ D. Your flight, hotel room, rental car, and meals are included in your prize package.

2. It requires more calories to eat a piece of celery than the celery has in it to begin with.

    ____ A. Celery has fewer calories than any other vegetable.

    ____ B. Celery can never cause a person to gain weight.

    ____ C. Celery is a nutritious addition to the diet.

    ____ D. The only reason people like celery is that it is so low in calories.

3. In casinos, there are no clocks or windows in areas where gambling is done.

    ____ A. Casino planners don't install clocks or windows to save money.

    ____ B. The sunlight coming through windows gets in gamblers' eyes and annoys them.

    ____ C. An old superstition says that gamblers will have bad luck if they play near a clock or a window.

    ____ D. Casino owners don't want gamblers to notice the passage of time.

INFERENCES IN READING

In reading, too, we make logical leaps from the information given in a straightforward way to ideas that are not stated directly. As one scholar has said, inferences are "statements about the unknown made on the basis of the known." To draw inferences, we use all the clues provided by the writer, our own experience, and logic.

☑ *Check Your Understanding*

Read the following passage and check (✓) the **three** inferences that can most logically be drawn from it. Then read the explanation that follows.

> [1]Early one morning, a man was walking along a sandy, deserted beach. [2]At least he thought it was deserted. [3]As he gazed ahead of him, he noticed that there was another human figure in sight. [4]It was a boy who kept bending down, picking something up, and throwing it into the sea. [5]He repeated the movement again and again and again.
>
> [6]As the man drew near, he saw that the sand surrounding the boy was covered with starfish that had been washed in by the waves. [7]It was these stranded starfish that the boy was throwing into the water.
>
> [8]"Why are you doing that?" the man asked.
>
> [9]Not pausing, the boy replied, "The tide is going out, and the sun is rising. [10]Soon the heat will be too much for the starfish, and they will die."
>
> [11]The man shook his head tolerantly. [12]"My dear boy," he said. [13]"There are miles of beach and hundreds, maybe thousands of starfish. [14]You can't save them all. [15]What you're doing can't make a difference!"

[16]The boy listened politely, then picked up the next starfish and threw it in the water. [17]"It makes a difference for this one," he answered.

____ 1. The boy knows he cannot save all the starfish.

____ 2. The man believes that the boy's efforts are admirable.

____ 3. Many starfish will die despite the boy's efforts.

____ 4. Starfish are very close to extinction.

____ 5. The man decides to help save some of the stranded starfish.

____ 6. The boy believes that a little help is better than nothing.

Explanation:

1. This is a logical inference. The boy doesn't show any surprise when the man tells him he can't save all the starfish. Also, the boy's obvious understanding of the shore cycles makes it clear he knew how few starfish he could save. He indicates he still wants to save the ones he can.

2. This is not a logical inference. The man is "tolerant" of what the boy is doing, but he suggests that the boy's actions are pointless.

3. This is a logical inference. As the man points out, there are perhaps thousands of starfish on the beach. The boy cannot save them all.

4. This is not a logical inference. Nothing in the passage suggests that starfish are near extinction.

5. This is not a logical inference. The man does not indicate that he will help save the starfish.

6. This is a logical inference. The boy's efforts to save as many starfish as he can indicate that he does believe a little help is better than none.

Guidelines for Making Inferences in Reading

The exercises in this chapter provide practice in making careful inferences when you read. Here are three guidelines to that process:

1 **Never lose sight of the available information.** As much as possible, base your inferences on the facts. For instance, in the paragraph about the starfish, we are told that the man questions the boy's efforts, even shaking his head in apparent disapproval. On the basis of those facts, we would not conclude that he sees the boy's efforts as admirable.

   It's also important to note when a conclusion lacks support. For instance, the statement that starfish are very close to extinction has no support in the paragraph. We can infer only that many will die.

2 **Use your background information and experience to help you in making inferences.** For instance, your sense of how much distance there is in a mile helps you conclude that the boy cannot possibly save all the starfish stranded on miles of beach.

The more you know about a subject, the better your inferences are likely to be. So keep in mind that if your background in an area is weak, your inferences may be shaky. If you have a rash and fever, a doctor's inferences about the cause are likely to be more helpful than your inferences.

3 **Consider the alternatives.** Don't simply accept the first inference that comes to mind. Instead, consider all of the facts of a case and all the possible explanations. For example, the doctor analyzing your rash and fever may first think of and then eliminate several possibilities before coming to the right conclusion.

➤ *Practice 2*

Read the following passages. Then, in the space provided, write the letter of the most logical answer to each question, based on the information given in the passage.

A.   ¹If you're a man, at some point a woman will ask you how she looks.

²"How do I look?" she'll ask.

³You must be careful how you answer this question. ⁴The best technique is to form an honest yet sensitive opinion, then collapse on the floor with some kind of fatal seizure. ⁵Trust me, this is the easiest way out. ⁶Because you will never come up with the right answer.

⁷The problem is that women generally do not think of their looks in the same way that men do. ⁸Most men form an opinion of how they look in seventh grade, and they stick to it for the rest of their lives. ⁹Some men form the opinion that they are irresistible stud muffins, and they do not change this opinion even when their faces sag and their noses bloat to the size of eggplants and their eyebrows grow together to form what appears to be a giant forehead-dwelling tropical caterpillar.

¹⁰Women do not look at themselves this way. ¹¹If I had to express, in three words, what I believe most women think about their appearance, those words would be: "not good enough." ¹²No matter how attractive a woman may appear to be to others, when she looks at herself in the mirror, she thinks: woof. ¹³She thinks that at any moment a municipal animal-control officer is going to throw a net over her and haul her off to the shelter.

_____ 1. The author (the well-known humorist Dave Barry) suggests that some men
    A. have an unrealistic view of their looks.
    B. don't care about women's looks.
    C. tend to think they look worse than they really do.

_____ 2. The author suggests that women
   A. don't like the way many men look.
   B. are never satisfied with their own looks.
   C. have worse judgment than men.

_____ 3. The author implies that
   A. most men are dishonest with women.
   B. most women, in fact, do not look good enough.
   C. no matter how a man answers a woman's question "How do I look?" she will be unhappy.

_____ 4. We can conclude that the author
   A. is only telling jokes.
   B. is taking something he has observed in real life and exaggerating it.
   C. actually feels that his own looks are "not good enough."

B.   ¹Not unlike drugs or alcohol, the television experience allows the participant to blot out the real world and enter into a pleasurable and passive mental state. ²The worries and anxieties of reality are as effectively put off by becoming absorbed in a television program as by going on a "trip" caused by drugs or alcohol. ³And just as alcoholics are only imperfectly aware of their addiction, feeling that they control their drinking more than they really do ("I can cut it out any time I want—I just like to have three or four drinks before dinner"), people similarly overestimate their control over television watching. ⁴Even as they put off other activities to spend hour after hour watching television, they feel they could easily resume living in a different, less passive style. ⁵But somehow or other while the television set is present in their homes, the click doesn't sound. ⁶With television pleasures available, those other experiences seem less attractive, more difficult somehow.

⁷A heavy viewer (a college English instructor) observes: "I find television almost irresistible. ⁸When the set is on, I cannot ignore it. ⁹I can't turn it off. ¹⁰I feel sapped, will-less, weakened. ¹¹As I reach out to turn off the set, the strength goes out of my arms. ¹²So I sit there for hours and hours."

_____ 5. The author (Marie Winn, in her book *The Plug-In Drug: Television, Children and Family*) compares being wrapped up in TV to
   A. the real world.
   B. a drug or alcohol "trip."
   C. more lively activities.

_____ 6. The author thus implies that watching television is
   A. addictive.
   B. easy to control.
   C. not pleasurable.

_____ 7. From the passage we can conclude that the author feels television
     A. is never really interesting.
     B. usually helps us face our problems.
     C. generally takes the place of more worthwhile activities.

_____ 8. From the passage we can conclude that educators
     A. are less likely to be TV addicts.
     B. can be TV addicts.
     C. are more likely to be TV addicts.

C. [1]Following the Civil War, the American pattern of food production and consumption changed dramatically as industrial development brought rural residents to cities, which depended on food from distant sources. [2]As American industry and cities grew, more and more people relied upon the foods produced and preserved by fewer and fewer people. [3]Instead of growing it in their backyards, urban folk got their food from stores. [4]Fewer women spent their days preparing meals "from scratch." [5]Instead, they got jobs and became increasingly dependent on canned and packaged convenience foods from the local market. [6]Today, 92 percent of Americans rely on foods grown and processed by others. [7]Even the remaining 8 percent who are still "down on the farm" don't really feed themselves. [8]They get most of their food from farms and factories hundreds or thousands of miles away. [9]Instead of making a daily trip to the local general store and greengrocer, most Americans shop for food once a week. [10]The food they buy may have left the factory weeks or months earlier, the farm even longer ago than that.

_____ 9. We can conclude that before industrial development, many people
     A. got their food from distant sources.
     B. grew much of their own food.
     C. had very little to eat.

_____ 10. The author suggests that because of industrial development, Americans
     A. cook more.
     B. buy less food.
     C. eat food that's less fresh.

_____ 11. We can infer that American industrial development
     A. led to a large food industry.
     B. caused cities to shrink.
     C. will mean the total disappearance of farms.

_____ 12. We can infer that the "8 percent who are still 'down on the farm'"
     A. specialize by growing only one or a few crops.
     B. grow a great variety of foods.
     C. will soon move to the city.

➤ *Practice 3*

Read the following textbook passages. Then put a check (✓) by the **three** inferences that are most logically based on the given facts in each passage.

A. Here is an excerpt from an actual home economics textbook printed in the 1960s:

> [1]Have dinner ready. [2]Plan ahead, even the night before, to have a delicious meal ready, on time for his return. . . .
>
> [3]Prepare yourself. [4]Take fifteen minutes to rest so you'll be refreshed when he arrives. [5]Touch up your make-up, put a ribbon in your hair, and be fresh-looking. . . . [6]Be a little gay and a little more interesting for him. [7]His boring day may need a lift and one of your duties is to provide it. . . . [8]After all, catering for his comfort will provide you with immense personal satisfaction. . . .
>
> [9]Listen to him. [10]You may have a dozen important things to tell him, but the moment of his arrival is not the time. [11]Let him talk first. [12]Remember, his topics of conversation are more important than yours. [13]Make the evening his. . . .
>
> [14]Speak in a low, soothing, and pleasant voice. [15]Don't ask him questions about his actions or question his judgment or integrity. [16]Remember, he is the master of the house and as such will always exercise his will with fairness and truthfulness. [17]You have no right to question him.
>
> [18]A good wife always knows her place.

____ 1. We can infer that the author of the 1960s passage believes a good wife dedicates herself to her husband's comfort and happiness.

____ 2. The author of the 1960s passage suggests that a good wife is intelligent and able to contribute to the family income.

____ 3. The author of the 1960s passage implies that a wife should speak up when her husband's judgment is questionable.

____ 4. The author of the 1960s passage implies that wives should be refreshed and attractive when their husbands return home from work.

____ 5. The author of the 1960s passage suggests that husbands prefer an obedient wife to an intelligent one.

____ 6. After reading the passage, we can conclude that views of marriage have not changed very much since the 1960s.

B. [1]Cholera is a severe, often fatal disease of the gastrointestinal system. [2]It is caused by bacteria, but before this cause was discovered, cholera epidemics often led to "blaming the victim." [3]During the epidemic of 1813, for example, Americans blamed those who fell ill, describing them as dirty, immoral, drunken, and lazy, and assumed that the disease was a punishment for low character. [4]Some time later, a doctor, John Snow, noticed that in London, victims of cholera were all getting their water from the same system; no one using another water system got sick. [5]Snow concluded, correctly, that the disease was being spread by bad water; but when the next epidemic broke out in America, in 1849, people paid no attention to his idea. [6]When the rich fled to the countryside, where the water was pure, this was taken as proof that clean, virtuous people did not get cholera. [7]In 1862 there was another epidemic, and by then enlightened people were beginning to think about Snow's discovery, but they had little power and little effect. [8]Not until the 1890s, when physicians accepted the germ theory of disease and the first public health laws were passed, would cholera epidemics end in the United States.

_____ 1. Most people who fell ill with cholera were in fact dirty, immoral, lazy, and drunken.

_____ 2. In the case of cholera, "blaming the victim" was at least partly due to ignorance of how the disease is caused and spread.

_____ 3. During the epidemic of 1849, rich people fled to the countryside precisely because they knew the water there was pure.

_____ 4. When the germ theory of disease was first proposed, people probably found it hard to believe that something they couldn't see could harm them.

_____ 5. Some of the public health laws mentioned in the final sentence may have dealt with ensuring a safe water supply.

_____ 6. Today, cholera has been wiped out worldwide.

C. [1]More than two hundred experiments reveal that, contrary to the old proverb about familiarity breeding contempt, familiarity breeds fondness. [2]Mere repeated exposure to all sorts of novel stimuli—nonsense syllables, Chinese characters, musical selections, faces—boosts people's ratings of them. [3]Do the supposed Turkish words *nansoma, saricik,* and *afworbu* mean something better or something worse than the words *iktitaf, biwojni,* and *kadirga?* [4]University of Michigan students tested by Robert Zajonc preferred whichever of these words they had seen most frequently. [5]Among the letters of the alphabet, people of differing nationalities, languages, and ages prefer the letters appearing in their own name and those that frequently appear in their own language. [6]French students rate capital *W,* the least frequent letter in French, as their least favorite letter.

[7]Many residents of Grand Rapids, Michigan, were not pleased when presented with their new downtown landmark, a huge metal sculpture created by the artist Alexander Calder. [8]Their reaction? [9]"An abomination," "an embarrassment," "a waste of money." [10]Other people were neutral; few seemed enthusiastic. [11]But within a decade, the sculpture had become an

object of civic pride: Its picture adorned bank checks, city posters, and tourist literature. [12]When completed in 1889, the Eiffel Tower in Paris was mocked as grotesque. [13]Today it is the beloved symbol of Paris.

____ 1. Young artists with new ideas are likely to appeal to more people than older artists whose work has been around for many years.

____ 2. University of Michigan students probably preferred Chinese characters to Turkish words.

____ 3. Americans probably tend to prefer the letter *S* to the letter *Y*.

____ 4. Familiarity influences people's taste in art and architecture.

____ 5. We always like someone or something we are familiar with.

____ 6. We may dislike something new just because it's unfamiliar.

INFERENCES IN LITERATURE

Inference is very important in reading literature. While writers of factual material usually state directly much of what they mean, creative writers often provide verbal pictures that *show* what they mean. It is up to the reader to infer the point of what the creative writer has said. For instance, a nonfiction writer might write the following:

The little boy was in a stubborn mood.

But the novelist might write:

When Todd's mother asked him to stop playing in the yard and come indoors, he didn't even look up but shouted "No!" and then spelled it out, "N . . . O!"

Rather than merely stating that Todd was stubborn, the author *shows* the stubbornness with specific details. To get the most out of literature, you must often infer meanings—just as you do in everyday life.

Now look at the following statement that a nonfiction writer might produce:

The more English I learned in school, the more separation I felt from my parents.

Compare the above line with the following excerpt from *Hunger of Memory*, a literary autobiography by Richard Rodriguez.

[1]Matching the silence I started hearing in public was a new quiet at home. [2]The family's quiet was partly due to the fact that, as we children learned more and more English, we shared fewer and fewer words with our parents. [3]Sentences needed to be spoken slowly when a child addressed his mother or

father. [4](Often the parent wouldn't understand.) [5]The child would need to repeat himself. [6](Still the parent misunderstood.) [7]The young voice, frustrated, would end up saying, "Never mind"—the subject was closed. [8]Dinners would be noisy with the clinking of knives and forks against dishes. [9]My mother would smile softly between her remarks; my father at the other end of the table would chew and chew his food, while he stared over the heads of his children.

[10]My mother! [11]My father! [12]After English became my primary language, I no longer knew what words to use in addressing my parents. [13]The old Spanish words (those tender accents of sound) I had used earlier— *mamá* and *papá*—I couldn't use anymore. [14]They would have been too painful reminders of how much had changed in my life. [15]On the other hand, the words I heard neighborhood kids call their parents seemed equally unsatisfactory. [16]Mother and Father; Ma, Papa, Pa, Dad, Pop (how I hated the all-American sound of that last word especially)—all those terms I felt were unsuitable, not really terms of address for my parents. [17]As a result, I never used them at home. [18]Whenever I'd speak to my parents, I would try to get their attention with eye contact alone. [19]In public conversations, I'd refer to "my parents" or "my mother and father."

☑ Check Your Understanding

See if you can answer the following inference questions about the excerpt.

_____ 1. From the passage we can infer that
   A. the Rodriguez children had never gotten along well with their parents.
   B. Rodriguez's father was very strict.
   C. Rodriguez's parents were not learning much English.

_____ 2. The passage suggests that
   A. the children's learning more English upset their relationship with their parents.
   B. the parents were not willing to have their home life disrupted to ensure that their children would fit in with mainstream America.
   C. the children were having problems in school.

_____ 3. We can conclude that Rodriguez's father stared over the heads of his children at the dinner table because he
   A. preferred not to speak while eating.
   B. felt alienated from his children.
   C. believed his children should not be speaking English.

_____ 4. The passage suggests that Rodriguez
   A. harbored a hatred of America.
   B. felt inferior to the other children in his neighborhood.
   C. felt some loyalty to the language and culture of his parents.

_____ 5. The passage suggests that Rodriguez's parents
   A. were angry and resentful when their children spoke English.
   B. patiently accepted their children's new language.
   C. were not interested in their children's well-being.

Explanation:

1. Rodriguez says that although he and his siblings spoke English slowly to their parents, their parents often did not understand them. This suggests that their parents did not know much English. The correct answer is C.

2. The passage shows that Rodriguez and his parents communicated less as the language gap between them grew. Instead of talking together over dinner, family members ate in silence, unable to share their thoughts. This is evidence that the relationship between parents and children was becoming difficult. Therefore, A is the correct answer.

3. Even if the author's father preferred not to speak while eating, he wouldn't have had to look over his children's heads. That he did so suggests he recognized that he could not interact with his children and thus felt distant, or alienated, from them. So answer A is wrong, and the correct answer is B. Answer C is wrong because there is nothing in the passage showing Rodriguez's father opposing his children going to an English-speaking school.

4. Rodriguez makes no negative comment about America, so answer A is incorrect. Also, he refers to "neighborhood kids" without revealing any sense of being intimidated by them, making answer B incorrect as well. Rodriguez's mention of the "tender accents of sound" of the Spanish words for "mother" and "father" shows he still has emotional ties to his parents' language.

5. At the dining table, Rodriguez' parents cannot understand much of what their children are saying. But Rodriguez says that his mother would "smile softly" and that his father would merely eat in silence. His parents' actions suggest, then, that they are patiently enduring the language changeover. The right answer, then, is B.

The excerpt from *Hunger of Memory* is a small example of how inference skills can increase your appreciation of literary forms—fiction, poetry, autobiography, and other imaginative literature.

A Note on Figures of Speech

Creative writers often use comparisons known as **figures of speech** to imply their meanings and give us a fresh and more informed way of looking at something. The two most common figures of speech are similes and metaphors.

- **Simile**—a comparison introduced with *like, as,* or *as if.*

  Instead of saying, "My stepfather shouted at me," you could express it vividly by saying, "When my stepfather shouted at me, it was like a fist in my face." The simile shows that the father's shout was shocking, violent, and painful. It gives us much more information than the line that simply tells us that the stepfather shouted.

Here are some other similes:

- Many of the players on the football team have arms *as big as tree trunks.*
- In the recently planted garden, I saw tomato plants starting to come out of the ground, curled up *like a hand unfolding.*
- I loved my mother, but she was about *as huggable as a cactus.*
- After I lost my job, my material possessions soon disappeared *like so much dandelion fluff in a wind.*
- When my new boyfriend arrived, my parents stared at him *as if he were a cockroach who had just come under the door.*

- **Metaphor**—an implied comparison, with *like, as,* or *as if* omitted.

  The thought "Life is a struggle" was memorably expressed in metaphor by the ancient writer Plotinus, who wrote: "Be kind, for everyone you meet is fighting a great battle." His comparison says that even though we may not be aware of it, everyone we meet is dealing with difficulties, just as we are.

Here are some other metaphors:

- From the airplane, I looked down on Manhattan, *an anthill of frantic life.*
- Looking westward, I saw an *army of dark clouds* massed on the horizon.
- Our boss is always a *bear* on Monday morning.
- None of the players on the demoralized football team were strong enough to withstand *the gale-force winds* of the coach's personality.
- My aunt's home was a *pack rat's nest* of everything she had collected during her life.

➤ *Practice 4*

Use a check (✓) to identify each figure of speech as a simile or a metaphor. Then, in the space provided, answer each inference question that follows.

_____ 1. The head of that corporation needs money as much as a bat needs sunglasses.

___ simile   ___ metaphor

You can infer that the head of the corporation
A. is bankrupt.
B. always has been wealthy.
C. doesn't need any more money.

_____ 2. When I emerged from the air-conditioned building, the air hit me in the face like a steaming washcloth.

___ simile   ___ metaphor

You can infer that the air outside was
A. cool and dry.
B. hot and humid.
C. hot and dry.

_____ 3. Marlo and Scott's relationship was first a racecar, then a stalled sedan, and finally scrap metal.

___ simile   ___ metaphor

You can infer that Marlo and Scott's relationship
A. started out strong but fell apart.
B. slowly grew to a strong and lasting one.
C. had a rapid start and an equally rapid end.

_____ 4. My job interview went as smoothly as a drive down a street filled with potholes.

___ simile   ___ metaphor

You can infer that the interview went
A. extremely well.
B. fairly well.
C. poorly.

_____ 5. There was nothing uncertain about the voice inside that told me what to do. It spoke with the clearness and certainty of church bells heard on bright Sundays.

___ simile   ___ metaphor

You can infer that the author
A. could not make up his mind.
B. felt very sure about what the voice was telling him to do.
C. experienced a moment of insanity.

> ## Practice 5

Following is a short story written by Langston Hughes, a poet and fiction writer who emerged as a major literary figure during the Harlem Renaissance of the 1920s. Read the story, and then write the letter of the most logical answer to each question, based on the information given in the story.

Early Autumn

[1]When Bill was very young, they had been in love. [2]Many nights they had spent walking, talking together. [3]Then something not very important had come between them, and they didn't speak. [4]Impulsively, she had married a man she thought she loved. [5]Bill went away, bitter about women.

[6]Yesterday, walking across Washington Square, she saw him for the first time in years.

[7]"Bill Walker," she said.

[8]He stopped. [9]At first he did not recognize her; to him she looked so old.

[10]"Mary! Where did you come from?"

[11]Unconsciously, she lifted her face as though wanting a kiss, but he held out his hand. [12]She took it.

[13]"I live in New York now," she said.

[14]"Oh"—smiling politely. [15]Then a little frown came quickly between his eyes.

[16]"Always wondered what happened to you, Bill."

[17]"I'm a lawyer. Nice firm, way downtown."

[18]"Married yet?"

[19]"Sure. Two kids."

[20]"Oh," she said.

[21]A great many people went past them through the park. [22]People they didn't know. [23]It was late afternoon. [24]Nearly sunset. [25]Cold.

[26]"And your husband?" he asked her.

[27]"We have three children. [28]I work in the bursar's office at Columbia."

[29]"You're looking very . . . " (he wanted to say old) ". . . well," he said.

[30]She understood. [31]Under the trees in Washington Square, she found herself desperately reaching back into the past. [32]She had been older than he then in Ohio. [33]Now she was not young at all. [34]Bill was still young.

[35]"We live on Central Park West," she said. [36]"Come and see us sometime."

[37]"Sure," he replied. [38]"You and your husband must have dinner with my family some night. [39]Any night. [40]Lucille and I'd love to have you."

[41]The leaves fell slowly from the trees in the Square. [42]Fell without wind. [43]Autumn dusk. [44]She felt a little sick.

[45]"We'd love it," she answered.

[46]"You ought to see my kids." [47]He grinned.

[48]Suddenly the lights came on up the whole length of Fifth Avenue, chains of misty brilliance in the blue air.

[49]"There's my bus," she said.

[50]He held out his hand. [51]"Good-by."

[52]"When . . ." she wanted to say, but the bus was ready to pull off. [53]The lights on the avenue blurred, twinkled, blurred. [54]And she was afraid to open her mouth as she entered the bus. [55]Afraid it would be impossible to utter a word.

[56]Suddenly she shrieked very loudly, "Good-by!" [57]But the bus door had closed.

[58]The bus started. [59]People came between them outside, people crossing the street, people they didn't know. [60]Space and people. [61]She lost sight of Bill. [62]Then she remembered she had forgotten to give him her address—or ask him for his— or tell him that her youngest boy was named Bill, too.

_____ 1. Authors of fiction often choose settings that symbolically reflect their story. In this case, the characters' stage of life is echoed in the author's choices of

A. city and park.

B. Season and time of day.

C. transportation and temperature.

_____ 2. Hughes portrayed the awkwardness of the meeting by indicating a contrast between

A. the woman's and Bill's jobs.

B. New York City and Ohio.

C. what Bill said and what he meant.

_____ 3. The suggestion that Bill was still young but the woman was not implies that

A. she was actually many, many years older than he.

B. her life has aged her more rapidly than his life has aged him.

C. he was an exercise buff who had taken especially good care of himself.

_____ 4. The story suggests that Bill

A. did not regret having married someone else.

B. plans on inviting the woman and her husband over for dinner.

C. still wished nothing had come between him and the woman when they were young.

_____ 5. The last few words of the story suggest that

A. the boy was really Bill's son.

B. the woman regretted naming her youngest son Bill.

C. the woman had thought of Bill with so much longing that she named a son after him.

INFERENCES IN TABLES AND GRAPHS

You have already tried your hand at making inferences from a picture, the cartoon of children "watching" a TV made of sand. Many of the cartoons in newspapers and magazines depend on your inference skills. Other "pictures" that require inferences are tables and graphs, which combine words with visual representations. Authors of textbooks, professional and newspaper articles, and other materials often organize large amounts of material into tables and graphs. Very often, the graphs and tables are used to show comparisons and changes that take place over time.

As with other reading material, to infer the ideas presented in tables and graphs, you must consider all the information presented.

Steps in Reading a Table or Graph

To find and make sense of the information in a table or graph, follow a few steps.

1 Read the title. It will tell you what the table or graph is showing in general.

- What is the title of the table below? _____

2 Check the source. At the bottom of a table or graph, you will usually find the source of the information, an indication of the reliability of its material.

- What are the sources for the table below? _____

_____

3 Read any labels or captions at the top, the side, or underneath that tell exactly what each column, line, bar, number, or other item represents. This information includes such things as quantities, percentages, and years.

The Bingeing Phenomenon

Many college students drink heavily;
shown below is the percentage of students in each category who binge.

Age	
Under 21	45%
21–23	48
24+	28

College residences	
Fraternity/sorority	84%
Coed dorm	52
Off-campus housing	40
Single-sex dorm	38

Race	
White	48%
Hispanic	33
Nat.Amer./Nat.Alask.	34
Asian/Pacific islander	21
African American	16

Gender	
Male	50%
Female	39

Participation in sports	
Nonparticipant	36%
Participant	54
Team leader	58

Attitude	
Frequent bingers who think they drink lightly/moderately	
Male	91%
Female	78

SOURCES: Harvard School of Public Health, *Journal of American College Health*

- How many student categories are presented in the table? _____
- What do the percentages refer to? _____
  _____

4 Once you have taken the above steps, you are ready to infer from the table or graph whatever information you seek from it.

☑ Check Your Understanding

See if you can put a check (✓) by the **three** inferences that are most logically based on the table.

_____ 1. The older students get, the more they tend to binge.

_____ 2. In general, students who live in fraternities or sororities drink more heavily than students who live elsewhere.

_____ 3. The percentage of white students who binge is three times as great as the percentage of African American students who binge.

_____ 4. Bingeing is not a problem for female students.

_____ 5. Bingeing is not popular among college athletes.

_____ 6. Most college students who binge are unaware of the true extent of their drinking.

Explanation:

1. From the section of the table labeled "Age," we can infer that once students become older than 23, their bingeing decreases—from 48 to 28 percent. So you should not have checked item 1.

2. A glance at the section labeled "College residences" tells us that fraternity and sorority members do drink more heavily than students who live in coed dorms, off-campus housing, and single-sex dorms. You should have checked item 2.

3. The section labeled "Race" tells us that 48 percent of white students and 16 percent of African American students binge. Since forty-eight is three times sixteen, you should have checked item 3.

4. The section labeled "Gender" shows that 39 percent of females binge, so you should not have checked item 4.

5. You also should not have checked item 5. The "Participation in sports" section shows that 54 percent of college athletes and 58 percent of team leaders binge.

6. The section labeled "Attitude" shows that most male and female bingers believe they drink only lightly or moderately. Thus item 6 is the third item you should have checked.

➤ *Practice 6*

Read the graph below, following the steps on pages 319–320. Then put a check
(✓) by the **three** inferences that are most logically based on the graph.

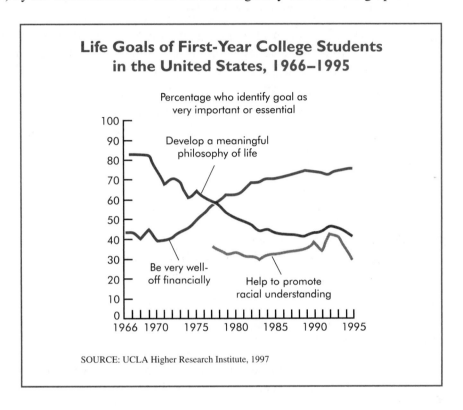

**Life Goals of First-Year College Students
in the United States, 1966–1995**

Percentage who identify goal as
very important or essential

SOURCE: UCLA Higher Research Institute, 1997

___ 1. From 1966 to 1995, the percentage of first-year college students who
cared strongly about developing a meaningful philosophy of life
went down by about half.

___ 2. From 1966 to 1995, the percentage of first-year students strongly
interested in becoming very well off financially changed very little.

___ 3. In general, from 1966 to 1995, as first-year students' interest in
developing a meaningful philosophy of life diminished, their interest
in being very well off increased.

___ 4. First-year college students' interest in promoting racial understanding
did not change in the 1990s.

___ 5. The researchers who gathered the data for this graph began asking
about racial understanding in the 1960s.

___ 6. The graph suggests that the values of first-year college students in
the United States in 1995 were quite different from the values of
first-year college students in the United States in 1966.

CHAPTER REVIEW

In this chapter, you learned the following:

- Many important ideas in reading are not stated directly, but must be inferred. To make inferences about implied ideas, use the information provided as well as your own experience and logic.

- Inferences are also a key part of reading literature and such visual materials as cartoons, tables, and graphs.

The next chapter—Chapter 9—will help make you aware of an author's purpose and tone.

On the Web: If you are using this book in class, you can visit our website for additional practice in making inferences. Go to **www.townsendpress.com** and click on "Online Exercises."

➤ Review Test 1

To review what you've learned in this chapter, answer each of the following questions about inferences.

1. We make inferences by "reading between the lines" and picking up ideas that are not directly _____ in what we are reading.

_____ 2. To draw sound inferences we must use
   A. all the information provided by the writer.
   B. our own experience.
   C. logic.
   D. all of the above.

3. A reader must make _____ when determining the meaning of words through context and when deciding on implied main ideas.

4. Creative writers often use comparisons to suggest what they mean. *Similes* are direct comparisons introduced with *like* or *as* or *as if*, and _____ are implied comparisons with *like* or *as* or *as if* omitted.

5. In textbooks we must often infer the ideas presented in diagrams called graphs and _____.

➤ Review Test 2

A. (1–4.) Put a check (✓) by the **four** inferences that are most logically based on the information given in the cartoon.

DILBERT reproduced by permission of United Feature Syndicate, Inc.

___ 1. The man in the chair is the supervisor of the man with the glasses.

___ 2. The man with glasses disapproves of his boss's behavior.

___ 3. The man with glasses would like to make his report more attractive.

___ 4. Reducing the type size and running the report through the fax machine will make the print lighter and harder to read.

___ 5. The seated man is using words to obscure, rather than clarify, meaning.

___ 6. Complicated language expresses ideas better than simple language.

___ 7. The cartoonist is criticizing how demanding bosses can be.

___ 8. The cartoonist is making fun of the way business communications are often written.

B. (5–8.) Read the following passage and then put a check (✓) by the **four** inferences that are most logically supported by the information given.

[1]As he lay dying, a friendless miser called to his bedside his doctor, pastor, and lawyer. [2]"They say you can't take it with you," the old skinflint began, "but I will prove them wrong. [3]Under my mattress, I've hidden $90,000. [4]Just before they throw the dirt into my grave, I want each of you to toss in an envelope containing $30,000." [5]At the funeral, the pastor, doctor, and lawyer secretly dropped their envelopes into the grave. [6]As they walked away from the burial plot, the pastor turned to the other two and said, "I have a confession. [7]My church desperately needs $10,000 to repair the roof, so there was only $20,000 in my envelope." [8]The doctor, moved by the pastor's admission, said, "I have to come clean as well. [9]We need $20,000 to buy equipment for the children's ward at the hospital. [10]So I only threw $10,000 into the grave." [11]The lawyer eyed both of his companions with disdain and said, "I'm appalled, outraged, and ashamed of you both. [12]My envelope contained my personal check for the entire amount."

____ 1. The miser felt he could trust the doctor, pastor, and lawyer.

____ 2. The miser secretly hoped that some of the money would go to a good cause.

____ 3. The doctor and pastor would have taken the money for only a good cause.

____ 4. The lawyer intended to use his $30,000 for a good cause as well.

____ 5. The pastor, doctor, and lawyer did not want anyone else to see them drop envelopes in the grave.

____ 6. Many people attended the funeral, glad the old man had died.

____ 7. The doctor and pastor actually took the remainder of their $30,000 for themselves.

____ 8. The lawyer is not sincere when he says he is "appalled, outraged, and ashamed."

C. (9–10.) Read the following textbook passage and then put a check (✓) by the **two** inferences that are most logically based on the information given.

> [1]The amount of eye contact differs from person to person and from setting to setting. [2]We tend to have better eye contact when we discuss topics that we are comfortable with or interested in. [3]Our eye contact also tends to be better when we are trying to influence the other person. [4]In contrast, we tend to avoid eye contact when discussing topics that make us uncomfortable or that we lack interest in. [5]We also tend to avoid eye contact when we are embarrassed, ashamed, or trying to hide something.

____ 1. A child who has "stolen" a cookie is likely to look his mother straight in the eye and deny taking the cookie.

____ 2. Salespeople are likely to have good eye contact with a person they wish to sell something to.

____ 3. A person who has asked his or her friend an important question is likely to have good eye contact when the answer is given.

____ 4. A defendant in court who wishes to be believed innocent should avoid eye contact with lawyers and the jury.

> ## Review Test 3

A. (1–4.) Read the graph below. Then put a check (✓) by the **four** statements that are most logically supported by the graph.

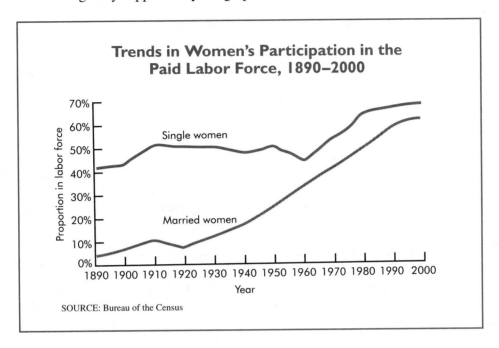

Trends in Women's Participation in the Paid Labor Force, 1890–2000

Single women

Married women

Proportion in labor force

Year

SOURCE: Bureau of the Census

_____ 1. The percentage of single women in the labor force kept growing from 1920 to 2000.

_____ 2. The percentage of married women in the labor force kept growing from 1920 to 2000.

_____ 3. From 1890 to 2000, the percentages of working married women and working single women have increased at about the same rate.

_____ 4. The percentage of single women who worked grew steadily from 1960 until about 1990.

_____ 5. The graph suggests that in 1890, a woman who got married was unlikely to work outside of the home.

_____ 6. The graph suggests that the average working single woman is making more money than the average working married woman.

_____ 7. In 1890, a majority of single women did not participate in the paid labor force.

_____ 8. In 1890, almost all single women worked for pay.

B. Identify each figure of speech as a simile or a metaphor. Then answer each inference question that follows.

_____ 5. The motivational speaker was like a cup of strong coffee for the drowsy audience.
   A. simile   B. metaphor

_____ 6. You can infer that the speaker in sentence 5 above
   A. was funny.   B. spoke clearly.   C. was energizing.

_____ 7. Paul flatters me so much that I feel as if I'm being force-fed cotton candy.
   A. simile   B. metaphor

_____ 8. You can infer that the speaker feels Paul's flattery is
   A. excessive.   B. deserved.   C. amusing.

_____ 9. The commissioner's explanations were a dense jungle to his listeners.
   A. simile   B. metaphor

_____ 10. You can infer that listeners found the commissioner's explanations to be
   A. distasteful.   B. unconvincing.   C. difficult to understand.

➤ Review Test 4

Here's a chance to apply your understanding of inferences to an excerpt from a recent, widely acclaimed memoir: *A Girl Named Zippy* by Haven Kimmel. To help you continue to strengthen your skills, the reading is followed by questions not only on what you've learned in this chapter but also on what you've learned in previous chapters.

Words to Watch

Below are some words in the reading that do not have strong context support. Each word is followed by the number of the paragraph in which it appears and its meaning there. These words are indicated in the article by a small circle (°).

evaporated (4): vanished
arced (5): moved in a curved line
deranged (7): insane
touchstone (8): a test for determining the quality of a thing
forewarned (8): warned ahead of time

A LEGENDARY MOMENT

Haven Kimmel

1   My mom and dad never fought, not really, which was a good thing, because my dad had a wicked, wicked bad temper, and if he'd married a woman who fought him, they probably would have killed each other. There was a great, legendary moment between them, though, which I'd heard about all my life.

2   One of the architectural marvels that were in my house in Mooreland was my parents' bedroom door, which was solid wood and heavy, and had a porcelain doorknob. It opened into the bedroom. At a forty-five-degree angle from the bedroom door was the closet door, which was solid wood and heavy, and had a porcelain doorknob. It also opened into the bedroom. If the closet door was open, the bedroom door could not be; if they were both halfway open, the doorknobs clinked together like little figurines in a rummage sale. It was possible, I had discovered through much trial and error, to get the doorknobs stuck together with neither door open enough to accommodate a grown person. Blocking the door in such a creative way was part of my mental plan for when and if the vampires came.

3   My mom was nine months pregnant with me, and hugely so, and she and my father were having an actual, vocal argument in their bedroom. My sister's friend Terri was visiting, and the two of them and my brother were all in the living room. The argument reached some critical phase and Mom walked out of the bedroom at the same moment that Dad decided to go in the closet, which caused the bedroom door to smack my mother in the back. She became so instantly enraged (she claimed it was pregnancy that did it) that she waited just a moment until she was sure Dad was halfway into the closet, and then she threw the bedroom door open, which sent my father flying headfirst into the closet at about sixty-four miles an hour, all the way back to where we kept the paint cans. My sister said they could hear him tumbling against the cans, and could actually discern the thick moment when he gathered himself up and prepared to face my mother.

4   He came out of the bedroom like a bullet, red-faced and with his eyebrows riding up his forehead. Mother was standing in the middle of the living room with her hands on her former hips, waiting for him. Melinda and Danny and Terri fled so quickly, and in so many different directions, that Mom later claimed they must have evaporated° into the walls. Dad finally came to a stop right in Mother's face, nose to nose, panting like a bull, with his fists clenched.

5   "Are you going to *hit* me?!?" my mother asked, pressing her forehead more aggressively into his. And before he could answer, she arced° out her own arm and slapped his right cheek, hard, He pulled away from her slightly, stunned.

6   "I said, are you going to hit me?!" and she raised her left arm, and got him on the other cheek, like a good Christian.

7   Miraculously, he walked away from her. Looking no less deranged° or murderous, he backed out of the house without taking his eyes off her, got in his truck, and drove away.

8   It became one of the touchstone° moments of their marriage, and afterward, there was never a threat of violence

between them again. Mom told me, when I was old enough to ask, that she had learned the lesson from Mom Mary, Dad's mother, who took her future daughter-in-law aside and told her that a woman has got to make herself absolutely clear, and early on. In Mom Mary's own case, she waited until she and my grandfather Anthel were just home from their honeymoon, and then sat him down and told him this: "Honey, I know you like to take a drink, and that's all right; but be forewarned° that I ain't your maid and I ain't your punching bag, and if you ever raise your hand to me, you'd best kill me. Because otherwise I'll wait till you're asleep, sew you into the bed, and beat you to death with a frying pan." Until he died, I am told, my grandfather was a gentle man.

Reading Comprehension Questions

Vocabulary in Context

_____ 1. In the sentence below, the word *discern* (dĭ-sûrn′) means:
   A. ignore.
   B. laugh at.
   C. detect.
   D. be mistaken about.

   "My sister said they could hear him tumbling against the cans, and could actually *discern* the thick moment when he gathered himself up and prepared to face my mother." (Paragraph 3)

Central Point and Main Ideas

_____ 2. Which sentence best expresses the central point of the selection?
   A. Because her parents fought so rarely, the author vividly remembers a time that they did.
   B. The author's father had a terrible temper and could have been capable of violence.
   C. The author's grandmother was a very strong woman.
   D. An argument between the author's parents made it clear that her mother would not be intimidated.

Supporting Details

_____ 3. TRUE OR FALSE? The author had personally witnessed this argument between her mother and father.

Transitions

_____ 4. The relationship between the two sentences on the next page is one of
   A. addition.
   B. time.
   C. comparison.
   D. cause and effect.

"Honey, I know you like to take a drink, and that's all right; but be forewarned that I ain't your maid and I ain't your punching bag, and if you ever raise your hand to me, you'd best kill me. Because otherwise I'll wait till you're asleep, sew you into the bed, and beat you to death with a frying pan." (Paragraph 8)

Patterns of Organization

_____ 5. Paragraph 1 contrasts
   A. this fight with all the big fights the author's parents had had before.
   B. the author's parents' tempers.
   C. the fact that the author's parents rarely fought with one occasion they did.
   D. a verbal argument with a physical fight.

Fact and Opinion

_____ 6. The sentence below contains
   A. a fact.
   B. an opinion.
   C. both a fact and an opinion.

   "At a forty-five-degree angle from the bedroom door was the closet door, which was solid wood and heavy, and had a porcelain doorknob." (Paragraph 2)

Inferences

_____ 7. The phrase "when and if the vampires came" suggests that, as a child, Kimmel
   A. believed in supernatural beings.
   B. thought that her parents were evil, like vampires.
   C. played a vampire game with other children.
   D. enjoyed reading about vampires.

_____ 8. The simile in "He came out of the bedroom like a bullet" indicates that the father
   A. had been badly wounded.
   B. was armed.
   C. had been thrust out.
   D. moved quickly toward his target.

_____ 9. The words of Kimmel's grandmother suggest that she
   A. disapproved of drinking.
   B. disliked her daughter-in-law.
   C. knew of marriages in which the husband was violent.
   D. was prone to violence.

_____ 10. A reasonable conclusion we can draw from the reading is that
- A. the author was deeply disturbed by the argument between her parents.
- B. the author thinks her mother and grandmother were abused women.
- C. the author thought her mother had gone too far in the argument with her father.
- D. the author admired her mother's spirit in standing up to her father.

Discussion Questions

1. The author describes this incident as "a great, legendary moment" that she had heard about all her life. Why do you think the incident was so important to the family? Do you have any family stories that people tell over and over again? Why do you think they are important to your family?

2. Do you think it was acceptable that the author's mother slapped her husband? Why or why not? Would you feel differently if the husband had slapped his wife? Why?

3. Within a marriage or other relationship, what would you say the rules for fair fighting should be? What kind of behavior is off-limits, in your opinion?

4. The author's mother and grandmother let their husbands know very clearly how they expected to be treated. Do you let other people know how you want them to treat you? What advice would you give people who, perhaps because of self-esteem problems, have trouble communicating their feelings and expectations?

Note: Writing assignments for this selection appear on page 631.

Check Your Performance   **INFERENCES**

Activity	Number Right	Points	Score
Review Test 1 (5 items)	_____	× 2 =	_____
Review Test 2 (10 items)	_____	× 3 =	_____
Review Test 3 (10 items)	_____	× 3 =	_____
Review Test 4 (10 items)	_____	× 3 =	_____
	TOTAL SCORE	=	_____%

Enter your total score into the **Reading Performance Chart: Review Tests** on the inside back cover.

INFERENCES: Mastery Test 1

A. (1–4.) Put a check (✓) by the **four** inferences that are most logically based on the details in the cartoon.

Copyright © 2002, The Washington Post Writers Group. Reprinted with permission.

___ 1. The cartoonist uses storks because they are associated with delivering babies.

___ 2. The cartoonist notes that most people are born into the middle class.

___ 3. She observes that many people are born into poverty.

___ 4. The cartoonist notes that a majority of people suffer from famine.

___ 5. The cartoonist is pleading for a cure for AIDS.

___ 6. She uses the wheel of fortune because it is a game of chance, not of skill.

___ 7. She is suggesting that the economic class one is born into is a matter of luck.

___ 8. The cartoonist implies that war is the cause of most poverty.

B. (5–6.) Read the passage below. Then check the **two** inferences that are most logically supported by the information given.

[1]"Does the chili have any meat in it?" the woman asked. [2]"No," answered the waiter. [3]"I'll have chili, then." [4]The waiter was disappointed, since chili was one of the restaurant's least expensive items. [5]"The lobster special is delicious," he suggested, "and healthy." [6]The woman shook her head and responded, "Not for the lobster."

(Continues on next page)

_____ 1. The woman is a vegetarian.

_____ 2. The woman was brought up as a vegetarian.

_____ 3. The waiter was hoping to get a larger tip for a more expensive meal.

_____ 4. The woman is on a tight budget.

_____ 5. The woman was alone.

C. (7–10.) Read the passage below. Then, in the spaces provided, write the letter of the most logical answer to each question, based on the information given in the passage.

[1]Mutual attraction may get us into a love relationship, but it is not the determining factor in making the relationship grow and last. [2]Two factors that make relationships endure have to do with expectations and equity. [3]When two people first fall in love, they often enjoy a mixture of romantic, sexual, and other intense feelings of love. [4]In healthy, lasting relationships this passionate love gradually shifts into compassionate love, which blends friendship, intimacy, commitment, and security. [5]If both people in the relationship anticipate and welcome this shift, the transition is managed comfortably. [6]Expectations are aligned with reality. [7]If not, the relationship can become troubled or even end because of this surprise about the nature of love or any number of other unrealistic expectations that can occur. [8]In addition, each person in the relationship needs to experience a balance between what he/she puts into the relationship and what he/she gets out of it. [9]Each needs to feel that neither too little nor too much is received when compared with what is given. [10]This equity helps make for a happy relationship.

_____ 7. We can infer that the author of this passage believes
   A. romantic love can be damaging to a relationship.
   B. the happiest couples are not physically attracted to one another.
   C. physical attraction is often strongest early in a relationship.

_____ 8. We can conclude that the author of this passage
   A. has learned through personal experience about the uncertainties in relationships.
   B. believes that realism about love increases the chance of happiness.
   C. believes that love inevitably fades after people have been together a long time.

_____ 9. We can infer from this passage that the author believes
   A. the changes that people in love go through are sad, but inevitable.
   B. compassionate love can be richly rewarding.
   C. people should change partners when feelings of romantic love fade.

_____ 10. We can conclude from the author's remarks that
   A. ideally, people in a relationship will enjoy both giving and receiving.
   B. a person who really wants a relationship to succeed will ignore his or her own needs.
   C. there is no such thing as receiving too much from a partner.

INFERENCES: Mastery Test 2

A. (1–2.) Read the passage below. Then check (✓) the **two** statements after the passage which are most logically supported by the information given.

> [1]In 1935, Harry S. Truman (who would become president eleven years later) had just been elected to the United States Senate. [2]As a brand-new senator from the Midwest, he was concerned that some of his more experienced colleagues might consider him "a sort of hick politician" who did not deserve to be part of such an important group of lawmakers. [3]But another senator, Ham Lewis, put him at his ease. [4]"Don't start out with an inferiority complex," Lewis told Truman. [5]"For the first six months, you'll wonder how you got here. [6]After that, you'll wonder how the rest of us got here."

_____ 1. This was Truman's first elected office.

_____ 2. Truman was concerned about what the other senators thought of him.

_____ 3. Truman felt he was not qualified to be a senator.

_____ 4. Ham Lewis was a close friend of Senator Truman.

_____ 5. Ham Lewis felt that after a while, Truman would not feel inferior.

B. (3–6.) Reach the passage below. Then check (✓) the **four** statements after the passage which are most logically supported by the information given.

> [1]Where does that road go? [2]How does a television set work? [3]What is that tool used for? [4]Answering these questions may have no obvious benefit for you. [5]You may not expect the road to take you anywhere you need to go, or the tool to be of any use to you. [6]Exploration and curiosity appear to be motives activated by the new and unknown and directed toward no more specific a goal than "finding out." [7]Even animals will learn a behavior just to be allowed to explore the environment. [8]The family dog will run around a new house, sniffing and checking things out, before it settles down to eat its dinner.
>
> [9]Animals also seem to prefer complexity, presumably because more complex forms take longer to know and are therefore more interesting. [10]Placed in a maze that is painted black, a rat will explore the maze and learn its way around. [11]The next time, given a choice between a black maze and a blue one, it will choose the blue one. [12]Apparently the unfamiliarity of the unknown maze has more appeal.

_____ 1. Curiosity is always stronger than great hunger.

_____ 2. We are curious about the unknown.

_____ 3. Curiosity is what separates people from animals.

_____ 4. Curiosity leads to exploration.

_____ 5. Rats are more curious than dogs.

_____ 6. Given a choice between a familiar blue maze and an unfamiliar white one, a rat will probably choose the white one.

_____ 7. Variety is interesting for its own sake.   *(Continues on next page)*

C. Read the passage below. Then, in the spaces provided, write the letter of the most logical answer to each question, based on the information given in the passage.

[1]While we say the future depends on our children, we don't feed all of them. [2]While the United States is the wealthiest nation in the world, more than 11 million American children are stuck below the poverty level. [3]Nor do we spend a lot of time with our children. [4]The time that parents spend with their children in meaningful interactions is measured in minutes per day, while the time children spend watching television is measured in hours. [5]We hope that our schools will do the job we aren't doing at home, but we pay schoolteachers a tiny percentage of what we pay professional athletes. [6]We graduate hundreds of thousands of students each year who cannot read their own high-school diplomas.

[7]We isolate our teenagers from the world, quarantining them in school buildings. [8]We give them little responsibility, and demand of them even less. [9]By cutting them off from the adult world, where they could develop a sense of competence and belonging, we leave them alienated and open to joining gangs that will give them a sense of belonging. [10]And many of us have turned away from the human values that have served all the generations that came before us. [11]We act as if enduring values are not important, and then we wonder why our children often seem so morally adrift.

_____ 7. You can infer that this author
   A. thinks society's attitude towards children is often hypocritical.
   B. does not believe our children are "morally adrift."
   C. is opposed to setting expectations for children.

_____ 8. You can infer that the author
   A. believes professional athletes are good role models for children.
   B. blames teachers for not doing a better job of teaching children to read.
   C. believes teachers deserve higher status in our society.

_____ 9. You can conclude that the author
   A. thinks teenagers need to learn to be more self-assertive.
   B. believes teenagers are hungry for a sense of belonging.
   C. does not understand why gangs are attractive to teenagers.

_____ 10. You can infer that the author of this passage is
   A. cautiously optimistic about the future of society.
   B. indifferent about the future of society.
   C. pessimistic about the future of society.

INFERENCES: Mastery Test 3

A. Read the passage below. Then, in the spaces provided, write the letter of the most logical answer to each question, based on the information given in the passage.

¹Theaters in ancient Greece, from around the fifth century B.C., were outdoors, lit only by the sun. ²A typical open-air theater was set into a hillside. ³At the base of the hill was the performance space, a flat circle about sixty feet across, paved with stone—this space was called the *orchestra,* and it served as a stage. ⁴Behind this was a stage house from which the actors (there were no actresses) made their entrances and exits. ⁵The audience seating was in a semicircle going up the slope of the hill; thus the actors were surrounded on three sides by the audience. ⁶At first, the audience probably sat in temporary wooden bleachers, but later, stone seats were used. ⁷A Greek theater was huge, holding perhaps as many as 17,000 people; in fact, the audience was a large proportion of the entire population of a city. ⁸But despite their size, these theaters had such good acoustics that an actor's whisper would carry clearly even to the top row of spectators. ⁹A striking feature of Greek theater was that each performer wore a mask covering the entire head; these masks included hair and beards as well as facial features.

_____ 1. We can infer that one reason the Greeks used a hillside for a theater was that

    A. the audience would then be too far away to notice that the actors were wearing masks.

    B. having the actors stand on a hilltop ensured that they could be plainly seen.

    C. the hill provided a convenient seating area for the audience.

_____ 2. From the passage, we can infer that the mask worn by a performer

    A. must have had a good mouth opening so that his voice could be plainly heard.

    B. had a face that was very similar to the face of the performer.

    C. was too heavy for a woman to wear.

_____ 3. The use of masks could have made it possible for

    A. one actor to take two or more roles in the same play.

    B. a male actor to take the part of a female.

    C. both of the above.

_____ 4. Performances at Greek theaters must have

    A. been too expensive for most citizens.

    B. taken place during the day.

    C. been of little interest to the average citizen.

(Continues on next page)

B. (5–10.) Ten statements follow the passage below, taken from *A Son of the Middle Border,* a literary autobiography by Hamlin Garland. The author grew up on a Midwestern farm in the 1860s and 1870s. First read the passage carefully, using the definitions as necessary. Then check (✓) the numbers of the **six** statements which are most logically supported by the information given.

> *imperative:* commanding   *resolution:* firm determination
> *impassive:* expressionless   *mused:* thought it over
> *countenance:* face

¹Slipping from my weary horse, I tied her to the rail and hurried up the walk toward the doctor's bell. ²I remembered just where the knob rested. ³Twice I pulled sharply, strongly, putting into it some part of the anxiety and impatience I felt. ⁴I could hear its imperative° jingle as it died away in the silent house.

⁵At last the door opened and the doctor, a big blond handsome man in a long nightgown, confronted me with an impassive° face. ⁶"What is it, my boy?" he asked kindly.

⁷As I told him he looked down at my water-soaked form and wild-eyed countenance° with gentle patience. ⁸Then he peered out over my head into the dismal night. ⁹He was a man of resolution°, but he hesitated for a moment. ¹⁰"Your father is suffering sharply, is he?"

¹¹"Yes, sir. I could hear him groan. ¹²Please hurry."

¹³He mused° a moment. ¹⁴"He is a soldier. ¹⁵He would not complain of a little thing—I will come."

____ 1. At the time of this narrative, the author is a boy.

____ 2. The author's ride had been a very short one.

____ 3. The author had been to the doctor's house before.

____ 4. The author was very afraid of the doctor.

____ 5. The author did not admire the doctor.

____ 6. The author's errand is an urgent one.

____ 7. The doctor was not expecting a visitor.

____ 8. The doctor did not want to go out at night for a little complaint.

____ 9. The doctor concluded that the soldier's problem deserved immediate attention.

___ 10. The doctor had been a soldier himself once.

INFERENCES: Mastery Test 4

A. Following is one of the most famous passages in the English language, from the play *The Tragedy of Macbeth* by William Shakespeare. Shakespeare has the king Macbeth speak the words below upon hearing of the death of his wife. Her death adds to the despair Macbeth feels as his power over the kingdom slips away from him.

First read the passage carefully, noting the definitions as necessary. Then, in the spaces provided, write the letter of the most logical answer to each question based on the information in the passage.

strut: walk pompously
fret: worry

. . . . Out, out, brief candle!
Life's but a walking shadow, a poor player
That struts° and frets° his hour upon the stage
And then is heard no more. It is a tale
Told by an idiot, full of sound and fury,
Signifying nothing.

_____ 1. The metaphor of the "brief candle" that goes out refers to
 A. the life of Macbeth's wife.
 B. any human life, including Macbeth's.
 C. both A and B.

_____ 2. In the metaphor of life as "a walking shadow," Macbeth suggests mainly that life is
 A. flimsy and insubstantial.
 B. ghostly.
 C. too mysterious to understand.

_____ 3. By saying life is a "poor player/that struts and frets his hour upon the stage/And then is heard no more," Macbeth implies that
 A. each life is too brief to be very significant.
 B. each person's life is of enormous value.
 C. he expects to die young.

_____ 4. By saying that life "struts and frets" upon the stage, Macbeth suggests that humanity is
 A. full of life and contentment.
 B. troubled and vain.
 C. important and special.

(Continues on next page)

337

_____ 5. When he then says that life is "a tale/Told by an idiot, full of sound and fury,/Signifying nothing," Macbeth implies that
   A. life is meaningless.
   B. people often pretend to care about things when they really do not.
   C. people of low intelligence are often angry.

B. (6–10.) Read the graph below. Then check the **five** statements that are most logically based on the graph.

World's Water Supply

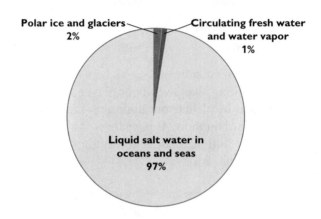

Polar ice and glaciers
2%

Circulating fresh water and water vapor
1%

Liquid salt water in oceans and seas
97%

____ 1. By far, the majority of the world's water is salt water.

____ 2. The pie graph represents 50 percent of the world's water supply.

____ 3. The pie graph represents 100 percent of the world's water supply.

____ 4. There is more water in polar ice and glaciers than there is fresh water and water vapor in the world.

____ 5. About 97 percent of the world is covered in water.

____ 6. About 1 percent of the world is covered in water.

____ 7. The water in the Pacific Ocean is part of the 97-percent section of the pie graph.

____ 8. The water that we shower in is represented in the 97-percent section of the pie graph.

____ 9. The humidity in the air is represented by the 2-percent section of the pie graph.

____ 10. Life processes of the plants and animals on land use the 1 percent of fresh water and water vapor in the world.

INFERENCES: Mastery Test 5

A. Read the following textbook passage. Then write the letter of the best answer to each question.

> [1]Scholars are limited in charting the details of early human social evolution because of the loss of evidence from natural causes. [2]But owing to the fortunate "airtight" atmospheric conditions in numerous caves of France and Spain, we know that between 33,000 and 12,000 years ago, humans produced some of the most stunning paintings in the entire history of human art. [3]In more than two hundred caves so far discovered (some as recently as 1991 and 1994), the earliest known artists painted breathtaking murals of prancing animals—bison, bulls, horses, stags, and even rhinoceroses. [4]The emphasis in this cave art was on movement. [5]Almost all of the murals depict game species running, leaping, chewing their cud, or facing the hunter at bay. [6]An ingenious device for giving the impression of motion was the drawing of additional outlines to indicate the areas in which the leg or the head of the animal had moved. [7]The cave painters sometimes achieved startling three-dimensional effects by using the natural bumps and indentations of the cave surfaces. [8]All in all, visitors today who are lucky enough to see the cave murals usually find them as stimulating as any paintings hanging in the world's foremost art museums.

_____ 1. The "natural causes" mentioned in the first sentence include
   A. religion and art.
   B. early human social evolution.
   C. weather and environmental elements that destroy evidence.
   D. animals that bury evidence.

_____ 2. The author refers to the "atmospheric conditions in numerous caves" as being fortunate because those conditions
   A. sheltered the ancient artists.
   B. kept the artwork from being washed away or disintegrating.
   C. were comfortable for the animal models.
   D. created the "natural bumps and indentations" that inspired the artists.

_____ 3. The author implies that
   A. artists have learned little throughout the centuries.
   B. the cave artists were creative and talented.
   C. the cave artwork was done quickly.
   D. at the time of the cave painters, interest in art was unusual.

_____ 4. The paintings reveal that
   A. hunting was a central activity of the time.
   B. meat was a major food of the time.
   C. rhinoceroses existed at the time in France and Spain.
   D. all of the above.

(Continues on next page)

_____ 5. We can conclude that
  A. the cave drawings were the first paintings in the history of human-kind.
  B. one or two artists made all of the drawings.
  C. the natural bumps of the caves may have been used to emphasize an animal's shape.
  D. all of the above.

B. (6–10.) Read the chart below. Then put a check (✓) by the **five** inferences that are most logically based on the chart.

The World of Prime-time TV Dramas versus the Real World

Compare the percentages of people and behaviors on American TV network dramas with those in the real world.

Item Viewed	Seen on Television (%)	In the Real World (%)
Female	33	51
Married	10	61
Blue-collar	25	67
Having a religious affiliation	6	88
Implied intercourse: partners unmarried	85	unknown
Beverages consumed: percentage alcoholic	45	16

SOURCE: *Social Psychology*, Sixth Edition (McGraw-Hill, 1999)

_____ 1. About a third of the characters on prime-time TV are females.

_____ 2. About a third of the real-world population is female.

_____ 3. TV producers must feel that prime-time audiences are more interested in women than in men.

_____ 4. TV producers probably feel that married life is less interesting to prime-time viewers than single life.

_____ 5. Almost all of the people in TV dramas drink alcohol.

_____ 6. Almost half of all the beverages consumed on TV are alcohol.

_____ 7. To prepare this table, someone must have counted the numbers of male and female, married, and blue-collar characters on prime-time shows.

_____ 8. The suggestion of sex among single people is avoided on prime-time television.

_____ 9. Religion is avoided on prime-time television.

_____ 10. Prime-time TV dramas are a mirror of real life in America.

INFERENCES: Mastery Test 6

A. (1–5.) Read the following editorial. Then check (✓) the **five** statements which are most logically supported by the information given.

> [1]The American health-care system is clearly in crisis. [2]But no one speaks of the obvious solution: a nationwide program of universal health care—one that covers every single American—administered by the federal government.
>
> [3]It's not that we could not establish such a system—dozens of countries have already managed to do so, with great success. [4]Americans simply have a gut-level conviction that competition and the profit motive—the free market, in other words—is the only way to maintain the "best health-care system in the world."
>
> [5]The truth of the matter is quite the contrary. [6]The American health-care system has the highest operating expenses (14 percent) among the systems of all other industrialized countries. [7]The obvious reason is that for-profit corporations run most of the system. [8]In contrast, the government system in Canada, often characterized here as "inefficient," runs with exactly 1 percent overhead. [9]Our own Social Security runs on about 2 percent overhead.
>
> [10]You see the overhead when you go to a medical facility and spend more time filling out forms than seeing the doctor; when you count the number of staff talking to insurance companies on the phone, and realize that they rival the number of medical personnel in the office. [11]You see the overhead in the salaries of the CEOs of health-related corporations. [12]In 2000 five top CEOs made annual salaries ranging from $11 million to $54 million. [13]A system is clearly broken that simultaneously produces huge salaries for executives and yet pays nurses' aides salaries that do not allow them to live above the poverty line, or to afford the very health care they are providing.

____ 1. The Canadian health-care system is run on a not-for-profit basis.

____ 2. Most American doctors oppose the idea of a universal health-care program.

____ 3. The current American health-care system is wasteful and inefficient.

____ 4. Executives of American health-related corporations oppose the idea of a universal health-care program.

____ 5. Canadian nurses' aides are more highly paid than American nurses' aides.

____ 6. The American Social Security program is run on a for-profit basis.

____ 7. The American public needs to make a more informed choice about health care.

____ 8. Many working Americans cannot afford health care.

(Continues on next page)

____ 9. The American health-care system helps promote good relationships between patients and doctors.

____ 10. Insurance companies are probably trying to convince the federal government to install a universal health-care system.

B. (6–10.) Read the following textbook passage. Then check (✓) the **five** statements which are most logically supported by the information given.

> ¹Humans are characterized by both biologically and socially determined wants. ²We seek food, clothing, shelter, and the many goods and services associated with a comfortable or affluent standard of living. ³We are also blessed with aptitudes and surrounded by quantities of property resources—both natural and manufactured. ⁴We use available human and property resources—labor and managerial talents, tools and machinery, land and mineral deposits—to produce goods and services which satisfy material wants. ⁵This is done through the organizational mechanism we call the economic system.
>
> ⁶Quantitative considerations, however, rule out an ideal solution. ⁷The blunt fact is that the total of all our material wants is beyond the productive capacity of available resources. ⁸Thus, absolute material abundance is not possible. ⁹This unyielding fact is the basis for our definition of economics: economics is concerned with the efficient use or management of limited productive resources to achieve maximum satisfaction of human material wants. ¹⁰Though it may not be self-evident, all the headline-grabbing issues of the day—inflation, unemployment, health care problems, government and international trade deficits, free-trade agreements among nations, poverty and inequality, pollution, and government regulation of business—are rooted in the one issue of using limited resources efficiently.

____ 1. The "biologically . . . determined wants" in paragraph 1 include cars.

____ 2. The "biologically . . . determined wants" in paragraph 1 include food.

____ 3. "Socially determined wants" might include sunshine.

____ 4. "Socially determined wants" might include television sets.

____ 5. Economics is based on absolute material abundance.

____ 6. Economics is based on the need to manage limited resources.

____ 7. Economics can lead to an ideal solution to resource management.

____ 8. Economic issues are rarely discussed in newspapers.

____ 9. The economic system organizes the way members of society share resources.

____ 10. Every society has some kind of economic system.

9
Purpose and Tone

There is an author—a person with thoughts, feelings, and opinions—behind everything you read. Whether this person is a sports writer, a newspaper columnist, a novelist, or a friend sending you a letter, he or she works from a personal point of view. That point of view is reflected in (1) the *purpose* of a piece of writing as well as (2) its *tone*—the expression of the author's attitude and feeling. Both purpose and tone are discussed in this chapter.

PURPOSE

Authors write with a reason in mind, and you can better evaluate their ideas by determining what that reason is. The author's reason for writing is also called the **purpose** of a selection. Three common purposes are as follows:

- To **inform**—to give information about a subject. Authors with this purpose wish to provide facts that will explain or teach something to readers.

  For example, the main idea of an informative paragraph about watching television might be "American children spend nearly as much time watching TV as they do in school." The author may then go on to provide evidence from research studies that show how many hours children watch TV.

- To **persuade**—to convince the reader to agree with the author's point of view on a subject. Authors with this purpose may give facts, but their main goal is to argue or prove a point to readers.

  The main idea of a persuasive passage about watching TV might be "Parents should not allow their children to watch more than two hours of TV each day." The author might then go on to support that main idea with details about the negative impact of such passive watching and the benefits of spending more time reading, studying, playing outdoors, and so on.

- To **entertain**—to amuse and delight; to appeal to the reader's senses and imagination. Authors with this purpose entertain in various ways, through fiction and nonfiction.

  The main idea of a humorous paragraph about watching TV might be "I'm very proud to say that my family always sits down to dinner together; there are five of us, my husband and me, our son and daughter, and the TV set."

While the cover and title of anything you read—books, articles, and so on—don't necessarily suggest the author's main purpose, often they do. Here are the covers of three books. See if you can guess the primary purpose of each of these books.

  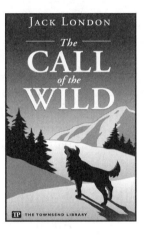

___ Primary purpose:	___ Primary purpose:	___ Primary purpose:
A. to inform	A. to inform	A. to inform
B. to persuade	B. to persuade	B. to persuade
C. to entertain	C. to entertain	C. to entertain

As you probably concluded, the main purpose of the textbook is to inform; the main purpose of *Fast-Food Nation* is to persuade (note the subtitle: "The Dark Side of the All-American Meal"); and the main purpose of the timeless story *The Call of the Wild* is to entertain.

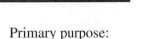 **Check Your Understanding**

Read each of the three paragraphs on the next page and decide whether the author's main purpose is to inform, to persuade, or to entertain. Write in your answers, and then read the explanation that follows.

1. Athletes should not earn millions of dollars a year. If they weren't paid so much, then tickets to sports events wouldn't have to be so expensive, and more people could enjoy sports more often. Also, more reasonable pay would make for better role models for young people, many of whom look up to sports figures.

   Purpose: _____

2. The Bubonic plague, also called the Black Death, swept Europe, Asia, and Africa from 1346 to 1353. So deadly was this disease that it killed one-third of the population of these continents. The plague was spread by fleas infected with bacteria from diseased rats. When it resulted in pneumonia, coughing spread the bacteria directly through the air.

   Purpose: _____

3. Men don't even notice 97 percent of the beauty efforts women make. For example, the average woman spends five thousand hours per year worrying about her fingernails. But I have never once, in more than forty years of listening to men talk about women, heard a man say, "She has a nice set of fingernails!" Many men would not notice if a woman had upward of four hands.

   Purpose: _____

Explanation:

In the first paragraph, the writer's purpose is *to persuade* readers that "athletes should not earn millions of dollars a year." The word *should* is a clue to the author's persuasive intention. Words like *should, ought,* and *must* are often meant to convince us rather than to inform us.

The purpose of the second paragraph is *to inform.* The author is providing readers with factual details about the Black Death.

In the third paragraph, the playful and exaggerated details about the beauty efforts of women tell us that the author's main goal is *to entertain* with humor.

Note: At times, writing may blend two or even three purposes. A persuasive article on the importance of avoiding junk foods, for example, might include a good many facts and even some comic touches. Remember in such cases to focus on the author's primary purpose. Ask yourself, "What is the author's main idea?"

➤ *Practice 1*

Label each item according to its main purpose: to inform (**I**), to persuade (**P**), or to entertain (**E**).

_____ 1. More than one-fourth of American children now live in single-parent families.

_____ 2. I read the obituaries every morning; if I don't find my name, I get dressed and go to work.

_____ 3. Television networks should reduce the number of commercials shown during children's programs.

_____ 4. Nowadays about half of U.S. marriages end in divorce.

_____ 5. American school systems must adopt a year-long schedule in order to become more competitive with international schools.

_____ 6. Many people in my family are seafood eaters. When they see food, they eat it.

_____ 7. The seeds of many fruits, including cherries, apples, plums, peaches and apricots, contain a form of cyanide that can be deadly when eaten in large amounts.

_____ 8. Cosmetic companies that test their products on animals don't deserve your business; please buy from cruelty-free companies instead.

_____ 9. The reason that koala bears appear so calm and sleepy-eyed is that they are slightly drugged from the eucalyptus leaves they feed on.

_____ 10. I had an uncle who knew when he was going to die; the warden told him.

➤ *Practice 2*

Following are three passages, one each from a textbook, a humor book, and a collection of essays. In the spaces provided, write the letter of the best description of the purpose of each passage.

_____ 1. ¹If we accept the notion that one goal of the judicial system is to rehabilitate people, our recidivism rate—the percentage of those released from prison who are later arrested for other crimes—shows how inadequate our criminal justice system really is. ²Depending on the particular study, this rate runs somewhere between 30 and 80 percent. ³The crime rate among former prisoners is actually much higher, for the recidivism rate represents only those who are rearrested. ⁴Part of the reason for recidivism is a penal system that produces contempt and hatred—attitudes hardly conducive to law-abiding behavior. ⁵To lower our recidivism rate, we must reform our penal system.

The main purpose of this passage is to
A. inform readers about the penal system.
B. convince readers that the penal system needs reforming.
C. amuse readers with an interesting view of human nature.

_____ 2. ¹I have thought about exercise. ²Read about it. ³Watched it. ⁴Even considered it. ⁵Doctors recommend it, especially when they can't think of anything else to say. ⁶When you're over fifty you go to the doctor and you're telling him that this hurts and that hurts and that you're tired all the time. ⁷You know the doctor just wants to blurt out: "What the blazes do you expect? ⁸You're o-l-d. ⁹Old!" ¹⁰But they don't say that, because they like to have you keep coming in so they can just kind of look you over and charge you three hundred bucks. ¹¹At my last checkup, I was complaining about a multitude of maladies visiting my body. ¹²(Most have since moved in.) ¹³And the doctor looked bored—kind of listless, like he might need a checkup himself—and said rotely what he always says, "Are you getting enough exercise?" ¹⁴I replied that I did not exercise at all, which I considered just about the right amount.

The main purpose of this passage is to
A. explain the drawbacks of exercise.
B. persuade people never to trust doctors.
C. entertain with humorous details about aging and doctors.

_____ 3. ¹At the beginning of the twentieth century, school administrators in Paris wanted to relieve overcrowding by removing youngsters who did not have the capacity to benefit from an academic education. ²They called in the psychologist Alfred Binet and asked him to devise a test to identify those children. ³The test that Binet developed was the precursor of a wide variety of tests that try to assign intelligence a numerical score. ⁴Binet's approach focused on finding children who were least likely to benefit from an education. ⁵Today, intelligence testing is also used to identify children with special strengths who can benefit from a richer teaching program.

The main purpose of this passage is to
A. inform readers about the origin and purpose of intelligence tests.
B. persuade readers to take intelligence tests.
C. entertain readers with a story about the origin of intelligence tests.

TONE

A writer's **tone** reveals the attitude that he or she has toward a subject. Tone is expressed through the words and details the writer selects. Just as a speaker's voice can project a range of feelings, a writer's voice can project one or more tones, or feelings: anger, sympathy, hopefulness, sadness, respect, dislike, and so on. Understanding tone is, then, an important part of understanding what an author has written.

To appreciate the differences in tone that writers can employ, read the following statements by employees of fast-food restaurants:

"I hate this job. The customers are rude, the managers are idiots, and the food smells like dog chow." (*Tone:* bitter, angry.)

"I have no doubt that flipping burgers and toasting buns will prepare me for a top position on Wall Street." (*Tone:* mocking, sarcastic.)

"I love working at Burger Barn. I meet interesting people, earn extra money, and get to eat all the chicken nuggets I want when I go on break." (*Tone:* enthusiastic, positive.)

"I'm not excited about wearing fluorescent green polyester uniforms, but the managers are willing to schedule me around my classes, and the company offers scholarships to hard-working employees." (*Tone:* fair-minded, objective.)

➤ Practice 3

Following are five reactions to an aggressive driver weaving his car dangerously in and out of traffic. Label each statement with the tone of voice that you think is present. Choose each tone from the following box, and use each tone only once.

A. angry	B. questioning	C. sarcastic
D. cautious	E. self-pitying	

_____ 1. "Oh my God—I hope he doesn't hit me. This always happens to me. No matter where I go, something like this happens."

_____ 2. "That lousy jerk—he acts like he owns the road! He'd better not try cutting in front of me."

_____ 3. "That man's driving a little dangerously. I'm going to slow down so there's some distance between his car and ours."

_____ 4. "What makes someone drive like that? Are they on drugs? Are they in emotional pain? Are they just flat-out crazy?"

_____ 5. "Well, there's a careful, considerate driver. I want everyone in this car to pay special attention to him, so you can learn how a mature driver acts."

Words That Describe Tone

Below and on the next page are two lists of words commonly used to describe tone. With the exception of the words *matter-of-fact* and *objective*, the words reflect a feeling or judgment. The words in the first list are more familiar ones. Brief meanings are given in parentheses for the words in the second list. Refer to these meanings as needed to learn any words you don't know yet.

Some Words That Describe Tone

admiring	cruel	loving
affectionate	curious	playful
amused	defensive	praising
angry	doubtful	respectful
apologetic	encouraging	self-pitying
ashamed	excited	serious
calming	forgiving	sorrowful
caring	frightened	sympathetic
cheerful	grateful	threatening
conceited	humorous	tragic
concerned	insulting	warm
critical	joyous	worried

More Words That Describe Tone—with Their Meanings

ambivalent	*(uncertain about a choice)*
arrogant	*(full of self-importance; conceited)*
bewildered	*(confused; puzzled)*
bitter	*(angry; full of hate)*
compassionate	*(deeply sympathetic)*
depressed	*(very sad or discouraged)*
detached	*(emotionally uninvolved)*
disbelieving	*(unbelieving)*
distressed	*(suffering sorrow, misery, or pain)*
hypocritical	*(false)*
impassioned	*(filled with strong feeling)*
indignant	*(angry about something unfair or mean)*
instructive	*(teaching)*
ironic	*(contrary to what is expected or intended)*

(Continues on next page)

More Words That Describe Tone—with Their Meanings

lighthearted	(*happy and carefree*)
matter-of-fact	(*sticking to facts; unemotional*)
mocking	(*making fun of and/or looking down upon something*)
nostalgic	(*longing for something or someone in the past*)
objective	(*not influenced by feelings or personal prejudices*)
optimistic	(*looking on the bright side of things*)
pessimistic	(*looking on the gloomy, unfavorable side of things*)
pleading	(*begging*)
prideful	(*full of pride or exaggerated self-esteem*)
remorseful	(*guilty over a wrong one has done*)
revengeful	(*wanting to hurt someone in return for an injury*)
sarcastic	(*sharp or wounding; ironic*)
scheming	(*tricky*)
scornful	(*looking down on someone or something*)
self-mocking	(*making fun of or looking down on oneself*)
sentimental	(*showing tender feelings; romantic; overly emotional*)
solemn	(*involved with serious concerns*)
straightforward	(*direct and honest*)
superior	(*looking down on others*)
tolerant	(*respectful of other views and behavior; patient about problems*)
uncertain	(*doubting*)

☑ Check Your Understanding

On the next page are five statements expressing different attitudes about an old car. Five different tones are used:

optimistic	disappointed	tolerant
humorous	angry	

Label each statement according to which of these five tones you think is present. Then read the explanation that follows.

_____ 1. Unfortunately, this car is a lot less reliable than I'd like.

_____ 2. It's not the greatest car in the world, but it usually takes me where I have to go.

_____ 3. If car dealers weren't so dishonest, I wouldn't have bought this piece of junk for so much money.

_____ 4. Even though the car has a problem now and then, I bet it'll keep running forever.

_____ 5. This car is so old it's eligible for an antique-vehicle license plate.

Explanation:

The first item has a disappointed tone because of the words *unfortunately* and *less reliable than I'd like.* In the second item, the phrase *usually takes me where I have to go* shows the writer's accepting attitude, giving the item a tolerant tone. The tone of the third item is angry because of the writer's clearly stated resentment of car dealers, of the car itself, and of its price tag. The bet in the fourth item that the car will "keep running forever" gives that item an optimistic tone. And finally, the obvious exaggeration in the last item imparts a humorous tone.

A Note on Irony and Sarcasm

One commonly used tone is **irony**, which involves a contrast between expectations and reality. This contrast often is humorous. Both language and situations can be ironic.

Following are a few examples of **sarcasm**, an often biting form of verbal irony. Notice that the irony of each quotation lies in the contrast between what is said and what is actually meant.

- If the price tag on a shirt you like is double what you'd expect, you might mutter, "What a bargain."

- After sitting through the first session of what is clearly going to be a very boring class, you say to a classmate, "I only hope I can stand all the excitement."

- If someone is unusually attractive and talented, we might remark, "Poor Laura. She's got absolutely nothing going for her."

- After seeing your favorite basketball team play its worst game ever, you might comment, "I knew they wouldn't disappoint me."

- Your sister comes home from a blind date, saying, "It was great once I understood the rules. You see, his job was to talk about himself 100 percent of the time, and my job was to nod."

As you can see, irony is a useful tone for humor and can be used to imply exactly the opposite of what is said or what is done.

Irony also refers to situations that involve a contrast between what is expected or intended and what actually happens. We could call it ironic, for example, if the arsonist responsible for a string of fires turned out to be a city firefighter, or if a bank is robbed by two guards that were hired to protect it. Here are a few more examples of this type of irony:

- An expensive computer system is installed to help a company manage its files. Several weeks later, it crashes, and all the files are lost.

- A doctor tells a man that he'd better exercise if he wants to stay healthy. So the man begins jogging. One day while jogging across a street, he is hit by a truck and dies instantly.

- A woman loved dancing, but her boyfriend did not dance well. So she insisted he take dancing lessons. After he started taking lessons, he fell in love with his dancing teacher.

- After being told they could never have children, a couple adopts a baby. A few months later, the wife becomes pregnant.

- In a story called "The Interlopers," two lifelong enemies are trapped when a tree falls upon them. Injured and helpless, they decide to forget their feud and become friends. Minutes later, they are attacked and killed by wolves.

The five examples above show that irony also describes meaningful situations that are contrary to what is intended or expected.

☑ Check Your Understanding

Look now at the cartoon below. Then identify the quotations from the cartoon as either straightforward or ironic (in which what is said is sarcastically the opposite of what is really meant) by circling the letter of your choice.

DILBERT reproduced by permission of United Feature Syndicate, Inc.

_____ 1. "If we know our senior executive is making a bad decision, shouldn't we tell her?"

   A. straightforward   B. ironic

_____ 2. "Let's end our careers by challenging a decision that won't change. That's a great idea."

   A. straightforward   B. ironic

_____ 3. "And let's pull our neckties until it hurts."

   A. straightforward   B. ironic

Explanation:

Note the contrast in tone within the cartoon:

1. In the first box, the tone of the words is straightforward—the speaker is serious.

2. What is said in the second box is ironic—it says the opposite of what the speaker really means. For instance, the speaker does not mean, "That's a great idea." The speaker is really saying, "That's a terrible idea."

3. The words on the right in the third box continue the irony by suggesting that causing themselves pain is as good an idea as challenging the boss's decision.

➤ Practice 4

A. Below and on the next page are five statements expressing different attitudes about going on a blind date. Five different tones are used:

A. pessimistic	B. self-pitying	C. ironic
D. enthusiastic	E. angry	

For each statement, write the letter of the tone that you think is present. Use each tone once.

_____ 1. Me go on a blind date? Oh sure, I've always wanted to meet Dracula's daughter.

_____ 2. I just know I'm going to hate this guy my mother's making me go out with. These things never work out.

_____ 3. No way I'm going on a blind date! You've got a lot of nerve trying to set me up. What do you think I am—desperate?

_____ 4. I'd love it if you'd fix me up with your cousin from out of state. It sounds like a lot of fun.

_____ 5. Oh, I suppose I'll go on a blind date. That's probably the only kind of date I can get.

B. The following conversation between an office worker and his boss involves five of the tones shown in the box below. For each statement, write the letter of the tone that you think is present. Five tones will be left over.

A. self-mocking	B. contented	C. indignant	D. sentimental
E. impatient	F. sarcastic	G. optimistic	H. lighthearted
I. apologetic	J. threatening		

_____ 6. "You're working too slow, Wilson! Where's that report? I'm tired of waiting for it!"

_____ 7. "Oh, I *am* sorry, Mr. Henderson. I can't imagine why I haven't finished the report in between the hours and hours of filing and typing you've asked me to do today, not to mention the two cross-town errands you've sent me on."

_____ 8. "Wilson, if you don't get that report done today, I'm going to fire you!"

_____ 9. "That's it, Mr. Henderson. I've taken all the stupid abuse I'm going to take. Your big mouth is making my life miserable! You can't fire me— because *I quit!*"

_____ 10. "Please, Wilson, don't be hasty. I fly off the handle sometimes and say things I don't mean. Listen—I'll clear your schedule tomorrow so you can finish the report."

➤ Practice 5

Each passage on the pages that follow illustrates one of the tones in the box below. In each space, put the letter of the one tone that best applies. Don't use any letter more than once. Three tones will be left over.

Remember that the tone of a selection reflects the author's attitude. To find the tone of a paragraph, ask yourself what attitude is revealed by its words and phrases.

A. admiring	B. bewildered	C. matter-of-fact	D. hopeful
E. nostalgic	F. uncertain	G. critical	H. playful

_____ 1. Clay comes out to meet Liston
And Liston starts to retreat.
If Liston goes back any further,
He'll end up in a ringside seat.
Clay swings with a left; 5
Clay swings with a right.
Look at young Cassius
Carry the fight.
Liston keeps backing
But there's not enough room. 10
It's a matter of time.
There, Clay lowers the boom.
Now Clay swings with a right.
What a beautiful swing.
And the punch raises the bear, 15
Clear out of the ring.
Liston is still rising
And the ref wears a frown,
For he can't start counting,
Till Sonny comes down. 20
Now Liston disappears from view.
The crowd is getting frantic,
But our radar stations have picked
   him up.
He's somewhere over the Atlantic.
Who would have thought 25
When they came to the fight
That they'd witness the launching
Of a human satellite?
Yes, the crowd did not dream
When they laid down their money 30
That they would see
A total eclipse of the Sonny!

(Recited by Cassius Clay, later known as Muhammad Ali, before his first fight with Sonny Liston)

_____ 2. [1]I never go back to my old neighborhood these days; it's changed for the worse, and now I hardly recognize it. [2]Instead, I prefer to visit that place in my memory. [3]There the old neighborhood lives on as it used to be. [4]Long-dead neighbors still sweep the sidewalks in front of their tidy rowhouses. [5]Children play stickball or jump "double dutch" in the narrow streets. [6]During the dog days of summer, all the kids from the block cool off at the fireplug. [7]In the evening the grownups sit out on the front steps sipping from beer cans. [8]Laughter echoes up and down the street. [9]The summer goes on forever, and we never have to go back to school. [10]Sure, it's all gone now, and I know it probably wasn't as wonderful as I recall it, but for me the memory of the old neighborhood is better than what it's become.

_____ 3. [1]Erik Erikson developed the dreary psychological theory that, from the moment of birth, life consists of a number of stages, each characterized by an issue to be resolved and a "virtue" to be obtained. [2]The task for newborns, to begin with, is to resolve the issue of "basic trust versus mistrust," though probably all they want to do is sleep, eat, and gurgle. [3]Toddlers are supposed to concentrate not on their teddy bears but on working out the issue of "autonomy versus shame and doubt"; preschoolers must take up the task of "initiative versus guilt." [4]And so it goes. [5]Erikson will not even let us die in peace. [6]Old folks, who might prefer just to put their feet up and relax after eighty years of confronting their dismal chores, are expected to resolve "integrity versus despair" before departing this world. [7]Erikson maintains that if we fail a task at any stage, we are in for serious trouble during the next, so those of us who manage to perish before completing this final task will have to face wrath in the afterlife.

_____ 4. [1]I have a dream that one day this nation will rise up and live out the true meaning of its creed: "We hold these truths to be self-evident; that all men are created equal."

[2]I have a dream that one day on the red hills of Georgia the sons of former slaves and the sons of former slave owners will be able to sit down together at the table of brotherhood.

[3]I have a dream that one day even the state of Mississippi, a desert state sweltering with the heat of injustice and oppression, will be transformed into an oasis of freedom and justice.

[4]I have a dream that my four little children will one day live in a nation where they will not be judged by the color of their skin but by the content of their character.

(From Dr. Martin Luther King, Jr.'s speech at the 1963 March on Washington)

_____ 5. [1]People's behavior is hard to understand. [2]To put it bluntly, every single one of us knows that every other one of us is going to die someday. [3]Our friends, our enemies, our family members, our classmates, our neighbors, our teachers, the guy who serves us our hamburger at McDonald's, ourselves, everybody. [4]Not only are we all aware of our own mortality, but we also know that every human being is dealing with painful, difficult realities of life every day. [5]We're all hurting; we're all struggling in some way or another. [6]Knowing all this, you'd think that people would go out of their way to be as kind and gentle to one another as they possibly could. [7]I mean, we're not here for very long—why not try to be a comfort to each another? [8]Instead, day after day, we beat each other up. [9]We do it on a personal level, on a community level, and certainly on a global level. [10]Why? [11]What is it we think we're gaining by being cruel to one another? [12]Can anyone explain this to me?

➤ Practice 6

Read the following short essay by noted science and science-fiction writer Isaac Asimov (1920–1992). Then answer the questions about purpose and tone that follow.

KP (1): work with the "kitchen police," soldiers who assist the army cooks
bents (2): tendencies
oracles (3): messages from the gods
foist (4): force
arbiter (4): judge

indulgently (6): done to go along with someone's wishes
raucously (6): loudly
smugly (6): in a self-satisfied way

What Is Intelligence, Anyway?

1   What is intelligence, anyway? When I was in the Army, I received a kind of aptitude test that all soldiers took and, against a normal of 100, scored 160. No one at the base had ever seen a figure like that, and for two hours they made a big fuss over me. (It didn't mean anything. The next day I was still a buck private with KP° as my highest duty.)

2   All my life I've been registering scores like that, so that I have the complacent feeling that I'm highly intelligent, and I expect other people to think so, too. Actually, though, don't such scores simply mean that I am very good at answering the type of academic questions that are considered worthy of answers by the people who make up the intelligence tests—people with intellectual bents° similar to mine?

3   For instance, I had an auto repairman once, who, on these intelligence tests, could not possibly have scored more than 80, by my estimate. I always took it for granted that I was far more intelligent than he was. Yet, when anything went wrong with my car, I hastened to him with it, watched him anxiously as he explored its vitals, and listened to his pronouncements as though they were divine oracles°—and he always fixed my car.

4   Well then, suppose my auto repairman devised questions for an intelligence test. Or suppose a carpenter did, or a farmer, or, indeed, almost anyone but an academician. By every one of those tests, I'd prove myself a moron. And I'd *be* a moron, too. In a world where I could not use my academic training and my verbal talents but had to do something intricate or hard, working with my hands, I would do poorly. My intelligence, then, is not absolute but is a function of the society I live in and of the fact that a small subsection of that society has managed to foist° itself on the rest as an arbiter° of such matters.

5   Consider my auto repairman, again. He had a habit of telling me jokes whenever he saw me. One time he raised his head from under the automobile hood to say, "Doc, a deaf-and-dumb guy went into a hardware store to ask for some nails. He put two fingers together on the counter and made hammering motions with the other hand. The clerk brought him a hammer. He shook his head and pointed to the two fingers he was hammering. The clerk brought him nails. He picked out the sizes he wanted, and left. Well, Doc, the next guy who came in was a blind man. He wanted scissors. How do you suppose he asked for them?"

6   Indulgently°, I lifted my right hand and made scissoring motions with my first two fingers. Whereupon my auto repairman laughed raucously° and said, "Why, you dumb jerk, he used his *voice* and asked for them." Then he said, smugly°, "I've been trying that on all my customers today." "Did you catch many?" I asked. "Quite a few," he said, "but I knew for sure I'd catch *you*." "Why is that?" I asked. "Because you're so goddamned educated, Doc, I *knew* you couldn't be very smart."

7   And I have an uneasy feeling he had something there.

_____ 1. In paragraph 4, the author refers to himself with a(n)
    A. egotistical tone.
    B. tragic tone.
    C. humble tone.

_____ 2. When discussing his auto repairman, the author generally uses a(n)
    A. loving tone.
    B. admiring tone.
    C. doubtful tone.

_____ 3. In referring to those who determine what intelligence is (in the last sentence of paragraph 4), the author uses a
    A. confused tone.
    B. lighthearted tone.
    C. critical tone.

_____ 4. In paragraph 6, the comments of the repairman have a
    A. straightforward tone.
    B. angry tone.
    C. superior tone.

_____ 5. Asimov's main purpose in this reading is to
    A. inform readers of the traditional view of intelligence tests.
    B. persuade readers that the traditional view of intelligence is inadequate.
    C. entertain readers with several colorful anecdotes.

CHAPTER REVIEW

In this chapter, you learned that part of reading critically is to do the following:

- Be aware of an author's **purpose**: the reason why he or she writes. Three common purposes are to inform, to persuade, and to entertain.

- Be aware of **tone**—the expression of the author's attitude and feeling about a subject. A writer's tone might be objective—the case in most textbook writing—or it might be lighthearted, sympathetic, angry, affectionate, respectful, or any of many other tones shown on pages 349–350.

    One important tone to recognize is **irony**: saying one thing but meaning the opposite.

    The final chapter in Part One—Chapter 10—will explain another part of reading critically: recognizing an author's point and evaluating the support for that point.

On the Web: If you are using this book in class, you can visit our website for additional practice in identifying an author's purpose and tone. Go to **www.townsendpress.com** and click on "Online Exercises."

➤ Review Test 1

To review what you've learned in this chapter, answer the following questions by filling in the blank or writing the letter of the correct answer.

_____ 1. The main purpose of a textbook is to
   A. inform.   B. persuade.   C. entertain.

_____ 2. The main purpose of an adventure story, mystery novel, or other work of fiction is to
   A. inform.   B. persuade.   C. entertain.

3. Just as a speaker's voice can project a range of feelings, a writer's voice can project one or more _____, attitudes, or feelings.

4. If a writer says one thing but means just the opposite, the writer's tone is _____.

_____ 5. TRUE OR FALSE? Textbook writing tends to be matter-of-fact and objective in tone, rather than reflecting feelings or judgments.

➤ Review Test 2: Purpose

In the space provided, indicate whether the primary purpose of each passage is to inform (**I**), to persuade (**P**), or to entertain (**E**).

_____ 1. ¹As a TIME subscriber, and one of our most valued customers, you are being extended this unusual invitation:
   ²When you pay early for your next one-year term, you can send a FREE yearlong gift to *anyone* you choose.
   ³You have several things to gain, should you accept:
   • ⁴The recipient of your gift is sure to appreciate your generosity and good taste.
   • ⁵The ULTRONIC AM/FM Radio—FREE!
   • ⁶You'll save 67% off the newsstand price on your own subscription.
   • ⁷We've also included a FREE gift card (enclosed) to announce your gift personally.

[8]Of course, TIME also has something to gain: the opportunity to acquaint your friend or relative with TIME. [9]We're confident that the person you choose will find that TIME'S perspective on the news is more valuable than ever before. [10]As a regular reader, you know that TIME'S analysis of world events offers unique insights into our ever-changing world so you can better determine how the news impacts your daily life.

[11]So let us hear from you *now*.

_____ 2. [1]Many people who have come close to death from drowning, cardiac arrest, or other causes have described near-death experiences—profound, subjective events that sometimes result in dramatic changes in values, beliefs, behavior, and attitudes toward life and death. [2]These experiences often include a new clarity of thinking, a feeling of well-being, a sense of being out of the body, and visions of bright lights or mystical encounters. [3]Such experiences have been reported by an estimated 30 to 40 percent of hospital patients who were revived after coming close to death and by about 5 percent of adult Americans in a nationwide poll. [4]Near-death experiences have been explained as a response to a perceived threat of death (a psychological theory); as a result of biological states that accompany the process of dying (a physiological theory); and as a foretaste of an actual state of bliss after death (a transcendental theory).

_____ 3. [1]Without question the most important invention in human history, next to frozen yogurt, is the computer. [2]Without computers, it would be virtually impossible for us to accomploiwer xow;gtkc,mg^&)

[3]Hold it, there seems to be a keyboard problem here. [4]Let me just try plugging this cable into . . .

[5]ERROR ERROR ERROR ALL FILES HAVE BEEN DESTROYED YOU STUPID BAZOOTYHEAD

[6]Ha ha! [7]Considering what a wonderful invention computers are, they certainly have a way of making you sometimes feel like pouring coffee into their private parts and listening to them scream. [8]Of course you should not do this. [9]The first rule of data processing is: "Never pour hot beverages into a computer, unless it belongs to somebody else, such as your employer."

_____ 4. [1]America—it's been the land of justice and opportunity. [2]It's been the land where you don't have to be born rich or privileged in order to get a fair chance in life. [3]This is the America that I've always believed in. [4]But Congress doesn't always work on behalf of everyday people. [5]The 2003 federal tax cut is a case in point. [6]A number of congressional members wanted more of the benefits of that tax cut to go to the country's millionaires, but they were restricted by their need to limit the cuts to $350 billion. [7]Then they made a shameful decision. [8]They had already created a $400-per-child tax credit. [9]With a few cold-hearted strokes of the pen, they added some fine print to that credit so that the poorest American families don't get that credit. [10]Many of these families belonged to military personnel who were fighting overseas for their country during the war in Iraq. [11]The result of the Congressional cuts was that American millionaires would get an extra $93,000 annually. [12]But American parents struggling to get by on $10,000 to $26,000 a year would get zero—nothing. [13]This reverse Robin Hood tactic on the part of Congress—stealing from the poor to give to the rich—was a heartless moment in our political history. [14]Let's not forget it the next time we vote for our representatives and senators.

_____ 5. [1]Mortal combat was one of the most popular sports in ancient Rome. [2]Bouts began with contestants—called gladiators—marching into the arena and acknowledging the Roman leader with the words "Hail, Caesar, we who are about to die salute you." [3]After this formality, the gladiators were given weapons as well as protective clothing. [4]Once armed, they began fighting. [5]Crowds enjoyed a skillful, courageous, and evenly matched fight. [6]If the loser was not killed, the event's sponsor decided his fate. [7]A thumbs-up sign meant the loser would be allowed to heal so he could fight another day. [8]Thumbs down meant that he would immediately have his throat cut by the winner's sword. [9]An actor dressed as a god would then emerge and spear the body to make certain he was dead. [10]The tattered body was then hooked behind a horse and dragged away and the entire arena sprayed with perfume, after which the crowd settled contentedly back for the next contest.

➤ **Review Test 3: Tone**

Each of the following five passages illustrates one of the tones in the box below. In the space provided, put the letter of the tone that best applies to each passage. Don't use any letter more than once. Three tones will be left over.

Remember that the tone of a selection reflects the author's attitude. To find the tone of a paragraph, ask yourself what attitude is revealed by its words and phrases.

A. admiring	B. ironic	C. frightened	D. regretful
E. forgiving	F. encouraging	G. puzzled	H. amused

_____ 1. ¹I wished the guy in the seat behind the bus driver would stop looking at me the way he did. ²He gave me the creeps. ³I was really glad when my stop came and I could get off the bus. ⁴It didn't take me long to realize, however, that he was getting off too. ⁵"Please, God, let him go the other way," I thought. ⁶I turned toward home. ⁷The streets were darker and emptier than I remembered they could be. ⁸His footsteps followed mine. ⁹When I walked faster, he did too. ¹⁰When I crossed to the other side, he crossed too. ¹¹Finally, I began to run. ¹²My vision was blurred by the tears in my eyes.

_____ 2. ¹Somewhere around midterm, almost every student feels like saying, "I just can't learn anything else. ²My brain is full!" ³Well, don't give up so easily—your brain has more room than you think. ⁴Scientists believe that memories are stored in the part of the brain called the cerebrum. ⁵If you were to store ten bits of information each second of your life, by your one-hundredth birthday, your memory-storage area would be only half full. ⁶So the next time you feel your brain is about to short circuit, take a break and then come back to those books, knowing you've got plenty of room in your head for more learning.

_____ 3. ¹Since the advent of voice mail and then e-mail, the concept of "business hours" has become obsolete. ²Before these technologies arrived on the scene, one telephoned office workers only between approximately 9 a.m. and 5 p.m. ³In fact, business etiquette dictated that one shouldn't call before 9:30 in the morning—this was to give the person one was calling time to settle in at his or her desk before having to answer the phone. ⁴Nor did a polite person call close to the end of the day, to avoid delaying people who might be clearing off their desks preparatory to going home. ⁵It was also thought inconsiderate to telephone during the lunch hour. ⁶All that has changed. ⁷Callers can now leave voice-mail messages at any time of the day or night, and e-mail arrives steadily around the clock. ⁸This is of course efficient, and a boon for people living and working in different time zones, but it has also meant the end of some practices that were once part of good manners.

_____ 4. ¹The Civil War general Stonewall Jackson had the odd belief that one of his arms was bigger than the other. ²As a result, he always walked and rode with that arm raised, so that his blood would drain into his body. ³He was a champion sleeper. ⁴More than once he fell asleep at the dinner table with food in his mouth. ⁵At one battle, his lieutenants found him all but impossible to awaken and lifted him, still asleep, onto his horse, where he continued to slumber while shells exploded around him. ⁶When awake, Jackson would often march his troops all over a battle area in such illogical and unexplainable ways that he earned a reputation among enemy officers for cleverness and cunning. ⁷Jackson owes some of his fame to the fact that he had the best nickname any soldier has ever enjoyed. ⁸That name may have come from his habit of standing inert, like a stone wall, when a charge was called for.

_____ 5. ¹Clare has a heart-shaped face with a lovely dimple when she smiles, a rosy complexion, and moon-shaped eyebrows over brown eyes that glisten when she's happy but become dark holes when she's not. ²She's seven inches taller than me—about five foot five—but my shortness has never seemed to faze her. ³She doesn't respond to the surface of things, to mere appearances. ⁴She connects on a different level. ⁵She speaks carefully, choosing words as if each one were a little vessel for carrying a thought from her mind to another's, and she likes nothing better than to probe deeply into another person's experiences or life history. ⁶She prefers to deal with no more than two or perhaps three people at a time. ⁷Crowds bewilder her. ⁸Cocktail parties and receptions make her impatient.

➤ Review Test 4

Here is a chance to apply your understanding of purpose and tone to a passage from a college textbook, *The Art of Public Speaking,* Sixth Edition, by Stephen E. Lucas (McGraw-Hill). This reading is about why and how to listen actively.

To help you continue to strengthen your skills, the reading is followed by questions not only on what you've learned in this chapter but also on what you've learned in previous chapters.

Words to Watch

Below are some words in the reading that do not have strong context support. Each word is followed by the number of the paragraph in which it appears and its meaning there. These words are indicated in the article by a small circle (°).

assess (5): evaluate
constituents (5): members of a group represented by an elected official
momentous (8): important
unduly (8): excessively
gaunt (8): bony and thin
finished (8): skilled
uncultivated (8): unpolished
unscrupulous (10): immoral
premise (15): argument
macabre (19): gruesome

HOW TO BECOME A BETTER LISTENER

Stephen E. Lucas

1   The first step to improvement is always self-awareness. Analyze your shortcomings as a listener and commit yourself to overcoming them. Good listeners are not born that way. They have *worked* at learning how to listen effectively. Good listening does not go hand in hand with intelligence, education, or social standing. Like any other skill, it comes from practice and self-discipline.

2   You should begin to think of listening as an active process. So many aspects of modern life encourage us to listen passively. We "listen" to the radio while studying or "listen" to the television while moving about from room to room. This type of passive listening is a habit—but so is active listening. We can learn to identify those situations in which active listening is important. If you work seriously at becoming a more efficient listener, you will reap the rewards in your schoolwork, in your personal and family relations, and in your career.

3   In an ideal world, we could eliminate all physical and mental distractions. In the real world, however, this is not possible. Because we think so much faster than a speaker can talk, it's easy to let our attention wander while we listen. Sometimes it's very easy—when the room is too hot, when construction machinery is operating right outside the window, when the speaker is tedious. But our attention can stray even in the best of circumstances—if for no other reason than a failure to stay alert and make ourselves concentrate.

4   Whenever you find this happening, make a conscious effort to pull your mind back to what the speaker is saying. Then force it to stay there. One way to do this is to think a little ahead of the speaker—try to anticipate what will come next. This is not the same as jumping to conclusions. When you jump to conclusions, you put words in the speaker's mouth and don't actually listen

to what is said. In this case you will listen—and measure what the speaker says against what you had anticipated.

5   Another way to keep your mind on a speech is to review mentally what the speaker has already said and make sure you understand it. Yet another is to listen between the lines and assess° what a speaker implies verbally or says non-verbally with body language. Suppose a politician is running for reelection. During a campaign speech to her constituents° she makes this statement: "Just last week I had lunch with the President, and he assured me that he has a special concern for the people of our state." The careful listener would hear this implied message: "If you vote for me, there's a good chance more tax money will flow into the state."

6   To take another example, suppose a speaker is introducing someone to an audience. The speaker says, "It gives me great pleasure to present to you my very dear friend, Nadine Zussman." But the speaker doesn't shake hands with Nadine. He doesn't even look at her—just turns his back and leaves the podium. Is Nadine really his "very dear friend"? Certainly not.

7   Attentive listeners can pick up all kinds of clues to a speaker's real message. At first you may find it difficult to listen so intently. If you work at it, however, your concentration is bound to improve.

8   If you had attended Abraham Lincoln's momentous° Cooper Union speech of 1860, this is what you would have seen:

The long, ungainly figure upon which hung clothes that, while new for this trip, were evidently the work of an unskilled tailor; the large feet and clumsy hands, of which, at the outset, at least, the orator seemed to be unduly° conscious; the long, gaunt° head, capped by a shock of hair that seemed not to have been thoroughly brushed out, made a picture which did not fit in with New York's conception of a finished° statesman.

But although he seemed awkward and uncultivated°, Lincoln had a powerful message about the moral evils of slavery. Fortunately, the audience at Cooper Union did not let his appearance stand in the way of his words.

9   Similarly, you must be willing to set aside preconceived judgments based on a person's looks or manner of speech. Einstein had frizzy, uncombed hair and wore sloppy clothes. Gandhi was a very unimpressive-looking man who often spoke dressed in a simple white cotton cloth. Helen Keller, deaf and blind from earliest childhood, always had trouble articulating words distinctly. Yet imagine if no one had listened to them. Even though it may tax your tolerance, patience, and concentration, don't let negative feelings about a speaker's appearance or delivery keep you from listening to the message.

10   On the other hand, try not to be misled if the speaker has an unusually attractive appearance. It's all too easy to assume that because someone is good-looking and has a polished delivery, he or she is speaking eloquently. Some of the most unscrupulous° speakers in history have been attractive people with hypnotic delivery skills. Again, be sure you respond to the message, not the package it comes in.

11   Unless we listen to people who think exactly as we do, we are going to hear things with which we disagree. When this happens, our natural inclination is to argue

mentally with the speaker or to dismiss everything he or she says. But neither response is fair—to the speaker or to ourselves. In both cases we blot out any chance of learning or being persuaded.

12   Does this mean you must agree with everything you hear? Not at all. It means you should hear people out *before* reaching a final judgment. Try to understand their point of view. Listen to their ideas, examine their evidence, assess their reasoning. *Then* make up your mind. If you're sure of your beliefs, you need not fear listening to opposing views. If you're not sure, you have every reason to listen carefully. It has been said more than once that a closed mind is an empty mind.

13   As we have seen, skilled listeners do not try to absorb a speaker's every word. Rather, they focus on specific things in a speech. Here are three suggestions to help you focus your listening.

14   Most speeches contain from two to four main points. Here, for example, are the main points of a speech by Raymond W. Kelly, former Police Commissioner of New York City.

1. The increasing level of crime and violence has become a serious problem throughout the United States.
2. The best way to deal with the problem at the national level is for Congress to pass strict gun control laws.
3. The best way to deal with the problem at the local level is by instituting community policing programs.

These main points are the heart of Kelly's message. As with any speech, they are the most important things to listen for.

15   Unless a speaker is terribly scatterbrained, you should be able to detect his or her main points with little difficulty. Often at the outset of the speech, a speaker will give some idea of the main points to be developed. For example, in his introduction Kelly said, "My premise° today is that we have gotten far too accustomed to, and accepting of, crime and violence." He also stated that "the vehicles to help us regain some ground over violent crime are there. One is gun control and the other is community policing." Noticing these remarks, a sharp listener would have been prepared for a speech with three main points—one dealing with the problem of crime and violence, one dealing with gun control, and one dealing with community policing.

16   Identifying a speaker's main points is not enough. You must also listen for supporting evidence. By themselves, Kelly's main points are only assertions. You may be inclined to believe them because they come from a respected law-enforcement official. Yet a careful listener will be concerned with evidence no matter who is speaking. Had you been listening to Kelly's speech, you would have heard him support his point about the problem of crime and violence with an abundance of verifiable evidence. Here's an excerpt:

17   There's no doubt about how violent we have become. The annual homicide rate in America is now about 22 for every 100,000 Americans. In Canada the rate is 3 for every 100,000 Canadians. In Japan it is less than 1. . . .

18   The number of guns in private hands about doubles in America every 20 years—to the point that there are now over 200 million guns in circulation. That compares to 54 million in 1950. . . . We confiscated

nearly 20,000 illegal guns in New York City last year. . . .

19 The fact is we have become too tolerant of murder. In New York City there has somehow arisen a new benchmark for homicides. Over 2,000 homicides is considered bad. Up to 2,000 is, well, somehow "expected," or acceptable. The old chestnut of laying things end-to-end to get a sense of proportion becomes frighteningly macabre° when you realize that 2,000 bodies end-to-end would stretch for over two miles.

20 There are four basic questions to ask about a speaker's evidence:

- Is it accurate?
- Is it taken from objective sources?
- Is it relevant to the speaker's claims?
- Is it sufficient to support the speaker's point?

21 In Kelly's case, the answer to each question is yes. His figures about guns in the United States, murders in New York City, and homicide rates for the United States, Canada, and Japan are well established in the public record and can be verified by independent sources. The figures are clearly relevant to Kelly's claim about the seriousness of crime and violence, and they are sufficient to support that claim. If Kelly's evidence were inaccurate, biased, irrelevant, or insufficient, you should be wary of accepting his claim.

22 You should be on guard against unfounded assertions and sweeping generalizations. Keep an ear out for the speaker's evidence and for its accuracy, objectivity, relevance, and sufficiency.

23 We said earlier that you should not let a speaker's delivery distract you from the message, and that is true. However, if you want to become an effective speaker, you should study the methods other people use to speak effectively. When you listen to speeches—in class and out—focus above all on the content of a speaker's message; but also pay attention to the techniques the speaker uses to get the message across.

24 Analyze the introduction: What methods does the speaker use to gain attention, to relate to the audience, to establish credibility and goodwill? Assess the organization of the speech: Is it clear and easy to follow? Can you pick out the speaker's main points? Can you follow when the speaker moves from one point to another?

25 Study the speaker's language: Is it accurate, clear, vivid, appropriate? Does the speaker adapt well to the audience and occasion? Finally, diagnose the speaker's delivery: Is it fluent, dynamic, convincing? Does it strengthen or weaken the impact of the speaker's ideas? How well does the speaker use eye contact, gestures, and visual aids?

26 As you listen, focus on the speaker's strengths and weaknesses. If the speaker is not effective, try to determine why. If he or she is effective, try to pick out techniques you can use in your own speeches. If you listen in this way, you will be surprised how much you can learn about successful speaking.

27 This is why many teachers require students to complete evaluation forms on their classmates' speeches. To fill in the form conscientiously, you must listen carefully. But the effort is well worth the rewards. Not only will you provide valuable feedback to your classmates about their speeches, you will also find yourself becoming a much more efficient listener.

Reading Comprehension Questions

Vocabulary in Context

_____ 1. In the excerpt below, the word *ungainly* (ŭn-gān′lē) means
   A. handsome.
   B. small.
   C. awkward.
   D. confident.

> "The long, ungainly figure, . . . the large feet and clumsy hands, . . . the long, gaunt head . . . made a picture that did not fit in with New York's conception of a finished statesman." (Paragraph 8).

Central Point and Main Ideas

_____ 2. Which sentence best expresses the central point of this selection?
   A. Physical appearance can greatly affect the impression a speaker makes on an audience.
   B. Good speeches usually contain between two to four main points.
   C. There are various techniques people can use to improve their ability to listen to others.
   D. Many speakers reveal much about their feelings through body language.

_____ 3. Which sentence best expresses the main idea of paragraphs 9–10?
   A. Einstein and Gandhi were not the most physically attractive people.
   B. You should avoid judging speakers by their appearance and manner of speech.
   C. Attractive people are often able to give very powerful speeches.
   D. Einstein, Gandhi, and Keller were worth listening to.

Supporting Details

_____ 4. According to the author, the main points of a speech are
   A. not as important as you might think.
   B. the only thing to listen for.
   C. usually saved for the conclusion.
   D. the most important thing to listen for.

Transitions

_____ 5. The relationship between the sentences on the next page is one of
   A. addition.
   B. cause and effect.
   C. comparison.
   D. contrast.

"We said earlier that you should not let a speaker's delivery distract you from the message, and that is true. However, if you want to become an effective speaker, you should study the methods other people use to speak effectively." (Paragraph 23)

Patterns of Organization

_____ 6. In paragraphs 4–6, the author
   A. describes a series of events in the order in which they happened.
   B. lists ways to keep your mind on a speech.
   C. discusses the effects of speeches.
   D. defines and illustrates a term.

Fact and Opinion

_____ 7. Which of the following is a statement of opinion?
   A. "The annual homicide rate in America is now about 22 for every 100,000 Americans."
   B. "The best way to deal with the problem at the national level is for Congress to pass strict gun control laws."
   C. "We confiscated nearly 20,000 illegal guns in New York City last year."
   D. "The number of guns in private hands about doubles in America every 20 years—to the point that there are now over 200 million guns in circulation."

Inferences

_____ 8. The author implies that active listening is
   A. a useful job skill.
   B. easy.
   C. hard to explain.
   D. encouraged in our society.

Purpose and Tone

_____ 9. The author's main purpose in writing this selection is to
   A. entertain readers with anecdotes about various speakers.
   B. convince readers of the importance of active listening and inform them how to become active listeners.
   C. persuade readers that they should never judge people by their appearance, whether seemingly attractive or unattractive.
   D. warn readers against making long speeches.

_____ 10. The author's tone throughout this selection may be characterized as
   A. sarcastic.
   B. uncertain.
   C. instructive.
   D. sentimental.

Discussion Questions

1. The author asserts that if you learn to be an active listener, you will be rewarded "in your schoolwork, in your personal and family relations, and in your career." What do you think might be some of the rewards of active listening in these areas? Be specific.

2. Which of Lucas's suggestions for active listening are most relevant and valuable for you? Be specific.

3. The author claims that "aspects of modern life encourage us to listen passively." Do you agree? Is the "listening" you do when watching TV different from the listening you do in a conversation with someone? How?

4. In explaining how to be a better listener, the author also suggests how to be a good speaker. On the basis of the reading, what are some guidelines for making a good speech?

Note: Writing assignments for this selection appear on page 632.

Check Your Performance   **PURPOSE AND TONE**

Activity	Number Right	Points	Score
Review Test 1 (5 items)	_____	× 2 =	_____
Review Test 2 (5 items)	_____	× 6 =	_____
Review Test 3 (5 items)	_____	× 6 =	_____
Review Test 4 (10 items)	_____	× 3 =	_____
		TOTAL SCORE =	_____%

Enter your total score into the **Reading Performance Chart: Review Tests** on the inside back cover.

PURPOSE AND TONE: Mastery Test 1

A. In the space provided, indicate whether the primary purpose of each item is to inform (**I**), to persuade (**P**), or to entertain (**E**).

_____ 1. More than half of adult Americans are overweight, and more than a fifth are obese.

_____ 2. Fast-food chains should not be allowed to advertise their high-fat, high-calorie products to children.

_____ 3. I get my exercise every day by lifting weights: my heavy arms and legs.

_____ 4. Medical problems associated with obesity include high cholesterol, high blood pressure, gallbladder disease, arthritis, diabetes, breast cancer, and colon cancer.

_____ 5. My son explained that the healthy vegetable side of his stomach felt full, but that the dessert side was very empty.

B. Each of the following passages illustrates better than the others one of the five different tones identified in the box below. In the space provided, put the letter of the tone that best applies to each passage. Use each tone once.

A. humble	B. objective	C. disappointed
D. compassionate	E. disbelieving	

_____ 6. [1]As I turned onto Stanton Street early one Sunday morning, I saw a chicken walking a few yards ahead of me. [2]"What's this about?" I thought. [3]The chicken seemed to know just where it was going. [4]I started walking faster than the chicken, so I gradually caught up. [5]"I am actually following a chicken," I said to myself. [6]The chicken turned south on Eighteenth. [7]At the fourth house along, it turned in at the walk, hopped up the front steps, and rapped sharply on the metal storm door with its beak. [8]After a moment, the door opened and the chicken went in. [9]I just stood there for a minute, looking at the closed door. [10]I didn't know what to think or say.

_____ 7. [1]America is losing one of its treasures. [2]In our efforts to have a world where everything we need is close at hand, we have allowed national retail chains like Burger King and Home Depot to spread across the country. [3]Sure, the stores make it easier to pick up a quick hamburger or buy a cheaper pair of pliers. [4]Yet the stores are causing the loss of

(Continues on next page)

small-town America. [5]Gone are the "mom and pop" stores and restaurants that used to be part of our neighborhoods. [6]Gone or dying are the regional differences that kept American culture so dynamic and vibrant. [7]Instead, America is becoming a nation of cookie-cutter Wal-Marts and stark, sprawling strip malls. [8]For each chain store that sprouts in our neighborhood like a weed, many small family-owned stores—old members of our communities—are forced to close forever.

_____ 8. [1]I guess it is hard for some people to understand why this was, why she kept going back to him when he treated her so badly. [2]I guess trying to explain it is futile, since it would be like trying to explain starving to someone who thinks hungry is being late for dinner. [3]Her life had slipped into a dull routine of sacrifice and loneliness, and these times with him offered at least a sliver of hope, a promise of what other people had. [4]She kept going back, even after she realized he might never change, not because she loved him in that pitiful way some women love bad men, but because there were whole months at a time when he did pay the electric bill, when he did give her money for groceries. [5]There were long months when he held his children with something very close to love, when he was sober, mostly, and kind. [6]There were nights at the table when he sat with a baby on his lap and spoon-fed him, and laughed when one of us daubed food in his face.

_____ 9. [1]The barber's red and white spiral-striped pole has its origins in bloodletting. [2]Bloodletting involves removal of small amounts of blood from the body. [3]During the Middle Ages it was considered a remedy for many ailments. [4]Barbers took up bloodletting as a result of their regular trips to monasteries. [5]Besides having the crowns of their heads shaved, medieval monks were required to undergo periodic bloodletting. [6]Barbers simply combined the two services. [7]In villages, barbers placed outside their doors white cloths reddened with blood to indicate the times thought best for bleeding (April, May, and September). [8]Today's barber pole reflects this early form of advertising.

_____ 10. [1]In Calcutta [wrote Mother Teresa], some time ago, we went out at night and picked up four or five people from the street and took them to our Home for the Dying. [2]One of them was in a very bad condition, and I wanted to take care of her myself. [3]I did for her all that my love could do. [4]When I put her into bed, she took hold of my hand, and there was such a wonderful smile on her face. [5]She said simply: "Thank you," and she died. [6]She gave me much more than I had given her. [7]She gave me her grateful heart, and I thought: What would I have done in her place? [8]My answer was: I would have tried to draw some attention to myself; I would have said: I am hungry or I am cold or I am dying. [9]But she, she was so great, she was so beautiful in her giving.

PURPOSE AND TONE: Mastery Test 2

A. In the space provided, indicate whether the primary purpose of each item is to inform (**I**), to persuade (**P**), or to entertain (**E**).

_____ 1. To reduce crime and make the city safer for residents, police must enforce the new curfew and keep teenagers off the streets at night.

_____ 2. My brother says that I was so ugly as a kid that my mother had to tie a pork chop around my neck to get our dog to play with me.

_____ 3. Scientists are almost certain that a catastrophic collision between the Earth and a large meteor will happen sometime in the next fifty thousand years.

_____ 4. Congress should focus its attention on passing laws to protect children from the spread of pornography on the Internet.

_____ 5. When I saw my daughter dumping large amounts of salt on her food, I asked, "Would you like a little dinner with your salt?"

_____ 6. [1]The shrew, a small animal similar to a mouse or a mole, measures two inches long from the tip of its nose to the tip of its tail. [2]It weighs only a few ounces. [3]Despite its small size, the shrew has a bite as deadly as that of a poisonous snake and eats as much as two times its own weight each day. [4]It attacks and kills animals much larger than itself. [5]Its main weapons are tiny needle-like teeth and a deadly saliva, which contains an unusually strong poison. [6]A special gland in the shrew's mouth produces this venom.

_____ 7. [1]If manufacturers of children's breakfast cereals were honest, they would call their products names like "Too Much Sugar Crisps" and "Fake Fruit Flakes." [2]Breakfast foods targeting children are filled with excess sugars and unnecessary chemical dyes. [3]Such foods condition young children to start their days with sweetened foods, making them more likely to continue eating heavily sugared foods as adults. [4]In addition, these cereals are often more expensive than healthier foods. [5]When shopping for children's breakfast foods, parents should leave these little boxes of sugar chips where they belong—on store shelves.

(Continues on next page)

B. Each of the following passages illustrates one of the tones identified in the box below. In each space provided, put the letter of the tone that applies to the passage. (Three tone choices will be left over.)

A. ambivalent	B. admiring	C. grim -
D. instructive	E. sarcastic	F. critical

_____ 8. ¹Throughout life, you are going to be lonely at times, you are going to have your heart broken on occasion, and you are going to feel as if something is missing from your life. ²No life is lived without some amount of pain and heartache. ³No matter how bad things get, however, make sure you are always developing into the kind of person you want to be, and the kind of person others will want to be around. ⁴It is important not to let external factors keep you from growing into a quality person—the type of person others will like and you will be proud of.

_____ 9. ¹Imagine a man who spends thirty years of his life in jail. ²The charge he was convicted of? ³Fighting to win equal rights for his people. ⁴Imagine that the years in prison were harsh. ⁵Among the tasks he was forced to do was breaking rocks, and the irritation of stone dust permanently damaged his eyesight. ⁶What kind of person would it take to endure this and much more and yet emerge unbroken in mind and spirit? ⁷Such a man is Nelson Mandela. ⁸And what is hardest of all to imagine is that he would become president of the nation that jailed him and that he would forgive those who did so. ⁹Truly, Mandela is an awesome person.

_____ 10. ¹The rise in personal debt in recent years is due largely to aggressive and unwarranted hustling by credit-card companies. ²In the last ten years, credit-card debt doubled. ³Today it is still rising. ⁴Credit cards with interest rates reaching nearly 20 percent are a remarkably lucrative part of the loan business. ⁵Debtors pay an average of a thousand dollars a year in interest and fees alone, money that could instead have been used for a college or retirement fund. ⁶Using subtle tactics to tempt unwary consumers to borrow, credit-card companies have led consumers to hold more cards and to fork over a bigger and bigger fraction of their income to the companies.

PURPOSE AND TONE: Mastery Test 3

A. Eight italicized quotations in the story below are preceded by a blank space. Identify the tone of each italicized quotation by writing in the letter of one of these tones. (Two tone choices will be left over.)

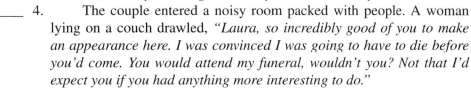

A. inviting	B. forgiving	C. disbelieving	D. sarcastic
E. outraged	F. optimistic	G. pessimistic	H. apologetic
I. malicious	J. matter-of-fact		

The family reunion was in full swing when Laura and her boyfriend, Brian, pulled up at the house. Laura looked at the street lined with cars and sighed.

_____ 1.   Brian smiled. *"Don't worry, Laura. The family that produced you has got to be great. It's going to be fun meeting them all, even crazy Uncle Erwin."*

_____ 2.   "That's Uncle Edwin, and I didn't say he was crazy. I said he was vicious," said Laura. *"You'll probably leave this reunion saying you want nothing to do with someone from such a crazy family."*

_____ 3.   Just then the front door swung open and a voice called out, *"It's Laura! Hi, honey. I'm so glad to see you. Come on in, you two."*

_____ 4.   The couple entered a noisy room packed with people. A woman lying on a couch drawled, *"Laura, so incredibly good of you to make an appearance here. I was convinced I was going to have to die before you'd come. You would attend my funeral, wouldn't you? Not that I'd expect you if you had anything more interesting to do."*

_____ 5.   "Hello, Mother," Laura answered. *"I'd like to introduce Brian Miller, my friend from college. Brian, this is my mother."*

_____ 6.   An enormous man then approached Brian and Laura. Glaring down at the couple, he laughed unpleasantly. *"What's the matter, Laura, couldn't you find a full-size boyfriend?"* he sneered. *"I think this one is the littlest shrimp I've seen you with yet!"*

_____ 7.   "Uncle Edwin!" shouted Laura. *"I have warned you before, and I'm not going to put up with your rudeness anymore!"* With those words, Laura picked up a pitcher of lemonade and dashed it in Uncle Edwin's face.

As if on signal, quarrels broke out all over the room. Shouts and then punches began to fly. The sound of breaking windows was heard over the hubbub.

(Continues on next page)

_____ 8.   Several hours later, sitting in the quiet of Laura's apartment, Brian was still shaking his head. *"Tell me again that all that wasn't staged just for my benefit,"* Brian said to Laura for the fifth time. *"Is it possible that people honestly act like that in real life?"*

"To tell you the truth," answered Laura, "that was one of the tamest reunions we've had in years."

B. In the space provided, indicate whether the primary purpose of each passage is to inform (**I**), to persuade (**P**), or to entertain (**E**).

_____ 9.   [1]Some students spend their first weeks in college lost in a dangerous kind of fantasy. [2]They feel, "All will be well, for here I am in college. [3]I have a student ID in my pocket, a sweatshirt with the college name on it, and textbooks under my arm. [4]All this proves I am a college student. [5]I have made it. [6]The worst is now behind me." [7]Such students have succumbed to a fantasy we all at times succumb to: the belief that we will get something for nothing. [8]But everyone knows from experience that this hope is a false one. [9]Life seldom gives us something for nothing—and students must understand that school won't either.

_____ 10.   [1]A community of nuns living in the Bronx faced a problem when their dog died. [2]There was too much tar and concrete in the Bronx for easy burial, so the nuns decided to put their old German shepherd in a big suitcase. [3]They would take their beloved pet to a convent in Yonkers, New York, where there was land enough for a decent burial. [4]Two of the sisters lugged the heavy suitcase to the subway. [5]At the station a courteous man helped the women in the brown Franciscan habits to lift the load onto the train. [6]On the crowded train two passengers gave up their seats to the sisters, and the kind man took a position with the suitcase not far behind them. [7]All seemed to be going well until they arrived at their stop, when a big surprise awaited them. [8]Their suitcase was gone, obviously stolen by the man who was not so nice after all. [9]Happily, their surprise was not the only surprise of the day.

PURPOSE AND TONE: Mastery Test 4

A. Eight quotations in the story below are preceded by a blank space. Identify the tone of each italicized quotation by writing in the letter of one of these tones. (Two tone choices will be left over.)

A. apologetic	B. relieved	C. joking	D. scolding
E. admiring	F. comforting	G. horrified	H. threatening
I. critical	J. downhearted		

Elena and Dan walked away from the movie theater discussing their reactions to the film they had just seen.

_____ 1. *"Didn't you think the acting was great? I just think the whole cast did a great job,"* Elena said.

_____ 2. *"The movie was short on plot, though. It really had no story at all,"* Dan said.

Before heading down the steps into the subway, Elena reached into her purse for her wallet.

_____ 3. *"Oh no!"* she cried. *"My wallet's gone!"*

_____ 4. *"Now, take it easy. You're probably just not spotting it,"* Dan said soothingly. *"Let's take a better look under the street light."*

"No, it's gone," Elena said after searching. "It must have fallen out when I put my purse down at our seats. We have to hurry back!"

When Elena and Dan arrived back at the theater, only the staff remained. "I've lost my wallet," Elena told an usher. "Please let us into the auditorium. We need to look for it at our seats."

The usher agreed.

_____ 5. *"I'm sorry about this, Dan,"* Elena said with some embarrassment as they searched.

"Hey, it could happen to anybody."

_____ 6. After searching without success, Elena said, *"I've lost thirty dollars and all my I.D. cards. What's most depressing is that somebody took my wallet—not just the money, but everything else too."*

Just then the usher approached them. "Would you describe your wallet for me?" she asked Elena.

"It was denim," Elena answered. "Blue denim with tan trim."

"Then here you are," the usher said with a grin, handing Elena her wallet.

_____ 7. *"That's it! Thank goodness!"* said Elena, beaming.

_____ 8. "Someone turned it in right after the movie." Then the usher giggled. *"I guess you're lucky the movie was* Act of Kindness. *That must have inspired the right emotion."*

(Continues on next page)

B. Read the passage below. Then carefully consider the questions that follow it, and, in the spaces provided, write the letters of the best responses.

[1]The United States has always been a diverse society. [2]In 1673, more than three centuries ago, a visitor to what is now New York City was astonished to find that eighteen languages were spoken among the city's eight thousand inhabitants. [3]By the middle of the nineteenth century, so many people from so many lands had come to the United States that the novelist Herman Melville exclaimed, "You cannot spill a drop of American blood without spilling the blood of the whole world."

[4]One can only imagine what Melville would say today! [5]The United States has become the most diverse society on the face of the Earth. [6]For more than a century, most immigrants to the United States were Europeans—Irish, Germans, English, Scandinavians, Greeks, Poles, Italians, and others. [7]Together with African Americans, they made America the "melting pot" of the world. [8]Today another great wave of immigration— more than one million people a year, mostly from Asia and Latin America— is transforming the United States into what one writer has called the "first universal nation," a multicultural society of unmatched diversity.

_____ 9. The primary purpose of this paragraph is to
  A. inform readers that the United States is and always was a diverse society.
  B. persuade readers that a multicultural society is the best type of society.
  C. entertain readers with colorful facts about the United States.

_____ 10. The tone of this paragraph is one of
  A. distress.
  B. amazement.
  C. tolerance.
  D. compassion.

PURPOSE AND TONE: Mastery Test 5

Read the paragraphs below. Then carefully consider the questions that follow, and, in the spaces provided, write the letters of the best responses.

A. ¹Habitat for Humanity is a program aimed at eliminating substandard housing and homelessness around the world. ²Habitat employees and dedicated volunteers work together to build new homes and renovate old ones that are then sold at no profit to families in need. ³The Habitat volunteers are rewarded with a keen sense of accomplishment and strong bonds of friendship. ⁴New volunteers are needed throughout the country to continue the work of this wonderful organization. ⁵No special building skills are required. ⁶Wouldn't you like to join the thousands who have enabled more than 300,000 people around the world to live in sturdy, decent housing?

_____ 1. The primary purpose of this paragraph is to
   A. inform readers about the existence and work of Habitat for Humanity.
   B. persuade readers to volunteer to help Habitat for Humanity.
   C. entertain readers with details about an interesting organization.

_____ 2. The main tone of this paragraph can be described as
   A. compassionate.   C. admiring.
   B. humble.   D. lighthearted.

B. ¹Our country has lost its head when it comes to gun control. ²When the framers of the United States Constitution said that people have the right to bear arms, they did not mean high-powered automatic rifles and assault weapons. ³Such guns are designed to kill—not defend. ⁴The long range and high power of these weapons jeopardize the safety of people miles away from where the gun is fired. ⁵No one is safe as long as these guns are available. ⁶And each time another one is manufactured and brought into a neighborhood, America's streets become more dangerous. ⁷We have a right to be safe at home, but these weapons do not guarantee safety. ⁸They prevent it. ⁹Until we outlaw them once and for all, we will have to live like prisoners in our own homes.

_____ 3. The primary purpose of this passage is to
   A. inform.
   B. persuade.
   C. entertain.

_____ 4. The tone of this paragraph can be described as
   A. objective.   C. sarcastic and revengeful.
   B. impassioned and indignant.   D. relaxed and chatty.

(Continues on next page)

C.   [1]During our daily bouts of pessimism, we can see its constructive role in our lives. [2]In these mild forms, pessimism serves the purpose of pulling us back a bit from the risky exaggerations of our optimism, making us think twice, keeping us from making rash, foolhardy gestures. [3]The optimistic moments of our lives contain the great plans, the dreams, and the hopes. [4]Reality is gently distorted to give the dreams room to flourish. [5]Without these times we would never accomplish anything difficult and intimidating; we would never even attempt the just barely possible. [6]Mount Everest would remain unscaled, the four-minute mile unrun; the jet plane and the computer would be blueprints sitting in some financial vice president's wastebasket.

_____   5. The primary purpose of this paragraph is to
     A. inform readers about research on pessimism and optimism.
     B. persuade readers of the usefulness of both pessimism and optimism.
     C. entertain readers with inspiring achievements.

_____   6. The author's tone can be described as
     A. critical but concerned.
     B. lighthearted and amused.
     C. cynical and disbelieving.
     D. serious and positive.

D.   [1]More and more, Americans have succumbed to treating their pets like people. [2]Dogs used to be called Rover or Spot or Fido; now they have people's names such as Ingrid, Stuart, or Alexander. [3]Pet food manufacturers no longer stick to dog biscuits—you can now buy your cat or dog a full-course meal that looks just like "people food." [4]Instead of putting plain water in the dog's bowl, you can offer Evian or broth or a soft drink. [5]Pet stores sell Christmas stockings for pets, filled with treats and toys. [6]Proving there is no end to this madness, pet health insurance is available, as is pet dentistry. [7]When your dog or cat becomes a senior citizen, you'll be overjoyed to hear that some veterinarians specialize in geriatrics. [8]And when life draws to a close for your pet, you can seek out a pet cemetery, unless you prefer to keep your pet's ashes at home in a special urn.

_____   7. The primary purpose of this paragraph is to
     A. inform readers about sensible ways of caring for their pets.
     B. persuade readers that the treatment of pets as people has gone too far.
     C. entertain readers with details about cute animals.

_____   8. The tone of the passage can be described as
     A. critical.   C. bewildered.
     B. hypocritical.   D. matter-of-fact.

PURPOSE AND TONE: Mastery Test 6

Read the paragraphs below. Then carefully consider the questions that follow, and, in the spaces provided, write the letters of the best responses.

A. ¹Dieting habits are heavily linked to culture. ²In the 1880s, the full-figured actress Lillian Russell was the epitome of beauty. ³Being overweight then was equated with wealth and success. ⁴Today, American culture has gone to the opposite extreme. ⁵Research shows that the body weight most American women want to achieve today is 13 to 19 percent below the expected weight for their age and height. ⁶Since a body weight below 15 percent of expected weight is one of the criteria for diagnosing anorexia nervosa, what does this say about our ideals? ⁷We must do something about those ideals. ⁸With extreme slimness as a cultural norm, it is no wonder that fad dieting, surgical fat removal, eating disorders, and fear of fat abound. ⁹Every day, magazines, TV, and movies send the message that "thin is in." ¹⁰Unfortunately, this obsession with thinness leads many people to feelings of guilt, despair, and inferiority. ¹¹Sadly, for some, this struggle ends in death. ¹²Isn't it time we taught our children not to emphasize their looks at the expense of their souls?

_____ 1. The primary purpose of this passage is to
   A. inform.   B. persuade.   C. entertain.

_____ 2. The tone of the passage can be described as
   A. puzzled and curious.   C. matter-of-fact.
   B. admiring and tolerant.   D. disapproving and distressed.

B. ¹Happiness is not a goal; it is a by-product. . . . ²Someone once asked me what I regarded as the three most important requirements for happiness. ³My answer was: "A feeling that you have been honest with yourself and those around you; a feeling that you have done the best you could both in your personal life and in your work; and the ability to love others."

⁴But there is another basic requirement, and I can't understand now how I forgot it at the time: that is the feeling that you are, in some way, useful. ⁵Usefulness, whatever form it may take, is the price we should pay for the air we breathe and the food we eat and the privilege of being alive. ⁶And it is its own reward, as well, for it is the beginning of happiness, just as self-pity and withdrawal from the battle are the beginning of misery.

_____ 3. The primary purpose of this paragraph is to
   A. inform with   B. persuade with   C. entertain with
      documented facts.   personal views.   charming anecdotes.

_____ 4. The tone of this paragraph can be described as
   A. lighthearted and cheerful.   C. serious and caring.
   B. indignant and scornful.   D. distressed and pessimistic.

(Continues on next page)

C.   [1]"Aravaipa" is an Apache name whose commonly accepted meaning is "laughing waters." [2]The Apaches who gave this name to a stream and a canyon are not around anymore. [3]Most of that particular band—unarmed old men, women, children—who huddled in a cave near the mouth of Aravaipa Canyon were exterminated in the 1880s by a death squad of American pioneers, aided by Mexican and Papagos, from the nearby city of Tucson. [4]The reason for this vigilante action is obscure (suspicion of murder and cattle stealing), but the results were clear: no more Apaches in Aravaipa Canyon. [5]During pauses in the gunfire, as the pioneers reloaded their rifles, the surviving Indians could have heard the sound of the laughing waters. [6]One hundred and twenty-five were killed, with the remainder relocated in the White Mountain Reservation to the northeast. [7]Since then those people have given us no back talk at all.

_____ 5. The primary purpose of this paragraph is to
    A. simply inform readers about what happened one day in Aravaipa Canyon in the 1880s.
    B. persuade readers that the band of Apaches in Aravaipa that day in 1880 were treated cruelly.
    C. entertain readers with a colorful story from the old Wild West.

_____ 6. The author's tone can be described as
    A. indignant and bitter.   C. forgiving and accepting.
    B. matter-of-fact and detached.   D. uncertain and worried.

D.   [1]In Africa's southernmost Lake Malawi swarm millions of shimmering fish in a rainbow of fluorescent colors that make them popular picks for aquariums. [2]Similar to perch, they belong to a family of fish called cichlids, of great interest to scientists because of the unusual variety of behavior they have developed in order to survive. [3]One brown and white species, for example, drops to the lake bottom, covers itself with sand, and plays dead. [4]When other fish come to scavenge, it leaps up and gobbles them. [5]The "upside down" species has reversed its coloration—light on top, dark on the bottom—so it can flip over and conceal itself from predators above or below. [6]And the sand dwellers are accomplished actors—cleverly masquerading as the opposite sex so they can steal eggs from other nests or misbehave on the sly.

_____ 7. The primary purpose of this paragraph is to
    A. inform.   C. entertain.
    B. persuade.

_____ 8. The tone of the passage can be described as
    A. concerned and sympathetic.
    B. mainly objective with a touch of wonder.
    C. mainly optimistic, with a touch of fear.
    D. formal and unimpressed.

10

Argument

Many of us enjoy a good argument. A good argument is not an emotional experience in which people allow their anger to get out of control, leaving them ready to start throwing things. Instead, it is a rational discussion in which each person advances and supports a point of view about some matter. We might argue with a friend, for example, about where to eat or what movie to go to. We might argue about whether a boss or a parent or an instructor is acting in a fair or unfair manner. We might argue about whether certain performers or sports stars deserve to get paid as much as they do. In an argument (such as the one going on in the above cartoon), the two parties each present their supporting evidence. The goal is to determine who has the more solid evidence to support his or her point of view.

Argumentation is, then, a part of our everyday dealings with other people. It is also an important part of much of what we read. Authors often try to convince us of their opinions and interpretations. Very often the most important things we must do as critical readers are

1 Recognize the **point** the author is making.

2 Decide if the author's support is **relevant**.

3 Decide if the author's support is **adequate**.

This chapter will give you practice in doing the above, first in everyday arguments and then in textbook material.

THE BASICS OF ARGUMENT: POINT AND SUPPORT

A good argument is one in which a point is stated and then persuasively and logically supported. Here is a point:

Point: Even though the apartment is nice, I don't think you should move there.

This statement hardly discourages us from moving into the apartment. "Why do you say that?" we might legitimately ask. "Give your reasons." Support is needed so we can decide for ourselves whether a valid argument has been made. Suppose the point is followed by these three reasons:

1. The closest washer and dryer are in a laundromat three miles away.

2. Close to the apartment building is an all-night bar.

3. Several bugs scurried into dark holes when the kitchen sink cabinet door was opened.

Clearly, the details provide solid support for the point. They give us a basis for understanding and agreeing with the point. In light of these details, we may consider looking for another apartment to rent.

We see here a small example of what clear thinking in an argument is about: making a point and then providing support that truly backs up that point. A valid argument may also be described as a conclusion supported by logical reasons, facts, examples, and other evidence.

Let's look at another example:

Point: The corner convenience store is run poorly.

We don't yet know if we would agree that the store is run poorly. We might trust the person who made the statement, but we can't judge for ourselves until supporting details are provided. Here are details:

1. Milk is routinely kept on the shelves several days after the suggested date of sale.

2. The "fresh" fruits and vegetables are often spotted and wrinkled.

3. At busy times of the day, there's not enough help in the store, so the lines are very long.

Again, the solid support convinces us that a logical point has been made.

The Point and Support of an Argument

In everyday life, of course, people don't simply say, "Here is my point" and "Here is my support." Nor do writers state their basic ideas so directly. Even so, the basic structure of point and support is still at work beneath the surface, and to evaluate an argument, you need to recognize that point.

The following activity will help you distinguish between a point and its support.

> *Practice 1*

In each group, one statement is the point, and the other statement or statements are support for the point. Identify each point with a **P** and each statement of support with an **S**.

> *Hint:* If it sounds right to insert the word *because* in front of a sentence, you probably have a statement of support. For example, we could say, *"Because* the closest washer and dryer are three miles away, *because* the apartment building is close to an all-night bar, and *because* several bugs were visible below the kitchen sink, I've come to the conclusion that I should not move into that apartment."

1. _____ A. You should learn how to budget your money.

   _____ B. You're always borrowing money from me.

2. _____ A. Our town ought to require all residents to recycle bottles and cans.

   _____ B. The more the town recycles, the less money it must pay for garbage removal.

3. _____ A. Use olive oil on your bread instead of butter, which can clog arteries.

   _____ B. You can eat a healthy diet in restaurants with a little care.

   _____ C. You can order sautéed or steamed dishes instead of fatty, high-cholesterol fried foods.

4. _____ A. A large new park will benefit the community.

_____ B. Joggers who risk accidents by running along the roadside will be able to run in the park.

_____ C. Kids who play ball in the streets can play in a safer place.

_____ D. A park provides good opportunities for people to meet their neighbors.

5. _____ A. Our mail carrier often puts our mail in someone else's mailbox.

_____ B. When our mail carrier delivers a package, he leaves it on our front stoop without ringing the doorbell to see if we're home.

_____ C. Our mail carrier is careless about delivering mail.

_____ D. After delivering our mail, the carrier often leaves our mailbox partially open.

6. _____ A. Mass transportation helps people who can't afford a car.

_____ B. Increased use of mass transportation would reduce air pollution from cars.

_____ C. The government should fund more mass transportation.

_____ D. Mass transportation is more energy-efficient than automobile use.

7. _____ A. Affordable daycare facilities often lack professionally trained staff and fail to follow adequate child-safety procedures.

_____ B. It's hard for working parents to find reliable, affordable daycare.

_____ C. Excellent daycare can cost $15,000–$20,000 a year per child.

_____ D. For many working parents, the oldest form of daycare—adult relatives who live nearby—is unavailable.

8. _____ A. A recent explosion of cable TV sports channels has brought a wider variety of sports events to the public, drawing viewers away from baseball's audience.

_____ B. Major league baseball is no longer the national pastime.

_____ C. Professional football and basketball have emerged as the sports of choice among spectators in their teens or twenties; baseball has dropped to third place.

_____ D. The popularity of major league baseball hasn't recovered from the 1994 players' strike that canceled the World Series.

9. ____ A. According to some medieval philosophers, laughing dishonored humans because it made them look like monkeys.

____ B. Some medieval theologians believed that all laughing mocked God's creation and therefore endangered the human soul.

____ C. Many people objected to comedy, believing that laughing encouraged drunkenness and improper behavior.

____ D. In the Middle Ages, many people considered laughing harmful.

10. ____ A. A bone marrow transplant can increase the chances of survival for thousands of people who are diagnosed with leukemia and other blood-related diseases each year.

____ B. More people should agree to donate bone marrow if their marrow matches the type of a patient in need.

____ C. Only about 30 percent of patients can find a match among their own family members.

____ D. People can donate marrow easily and safely: it can be collected in about forty-five minutes and is naturally replaced by the body within two to three weeks.

RELEVANT SUPPORT

Once you identify the point and support of an argument, you need to decide if each piece of evidence is **relevant**—in other words, if it really applies to the point. The critical reader must ask, "Is this reason relevant support for the argument?" In their enthusiasm for making an argument, people often bring up irrelevant support. For example, in trying to get your cousin to take you to dinner, you might say, "You just got your paycheck." The fact that she just got her paycheck is beside the point; the question is whether she wants or is able to spend any of it on you.

An excellent way to develop your skill in recognizing relevant support is to work on simple point-support outlines of arguments. By isolating the reasons of an argument, such outlines help you think about whether each reason is truly relevant. Paying close attention to the relevance of support will help you not only in your reading, but also in making and supporting points in your own writing.

☑ *Check Your Understanding*

Consider the following outline. The point is followed by six facts, only three of which are relevant support for the point. See if you can check (✓) the numbers of the **three** relevant statements of support.

> **Point:** Pigs make good pets.
>
> ____ 1. When a pig weighs over 180 pounds, it is called a hog.
>
> ____ 2. Pigs are friendly and intelligent.
>
> ____ 3. In 1965, a pig named "Old Faithful" gave birth to thirty-six piglets in one litter.
>
> ____ 4. Pigs are easily housebroken.
>
> ____ 5. Pigs, like people, can get sunburn.
>
> ____ 6. Pigs can be taught to walk on a leash.

Now read the following comments on the six items to see which numbers you should have checked and why.

Explanation:

1. What an animal is called has no bearing on how good a pet it will make. And for many people, the fact that pigs can weigh over 180 pounds is a reason they are *not* good pets. So you should not have checked number 1.

2. People tend to like pets who like them back and with whom they can interact. You should have checked number 2.

3. Admittedly, Old Faithful's accomplishment is nothing to oink at, but how many pet owners want thirty-six more pets than they started out with? You should not have checked number 3.

4. Given modern standards of cleanliness, being easily housebroken is even more attractive to many pet owners than friendliness or a genius IQ. You should have checked number 4.

5. Most people would prefer a pet for whom they wouldn't have to buy a lifetime supply of sunscreen. Therefore, you should not have checked number 5.

6. Since humans enjoy taking walks with their pets, the ability to keep an animal under control outdoors is important. Number 6 is the third number you should have checked.

> **Practice 2**

Each point is followed by three statements that provide relevant support and three that do not. In the spaces, write the letters of the **three** relevant statements of support.

> *Hint*: To help you decide if a sentence is relevant, ask yourself, "Does this provide logical support for the point being argued?"

1. **Point:** High-heeled shoes are a health risk.
   A. It is difficult to walk fast in high-heeled shoes.
   B. Although males have worn high-heeled shoes in some cultures and historical periods, they do not wear high-heeled shoes in our society.
   C. Long-term wearing of high-heeled shoes increases the likelihood of developing back and foot disorders.
   D. Many women wear high-heeled shoes to work.
   E. High-heeled shoes increase the risk of falling on a slippery surface.
   F. High, narrow heels easily catch in sidewalk cracks and gratings, resulting in falls.

   Items that logically support the point: _____   _____   _____

2. **Point:** Cities should build more bicycle lanes.
   A. Some roads are too narrow to make room for bicycle lanes.
   B. There are bicycles for every age and pocketbook.
   C. More bicycle lanes would reduce pollution by encouraging people to bike more and drive less.
   D. Cyclists would be safer if they could ride in lanes separate from automobile traffic.
   E. Bicycles can have different gears.
   F. With cycling lanes, more people would be encouraged to get beneficial exercise from cycling.

   Items that logically support the point: _____   _____   _____

3. **Point:** People who do not enjoy flying can do a number of things to make flying less unpleasant. .
   A. Fear of flying is a relatively common phobia.
   B. People who suffer from motion sickness during air travel can take over-the-counter medications such as Dramamine.
   C. Media reports of airline crashes serve to increase people's fear of flying.
   D. Fearful flyers can use visualization to feel more in control of the flying experience.
   E. Hypnosis has helped some fearful flyers to control their anxiety about air travel.
   F. Motion-sickness medication can leave a traveler feeling unpleasantly drugged.

   Items that logically support the point: _____   _____   _____

4. **Point:** The flu epidemic of 1918 was horrendous.
   A. Worldwide, 40 million people died of the 1918 flu—more than the number killed in World War I.
   B. Because of the flu epidemic, in 1918 many public events, including funerals, were restricted or canceled, and bodies piled up in city morgues.
   C. The flu strain that swept the world in 1918 was so severe that people would show the first symptoms in the morning and be dead by nightfall.
   D. Bubonic plague, another terrible disease, killed about 70,000 people in London between 1664 and 1666.
   E. Ordinary flu usually results in fever, coughing, and headache for three or four days.
   F. A contagious disease that covers a large part of the world is properly called a "pandemic."

   Items that logically support the point: _____ _____ _____

5. **Point:** People should consider alternatives to traditional burial practices.
   A. A sympathetic, well-trained funeral director can be very helpful during a difficult time.
   B. A biodegradable coffin buried in a plot marked by shrubbery is easier on the environment than a traditional coffin and headstone.
   C. People may feel that giving their loved ones anything other than an expensive, conventional burial is somehow disrespectful.
   D. Families can avoid the expense of maintaining a cemetery plot by cremating, instead of burying, the dead.
   E. Many states permit burial on home property, which can be a more convenient burial location than a cemetery.
   F. Burial grounds provide valuable information to genealogists, sociologists, and other people interested in the past.

   Items that logically support the point: _____ _____ _____

Relevant Support in Paragraphs

The point, or main idea, of the argument in the paragraph below is stated in the first sentence. One of the other sentences is not relevant support for that point.

☑ *Check Your Understanding*

Read the paragraph that follows and see if you can find the statement that does **not** support the point of the argument.

> [1]When you go to college, you should live off campus. [2]In a rented apartment you can enjoy the privacy and convenience of your own kitchen and bathroom. [3]If you live off campus, getting to and from classes will take more time. [4]However, off-campus apartments give you more living space than a dormitory room for the same price or less. [5]An off-campus apartment is usually quieter than a dorm. [6]It also gives you a better chance to develop a sense of the larger community, the town or city in which your college is located.

The number of the irrelevant sentence: _____

Explanation:

The point of this argument is stated in the first sentence: "When you go to college, you should live off campus." Any statement that doesn't help prove this point is irrelevant. Sentences 2, 4, 5, and 6 provide advantages of living off campus. However, having to spend more time getting to and from classes would generally be considered undesirable since it takes time away from other activities. Therefore sentence 3 is irrelevant to the argument in this paragraph—it changes the subject to a disadvantage of living off campus.

➤ *Practice 3*

The point of the argument in each paragraph that follows is stated in the first sentence. One sentence in the paragraph does not support that point. Read each paragraph, and decide which sentence is **not** relevant evidence. Then write its letter in the space provided.

Hint: To decide if a sentence is irrelevant, ask yourself, "Does this *really* provide logical support for the point being argued?"

_____ 1. [1]What people consider masculine and feminine behavior is actually quite variable. [2]Americans, for instance, think of men as naturally stronger and tougher than women and better suited to perform the most strenuous physical labor. [3]In many traditional societies, however, particularly in sub-Saharan Africa and South America, women do most of the heavy work—carrying goods to market, hauling firewood, and constructing houses. [4]Men hunt—and spend a lot of time talking. [5]Americans can learn something from looking at such traditional societies. [6]Among some peoples, agriculture is restricted to men, while in other societies farming is regarded as women's work. [7]In still other societies, men and women work in the fields side by side.

Which of the following sentences does **not** support the argument that what people consider masculine and feminine behavior can vary?

A. Sentence 3   C. Sentence 5
B. Sentence 4   D. Sentence 6

_____ 2. [1]Cities should give privately run schools a try. [2]Private companies that run school districts are a relatively recent development. [3]Educational companies have done much to upgrade the physical condition of schools that school boards have allowed to decay. [4]One company that was hired to run an East Coast school district, for example, began by immediately painting and repairing local schools that had become so rundown that they challenged any sense of pride that teachers and students might have had in their schools. [5]Graffiti were painted over and kept clean; the only "art work" in hallways was student work and colorful upbeat posters. [6]Furthermore, any nonstudents who used to wander the hallways looking for trouble as well as for customers for drugs were immediately eliminated by a strong disciplinary system that included professional guards. [7]In addition, year-end reading and math scores of students in the privately run schools improved in many cases.

Which of the following sentences does **not** support the argument that cities should give privately run schools a try?

A. Sentence 2   C. Sentence 5
B. Sentence 3   D. Sentence 7

ADEQUATE SUPPORT

A valid argument must include not only relevant support but also **adequate** support—substantial enough to prove the point. For example, it would not be valid to argue "A government tax cut is a bad idea" if one's only support was "My taxes will still be too high." Such an important issue would require more support than one person's tax situation. Arguing a point that doesn't have adequate support is called "jumping to a conclusion."

☑ *Check Your Understanding*

In the argument below, three supporting reasons are given, followed by four possible conclusions. The evidence (that is, the supporting reasons) adequately supports only one of the points; it is insufficient to support the other three. Choose the **one** point that you think is adequately supported, and put a check mark (✓) beside it.

Support:

> • Lately Valerie has looked thinner and paler than usual.
> • She used to go to all the parties, but now she stays home in the evenings.
> • At work, she has been seen crying in the ladies' room.

Which **point** is adequately supported by all the evidence above?

____ A. Valerie is seriously ill.

____ B. Something is troubling Valerie.

____ C. Valerie has broken up with her boyfriend.

____ D. Valerie owes a great deal of money.

Explanation:

The correct answer is B. From her behavior, we can safely conclude that something is troubling Valerie, but we have very little evidence about what is troubling her. Answer A is not well supported. The fact that Valerie hasn't been looking well makes us wonder if she's seriously ill, but we have no other evidence for that conclusion. Answer C is also poorly supported. The fact that Valerie hasn't been going to parties does make us wonder whether or not she's broken up with her boyfriend, but we have absolutely no other evidence to support that conclusion. Finally, except for the evidence showing that Valerie is troubled in some way, answer D has no evidence at all to support it, so it too is a poorly supported conclusion. We simply have insufficient information to decide anything more than that something is troubling Valerie.

➤ **Practice 4**

For each group, read the three items of support (the evidence). Then check (✓) the **one** point that is adequately supported by that evidence.

Group 1

Support:

> - In one study, fifteen of the thirty women who listened to music during childbirth labor had no need for anesthesia.
> - Studies indicate that the body produces pain-reducing hormones when a person listens to enjoyable music.
> - Patients who had suffered a stroke gained lasting benefits after listening for three weeks to recorded music.

Point: Which of the following conclusions is best supported by all the evidence above?

____ A. Music can have a role in curing diseases of all types.

____ B. Music can be a helpful tool in dealing with some physical problems.

____ C. Music should be a resource in every medical office.

____ D. Music can also have negative effects on our physical well-being.

Group 2

Support:

> - "Living out of a suitcase"—being away from home and our familiar routine—and coping with planes, trains, buses, and rental cars can be exhausting.
> - While on vacation, we often eat too much, drink too much, get too little sleep, work too hard at sightseeing, and in general overextend ourselves.
> - Also, we tend to expect a vacation to be a "dream come true," and so we feel frustrated, angry, and let down if anything is less than perfect.

Point: Which of the following conclusions is best supported by all the evidence above?

___ A. A vacation trip with young children can be very difficult.

___ B. A vacation trip isn't always restful.

___ C. The expense of a vacation trip is a big worry for most people.

___ D. The best vacation is one spent dieting and exercising.

ARGUMENT IN TEXTBOOK WRITING

In most textbook writing, argument takes the form of well-developed ideas or theories presented with experiments, surveys, studies, reasons, examples, or other supporting evidence. Textbook arguments generally have solid support, but recognizing the author's point and watching for relevant and adequate support will help you become a more involved and critical reader. Following are two exercises that will give you practice in thinking through the arguments in textbooks.

➤ *Practice 5*

The point of the argument in each of the textbook paragraphs below is stated in the first sentence. One sentence in each paragraph does not support the point. Read each paragraph, and then decide which sentence is **not** relevant to the argument. Then, in the space provided, write the letter of that sentence.

To help you decide if a sentence is irrelevant or not, ask yourself, "Does this *really* provide logical support for the point being argued?"

_____ 1. ¹Science and technology, while they help solve societal problems, are themselves responsible for many of our problems. ²Before scientific advances in weaponry, humans were limited to bows and arrows and swords. ³Now, however, we can kill many more people with the destructive guns and bombs that science has given us. ⁴Today we save or extend the lives of countless people because of medical advances that science has provided, but the hazardous waste products that result from medicine pollute our air, streams, and oceans and threaten our health. ⁵The world's political leaders must join together to deal with the continuing pollution of our planet. ⁶And the tear in the ozone layer caused by gases we've unleashed into the environment through such scientific advances as air conditioning and spray cans allows more ultraviolet rays to reach our skin, resulting in more skin cancer.

Which sentence is **not** relevant support for the argument that science and technology are responsible for many of society's problems?

A. Sentence 3   C. Sentence 5

B. Sentence 4   D. Sentence 6

_____ 2. [1]The safe disposal of toxic chemicals is a huge problem. [2]The amount of hazardous waste produced in the United States rose from about 9 million metric tons in 1970 to 300 million less than 20 years later—enough to fill a line of railroad cars that would stretch around the world, with several thousand miles to spare. [3]Typically, corporations choose the cheapest means of disposal, which are to release the waste products into the air and waterways and to bury the materials in dump sites. [4]Corporations should face heavy fines whenever they are caught favoring profits over public health. [5]In one infamous instance of irresponsible disposal, the Hooker Chemical and Plastics Corporation over a number of years dumped 43.6 million pounds of eighty-two different chemical substances into Love Canal, New York, near Niagara Falls. [6]Among the chemicals dumped were 200 tons of trichlorophenol, which included an estimated 130 pounds of one of the most toxic and carcinogenic substances known—dioxin. [7]Three ounces of this substance can kill more than a million people. [8]As a result of exposure to the various chemicals dumped at Love Canal, nearby residents have an unusual number of serious illnesses, a high incidence of miscarriages, and a significant number of children born with birth defects.

Which sentence is **not** relevant support for the argument that safe disposal of toxic chemicals is a huge problem?

A. Sentence 3   C. Sentence 6
B. Sentence 4   D. Sentence 7

➤ Practice 6

In each group, the support is from studies reported in a textbook. Check (✓) the point in each case that is adequately supported by that evidence.

Group 1

Support:

- An increased amount, or volume, of blood in the circulatory system can elevate blood pressure.
- If the heart is pumping with too much force, that increases blood pressure by straining the circulation.
- The condition of the artery wall is also important: when the wall thickens, the artery becomes narrower, and the pressure of the blood flowing through it rises.

Which **point** is adequately supported by all the evidence above?

____ A. High blood pressure is a mysterious, silent killer.

____ B. Factors in high blood pressure include stress, a fatty diet, and lack of exercise.

____ C. Factors in high blood pressure include the blood, the heart, and the arteries.

____ D. High blood pressure can be controlled by medications and lifestyle changes.

Group 2

Support:

> - Athletes often privately credit their victories to their own ability and their losses to bad breaks, lousy officiating, or the other team's exceptional performance.
> - After receiving poor exam grades, most students in a half dozen studies criticized the exam, not themselves; generally, students interpret good grades to be the result of their own efforts.
> - On insurance forms, drivers have explained accidents in such words as these: "An invisible car came out of nowhere, struck my car, and vanished"; "As I reached an intersection, a hedge sprang up obscuring my vision, and I did not see the other car"; "A pedestrian hit me and went under my car."

Which **point** is adequately supported by the evidence above?

____ A. Most people lack the skills they need to perform well at work and school.

____ B. People accept more responsibility for good deeds than for bad ones.

____ C. People tend to perform at a rather high level most of the time.

____ D. People accept more responsibility for successes than for failures.

A Final Note

This chapter has dealt with the basics of argument, including the need for relevant and adequate support. If time permits, you may want to turn to pages 603–614 to consider common errors in reasoning—also known as **logical fallacies**—that people may make when advancing an argument.

CHAPTER REVIEW

In this chapter, you learned the following:

- A good argument is made up of a point, or a conclusion, and logical evidence to back it up.

- To critically read an argument, you must recognize the **point** the author is making.

- To think through an argument, you need to decide if each piece of evidence is **relevant**.

- To think through an argument, you also need to decide if the author's support is **adequate**.

- Textbook arguments generally have solid support, but recognizing the author's point and watching for relevant and adequate support will help you become a more involved and critical reader.

 On the Web: If you are using this book in class, you can visit our website for additional practice in evaluating arguments. Go to **www.townsendpress.com** and click on "Online Exercises."

➤ Review Test 1

To review what you've learned in this chapter, fill in the blanks.

1. When two people argue a point, the goal is to see who has the more compelling _____ for his or her point.

_____ 2. TRUE OR FALSE? A good argument should be more than a rational discussion: it should also be an emotional one as well.

3. It is important to consider whether each piece of evidence in an argument logically supports the point—in other words, that it is (*relevant, adequate*) _____.

4. It is equally important to consider that an argument includes a(n) (*relevant, adequate*) _____ amount of support—enough to convincingly prove the point.

5. To become a more effective reader (or listener or speaker or writer), you should make a habit of asking yourself two questions: 1) What is the point? and 2) _____?

➤ *Review Test 2*

A. In each group, one statement is the point, and the other statements are support for that point. Write the letter of the point in the space provided.

> *Hint:* If it sounds right to insert the word *because* in front of a sentence, you probably have a statement of support.

_____ 1. A. Ancient Egyptian law protected cats from harm.
B. The ancient Egyptians must have honored cats.
C. Archaeologists have uncovered entire cemeteries in Egypt devoted to mummified cats.

_____ 2. A. Books can be gotten free from public libraries.
B. Many delicious, healthy meals can be made out of inexpensive ingredients, such as beans and grains.
C. One does not have to be rich to have rich experiences.
D. Beautiful public parks throughout the country can be enjoyed free or for a small fee.

_____ 3. A. Thirty-five percent of America's endangered species live in tidal wetlands.
B. Tidal wetlands provide a natural way to control flooding and storm damage.
C. Plants that grow only in wetlands are essential to the food chain.
D. Preserving tidal wetlands from overdevelopment should be a national priority.

_____ 4. A. Various powerful social forces are behind the current high rate of divorce.
B. Women are no longer financially dependent upon their husbands.
C. There is no longer as much social disapproval of divorce.
D. No-fault divorce laws make divorce much easier to obtain.

B. Each point is followed by three statements that provide relevant support and three that do not. In the spaces, write the letters of the **three** relevant statements of support.

5–7. **Point:** "Dress-down" Friday in offices has positive effects.

    A. No one knows exactly how the custom of dressing casually on Fridays started.

    B. Whatever its origins, dressing casually on Fridays has become very widespread.

    C. Dressing casually on Fridays provides a break in the routine, which energizes workers.

    D. Casual dress seems to reduce stress by creating a more relaxed atmosphere.

    E. Informality also seems to lead to more friendliness and cooperation between employees.

    F. Some employers complain that workers abuse the custom by wearing outfits that belong on the beach—or in the bedroom.

Items that logically support the point: _____ _____ _____

8–10. **Point:** We should use more solar energy.

    A. Unlike oil and coal, energy from the sun is unlimited.

    B. The sun nourishes plants and animals.

    C. Solar energy is nonpolluting.

    D. Wind and water power have been used for centuries.

    E. Solar energy is less effective in cloudy climates.

    F. Solar energy is extremely cost-effective.

Items that logically support the point: _____ _____ _____

➤ Review Test 3

A. In the space provided, write the letter of the irrelevant sentence in each paragraph—the sentence that changes the subject.

_____ 1. ¹The current generation of young workers will have a better financial future if workers save for retirement instead of counting on the Social Security program. ²Saving will also provide today's workers with some of the discipline their "I want it all now" generation so sorely needs. ³Social Security benefits already have been reduced to accommodate a shrinking labor pool and a growing number of retirees. ⁴In addition, the government has had to start taxing a percentage of the benefits, lessening them even more. [5]At this rate, if the program isn't completely bankrupt by the early twenty-first century, monthly Social Security checks will be very small.

Which of the following is **not** relevant to the author's conclusion that workers must save for retirement instead of counting on Social Security?

A. Sentence 2   C. Sentence 4
B. Sentence 3   D. Sentence 5

2. [1]The death penalty is a vital tool in the fight against crime. [2]Knowing that they will die if they are caught, potential killers will think twice about committing murder. [3]And when murderers are caught, the death penalty is the only sure guarantee that these criminals will not escape or be released to repeat their crimes. [4]Some murderers who have not been executed and instead were released on parole went on to kill other victims. [5]Finally, let us remember that the victims of murder were shown no mercy and given no second chance.

Which of the following is **not** relevant to the author's conclusion that the death penalty is a vital tool in the fight against crime?

A. Sentence 2   C. Sentence 4
B. Sentence 3   D. Sentence 5

3. [1]The quest for the ideal body can become physically unhealthy. [2]At one time or other, almost every American girl undereats for an extended period, sometimes drastically, in order to be thinner. [3]And roughly 5 percent of male high-school seniors use steroids to build up their muscles. [4]These young men risk a variety of serious health problems, especially if they obtain steroids illegally and "stack" one drug with another, as many do. [5]Although one misguided motivation for taking steroids is probably to excel at sports, one survey found that a third of steroid users did not participate at all in interscholastic athletics, apparently taking steroids solely for the sake of appearance. [6]Further, although most adolescents believe that smoking cigarettes puts their health "at risk," at least one in five high-school seniors is a daily smoker, partly because smoking reduces appetite. [7]Interestingly, with most drugs, girls are much more cautious than boys and hence less likely to be users. [8]But largely because of the suppressant effect that smoking has on appetite and weight gain, the rate of cigarette smoking over the past twenty years has been slightly higher among girls than among boys.

Which of the following is **not** relevant to the author's conclusion that the quest for the ideal body can become physically unhealthy?

A. Sentence 2   C. Sentence 7
B. Sentence 6   D. Sentence 8

B. For each group, read the three items of support (the evidence). Then, in the space provided, write the letter of the **one** point that is adequately supported by that evidence.

Remember that the point, or conclusion, should follow logically from the evidence. Do not jump to a conclusion that is not well supported.

Group 1

Support:

> - The weather bureau said this would be a mild winter, but for weeks, temperatures have been well below normal.
> - There was no storm warning in the forecast today, but the winds were so severe our fishing boat almost capsized.
> - The forecast on the radio said it would be sunny all day, but the ball game was rained out.

_____ 4. Which **point** is adequately supported by all the evidence above?
   A. People's poor treatment of the environment affects the ozone layer and causes changes in the weather.
   B. Always expect the opposite weather from what the weather reports predict.
   C. It is impossible to ever correctly predict the weather.
   D. Weather predictions are not always accurate.

Group 2

Support:

> - "Ring Around a Rosy" was originally sung about the rose-colored rash that was a symptom of the deadly Great Plague; "they all fall down" meant that they died.
> - In "Three Blind Mice," the farmer's wife cuts off the mice's tails with a carving knife.
> - In "Ladybug, Ladybug," the ladybug is told to fly away home because "your house is on fire, and your children—they will burn."

_____ 5. Which **point** is adequately supported by all the evidence above?
   A. Violence on TV can't be so bad for kids.
   B. All nursery rhymes are morbid and depressing.
   C. Some traditional children's verses refer to gruesome events.
   D. Violent criminals are created in early childhood.

➤ Review Test 4

When does obedience go too far? Here is a chance to apply your understanding of arguments to a selection from the textbook *Psychology*, by Mary M. Gergen and others (Harcourt Brace Jovanovich) that addresses that question.

To help you continue to strengthen your skills, the reading is followed by questions not only on what you've learned in this chapter but also on what you've learned in previous chapters.

Words to Watch

Below are some words in the reading that do not have strong context support. Each word is followed by the number of the paragraph in which it appears and its meaning there. These words are indicated in the article by a small circle (°).

critical (1): crucial
solicited (3): sought
confederate (3): associate
sadistic (7): cruel

OBEDIENCE: MILGRAM'S CONTROVERSIAL STUDIES

Mary M. Gergen et al.

1   One of the most direct forms of social influence is the demand for *obedience:* people follow orders because an authority figure tells them to. In most societies, obedience plays a critical° role in social control. We obey parents, teachers, police, and other officials. Since many rules, laws, and commands from authority have a positive value, obedience is a major foundation of social life and behavior. However, obedience can go too far! Soldiers in Nazi Germany obeyed the orders of their superiors and, as a result, millions of people were slaughtered. More recently, nine hundred men, women, and children died in a mass suicide in Guyana. The leader of the community, James Jones, gave the order for his followers to drink a poisoned juice, and they did.

2   In these two instances, we seem to be observing extreme cases of blind obedience. Some might say that instances of blind obedience, where the commands of authority contradict moral and human principles, are extremely rare. But are they? Social psychologist Stanley Milgram set out to find out.

3   In a series of experiments, Milgram solicited° subjects drawn from all walks of life through newspaper advertisements. In the ads, subjects were told they would be paid for participating in a psychology study at Yale University. Volunteers were paired and were told that one would be the "teacher" and the other the "learner" in a study to test the effect of shock on learning. The person designated as learner and the person designated as teacher were seemingly

determined by a random draw. Then the learner was seated in an adjoining room, and his arms were strapped to his chair. Electrodes were attached to his arms. At this point, the learner (actually a confederate° of Milgram's) mentioned that he had a slight heart condition.

4   The teacher was then escorted to a separate room and seated in front of an impressive, complicated-looking machine, which the experimenter referred to as a shock generator. The machine had a series of switches with labels from 15 volts ("slight shock") to 450 volts ("danger— severe shock").

5   The teacher was given a somewhat painful sample shock (45 volts) so he or she could have an idea of what the learner would be experiencing. After the sample shock, the experimenter told the teacher to read over the intercom a list of pairs of words so the learner could memorize them. The experimenter then instructed the teacher to read one word of each pair along with four alternatives. It was now the learner's job to pick out the right response. If the response was correct, the teacher was to proceed to the next word. If the response was incorrect, the teacher's task was to give the learner a shock. The teacher was told to start at 15 volts and to proceed up the scale toward 450 volts.

6   During the experiment, the learner got some items right and others wrong. However, as the experiment progressed, the learner made errors more and more frequently. Each error increased the amount of shock given. In one condition of this experiment, the learner made no response to the shocks until they reached the 300-volt level; then he yelled and complained about the shock and pounded on the wall, shouting "Let me out of here." The learner did this on several occasions. Finally, he stopped responding to the test. Regardless of what the learner said or did, the experimenter told the teacher to continue to read the words and to test for the right answer; if the learner gave an incorrect answer or no answer, the teacher was instructed to administer the next higher level of shock.

7   As the learner began to scream with pain, the teachers usually became upset and jittery. Many broke out in nervous laughter. Some threatened to quit the experiment. What would you have done? What do you think the average subjects did? Would they go on or would they stop? Milgram was curious about this question and asked a group of psychiatrists to predict what percentage they thought would obey the experimenter's demands. They estimated that only half of 1 percent (that is, one person in two hundred) of the population would be sadistic° enough to obey. But they were clearly wrong.

8   Readers are usually surprised to learn that 65 percent of the subjects who served as teachers obeyed the experimenter's commands and delivered shocks up to the maximum (450 volts), even though the learner objected, screamed, and begged to be released. Of course, in actuality, the learner was a confederate of Milgram's, never actually received any shocks, and answered the word-pair questions according to a prearranged schedule. However, the confederate was well-trained, and his faked pain and protests were well-staged and seemed quite real to the subject.

9   The finding that two-thirds of the subjects went along with the experimenter's commands suggests that obedience is not just to be found in Nazi Germany or in Jonestown. Rather, obedience seems to be a common response

to the commands of authorities. In fact, after examining hundreds of sessions, Milgram failed to find any background, socioeconomic, or personality factors that predicted who would obey the experimenter's commands and who would not.

10   The important question, of course, is why did so many people obey? Milgram thought that people obeyed because they perceived the experimenter to be a legitimate authority; he had the right to dictate behaviors and demands because he was in the role of a scientist. Presumably, obedience to legitimate authorities is something we learn early in life and retain throughout adulthood. As long as we recognize the authority as legitimate, we are subject to its influence.

11   Milgram's research has been strongly criticized for being unethical and misleading. Certain critics have objected to his misuse of people as subjects. They argue that the subjects should not have been led to believe that they may have killed someone. Other critics have suggested that the laboratory experiments were not adequate demonstrations of obedience in real life because the subjects would have felt it was a "science game" and would simply have been playing a cooperative role. However, despite these objections, Milgram's work seems to have had a substantial social impact. It would appear that people rather readily acquiesce to authority figures, whether they are army officers, religious leaders, or scientists. Given the consequences of obedience, Milgram's works stand out as an important contribution to psychology and as a warning for our society.

Reading Comprehension Questions

Vocabulary in Context

_____ 1. In the sentence below, the words *acquiesce to* (ăk′wē-ĕs′ too̅) mean
   A. oppose.
   B. obey.
   C. question.
   D. converse with.

"It would appear that people rather readily acquiesce to authority figures, whether they are army officers, religious leaders, or scientists." (Paragraph 11)

Central Point and Main Ideas

_____ 2. Which sentence best expresses the central point of the selection?
   A. Psychological experiments can reveal much about human behavior in various situations.
   B. Stanley Milgram has conducted psychological research that has been strongly criticized for being unethical and misleading.
   C. An important experiment conducted by Stanley Milgram showed that people will often blindly obey authority.
   D. Electrical shocks should not be administered as part of a psychological experiment.

_____ 3. Which sentence best expresses the main idea of paragraph 10?
   A. Scientists are authority figures.
   B. Milgram concluded that people tend to obey anyone they recognize as a legitimate authority.
   C. Milgram wondered why so many people obeyed the experimenter in his experiment.
   D. Milgram was surprised to be considered a legitimate authority figure.

Supporting Details

_____ 4. According to the author, obedience to legitimate authority is probably
   A. always dangerous.
   B. often painful.
   C. learned early in life.
   D. senseless.

Transitions

_____ 5. The relationship expressed by the sentence below is one of
   A. time.
   B. addition.
   C. contrast.
   D. cause and effect.

   "Soldiers in Nazi Germany obeyed the orders of their superiors and, as a result, millions of people were slaughtered." (Paragraph 1)

Patterns of Organization

_____ 6. The overall pattern of organization of paragraphs 3–6 is
   A. steps in a process.
   B. list of items.
   C. cause and effect.
   D. definition and example.

Fact and Opinion

_____ 7. The statement that "Milgram's works stand out as an important contribution to psychology" (paragraph 11) is
   A. a fact.
   B. an opinion.

Inferences

_____ 8. The author suggests that
   A. Milgram's research sheds little light on obedience.
   B. paid volunteers are more likely to obey than nonpaid volunteers.
   C. people should be more questioning of authority figures.
   D. there is little reason for obedience in contemporary societies.

Purpose

_____ 9. On the basis of the reading—including its last sentence—we might conclude that the author's intention was
   A. only to inform.
   B. both to inform and to persuade.
   C. to entertain and to persuade.

Argument

10. Label the point of the following argument based on the reading with a **P**; label the two statements of support for the point with an **S**. Label with an **X** the one statement that is neither the point nor the support of the argument.

   ____ A. Participants may have felt that academic researchers would not allow anyone to be genuinely hurt.

   ____ B. Obedient soldiers in Nazi Germany killed millions of people.

   ____ C. Milgram's experiment does not represent obedience in real life.

   ____ D. Participants in the experiment may have felt they were simply cooperating in a "science game."

Discussion Questions

1. Imagine that you were a subject in Milgram's experiment. How do you think you would have responded to the experimenter's commands? Why?

2. The authors write, "Presumably, obedience to legitimate authorities is something we learn early in life and retain throughout adulthood." Why do you think people develop an obedience to authority?

3. What might the authors have been thinking of when they wrote that Milgram's experiments "stand out as . . . a warning for our society"? Can you think of any events that reflect unwise obedience to authority?

4. The reading refers to what is negative about obedience to authority. What do you think might be the positive aspects of such obedience?

Note: Writing assignments for this selection appear on page 632.

Check Your Performance   ARGUMENT

Activity	Number Right	Points	Score
Review Test 1 (5 items)	_____	× 2 =	_____
Review Test 2 (10 items)	_____	× 3 =	_____
Review Test 3 (5 items)	_____	× 6 =	_____
Review Test 4 (10 items)	_____	× 3 =	_____
		TOTAL SCORE =	_____%

Enter your total score into the **Reading Performance Chart: Review Tests** on the inside back cover.

ARGUMENT: Mastery Test 1

A. In each group, one statement is the point of an argument, and the other statements are support for that point. In the space provided, write the letter of the point of each group.

_____ 1. A. TV surveillance cameras are positioned throughout the stores.

B. Security guards watch customers through one-way mirrors.

C. Retail merchants are trying to combat shoplifting.

D. Merchandise has special tags that trigger an alarm if not removed by a salesclerk.

_____ 2. A. Many adult sons and daughters must work and are unable to stay home to care for their parents.

B. Caring for elderly parents presents problems for adult children.

C. Adult children often live too far away to assist their elderly parents.

D. Providing paid caregivers is beyond the financial ability of most children.

_____ 3. A. When a computer chip is added to a hearing aid, it is possible to enhance the human voice and reduce background noise.

B. A surgically implanted processor permits some profoundly deaf people to hear sounds.

C. A computer can help deaf people speak more clearly by having them imitate speech patterns they see on the display screen.

D. New technology is helping deaf and hearing-impaired people.

_____ 4. A. The Internal Revenue Service is the only government agency with the power to take people's property and salaries without a hearing or court order.

B. Legal loopholes allow wealthy, well-connected Americans to avoid paying their fair share of income tax.

C. The U.S. income tax system needs to be reformed.

D. The current tax on interest earned in bank accounts punishes people for saving their money.

(Continues on next page)

B. Each point is followed by three statements that provide relevant support and three that do not. In the spaces, write the letters of the **three** relevant statements of support.

5–7. **Point:** Cats and dogs benefit from being neutered.

    A. Cats and dogs should be taken to a veterinarian at least once a year for a checkup and vaccinations.

    B. Neutering reduces the likelihood that a cat or dog will develop certain common forms of cancer.

    C. If you adopt an animal from a local shelter, the shelter may neuter your new pet.

    D. Neutered cats and dogs tend to be more content to stay at home, where they're safest.

    E. On average, neutered cats and dogs live longer than unneutered ones.

    F. Purebred cats and dogs are more likely than mixed breeds to suffer from inherited disorders.

Items that logically support the point: _____ _____ _____

8–10. **Point:** Many women lack healthy strategies for dealing with their anger.

    A. Women with violent partners often blame themselves for the abuse rather than becoming angry with the man.

    B. Men are typically able to express anger with one another without fearing their relationship will be destroyed.

    C. Rather than showing anger, many women let anger build up and become very stressful.

    D. Being too ready to express one's anger can be as mentally unhealthy as repressing it.

    E. Women commit violent, anger-related crimes far less frequently than men.

    F. Some women become so afraid of their own anger that they lose the ability to know when they're angry.

Items that logically support the point: _____ _____ _____

ARGUMENT: Mastery Test 2

A. In each group, one statement is the point of an argument, and the other statements are support for that point. In the space provided, write the letter of the point of each group.

_____ 1. A. A defendant charged with assault and battery would be foolish to show up in the courtroom wearing a black leather jacket, jeans, and boots.
   B. The woman who dresses in sweatpants for a job interview with a major retail company isn't likely to be hired.
   C. Someone who shows up at a wedding wearing jeans and tennis shoes is likely to be considered rude.
   D. People make judgments about us based on the way we dress.

_____ 2. A. Bureaucratic "red tape" may call attention to an undesirable community project so that people can take steps to oppose it.
   B. The impersonality of bureaucracy means equal treatment for all who seek benefits.
   C. One researcher found that bureaucrats perform at a higher intellectual level than nonbureaucrats.
   D. Despite the popular idea of bureaucracies as places where workers are unthinking and nothing gets done, bureaucracies are not all bad.

_____ 3. A. Our schools must spend time dealing with such social problems as substance abuse and teenage pregnancy, which Japanese schools are not expected to do.
   B. U.S. schools are not entirely to blame for the lower achievement of their students compared with the skills of Japanese students.
   C. Many U.S. teenagers cut back on their study time by taking a part-time job, which is virtually unheard of in Japan.
   D. Many U.S. parents work full-time and leave homework decisions to their children, whereas Japanese mothers make sure their children study several hours each night.

_____ 4. A. Some nutritionists believe that dividing food intake into "three square meals a day" is a poor way to fuel metabolism.
   B. Many healthcare professionals now consider traditional American eating and activity patterns unhealthy.
   C. Heart specialists say today's jobs involve insufficient physical activity.
   D. According to healthcare professionals, fast food eaten "on the run" contributes to dangerously high levels of fat and cholesterol and forces the digestive system to work too hard and too fast.

(Continues on next page)

B. Each point is followed by three statements that provide relevant support and three that do not. In the spaces, write the letters of the **three** relevant statements of support.

5–7. **Point:** The ruby-throated hummingbird is an extraordinary bird.

   A. One of the world's smallest birds, it weighs only one-tenth of an ounce!

   B. It can be found in woods, orchards, and gardens.

   C. It can fly backward and upside down.

   D. Despite its tiny size, it migrates more than 1,850 miles.

   E. Its main food is nectar, but it also eats some insects and spiders.

   F. During the Victorian era, people often displayed stuffed hummingbirds in glass cases in their living rooms.

   Items that logically support the point: _____   _____   _____

8–10. **Point:** Wolfgang Amadeus Mozart was a musical genius.

   A. He started composing symphonies at age 9 and by age 13 had written his first opera.

   B. Many of Mozart's compositions are universally regarded as masterpieces.

   C. Even after being appointed to the prestigious position of concertmaster to the archbishop of Salzburg, Mozart made little money.

   D. Mozart composed at superhuman speed; for example, he wrote the overture to his opera *Don Giovanni* the night before its first performance.

   E. Mozart was eventually kicked out of the archbishop's palace by the successor to the man who had hired him.

   F. Like so many great artists, Mozart died in poverty.

   Items that logically support the point: _____   _____   _____

ARGUMENT: Mastery Test 3

A. Each point is followed by three statements that provide relevant support and three that do not. In the spaces, write the letters of the **three** relevant statements of support.

1–3. **Point:** When naming a baby, parents should consider the effect that a name may have on their child.

    A. Michael, Christopher, and Jessica are among the most popular children's names today.

    B. Unusual or out-of-date names such as Zipperath and Ubaldus may make a child a target for teasing by classmates.

    C. Children's initials have been known to have a negative impact on them. Patricia Irene Graham and Anthony Steven Smith are fine names, but when these children's friends realize what the initials spell, Patricia and Anthony may never hear the end of it.

    D. Some people change their names when they get older.

    E. Names like Buffy and Missy may be perfect for a baby, but they may not inspire confidence in the same person when she or he later runs for Congress or does heart surgery.

    F. The most common family name in the world is the Chinese name Chung, shared by at least 104 million people.

Items that logically support the point: _____ _____ _____

4–6. **Point:** Cutting down on fats in the diet is not easy.

    A. Fats are flavor carriers, so foods such as baked goods often seem tasteless without fat.

    B. Fats satisfy hunger, so people get hungrier more often on a very low-fat diet.

    C. Americans, on average, consume far too much fat, as a percentage of total calories.

    D. There are several different kinds of fats, some more harmful to health than others.

    E. Many popular frozen desserts contain large amounts of fat.

    F. Fat cells insulate the body from cold and help protect it from injury.

Items that logically support the point: _____ _____ _____

(Continues on next page)

B. For each group, read the three items of support (the evidence). Then, in the space provided, write the letter of the point that is adequately supported by that evidence.

Group 1

Support:

> • White settlers in North America were called pioneers rather than invaders; their conquest of the Native Americans' lands was called homesteading, not robbery.
> • Whites stereotyped the Native Americans as "lazy," although it was whites who forced them to give up their traditional occupations.
> • Whites called Native Americans savages, yet it was whites who slaughtered hundreds of thousands of Native Americans.

_____ 7. Which **point** is adequately supported by all the evidence above?
  A. When white people came to North America, they and the Native Americans were always enemies.
  B. Contrary to how they were stereotyped, Native Americans were not lazy.
  C. Language was used to hide the truth of the unjust treatment of Native Americans by white settlers.
  D. Native Americans naturally resisted the invasion of the white "settlers."

Group 2

Support:

> • In France, no house is given the number 13, and in Italy, the national lottery omits the number 13.
> • Friday the 13th is often considered the unluckiest of days; some believe it to be the day that Eve tempted Adam with the apple, the day the Great Flood began, and the day Jesus died.
> • In America, many modern skyscrapers, condos, coops, and apartments skip the number 13; the floor above level 12 is numbered 14.

_____ 8. Which **point** is adequately supported by all the evidence above?
  A. Thirteen is an unlucky number, and if you use it, you are just asking for trouble.
  B. Everyone is superstitious about something.
  C. Many people throughout the world are superstitious about the number 13.
  D. Another common superstition is the fear of walking under a ladder.

ARGUMENT: Mastery Test 4

A. The point below is followed by three statements that provide relevant support and three that do not. In the spaces, write the letters of the **three** relevant statements of support.

1–3. **Point:** Not all stereotypes are negative views of groups.

A. Asians are often stereotyped as a "model minority," presumably smarter and harder-working than others.

B. Redheaded women are supposed to be sultry, sexy, and gorgeous.

C. On the other hand, redheads are also supposed to be hot-tempered— a negative stereotype.

D. Women in general are stereotyped as having a "maternal instinct" and nurturing: in other words, as good mothers and good caregivers.

E. Other stereotypes of women depict them as being illogical and weak.

F. Most stereotypes are oversimplified at best and outright false at worst.

Items that logically support the point: _____   _____   _____

B. For each group, read the three items of support (the evidence). Then, in the space provided, write the letter of the point that is adequately supported by that evidence.

Group 1

Support:

> • In the early 1900s, classrooms were crowded, stuffy, poorly lit, and conducive to the spread of disease.
> • Classroom "learning" consisted mainly of memorizing questionable facts.
> • Physical punishment was commonly considered the best way to teach good behavior.

_____ 4. Which **point** is adequately supported by all the evidence above?

A. A century ago, most child education was an overwhelmingly negative experience.

B. Teachers in the early 1900s were poorly trained.

C. Parents of students a century ago objected to physical punishment of their children.

D. A century ago, few students completed high school.

(Continues on next page)

Group 2

Support:

> - At Western University last year, seven students were expelled for stealing the answer key to the final biology exam.
> - Many teachers report that when they leave the room during a test, students began to compare answers.
> - At some schools, students tape the answers for tests to their forearms and the palms of their hands.

_____ 5. Which **point** is adequately supported by all the evidence above?
   A. Kids today can't be trusted—they'll cheat every chance they get.
   B. Students today cheat more than their parents and grandparents did.
   C. High-school students are more likely to cheat than college students.
   D. Cheating has been a problem at some schools.

C. Read the paragraphs below and then answer the questions that follow.

¹The lack of childcare places women at a disadvantage in the workplace. ²First of all, women are sometimes prevented from taking paid positions when good childcare is unavailable. ³Participation in many social activities is also difficult for these same women. ⁴In addition, childcare problems force women to stay in part-time jobs with lower pay, little career mobility, and no fringe benefits. ⁵Finally, the childcare dilemma discourages women from putting in the time necessary to seek and accept job promotions. ⁶Women with childcare responsibilities thus often have no choice but to remain in jobs for which they are overqualified.

_____ 6. Which sentence is the point of the argument?

_____ 7. Which sentence is **not** relevant support for the author's argument?
   A. Sentence 2   C. Sentence 4
   B. Sentence 3   D. Sentence 5

¹Animals can be useful in promoting mental stability and health. ²By forming close relationships with animals, we can demonstrate the kinship of all living things. ³Experiments in prisons have shown that convicts who are allowed pets become less violent. ⁴Also, patients in nursing homes show greater responsiveness and a more positive attitude when they have an opportunity to share affection with dogs and cats. ⁵When some autistic children were given the opportunity to interact with dolphins, they made great strides, including speaking for the first time in their lives.

_____ 8. Which sentence is **not** relevant support for the author's argument?
   A. Sentence 2   C. Sentence 4
   B. Sentence 3   D. Sentence 5

ARGUMENT: Mastery Test 5

A. Read the paragraphs below and then answer the questions that follow.

[1]The age of required retirement in companies should be raised, and the age at which Social Security begins should be raised. [2]First of all, older workers who remain healthy are valuable workers. [3]Although they may lose some mental speed, their accumulated experience more than compensates for the loss of quickness. [4]In fact, compared with youngsters, older persons may take longer to make a decision, but it is usually a better one. [5]Many studies have shown that the quality of job performance improves with age. [6]Furthermore, raising the retirement age would prevent some of the dire economic consequences that older workers face when they are forced to retire before they need to. [7]Nearly 60 percent of workers in the private sector reach retirement age without any pension from their lifelong work, so they should be allowed to continue working for economic reasons. [8]Luckily, older people don't have to furnish a home, raise children, and pay for educational expenses. [9]Finally, raising the age of required retirement could also mean raising the age that Social Security payments begin. [10]As a result, the cost of one of our country's biggest financial burdens will go down.

_____ 1. Which sentence is the point of the argument?
   A. Sentence 1   C. Sentence 5
   B. Sentence 2   D. Sentence 9

_____ 2. Which sentence is **not** relevant support for the point of the argument?
   A. Sentence 3   C. Sentence 5
   B. Sentence 4   D. Sentence 8

(Continues on next page)

[1]Victimless crimes involving drug use or sexual activity should be decriminalized. [2]These crimes consume an inordinate amount of the time and resources of the criminal justice system and clog already congested courts and jails. [3]Additionally, the laws against drug use and sexual activity almost invariably lead to the development of a black market supplied by organized crime. [4]Victimless crimes are often related to the corruption of police officers and others in the criminal justice system who receive bribes and payoffs from illegal suppliers and practitioners. [5]Of course, if police officers were honest, then bribery would not be a problem. [6]Finally, victimless crime involves acts that are private matters, acts that are not rightfully the concern of government or other people.

_____ 3. Which sentence is the point of the argument?
   A. Sentence 1   C. Sentence 3
   B. Sentence 2   D. Sentence 4

_____ 4. Which sentence is **not** relevant support for the point of the argument?
   A. Sentence 3   C. Sentence 5
   B. Sentence 4   D. Sentence 6

B. In the group below, read the three items of support (the evidence). Then, in the space provided, write the letter of the point that is adequately supported by that evidence.

Support:

> • In 1927, Charles Lindbergh flew from New York to Paris, France, in 33 hours, 29 minutes; in 1978, the Concorde supersonic airliner made the same trip in 3 hours, 30 minutes.
> • In 1825, an early steam-engine train, Locomotion I, pulled 48 tons at a speed of 15 miles per hour; in 1988, West Germany's Intercity Experimental train attained the fastest speed for a train carrying passengers—252 miles per hour.
> • The first gasoline-driven car, built by Karl Friedrich Benz in 1885, was a three-wheeler that reached 8–10 miles per hour; in 1997, Andy Green drove his jet-engined car at a speed of over 763 miles per hour.

_____ 5. Which **point** is adequately supported by all the evidence above?
   A. Someday soon, trains will go faster than airplanes.
   B. The American cars of the future will run on jet engines.
   C. Transportation speeds have greatly increased over the past two centuries.
   D. No airliner will ever fly faster than the Concorde.

ARGUMENT: Mastery Test 6

A. Read the paragraphs below and then answer the questions that follow.

[1]The Civil War brought slavery to an end. [2]However, when Reconstruction ended in 1877 with the withdrawal of federal troops from the South, whites in the region regained power and gradually reestablished racial segregation. [3]They enacted a variety of laws that prohibited black citizens from using the same public facilities as whites. [4]During that same time, however, positive milestones such as the founding of the Tuskegee Institute occurred. [5]In *Plessy v. Ferguson* (1896), the Supreme Court endorsed these laws, ruling that "separate" facilities for the two races did not violate the Constitution as long as the facilities were "equal." [6]The Plessy decision, in practice, became a justification for the separate and unequal treatment of African Americans. [7]Black children, for instance, were forced into separate schools that rarely had libraries and had few teachers. [8]They were given worn-out books that had been used previously in white schools.

_____ 1. Which sentence is the point of the argument?
  A. Sentence 1   C. Sentence 3
  B. Sentence 2   D. Sentence 5

_____ 2. Which sentence is **not** relevant support for the point of the argument?
  A. Sentence 3   C. Sentence 5
  B. Sentence 4   D. Sentence 6

[1]Many Westerners are uncomfortable with silence, which they find embarrassing and awkward. [2]In contrast, Asian cultures have for thousands of years promoted quiet and discouraged the expression of thoughts and feelings. [3]Silence is valued. [4]Asian proverbs support this point of view, saying, "In much talk there is great weariness," and "One who speaks does not know; one who knows does not speak." [5]Unlike Westerners who tend to chatter nervously to fill up silence, Japanese and Chinese believe that remaining quiet is the proper state when there is nothing essential to be said. [6]Of course, individual quirks may make a Westerner very quiet or an Asian person talkative. [7]To Asians, a talkative person is often considered to be showing off or insincere.

_____ 3. Which sentence is the point of the argument?
  A. Sentence 1   C. Sentence 5
  B. Sentence 3   D. Sentence 7

_____ 4. Which sentence is **not** relevant support for the point of the argument?
  A. Sentence 3   C. Sentence 5
  B. Sentence 4   D. Sentence 6

(Continues on next page)

B. In the group below, read the three items of support (the evidence). Then, in the space provided, write the letter of the point that is adequately supported by that evidence.

Support:

- Laughter has been called "inner jogging"—a hearty laugh gives a good workout to some muscles, such as those in the face, shoulders, and abdomen.
- A robust laugh initiates rushes of hormones that numb pain and that lift you to a high level of alertness.
- In one study, watching a funny tape of a comedian's performance temporarily raised saliva levels of antibodies, which help defend against infection.

_____ 5. Which **point** is adequately supported by all the evidence above?
  A. Laughter prevents a wide range of diseases.
  B. Laughter is a way to overcome our anxieties and fears.
  C. Laughter leads to sound sleep.
  D. Laughter is good for our health.

Part II

TEN READING SELECTIONS

1

The Professor Is a Dropout
Beth Johnson

Preview

After being mistakenly labeled "retarded" and humiliated into dropping out of first grade, Lupe Quintanilla knew she wanted nothing more to do with formal education. Life as a wife and mother would satisfy her . . . and it did, until she saw her own children being pushed aside as "slow learners." Driven to help them succeed, Lupe took steps that dramatically changed her life.

Words to Watch

radical (16): extreme
plant (29): a person put somewhere to spy
renowned (36): famous

1   Guadalupe Quintanilla is an assistant professor at the University of Houston. She is president of her own communications company. She trains law enforcement officers all over the country. She was nominated to serve as the U.S. Attorney General. She's been a representative to the United Nations.

2   That's a pretty impressive string of accomplishments. It's all the more impressive when you consider this:

"Lupe" Quintanilla is a first-grade dropout. Her school records state that she is retarded, that her IQ is so low she can't learn much of anything.

How did Lupe Quintanilla, "retarded" nonlearner, become Dr. Quintanilla, respected educator? Her remarkable journey began in the town of Nogales, Mexico, just below the Arizona border. That's where Lupe first lived with her grandparents. (Her parents had divorced.) Then an uncle who had just finished medical school made her grandparents a generous offer. If they wanted to live with him, he would support the family as he began his medical practice.

4   Lupe, her grandparents, and her uncle all moved hundreds of miles to a town in southern Mexico that didn't even have paved roads, let alone any schools. There, Lupe grew up helping her grandfather run his little pharmacy and her grandmother keep house. She remembers the time happily. "My grandparents were wonderful," she said. "Oh, my grandfather was stern, authoritarian, as Mexican culture demanded, but they were also very kind to me." When the chores were done, her grandfather taught Lupe to read and write Spanish and do basic arithmetic.

5   When Lupe was 12, her grandfather became blind. The family left Mexico and went to Brownsville, Texas, with the hope that doctors there could restore his sight. Once they arrived in Brownsville, Lupe was enrolled in school. Although she understood no English, she was given an IQ test in that language. Not surprisingly, she didn't do very well.

6   Lupe even remembers her score. "I scored a sixty-four, which classified me as seriously retarded, not even teachable," she said. "I was put into first grade with a class of six-year-olds. My duties were to take the little kids to the bathroom and to cut out pictures." The classroom activities were a total mystery to Lupe—they were all conducted in English. And she was humiliated by the other children, who teased her for being "so much older and so much dumber" than they were.

7   After four months in first grade, an incident occurred that Lupe still does not fully understand. As she stood in the

Guadalupe Quintanilla today

doorway of the classroom waiting to escort a little girl to the bathroom, a man approached her. He asked her, in Spanish, how to find the principal's office. Lupe was delighted. "Finally someone in this school had spoken to me with words I could understand, in the language of my soul, the language of my grandmother," she said. Eagerly, she answered his question in Spanish. Instantly her teacher swooped down on her, grabbing her arm and scolding her. She pulled Lupe along to the principal's office. There, the teacher and the principal both shouted at her, obviously very angry. Lupe was frightened and embarrassed, but also bewildered. She didn't understand a word they were saying.

8   "Why were they so angry? I don't know," said Lupe. "Was it because I spoke Spanish at school? Or that I spoke to the man at all? I really don't know. All I know is how humiliated I was."

9   When she got home that day, she cried miserably, begging her grandfather not to make her return to school. Finally he agreed.

10   From that time on, Lupe stayed at home, serving as her blind grandfather's "eyes." She was a fluent reader in Spanish, and the older man loved to have her read newspapers, poetry, and novels aloud to him for hours.

11   Lupe's own love of reading flourished during these years. Her vocabulary was enriched and her imagination fired by the novels she read—novels which she learned later were classics of Spanish literature. She read *Don Quixote,* the famous story of the noble, impractical knight who fought against windmills. She read thrilling accounts of the Mexican revolution. She read *La Prensa,* the local Spanish-language paper, and *Selecciones,* the Spanish-language version of *Reader's Digest.*

12   When she was just 16, Lupe married a young Mexican American dental technician. Within five years, she had given birth to her three children, Victor, Mario, and Martha. Lupe's grandparents lived with the young family. Lupe was quite happy with her life. "I cooked, sewed, cleaned, and cared for everybody," she said. "I listened to my grandmother when she told me what made a good wife. In the morning I would actually put on my husband's shoes and tie the laces—anything to make his life easier. Living with my grandparents for so long, I was one generation behind in my ideas of what a woman could do and be."

13   Lupe's contentment ended when her children started school. When they brought home their report cards, she struggled to understand them. She could read enough English to know that what they said was not good. Her children had been put into a group called "Yellow Birds." It was a group for slow learners.

14   At night in bed, Lupe cried and blamed herself. It was obvious—not only was *she* retarded, but her children had taken after her. Now they, too, would never be able to learn like other children.

15   But in time, a thought began to break through Lupe's despair: Her children didn't seem like slow learners to *her.* At home, they learned everything she taught them, quickly and easily. She read to them constantly, from the books that she herself had loved as a child. *Aesop's Fables* and stories from *1,001 Arabian Nights* were family favorites. The children filled the house with the sounds of the songs, prayers, games, and rhymes they had learned from their parents and grandparents. They were smart children, eager to learn. They learned quickly—in Spanish.

16   A radical° idea began to form in Lupe's mind. Maybe the school was *wrong* about her children. And if the school system could be wrong about her children—maybe it had been wrong about her, too.

17   Lupe visited her children's school, a daring action for her. "Many Hispanic parents would not dream of going to the classroom," she said. "In Hispanic culture, the teacher is regarded as a third parent, as an ultimate authority. To question her would seem most disrespectful, as though you were saying that she didn't know her job." That was one reason Lupe's grandparents had not interfered when Lupe was classified as retarded. "Anglo

teachers often misunderstand Hispanic parents, believing that they aren't concerned about their children's education because they don't come visit the schools," Lupe said. "It's not a lack of concern at all. It's a mark of respect for the teacher's authority."

18 At her children's school, Lupe spoke to three different teachers. Two of them told her the same thing: "Your children are just slow. Sorry, but they can't learn." A third offered a glimmer of hope. He said, "They don't know how to function in English. It's possible that if you spoke English at home they would be able to do better."

19 Lupe pounced on that idea. "Where can I learn English?" she asked. The teacher shrugged. At that time there were no local English-language programs for adults. Finally he suggested that Lupe visit the local high school. Maybe she would be permitted to sit in the back of a classroom and pick up some English that way.

20 Lupe made an appointment with a counselor at the high school. But when the two women met, the counselor shook her head. "Your test scores show that you are retarded," she told Lupe. "You'd just be taking space in the classroom away from someone who could learn."

21 Lupe's next stop was the hospital where she had served for years as a volunteer. Could she sit in on some of the nursing classes held there? No, she was told, not without a diploma. Still undeterred, she went on to Texas Southmost College in Brownsville. Could she sit in on a class? No; no high-school diploma. Finally she went to the telephone company, where she knew operators were being trained. Could she listen in on the classes? No, only high-school graduates were permitted.

22 That day, leaving the telephone company, Lupe felt she had hit bottom. She had been terrified in the first place to try to find an English class. Meeting with rejection after rejection nearly destroyed what little self-confidence she had. She walked home in the rain, crying. "I felt like a big barrier had fallen across my path," she said. "I couldn't go over it; I couldn't go under it; I couldn't go around it."

23 But the next day Lupe woke with fresh determination. "I was motivated by love of my kids," she said. "I was not going to quit." She got up; made breakfast for her kids, husband, and grandparents; saw her children and husband off for the day; and started out again. "I remember walking to the bus stop, past a dog that always scared me to death, and heading back to the college. The lady I spoke to said, 'I told you, we can't do anything for you without a high-school degree.' But as I left the building, I went up to the first Spanish-speaking student I saw. His name was Gabito. I said, 'Who really makes the decisions around here?' He said, 'The registrar.'" Since she hadn't had any luck in the office building, Lupe decided to take a more direct approach. She asked Gabito to point out the registrar's car in the parking lot. For the next two hours she waited beside it until its owner showed up.

24 Impressed by Lupe's persistence, the registrar listened to her story. But instead of giving her permission to sit in on a class and learn more English, he insisted that she sign up for a full college load. Before she knew it, she was enrolled in four classes: basic math, basic English, psychology, and typing. The registrar's parting words to her were, "Don't come back if you don't make it through."

Lupe enjoys a story with (left to right) her twin grandchildren,
Alyssa and Christian, and a visiting friend.

25   With that "encouragement," Lupe began a semester that was part nightmare, part dream come true. Every day she got her husband and children off to school, took the bus to campus, came home to make lunch for her husband and grandparents, went back to campus, and was home in time to greet Victor, Mario, and Martha when they got home from school. In the evenings she cooked, cleaned, did laundry, and got the children to bed. Then she would study, often until three in the morning.

26   "Sometimes in class I would feel sick with the stress of it," she said. "I'd go to the bathroom and talk to myself in the mirror. Sometimes I'd say, 'What are you doing here? Why don't you go home and watch *I Love Lucy?*' "

27   But she didn't go home. Instead, she studied furiously, using her Spanish-English dictionary, constantly making lists of new words she wanted to understand. "I still do that today," she said. "When I come across a word I don't know, I write it down, look it up, and write sentences using it until I *own* that word."

28   Although so much of the language and subject matter was new to Lupe, one part of the college experience was not. That was the key skill of reading, a skill Lupe possessed. As she struggled with English, she found the reading speed, comprehension, and vocabulary that she had developed in Spanish carrying over into her new language. "Reading," she said, "reading was the vehicle. Although I didn't know it at the time, when I was a

girl learning to love to read, I was laying the foundation for academic success."

29   She gives credit, too, to her Hispanic fellow students. "At first, they didn't know what to make of me. They were eighteen years old, and at that time it was very unfashionable for an older person to be in college. But once they decided I wasn't a 'plant'° from the administration, they were my greatest help." The younger students spent hours helping Lupe, explaining unfamiliar words and terms, coaching her, and answering her questions.

30   That first semester passed in a fog of exhaustion. Many mornings, Lupe doubted she could get out of bed, much less care for her family and tackle her classes. But when she thought of her children and what was at stake for them, she forced herself on. She remembers well what those days were like. "Just a day at a time. That was all I could think about. I could make myself get up one more day, study one more day, cook and clean one more day. And those days eventually turned into a semester."

31   To her own amazement perhaps as much as anyone's, Lupe discovered that she was far from retarded. Although she sweated blood over many assignments, she completed them. She turned them in on time. And, remarkably, she made the dean's list her very first semester.

32   After that, there was no stopping Lupe Quintanilla. She soon realized that the associate's degree offered by Texas Southmost College would not satisfy her. Continuing her Monday, Wednesday, and Friday schedule at Southmost, she enrolled for Tuesday and Thursday courses at Pan American University, a school 140 miles from Brownsville. Within three years, she had earned both her junior-college degree and a bachelor's degree in biology. She then won a fellowship that took her to graduate school at the University of Houston, where she earned a master's degree in Spanish literature. When she graduated, the university offered her a job as director of the Mexican American studies program. While in that position, she earned a doctoral degree in education.

33   How did she do it all? Lupe herself isn't sure. "I hardly know. When I think back to those years, it seems like a life that someone else lived." It was a rich and exciting but also very challenging period for Lupe and her family. On the one hand, Lupe was motivated by the desire to set an example for her children, to prove to them that they could succeed in the English-speaking academic world. On the other hand, she worried about neglecting her family. She tried hard to attend important activities, such as parents' meetings at school and her children's sporting events. But things didn't always work out. Lupe still remembers attending a baseball game that her older son, Victor, was playing in. When Victor came to bat, he hit a home run. But as the crowd cheered and Victor glanced proudly over at his mother in the stands, he saw she was studying a textbook. "I hadn't seen the home run," Lupe admitted. "That sort of thing was hard for everyone to take."

34   Although Lupe worried that her children would resent her busy schedule, she also saw her success reflected in them as they blossomed in school. She forced herself to speak English at home, and their language skills improved quickly. She read to them in English instead of Spanish—gulping down her pride as their pronunciation became better than hers and they began correcting her. (Once the children were in high school and fluent in English, Lupe switched back to Spanish

*Two members of the Houston police department learn job-specific Spanish phrases
from Lupe. Lupe also trains the officers in cultural awareness.*

at home, so that the children would be fully comfortable in both languages.) "I saw the change in them almost immediately," she said. "After I helped them with their homework, they would see me pulling out my own books and going to work. In the morning, I would show them the papers I had written. As I gained confidence, so did they." By the next year, the children had been promoted out of the Yellow Birds.

35   Even though Victor, Mario, and Martha all did well academically, Lupe realized she could not assume that they would face no more obstacles in school. When Mario was in high school, for instance, he wanted to sign up for a debate class. Instead, he was assigned to woodworking. She visited the school to ask why. Mario's teacher told her, "He's good with his hands. He'll be a great carpenter, and that's a good thing for a

Mexican to be." Controlling her temper, Lupe responded, "I'm glad you think he's good with his hands. He'll be a great physician someday, and he *is* going to be in the debate class."

Today, Lupe Quintanilla teaches at   36 the University of Houston, where she has developed several dozen courses concerning Hispanic literature and culture. Her cross-cultural training for law enforcement officers, which helps bring police and firefighters and local Hispanic communities closer together, is renowned° throughout the country. Former President Ronald Reagan named her to a national board that keeps the White House informed of new programs in law enforcement. She has received numerous awards for teaching excellence, and there is even a scholarship named in her honor. Her name appears in the Hispanic Hall of Fame, and she has been co-chair of the White House Commission on Hispanic Education.

37   The love of reading that her grandfather instilled in Lupe is still alive. She thinks of him every year when she introduces to her students one of his favorite poets, Amado Nervo. She requires them to memorize these lines from one of Nervo's poems: "When I got to the end of my long journey in life, I realized that I was the architect of my own destiny." Of these lines, Lupe says, "That is something that I deeply believe, and I want my students to learn it *before* the end of their long journey. We create our own destiny."

Her love of reading and learning has helped Lupe create a distinguished destiny. But none of the honors she has received means more to her than the success of her own children, the reason she made that frightening journey to seek classes in English years ago. Today Mario *is* a physician. Victor and Martha are lawyers, both having earned doctor of law degrees. And so today, Lupe likes to say, "When someone calls the house and asks for 'Dr. Quintanilla,' I have to ask, 'Which one?' There are four of us—one retarded and three slow learners." 38

Lupe surrounded by her children: Martha, Victor, and Mario.

BASIC SKILL QUESTIONS

Vocabulary in Context

_____ 1. In the excerpt below, the word *flourished* (flûr′ĭsht) means
- A. grew.
- B. stood still.
- C. was lost.
- D. remained.

> "Lupe's own love of reading flourished during these years. Her vocabulary was enriched and her imagination fired by the novels she read. . . . " (Paragraph 11)

_____ 2. In the excerpt below, the word *vehicle* (vē′ĭ-kəl) means
- A. obstacle.
- B. loss.
- C. means.
- D. place.

> "Reading," she said, "reading was the vehicle. Although I didn't know it at the time, when I was a girl learning to love to read, I was laying the foundation for academic success." (Paragraph 28)

_____ 3. In the sentence below, the word *instilled* (ĭn-stĭld′) means
- A. frightened.
- B. established.
- C. forced.
- D. forgot.

> "The love of reading that her grandfather instilled in her is still alive." (Paragraph 37)

Central Point and Main Ideas

_____ 4. Which sentence best expresses the central point of the selection?
- A. Lupe, a first-grade dropout, eventually earned a doctoral degree and created a professional career.
- B. Lupe Quintanilla's experience proves that the educational system must be set up to accommodate somehow children who speak languages other than English.
- C. Through hard work and persistence combined with a love of reading and learning, Lupe has created a distinguished career and helped her children become professionals.
- D. In school, Spanish-speaking students may experience obstacles to aiming for a professional career.

_____ 5. Which of the following sentences expresses the main idea of paragraphs 19–24?

   A. People at school, a hospital, and a telephone company rejected Lupe's requests for an education.

   B. Overcoming rejections and disappointment, Lupe finally found someone who gave her a chance to learn English by enrolling at a college.

   C. Lupe discovered that the person who made decisions about who could go to college and who could not was the registrar of the college.

   D. The tests Lupe took in first grade indicating that she was retarded were a barrier to her desire to learn English.

_____ 6. Which of the following sentences expresses the main idea of paragraph 34?

   A. Lupe's children blossomed in school as she continued to speak English to them and was a role model for them.

   B. Lupe was afraid that her children would resent the busy schedule that kept her from spending as much time with them as she would have liked.

   C. Wanting her children to know both English and Spanish, Lupe spoke Spanish at home once her children knew English.

   D. After helping her children with their homework, Lupe would do her own homework.

Supporting Details

_____ 7. Lupe realized that her children were not retarded when

   A. they got good grades at school.

   B. they were put in the group called "Yellow Birds."

   C. she saw how quickly they learned at home.

   D. they read newspapers, poetry, and novels to her.

_____ 8. Lupe's training for law enforcement officers

   A. teaches them to speak Spanish.

   B. brings police, firefighters, and local Hispanic communities together.

   C. offers a scholarship named in her honor.

   D. teaches Hispanic literature and culture.

Transitions

_____ 9. The relationship between the last sentence below and the two that come before it is one of

   A. time.

   B. addition.

   C. illustration.

   D. cause and effect.

   " 'In Hispanic culture, the teacher is regarded as a third parent, as an ultimate authority. To question her would seem most disrespectful, as though you were saying that she didn't know her job.' That was one reason Lupe's grandparents had not interfered when Lupe was classified as retarded." (Paragraph 17)

_____ 10. The relationship between the two sentences below is one of
A. addition.
B. illustration.
C. contrast.
D. cause and effect.

"When Mario was in high school . . . he wanted to sign up for debate class. Instead, he was assigned to woodworking." (Paragraph 35)

Patterns of Organization

_____ 11. The pattern of organization of Paragraph 1 is
A. time order.
B. list of items.
C. contrast.
D. comparison.

_____ 12. The main pattern of organization of paragraphs 3–35 is
A. time order.
B. list of items.
C. definition and example.
D. contrast.

ADVANCED SKILL QUESTIONS

Fact and Opinion

_____ 13. The statement below is
A. a fact.
B. an opinion.
C. both fact and opinion.

"Today, Lupe Quintanilla teaches at the University of Houston, where she has developed several dozen courses concerning Hispanic literature and culture." (Paragraph 36)

_____ 14. The word that makes the statement below an opinion is
A. *reading.*
B. *learning.*
C. *create.*
D. *distinguished.*

"Her love of reading and learning has helped Lupe create a distinguished destiny." (Paragraph 38)

Inferences

_____ 15. From the sentences below, we might conclude that

    A. although Lupe was not very intelligent at first, she became more intelligent once she learned English.

    B. Lupe really did know English.

    C. there are no IQ tests in Spanish.

    D. an IQ test in a language that the person tested doesn't know is useless.

> "Once they arrived in Brownsville, Lupe was enrolled in school. Although she understood no English, she was given an IQ test in that language. Not surprisingly, she didn't do very well." (Paragraph 5)

_____ 16. We might conclude from the reading that

    A. a school system's judgment about an individual is always accurate.

    B. it is often better for a child to stay home rather than attend school.

    C. by paying attention and speaking up, parents may remove obstacles to their children's education.

    D. working parents should accept the fact that they cannot attend important events in their children's lives.

_____ 17. The last line of the reading suggests that

    A. retarded people can become successful professionals.

    B. people should not blindly accept other people's opinion of them.

    C. Lupe's children are smarter than she is.

    D. all of the above.

Purpose and Tone

_____ 18. The author's main purpose is to

    A. inform readers of the struggle Lupe and her children endured to gain an education and accomplish their goals.

    B. persuade readers that the educational system needs to be reformed.

    C. entertain readers with anecdotes about Lupe's adventures in school.

_____ 19. The general tone of the reading is

    A. instructive.

    B. sentimental.

    C. admiring.

    D. uncertain.

Argument

_____ 20. One of the following statements is the point of an argument. The other statements are support for that point. Write the letter of the point of the argument.

    A. Lupe and others thought of her as being retarded because an educator gave her an IQ test in a language she didn't know.

B. Putting Mario in a stereotypical career category, one teacher said, "He'll be a great carpenter, and that's a good thing for a Mexican to be."

C. Through lack of insight and perpetuation of stereotypes, educators became obstacles to Lupe's and her children's education.

D. A teacher and principal shouted at young Lupe in a language she didn't understand, bewildering and embarrassing her so much that she dropped out of school.

SUMMARIZING

Add the ideas needed to complete the following summary of "The Professor Is a Dropout."

When Lupe Quintanilla was very young, she and her grandparents moved from Nogales, Mexico, to live with her uncle in a small town in southern Mexico that had no schools. When she was 12, _____ _____ _____.

In Brownsville, Lupe was enrolled in school. After scoring poorly on an IQ test that was given in English, which she did not speak, Lupe was put in first grade. When _____ _____, Lupe begged her grandfather not to send her back to school. Lupe stayed home, where she read newspapers, poetry, and novels to her grandfather. At 16, she married, and within five years, she had three children. When her children were enrolled in school, they were grouped as slow learners, a fact that depressed Lupe—until she realized that at home, they didn't seem like slow learners. That gave her courage to go to school and talk to her children's teachers. When one suggested that _____ might help her children, Lupe began a search for a way to learn English that ended in attending college and then a university, where she earned a doctoral degree in education. And by speaking English at home, helping her children with their homework, and serving as a good role model, Lupe encouraged her children to do well in school as well. Today, Lupe has a distinguished career as a professor and emphasizes to her students that they create their own destinies. She is also a communications company president and law enforcement trainer. She has been a representative to the United Nations. But what means most to her is _____ _____.

DISCUSSION QUESTIONS

1. Lupe credits her fellow Hispanic students with being a great help to her in college. Is there anyone in your life—a teacher, family member, or friend—who has helped you through challenging times during your education? Explain what your obstacle was and how this person helped you to overcome it.

2. Lupe found that her school responsibilities conflicted with her duties as wife and mother. What kinds of personal responsibilities have you had to juggle as a student? These may include parenthood, a job, a difficult home situation, extracurricular school activities, or anything else that poses a challenge to your academics. How have you balanced these obligations with your role as student?

3. Lupe is an outstanding example of a person who took charge of her life. Would you say that you have taken charge of your life? Describe how, or describe what you think you must yet do to take charge of your life.

4. By the end of Lupe's story, we see the serious mistakes made by those who called her "retarded" and her children "slow learners." Was there ever a time when you felt people misjudged you? What did they say about you that was wrong, and how did it make you feel? Explain how you reacted to their judgments—did you accept their remarks, or did you fight to disprove them?

Note: Writing assignments for this selection appear on page 633.

Check Your Performance	THE PROFESSOR IS A DROPOUT		
Activity	*Number Right*	*Points*	*Score*
BASIC SKILL QUESTIONS			
Vocabulary in Context (3 items)	_____	× 4 =	_____
Central Point and Main Ideas (3 items)	_____	× 4 =	_____
Supporting Details (2 items)	_____	× 4 =	_____
Transitions (2 items)	_____	× 4 =	_____
Patterns of Organization (2 items)	_____	× 4 =	_____
ADVANCED SKILL QUESTIONS			
Fact and Opinion (2 items)	_____	× 4 =	_____
Inferences (3 items)	_____	× 4 =	_____
Purpose and Tone (2 items)	_____	× 4 =	_____
Argument (1 item)	_____	× 4 =	_____
SUMMARIZING (4 items)	_____	× 5 =	_____
	TOTAL SCORE =		_____ %

Enter your total score into the **Reading Performance Chart: Ten Reading Selections** on the inside back cover.

2

Taming the Anger Monster

Anne Davidson

Preview

Many of us have an anger problem. We may snap at slow-moving clerks, swear at aggressive drivers, or steam at the general incompetence that many people (including ourselves) show in the matters of everyday life. Why are we so irritable? Is there anything we can do about it? This article explores the roots of our anger and suggests some ways of coping.

Words to Watch

designated (3): set apart for a particular purpose
petty (5): insignificant
chronic (15): continuous
diffuse (15): not confined to one area; present everywhere
self-perpetuating (15): causing itself to continue
catharsis (15): a release of tension

1   Laura Houser remembers the day with embarrassment.

2   "My mother was visiting from Illinois," she says. "We'd gone out to lunch and done some shopping. On our way home, we stopped at an intersection. When the light changed, the guy ahead of us was looking at a map or something and didn't move right away. I leaned on my horn and automatically yelled—well, what I generally yell at people who make me wait. I didn't even think about what I was doing. One moment I was talking and laughing with my mother, and the next I was shouting curses at a stranger. Mom's jaw just dropped. She said, 'Well,

I guess *you've* been living in the city too long.' That's when I realized that my anger was out of control."

3   Laura has plenty of company. Here are a few examples plucked from the headlines of recent newspapers:

- Amtrak's Washington-New York train: When a woman begins to use her cell phone in a designated° "quiet car," her seatmate grabs the phone and smashes it against the wall.

- Reading, Massachusetts: Arguing over rough play at their ten-year-old son's hockey practice, two fathers begin throwing punches. One of the dads beats the other to death.

- Westport, Connecticut: Two super-market shoppers get into a fistfight over who should be first in a just-opened checkout line.

4   Reading these stories and countless others like them which happen daily, it's hard to escape the conclusion that we are one angry society. An entire vocabulary has grown up to describe situations of out-of-control fury: road rage, sideline rage, computer rage, biker rage, air rage. Bookstore shelves are filled with authors' advice on how to deal with our anger. Court-ordered anger management classes have become commonplace, and anger-management workshops are advertised in local newspapers.

5   Human beings have always experienced anger, of course. But in earlier, more civil decades, public displays of anger were unusual to the point of being aberrant. Today, however, whether in petty° or deadly forms, episodes of unrepressed rage have become part of our daily landscape.

6   What has happened to us? Are we that much angrier than we used to be?

[left margin, handwritten:] aberrant – defect in focus, blurring in an image

Have we lost all inhibitions about expressing our anger? Are we, as a society, literally losing our ability to control our tempers?

WHY ARE WE SO ANGRY?

7   According to Sybil Evans, a conflict-resolution expert in New York City, there are three components to blame for our societal bad behavior: time, technology and tension.

8   What's eating up our time? To begin with, Americans work longer hours and are rewarded with less vacation time than people in any other industrial society. Over an average year, for example, most British employees work 250 hours less than most Americans; most Germans work a full 500 hours less. And most Europeans are given four to six weeks of vacation each year, compared to the average American's two weeks. And to top it all off, many Americans face long, stressful commutes at the beginning and end of each long workday.

9   Once we Americans do get home from work, our busy day is rarely done. We are involved in community activities; our children participate in sports, school programs, and extracurricular activities; and our houses, yards and cars cry out for maintenance. To make matters worse, we are reluctant to use the little bit of leisure time we do have to catch up on our sleep. Compared with Americans of the nineteenth and early twentieth centuries, most of us are chronically sleep-deprived. While our ancestors typically slept nine and a half hours a night, many of us feel lucky to get seven. We're critical of "lazy" people who sleep longer, and we associate naps with toddlerhood. (In doing so, we ignore the examples of successful people, including

Winston Churchill, Albert Einstein, and Napoleon, all of whom were devoted to their afternoon naps.)

10   The bottom line: we are time-challenged and just plain tired—and tired people are cranky people. We're ready to blow—to snap at the slow-moving cashier, to tap the bumper of the slowpoke ahead of us, or to do something far worse.

11   Technology is also to blame for the bad behavior so widespread in our culture. Amazing gadgets were supposed to make our lives easier—but have they? Sure, technology has its positive aspects. It is a blessing, for instance, to have a cell phone on hand when your car breaks down far from home or to be able to "instant message" a friend on the other side of the globe. But the downsides are many. Cell phones, pagers, fax machines, handheld computers and the like have robbed many of us of what was once valuable downtime. Now we're *always* available to take that urgent call or act on that last-minute demand. Then there is the endless pressure of feeling we need to keep up with our gadgets' latest technological developments. For example, it's not sufficient to use your cell phone for phone calls. Now you must learn to use the phone for text-messaging and downloading games. It's not enough to take still photos with your digital camera. You should know how to shoot ultra high-speed fast-action clips. It's not enough to have an enviable CD collection. You should be downloading new songs in MP3 format. The computers in your house should be connected by a wireless router, and online via high-speed DSL service. In other words, if it's been more than ten minutes since you've updated your technology, you're probably behind.

12   In fact, you're not only behind; you're a stupid loser. At least, that's how most of us end up feeling as we're confronted with more and more unexpected technologies: the do-it-yourself checkout at the supermarket, the telephone "help center" that offers a recorded series of messages, but no human help. And feeling like losers makes us frustrated and, you guessed it, angry. "It's not any one thing but lots of little things that make people feel like they don't have control of their lives," says Jane Middleton-Moz, an author and therapist. "A sense of helplessness is what triggers rage. It's why people end up kicking ATM machines."

13   Her example is not far-fetched. According to a survey of computer users in Great Britain, a quarter of those under age 25 admitted to having kicked or punched their computers on at least one occasion. Others confessed to yanking out cables in a rage, forcing the computer to crash. On this side of the Atlantic, a Wisconsin man, after repeated attempts to get his daughter's malfunctioning computer repaired, took it to the store where he had bought it, placed it in the foyer, and attacked it with a sledge-hammer. Arrested and awaiting a court appearance, he told local reporters, "It feels good, in a way." He had put into action a fantasy many of us have had—that of taking out our feelings of rage on the machines that so frustrate us.

14   Tension, the third major culprit behind our epidemic of anger, is intimately connected with our lack of time and the pressures of technology. Merely our chronic exhaustion and our frustration in the face of a bewildering array of technologies would be enough to cause our stress levels to skyrocket, but we are dealing with much more. Our tension is often fueled by a reserve of anger that might be the result of a critical boss, marital discord, or (something that

many of today's men and women experience, if few will admit it) a general sense of being stupid and inadequate in the face of the demands of modern life. And along with the annoyances of everyday life, we now live with a widespread fear of such horrors as terrorist acts, global warming, and antibiotic-resistant diseases. Our sense of dread may be out of proportion to actual threats because of technology's ability to so constantly bombard us with worrisome information. Twenty-four-hour-a-day news stations bring a stream of horror into our living rooms. As we work at our computers, headlines and graphic images are never more than a mouse click away.

THE RESULT OF OUR ANGER

15 Add it all together—our feeling of never having enough time; the chronic° aggravation caused by technology; and our endless, diffuse° sense of stress—and we become time bombs waiting to explode. Our angry outbursts may be briefly satisfying, but afterwards we are left feeling—well, like jerks. Worse, flying off the handle is a self-perpetuating° behavior. Brad Bushman, a psychology professor at Iowa State University, says, "Catharsis° is worse than useless." Bushman's research has shown that when people vent their anger, they actually become more, not less, aggressive. "Many people think of anger as the psychological equivalent of the steam in a pressure cooker. It has to be released, or it will explode. That's not true. The people who react by hitting, kicking, screaming, and swearing just feel more angry."

16 Furthermore, the unharnessed venting of anger may actually do us physical harm. The vigorous expression of anger pumps adrenaline into our system and raises our blood pressure, setting the stage for heart attack and strokes. Frequently angry people have even been shown to have higher cholesterol levels than even-tempered individuals.

HOW TO DEAL WITH OUR ANGER

17 Unfortunately, the culprits behind much of our anger—lack of time, frustrating technology, and mega-levels of stress—are not likely to resolve themselves anytime soon. So what are we to do with the anger that arises as a result?

18 According to Carol Tavris, author of *Anger: The Misunderstood Emotion*, the keys to dealing with anger are common sense and patience. She points out that almost no situation is improved by an angry outburst. A traffic jam, a frozen computer, or a misplaced set of car keys is annoying. To act upon the angry feelings those situations provoke, however, is an exercise in futility. Shouting, fuming, or leaning on the car horn won't make traffic begin to flow, the screen unlock, or keys materialize.

19 Patience, on the other hand, is a highly practical virtue. People who take the time to cool down before responding to an anger-producing situation are far less likely to say or do something they will regret later. "It is true of the body as of arrows," Tavris says, "that what goes up must come down. Any emotional arousal will simmer down if you just wait long enough." When you are stuck in traffic, in other words, turn on some soothing music, breathe deeply, and count to ten—or thirty or forty, if need be.

20 Anger-management therapist Doris Wild Helmering agrees. "Like any

feeling, anger lasts only about three seconds," she says. "What keeps it going is your own negative thinking." As long as you focus on the idiot who cut you off on the expressway, you'll stay angry. But if you let the incident go, your anger will go with it. "Once you come to understand that you're driving your own anger with your thoughts," adds Helmering, "you can stop it."

21   Experts who have studied anger also encourage people to cultivate activities that effectively vent their anger. For some people, it's reading the newspaper or watching TV, while others need more active outlets, such as using a treadmill, taking a walk, hitting golf balls, or working out with a punching bag. People who succeed in calming their anger can also enjoy the satisfaction of having dealt positively with their frustrations.

For Laura Houser, the episode in the car with her mother was a wake-up call. "I saw myself through her eyes," she said, "and I realized I had become a chronically angry, impatient jerk. My response to stressful situations had become habitual—I automatically flew off the handle. Once I saw what I was doing, it really wasn't that hard to develop different habits. I simply decided I was going to treat other people the way I would want to be treated." The changes in Laura's life haven't benefited only her former victims. "I'm a calmer, happier person now," she reports. "I don't lie in bed at night fuming over stupid things other people have done and my own enraged responses." Laura has discovered the satisfaction of having a sense of control over her own behavior—which ultimately is all any of us can control.   22

BASIC SKILL QUESTIONS

Vocabulary in Context

_____   1. In the sentence below, the word *aberrant* (ă-bĕr′ənt) means
    A. amusing.
    B. abnormal.
    C. common.
    D. beneficial.

    "But in earlier, more civil times, public displays of anger were unusual to the point of being <u>aberrant</u>." (Paragraph 5)

_____   2. In the sentence below, the word *discord* (dĭs′kôrd′) means
    A. disagreement.
    B. harmony.
    C. absence.
    D. energy.

    "Our tension is often fueled by a reserve of anger that might be the result of a critical boss, marital discord, or (something that many of today's men and women experience, if few will admit it) a general sense of being stupid and inadequate in the face of the demands of modern life." (Paragraph 14)

discord - conflict; disagreement

Central Point and Main Ideas

_____ 3. Which sentence best expresses the central point of the selection?
A. People today have lost their ability to control their anger and behave in a civil fashion.
B. Our out-of-control anger has understandable causes, but common sense and patience are more satisfying than outbursts of rage.
C. Anger would last only a few seconds if we didn't keep it going with negative thinking.
D. While technology has its positive aspects, it has made us constantly available to others and challenged us to master the endless new developments.

_____ 4. The main idea of paragraph 9 is expressed in its
A. first sentence.
B. second sentence.
C. third sentence.
D. fourth sentence.

_____ 5. Which sentence best expresses the implied main idea of paragraph 11?
A. Cell phones, computers, and other technological gadgets can be very convenient.
B. We would all be better off living without technological gadgets.
C. Despite their good points, technological gadgets have added stress to our lives.
D. Cell phones, digital cameras, and computers need to be made simpler to use.

Supporting Details

_____ 6. Sybil Evans says that the three forces to blame for our anger are
A. finances, technology, and tension.
B. technology, marital discord, and money.
C. time, technology, and tension.
D. tension, incompetence, and critical employers.

_____ 7. A number of respondents to a survey of computer users in Great Britain admitted that
A. they had kicked or punched their computers.
B. their computers made them feel stupid.
C. they often sent and received personal e-mails at work.
D. they had accidentally deleted important work files and lied about it.

_____ 8. According to psychology professor Brad Bushman,
A. "blowing off steam" is a psychological necessity.
B. people who do not express their anger become seriously depressed.
C. the emotion of anger lasts only a few seconds.
D. venting our anger does us more harm than good.

Transitions

_____ 9. The relationship of the second sentence below to the first is one of
    A. time order.
    B. cause and effect.
    C. illustration.
    D. comparison.

    "Unfortunately, the culprits behind most of our anger . . . are not likely to resolve themselves anytime soon. So what are we to do with the anger that arises as a result?" (Paragraph 17)

_____ 10. What is the relationship of the second sentence below to the first?
    A. Contrast
    B. Illustration
    C. Comparison
    D. Cause and effect

    "[Tavris] points out that almost no situation is improved by an angry outburst. . . . Patience, on the other hand, is a highly practical virtue." (Paragraphs 18 and 19)

Patterns of Organization

_____ 11. The pattern of organization of paragraph 2 is
    A. comparison.
    B. list of items.
    C. definition and example.
    D. time order.

_____ 12. The section "Why Are We So Angry?" (paragraphs 7–14)
    A. compares people's reasons for being angry.
    B. presents a series of steps in the process of becoming angry.
    C. lists and discusses causes of the angry behavior in our society.
    D. contrasts time with technology.

_____ 13. Paragraph 22
    A. explains changes that Laura has made and the effects of those changes.
    B. contrasts Laura's and her mother's ways of handling anger.
    C. lists ways that Laura has changed her behavior.
    D. defines *patience* and illustrates the term.

ADVANCED SKILL QUESTIONS

Fact and Opinion

_____ 14. Paragraph 8 is made up of
    A. facts.
    B. opinions.
    C. a mixture of facts and opinions.

Inferences

_____ 15. From paragraph 2 we can infer that
    A. Laura's mother was a bad-tempered woman.
    B. Laura's mother was proud of her daughter's behavior.
    C. Laura's mother knew the driver of the car ahead of them.
    D. Laura had not always been so quick-tempered.

_____ 16. In paragraph 11, the author suggests that
    A. it is nearly impossible to keep up with technological advances.
    B. only lazy people ignore the wonderful advantages of technology.
    C. text messaging is a waste of time.
    D. most digital cameras and cell phones do not work very well.

_____ 17. We can infer from the excerpt that follows that
    A. being well-informed about bad news gives us a sense of control.
    B. we would be less worried about problems if we were not constantly reminded of them.
    C. the news media deliberately exaggerate the problems in the world.
    D. it is irresponsible not to keep up with world news.

> "Our sense of dread may be out of proportion to actual threats because of technology's ability to so constantly bombard us with worrisome information. Twenty-four-hour-a-day news stations bring a stream of horror into our living rooms. As we work at our computers, headlines and graphic images are never more than a mouse click away." (Paragraph 14)

Purpose and Tone

_____ 18. The main purpose of this selection is to
    A. entertain readers with anecdotes about people whose tempers are out of control.
    B. inform readers about the epidemic of anger and ways to handle anger.
    C. persuade readers to get more sleep at night and to nap during the day.

_____ 19. The author's tone when discussing technology is largely
   A. admiring.
   B. amused.
   C. concerned.
   D. thankful.

Argument

_____ 20. Three of the items below are supporting details for an argument. Write the letter of the statement that represents the point of these supporting details.
   A. Modern technological gadgets often make us feel stupid or inadequate.
   B. A hundred years ago, most people got several hours more sleep a night than people do today.
   C. Twenty-four-hour news sources keep us constantly aware of scary or worrisome stories.
   D. Modern-day people have to deal with sources of anger that earlier people did not.

OUTLINING

Complete the outline by filling in the four missing major details.

Central point: There is an epidemic of anger in today's society, but people can learn to deal with their anger.

   A. Introduction: Laura Houser anecdote and other examples of widespread public anger

   B. Causes of our anger

      1. _____

      2. _____

      3. _____

   C. Solutions to our anger

      1. _____

      2. Finding activities that vent our anger

DISCUSSION QUESTIONS

1. What kinds of things make you most angry? Is your anger directed mostly at others, or at yourself? What steps do you think you should take, or what steps have you taken, to control anger?

2. If you were teaching a class to students on what they should do to control anger, what would be your advice?

3. Of the three sources of our anger identified in the reading—time, technology, and tension—which do you think is the greatest problem for you? Why?

4. Do you agree with Carol Tavris, author of *Anger: The Misunderstood Emotion*, that almost no situation is improved by an angry outburst? Is anger ever helpful? Explain your answer.

Note: Writing assignments for this selection appear on page 633.

Check Your Performance   **TAMING THE ANGER MONSTER**

Activity	Number Right	Points	Score
BASIC SKILL QUESTIONS			
Vocabulary in Context (2 items)	_____	× 4 =	_____
Central Point and Main Ideas (3 items)	_____	× 4 =	_____
Supporting Details (3 items)	_____	× 4 =	_____
Transitions (2 items)	_____	× 4 =	_____
Patterns of Organization (3 items)	_____	× 4 =	_____
ADVANCED SKILL QUESTIONS			
Fact and Opinion (1 item)	_____	× 4 =	_____
Inferences (3 items)	_____	× 4 =	_____
Purpose and Tone (2 items)	_____	× 4 =	_____
Argument (1 item)	_____	× 4 =	_____
OUTLINING (4 items)	_____	× 5 =	_____
		TOTAL SCORE =	_____%

Enter your total score into the **Reading Performance Chart: Ten Reading Selections** on the inside back cover.

3

He Was First
John Kellmayer

Preview

Until the year 1947, major-league baseball was "for whites only." It took the willingness of Branch Rickey, and the talent and spirit of Jackie Robinson, to break baseball's color line and to open up professional sports for all Americans. Robinson, born in the rural South, the son of a sharecropper, was to die prematurely at the age of 52. But his life was a study in courage and achievement, as described in this reading.

Words to Watch

rampant (6): widespread
staunch (7): strong
raucous (14): harsh-sounding
cantankerous (21): ill-tempered
tumultuous (31): noisy
adulation (31): great admiration

1   Today few people under 60 can remember what it was like *not* to see blacks in professional baseball.

2   But until April 15, 1947, when Jackie Robinson played his first game with the Brooklyn Dodgers, the world of major-league baseball was a whites-only world.

3   The transition was not an easy one. It took place largely because Branch Rickey, owner of the Dodgers, held on to a dream of integrating baseball and because Jackie Robinson had the character, talent, and support to carry him through an ugly obstacle course of racism.

4   Even before he arrived in professional baseball, Robinson had to combat discrimination. Robinson entered the army with a national college reputation as an outstanding athlete. Still, he was

denied permission to play on the football and baseball teams at Fort Riley, Kansas, where he was stationed. He had been allowed to practice with the football team, but when the first game against an opposing team came up, Robinson was sent home on a pass. His exclusion from the baseball team there was more direct. A member of that team recalls what happened: "One day we were out at the field practicing when a Negro lieutenant tried out for the team. An officer told him, 'You have to play with the colored team.' That was a joke. There was no colored team." Robinson walked silently off the field.

5   Eventually, Robinson was granted an honorable discharge, and soon after he signed a contract to play baseball in the Negro American League.

6   At this time Branch Rickey was waiting for his opportunity to sign a black ballplayer and to integrate major-league baseball. He understood not only that the black ballplayer could be good box office but that bigotry had to be fought. While involved with his college baseball team, he had been deeply moved by a nasty scene in which his star catcher, an outstanding young black man, was prohibited from registering at a hotel with the rest of the team. Rickey then became determined to do something about the rampant° racism in baseball.

7   By 1944, the social climate had become more accepting of integration, in large part because of the contribution of black soldiers in World War II. Also, when the commissioner of baseball, a staunch° opponent of integration, died in 1944, he was replaced by a man named Happy Chandler. Chandler was on record as supporting integration of the game— "If a black man can make it at Okinawa and go to Guadalcanal, he can make it in baseball."

Rickey knew the time had come. He   8
began searching for the special black ballplayer with the mix of talent and character necessary to withstand the struggles to follow. When he learned about a star player in the Negro American League named Jackie Robinson, he arranged to meet with him.

At their meeting, Rickey said, "Jack,   9
I've been looking for a great colored ballplayer, but I need more than a great player. I need a man who will accept insults, take abuse, in a word, carry the flag for his race. I want a man who has the courage not to fight, not to fight back. If a guy slides into you at second base and calls you a black son of a bitch, I wouldn't blame you if you came up swinging. You'd be right. You'd be justified. But you'd set the cause back twenty years. I want a man with courage enough not to fight back. Can you do that?"

Robinson thought for a few minutes   10
before answering, "If you want to take this gamble, I promise you there'll be no incidents." The promise was not easily made. Robinson had encountered plenty of racism in his life, and he was accustomed to fighting for black rights. He was known by his teammates in the Negro American League to have a fast temper. Consequently, keeping his promise to Rickey was going to require great personal will.

After signing with the Dodgers in   11
October 1945, Robinson did not have to wait long to put his patience to the test. Even before he began to play with the Dodger organization, he and his wife, Rachel, encountered the humiliation of Southern racism.

It began when the Robinsons flew   12
from Los Angeles to spring training in Florida, two weeks after they got

married. On a stop in New Orleans, they were paged and asked to get off the plane. They later learned that, in the South, whites who wanted seats on a flight took preference over blacks already seated. Their places had been given to a white couple. They had to wait a day to get another flight and then were told to get off for yet another white couple at a stop in Pensacola, Florida. The Robinsons then had to take a segregated bus the rest of the way to Jacksonville, where Branch Rickey had a car waiting for them. Of that trip, Rachel Robinson later said, "It sharpened for us the drama of what we were about to go into. We got a lot tougher thereafter."

13   Soon after, during an exhibition game in Florida, Jackie suffered another humiliation, the first of many more to come on the diamond. During the first inning of that game, a police officer came onto the field and told Jackie, "Your people don't play with no white boys. Get off the field right now, or you're going to jail." Jackie had no choice but to walk quietly off the field. Not one of his teammates spoke up for him then.

14   Robinson's assignment to the Dodger minor-league team in Montreal was evidence of Rickey's careful planning for the breaking of the color barrier, as there was little racism in the Canadian city. That fact became important in supporting the spirits of Jackie and Rachel against the horrible outpouring of hate that greeted him at each stop on the road. Baseball historian Robert Smith wrote that when Robinson first appeared in Syracuse, "the fans reacted in a manner so raucous°, obscene, and disgusting that it might have shamed a conclave of the Ku Klux Klan." It was during this game that a Syracuse player threw a black cat at Jackie and yelled, "Hey, Jackie, there's your cousin."

In Baltimore, the players shouted racist insults, threw balls at his head, and tried to spike him. In addition, as would be the case at many stops through the years, Jackie wasn't allowed to stay at the same hotel as the rest of the team.

Robinson's manager at Montreal was   15 Clay Hopper, a Mississippi native adamantly opposed at first to the presence of Robinson on his ball club. Rickey once stood near Hopper during a game when Robinson made a superb dive to make an out, and Rickey commented that Robinson seemed "superhuman." Hopper's reply was, "Do you really think he's a human being?"

No civil rights legislation could have   16 turned Clay Hopper around the way Jackie Robinson did. By the end of a season in which Robinson led his team to the minor-league World Series, Hopper told Robinson, "You're a great ballplayer and a fine gentleman. It's been wonderful having you on the team." Hopper would later remark to Rickey, "You don't have to worry none about that boy. He's the greatest competitor I ever saw, and what's more, he's a gentleman."

It was clear that Jackie Robinson's   17 next stop was the big leagues, the Brooklyn Dodgers. Not surprisingly, though, the prospect of a black major-league player was not met by all with open arms. Just how much resistance there was, however, could be seen in the meeting of the baseball club owners in January of 1947 in which every owner but Rickey voted against allowing Jackie to play.

Fortunately, commissioner Happy   18 Chandler had another point of view. He later told Rickey, "Mr. Rickey, I'm going to have to meet my maker some day. If He asked me why I didn't let this man play, and I answered, 'Because he's a Negro,' that might not be a sufficient answer. I will approve of the transfer of Robinson's contract from Montreal to Brooklyn." So the color barrier was broken, and Robinson became a member of the Brooklyn Dodgers.

19   Robinson's talent meant less to some of the Brooklyn players than race. The prospect of a black teammate prompted a Dodger outfielder, a Southerner by the name of Dixie Walker, to pass among the other Southern players a petition urging Rickey to ban Robinson from their team. Walker gathered signatures and his petition gained momentum until he approached shortstop Pee Wee Reese, a Kentucky native. Robinson had originally been signed on as a shortstop and could have posed a real threat to Reese's job. Nonetheless, Reese refused to sign the petition. Reese was one of the leaders of the Brooklyn "Bums," so his acceptance of Robinson was of great importance in determining how the rest of the Dodgers would react.

20   As expected, Robinson's presence triggered an ugly racial response. It began with hate mail and death threats against him and his wife and baby boy. In addition, some of his teammates continued to oppose him. Some even refused to sit near him.

21   The opposing teams, however, were much worse, and the hatred was so intense that some of the Dodger players began to stand up for Jackie. In Philadelphia, players cried out such insults as, "They're waiting for you in the jungles, black boy," and "Hey, snowflake, which one of you white boys' wives are you dating tonight?" The first Dodger to stand up for Robinson on the field was a Southerner, the cantankerous° Eddie "The Brat" Stankey. When the Phillies pointed their bats at Robinson and made machine-gun-like noises in a cruel reference to the threats on his and his family's lives, Stankey shouted, "Why don't you yell at someone who can answer back?"

22   Other opposing teams were no better. In an early-season game in Cincinnati, for instance, players yelled racial epithets at Jackie. Rex Barney, who was a Dodger pitcher then, described Pee Wee Reese's response: "While Jackie was standing by first base, Pee Wee went over to him and put his arm around him, as if to say, 'This is my man. This is the guy. We're gonna win with him.' Well, it drove the Cincinnati players right through the ceiling, and you could have heard the gasp from the crowd as he did it."

23   In the face of continuing harassment, Jackie Robinson, a hot-tempered young man who had struggled against racism all his life, chose to fight his toughest battle, not with his fists or foul language, but with the courage not to fight back. Instead, he answered his attackers with superior play and electrifying speed.

24   Within the first month of the 1947 season, it became apparent that Robinson could be the deciding factor in the pennant race. His speed on the base paths brought an entirely new dimension to baseball. Robinson used bunts and fake bunts and steals and fake steals to distract opposing pitchers and force basic changes in strategy in the game.

25   Undoubtedly, one reason many Dodger players rallied around Robinson was that they saw him as a critical, perhaps *the* critical, factor in their pursuit of the pennant. Like Rickey's, their motives reflected a mixture of personal ambition and a genuine concern for doing what was right.

26   And many did do what was right, even off the field. For example, Robinson at first waited until all his teammates had finished their showers before he would

take his. One day, outfielder Al Gionfriddo patted Robinson on the butt and told him to get into the showers with everybody else, that he was as much a part of the team as anyone. Robinson smiled and went to the showers with Gionfriddo.

27   The ballplayers' wives also extended the hand of friendship to Robinson and his wife. Pitcher Clyde King related an incident that was typical of the efforts put forth to make the Robinsons feel part of the Dodger family. At Ebbets Field, an iron fence ran from the dugout to the clubhouse, keeping the fans from the players. After the games, the Dodger wives would be allowed inside the fence to wait for their husbands. Rachel Robinson, reluctant to join the other wives, would wait for Jackie outside the fence among the fans. King remembers that his own wife, Norma, a North Carolina girl, made sure that Rachel join her and the other Dodger wives inside.

28   For Jackie, a series of such small but significant events may have meant the difference between making it and exploding under the enormous pressure that followed him throughout that first baseball season.

29   As the season passed, he gained the support not only of many of his teammates but of much of the baseball world in general. On September 12, *Sporting News,* the leading publication in baseball, selected Robinson as its Rookie of the Year—the first of many prestigious awards he would receive during his term with the Dodgers.

30   In the article announcing the award, there was a quote from none other than Dixie Walker, the same Dodger who had started the petition in the spring to ban Robinson from playing for Brooklyn.

Walker praised Robinson for his contributions to the club's success, stating that Robinson was all that Branch Rickey had said and more.

31   On September 22, the Dodgers defeated the St. Louis Cardinals to clinch the National League pennant—against a team in whose town Jackie had to stay in a "colored" hotel. Fittingly enough, the following day was proclaimed Jackie Robinson Day at the Dodger ballpark. Robinson was honored with a tumultuous° outpouring of affection from the Brooklyn fans, an unbroken peal of adulation° that shook the very foundations of Ebbets Field.

32   Americans learned something that year about competition and excellence, about character and race. The fire that Jackie Robinson fanned swept across the years to follow, resulting in a permanent change in the makeup of the game. He had demonstrated that not only could blacks play on the same field with white players; they could excel. People brought their families hundreds of miles to see him play. The floodgates opened for the signing of the black ballplayer. The same major-league team owners who had voted against hiring blacks soon followed Rickey's lead. In the next few years came Willie Mays, Ernie Banks, Henry Aaron, and more—an endless list of black stars.

33   For some, Jackie Robinson is simply one of the greatest second basemen of all time. For others, he is much more. He is an individual who stood up and opposed the ugliness of racism with a relentless intensity. He was the first to brave the insults and the ignorance, the first to show that major-league baseball could be raised from the depths of segregation. His victory is a model of what one determined person can accomplish.

BASIC SKILL QUESTIONS

Vocabulary in Context

_____ 1. In the sentence below, the word *adamantly* (ăd′ə-mənt-lē) means
   A. weakly.
   B. stubbornly.
   C. secretly.
   D. pleasantly.

> "Robinson's manager at Montreal was Clay Hopper, a Mississippi native adamantly opposed at first to the presence of Robinson on his ball club." (Paragraph 15)

_____ 2. In the excerpt below, the word *momentum* (mō-měn′təm) means
   A. money.
   B. opposition.
   C. forward movement.
   D. defeat.

> "Walker gathered signatures and his petition gained momentum until he approached shortstop Pee Wee Reese. . . ." (Paragraph 19)

Central Point and Main Ideas

_____ 3. Which sentence best expresses the central point of this selection?
   A. Until 1947, there were no blacks in professional baseball.
   B. Jackie Robinson, a man of principle and courage, became the best second baseman in baseball.
   C. Baseball became integrated because of the courage of Branch Rickey and Jackie Robinson, who proved blacks could excel in major-league baseball.
   D. The integration of American society was not easily accomplished.

_____ 4. Which sentence best expresses the main idea of paragraph 7?
   A. Happy Chandler became baseball commissioner in 1944.
   B. Black soldiers fought for the United States during World War II.
   C. A commissioner of baseball who was opposed to integration died in 1944.
   D. By 1944, society had become more open to integrating baseball.

Supporting Details

_____ 5. Robinson encountered racism
   A. on and off the field in both the North and the South.
   B. only during baseball games.
   C. mainly in Canada.
   D. until he joined the major leagues.

_____ 6. TRUE OR FALSE? During Robinson's first year with the Dodgers, none of his teammates accepted him.

Transitions

_____ 7. The sentence below expresses a relationship of
   A. addition.
   B. comparison.
   C. cause and effect.
   D. illustration.

   ". . . the social climate had become more accepting of integration, in large part because of the contribution of black soldiers in World War II." (Paragraph 7)

_____ 8. The relationship of the second sentence below to the first is one of
   A. contrast.
   B. illustration.
   C. cause and effect.
   D. time order.

"Other opposing teams were no better. In an early-season game in Cincinnati, for instance, players yelled racial epithets at Jackie." (Paragraph 22)

_____ 9. The relationship of paragraph 27 to paragraph 26 is one of
   A. time.
   B. illustration.
   C. addition.
   D. contrast.

Patterns of Organization

_____ 10. The pattern of organization of paragraph 3 is
   A. time order.
   B. definition and example.
   C. cause and effect.
   D. comparison and/or contrast.

_____ 11. The pattern of organization of paragraph 12 is
   A. time order.
   B. list of items.
   C. definition and example.
   D. comparison and/or contrast.

ADVANCED SKILL QUESTIONS

Fact and Opinion

_____ 12. Which of the following is a statement of opinion?
A. "The transition was not an easy one."
B. "Robinson walked silently off the field."
C. "In addition, as would be the case at many stops through the years, Jackie wasn't allowed to stay at the same hotel as the rest of the team."
D. "On September 12, *Sporting News,* the leading publication in baseball, selected Robinson as its Rookie of the Year. . . ."

_____ 13. Which of the following is a statement of fact?
A. "No civil rights legislation could have turned Clay Hopper around the way Jackie Robinson did."
B. "Other opposing teams were no better."
C. "King remembers that his own wife, Norma, a North Carolina girl, made sure that Rachel join her and the other Dodger wives inside."
D. "For Jackie, a series of such small but significant events may have made the difference between making it and exploding under the enormous pressure. . . ."

Inferences

_____ 14. The author implies that some of Robinson's Dodger teammates
A. resented the intense racism of the opposing teams and fans.
B. taught him a lot about baseball strategy.
C. opposed him more as they won more games.
D. had little influence on how he stood the pressure of his first major-league season.

_____ 15. TRUE OR FALSE? The author implies that the Dodgers won the 1947 National League pennant largely because of Jackie Robinson.

_____ 16. Which of the following inferences is best supported by paragraph 19?
A. All Southern players were racist.
B. Pee Wee Reese felt no threat from Jackie Robinson.
C. Reese put principle ahead of personal concern.
D. Without Pee Wee Reese, baseball would not have become integrated.

Purpose and Tone

_____ 17. The main purpose of this selection is to
A. inform readers about how major-league baseball became integrated.
B. persuade readers that Jackie Robinson was the greatest second baseman of all time.
C. simply entertain readers with an account of Jackie Robinson's first major-league season.

_____ 18. The author's tone when discussing Robinson is
  A. totally objective.
  B. admiring.
  C. lighthearted.
  D. sentimental.

19. In which paragraph of the reading does the author first show, through his choice of words, his attitude toward Jackie Robinson? Paragraph _____

Argument

20. Label the point of the following argument with a **P** and the two statements of support with an **S**. Label with an **X** the one statement that is neither the point nor the support of the argument.
  ____ A. Robinson had the inner strength to take racial insults with patience.
  ____ B. Robinson was the perfect person to break the color barrier.
  ____ C. Robinson had played in the Negro American League before he was hired by Rickey.
  ____ D. Robinson was a great enough ballplayer to be welcomed by baseball fans.

SUMMARIZING

Add the ideas needed to complete the following summary of "He Was First."

Because of the contributions of black soldiers, the social climate in the United States was more favorable to integration after World War II. Hoping to break the color barrier in baseball, Branch Rickey, owner of the Dodgers, hired Jackie Robinson in 1945 after Robinson agreed _____

_____.

Rickey assigned him to the minor-league team in Montreal, a town with little racism. Robinson led the team to the minor-league World Series and won over his manager, Clay Hopper, whose reaction to Robinson was at first racist. In 1947, after the baseball commissioner approved his transfer to Brooklyn, Robinson joined the Brooklyn Dodgers. Robinson immediately encountered racism, both from his own team and from opposing teams. But within the first month of the season, it became clear that Robinson's superior play could help the team reach the pennant. The ballplayers and their wives soon _____

_____.

As the season progressed, Robinson also gained the support of much of the baseball world and was named Rookie of the Year by the prestigious *Sporting News.* On September 22, the Dodgers beat the St. Louis Cardinals to win the National League pennant, in a town, ironically, where _____

_____.

At home in Brooklyn, Jackie Robinson Day was proclaimed at the Dodgers' ballpark. Within a few years, _____

_____.

DISCUSSION QUESTIONS

1. Kellmayer writes, "By 1944, the social climate had become more accepting of integration, in large part because of the contribution of black soldiers in World War II." Why do you think the contribution of black soldiers in World War II would be such an influence on the progress of integration in the United States?

2. An ongoing question about history is whether individuals cause important changes in society or whether it is circumstances that lead to changes— once the circumstances are right, the right individuals will emerge. In the integration of baseball, how important do you think the times were? How important were the individuals involved?

3. Do you think Branch Rickey was right to make Robinson agree "not to fight back"? Explain your answer.

4. Robinson had to face a great deal of racism. Unfortunately, despite the greater integration of today, there is still racism. Have you experienced any racial insults yourself or seen anyone else treated badly because of the racial or ethnic group he or she belongs to? Tell what happened, and how you or the other person reacted.

Note: Writing assignments for this selection appear on page 634.

Check Your Performance   **HE WAS FIRST**

Activity   *Number Right*   *Points*   *Score*

BASIC SKILL QUESTIONS

    Vocabulary in Context (2 items)   _____   × 4 = _____

    Central Point and Main Ideas (2 items)   _____   × 4 = _____

    Supporting Details (2 items)   _____   × 4 = _____

    Transitions (3 items)   _____   × 4 = _____

    Patterns of Organization (2 items)   _____   × 4 = _____

ADVANCED SKILL QUESTIONS

    Fact and Opinion (2 items)   _____   × 4 = _____

    Inferences (3 items)   _____   × 4 = _____

    Purpose and Tone (3 items)   _____   × 4 = _____

    Argument (1 item)   _____   × 4 = _____

SUMMARIZING (4 items)   _____   × 5 = _____

                             TOTAL SCORE = _____%

Enter your total score into the **Reading Performance Chart: Ten Reading Selections** on the inside back cover.

4

Keys to College Success
Sheila Akers

Preview

Some students feel that the ability to do well in school is a natural gift, something one is born with. They don't realize that ability is in large part learned. If you haven't yet picked up ways to succeed in college, or if you've forgotten what you once knew, this article can help. The strategies described here can mean the difference between wasting time and making the most of it.

Words to Watch

fixed (5): not varying
floundering (8): struggling

1   Every year, college catches numerous first-year students by surprise. They simply don't realize how much more difficult college can be than high school. Not ready to take responsibility for their own learning, they discover too late that instructors may not remind them to complete an assignment or prepare for a test. Some give up and drop out before they learn that there are keys to college success—practical ways for any student to take charge of his or her college life and do well. There are four keys to becoming a smart student and a power learner.

MANAGE YOUR TIME

2   Gordon had a typically busy college schedule. He was taking four classes, as well as working in a local fast-food restaurant. He liked to play basketball at least one night a week and go out on a date or to a party two or three times a week. Five weeks into the semester, Gordon realized that he was in serious trouble. He was behind in his reading in every class. A major midterm paper was due soon, and he had only a vague idea what his topic would be. Nevertheless, he felt that he was constantly studying.

Other people he knew had schedules as busy as his, and yet they were keeping up. What was wrong?

3   Gordon's sense that he was "always studying" came from the fact that he generally carried his books around with him. And, in fact, he did glance at them every so often. But those few minutes of reading were sandwiched between a hundred other tasks: eating lunch, talking with friends, making phone calls. Rarely did Gordon sit down with the specific intention of studying a particular topic for a planned period of time. The hours, days, and weeks were slipping away, leaving Gordon with very little to show for them.

4   Gordon needed some education in the first key to success in college: managing time. There are three steps involved in time control. The *first step* is to have a large monthly calendar. Buy a calendar with a large white block around each date, or make one yourself. At the beginning of the college semester, mark important dates on this calendar: days on which tests are scheduled and papers are due. Be sure to hang this calendar in a place where you can see it every day— your kitchen, your bedroom, even your bathroom!

5   The *second step* in time control is to prepare a weekly study schedule for the semester. Make up a chart that covers all the days of the week and all the waking hours in each day. On the chart, mark in all the fixed° hours in each day—hours for meals, classes, job (if any), and travel time. Next, mark in time blocks that you can *realistically* use for study each day. Depending on the number of courses you are taking and the demands of the courses, you may want to block off five, ten, even twenty or more hours of study time a week. Keep in mind that you should not block off time for study that you do not truly intend to use for study. Otherwise,

your schedule will be a meaningless gimmick. Also, remember that you should leave time for some relaxation in your schedule. You will be happiest, and able to accomplish the most, when you have time for *both* work and play. Keep this schedule next to your calendar and use it as a daily guide.

6   The *third step* in time control is to make up a daily or weekly "to do" list. This may be the most valuable time-control method you ever use. On this list, write down the things you need to do for the following day or the following week. If you choose to write a weekly list, do it on Sunday night. If you choose to write a daily list, do it the night before. You may use a three- by five-inch note pad or a small spiral-bound notebook for this list. Carry the list with you during the day.

7   Always concentrate on doing first the most important items on your list. Mark high-priority items with an asterisk and give them precedence over low-priority items in order to make the best use of your time. For instance, you may find yourself deciding what to do after dinner on Thursday evening. Among the items on your list are "Clean inside of car" and "Review class notes for math quiz." It is obviously more important for you to review your notes at this point; you can clean the car some other time. As you complete items on your "to do" list, cross them out. Unfinished items can be rescheduled for the next day. By using a "to do" list, along with a monthly calendar and a weekly study schedule, you will begin to take control of your studies and your life!

ATTEND CLASS AND TAKE NOTES

8   Tracy had always done pretty well in high school. When there were ideas that

students were expected to remember, the teacher carefully wrote those ideas on the board or repeated them aloud so that students would have plenty of time to write them down. Sometimes teachers even distributed handouts that summarized materials or made it clear just what students would be expected to study for a test. Tracy was unhappily surprised, then, to find herself floundering° in college.

9   Her professors lectured at what seemed to Tracy an astonishing pace. She was never sure when to write and when to just listen. Sometimes she lost the professor's train of thought and just sat there semiparalyzed, vaguely aware that facts and concepts she would never hear again were just flowing down the drain because she had no idea of what to write. Sometimes she began to daydream, and when the class ended, she would have only a quarter of a page of notes as a record of the information presented on that day. "All this is in the textbook," she would think uneasily. "I'll be able to get anything I've missed by just reading the book." Since most of her professors did not take attendance, Tracy began missing classes, especially on warm, sunny days or on Fridays. With each absence, she said the same thing to herself: "I'll just get any material I need by using the book." When her first exams came, Tracy's uneven and sketchy classroom notes were of little help, and the textbooks were too much to cover at the last minute. As a result, she failed those exams.

10   Tracy badly needed to learn about the second key to college success—taking effective class notes. The following hints will help make you a good note-taker.

11   • First, attend class faithfully. In class lectures and discussions, your instructor typically presents and develops the main ideas and facts of the course—the ones you will be expected to know on exams. Going to classes is the heart of the college experience, and if you miss classes, the cold, hard fact is that you may be a college student in name only.

12   • Take a lot of notes in class. It is often better to write down too much than too little. You must get down a written record because forgetting sets in almost immediately. Studies have made it very clear that after a month, you would be lucky to remember 5 percent of what you have heard! On the other hand, if you take extensive notes, you can review class material and go into a test knowing almost 100 percent of what an instructor has said.

13   • To save time, use abbreviations while taking notes. Abbreviate terms that recur frequently in a lecture, and put a key to your abbreviations at the top of your notes. For example, in a sociology class, *eth* could stand for *ethnocentrism;* in a psychology class, *STM* could stand for *short-term memory.*

14   • Another hint for taking notes is to look for signals of importance. Write down whatever your instructor puts on the board. If he or she takes time to put material on the board, it is probably important, and the chances are very good that it will come up later on exams. In addition, always write down definitions, examples, and lists of items. Lists of items are signaled in such ways as "The two effects were . . . ," "There were three reasons for . . . ," "The four steps in the process are . . . ," and so on. Always number such lists in your notes: 1, 2, 3, and so on. They will help you understand relationships among ideas and organize the material of the lecture. Finally, if your instructor repeats a

point, you can assume it is important. You might put an *R* for *repeated* in the margin, so that later you will know that your instructor has stressed it.

15 • Review your notes as soon as possible after class. Make the notes as clear as possible while they are fresh in your mind. A day later may be too late, because forgetting sets in very quickly. Make sure that punctuation is clear, that all words are readable and correctly spelled, and that unfinished sentences are completed (or at least marked off so that you can check your notes with another student's). Add clarifying or connecting comments whenever necessary. Make sure important ideas are clearly marked. Improve the organization if necessary, so that you can see at a glance main points and relationships among them.

READ YOUR TEXTBOOK IN AN ORGANIZED WAY

16   For her first college exam, Laura was responsible for three chapters of her introductory sociology text. She began to read the chapters, using a purple highlighting pen. After ten pages, most of the pages were purple, and she realized that her method of highlighting was going to be of little help. She then read another ten pages without using the pen. At the end of those pages, too, she wondered just what she had accomplished. Then she decided that maybe she should take notes as she read, but she didn't know how many notes to take. Discouraged, she starting flipping through pages at random, reading a bit here or there. She felt frustrated and confused about just what she needed to do to read and study the book, and she began to wonder if she really belonged in college.

17   Laura needed to learn the third key to college success—reading textbook material in a systematic way. Here is a four-step process called PRWR (Preview, Read, Write, Recite) that will boost your study power.

1. Preview the reading.

18   A two- or three-minute preview or survey of a reading gives you a general overview of the selection before you begin a careful reading. By "breaking the ice" and providing a quick sense of the new material, the preview will help you get into the reading more easily. There are four parts to a preview:

19 • *Consider the title.* The title is often a tiny summary of the chapter. Use it to help you focus in on the central idea of the material. For instance, a chapter titled "Aggression: Origins and Responses" suggests that you will be reading theories about what causes aggression and what can be done to control it.

20 • *Read over the first and last paragraphs of the selection.* The first paragraph or so of a reading is often written as an introduction. It may thus present the main ideas, giving you an overview of what's coming. The last paragraphs may be a summary of a reading and thus give you another general view of the main ideas.

21 • *Note headings and their relationships.* Main headings tell you what sections of a chapter are about. They are generally printed in darker or larger type; they may appear in capital letters or in a different color. The main headings under the section title "Theories of Aggression," for example, would probably tell you which theories are being covered.

22   Subheadings fall under main headings and help identify and organize the material under main heads. Sub-heads are printed in a way that makes them more prominent than the text but less prominent than the main headings. A selection may even contain sub-subheadings that label and organize material under the subheads. Here is how a series of heads might look:

MAIN HEAD (at the margin in larger type)

   Subhead (indented and in slightly smaller type)

      Sub-subhead (further indented and in even smaller type)

23   • *Note material that is set off in some way.* Words in *italic* or **boldface** type often indicate important terms and topics. Tables, graphs, and pictures are often used to illustrate key concepts.

2. Read the material and mark important parts.

24   After previewing a selection, take the time to read it through from start to finish. Keep reading even if you run into some parts you don't understand. You can always come back to those parts. By reading straight through, you'll be in a better position to understand the difficult parts later.

25   As you read, mark points you feel are especially significant. This marking will make it easy for you to find the points later when you take study notes. The goal is to mark the most important ideas of a selection. They include the following:

• Definitions

• Helpful examples

• Major lists of items

• Points that receive the most space, development, and attention.

26   Here are some ways to mark off important ideas:

• Underline definitions and identify them by writing *DEF* in the margin.

• Identify helpful examples by writing *EX* in the margin.

• Number *1, 2, 3,* etc. the items in lists.

• Underline obviously important ideas. You can further set off important points by writing *IMP* in the margin. If important material is several lines long, do not underline it all; instead, draw a vertical line alongside the material.

27   As you mark a selection, remember to be selective. Your marking should help you set off the most significant parts of the reading; if everything in a reading is marked, you won't have separated out the most important ideas. Often you won't know what the most important ideas in a paragraph or a section are until you've read all of it. So it's good to develop a habit of reading a bit and then going back to do the marking.

3. Write study notes.

28   After reading and marking a selection, you are ready to take study notes. *Taking notes is the key to successful learning.* In the very act of deciding what is important enough to write down and then writing it down, you begin to learn and master the material.

   Here are some guidelines to use in writing study notes:

• After you have previewed, read, and marked the selection, reread it. Then write out the important information on 8½-by-11-inch sheets of paper. Write on only one side of each page.

• Write clearly. Then you won't waste valuable study time trying to decipher your handwriting.

- Use a combination of the author's words and your own words. Using your own words at times forces you to think about and work at understanding the material.

- Organize your notes into a rough outline that will show relationships between ideas. Write main headings at the margin of your notes. Indent subheads about half an inch away from the margin. Indent sub-subheads even more.

- Also, number items in a list, just as you did when marking important items in a list in the text. Be sure each list in your notes has a heading. To illustrate, here is the start for a sheet of study notes on a chapter in a communications textbook:

> *Five ways to send messages:*
> 1. *Face-to-face communication—most effective means; gives maximum feedback.*
> 2. *Face-to-group communication . . .*

4. Recite the ideas in your notes.

30   After writing your study notes, go through them and write key words in the margin of your notes. The words will help you study the material. For example, here are the key words you might write in the margin of the above notes taken on the communications text:

> *5 ways to send messages:*

31   To study your notes, turn the words in the margin into questions. First ask yourself, for instance, "What are five ways to send messages?" Then recite the answer until you can say it without looking at your notes. Then ask yourself, "Why is face-to-face communication best?" Then recite that answer until you can say it without looking at your notes.

32   Finally—and this is a key point—go back and review your answer to the first question. Test yourself—see if you can say the answer without looking at it. Then test yourself on the second answer. *As you learn each new bit of information, go back and test yourself on the previous information.* Such repeated self-testing is at the heart of effective memorization.

33   In summary, then, you should preview, read, write, and recite your college reading assignments. By doing so, and by also reciting and learning your classroom notes, you will be well prepared to deal with college exams.

TAKE RESPONSIBILITY FOR YOUR STUDIES

34   Not long into his first college semester, Ronald gave up on his classes. He was in college, but he stopped being a student. He spent his time playing sports, sleeping, watching a lot of television, and socializing with old and new friends. He wasn't ready to be an active student, but he played the game of being one. He carried books around and occasionally went to a class or two and doodled in his notebook or dreamed about the great job he would have some day. Ronald wanted to enjoy his life and freedom, and after all his years of moving passively along from one grade to another in high school, he was not prepared to be an active learner in college.

35   The final key to success is deciding that a college degree can help you get where you want to go in your life. If you realize that earning a college degree is an important step you must take to achieve your career goals, you will take responsibility for your studies. You'll become an active learner, applying the skills in this article to make yourself as good a student as possible. Chances are

you'll then discover that you enjoy learning for its own sake, and that even though you have to work hard, you'll be pleased and proud at what you are doing. You'll know that you have taken charge of your life, and that the final key to success lies in your hands and your heart.

BASIC SKILL QUESTIONS

Vocabulary in Context

_D_ 1. In the excerpt below, the words *precedence over* (prĕs'ĭ-dəns ō'vər) mean
   A. a way to.
   B. a name for.
   C. less time than.
   D. more importance than.

   "Always concentrate on doing first the most important items on your list. Mark high-priority items with an asterisk and give them precedence over low-priority items in order to make the best use of your time." (Paragraph 7)

_C_ 2. In the excerpt below, the word *decipher* (dĭ-sī'fər) means
   A. improve.
   B. defend.
   C. figure out.
   D. misunderstand.

   "Write clearly. Then you won't waste valuable study time trying to decipher your handwriting." (Paragraph 29)

Central Point and Main Ideas

_B_ 3. The author expresses her central point in the
   A. first sentence of paragraph 1.
   B. last sentence of paragraph 1.
   C. second sentence of paragraph 4.
   D. second sentence of paragraph 35.

_D_ 4. Which statement best expresses the main idea of paragraphs 4–7?
   A. Gordon managed his time poorly.
   B. The first key to success in college is managing time, which involves three steps.
   C. The first step in managing time is filling in a monthly calendar.
   D. A large monthly calendar allows you to keep track of important due dates and tests.

_____ 5. Which statement best expresses the main idea of paragraph 9?

    A. Because of problems with note-taking, class attendance, and keeping up with the reading, Tracy failed her first set of college exams.

    B. Tracy discovered that it was impossible to read all her textbooks at the last minute.

    C. Tracy's professors lectured so quickly and said so much that Tracy had no idea of what to write down in her notes.

    D. Tracy decided that reading her textbooks would give her more information than attending or taking notes in class.

Supporting Details

_____ 6. According to the author, "to-do" lists

    A. should contain only schoolwork.

    B. will help students remember when long-term projects are due.

    C. should be written a month at a time.

    D. help students to achieve daily goals.

_____ 7. When previewing a selection, you should _not_

    A. look at the title.

    B. read the first and last paragraphs.

    C. read every word.   .

    D. check the headings and their relationships.

_____ 8. TRUE OR FALSE? According to the author, when you are reading a selection for the first time, you should stop to reread parts you don't understand.

Transitions

_____ 9. The relationship of the second sentence below to the first is one of

    A. time.

    B. addition.

    C. comparison.

    D. contrast.

> "Studies have made it very clear that after a month, you would be lucky to remember 5 percent of what you have heard! On the other hand, if you take extensive notes, you can review class material and go into a test knowing almost 100 percent of what an instructor has said." (Paragraph 12)

Patterns of Organization

_____ 10. The overall pattern of organization of the entire selection is

    A. list of items.

    B. time order.

    C. definition and example.

    D. contrast.

_C_ 11. The main pattern of organization of paragraphs 31 and 32 is
  A. list of items.
  B. time order.
  C. cause and effect.
  D. definition and example.

ADVANCED SKILL QUESTIONS

Fact and Opinion

_A_ 12. The words that makes the statement below an opinion are
  A. *often better.*
  B. *write down.*
  C. *too much.*
  D. *too little.*

> "It is often better to write down too much than too little."
> (Paragraph 12)

_A_ 13. The statements below are
  A. facts.
  B. opinions.
  C. both facts and opinions.

> "Main headings tell you what sections are about. They are generally
> printed in darker or larger type; they may appear in capital letters or
> in a different color." (Paragraph 21)

Inferences

_D_ 14. We can infer that this article was probably written for college
  A. instructors.
  B. seniors.
  C. graduates.
  D. first-year students.

 True 15. TRUE OR FALSE? From the final paragraph of the selection, we can
  conclude that the first three keys to college success are useless without
  this fourth one.

_D_ 16. We can infer from the reading that
  A. the PRWR system is very easy to do.
  B. it is best to reread entire textbook assignments the night before an
  exam.
  C. if one takes excellent lecture notes, textbook notes are unnecessary.
  D. students who do well are very organized in their approach to study.

Purpose and Tone

_____A___ 17. The purpose of this selection is

    A. both to inform and to persuade.

    B. both to persuade and to entertain.

    C. only to persuade.

_____C___ 18. The author's tone can be described as

    A. ironic and ambivalent.

    B. distressed but informal.

    C. encouraging and optimistic.

    D. sympathetic and lighthearted.

Argument

_____A___ 19. Which item does *not* support the following point?

    Point: A large monthly calendar will help you manage your study time.

    A. The calendar can be purchased, or you can make it yourself.

    B. The large white squares on the calendar leave plenty of room to write in long-term assignments.

    C. You can use the calendar to record days on which tests are scheduled or papers are due.

    D. The calendar can be hung somewhere where you will see it every day—your kitchen, bedroom, or bathroom—thereby preventing you from forgetting a major due date.

_____D___ 20. Write the letter of the statement that is the point of the following argument. The other statements are support for that point.

    A. Study notes of a selection are easier to review than the entire selection itself.

    B. Writing study notes on a reading selection is a good study technique.

    C. Writing study notes forces you to think about what is important in a reading.

    D. You are more likely to remember a point when you take the time to write it in your study notes.

OUTLINING

Fill in the points that are missing in the following outline based on "Keys to College Success." (The numbers of the paragraphs covered by the outline are included.)

Central point: Students can do well in college by learning the four keys to college success.

1. Manage your time. *(Paragraphs 2–7)*

   a. Mark a large monthly calendar with due dates.

   b. _____

   c. Use daily or weekly "to-do" lists.

2. _____

   _____ *(Paragraphs 8–15)*

   a. Attend class faithfully.

   b. Take a lot of class notes.

   c. _____

   d. Look for signals of importance.

   e. Review your notes as soon as possible after class.

3. Use the PRWR method to study your reading assignments. *(Paragraphs 16–33)*

   a. *Step 1:* _____

      1) Consider the title.

      2) Read over the first and last paragraphs of the selection.

      3) Note headings and their relationships.

      4) Note material that is set off.

   b. *Step 2:* _____

      1) Read the material from start to finish, even if you run into parts you don't understand.

      2) Mark significant parts—definitions, examples, major lists of items.

      3) Use various ways of marking.

      4) Be selective in marking.

c. *Step 3:* _____

   1) Reread the selection and write out important information.

   2) _____

   3) Use a combination of the author's and your own words.

   4) _____

   5) Number items in a list.

d. *Step 4:* Recite the ideas in your notes.

   1) Write key words in the margins of your notes.

   2) Turn key words into questions, and recite the answers.

   3) _____

   _____

4. _____

(Paragraphs 34–35)

DISCUSSION QUESTIONS

1. In general, would you say that your high-school experience prepared you adequately for the demands of college learning? Why or why not?

2. Could your studying benefit from time-control measures? What steps do you already take to manage your time? When do you do most of your studying? Are there hours that slip away because you get distracted? Explain.

3. What study system or approach to studying textbooks do you use? How does it compare or contrast with the PRWR approach? Now that you have read about the PRWR approach, do you plan to use all or part of it? (Be honest.) Why or why not?

4. The author states, "If you realize that earning a college degree is an important step you must take to achieve your career goals, you will take responsibility for your studies." What are your career goals, and how will a college degree help you achieve them?

Note: Writing assignments for this selection appear on page 635.

Check Your Performance   **KEYS TO COLLEGE SUCCESS**

Activity	Number Right	Points	Score

BASIC SKILL QUESTIONS

Vocabulary in Context (2 items)   _____   × 4 =   _____

Central Point and Main Ideas (3 items)   _____   × 4 =   _____

Supporting Details (3 items)   _____   × 4 =   _____

Transitions (1 item)   _____   × 4 =   _____

Patterns of Organization (2 items)   _____   × 4 =   _____

ADVANCED SKILL QUESTIONS

Fact and Opinion (2 items)   _____   × 4 =   _____

Inferences (3 items)   _____   × 4 =   _____

Purpose and Tone (2 items)   _____   × 4 =   _____

Argument (2 items)   _____   × 4 =   _____

OUTLINING (10 items)   _____   × 2 =   _____

TOTAL SCORE =   _____%

Enter your total score into the **Reading Performance Chart: Ten Reading Selections** on the inside back cover.

5

Motivation and Needs
Virginia Quinn

Preview

If you had to choose between friendship and achievement, which would you pick? And how much security would you give up in order to avoid boredom? According to psychologist Abraham Maslow, we all would answer these questions in more or less the same way—because we all share the same basic human needs. In this selection from her textbook *Applying Psychology* (McGraw-Hill), Virginia Quinn explains Maslow's view of human motivation and needs.

Words to Watch

hierarchy (2): a group arranged in order of rank
et al. (7): an abbreviation of a Latin phrase meaning "and others"
apathetic (7): having little interest
dispirited (7): discouraged
novelty (10): something new
fluctuate (10): alternate
affiliation (13): social connection
superficial (13): shallow
implications (15): inferences
refraining from (15): not using
capitalize on (18): take advantage of
spontaneous (31): behaving freely

1   Whether their motivation is conscious or unconscious, people have a broad range of needs. Some needs are shared by everyone. For example, everyone is motivated to stay alive and survive. Food, rest, oxygen, and other

necessities for life are common to all people. Other needs vary from one person to the next. For example, some people need to drive a fancy sports car and wear designer clothes. Others may need to travel to far-off lands and live among different cultures. Undoubtedly, you have heard of individuals who had a need to climb high mountains or do missionary work in underdeveloped countries. Strangely, some people even feel a need to write psychological books!

2   Trying to sort and organize every possible need seems like a monstrous task. Yet Abraham Maslow, one of the most important contributors to the field of motivation, managed to classify human needs or motivations into a pyramid-like hierarchy°. In order to progress upward to the top of the pyramid, you need to satisfy each need along the way.

3   At the base of his pyramid, Maslow placed everyday physiological needs required for survival—needs for food, drink, rest, elimination, etc. On the next level, Maslow put need for stimulation and escape from boredom. The need to explore and satisfy curiosity would be included on this second level. Safety and security needs follow. As you continue up his pyramid, you develop a need for love and a sense of belonging. At this fourth level, friendships become important. As you move to the upper levels of the hierarchy, you need to feel respected by others. The final level is reached by very few people. It involves carrying out one's total potential. Maslow labeled the top step of his hierarchy "self-actualization."

4   Maslow felt that people move up and down this pyramid throughout their lives. Indeed, people can move to different steps or needs on the pyramid within a single day. His pyramid is like a ladder you climb throughout your life. You must step on each rung to reach the next. But suppose a person is on a high rung. For example, a woman may have progressed to the point where she is looking for approval and self-esteem. Suddenly, a man points a gun in her back. She will abruptly descend the hierarchy to satisfy her need for safety and security. Whenever a rung in the hierarchy "breaks," the person must return down to that level to satisfy the need. However, usually the person's progress back up to the higher level will occur rapidly.

5   In the next sections, you will focus on what specifically is encountered at each step of Maslow's hierarchy of needs.

SURVIVAL NEEDS

6   Most Americans experience only a mild form of survival need. Survival needs are biological necessities required to continue living. You may have believed yourself starving or dying of thirst. But chances are your needs were minimal when compared with people who had beyond doubt been without water or food for days.

7   During World War II, Keys et al.° studied men who had been fed just enough to stay alive. They found that the men became preoccupied with food thoughts and fantasies. The men delighted in reading cookbooks and exchanging favorite recipes. They forgot about wives, girlfriends, and sex. They became apathetic°, dispirited°, and irritable.

8   There has been considerable evidence that thirst needs are even stronger than hunger needs. When any physiological needs are not satisfied, personality changes generally result. Persons who have been without sleep for extended periods have been known to become anxious and hallucinate. Have you ever been in steady, persistent pain

for a prolonged time? You probably noticed your own personality change. In all likelihood, you were easily irked and had difficulty concentrating. Your interest and motivation were concentrated on how to relieve yourself of some pain and become more comfortable.

9   Newborn infants are motivated on this lowest level of Maslow's hierarchy. Initially their concerns are biological. If newborn infants are provided with food, drink, and comfortable, restful surroundings where they are free from pain, their motivational needs will be satisfied. But not for long! Once this step is met, the infant quickly progresses to the next level, stimulation needs.

STIMULATION NEEDS

10   Just as the infant who is fed, rested, and comfortable begins to look for something of interest, all children and adults also seek ways to escape boredom. However, as you might have suspected, the rattles and mobiles that satisfy the infant's need for novelty° and stimulation rarely, if ever, excite interest in adults. As you grow older, your interests and stimulation needs change and fluctuate°. Maslow would consider that sexual interest, curiosity, and pleasure were stimulation needs. Although sexual activity is biological or physiological in nature, it is not essential for survival. Consequently, the need for sex is on the second step of Maslow's hierarchy and is classified as a stimulation or psychological need.

SAFETY AND SECURITY NEEDS

11   Chances are you take many precautions to be certain you are safe and secure. You live in some type of shelter, whether it be an apartment, a house, a teepee, or a barn. This shelter protects you from rain, snow, and other unfavorable elements. But undoubtedly, your motivations and concerns for safety and security extend well beyond your need for shelter. Do you have locks on your doors and windows? How about flashlights and hurricane lanterns? If you keep a spare tire in your car and maintain health and auto insurance, you are responding to your motivation to satisfy safety and security needs. Our country supports a national military force; towns and cities have police and fire departments. These people in uniform all attest to our needs for safety and security.

LOVE AND BELONGINGNESS NEEDS

12   The first three levels of Maslow's hierarchy may have seemed selfish to you. Indeed, the needs described are basic, self-centered, and narrow. Physiological, curiosity, and security needs may be satisfied without calling on other people. However, these basic needs must be met before the need for other individuals can be recognized and accepted.

13   The needs for love and belongingness are sometimes called "affiliation° needs." If you have ever felt lonely or isolated, you have experienced a need to affiliate. Affiliation is not limited to romantic or parental love. You also need friends who accept you. There are immense differences in affiliation needs. Some people are satisfied with one or two close, deep friendships. Others crave superficial° relationships with large groups. Some fluctuate between group and individual friendships. Selection of friends usually changes with development.

14   At this level of the hierarchy, people look for ways to please others and win

their approval. Most are selective, seeking acceptance from only certain friends and associates. It would clearly be impossible to win everyone's approval!

15   Clubs such as Alcoholics Anonymous and Weight Watchers are designed to motivate people through their need for affiliation and social approval. Many individuals drink or eat because they feel unwanted or lonely. Although eating and drinking are physiological needs, they are often also associated with affiliation. Whether we are enjoying a formal dinner party or a few beers with some friends, the purpose is not solely satisfying hunger and thirst needs. Alcoholics Anonymous and Weight Watchers recognize the social implications° of eating and drinking. The groups were formed to approve refraining from° alcohol and excessive food. To win acceptance from the groups, you must keep sober and thin.

16   Just as there are differences in the type and number of friends needed, there are also wide variations in the intensity and strength of the need to belong and be accepted by others. Crowne and Marlowe developed a test to measure the need for social approval. They then used subjects who had either extremely high or extremely low scores on their tests. Next, the high and low scorers were asked to do a chore. They were told to put twelve spools in a box, lifting only one at a time. When the box was full, they had to empty it and repeat placing each spool back in the box. Sound like fun? Interestingly, the subjects who had high scores on the need-for-approval test claimed they enjoyed the task. They were also far more enthusiastic about the scientific usefulness of the experiment than were the low scorers. High scorers even stated they had learned something from the experiment. Evidently the low scorers had less need to be approved and could recognize a dull chore!

17   High needs for approval and affiliation can also be identified through clothes. Sorority and fraternity pins, team or club windbreakers, and dressing alike are ways of demonstrating a need to belong. Adolescents often show remarkable conformity in their dress. Men and women who frequent singles bars or attend every mixer and dance usually have strong affiliation needs.

18   Advertisers capitalize on° the need for love and belongingness. Many ads begin with a negative appeal. Jim is lonely and disapproved of by everyone. He has either dandruff, messy hair, bald spots, bad breath, a bad odor, or ill-fitting underwear. However, after he uses the advertised product, his problem is solved and he gains popularity. The advertisers are appealing to your need for approval. They hope you will believe their product will gain you the same popularity as Jim. Check magazines, newspapers, and your television for this type of ad.

ESTEEM AND SELF-ESTEEM NEEDS

19   Once you feel approved of and accepted by others, you are prepared to progress to the next step in the hierarchy, esteem and self-esteem. At this level you seek what both Rodney Dangerfield and Charlie Brown never get, namely, "respect." To satisfy the need for esteem, you need more than acceptance and belonging. You have to be held in high regard and have some status in your group.

20   How can you convince others that you are worthy of their respect? Usually an outstanding achievement will win some praise and prestige. If you score a goal in a soccer game, win a beauty contest, create an outstanding mural, or

produce a perfect exam paper, you will usually win the esteem of others. Achievements also improve your own self-esteem. When you convince others that you deserve respect, you also convince yourself.

21 **The need to achieve.** Clearly, esteem and self-esteem needs are related to each other. And achievements are a key way to satisfy the need for both. Achievements can be any accomplishment, from getting an office with a view or a personal secretary to maintaining the clearest complexion on campus. An achievement is a demonstration of success. Think of some achievements that you felt gave you status among others. Did you ever receive the highest grade on an exam or earn enough money for a car or an unusual vacation? Perhaps you have won a contest!

22 Some contests require an accomplishment while others are based strictly on luck. Often people feel a sense of achievement in winning contests based more on chance than on actual accomplishments. Bingo and sweepstake addicts delight in the possibility of winning huge sums of money easily. Studies have shown that only rarely are these individuals strong achievers at work. Strong achievers usually want to feel personally responsible for their own success.

23 Games of chance do not require individual efforts. According to McClelland, people with strong needs for achievement like to use their own skills and want to improve themselves. They prefer tasks that require some effort but are not impossible. If they have control of their jobs and set their own goals, they feel more satisfied with themselves. A high achiever would prefer a game of chess to a game of poker.

24 Achievers usually set goals for themselves that everyone else will believe are symbols or signs of success. They want to do well and enjoy getting positive feedback from others. Men and women with strong needs for achievement like to get pats on the back. Feedback from others is more important than money. Adams and Stone reported that high achievers will even spend their leisure time in activities that will reflect achievement.

25 Why do some people have strong needs for achievement? McClelland found that the need for achievement is related to parents' attitudes. Parents who are high achievers themselves usually demand independence from their children. The children must become self-reliant at a relatively early age. As a result, the children develop a sense of confidence and find enjoyment in their own achievements.

26 On the other hand, parents who have low needs for achievement are more protective of their children. They help their children perform everyday tasks such as dressing and feeding far more than necessary. Their children have less freedom and usually have low achievement needs.

27 **Fear of success.** What about people who are afraid to achieve? Psychologists believe the fear of success is usually related to a lower need, the need for love and belongingness. People who fear success are afraid they will lose valued friendships and affection if they become successful.

28 Horner was a pioneer in the study of fear of success in women. She gave college students one sentence and asked them to complete an essay. Male students were given the sentence: "After first-term finals, John finds himself at the top of his medical school class." Female students

were given the same sentence, with the name "Ann" substituted for "John." The men had a positive attitude toward "John." Only about 10 percent of the male students had any negative comments. Interestingly, almost two-thirds of the women had a negative attitude toward "Ann." They described her as either unpopular and rejected, or a guilty cheat, or a hoax.

29 Recent studies by Maccoby and Jacklin and Monahan and Shaver have supported Horner's findings. In our society, fear of success is common among women. Successful competitive women are often not socially acceptable. Although more prevalent in women, fear of success has also been found to occur in men. Many men feel insecure about achieving and losing the friendship of their coworkers and their acquaintances in their own economic group. Again, from Maslow's point of view, unless the need for love and belonging is met fully, achievement will not be possible.

SELF-ACTUALIZATION

30 At last to the top of the pyramid! But only when every imaginable need has been met is a person ready for the maximum growth through self-actualization. Maslow himself had difficulty finding a precise definition for self-actualization. He felt that all people have some inner talents or abilities that they want to use or actualize. If all lower needs are met, people can grow and develop by using these abilities. This growth is a continuous process that allows individuals to find self-fulfillment and realize their full potential.

31 In his attempt to identify some characteristics of people who have reached the level of self-actualization, Maslow studied the lives of forty-nine people that he believed to be self-actualizers. Among those studied were Albert Einstein, Eleanor Roosevelt, Abraham Lincoln, Thomas Jefferson, William James, and Jane Addams. Among the common characteristics of self-actualizers were:

- *Honesty* They have an ability to be objective and do not show selfish interest.
- *Creativity* They are spontaneous° and natural and enjoy trying new approaches.
- *Acceptance* They have total acceptance of themselves and are willing to accept others for what they are.
- *Appreciation* They possess an ability to become fully absorbed, enjoying even simple and basic experiences.
- *Sense of humor* They can recognize cleverness and whimsy and will laugh easily.
- *Sensitivity* They experience a deep feeling of sympathy for other people.

32 According to Maslow, self-actualization is extremely rare. He screened about three thousand students and found only one self-actualized person. Although self-actualization is slightly more likely among older individuals, it is far from common. Most people never move above the level of esteem. They never reach self-actualization and fully develop their potential.

33 Slightly more common than self-actualization are what Maslow called "peak experiences." A peak experience is an extremely brief, momentary sense of total happiness or fulfillment. For a few seconds or perhaps a minute, you have a sense of self-actualization. This feeling could come from such experiences as

watching a spectacular sunset, holding a baby, running a marathon, creating a sculpture, or greeting a returned love. Peak experiences give the same feeling of aliveness and wholeness that self-actualizers encounter. However, the feeling ends abruptly.

BASIC SKILL QUESTIONS

Vocabulary in Context

_____ 1. In the excerpt below, the word *irked* (ûrkt) means
  A. pleased.
  B. informed.
  C. annoyed.
  D. entertained.

  "Have you ever been in steady, persistent pain for a prolonged time? . . . In all likelihood, you were easily irked and had difficulty concentrating." (Paragraph 8)

_____ 2. In the excerpt below, the words *attest to* (ə-tĕst′ tōō) mean
  A. are evidence of.
  B. remain ignorant.
  C. become silent.
  D. make complaints.

  ". . . towns and cities have police and fire departments. These people in uniform all attest to our needs for safety and security." (Paragraph 11)

Central Point and Main Ideas

_____ 3. Which sentence best expresses the central point of the selection?
  A. Everyone has various needs to satisfy.
  B. Motivation can be conscious or unconscious.
  C. Maslow classified human motivations into six levels through which people progress.
  D. The most fundamental needs, according to Maslow, are physiological survival needs.

_____ 4. Which sentence best expresses the main idea of paragraph 1?
  A. Our motivations may be conscious or unconscious.
  B. Some needs, such as the need to stay alive and survive, are shared by everyone.
  C. Some needs, such as the need to drive a fancy sports car, vary from one person to the next.
  D. People have a broad range of needs, some of which are shared by everyone and some of which vary from person to person.

_____ 5. The main idea of paragraph 18 is stated in its
 A. first sentence.
 B. second sentence.
 C. third sentence.
 D. last sentence.

Supporting Details

_____ 6. The first three levels of Maslow's hierarchy
 A. depend on other people.
 B. are self-centered.
 C. are always fully met.
 D. result in "peak experiences."

_____ 7. TRUE OR FALSE? According to Maslow, most people never reach the level of self-actualization.

Transitions

_____ 8. The transition beginning paragraph 26 signals
 A. addition.
 B. time.
 C. contrast.
 D. cause and effect.

_____ 9. The relationship of the second sentence below to the first is one of
 A. addition.
 B. illustration.
 C. contrast.
 D. cause and effect.

 "The children must become self-reliant at a relatively early age. As a result, the children develop a sense of confidence and find enjoyment in their own achievements." (Paragraph 25)

Patterns of Organization

_____ 10. The pattern of organization of paragraph 31 is
 A. a series of events.
 B. steps in a process.
 C. list of items.
 D. cause and effect.

 11. The term being defined in paragraph 33 is "_____."

 The paragraph provides *(how many?)* _____ examples of that term.

ADVANCED SKILL QUESTIONS

Fact and Opinion

_____ 12. The author's statement that Abraham Maslow is "one of the most important contributors to the field of motivation" (paragraph 2) is a statement of
   A. fact.
   B. opinion.

_____ 13. TRUE OR FALSE? The statement below is an opinion.

"Some contests . . . are based strictly on luck." (Paragraph 22)

Inferences

_____ 14. We can infer that Maslow's hierarchy is considered to be like a ladder because
   A. ladders come in different heights.
   B. Maslow was influenced by house-building techniques.
   C. one can begin with the top need and work downward.
   D. one must "climb" from the lower needs to the higher ones.

_____ 15. Paragraph 3 implies that Maslow felt
   A. the need for love is as important as the need for survival.
   B. a person is more likely to seek friendship than security.
   C. curiosity is more fundamental than the need for safety.
   D. people will seek respect before they seek food and drink.

_____ 16. From the reading we can conclude that
   A. people's needs for esteem can be met in different ways.
   B. upbringing greatly influences how people meet their needs for esteem.
   C. people who have not met all their esteem needs may still enjoy peak experiences at times.
   D. all of the above.

_____ 17. TRUE OR FALSE? From paragraphs 27–29, we might conclude that children who gain a strong sense of being loved and belonging are more likely than other children to seek success as adults.

Purpose and Tone

_____ 18. The main purpose of this selection is to
   A. inform.
   B. persuade.
   C. entertain.

_____ 19. From the tone of paragraph 2, we can infer that the author
   A. is critical of Maslow's pyramid.
   B. is amused by Maslow's pyramid.
   C. accepts Maslow's pyramid.
   D. rejects Maslow's pyramid.

Argument

20. Label the point of the following argument with a **P** and the two statements of support with an **S**. Label with an **X** the one statement that is neither the point nor the support of the argument.

   _S_ A. Sexual interest and curiosity help fulfill adults' stimulation needs.

   _X_ B. Sexual activity is not essential for survival.

   _S_ C. Well-fed, comfortable babies may meet their stimulation needs with rattles and mobiles.

   _P_ D. Our stimulation needs change throughout our lives.

MAPPING

Using the headings and other boldfaced words in the selection, complete the map below.

Central point: According to Abraham Maslow, there are six levels of human needs.

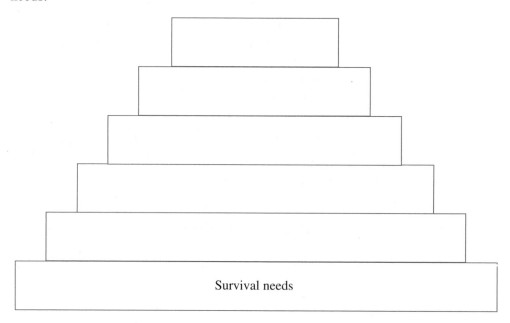

Survival needs

DISCUSSION QUESTIONS

1. Do you know a workaholic, a compulsive gambler, a television addict, or a joiner? Which of Maslow's needs do you think each of these people is trying to meet?

2. What ads have you seen recently that appeal to our need for approval? Which ones begin with a "negative appeal," as Quinn describes it in paragraph 18?

3. On the basis of your own experience, why might some people fear success? And what reasons can you see for the fear of success being much more common among women than among men?

4. According to the reading, achievements are a key way to satisfy the need for esteem and self-esteem. What achievements of yours have most strengthened your esteem and self-esteem? What achievement goals do you have for the future?

Note: Writing assignments for this selection appear on page 635.

Check Your Performance	MOTIVATION AND NEEDS		
Activity	*Number Right*	*Points*	*Score*
BASIC SKILL QUESTIONS			
Vocabulary in Context (2 items)	_____	× 4 =	_____
Central Point and Main Ideas (3 items)	_____	× 4 =	_____
Supporting Details (2 items)	_____	× 4 =	_____
Transitions (2 items)	_____	× 4 =	_____
Patterns of Organization (2 items)	_____	× 4 =	_____
ADVANCED SKILL QUESTIONS			
Fact and Opinion (2 items)	_____	× 4 =	_____
Inferences (4 items)	_____	× 4 =	_____
Purpose and Tone (2 items)	_____	× 4 =	_____
Argument (1 item)	_____	× 4 =	_____
MAPPING (5 items)	_____	× 4 =	_____
	TOTAL SCORE =	_____	%

Enter your total score into the **Reading Performance Chart: Ten Reading Selections** on the inside back cover.

6

Effects of the Automobile
James M. Henslin

Preview

"Well, of course cars have had an effect on society," you may be thinking. "They've allowed us to move from place to place much more easily." But like most important technological breakthroughs, the automobile has affected society in far more subtle ways than meet the eye. When you read this excerpt from the textbook *Sociology: A Down-to-Earth Approach* (Allyn & Bacon), you may be surprised to learn how the world we live in has been shaped by the automobile.

Words to Watch

in earnest (2): seriously
prospect (2): possibility
cumbersome (6): awkward
flourishing (6): thriving
urban sprawl (9): the spread of urban development into areas adjoining the city's edge
trysting (9): meeting
forays (12): attempts to leave one's usual area

1   If we try to pick the single item that has had the greatest impact on social life in the twentieth century, among the many candidates the automobile stands out. Let us look at some of the ways in which it changed U.S. society.

The automobile gradually pushed aside the old technology, a replacement that began in earnest° when Henry Ford began to mass produce the Model T in 1908. People immediately found automobiles attractive. They considered them

2

cleaner, safer, more reliable, and more economical than horses. Cars also offered the appealing prospect° of lower taxes, for no longer would the public have to pay to clean up the tons of horse manure that accumulated in the city streets each day. Humorous as it sounds now, it was even thought that automobiles would eliminate the cities' parking problems, for an automobile took up only half as much space as a horse and buggy.

3 The automobile also replaced a second technology. The United States had developed a vast system of urban transit, with electric streetcar lines radiating outward from the center of our cities. As the automobile became affordable and more dependable, Americans demonstrated a clear preference for the greater convenience of private transportation. Instead of walking to a streetcar and then having to wait in the cold and rain, people were able to travel directly from home on their own schedule.

4 The decline in the use of streetcars actually changed the shape of U.S. cities. Before the automobile, U.S. cities were web-shaped, for residences and businesses were located along the streetcar lines. When freed by automobiles from having to live so close to the tracks, people filled in the area between the "webs."

5 The automobile also stimulated mass suburbanization. Already in the 1920s, U.S. residents had begun to leave the city, for they found that they could commute to work in the city from outlying areas where they benefited from more room and fewer taxes. Their departure significantly reduced the cities' tax base, thus contributing to many of the problems that U.S. cities experience today.

6 The automobile had a profound impact on farm life and villages. Prior to the 1920s, most farmers were isolated from the city. Because using horses for a trip to town was slow and cumbersome°, they made such trips infrequently. By the 1920s, however, the popularity and low price of the Model T made the "Saturday trip to town" a standard event. There, farmers would market products, shop, and visit with friends. As a consequence, farm life was altered; for example, mail-order catalogues stopped being the primary source of shopping, and access to better medical care and education improved. Farmers were also able to travel to bigger towns, where they found a greater variety of goods. As farmers began to use the nearby villages only for immediate needs, these flourishing° centers of social and commercial life dried up.

7 The automobile's effects on commercial architecture are clear—from the huge parking lots that decorate malls like necklaces to the drive-up windows of banks and restaurants. But the automobile also fundamentally altered the architecture of U.S. homes. Before the car, each home had a stable in the back where the family kept its buggy and horses. The stable was the logical place to shelter the family's first car, and it required no change in architecture. The change occurred in three steps. First, new homes were built with a detached garage located like the stable, at the back of the home. Second, as the automobile became a more essential part of the U.S. family, the garage was incorporated into the home by moving it from the backyard to the side of the house, and connecting it by a breezeway. In the final step the breezeway was removed, and the garage integrated into the home so that Americans could enter their automobiles without even going outside.

8 By the 1920s, the automobile was used extensively for dating. This removed

children from the watchful eye of parents and undermined parental authority. The police began to receive complaints about "night riders" who parked their cars along country lanes, "doused their lights, and indulged in orgies." Automobiles became so popular for courtship that by the 1960s about 40 percent of marriage proposals took place in them.

9   In 1925 Jewett introduced cars with a foldout bed, as did Nash in 1937. The Nash version became known as "the young man's model." Since the 1970s, mobile lovemaking has declined, partly because urban sprawl° (itself due to the automobile) left fewer safe trysting° spots, and partly because changed sexual norms made beds more accessible.

10   The automobile may also lie at the heart of the changed role of women in U.S. society. To see how, we first need to see what a woman's life was like before the automobile. Historian James Flink described it this way:

11   Until the automobile revolution, in upper-middle-class households, groceries were either ordered by phone and delivered to the door or picked up by domestic servants or the husband on his way home from work. Iceboxes provided only very limited space for the storage of perishable foods, so shopping at markets within walking distance of the home was a daily chore. The garden provided vegetables and fruits in season, which were home-canned for winter consumption. Bread, cakes, cookies, and pies were home-baked. Wardrobes contained many home-sewn garments.

12   Mother supervised the household help and worked alongside them preparing meals, washing and ironing, and house cleaning. In her spare time she mended clothes, did decorative needlework, puttered in her flower garden, and pampered a brood of children. Generally, she made few family decisions and few forays° alone outside the yard. She had little knowledge of family finances and the family budget. The role of the lower-middle-class housewife differed primarily in that far less of the household work was done by hired help, so that she was less a manager of other people's work, more herself a maid-of-all-work around the house.

13   Because automobiles required skill rather than strength, women were able to drive as well as men. This new mobility freed women physically from the narrow confines of the home. As Flink observed, the automobile changed women "from producers of food and clothing into consumers of national-brand canned goods, prepared foods, and ready-made clothes. The automobile permitted shopping at self-serve supermarkets outside the neighborhood and in combination with the electric refrigerator made buying food a weekly rather than a daily activity." When women began to do the shopping, they gained greater control over the family budget, and as their horizons extended beyond the confines of the home, they also gained different views of life.

14   In short, the automobile changed women's roles at home, including their relationship with their husbands, altered their attitudes, transformed their opportunities, and stimulated them to participate in areas of social life not connected with the home.

15   With changes this extensive, it would not be inaccurate to say that the automobile also shifted basic values and changed the way we look at life. No longer isolated, women, teenagers, and farmers began to see the world differently.

So did husbands and wives, whose marital relationship had also been altered. The automobile even transformed views of courtship, sexuality, and gender relations.

16   No one attributes such fundamental changes solely to the automobile, of course, for many historical events, as well as other technological changes, occurred during this same period, each making its own contribution to social change. Even this brief overview of the social effects of the automobile, however, illustrates that technology is not merely an isolated tool but exerts a profound influence on social life.

BASIC SKILL QUESTIONS

Vocabulary in Context

_____ 1. In the sentence below, the word *confines* (kŏn′fīnz′) means
     A. thrills.
     B. limits.
     C. bedrooms.
     D. emotional attachments.

> "This new mobility freed women physically from the narrow confines of the home." (Paragraph 13)

Central Point and Main Ideas

_____ 2. Which sentence best expresses the central point of the selection?
     A. The automobile has been the source of all social change during the twentieth century.
     B. Automobiles are responsible for the decline of traditional farm communities.
     C. The automobile has had a profound impact on American culture and society.
     D. Women's liberation could never have occurred without the automobile.

_____ 3. The main idea of paragraphs 2 and 3 is stated in the
     A. first sentence of paragraph 2.
     B. last sentence of paragraph 2.
     C. first sentence of paragraph 3.
     D. second sentence of paragraph 3.

_____ 4. The main idea of paragraph 4 is
     A. stated in its first sentence.
     B. stated in its second sentence.
     C. stated in its third sentence.
     D. unstated.

_____ 5. The main idea of paragraph 6 is stated in its
    A. first sentence.
    B. second sentence.
    C. third sentence.
    D. last sentence.

_____ 6. Which sentence best expresses the implied main idea of paragraph 7?
    A. The automobile had numerous important effects.
    B. The automobile affected both commercial and home architecture.
    C. The automobile led to huge parking lots and drive-up windows.
    D. At first, the stable was the logical place to keep the automobile.

_____ 7. Which sentence best expresses the implied main idea of paragraph 13?
    A. Being physically strong is not a necessity when it comes to driving a car.
    B. Before the invention of the car, women produced more of their own food.
    C. Men's authority was not affected as the result of the automobile.
    D. The automobile transformed women's lives in several ways.

Supporting Details

_____ 8. According to the author, the automobile changed the shape of U.S. cities because
    A. cars severely damaged the old cobblestone and dirt streets.
    B. auto accidents required the installation of traffic lights.
    C. many buildings were demolished in order to build wider streets.
    D. cars enabled residents to settle in areas away from streetcar tracks.

_____ 9. Villages near farming families lost their place as "centers of social and commercial life" because
    A. farmers could not afford to shop in those centers after buying cars.
    B. farmers used mail-order catalogues instead of shopping in the nearby villages.
    C. once they had cars, farmers could drive to the city both to socialize and to shop.
    D. there wasn't enough room in the nearby villages to park the farmers' cars.

Transitions

_____ 10. The relationship expressed in the sentence below is one of
   A. comparison.
   B. illustration.
   C. contrast.
   D. cause and effect.

   "Their departure significantly reduced the cities' tax base, thus contributing to many of the problems that U.S. cities experience today." (Paragraph 5)

_____ 11. The relationship of the last sentence of paragraph 12 to the sentences before it is one of
   A. comparison.
   B. contrast.
   C. illustration.
   D. effect.

Patterns of Organization

_____ 12. The selection mainly
   A. presents a definition with many kinds of examples.
   B. narrates a series of events in time order.
   C. discusses many different effects that had the same cause.
   D. compares and contrasts the automobile with other new technologies.

_____ 13. Paragraph 2 in large part
   A. compares the use of horses and cars.
   B. contrasts people's views of horses and cars.
   C. lists modes of transportation.
   D. defines and illustrates a new term.

ADVANCED SKILL QUESTIONS

Fact and Opinion

_____ 14. The sentence below is
   A. factual.
   B. opinion.
   C. both fact and opinion.

   "Already in the 1920s, U.S. residents had begun to leave the city, for they found that they could commute to work in the city from outlying areas where they benefited from more room and fewer taxes." (Paragraph 5)

Inferences

_____ 15. From the sentences below, we might conclude that
   A. before the 1920s, arranged marriages were common in the U.S.
   B. before the 1920s, most dating was done in the home.
   C. people married at a younger age before the 1920s than after it.
   D. the practice of dating was almost unknown before the 1920s.

> "By the 1920s, the automobile was used extensively for dating. This removed children from the watchful eye of parents and undermined parental authority." (Paragraph 8)

_____ 16. We might conclude after reading paragraph 13 that
   A. women were at first reluctant to try out the new automotive technology.
   B. men welcomed the changes that the automobile created in women's lives.
   C. the introduction of the car made women less dependent on their husbands.
   D. women grew more socially conservative as a result of the introduction of the car.

Purpose and Tone

_____ 17. The author's main purpose is to
   A. inform readers of ways in which the introduction of the automobile affected U.S. society.
   B. persuade readers that the automobile was the only important influence on social life in the twentieth century.
   C. entertain readers with anecdotes about why people loved the automobile when it first appeared.

_____ 18. From the tone of paragraphs 10 and 13, we can conclude that the author
   A. is skeptical about Flink's conclusions.
   B. disagrees with Flink's observations.
   C. is scornful of Flink's scholarship.
   D. accepts Flink's observations.

Argument

   19. The following argument is based on the reading. Label the point of the argument with a P and the two statements of support with an S.
   ____ A. The automobile has made people less community-oriented and more independent.

   ____ B. People travel outside their neighborhoods for shopping and entertainment.

   ____ C. Instead of using public transportation to commute to work with their neighbors, people drive alone in cars.

_____20. The point below is followed by four statements, three of which logically support the point. Which of the statements does **not** support the point of the argument?

Point: The automobile affected the way that the United States looks.

A. Houses are now built with garages attached.

B. Shopping centers are surrounded by huge parking lots.

C. Once they could drive, women began to make more family decisions.

D. Suburban developments have grown to house people who commute long distances to work.

SUMMARIZING

Add the five ideas needed to complete this summary of "Effects of the Automobile." Read the entire passage before deciding what fits in each blank.

The automobile quickly replaced two technologies: _____ _____. The decline of streetcars affected the appearance of cities because residents no longer had to live close to streetcar lines. Many residents left the cities for the suburbs, attracted by the suburbs' greater space and _____. The lives of farmers were dramatically changed, as they could now easily travel to distant towns to market products, shop, or visit friends. As a result, local villages dried up. The automobile affected both commercial and residential architecture. For instance, businesses installed large parking lots and drive-up windows. Houses were now built with attached garages. By the 1920s, the car was used extensively for dating. This increased freedom for young people undermined the authority of _____. The automobile may also lie at the heart of the changed role of women in U.S. society. Before the advent of automobiles, women did their shopping on a daily basis at stores that were within walking distance of their homes. They produced a good deal of their own food and often sewed the family's clothes. The use of the automobile changed _____ from producers of food and clothing into consumers of store-bought food and clothing. As a result, women gained greater control over the family budget. The automobile led to the end of isolation for women, teenagers, and farmers, thus illustrating that changes in _____ have a profound effect on social life.

DISCUSSION QUESTIONS

1. The author lists numerous effects of the automobile, but does he think any of those effects are positive or negative? Look at the reading and try to determine the author's opinion of the various effects he describes.

2. Most people's lives would be different without the automobile and its automotive "relatives," such as the van, truck, bus, tractor, and motorcycle. How would your life change if there were suddenly no automobiles?

3. The selection explains that domestic chores were greatly changed with the introduction of the car and the electric refrigerator. Give some examples of other technological inventions that have changed domestic chores.

4. The passage argues that the automobile stands out as a candidate for the "single item that has had the greatest impact on social life in the twentieth century." Can you think of another item that has also had—or will have—a tremendous impact on society? What is it, and what are some of its more important effects?

Note: Writing assignments for this selection appear on page 636.

Check Your Performance   **EFFECTS OF THE AUTOMOBILE**

Activity	*Number Right*	*Points*	*Score*
BASIC SKILL QUESTIONS			
Vocabulary in Context (1 item)	_____	× 4 =	_____
Central Point and Main Ideas (6 items)	_____	× 4 =	_____
Supporting Details (2 items)	_____	× 4 =	_____
Transitions (2 items)	_____	× 4 =	_____
Patterns of Organization (2 items)	_____	× 4 =	_____
ADVANCED SKILL QUESTIONS			
Fact and Opinion (1 item)	_____	× 4 =	_____
Inferences (2 items)	_____	× 4 =	_____
Purpose and Tone (2 items)	_____	× 4 =	_____
Argument (2 items)	_____	× 4 =	_____
SUMMARIZING (5 items)	_____	× 4 =	_____
	TOTAL SCORE =	_____ %	

Enter your total score into the **Reading Performance Chart: Ten Reading Selections** on the inside back cover.

7

Rabies
Robert Berkow, M.D., ed.

Preview

Rabies has long been regarded as one of the most horrifying diseases to afflict animals and humans. Its frightening symptoms—agitation, foaming at the mouth, crazed behavior—have contributed to its fearsome status as much as its usually fatal outcome. Stories including the childhood classic "Old Yeller" and Stephen King's *Cujo* have added to rabies' terrifying reputation. This excerpt from *The Merck Manual of Medical Information, Home Edition*—based on *The Merck Manual*, the most widely used medical textbook in the world—provides an objective look at this dreaded disease.

Words to Watch

inoculation (2): penetration
agitated (3): disturbed
nocturnal (4): most active at night
incubation (6): the time period between infection and the appearance of the first symptoms
excruciatingly (7): intensely; extremely
vaccine (10): a preparation that when introduced into the body produces immunity to a specific illness by causing antibodies to form
antibody (10): a substance that provides immunity to a specific disease
immunoglobulin (12): an antibody

1   Rabies is a viral infection of the brain that causes irritation and inflammation of the brain and spinal cord.

2   The rabies virus is present in the saliva of infected animals. An animal with rabies transmits the infection to other animals or humans by biting and sometimes licking. The virus travels from the site of initial inoculation° along the nerves to the spinal cord and the brain,

where it multiplies. It subsequently travels down the nerves to the salivary glands and into the saliva.

3   Many different animals can transmit rabies to people. Although dogs are frequently the source of infection for people, cats, bats, raccoons, skunks, foxes, and others may be responsible. It is unusual for mice, rats, or other small mammals to be rabid, partly because the bite of another animal is usually fatal for them. In the United States, vaccination has largely eliminated rabies in dogs. However, rabies in dogs is still fairly common in most countries of Latin America, Africa, and Asia, where pets aren't always vaccinated against the disease. Infected animals may have either "furious" rabies or "dumb" rabies. In furious rabies, the animal is agitated° and vicious, then later becomes paralyzed and dies. In dumb rabies, the localized or generalized paralysis is prominent from the beginning.

4   In the United States, most cases of human rabies during the last thirty years have been caused by bites of infected wild animals. Rabid wild animals may show furious behavior, but less obvious changes in behavior are more likely. Nocturnal° animals (bats, skunks, raccoons, and foxes) infected with rabies may come out during the day and may not show the normal fear of humans.

5   Though extremely rare, rabies may be acquired by breathing infected air. Two cases occurred when explorers breathed the air of a bat-infested cave.

SYMPTOMS

6   Symptoms usually begin 30 to 50 days after infection, but the incubation° period varies from ten days to more than a year. The incubation period is usually shortest in people who were bitten on the head or trunk or who received many bites.

7   In 20 percent of people, rabies starts with paralysis in the lower legs that moves up through the body. However, the disease commonly starts with a short period of mental depression, restlessness, a sick feeling, and a fever. Restlessness increases to uncontrollable excitement, and the person produces a lot of saliva. Spasms of the muscles of the throat and voice box can be excruciatingly° painful. These spasms are caused by irritability of the area in the brain responsible for swallowing and breathing. A slight breeze or an attempt to drink water can induce these spasms. Thus, a person with rabies can't drink. For this reason, the disease is sometimes called hydrophobia (fear of water).

DIAGNOSIS

8   When a person is bitten by a sick or wild animal, the biggest concern is rabies. Determining whether an animal has rabies usually requires an examination of a brain tissue sample. The animal should be captured and observed. Typically, the animal must be killed to examine the brain. If a dog or cat without symptoms bites a person, however, a veterinarian may confine and observe the animal for ten days. If the animal remains healthy, the veterinarian can safely conclude that the animal didn't have rabies at the time of the bite.

9   If a person who has been bitten by an animal develops symptoms of progressive brain inflammation (encephalitis), rabies is the likely cause. Viral testing of the person isn't helpful until symptoms appear. A skin biopsy, in which a sample of skin is taken (usually from the neck) for examination under a microscope, can reveal the virus.

PREVENTION AND TREATMENT

10   Steps to prevent rabies can be taken before exposure to the rabies virus or immediately after exposure. For example, a vaccine° can be administered to people at high risk for exposure to the virus. These people include veterinarians, laboratory workers who handle potentially infected animals, people who live or stay more than thirty days in developing countries where rabies in dogs is widespread, and people who explore bat caves. Vaccination gives most people some degree of protection for the rest of their lives. However, antibody° levels fall with time, and people at high risk of further exposure should receive a booster dose of vaccine every two years.

11   People who have been bitten by a rabid animal rarely develop rabies if appropriate preventive steps are taken immediately. People bitten by rabbits and rodents (including squirrels, chipmunks, rats, and mice) require no further treatment unless there is definite suspicion of rabies; these animals are rarely infected. However, people bitten by wild animals such as skunks, raccoons, foxes, and bats need further treatment unless the biting animal can be captured and proved to be free of rabies.

12   Treating a bite wound immediately may be the most valuable preventive measure. The contaminated area is cleaned thoroughly with soap. Deep puncture wounds are flushed out with soapy water. Once the wound has been cleaned, people not previously immunized with rabies vaccine are given an injection of rabies immunoglobulin°, with half of the dose given at the location of the bite. For people who have not been previously immunized, rabies vaccine injections are given on the day of exposure and on days three, seven, fourteen, and twenty-eight.

13   Pain and swelling at the injection site are usually minor. Serious allergic reactions are rare during the series of five injections; fewer than 1 percent of people develop a fever when they receive the vaccine.

14   If a person who is bitten has already been vaccinated, the risk of acquiring rabies is reduced, but the wound still needs to be cleaned promptly and two doses of vaccine must be given (on days zero and two).

15   Before current therapy was available, death usually occurred in three to ten days. Most people died of blocked airways (asphyxia), convulsions, exhaustion, or widespread paralysis. Although death from rabies was once considered inevitable, a few people did survive. Survival in those instances can be attributed to intensive care to control symptoms affecting the heart, lungs, and brain. Neither vaccine nor rabies immunoglobulin appears to be helpful once a person develops symptoms.

BASIC SKILL QUESTIONS

Vocabulary in Context

_____ 1. In the sentence below, the phrase *incubation period* (ĭn'kyə-bā'shən pĭr'ē-əd) means the period of time
A. when the animal bites.
B. after infection when the illness is developing but before symptoms appear.
C. during which the illness lasts.
D. before the animal bites.

> "Symptoms usually begin 30 to 50 days after infection, but the incubation period varies from ten days to more than a year." (Paragraph 6)

_____ 2. In the excerpt below, the word *induce* (ĭn-dōos') means
A. temporarily stop.
B. cause.
C. cure.
D. mask.

> "A slight breeze or an attempt to drink water can induce these spasms. Thus, a person with rabies can't drink." (Paragraph 7)

Central Point and Main Ideas

3. *Fill in the blank:* The implied central point of this selection is that rabies must be taken very seriously; the reading presents information about the

_____, diagnosis, prevention and treatment of rabies.

_____ 4. Which sentence best expresses the main idea of paragraph 7?
A. The first symptoms of rabies vary.
B. A series of symptoms appears as rabies develops within a person.
C. One of the worst symptoms of rabies is spasms of the muscles of the throat and voice box.
D. Rabies is sometimes called hydrophobia, which means "fear of water."

_____ 5. Which sentence best expresses the main idea of paragraph 12?
A. Rabies vaccine injections are given to bite victims several times and at varying intervals.
B. The spot where the virus has entered the body is referred to as the contaminated area.
C. Deep puncture wounds resulting from animal bites should be rinsed thoroughly with soapy water.
D. Preventive measures against rabies in people who have not been immunized consist of immediate, careful washing of the bite wound and vaccination.

Supporting Details

_____ 6. An animal or human can get infected with the rabies virus by direct contact with an infected animal or even by
  A. breathing it in.
  B. being bitten by an uninfected animal.
  C. eating spoiled food.
  D. simply touching someone with the virus.

_____ 7. To determine whether an animal is rabid, it often must be killed so that there can be an examination of a sample of its
  A. teeth.
  B. stomach.
  C. brain.
  D. intestines.

_____ 8. For a person who is bitten and has already been vaccinated against rabies,
  A. no further treatment is needed.
  B. serious allergic reactions are rare.
  C. the wound still must be promptly cleaned and two doses of vaccine must be given.
  D. a brain tissue sample must be examined under a microscope.

_____ 9. Once a person develops symptoms of rabies,
  A. it is time to wash out the wound.
  B. a vaccine must be given.
  C. an injection of rabies immunoglobulin must be given.
  D. neither the vaccine nor rabies immunoglobulin appears to help.

Transitions

_____ 10. The relationship between the two sentences below is one of
  A. comparison.
  B. contrast.
  C. illustration.
  D. cause and effect.

  "A slight breeze or an attempt to drink water can induce these spasms. Thus, a person with rabies can't drink." (Paragraph 7)

_____ 11. The relationship between the two parts of the sentence below is one of
  A. illustration.
  B. time.
  C. addition.
  D. cause and effect.

  "Before current therapy was available, death usually occurred in three to ten days." (Paragraph 15)

Patterns of Organization

_____ 12. The main pattern of organization of paragraph 12 is
   A. time order.
   B. definition and example.
   C. comparison-contrast.
   D. addition.

ADVANCED SKILL QUESTIONS

Fact and Opinion

_____ 13. The reading is
   A. all fact.
   B. all opinion.
   C. about half fact and half opinion.

_____ 14. The facts of the reading are probably based on
   A. the author's observation of his or her own family members.
   B. one or two well-known cases of rabies.
   C. a great deal of research and physician experience.
   D. only animal observations.

Inferences

_____ 15. We might infer that in the popular image of a dog with rabies foaming at the mouth,
   A. the dog really does not have rabies.
   B. the dog has been mistreated.
   C. the foam is saliva.
   D. the image is incorrect.

_____ 16. TRUE OR FALSE? We can conclude that the main reason cleaning a bite wound is so important is that soap and water can remove much of the infectious material.

_____ 17. We can conclude that in the phrase "on days zero and two" (paragraph 14), *day zero* refers to
   A. the time before someone is exposed to rabies.
   B. the day someone is exposed to rabies.
   C. the day after someone is exposed to rabies.
   D. two days after someone is exposed to rabies.

Purpose and Tone

_____ 18. The author's primary purpose in this selection is to
   A. inform.
   B. persuade.
   C. entertain.

_____ 19. The tone of the selection is
    A. ambivalent.   C. prideful.
    B. sympathetic.   D. objective.

Argument

_____ 20. Write the letter of the statement that is the point of the following argument. The other statements are support for that point.
    A. Bats can transmit rabies through a bite or through the air.
    B. Rabies is deadly.
    C. People who explore bat caves should get vaccinated against rabies.
    D. The rabies vaccination causes protective antibodies to form.

OUTLINING

Complete the outline of paragraphs 10–14 by filling in the missing major and minor details. The missing items are listed in random order below.

Items Missing from the Outline

- For people not previously immunized
- Vaccine injections on days 0 and 2
- A booster dose every two years, since antibody levels fall with time
- Prevention for people already bitten by an animal that may have rabies

Main idea: There are ways to prevent and treat rabies.

  A. Prevention before exposure for people at high risk of exposure (vets, workers in animal labs, etc.)

    1. Vaccination for some degree of lifelong protection

    2. _____

       _____

  B. _____

    _____

    1. _____

      a. Prompt, thorough cleaning

      b. Injection of rabies immunoglobulin, half at site of bite

      c. Vaccine injections on day of exposure and days 3, 7, 14, and 28 (few serious reactions)

    2. For people previously immunized

      a. Prompt, thorough cleaning

      b. _____

DISCUSSION QUESTIONS

1. The tone of this essay can best be described as objective. Why has the author chosen to treat the subject matter in such a way?

2. According to the article, many of the animals people typically associate with rabies—rats, mice, and other small mammals—rarely carry the disease. Have you ever had an idea about a disease, or a treatment for a disease, that you discovered to be false? Explain. What do you think causes people to believe false ideas?

3. This essay appears in a current medical reference book designed for home use. Do you have such a medical reference book at home? How do you typically get medical information when you need it?

4. A major section of this essay concerns prevention. What steps, if any, do you take in your life to prevent general health problems? When did you become aware of the value of preventive medicine? If you take no everyday steps to prevent illness, why have you chosen not to protect yourself?

Note: Writing assignments for this selection appear on page 636.

Check Your Performance   **RABIES**

Activity	Number Right	Points	Score
BASIC SKILL QUESTIONS			
Vocabulary in Context (2 items)	_____	× 4 =	_____
Central Point and Main Ideas (3 items)	_____	× 4 =	_____
Supporting Details (4 items)	_____	× 4 =	_____
Transitions (2 items)	_____	× 4 =	_____
Patterns of Organization (1 item)	_____	× 4 =	_____
ADVANCED SKILL QUESTIONS			
Fact and Opinion (2 items)	_____	× 4 =	_____
Inferences (3 items)	_____	× 4 =	_____
Purpose and Tone (2 items)	_____	× 4 =	_____
Argument (1 item)	_____	× 4 =	_____
OUTLINING (4 items)	_____	× 5 =	_____
	TOTAL SCORE =		_____%

Enter your total score into the **Reading Performance Chart: Ten Reading Selections** on the inside back cover.

8

Bad Managers
Michael W. Drafke and Stan Kossen

Preview

We often hear about workers who make life hard for their managers in various ways—coming in late, leaving early, taking no pride in their work. But just as there are bad workers, there are bad managers as well, and they come in various forms. In this reading from *The Human Side of Organizations,* Seventh Edition (Addison-Wesley, 1998), Michael W. Drafke and Stan Kossen describe various troublesome behaviors of bad managers. See if any of these bosses sound familiar to you.

Words to Watch

laterally (1): to a position at a similar level
entrenched (3): securely established
dysfunctional (3): not working normally or correctly
anticlimactic (8): disappointing after a big buildup
malicious (9): deliberately harmful
manifests (9): makes known
Machiavellian (14): characterized by selfishness and deceit, from Niccolò Machiavelli, who described in his book *The Prince* (1513) a king who gained and kept power with no concern for moral principles

1   The incompetent manager is a victim of the Peter Principle or a psychological deficiency. The Peter Principle states that people are promoted to their level of incompetence. In other words, when people do well in a job, they are rewarded with a promotion. If they do well in the next job, they are promoted again. The cycle repeats itself until they are placed in a job that they can't perform. Then they

are demoted, moved laterally°, or fired. The level at which the Peter Principle applies is different for each person. Some people reach competence with an entry-level position; others reach it after ten promotions.

2   Some managers are incompetent not because of a lack of ability but because of a psychological defect. The only result of their actions that they foresee is failure. They are unable to decide because they are convinced that whatever they choose will be wrong. Several warning signs can identify the psychologically impaired incompetent manager:

- denial
- playing it by the numbers
- buck passing
- abdication
- obfuscation
- delaying tactics
- escaping

Managees should be alert to these warning signs, for it is hard for a managee to do his or her job, much less progress, with an incompetent manager.

3   Managers using denial will insist that there are no problems. Problems brought to their attention either don't exist, will go away by themselves, or were solved long ago. If there are no problems, no decision needs to be made or action taken. Managers playing it by the numbers always consult the rule book. If the answer is in the book, then they do not have to devise any solutions, and if the problem is not in the book, then it is not a problem. This can often be seen in the firmly entrenched°, and dysfunctional°, bureaucratic mind.

4   Buck passing (passing a problem along to someone else) is a strong sign of incompetence, but it may also be a characteristic of new managers. Some-times a manager has not been managing

or is so new to the organization that he or she really doesn't know the answer and must pass the decision along. If the manager is experienced, then buck passing can be a sign of incompetence. The issue may be passed to other areas or departments, or it may be passed up to the manager's manager. In either case, the incompetent manager can never seem to decide anything on his or her own authority.

5   An incompetent manager who can't give a problem to another manager may try giving it to managees. Whereas buck passing removes the decision from one manager to another, abdication passes authority off to others with less power or with no official power. Abdication can involve passing authority to a committee, to subordinates, or to a third party. Passing authority to subordinates may look like participative management, but a behavioral manager acts as a group leader, not an absent leader. When unable to form a committee and when unable to have managees make decisions, the abdicator may bring in consultants. Whatever form of abdication is chosen, there are two goals: avoid making the decision, and ensure that there is someone else to blame if things go wrong.

6   Some incompetent managers use obfuscation, clouding and confusing the issue to the point that people walk away too embarrassed to admit they are confused, or they give up in frustration. If the problem cannot be clouded or given to someone else, then the incompetent manager may try to delay any involvement. Managers have a number of effective delaying tactics. One reason many of them are effective is that sometimes there are valid excuses for waiting. However, delaying tactics become warning signs of incompetence when they constantly recur. One common delaying tactic is to ask for the problem

in writing. This works quite often. Sometimes managees are reluctant to create evidence that they are afraid may be used against them, or they may believe that writing the incident down will be a waste of time because nothing will happen anyway (which with incompetent managers is usually true). This reinforces the manager's mental problems because the manager can now rationalize the avoidance of decision making by saying that it couldn't have been much of a problem if the managee wasn't willing to put it in writing.

7   Caution is another delaying tactic used by incompetent managers. Here the manager always warns managees that "We'd better not move too quickly. Slow and steady wins the race." Another form of using caution to delay is to wait for new technology. But because technology is always improving, the manager is always waiting and never has to decide. Another delaying tactic involves insisting that problems must be handled on a first-come, first-served basis. Because this manager still has his or her first problem to decide, this in effect bars all future decisions until the past ones are decided. Sometimes the problem is insufficient information. Therefore, the situation will have to be studied and some research done. Of course the information is never gathered, or there is always more to get.

8   The final signal that a manager may be incompetent is escaping, or running away from the entire situation. Some managers escape by leaving for a business trip, going home, arranging to be too busy or always in a meeting, or going on vacation. In one situation involving an abusive health care managee, the day finally came when physicians, an outside agency, co-managees, and a particularly spineless manager were to present a large volume of information

and the managee was to be fired. As the appointed hour on a Wednesday afternoon came, all were gathered except the manager. After several minutes of this high-tension atmosphere, the manager's secretary came in to announce that the manager had just called to say he had decided to start a vacation that day. About two months after the abusive managee was fired, many of the same people and top administrators gathered for the firing of the manager (for this and other acts of incompetence). The event was somewhat anticlimactic° because the manager had taken an unannounced "personal day."

9   Incompetent managers are just one type of generally poor managers; other bad managers can actually be classified as malicious°. Malicious managers actively cause harm or distress to managees. Typically this is mental distress, but sometimes sexual and physical harassment is involved. Whatever stressful behavior is exhibited by these managers, they can be classified by the manner in which the maliciousness manifests° itself. Some of the mostly unsuccessful malicious managers are:

- clueless
- Janus-type
- grumps
- spineless

[Three] other types are often highly successful, but their tactics are typically unnecessarily harsh or stressful. These types can be classified as:

- first-in, last-out managers
- perfectionists
- intimidators

If you are being managed, learn to differentiate between these types because your responses should differ depending on the type.

10   Clueless managers are living in the dark ages. They have missed or ignored behavioral management, women's rights, diversity and minority rights, and the Americans with Disabilities Act. Clueless managers may stun you with behavior so out of date that you have no immediate response. Sexual advances; stereotypical comments concerning race, gender, or ability; and a lack of any sense of what is appropriate in the workplace are symptoms of managerial cluelessness. Typically, the clueless manager is consistently clueless, whereas the Janus types are unpredictable.

11   Janus, the Roman god of gates and doorways, had two faces. Janus-type managers have two faces, and managees never know which to expect, the good side or the bad side. The disturbing aspect to Janus-type behavior is that the mood can change from day to day or even from hour to hour. Many consider Janus-types to be more difficult than grumps, who are always in a bad mood. They seem to hate everything and almost everybody, seem to never be happy, and think that nothing is ever going to improve or to work properly. However, at least the grumps are consistent. You know what you are getting when you have to talk with one. People fear the unknown, and the Janus-types touch this with their unpredictability. . . .

12   Spineless managers choose to avoid issues and deny problems, and they are quite adept at it. To avoid being held accountable later, the spineless never take a stand or express a strong opinion. These managers seem to walk around holding their breath, fearful that someone might ask them a pointed question. Once, during a heated discussion involving much yelling and gesturing, two people who were arguing turned to a third colleague, each looking for support. The colleague was almost totally spineless even though the outcome of the argument was going to affect him directly. Instead of choosing sides, offering a compromise, or even offering a third option, he just stood there staring at the floor. After more than a few moments with no response, the two that had been arguing looked at him, looked at each other, looked at him again, and looked at each other once more; finally one said, "Hello? Anyone home?" The entire argument stopped cold while Mr. Spineless stared at the floor. Finally the two settled the argument and things broke up. Later Mr. Spineless said that he was so shocked to see the other two yelling that he couldn't respond. The problem was that he couldn't decide who was going to win, and rather than take a chance or try to figure out who was right, he pretended that his brain had locked up on him.

13   Because of their insecurities, the spineless will not commit to things and will not direct people in what to do. As with the other signs of maliciousness, this one is self-evident. Because this behavior is seen, the incompetence of spineless managers eventually is exposed, and few last long in any one place. This is not to say that they can't, for reasons strange and bizarre, be found in upper management. They can. However, you would not find as many of these as you would the next [three] types.

14   Some successful managers can still be classified as malicious. This is so because, when dealing with other people, sometimes "It's not whether you win or lose; it's how you play the game." Some malicious people (Hitler, Attila the Hun, Stalin) had what they would argue was some degree of success. We typically

reject a Machiavellian° world in which anything goes in the name of winning (winning typically meaning that the individual gets what he or she wants regardless of what happens to others). The ends do not justify the means. An example of one who sometimes succeeds is the FILO manager.

15 FILO is an accounting term meaning "first in, last out." FILO managers are the first to arrive and the last to leave. They often work on Saturdays, Sundays, and holidays. This would be fine, except that most FILO managers expect their managees to do the same. One FILO manager put up cots in the workplace to remind people that their twelve- to fourteen-hour workdays could be worse—they could be twenty-four-hour workdays. Worse yet, FILOs seem to travel in groups. Entire organizations can be composed of these workaholics, so it is important to know whether or not you can fit in with these people before making a major commitment to what is essentially an entire lifestyle. . . .

16 Perfectionists seem to think that everyone must share in their compulsion. The malicious perfectionist with power often victimizes managees with numerous, highly detailed questions that it is unlikely any one person could answer. Other perfectionists may make completely unreasonable demands of managees and then berate them publicly for not being able to complete the task. One perfectionist who sometimes screams at people with veins popping out of his head and fists banging on the desk until they leave in tears has a sign on the wall, "Be realistic. Demand the impossible." Although we should strive to do the job right, perfectionist standards are unrealistically high, and they perceive anything less, no matter how close to perfect it comes, as failure. In school, these people consider missing one item on a test with fifty or one hundred questions a failure. It is not just their having high standards that stresses other people, but rather the anything-less-is-totally-unacceptable attitude that accompanies it that seems to push these people into the poor manager category.

17 The final general type of malicious manager includes behavior that is often exhibited with that of other types. Whether as a means to push their perfectionist ideals or as part of mind games or to make up for their own deficiencies or mental inadequacies, some managers may become intimidators. Intimidators do not lead (at least not in the typical way), they do not persuade, they do not request. Instead, they bully people. They yell, insult, or scream to get what they want. Some intimidators return work they don't like torn into tiny pieces. Others throw things, make managees stay in meetings past midnight, withhold paychecks, or keep people waiting simply to demonstrate their power. A few even work with a partner. While one plays the bad guy, screams and yells and stomps out of the room, the other plays good guy, staying behind and remaining calm so as to smooth over the intimidation of the one playing the bad guy. The intimidators are not just intelligent or tough; they can be either or both, and they want to display their power and position. Maybe they like to be bullies, maybe they can't think of another, more civil way to act, or maybe they don't believe other tactics will work. In any case, they and the other malicious and incompetent managers need to be dealt with.

BASIC SKILL QUESTIONS

Vocabulary in Context

_____ 1. In the excerpt below, the word *managee* (măn-ə-jē′) means
  A. someone who works under a manager.
  B. an incompetent worker.
  C. a highly competent worker.
  D. a manager.

  ". . . it is hard for a managee to do his or her job, much less progress, with an incompetent manager." (Paragraph 2)

_____ 2. In the excerpt below, the word *rationalize* (răsh′ə-nə-līz) means
  A. explain away.
  B. predict.
  C. notice.
  D. imitate.

  "This reinforces the manager's mental problems because the manager can now rationalize the avoidance of decision making by saying that it couldn't have been much of a problem . . . ." (Paragraph 6)

Central Point and Main Ideas

_____ 3. Which sentence best expresses the central point of the selection?
  A. It is hard for a managee to do his or her job with an incompetent manager.
  B. Incompetent and malicious managers can be identified by a number of warning signs, which managees should learn to identify.
  C. Denial, buck-passing, abdication, and escaping are all signs of incompetence in managers.
  D. Many managers are placed in jobs that they're not capable of performing.

_____ 4. Which sentence best expresses the main idea of paragraph 4?
  A. Buck-passing is passing a problem along to someone else rather than solving it oneself.
  B. Although buck-passing is understandable in new managers, it can be a sign of incompetence in an experienced manager.
  C. Managers who are new should not be expected to deal with problems that go beyond their experience.
  D. Buck-passing may involve passing the problem along to other areas or up to the manager's manager.

_____ 5. Which of these sentences best expresses the main idea of paragraph 7?

    A. There are no valid reasons to warn employees against moving too quickly.

    B. If a manager insists on a "first-come, first-served" policy but never deals with the first problem, the later problems will never be addressed either.

    C. There are several ways an incompetent manager can justify using "caution" as a reason not to address a problem.

    D. Because technology is constantly changing, a manager can put off a decision for a long time while waiting for "new technology."

Supporting Details

_____ 6. Write the letter of the best general outline of the reading.

    A. 1. Victims of the Peter Principle
         2. Incompetent managers
         3. Warning signs
         4. Escaping

    B. 1. Incompetent managers
           a. Victims of the Peter Principle
           b. Victims of a psychological deficiency, who can be identified by various warning signs
         2. Malicious managers
           a. Unsuccessful malicious managers
           b. Successful malicious managers

    C. 1. denial, playing it by the numbers, buck passing, abdication
         2. obfuscation, delaying tactics, escaping
         3. clueless, Janus-type, grumps, spineless
         4. first-in, last-out managers; perfectionists; intimidators

_____ 7. Managers who "play by the numbers"

    A. pass authority along to others with less power.

    B. deny that a problem exists if they can't find it in the rule book.

    C. are generally less experienced than other managers.

    D. rewrite the rule book so that it reflects their own preferences.

_____ 8. The authors refer to managers who bully managees by yelling, insulting, and screaming as

    A. clueless.

    B. spineless.

    C. grumps.

    D. intimidators.

Transitions

_____ 9. The relationship of the second sentence below to the first is one of
   A. contrast.
   B. time.
   C. addition.
   D. illustration.

   "One reason many of them are effective is that sometimes there are valid excuses for waiting. However, delaying tactics become warning signs of incompetence when they constantly recur." (Paragraph 6)

_____ 10. The sentence below expresses a relationship of
   A. illustration.
   B. addition.
   C. comparison.
   D. cause and effect.

   "The event was somewhat anticlimactic because the manager had taken an unannounced 'personal day.'" (Paragraph 8)

Patterns of Organization

_____ 11. The main pattern of organization of "Bad Managers" is
   A. list of items.
   B. time order.
   C. cause and effect.
   D. comparison-contrast.

_____ 12. The main patterns of organization of paragraph 2 are
   A. cause-effect and list of items.
   B. definition-example and comparison.
   C. cause-effect and contrast.
   D. definition and example.

ADVANCED SKILL QUESTIONS

Fact and Opinion

_____ 13. In the sentence below, words that reflect opinions are
   A. *managers, type.*
   B. *one, other.*
   C. *just, be classified.*
   D. *poor, bad, malicious.*

   "Incompetent managers are just one type of generally poor managers; other bad managers can actually be classified as malicious." (Paragraph 9)

_____ 14. The reading is
- A. all fact.
- B. all opinion.
- C. both fact and opinion.

Inferences

_____ 15. We can infer that the manager in the anecdote in paragraph 8
- A. believed the managee to be fired was not truly abusive.
- B. had planned his vacation weeks in advance.
- C. began his vacation in order to avoid being involved in the firing.
- D. believed that the firing would be less painful for the managee if he was not present.

_____ 16. The selection suggests that
- A. managers who are psychologically impaired often become more competent as time goes on.
- B. working for an incompetent manager can be difficult.
- C. all managers suffer from some degree of psychological impairment.
- D. managees can usually find ways to effectively deal with an incompetent manager and so find great satisfaction in working under him or her.

Purpose and Tone

_____ 17. TRUE OR FALSE? The main purpose of this selection is to inform the reader about psychological impairment or maliciousness in various types of poor managers.

_____ 18. Which sentence reveals a persuasive element in the reading?
- A. "The level at which the Peter Principle applies is different for each person."
- B. "Managers using denial will insist that there are no problems."
- C. "Some managers escape by leaving for a business trip, going home, arranging to be too busy or always in a meeting, or going on vacation."
- D. "If you are being managed, learn to differentiate between these types because your responses should differ depending on the type."

_____ 19. The authors' tone in the discussion of malicious managers (paragraphs 14–17) is
- A. tolerant.
- B. threatening.
- C. critical.
- D. curious.

Argument

_____ 20. TRUE OR FALSE? The authors support their point that managers may be incompetent or malicious by explaining specific types of incompetence and malice.

MAPPING

Complete the map of "Bad Managers" by filling in the rest of the main idea and the missing major and minor supporting details.

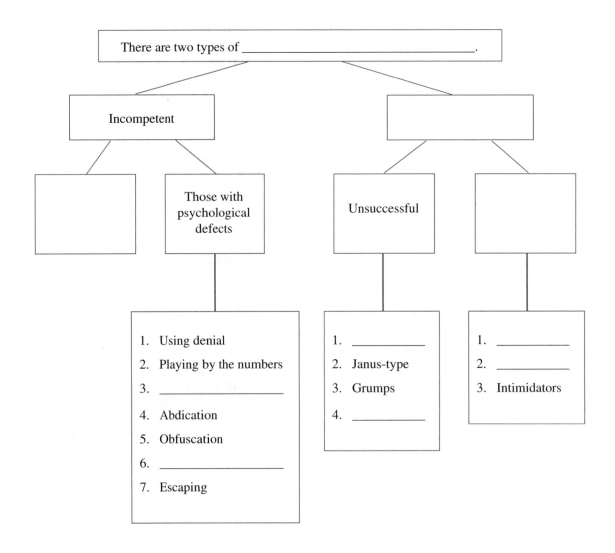

DISCUSSION QUESTIONS

1. Describe the worst boss you ever had. Which of the behaviors described in this selection did your boss exhibit? How did those behaviors affect you and other employees?

2. The reading describes problem managers but gives no advice on how workers should deal with them. Select one of the incompetent or malicious managers described in the reading. What advice would you give to someone who was trying to deal with such a boss?

3. On the basis of the information in this article and your own experience, describe the qualities of a person you would consider an ideal boss.

4. What steps do you think companies should take to protect employees from incompetent or malicious bosses?

Note: Writing assignments for this selection appear on page 637.

Check Your Performance		BAD MANAGERS	
Activity	*Number Right*	*Points*	*Score*
BASIC SKILL QUESTIONS			
Vocabulary in Context (2 items)	_____	× 4 =	_____
Central Point and Main Ideas (3 items)	_____	× 4 =	_____
Supporting Details (3 items)	_____	× 4 =	_____
Transitions (2 items)	_____	× 4 =	_____
Patterns of Organization (2 items)	_____	× 4 =	_____
ADVANCED SKILL QUESTIONS			
Fact and Opinion (2 items)	_____	× 4 =	_____
Inferences (2 items)	_____	× 4 =	_____
Purpose and Tone (3 items)	_____	× 4 =	_____
Argument (1 item)	_____	× 4 =	_____
MAPPING (10 items)	_____	× 2 =	_____
		TOTAL SCORE =	_____ %

Enter your total score into the **Reading Performance Chart: Ten Reading Selections** on the inside back cover.

9

Busy As a Bee? Then Who's Doing the Work?
Natalie Angier

Preview

The next time people praise you for "working like a beaver" or scold you for being "lazy as a sloth," refer them to this essay, first published in the science section of the *New York Times*. In it, Natalie Angier challenges the myth about the supposed industriousness of our fellow creatures—and she explains how doing nothing much at all can accomplish a great deal.

Words to Watch

ambling (4): walking leisurely
indolence (6): laziness
pride's (8): belonging to a group of lions
spate (9): sudden outpouring
foraging (12): looking for food
perimeter (24): outer boundary
herbivores (28): animals that eat only plants
maligned (34): falsely spoken of in a negative way
evocative (34): filled with emotion as well as meaning
loath (34): very unwilling
perverse (35): stubbornly wrong
niche (35): an animal's place in its habitat

1   During midsummer days, humans who feel the urge to take it easy but remain burdened by a work ethic might do well to consider that laziness is perfectly natural, perfectly sensible, and shared by nearly every other species on the planet.

2 Contrary to the old fables about the unflagging industriousness of ants, bees, beavers, and the like, field biologists engaged in a new specialty known as time-budget analysis are discovering that the great majority of creatures spend most of their time doing nothing much at all.

3 They eat when they must or can. They court and breed when driven by seasonal impulses. Some species build a makeshift shelter now and again, while others fulfill the occasional social obligation, like picking out fleas from a fellow creature's fur.

4 But more often than not, most creatures engage in any number of inactive activities: sitting, sprawling, dozing, rocking back and forth, ambling° around in purposeless circles. . . .

5 In fact, compared with other creatures, human beings spend anywhere from two to four times as many hours working, particularly if family, household, and social duties are taken into account.

6 But lest people feel smug about their diligence, evolutionary biologists are discovering that animal inactivity is almost never born of aimless indolence°, but instead serves a broad variety of purposes. Some animals sit around to conserve precious calories, others to improve digestion of the calories they have consumed. Some do it to stay cool, others to keep warm. Predators and prey alike are best camouflaged when they are not fidgeting or fussing. Some creatures linger quietly in their territory to guard it, and others stay home to avoid being cannibalized by their neighbors.

7 So while there may not be a specific gene for laziness, there is always a good excuse. . . .

HOW THEY DO IT

A Repertory of Resting

8 Dr. Craig Packer and Dr. Anne Pusey, zoologists with the University of Minnesota in Minneapolis, have studied lions in the Serengeti since the 1970s, and they said nearly all of that time has been spent staring through binoculars at tawny heaps of fur, the pride's° collective immobility broken only by the intermittent twitch of an ear.

9 "A lion can lie in the same spot, without budging, for twelve hours at a stretch," said Dr. Pusey. "They're active on their feet maybe two or three hours a day." In that brief spate° of effort, they are likely to be either hunting or devouring the booty of that hunt, which is one reason they need so much downtime.

10 "A lion can eat an enormous amount in one sitting, maybe seventy pounds of meat," said Dr. Pusey. "Their bellies get extremely fat, and they look incredibly uncomfortable and incredibly immobile, lying on their backs and panting in the heat."

11 Monkeys are commonly thought of as nature's indefatigable acrobats, but many species sit around as much as three-quarters of the day, not to mention the twelve hours of the night they usually spend sleeping.

'Monkeys Were Still Sleeping'

12 Dr. Frans de Waal, a primatologist at the Yerkes Regional Primate Center in Atlanta and author of *Peacemaking Among Primates,* said that he was amused to discover the lax habits of the woolly spider monkey, which he observed in Brazil with Dr. Karen Stryer. One morning the two researchers awoke before dawn to get out to a distant observation site by 7 a.m., when they

assumed the monkeys would begin their day's foraging°.

13   "We were sitting there and sitting there," said Dr. de Waal. "By eleven o'clock, the monkeys were still sleeping, at which point I fell asleep myself."

14   Hummingbirds are the world's most vigorous and energy-intensive fliers—when they are flying. The birds turn out to spend 80 percent of their day perched motionless on a twig; at night, they sleep.

15   Beavers are thought to bustle about so singlemindedly that their name is often used as a synonym for work. But beavers emerge from the safe haven of their lodge to gather food or to patch up their dam for only five hours a day, give or take a few intermissions. "Even when they're supposed to be most active, they'll retreat back into the lodge for long periods of time, and rest," said Dr. Gerald E. Svendsen, a zoologist at Ohio University in Athens who studies beavers. . . .

16   Even the busy bees or worker ants of Aesopian fame dedicate only about 20 percent of the day to doing chores like gathering nectar or tidying up the nest. Otherwise, the insects stay still. "They seem to have run out of work to do," said Dr. Gene E. Robinson, an entomologist at the University of Illinois in Urbana-Champaign. "They really do look lazy."

WHY THEY DO IT

Cost-Benefit Study Shows Rest Is Best

17   In his view, the myth of the tireless social insect probably arose from observations of entire hives or anthills, which are little galaxies of ceaseless activity. "Human fascination with the industriousness of social insects probably comes from considering whole colonies rather than from considering what individuals in those colonies do," he said. "But since we've been tagging individuals to see what each bee does, we've found that any individual has a lot of surplus time."

18   Biologists studying animals at rest turn to sophisticated mathematical models resembling those used by economists, which take into account an animal's energy demands, fertility rate, the relative abundance and location of food and water, weather conditions, and other factors. They do extensive cost-benefit analyses, asking questions like: How high is the cost of foraging compared with the potential calories that may be gained?

The Cost of Moving

19   Such a calculation involves not only a measure of how much more energy an animal burns as it rummages about relative to what it would spend resting, but aiso a consideration of, for example, how hot it will become in motion, and how much of its stored water will then be needed to evaporate away heat to cool the body. Overheating can be a deadly threat for many animals.

20   When they complete their computations, biologists usually end up respecting an animal's decision to lie low.

21   "Let's say a moose spends so much time foraging that its body temperature rises close to the lethal maximum," said Dr. Gary E. Belovsky, associate professor of wildlife ecology at the University of Michigan in Ann Arbor. "And let's say a wolf comes along and chases it. Well, that raises the moose's body temperature further, and it's likely to drop over dead. The moose must stay cool if it is to survive." . . .

Flying Is So Draining

22   Researchers who have looked at hummingbird behavior have also concluded that the tiny birds are perfectly justified in taking frequent breaks. To hover in midair while sipping from long-tubed flowers, they must beat their wings in elaborate figure-eight patterns at a rate of sixty times a second.

23   "The cost of their flight is among the greatest of any type of movement in the animal kingdom," said Dr. Frank B. Gill, curator of ornithology at the Academy of Natural Sciences of Philadelphia. "They burn more fuel in calories per gram of body weight when flying than anything else ever studied."

24   Flying is so draining that many hummingbirds and their African relatives, the sunbirds, are better off staying motionless unless the food they can obtain is very rich indeed. To help ensure that they can get nectar without having to travel too far for their dinner, sunbirds will choose a territory and stand around on the perimeter°, waiting for the flowers within to become plump with nectar.

HOW THEY BENEFIT

Conserving Water and Heat

25   For some creatures, immobility carries so many benefits that they become almost Buddha-like in their stillness. The fringe-toed lizard, which lives in the desert of the southwest United States, sits motionless just below the surface of the sand for hours, with nothing sticking up but its eyes. As the lizards sit, the sand warms and invigorates them. "They're ready to lurch out at anything edible that passes by, like a butterfly," said Dr. Philip Brownell, a biologist at Oregon State University in Corvallis.

26   And should it see a predatory snake approaching, the lizard can further immobilize itself by suppressing its breathing. "The lizard just shuts off its engines," Dr. Brownell said.

27   What is more, by staying snug in its sandy blanket, the lizard cuts down on water loss, a constant threat to desert creatures. . . .

28   Several hundred species of mammals go into hibernation each winter, cutting down on energy expenditure by dramatically lowering their metabolic rates. In hibernating ground squirrels, for example, the heart rate slows to only one or two beats a minute, and the body temperature goes down to near freezing. For herbivores°, winter hibernation makes sense. "There's nothing for you to eat, the weather's bad, you can't reproduce, and there are still predators trying to eat you," said Dr. Sherman. "The best thing to do is go into suspended animation."

WHEN THEY MOVE

Vigilant Resters Spring to Life

29   But sometimes a biologist is stumped over apparent indolence that cannot be explained by obvious things like inclement weather. Dr. Sherman has been studying the naked mole rat, a peculiar social mammal that spends its entire life underground. He long wondered why the largest mole rats in a group did the least and seemed to sleep the most, but he found out one day when he introduced a snake into the colony he had set up in his lab.

30   "The big ones instantly sprang into action, and attacked the snake," he said. "We'd thought they were sleeping, but they were just maintaining quiet vigilance."

31   Such a need for vigilance may help explain why bees and ants spend so much time resting. Dr. Robinson recently has learned that honeybees have a soldier caste; members do little or nothing around the hive but are the first to act should the hive be disturbed. "They're like a standing army," he said. "They're hanging around the colony, not doing anything in particular, but they can be immediately mobilized."

32   Other bees and ants may be saving their energy for a big job, like the discovery of an abundant new source of food, which requires overtime effort to harvest it, or the intermittent splitting of one hive into two, which suddenly leaves fewer workers to do the same tasks. "A colony has a labor force bigger than it really needs to get through those critical episodes," said Dr. Robinson.

33   New studies show that social insects cannot afford to waste their energy on noncritical activities. It turns out ants and bees are born with a set amount of energy to devote to their colony, which for reasons that remain mysterious seems to have less to do with the amount of food they eat than with an inborn genetic program. "They're like batteries," said Dr. Peter Nonacs, who studies ants with Dr. Edward O. Wilson at Harvard University. "They have a fixed amount of energy in them, which they can use up quickly or slowly. The harder they work, the quicker they die." . . .

34   And perhaps biologists who study inactivity can even lend luster to the much maligned° creature that gave laziness its most evocative° term: the sloth. Found throughout Central and South America, the sloth hangs from trees by its long rubbery limbs, sleeping fifteen hours a day and moving so infrequently that two species of algae grow on its coat and between its claws. A newborn sloth sits atop its mother's belly and is so loath° to move that it freely defecates and urinates onto her fur, which she will only intermittently bother to clean.

35   But lest such sluggishness seem almost perverse°, the sloth is suited to its niche°. By moving so slowly, it stays remarkably inconspicuous to predators. Even its fungal coat serves a camouflaging purpose. With the algae glinting greenish-blue in the sunlight, the sloth resembles the hanging plant it has very nearly become.

BASIC SKILL QUESTIONS

Vocabulary in Context

_____ 1. In the excerpt below, the word *unflagging* (ŭn-flăg′ĭng) means
   A. new.
   B. hidden.
   C. poor.
   D. tireless.

"Contrary to the old fables about the unflagging industriousness of ants, bees, beavers, and the like, field biologists . . . are discovering that the great majority of creatures spend most of their time doing nothing much at all." (Paragraph 2)

_____ 2. In the excerpt below, the word *intermittent* (ĭn′tər-mĭt′nt) means
    A. violent.
    B. occasional.
    C. constant.
    D. threatening.

> "Dr. Craig Packer and Dr. Anne Pusey . . . have studied lions in the Serengeti since the 1970s, and they said nearly all of that time has been spent staring through binoculars at tawny heaps of fur, the pride's collective immobility broken only by the intermittent twitch of an ear." (Paragraph 8)

_____ 3. In the excerpt below, the word *vigilance* (vĭj′ə-ləns) means
    A. watchfulness.
    B. sleeping.
    C. avoidance.
    D. delay.

> "He long wondered why the largest mole rats in a group did the least and seemed to sleep the most, but he found out one day when he introduced a snake into the colony he had set up in his lab.
>
> "'The big ones instantly sprang into action, and attacked the snake,' he said. 'We'd thought they were sleeping, but they were just maintaining quiet vigilance.'" (Paragraphs 29–30)

Central Point and Main Ideas

_____ 4. Which sentence best expresses the central point of the selection?
    A. There are various reasons for animal behavior.
    B. Some species build makeshift shelters now and then, while others fulfill the occasional social obligation.
    C. Animals spend most of their time in inactivity, which serves various important purposes.
    D. Some biologists use mathematical models to figure out the factors behind animal inactivity.

_____ 5. The main idea of paragraphs 25–28 is stated in the
    A. last sentence of paragraph 24.
    B. first sentence of paragraph 25.
    C. first sentence of paragraph 26.
    D. sentence that makes up paragraph 27.

_____ 6. Which sentence best expresses the main idea of paragraphs 34–35?
   A. The sloth appears to be too sluggish for its own good.
   B. The sloth is not nature's most clean animal.
   C. The sloth moves so infrequently that algae grows on its coat and between its claws.
   D. The sloth's inactivity turns out to have a good purpose: to protect it from its predators.

Supporting Details

_____ 7. According to one scientist, the notion that social insects are tireless probably comes from
   A. how busy a single bee or ant is.
   B. the busy sound of a bee buzzing.
   C. the busyness of an entire colony of ants or bees.
   D. fiction.

_____ 8. Hibernation
   A. is an extreme form of rest.
   B. occurs when food may be scarce.
   C. keeps an animal away from predators.
   D. all of the above.

_____ 9. TRUE OR FALSE? The main reason most animals are inactive is that they are watching out for enemies.

Transitions

_____ 10. The excerpt below expresses a relationship of
   A. time.
   B. addition.
   C. contrast.
   D. comparison.

   "It turns out ants and bees are born with a set amount of energy to devote to their colony. . . . 'They're like batteries,' said Dr. Peter Nonacs. . . ." (Paragraph 33)

Patterns of Organization

_____ 11. Paragraph 6 lists
   A. animals.
   B. activities.
   C. purposes.
   D. comparisons.

_____ 12. In paragraphs 8–16, the author
  A. narrates a series of events in the order in which they happened.
  B. lists examples.
  C. contrasts animals.
  D. defines and illustrates a term.

_____ 13. TRUE OR FALSE? After listing examples of inactivity among animals, the article goes on to discuss reasons for that inactivity.

ADVANCED SKILL QUESTIONS

Fact and Opinion

_____ 14. The supporting details of this article are mainly
  A. facts.
  B. opinions.

Inferences

_____ 15. From paragraph 17, we can conclude that
  A. bees are more active than ants.
  B. ants are more active than bees.
  C. hives and anthills are really quiet places much of the time.
  D. at any given moment, while some bees and ants are busy, others are resting.

_____ 16. We can conclude that animals must conserve their energy
  A. in the morning.
  B. when they are being observed.
  C. for life-sustaining activities.
  D. occasionally.

_____ 17. From the selection, we can conclude that animals
  A. are all alike.
  B. have few needs.
  C. should be busier than they are.
  D. tend to behave in ways that benefit their species.

Purpose and Tone

_____ 18. The article's main purpose is to
  A. inform readers about the reasons for and benefits of rest for animals.
  B. persuade readers that they should get as much rest as animals.
  C. entertain readers with a series of amusing stories about animal behavior.

_____ 19. The tone of the article can be described as
   A. very skeptical.
   B. somewhat alarmed.
   C. informal but objective.
   D. somewhat apologetic.

Argument

20. Label the point of the following argument with a **P** and the two statements of support with an **S**. Label with an **X** the one statement that is neither the point nor the support of the argument.
   ____ A. The myth of the tireless social insect may have arisen from the ceaseless activity in hives and anthills.

   ____ B. The sloth's inactivity makes it inconspicuous to predators.

   ____ C. Inactivity among animals is helpful for a variety of reasons.

   ____ D. To digest its food, the moose must rest for four hours for every hour of grazing.

OUTLINING

Circle the letter of the outline notes that best cover "Busy As a Bee? Then Who's Doing the Work?"

A. Researchers are finding that most animals are inactive much of the time.
   1. Lions, monkeys, hummingbirds, beavers, bees, and ants
   2. Moose and hummingbirds
   3. Fringe-toed lizards and hibernating herbivores
   4. Naked mole rat, bees, and ants
   5. Bees and ants, social insects
   6. Sloths

B. Researchers are finding that most animals are inactive much of the time for various reasons.
   1. Much more inactivity among animals than previously realized
      Examples: lions, monkeys, hummingbirds, beavers, bees, and ants
   2. Benefits of inactivity
      a. Balance energy intake and expenditure
         Examples: moose, hummingbird
      b. Adaptation to weather and its effects
         Examples: fringe-toed lizards, hibernating herbivores

     c. Maintenance of vigilance and energy for protection
       Examples: naked mole rat, bees and ants
     d. Energy conservation for future needs and longer life span
       Examples: bees and ants, social insects
     e. Camouflage
       Example: sloths

  C. Researchers are finding that animals benefit from inactivity.
     1. Balance energy intake and expenditure
       Examples: moose, hummingbird
     2. Adaptation to weather and its effects
       Examples: fringe-toed lizards, hibernating herbivores
     3. Maintenance of vigilance and energy for protection
       Examples: naked mole rat, bees, and ants
     4. Energy conservation for future needs and longer life span
       Examples: bees and ants, social insects
     5. Camouflage
       Example: sloths

DISCUSSION QUESTIONS

1. Books, articles, and television shows about animal behavior are often very popular. How would you explain the fascination that animal behavior holds for people?

2. Do you have a pet? If so, how inactive is that animal? What do you think might be the similarities and differences between your pet's needs and the needs of animals living in the wild?

3. The article mentions that some scientists object to the term "laziness" being applied to animals and insects. The concept of laziness may apply only to humans. Can you think of any other human characteristics that are frequently attributed to animals? Do you believe the animals actually have those characteristics?

4. In writing about the animal researchers and their work, the author could have used a formal, scientific tone or a lighter, more informal approach. Which tone did she use, and why do you think she made that choice? Find examples to support your opinion.

Note: Writing assignments for this selection appear on page 638.

Check Your Performance   BUSY AS A BEE?

Activity	Number Right	Points	Score

BASIC SKILL QUESTIONS

Vocabulary in Context (3 items)   _____ × 4 = _____

Central Point and Main Ideas (3 items)   _____ × 4 = _____

Supporting Details (3 items)   _____ × 4 = _____

Transitions (1 item)   _____ × 4 = _____

Patterns of Organization (3 items)   _____ × 4 = _____

ADVANCED SKILL QUESTIONS

Fact and Opinion (1 item)   _____ × 4 = _____

Inferences (3 items)   _____ × 4 = _____

Purpose and Tone (2 items)   _____ × 4 = _____

Argument (1 item)   _____ × 4 = _____

OUTLINING (1 item)   _____ × 20 = _____

                              TOTAL SCORE = _____%

Enter your total score into the **Reading Performance Chart: Ten Reading Selections** on the inside back cover.

10

The Life of the
Urban Working Class
Robert E. Lerner,
Standish Meacham,
and Edward McNall Burns

Preview

Today we take large, crowded cities for granted. But just two centuries ago, many people lived and worked in the countryside. Industrialization and rapid population growth then started bringing more and more people to the cities, which offered a radically different way of living. This selection from the widely used college and university textbook *Western Civilizations: Their History and Their Culture,* Thirteenth Edition (W. W. Norton & Co.) vividly describes city life for the working class in the nineteenth century.

Words to Watch

acclimatization (2): adjustment to a new environment
amenities (3): features; attractions
adulterated (4): made impure with the addition of foreign substances
promiscuous (6): morally loose
precursor (6): something that comes before and suggests something to come
coarser (6): less refined
curtailed (8): limited

1   Like the middle class, the working class was divided into various subgroups and categories, determined in this case by skill, wages, and workplace. The working class included skilled workers in crafts that were centuries old—glassblowing

and cabinetmaking, for example. It included as well mechanics equally skilled in new industrial technology. It included the men, women, and children who together worked in mines and quarries. And it included the countless millions who labored at unskilled jobs—dock workers, coal porters, cleaning women, and the like. The nature of workers' experiences naturally varied, depending upon where they worked, where they lived, and, above all, how much they earned. A skilled textile worker lived a life far different from that of a ditch digger, the former able to afford the food, shelter, and clothing necessary for a decent existence, the latter so busy trying to keep himself and his family alive that he would have little time to think about anything but the source of their next meal.

2   Some movement from the ranks of the unskilled to the skilled was possible, if children were provided, or provided themselves, with at least a rudimentary education. Yet education was considered by many parents a luxury, especially since children could be put to work at an early age to supplement a family's meager earnings. There was movement from skilled to unskilled also, as technological change—the introduction of the power loom, for example—drove highly paid workers into the ranks of the unskilled and destitute. Further variations within the working class were the result of the fact that though every year more men, women, and children were working in factories, the majority still labored either in workshops or at home. These variations mean that we cannot speak of a common European working-class experience during the years from 1800 to 1850. The life we shall be describing was most typical of British workers, during

the first half-century of their exposure to industrialization. Only later in the century did most Continental workers undergo this harsh process of urban acclimatization°.

3   Life in industrial cities was, for almost all workers, uncomfortable at best and unbearably squalid at worst. Workers and their families lived in housing that failed to answer the needs of its inhabitants. In older cities single-family dwellings were broken up into apartments of often no more than one room per family. In new manufacturing centers, rows of tiny houses, located close by smoking factories, were built back-to-back, thereby eliminating any cross-ventilation or space for gardens. Whether housing was old or new, it was generally poorly built. Old buildings were allowed by landlords to fall into disrepair; new houses, constructed of cheap material, decayed quickly. Water often came from an outdoor tap, shared by several houses and adjacent to an outdoor toilet. Crowding was commonplace. Families of as many as eight lived in two or, at the most, three rooms. A newspaper account from the 1840s noted that in Leeds, a textile center in northern Britain, an "ordinary" worker's house contained no more than 150 square feet, and that in most cases those homes were "crammed almost to suffocation with human beings both day and night." When, after 1850, governments began to rid cities of some of their worst slums, many working-class men and women discovered that urban "improvement" meant relocation into dreary "model" tenements whose amenities° were matched by their barracklike anonymity; or removal from one dilapidated structure to another in the wake of a clearance scheme—the nineteenth century called it

"ventilation"—that replaced ancient, overcrowded housing with a more sanitary—and, for the landlord, more profitable—railway switching yard.

4   The life of working-class wives and mothers was hard. Lack of cheap contraceptive devices and a belief that these devices were immoral helped to keep women pregnant through most of their childbearing years, thus endangering their general health and adding to the burden of their lives. Wives were usually handed a portion of the weekly wage packet by their husbands, and were expected to house, feed, and clothe the family on the very little they were given. Their daily life was a constant round of cooking, cleaning, shopping, and washing—in a tiny space and without enough money. Housewives could not rely, as in the country, on their own gardens to help supply them with food. Instead, they went to markets that catered to their needs with cheap goods, often stale or nearly rotten, or dangerously adulterated°. Formaldehyde was added to milk to prevent spoilage. Pounded rice was mixed into sugar. Fine brown earth was mixed into cocoa. A woman's problems were compounded, of course, when she had to work, and therefore had far less time to accomplish the household tasks she was still expected to perform.

5   Women were employed in growing numbers—along with children—in factories during the nineteenth century. Yet many more labored at home or in small workshops—"sweatshops," as they came to be called—for wretchedly low wages based not on the hours they worked but on the amount of work they did: so much per shirt stitched or matchbox glued. By far the greatest number of unmarried working-class young women worked as domestic servants, often a lonely occupation and one that occasionally trapped female servants into undesired sexual relationships with their male employers or their employers' sons.

6   Female sexuality within the working classes of western Europe was acknowledged in a way that it was not within the middle class. Demographic evidence reveals a sharp rise in illegitimacy between 1750 and 1850. In Frankfurt, Germany, for example, where the illegitimacy rate had been a mere 2 percent in the early 1700s, it reached 25 percent in 1850. In Bordeaux, France, in 1840, one-third of the recorded births were illegitimate. Reasons for this increase are difficult to establish. Illegitimacy in Germany may have been the result of laws forbidding the poor to marry. Certainly, increased mobility meant weaker family ties, less parental supervision, and greater opportunity for an unrestricted life. This is not to say that the majority of working-class women were sexually promiscuous°. Premarital intercourse was an accepted practice in preindustrial villages, but, because of the social controls that dominated village life, it was almost always a precursor° to marriage. In the far more anonymous setting of a factory town, such controls often did not exist. In addition, the economic uncertainties of the early industrial age meant that a young workingman's promise of marriage based on his expectation of a job might frequently be difficult to fulfill. The same economic uncertainty led some young working-class women to careers—usually temporary—as prostitutes. The anonymity of city life encouraged prostitution. Middle-class men, prepared to postpone marriage until they could afford a house and furnishings reflecting the social position to which they aspired, turned to the

sexual underworld to satisfy their desires. Class consciousness encouraged them to regard working-class women—prostitutes or not—as easy prey, possessed of coarser° natures and therefore a lesser breed of womankind than the middle-class "ladies" they intended eventually to marry.

7 New cities could be lonely places, particularly for working-class men and women struggling to cope with an alien environment. If possible, they would live near relatives who had already made the transition and who could assist the newcomers in adjusting to their very different existence. In many cities working-class families lived in districts inhabited primarily by others working at the same trade—weavers in one place, miners in another—and in this was achieved some sense of commonality.

8 Adjustment to the demands of the factory was every bit as difficult for workers as was acceptance of urban living patterns. The factory system, emphasizing as it did standard rather than individual work patterns, denied skilled laborers the pride in craft that had previously been theirs. Many workers found themselves stripped of the reassuring protection of guilds and formal apprenticeships that had bound their predecessors to a particular trade or place, and that were outlawed or sharply curtailed° by legislation in France, Germany, and Britain in the first half of the nineteenth century. Factory hours were long; before 1850 usually twelve to fourteen hours a day. Conditions were dirty and dangerous. Textile mills remained unventilated, so that bits of material lodged in workers' lungs. Machines were unfenced and were a particular danger to child workers, often hired, because of their supposed agility, to clean under and around the moving parts. Manufacturing processes were unhealthy. The use of poisonous lead in the making of glazed pottery, for example, was a constant hazard to men and women workers in that industry. Surveys by British physicians in the 1840s catalogued the toll that long factory hours and harsh working conditions were taking, particularly on young workers. Spinal curvature and other bone malformations resulted from standing hour after hour in unnatural positions at machines. Varicose veins and fallen arches were also common. One concerned doctor stated his belief that "from what I saw myself, a large mass of deformity has been produced by the factory system." And what was true of factories was true as well of mines, in which over fifty thousand children and young people were employed in Britain in 1841. Children were used to haul coal to underground tramways or shafts. The youngest were set to work—often for as long as twelve hours at a stretch—operating doors that regulated the ventilation in the mines. When they fell asleep, which, because of long hours, they frequently did, they jeopardized the safety of the entire work force. Women—sometimes pregnant women—were employed to haul coal and perform other strenuous underground tasks. Lung diseases—popularly known as "black spittle"—and eye infections, not to mention the danger of explosions caused by trapped gas, were constant threats to life and limb in the mines.

9 As upsetting as the physical working conditions was the psychological readjustment demanded of the first-generation workers in the factories. Preindustrial laborers had to work long hours and for very little monetary reward.

Yet, at least to some degree, they were free to set their own hours and structure their own activities, to move from their home workshops to their small garden plots and back again as they wished. In a factory, all "hands" learned the discipline of the whistle. To function efficiently, a factory demanded that all employees begin and end work at the same time. Most workers could not tell time; fewer possessed clocks. None was accustomed to the relentless pace of the machine. In order to increase production, the factory system encouraged the breaking down of the manufacturing process into special-ized steps, each with its own assigned time, an innovation that upset workers accustomed to completing a task at their own pace. The employment of women and children was a further disturbing innovation. In preindustrial communities, women and children had worked, as well as men, but usually all together and at home. In factory towns women and chil-dren were frequently hired instead of men: they could be paid less and were declared to be easier to manage. When this happened, the pattern of family life was severely disrupted, and a further break with tradition had to be endured. It is no wonder that workers began to see machinery itself as the tyrant that had changed their lives and bound them to a kind of industrial slavery. A radical working-class song written in Britain in the 1840s expressed the feeling: "There is a king and a ruthless king; / Not a king of the poet's dream; / But a tyrant fell, white slaves know well, / And that ruthless king is steam."

Faced with a drastic reordering of their lives, working-class men and women reacted in various ways. Some sought "the shortest way out of Manchester"* by taking to drink (there were 1,200 public houses in that city in 1850). Many more men and women struggled to make some sort of community out of the street where they lived or the factory where they worked. It was a long and discouraging process. Yet by midcentury their experi-ences were beginning to make them conscious of themselves as different from and in opposition to the middle class that was imposing a new way of life on them.

10

---

*Manchester is a highly industrialized city, so "the shortest way out of Manchester" is a way of saying "a quick escape from the pressures of industrial life."

BASIC SKILL QUESTIONS

Vocabulary in Context

_____ 1. In the sentence below, the word *rudimentary* (roō′də-měn′tə-rē) means
   A. basic.
   B. expensive.
   C. complicated.
   D. unnecessary.

"Some movement from the ranks of the unskilled to the skilled was possible, if children were provided, or provided themselves, with at least a rudimentary education." (Paragraph 2)

_____ 2. In the sentence below, the word *compounded* (kŏm-pound′ĭd) *means*
A. known.
B. forgotten.
C. improved.
D. made bigger.

> "A woman's problems were compounded, of course, when she had to work, and therefore had far less time to accomplish the household tasks she was still expected to perform." (Paragraph 4)

_____ 3. In the sentence below, the word *agility* (ə-jĭl′ĭ-tē) means
A. ability to move easily and quickly.
B. stubbornness.
C. interest in cleanliness.
D. ability to lift heavy objects.

> "Machines were unfenced and were a particular danger to child workers, often hired, because of their supposed agility, to clean under and around the moving parts." (Paragraph 8)

Central Point and Main Ideas

_____ 4. Which sentence best expresses the central point of the selection?
A. Members of the working class in the nineteenth century often lived in overcrowded, unsanitary conditions.
B. The roles of women and children underwent substantial change as a result of the move to the cities by much of the British working class.
C. In nineteenth-century industrial cities, life at home and at work ranged from uncomfortable to terrible for almost all workers.
D. The industrialization of the first half the nineteenth century led to many changes worldwide.

_____ 5. The main idea of paragraph 4 is best expressed in its
A. first sentence.
B. second sentence.
C. third sentence.
D. last sentence.

_____ 6. The main idea of paragraph 9 is best expressed in its
A. first sentence.
B. second sentence.
C. third sentence.
D. last sentence.

Supporting Details

_____ 7. The main time period covered in the selection is
   A. 1800–1850.
   B. 1850–1900.
   C. 1750–1850.
   D. 1800–1950.

_____ 8. The supporting details in paragraph 3 are
   A. reasons workers accepted poor housing conditions.
   B. the differences between older and newer housing.
   C. evidence that housing conditions during the 1800s were poor.
   D. facts showing how difficult all aspects of life were in industrial cities.

_____ 9. TRUE OR FALSE? Women were often hired to work in factories because they were better able to do the work.

Transitions

_____ 10. The relationship of the second sentence below to the first is one of
   A. time.
   B. contrast.
   C. addition.
   D. illustration.

   "Some movement from the ranks of the unskilled to the skilled was possible, if children were provided . . . with at least a rudimentary education. Yet education was considered by many parents a luxury . . ." (Paragraph 2)

_____ 11. In the excerpt below, the cause-effect transition is
   A. *of course.*   C. *therefore.*
   B. *when.*   D. *still.*

   "A woman's problems were compounded, of course, when she had to work and therefore had far less time to accomplish the household tasks she was still expected to perform." (Paragraph 4)

Patterns of Organization

_____ 12. On the whole, the reading is organized as a
   A. series of events during the 1800s.
   B. contrast between the middle class and the working class during the 1800s.
   C. comparison between life in various locations during the 1800s.
   D. list of details about the difficulty of life for the working class in the 1800s.

_____ 13. The main pattern of organization of the final paragraph is
   A. series of stages.
   B. list of items.
   C. comparison.
   D. definition and example.

ADVANCED SKILL QUESTIONS

Fact and Opinion

_____ 14. Most of the information in the reading is
   A. factual.
   B. opinions.

_____ 15. The word that expresses an opinion in the excerpt below is
   A. *labored.*
   B. *wretchedly.*
   C. *wages.*
   D. *glued.*

> "Yet many more labored at home or in small workshops—
> 'sweatshops,' as they came to be called—for wretchedly low wages
> based not on the hours they worked but on the amount of work they
> did: so much per shirt stitched or matchbox glued." (Paragraph 5)

Inferences

_____ 16. From the final paragraph of the reading, we might infer that
   A. the working class admired and imitated the middle class.
   B. alcohol abuse did not occur in Britain before industrialization.
   C. in the second half of the century, the working class became
      significantly richer.
   D. conflict between the working class and middle class in Britain
      increased after 1850.

_____ 17. The reading suggests that
   A. skilled craftspeople, such as glassblowers, quickly became wealthy
      in the cities.
   B. living conditions in villages were worse than those in the city.
   C. dishonesty was rare in the nineteenth-century marketplace.
   D. class and economics can influence sexual behavior.

Purpose and Tone

_____ 18. The main purpose of this selection is to
   A. inform the reader about what life was like for the working class in Europe in the 1800s after industrialization.
   B. persuade the reader to support the working classes throughout the world.
   C. entertain the reader with colorful details of a long-ago way of life.

_____ 19. The authors' tone is
   A. somewhat confused when discussing the facts.
   B. matter-of-fact, but somewhat amused.
   C. generally nostalgic, but somewhat angry and sarcastic.
   D. largely objective, but strongly sympathetic to the working class.

Argument

_____ 20. One of the following statements is the point of an argument. The other statements support that point. Write the letter of the point.
   A. Before 1850, factory hours were long: usually twelve to fourteen hours a day.
   B. Conditions were dirty and dangerous, with textile mills unventilated and machines unfenced.
   C. Skilled workers were denied the pride in craft that had previously been theirs.
   D. Adjustments to the demands of the factory were difficult.

SUMMARIZING

Circle the letter of the paragraph that best summarizes the reading "The Life of the Urban Working Class."

As you read the three choices, keep in mind that a good summary will include general statements that sum up the selection. It will cover the key elements of the reading. Some specific details may be included as well.

A. During the nineteenth century, the working class underwent dramatic changes as members became accustomed to urban life. Instead of laboring primarily in small home-based workshops as they had done in the past, many workers found employment in industrial cities. The adjustment was both physically and psychologically harsh. Housing conditions in the cities were appalling. Women were particularly hard-hit by the adjustment to urban life because they had to work out of the home during frequent pregnancies, because the traditional family structure was lost, and because of a belief that working-class women were sexually available to middle-class men. The physical health of many workers was compromised by dangerous conditions in factories. And the demands of the factory system meant that workers had to give up a pride in craft and the freedom to set their own hours and pace. Family life suffered as women and children were employed in large numbers. As workers struggled to adjust to their harsh new circumstances, they began to perceive themselves as separate from and in conflict with the higher classes.

B. Within the British working class of 1800–1850, skilled workers lived better than unskilled factory laborers. But life for almost all was uncomfortable. New cities could be lonely places. Many families lived in small, one-room apartments. For example, a newspaper story from the city of Leeds said an average worker's home contained no more than 150 square feet. Even when governments began to get rid of some of the worst slums, the replacements were generally just as bad. The "improved" housing was ugly tenements. Unscrupulous merchants added formaldehyde to milk to keep it from spoiling. Many women worked in sweatshops or as servants. Factory life was difficult, as was life in the mines. Some workers began drinking to cope with the stress. There were 1,200 pubs in Manchester in 1850.

C. Although workers on the Continent went through the process of urban acclimatization in the years 1850–1900, the British working class experienced the adjustment during the first half of the 1800s. Housing for workers in the city was unpleasant and inadequate. Government attempts to improve the housing situation were badly planned. The move to the cities was particularly hard on women. They had to deal with frequent pregnancies, because contraception was considered immoral. Many had to work in factories as well as keep up with housekeeping. They had to buy cheap marketplace goods, often adulterated, rather than raising their own food. They worked in wretched sweatshops or as servants, and they were sometimes expected to be sexually available to their employers. The rate of illegitimate births rose sharply during these years. Although premarital sexual relationships were common in village life, they were almost always followed by marriage. Workers tried to ease the transition to the city by living near relatives or near people working in the same trade.

DISCUSSION QUESTIONS

1. If you had lived in the period described in this article, what would have been the hardest parts of everyday life for you? What parts would be most different from your life in the world today?

2. The reading suggests that the demands of the urban environment had a dramatic effect on traditional family life. What details in the reading support the idea that family life was affected by the move to the industrial city?

3. Find details in the selection that suggest how children were regarded in the early 1800s. Judging from those details, how would you say the perception of childhood has changed between then and now? Explain your answer.

4. The selection ends with the idea that by midcentury, the working class was beginning to see itself as having an identity of its own. Why do you think the workers saw themselves as "different from and in opposition to the middle class"?

Note: Writing assignments for this selection appear on page 639.

Check Your Performance   THE LIFE OF THE URBAN WORKING CLASS

Activity	Number Right	Points	Score
BASIC SKILL QUESTIONS			
Vocabulary in Context (3 items)	_____	× 4 =	_____
Central Point and Main Ideas (3 items)	_____	× 4 =	_____
Supporting Details (3 items)	_____	× 4 =	_____
Transitions (2 items)	_____	× 4 =	_____
Patterns of Organization (2 items)	_____	× 4 =	_____
ADVANCED SKILL QUESTIONS			
Fact and Opinion (2 items)	_____	× 4 =	_____
Inferences (2 items)	_____	× 4 =	_____
Purpose and Tone (2 items)	_____	× 4 =	_____
Argument (1 item)	_____	× 4 =	_____
SUMMARIZING (1 item)	_____	× 20 =	_____
		TOTAL SCORE =	_____%

Enter your total score into the **Reading Performance Chart: Ten Reading Selections** on the inside back cover.

Part III

FOR FURTHER STUDY

1

Combined-Skills Tests

Following are fifteen tests that cover the skills taught in Part I of this book. Each test consists of a short reading passage followed by questions on any of the following: vocabulary in context, main ideas, supporting details, relationships, fact and opinion, inferences, purpose and tone, and argument.

COMBINED SKILLS: Test 1

Read the passage below. Then write the letter of the best answer to each question that follows.

[1]Exact figures on the number of poor are difficult to determine. [2]For one thing, the amount of money needed for subsistence varies by locality. [3]For example, the money needed for rent in New York City is much greater than the money needed in rural Arkansas. [4]Another difficulty is that those most likely to be missed by the U.S. census are the poor. [5]People most likely to be missed in the census live in ghettos (where several families may be crowded into one apartment) or in rural areas, where some homes are inaccessible and where some workers follow the harvest from place to place and therefore have no permanent home. [6]Transients of any kind are sometimes missed by the census. [7]The conclusion is inescapable that the proportion of the poor in the United States is underestimated because the poor tend to be invisible, even to the government.

_____ 1. The word *subsistence* in sentence 2 means
   A. food.
   B. basic shelter and food needs.
   C. moving.
   D. work needs.

_____ 2. According to the author, census workers are likely to miss
   A. people in the suburbs.
   B. people who live in small towns.
   C. farm workers who follow harvests.
   D. all of the above.

_____ 3. The main pattern of organization of the passage is
   A. a series of events.
   B. a list of reasons.
   C. a comparison and contrast.
   D. steps in a process.

_____ 4. One can conclude from this passage that
   A. there are probably fewer poor people in the United States than the number reported in the U.S. census.
   B. poor people deliberately avoid being counted by census workers.
   C. there are fewer poor people in New York City than in Arkansas.
   D. more poor people live in the United States than the census indicates.

_____ 5. You might infer that the author feels people should be classified as poor
   A. according to their income only.
   B. according to income and cost of living.
   C. only according to the state they live in.
   D. according to whether they are transient or not.

_____ 6. TRUE OR FALSE? The author uses mostly opinions to support the main idea of the passage.

_____ 7. Which sentence best expresses the main idea of the passage?
   A. The amount of money needed for food and shelter varies greatly from place to place in the United States.
   B. The census is likely to underestimate the numbers of transients in the country.
   C. Because it is difficult to determine the exact number of poor people in the United States, the proportion of the poor is underestimated.
   D. There are various reasons for poverty throughout our country.

_____ 8. Which outline best organizes the material in the passage?

   A. There are two reasons why we greatly underestimate the exact number of poor in our country.
      1. It can be unclear who is poor because the income needed to live above poverty varies from place to place.
      2. The United States census is likely to greatly undercount the poor.

   B. There are reasons for poverty throughout our country.
      1. More reasons can be found in New York City than in rural Arkansas.
      2. Poverty is sustained by various lifestyles, including rural life and following the harvest from place to place.

   C. Food and shelter needed to avoid poverty
      1. New York City
      2. Arkansas
      3. Ghettos
      4. Rural areas
      5. Transients

COMBINED SKILLS: Test 2

Read the passage below. Then write the letter of the best answer to each question that follows.

[1]Monkey researchers have observed the process by which behavioral innovations spread from individual to individual and become part of a troop's culture independently of genetic transmission. [2]Consider the case of Imo, a two-year-old female monkey. [3]Imo and her troop of free-ranging monkeys live on the small Japanese island of Koshima, a high, wooded mountain with a surrounding beach. [4]Researchers enticed Imo and a number of other younger monkeys out of the forest by leaving sweet potatoes on a stretch of open beach. [5]In due course Imo began doing something that no other monkey had done. [6]She would carry her sweet potatoes to a freshwater pool, dip them in the water with one hand, and brush the sand off with the other. [7]Soon her companions began copying her. [8]The behavior spread to the playmates' siblings and mothers. [9]However, adult males, who rarely participated in the group's behavior, did not acquire the habit. [10]When the young females who engaged in potato-washing matured and had offspring of their own, all of the offspring learned to wash potatoes from their mothers. [11]Then Imo undertook another new behavior. [12]She took the potatoes that she had cleaned in the fresh water and washed them anew in the sea. [13]Imo apparently liked the flavor of the salt water. [14]Within ten years, the practice of washing sweet potatoes in the sea had spread to two-thirds of the monkeys.

_____ 1. In sentence 1, *behavioral innovations* means
   A. noisy behaviors.
   B. old behaviors.
   C. new behaviors.
   D. genetic behaviors.

_____ 2. Imo's practice of washing her potatoes in fresh water was first copied by
   A. fathers of the group.
   B. Imo's children.
   C. mothers of the group.
   D. Imo's companions.

_____ 3. What is the relationship of sentence 9 to sentence 8?
   A. Addition
   B. Contrast
   C. Illustration
   D. Time

_____ 4. Sentence 10 is a statement of
   A. fact.
   B. opinion.
   c. fact and opinion.

_____ 5. From this passage, you could infer that
   A. monkeys are solitary animals by nature.
   B. most monkeys dislike the taste of salt.
   C. Imo was a monkey of average intelligence.
   D. the monkeys learned by watching.

_____ 6. The purpose of this passage is mainly to
   A. inform.
   B. entertain.
   C. persuade.

_____ 7. Which title best summarizes the selection?
   A. Genetic Influences on Animal Cultures
   B. A Diet for Monkeys: Sweet Potatoes
   C. How a Young Monkey Changed Her Troop's Culture
   D. Animal Researchers and Subjects in Native Environments

_____ 8. Which of the following is the best outline of the selection?

   A. Scientists observed behaviors among members of a monkey troop in Japan.
      1. Young and female monkeys copied a young female monkey's ideas in preparing sweet potatoes for eating—washing the potatoes in fresh water and then in salt water.
      2. Adult male monkeys did not copy the new behaviors, presumably because they rarely participated in the group's behaviors.

   B. Monkeys' innovative behavior
      1. Japanese island of Koshima
         a. a high, wooded mountain
         b. a surrounding beach
      2. Imo and her troop of free-ranging monkeys

   C. New behaviors have been observed to spread from individual to individual to become part of a group's culture.
      1. Imo's washing of sweet potatoes in fresh water became a common behavior in her monkey troop.
      2. Imo's practice of washing sweet potatoes a second time in salt water also spread throughout much of the troop.

COMBINED SKILLS: Test 3

Read the passage below. Then write the letter of the best answer to each question that follows.

[1]Humans generally spend more time working than do other creatures, but there is greater variability in industriousness from one human culture to the next than is seen in subgroups of any other species. [2]For instance, the average French worker toils for 1,646 hours a year; the average American for 1,957 hours; and the average Japanese for 2,088.

[3]One reason for human diligence is that people, unlike animals, can often override the impulses they may feel to slow down. [4]They can drink coffee when they might prefer a nap or flick on the air-conditioning when the heat might otherwise demand torpor. [5]Many humans are driven to work hard by a singular desire to gather resources far beyond what is required for survival. [6]Squirrels may collect what they need to make it through one winter, but only humans worry about college bills, retirement, or replacing their old record albums with compact discs.

[7]"Among other primates, if you don't need to travel around to get food for that day, you sit down and relax," said Dr. Frans de Waal of Emory University in Atlanta. [8]"It's typically human to try to accumulate wealth and get more and more."

[9]Much of the acquisitiveness is likely to be the result of cultural training. [10]Anthropologists have found that most hunter-gatherer groups, who live day to day on the resources they can kill or forage and who stash very little away for the future, generally work only three to five hours daily.

[11]Indeed, an inborn temptation to slack off may lurk beneath even the most work-obsessed people, which could explain why sloth ranks with lust and gluttony as one of the seven deadly sins.

_____ 1. The word *torpor* in sentence 4 means
  A. increased activity.
  B. extreme heat.
  C. industriousness.
  D. inactivity.

_____ 2. The relationship of sentence 2 to sentence 1 is one of
  A. time.
  B. illustration.
  C. contrast.
  D. cause and effect.

_____ 3. According to the author, humans are so industrious because
  A. they are stronger and better protected than animals.
  B. they can overcome the impulse to slow down, and they work for gains beyond survival.
  C. they have an inborn temptation to take it easy.
  D. they need much more than animals need in order to survive.

_____ 4. The pattern of organization of the passage is a combination of contrast and
  A. a series of events.
  B. steps in a process.
  C. definition and example.
  D. cause and effect.

_____ 5. Sentence 2 is a statement of
  A. fact.
  B. opinion.
  C. both fact and opinion.

_____ 6. The author implies that most hunter-gatherer groups
  A. have not been culturally conditioned to desire many possessions.
  B. often go hungry.
  C. would be happier if they worked more hours each day.
  D. are more industrious than many French people.

_____ 7. The tone of this passage is
  A. critical and anxious.
  B. disbelieving and excited.
  C. straightforward and analytical.
  D. ambivalent yet optimistic.

_____ 8. Which title best summarizes the selection?
  A. Sloth: One of the Seven Deadly Sins
  B. Work Among Humans and Animals
  C. The Accumulation of Wealth
  D. Cultural Training

COMBINED SKILLS: Test 4

Read the passage below. Then write the letter of the best answer to each question that follows.

[1]Our first year in New York we rented a small apartment with a Catholic school nearby, taught by the Sisters of Charity, hefty women in long black gowns and bonnets that made them look peculiar, like dolls in mourning. [2]I liked them a lot, especially my grandmotherly fourth-grade teacher, Sister Zoe. [3]I had a lovely name, she said, and she had me teach the whole class how to pronounce it. [4]*Yo-lan-da.* [5]As the only immigrant in my class, I was put in a special seat in the first row by the window, apart from the other children so that Sister Zoe could tutor me without disturbing them. [6]Slowly, she enunciated the new words I was to repeat: *laundromat, corn flakes, subway, snow.*

[7]Soon I picked up enough English to understand a threat of war was in the air. [8]Sister Zoe explained to a wide-eyed classroom what was happening in Cuba. [9]Russian missiles were being assembled, trained supposedly on New York City. [10]President Kennedy, looking worried too, was on television at home, explaining we might have to go to war against the Communists. [11]At school, we had air-raid drills: an ominous bell would go off and we'd file into the hall, fall to the floor, cover our heads with our coats, and imagine our hair falling out, the bones in our arms going soft. [12]At home, Mami and my sisters and I said a rosary for world peace. [13]I heard new vocabulary: *nuclear bomb, radioactive fallout, bomb shelter.* [14]Sister Zoe explained how it would happen. [15]She drew a picture of a mushroom on the blackboard and dotted a flurry of chalkmarks for the dusty fallout that would kill us all.

[16]The months grew cold, November, December. [17]It was dark when I got up in the morning, frosty when I followed my breath to school. [18]One morning as I sat at my desk daydreaming out the window, I saw dots in the air like the ones Sister Zoe had drawn—random at first, then lots and lots. [19]I shrieked, "Bomb! Bomb!" [20]Sister Zoe jerked around, her full black skirt ballooning as she hurried to my side. [21]A few girls began to cry.

[22]But then Sister Zoe's shocked look faded. [23]"Why, Yolanda dear, that's snow!" [24]She laughed. [25]"Snow."

[26]"Snow," I repeated. [27]I looked out the window warily. [28]All my life I had heard about the white crystals that fell out of American skies in the winter. [29]From my desk I watched the fine powder dust the sidewalk and parked cars below. [30]Each flake was different, Sister Zoe had said, like a person, irreplaceable and beautiful.

_____ 1. In sentence 6, *enunciated* means

    A. knew.   C. pronounced.

    B. shouted.   D. listened to.

_____ 2. The author was seated apart from the other children
   A. to punish her for not speaking English.
   B. because she had trouble hearing the teacher otherwise.
   C. so the teacher could give her special help.
   D. because she was afraid of the other children.

_____ 3. During an air-raid drill, the children
   A. crouched under their desks.
   B. ran to their homes.
   C. said a rosary for world peace.
   D. went into the hall and covered themselves with their coats.

_____ 4. When Yolanda mistook snow for radioactive fallout, Sister Zoe
   A. laughed and reassured her.
   B. scolded her for frightening the others.
   C. burst into tears.
   D. announced an air-raid drill.

_____ 5. The main pattern of organization used in this passage is
   A. time order.
   B. definition and example.
   C. comparison and contrast.
   D. cause and effect.

_____ 6. We can infer from this passage that
   A. Sister Zoe resented having to deal with an immigrant student.
   B. the author's fellow students made fun of her inability to speak English.
   C. the Cuban government supported President Kennedy.
   D. before moving to New York City, the author had never seen snow.

_____ 7. It is reasonable to conclude that Sister Zoe
   A. spoke Yolanda's native language.
   B. was a kind and caring teacher.
   C. had not been a nun very long.
   D. was an immigrant herself.

_____ 8. Which of the following is the best title for the selection?
   A. Sister Zoe and My First Snowfall
   B. The Sisters of Charity
   C. Air-Raid Drills
   D. The Cuban Missile Crisis

COMBINED SKILLS: Test 5

Read the passage below. Then write the letter of the best answer to each question that follows.

[1]South Pole explorer Ernest Shackleton never reached his goal of crossing Antarctica, but the circumstances that prevented him from reaching that goal pushed him to achieve an even more amazing feat. [2]In January 1915 Shackleton's ship *Endurance* became trapped in ice off Antarctica. [3]He and his crew of twenty-seven lived on the ship trapped in the ice floes for nine months, until they had to abandon ship when the ice crushed the boat. [4]The day the boat sank, Shackleton wrote his new goal: "The task is to reach land with all members of the Expedition." [5]The group camped on the ice floes for six months, until the ice broke up and they took small lifeboats to nearby uninhabited Elephant Island. [6]During their time on the boat, ice, and island, Shackleton's group endured temperatures as low as twenty degrees below zero and had no daylight from May to July. [7]They had to hunt scarce seals and penguins for food, and were hunted themselves by killer whales and sea leopards, which would rise through the ice in search of prey. [8]Throughout this time, Shackleton demonstrated his leadership by rationing food, rotating use of the warmer sleeping bags, and keeping a calm, positive attitude that helped morale. [9]He also showed great courage as he and five of his men crossed eight hundred miles of dangerous ocean to the nearest inhabited island to seek help. [10]Despite no maps and terrible weather, Shackleton's small boat reached the island where Shackleton and an even smaller group crossed unexplored, jagged mountains to reach a whaling station. [11]He organized a rescue party to retrieve the rest of his crew, and despite the perils of living in south polar waters for almost two years, all twenty-seven men came back from the expedition. [12]Shackleton never crossed the South Pole, but he completed the task of bringing back all of his crew alive.

_____ 1. Shackleton and his men had to abandon the *Endurance* when
     A. killer whales attacked the ship.
     B. the ship ran aground on Elephant Island.
     C. they ran out of food and had to leave to hunt for more.
     D. ice crushed the ship.

_____ 2. The "more amazing feat" referred to in sentence 1 is Shackleton's
     A. ability to withstand severe cold.
     B. managing to get all crew members back alive.
     C. crossing jagged, unexplored mountains.
     D. crossing eight hundred miles of ocean.

_____ 3. The main pattern of organization used in the passage is one of
   A. list of items.
   B. definition and example.
   C. time order.
   D. cause and effect.

_____ 4. Sentence 1 is made up of
   A. fact.
   B. opinion.
   C. fact and opinion.

_____ 5. The author's main purpose in this passage is to
   A. inform readers about the facts of the Shackleton expedition.
   B. persuade readers that Shackleton was responsible for the failure of the expedition.
   C. entertain readers with anecdotes about the hardships of the Shackleton expedition.

_____ 6. The author's tone is
   A. detached.
   B. admiring.
   C. doubtful.
   D. sentimental.

_____ 7. The author implies that
   A. Shackleton's men were generally cowardly and poor sailors.
   B. Shackleton carelessly began the voyage without adequate preparation.
   C. he considers Shackleton's voyage a failure because it did not reach the South Pole.
   D. Shackleton's men would likely have perished if not for his courage.

_____ 8. The main idea of the passage is
   A. stated in sentence 1.
   B. stated in sentence 4.
   C. stated in sentence 8.
   D. not stated.

COMBINED SKILLS: Test 6

Read the passage below. Then write the letter of the best answer to each question that follows.

¹In a song of many years past, Bob Dylan sang, "The times, they are a-changing." ²Well, the times have changed dramatically, making a parent's job today much more challenging than it was a generation ago. ³Today's parents must try, first of all, to control all the new distractions that tempt children away from schoolwork. ⁴At home, a child may have a room furnished with a stereo, personal computer, and television. ⁵Not many young people can resist the urge to listen to a CD, surf the Internet, or watch MTV—especially if it is time to do schoolwork. ⁶Outside the home the distractions are even more alluring. ⁷Children no longer "hang out" on a neighborhood corner within earshot of Mom or Dad's reminder to come in and do homework. ⁸Instead, they congregate in vast shopping malls, buzzing video arcades, and gleaming fast-food restaurants. ⁹Parents and school assignments have obvious difficulty competing with such enticing alternatives.

¹⁰Besides dealing with these distractions, parents have to shield their children from a flood of sexually explicit materials. ¹¹Today, children can download pornographic pictures from the Internet or find sex magazines in a nearby convenience store. ¹²Children will not see the fuzzily photographed nudes that a previous generation did but will encounter the hard-core raunchiness of *Playboy* or *Hustler.* ¹³Moreover, the movies young people attend often focus on highly sexual situations. ¹⁴It is difficult to teach children traditional values when films show young people treating sex as a casual sport. ¹⁵An even more difficult matter for parents is the heavily sexual content of programs on television. ¹⁶With just a flick of the dial, children can see soap-opera stars cavorting in bed, watch music videos with all-too-explicit lyrics, or view cable programs where nudity is common. ¹⁷And even national TV news shows expose children to raw details about sexual misbehaviors of celebrities or national politicians.

¹⁸Most disturbing to parents is the increase in life-threatening dangers that face young people. ¹⁹When children are small, their parents fear that their youngsters may be victims of violence. ²⁰Every news program seems to carry a report about predators who molest or exploit children. ²¹When children are older, parents begin to worry about their kids' use of drugs. ²²Peer pressure to experiment with drugs is often stronger than parents' warnings. ²³This pressure to experiment can be fatal. ²⁴Finally, kids must still resist the pressure to drink. ²⁵Although alcohol has always held an attraction for teenagers, reports indicate that they are drinking even more than before. ²⁶As many parents know, the consequences of this attraction can be deadly—especially when drinking is combined with driving.

_____ 1. In sentence 9, *enticing* means
    A. low-cost.
    B. uncommon.
    C. educational.
    D. tempting.

_____ 2. The three major supporting details in this reading concern
    A. malls, arcades, and drugs.
    B. new temptations, former temptations, and life-threatening dangers.
    C. stereo and television, sexually explicit materials, and drinking and driving.
    D. new distractions from schoolwork, sexually explicit materials, and life-threatening dangers.

_____ 3. The relationship of sentence 13 to sentence 12 is one of
    A. addition.
    B. contrast.
    C. time order.
    D. illustration.

_____ 4. The main organizational pattern of the second paragraph is
    A. time order.
    B. list of items.
    C. comparison.
    D. definition and example.

_____ 5. Sentence 18 is a(n)
    A. fact.
    B. opinion.

_____ 6. From reading the passage, one can conclude that the author believes
    A. children today are less moral and more irresponsible than children of past generations.
    B. parents should not allow their children to ask questions about sex, drugs, or alcohol.
    C. children who are raised properly will not be affected by the pressures of modern life.
    D. children today are faced with situations they are not mature enough to deal with.

_____ 7. The tone of this passage can be described as primarily
    A. revengeful.
    B. concerned.
    C. reassuring.
    D. ambivalent.

_____ 8. The central point of the selection is stated in sentence
    A. 2.
    B. 10.
    C. 18.
    D. 26.

COMBINED SKILLS: Test 7

Read the passage below. Then write the letter of the best answer to each question that follows.

[1]Late in the year, we tackled the informal essay. [2]"The essay, don't you see, is the . . ." [3]My mind went numb. [4]Of all the forms of writing, none seemed so boring as the essay. [5]Naturally we would have to write informal essays. [6]Mr. Fleagle distributed a homework sheet offering us a choice of topics. [7]None was quite so simple-minded as "What I Did on My Summer Vacation," but most seemed to be almost as dull. [8]I took the list home and dawdled until the night before the essay was due. [9]Sprawled on the sofa, I finally faced up to the grim task, took the list out of my notebook, and scanned it. [10]The topic on which my eye stopped was "The Art of Eating Spaghetti."

[11]This title produced an extraordinary sequence of mental images. [12]Surging up out of the depths of memory came a vivid recollection of a night in Belleville when all of us were seated around the supper table— Uncle Allen, my mother, Uncle Charlie, Doris, Uncle Hal—and Aunt Pat served spaghetti for supper. [13]Spaghetti was an exotic treat in those days. [14]Neither Doris nor I had ever eaten spaghetti, and none of the adults had enough experience to be good at it. [15]All the good humor of Uncle Allen's house reawoke in my mind as I recalled the laughing arguments we had that night about the socially respectable method for moving spaghetti from plate to mouth.

[16]Suddenly I wanted to write about that, about the warmth and good feeling of it, but I wanted to put it down simply for my own joy, not for Mr. Fleagle. [17]It was a moment I wanted to recapture and hold for myself. [18]I wanted to relive the pleasure of an evening at New Street. [19]To write it as I wanted, however, would violate all the rules of formal composition I'd learned in school. . . .

[20]Two days passed before Mr. Fleagle returned the graded papers, and he returned everyone's but mine. [21]I was bracing myself for a command to report to Mr. Fleagle immediately after school for discipline when I saw him lift my paper from his desk and rap for the class's attention.

[22]"Now, boys," he said, "I want to read you an essay. [23]This is titled 'The Art of Eating Spaghetti.'"

[24]And he started to read. [25]My words! [26]He was reading *my words* out loud to the entire class. [27]What's more, the entire class was listening. [28]Listening attentively. [29]Then somebody laughed; then the entire class was laughing. . . .

[30]When Mr. Fleagle finished, he put the final seal on my happiness by saying, "Now that, boys, is an essay, don't you see. [31]It's—don't you see— it's of the very essence of the essay, don't you see. [32]Congratulations, Mr. Baker."

_____ 1. The word *exotic* in sentence 13 means
   A. boring.
   B. well-known.
   C. favorite.
   D. excitingly unfamiliar.

_____ 2. Sentences 10–12
   A. define a term.
   B. compare two things.
   C. describe a cause-effect relationship.
   D. list several items.

_____ 3. According to the author, the choices for an essay topic
   A. featured "What I Did on My Summer Vacation."
   B. were hard to choose from because so many were interesting.
   C. were mostly about food.
   D. seemed quite dull at first.

_____ 4. When Mr. Fleagle returned the students' papers, he
   A. held back several of the best ones.
   B. congratulated Baker as he handed him his paper.
   C. held back only Baker's.
   D. announced that Baker had gotten the only A.

_____ 5. From reading this passage, one can conclude that
   A. Mr. Fleagle was an extraordinarily good teacher.
   B. Baker had always enjoyed writing essays.
   C. a simple experience can be a good topic for an essay.
   D. it was painful for the author when the entire class laughed.

_____ 6. Young Baker
   A. had expected Mr. Fleagle to like his essay.
   B. enjoyed the dinner at his aunt's, and his essay showed that enjoyment.
   C. invented many of the details that appeared in his essay.
   D. did not intend his essay to be amusing.

_____ 7. From the passage, we can conclude the author would agree that
   A. students should not be required to write informal essays.
   B. students should not be subjected to hearing their work read aloud in front of a class.
   C. people who are not "born writers" will never learn to enjoy writing.
   D. one key to good writing is finding the right topic.

_____ 8. Which statement best expresses the main idea of this selection?
   A. An interesting assignment and others' approval gave the author a joyful writing experience.
   B. The informal essay is more useful than the formal essay for getting students excited about their assignments.
   C. A writing assignment brought to the author's mind a funny spaghetti dinner at his aunt's house.
   D. Teachers should create interesting writing assignments if they expect their students to care about writing.

COMBINED SKILLS: Test 8

Read the passage below. Then write the letter of the best answer to each question that follows.

[1]Optimism predisposes a positive approach to life. [2]"The optimist," notes researcher H. Jackson Brown, "goes to the window every morning and says, 'Good morning, God.' [3]The pessimist goes to the window and says, 'Good God, morning.'" [4]Many of us, however, have what researcher Neil Weinstein terms "an unrealistic optimism about future life events." [5]At Rutgers University, for example, students perceive themselves as far more likely than their classmates to get a job, draw a good salary, and own a home, and as far less likely to experience negative events, such as developing a drinking problem, having a heart attack before age 40, or being fired. [6]In Scotland, most late adolescents think they are much less likely than their peers to become infected by the AIDS virus. [7]After experiencing the 1989 earthquake, San Francisco Bay area students did lose their optimism about being less vulnerable than their classmates to injury in a natural disaster, but within three months their illusory optimism had rebounded.

[8]Another researcher notes how illusory optimism increases our vulnerability. [9]Believing ourselves immune to misfortune, we do not take sensible precautions. [10]In one survey, 137 marriage license applicants accurately estimated that half of marriages end in divorce, yet most assessed their chance of divorce as zero percent. [11]Sexually active undergraduate women who don't consistently use contraceptives perceive themselves, compared with other women at their university, as much less vulnerable to unwanted pregnancy. [12]Those who cheerfully shun seatbelts, deny the effects of smoking, and stumble into ill-fated relationships remind us that blind optimism, like pride, may, as the ancient proverb warns, go before a fall.

[13]Optimism definitely beats pessimism in promoting self-efficiency, health, and well-being. [14]Yet a dash of realism can save us from the perils of unrealistic optimism. [15]Self-doubt can energize students, most of whom—especially those destined for low grades—exhibit excess optimism about upcoming exams. [16](Such illusory optimism often disappears as the time approaches for receiving the exam back.) [17]Students who are overconfident tend to underprepare. [18]Their equally able but more anxious peers, fearing that they are going to bomb on the upcoming exam, study furiously and get higher grades. [19]The moral: Success in school and beyond requires enough optimism to sustain hope and enough pessimism to motivate concern.

_____ 1. In sentences 7 and 8, *illusory* means

A. proven.

B. carefully considered.

C. helpful.

D. based on error.

_____ 2. The relationship of sentence 8 to the several sentences before it is one of
   A. time.
   B. cause-effect.
   C. addition.
   D. contrast.

_____ 3. Which of the following is in a contrast relationship to the sentence preceding it?
   A. Sentence 10
   B. Sentence 11
   C. Sentence 12
   D. Sentence 14

_____ 4. The third paragraph
   A. lists several causes of optimism.
   B. contrasts optimism with realism and pessimism.
   C. defines and illustrates optimism.
   D. all of the above.

_____ 5. The passage suggests that
   A. many people unrealistically think themselves safe from harm.
   B. both optimism and pessimism are useful.
   C. unrealistic optimism can create problems.
   D. all of the above.

_____ 6. The author of this passage would probably agree with which of the following statements?
   A. Children should be encouraged to be as optimistic as possible.
   B. It is better to be 100 percent realistic.
   C. Negative experiences make people temporarily more realistic.
   D. Optimists are more likely than pessimists to take precautions.

_____ 7. Which sentence best expresses the central point of the selection?
   A. Sentence 1
   B. Sentence 8
   C. Sentence 15
   D. Sentence 19

_____ 8. Which title best summarizes the passage?
   A. Optimism Affects Grades
   B. A Dash of Realism
   C. Unrealistic Optimism
   D. Think Positive!

COMBINED SKILLS: Test 9

Read the passage below. Then write the letter of the best answer to each question that follows.

[1]Those with closed minds refuse to consider any contradictory facts, and they proceed with their planned course of action, full speed ahead, with their "minds made up" and tightly shut. [2]As an illustration, consider the situation in 1986, prior to the space shuttle *Challenger*'s disastrous launch that killed all seven astronauts aboard. [3]There was a heated telephone debate between two engineers for the company that produced the shuttle booster rockets and top officials of NASA (the federal government's space agency). [4]The engineers insisted that the flight was too risky because of freezing temperatures at the Florida launch site. [5]They explained that some of the seals on the fuel tanks were not designed to withstand such low temperatures and might leak under pressure, thus endangering the craft and crew.

[6]Despite the pleas to abort the flight, officials at NASA overruled the engineers, who were best qualified to make judgments about the complex technical problems of space flight. [7]What caused the officials to ignore the engineers? [8]Several flights had already been postponed, and it would not look good to postpone another. [9]It would be bad public relations to disappoint the crowds of people and news reporters waiting for the launch. [10]Top government officials were ready to appear on national television and take the credit for another safe flight. [11]As a result, with their minds absolutely closed to the facts presented by the engineers, NASA officials ordered the *Challenger* to take off. [12]Seventy-three seconds later, the spacecraft was enveloped in flame.

[13]Incredibly, seventeen years later, the lesson of the *Challenger* disaster was repeated. [14]In 2003, the space shuttle *Columbia* broke apart while re-entering the earth's atmosphere, killing another crew of seven. [15]During the shuttle's liftoff, a piece of foam insulation had broken off, hitting the shuttle's wing at five hundred miles per hour. [16]Lower-level engineers at NASA begged for photographs of the *Columbia* in orbit, which might have shown the extent of the damage, but their closed-minded superiors ignored their requests. [17]It was the damage caused by the 1.7-pound chunk of insulation that doomed the *Columbia*.

[18]There is no virtue in ignoring contradictory facts and "sticking to your guns" when the course taken shows all the signs of being the wrong one. [19]Closed minds are especially noticeable in political campaigns and debates. [20]Many people line up to support one candidate or another and won't listen to any facts presented by the opposing candidate.

[21]All those with an open mind say is this: "I don't know everything, so I'd better keep my mind, eyes, and ears open to any new facts that may come along." [22]The world would be a much better and safer place if everyone had this attitude.

_____ 1. In sentence 6, the word *abort* means
  A. take.   C. watch.
  B. rush.   D. stop.

_____ 2. The pattern of organization used in the second paragraph is
  A. cause and effect.   C. comparison.
  B. illustration.   D. contrast.

_____ 3. The *Challenger*'s weak point was
  A. its crew.   C. the fuel tanks' seals.
  B. the fuel.   D. the size of its rockets.

_____ 4. The author implies that
  A. the *Columbia* disaster was impossible to foresee.
  B. incompetent engineers were to blame for the *Columbia* explosion.
  C. the *Columbia*'s damaged wing could not withstand the stress of re-entering the earth's atmosphere.
  D. the *Columbia* was deliberately sabotaged.

_____ 5. The author of this passage would probably agree with which of the following statements?
  A. People with open minds make more responsible citizens than those with closed minds.
  B. NASA should abandon its space-shuttle campaign.
  C. Once a person makes a decision, he or she should stick to it.
  D. The *Challenger* and *Columbia* explosions may have been caused by deliberate foul play.

_____ 6. The author's main purpose is to
  A. inform readers about what an open mind is.
  B. entertain the reader with two stories of tragedies in space.
  C. persuade readers of the importance of an open mind.

_____ 7. The tone of the second and third paragraphs can be described as
  A. amused.
  B. critical.
  C. revengeful.
  D. uncertain.

_____ 8. Which sentence best expresses the main idea of the passage?
  A. There is a great deal of closed-minded thinking in the federal government.
  B. One is more likely to see closed-minded thinkers in science and politics.
  C. An open mind is more logical and safer than a closed mind.
  D. Closed-minded thinking is a widespread phenomenon.

COMBINED SKILLS: Test 10

Read the passage below. Then write the letter of the best answer to each question that follows.

[1]It is clear that advertisements work. [2]Attention is caught, communication occurs between producers and consumers, and sales result. [3]It turns out to be difficult to detail the exact relationship between a specific ad and a specific purchase, or even between a campaign and subsequent sales figures, because advertising is only one of a host of influences upon consumption. [4]Yet no one is fooled by this lack of perfect proof; everyone knows that advertising sells. [5]If this were not the case, then tightfisted American businesses would not spend a total of fifty billion dollars annually on these messages.

[6]But before anyone despairs that advertisers have our number to the extent that they can marshal us at will and march us like automatons to the checkout counters, we should recall the resiliency and obduracy of the American consumer. [7]Advertisers may have uncovered the softest spots in our minds, but that does not mean they have found truly gaping holes. [8]There is no evidence that advertising can get people to do things contrary to their self-interests. [9]Despite all the finesse of advertisements, and all the subtle emotional tugs, the public resists the vast majority of the petitions. [10]According to the marketing division of the ACNielsen Company, a whopping 75 percent of all new products die within a year in the marketplace, the victims of consumer disinterest, which no amount of advertising could overcome. [11]The appeals in advertising may be the most captivating there are to be had, but they are not enough to entrap the wily consumer.

[12]The key to understanding the discrepancy between, on the one hand, the fact that advertising truly works, and, on the other, the fact that it hardly works, is to take into account the enormous numbers of people exposed to an ad. [13]Modern-day communications permit an ad to be displayed to millions upon millions of individuals; if the smallest fraction of that audience can be moved to buy the product, then the ad has been successful. [14]When 1 percent of the people exposed to a television advertising campaign reach for their wallets, that could be one million sales, which may be enough to keep the product and the advertisements coming.

_____ 1. In sentence 3, the word *host* means a
    A. lack.
    B. question.
    C. fear.
    D. large number.

_____ 2. The word *discrepancy,* in sentence 12, means
   A. similarity.
   B. inconsistency.
   C. marketing.
   D. delay.

_____ 3. According to the passage, the American consumer is
   A. a sucker for ads.
   B. stingy.
   C. willing to try anything new.
   D. motivated by self-interest.

_____ 4. The reading
   A. contrasts advertisements with consumers.
   B. discusses the effectiveness of ads.
   C. lists reasons for advertising.
   D. narrates a series of events in the history of advertising.

_____ 5. According to the A.C. Nielson Company, the percentage of new products that survive their first year in the marketplace is
   A. 15.
   B. 25.
   C. 50.
   D. 75.

_____ 6. The passage suggests that an ad may be considered successful if it
   A. makes people laugh or cry.
   B. moves 1 percent of viewers to buy the product advertised.
   C. is remembered by 75 percent of the viewers.
   D. costs a great deal.

_____ 7. One can conclude from reading this passage that
   A. advertisements aren't worth their enormous cost.
   B. advertising is the single most important influence on a consumer's decision to buy.
   C. an ad cannot get people to buy a product they aren't otherwise interested in.
   D. companies are generally reluctant to spend money on advertising.

_____ 8. Which title best summarizes the passage?
   A. The Role of Advertising in Modern Life
   B. Advertising: Effective but Not Foolproof
   C. Why Advertising Fails
   D. What Makes for a Good Advertisement?

COMBINED SKILLS: Test 11

Read the passage below. Then write the letter of the best answer to each question that follows.

[1]We tend to think of America's early European settlers, who came seeking religious freedom, as solemn, sober folk. [2]So it is surprising to learn that in the seventeenth and eighteenth centuries, beer consumption was a big part of daily life, and it is even more surprising to learn that beer was considered a health drink! [3]In the seventeenth century, even adult Quakers (religious refugees from England who were known for their devout and simple lifestyle) typically drank three to four quarts of beer a day. [4]Their children drank one to two quarts of "small beer"—a very weak brew with a low alcohol content. [5]Large estates, such as the home of wealthy William Penn, Pennsylvania's founder, included a brew house. [6]In humbler households, the housewife brewed beer in a big iron kettle in the yard. [7]The colonists considered beer a necessity because they believed it was healthier than water— and indeed it was, though for reasons that were not understood at the time. [8]In early American towns and homesteads, wells were not lined. [9]As a result, drinking water was often contaminated with animal manure and human waste. [10]The early settlers did not know that their water was full of bacteria; it was not until the mid-nineteenth century that scientists began to understand that invisible germs cause much disease, and that boiling water kills these germs. [11]The colonists did not realize that the several rounds of boiling that are part of the brewing process sterilized their dirty water. [12]But they did realize that they stayed healthier drinking beer than drinking well water. [13]Tea—also made with boiled water—was also considered a healthy drink; but tea was an expensive product imported from China or India, out of reach of many homesteaders, and reserved for guests and special occasions even in wealthy homes. [14]Thus, while the colonists condemned and punished public drunkenness, it is likely that they frequently went about their business feeling something of an alcohol "buzz"—which they undoubtedly preferred to the stomach sickness they might have gotten from a plain glass of their unsanitary well water.

_____ 1. According to the passage,
   A. rich settlers had their own brew houses.
   B. rich households drank only tea rather than beer.
   C. wealthy settlers usually lined their wells and drank water.
   D. non-wealthy settlers could afford only "small beer."

_____ 2. Beer actually was healthier than water in colonial times because
   A. the alcohol in the beer killed bacteria.
   B. the boiling involved in the brewing process killed bacteria.
   C. the linings of wells polluted the water with lead.
   D. high-quality ingredients for brewing beer were imported from China and India.

_____ 3. The relationship between sentences 8 and 9 is one of
   A. time order.
   B. cause and effect.
   C. comparison.
   D. contrast.

_____ 4. The relationship of sentence 12 to sentence 11 is one of
   A. time order.
   B. cause and effect.
   C. comparison.
   D. contrast.

_____ 5. The author's tone can be described as
   A. admiring and amused.
   B. objective and informal.
   C. scholarly, but critical.
   D. unkind and sarcastic.

_____ 6. The author implies that
   A. drunkenness was unknown in the colonies.
   B. the Quakers did not realize beer could lead to intoxication.
   C. beer was simply considered a beverage, not a sure way to become intoxicated.
   D. the beer the colonists brewed contained little water.

_____ 7. Which is the most appropriate title for this selection?
   A. The Surprising Quakers
   B. Life in the Early Colonies
   C. Beer Consumption in Colonial America
   D. Benefits of Beer and Tea

_____ 8. Which of the following statements best expresses the main idea of the passage?
   A. Quakers, religious refugees from England known for their devout and simple lifestyle, drank a lot of beer.
   B. The American colonists knew that drinking water was unhealthy, but they didn't know why.
   C. The well water in early-American towns and homesteads was often contaminated by manure and human waste.
   D. Early American colonists found beer to be more healthful than water.

COMBINED SKILLS: Test 12

Read the passage below. Then write the letter of the best answer to each question that follows.

[1]The case for making a distinction between good and bad laws is well stated by Henry David Thoreau, Martin Luther King, Jr., and others. [2]No matter how strongly one advocates lawful obedience to the state and its laws, it is inevitable that some laws will turn out to be bad ones. [3]Lawmakers are not only human—which is sufficient cause for having a few bad laws—but a percentage of them will always be self-centered in their interests, shortsighted or dead wrong in their opinion of what constitutes justice, mentally out of touch with reality, and woefully uninformed on the nature of values and value judgments (and after all, laws are the legislation of human values). [4]These statements can be made with some certainty simply because the leaders of men are not immune to the reasoning and emotional problems shared by the populace as whole.

[5]Therefore, in any legal system, it is quite possible to point to laws that range from the mildly unjust to the terribly inhuman, and such laws should promote a feeling of outrage in individuals who are victimized by them or see others hurt by them. [6]More important, perhaps, is the fact that unless laws are periodically challenged—as the authors of the American system recognized—then they don't get improved. [7]In 1787 Thomas Jefferson said, "God forbid, we should ever be twenty years without such a rebellion." [8]Elsewhere he elaborated: "What country can preserve its liberties, if its rulers are not warned from time to time, that this people preserve the spirit of resistance?" [9]Among mature people criticism is cherished: it is through the assessment of wise criticism that more just laws can be formulated and antiquated laws updated. [10]Also, it is through open criticism that the selfish interests of those in power can be rapidly brought to the attention of enough citizens who can object and, if necessary, dissent before a deeper tyranny sets in.

_____ 1. As used in sentence 9, the word *cherished* means
   A. questioned.
   B. valued greatly.
   C. rejected.
   D. distrusted.

_____ 2. The details in sentences 3, 4, and 5 support the point made in sentence
   A. 1.
   B. 2.
   C. 6.
   D. 7.

_____ 3. The author believes that
   A. people always should obey the law.
   B. only lawyers and judges know enough to determine whether a particular law is just.
   C. most people have little respect for the law.
   D. there will always be unjust laws.

_____ 4. The relationship of the first sentence in paragraph 2 to the sentences that come before it is one of
   A. time.
   B. addition.
   C. cause and effect.
   D. contrast.

_____ 5. The tone of the passage is
   A. angry and bitter.
   B. ironic.
   C. serious and analytical.
   D. detached and uncaring.

_____ 6. We can infer that the type of criticism referred to in the passage is found today
   A. on editorial pages of newspapers.
   B. in television news commentary.
   C. in magazine columns.
   D. all of the above.

_____ 7. We can conclude that the author admires
   A. lawmakers.
   B. reformers such as Martin Luther King, Jr.
   C. judges.
   D. people who break the law.

_____ 8. Which of the following sentences best expresses the main idea of the passage?
   A. Some laws are unjust, and people have the right and duty to challenge them.
   B. Despite the best intentions, lawmakers will occasionally pass an unjust law.
   C. The law is a constantly changing thing.
   D. Thomas Jefferson expected and welcomed occasional rebellion.

COMBINED SKILLS: Test 13

Read the passage below. Then write the letter of the best answer to each question that follows.

[1]Resources are the things or services used to produce goods, which then can be used to satisfy wants. [2]Economic resources are scarce; free resources, such as air, are so abundant that they can be obtained without charge. [3]The test of whether a resource is an economic resource or a free resource is price: scarce economic resources command a price; abundant free resources do not. [4]The number of free resources is actually quite limited. [5]For instance, although the Earth contains a huge amount of water, it is not a free resource to typical urban or suburban homeowners, who must pay a local water authority for providing and maintaining their water supply. [6]In a world where all resources were free, there would be no economic problems, since all wants could be satisfied.

[7]Economic resources can be classified into three categories:

Land. [8]A shorthand expression for natural resources, land includes minerals as well as plots of ground. [9]Clearly, land is an important and valuable resource in both agriculture and industry. [10]Think of the fertile soil of Iowa or Kansas, which produces such abundant crops. [11]Or consider Manhattan Island, which supports the skyscrapers, shops, and theaters in the heart of New York. [12]In addition, land is an important part of our environment, and it provides enjoyment above and beyond its contribution to agricultural and industrial output.

Labor. [13]Human efforts, both physical and mental, are included in the category of labor. [14]Thus, when you study for a final examination or make out an income tax return, this is as much labor as if you were to dig a ditch. [15]In 2003, over 140 million people were employed (or looking for work) in the United States. [16]This vast labor supply is, of course, an extremely important resource, without which our nation could not maintain its current output level.

Capital. [17]Buildings, equipment, inventories, and other nonhuman producible resources that contribute to the production, marketing, and distribution of goods and services all fall within the economist's definition of capital. [18]Examples are machine tools and warehouses; but not all types of capital are big and bulky: for example, a hand calculator, or a pencil for that matter, is a type of capital. [19]Workers in the United States have an enormous amount of capital to work with. [20]Think of the oil refineries in New Jersey and Philadelphia, the electronics factories near Boston and San Francisco, the aircraft plants in California, and all of the additional types of capital we have and use in this country. [21]Without this capital, the nation's output level would be a great deal less than it is.

_____ 1. In sentence 3, the word *command* means
A. give an order.   C. escape.
B. have authority over.   D. can get.

_____ 2. Labor is defined as
A. a form of capital.
B. mental and physical efforts.
C. only physical efforts.
D. excluding persons looking for work.

_____ 3. According to the passage, the number of free resources is
A. limited.
B. determined by the availability of labor.
C. the same the world around.
D. growing.

_____ 4. The passage lists several
A. definitions and examples.
B. comparisons.
C. events in time order.
D. causes and effects.

_____ 5. The relationship of sentence 5 to sentence 4 is one of
A. addition.
B. comparison.
C. contrast.
D. illustration.

_____ 6. The author's main purpose is to
A. inform.
B. persuade.
C. entertain.

_____ 7. Sentence 3 is a statement of
A. fact.
B. opinion.
C. fact and opinion.

_____ 8. Which statement best expresses the central point of the passage?
A. Economic resources are scarce and cost money, unlike free resources such as air.
B. Economic resources—resources that aren't free—can be classified into three categories: land, labor, and capital.
C. Resources are things and services used to produce goods, which may then be used to fulfill wants.
D. Such things as buildings, equipment, and pencils are among the nonhuman producible resources that contribute to the economy.

COMBINED SKILLS: Test 14

Read the passage below. Then write the letter of the best answer to each question that follows.

[1]In seeking to explain belief in witchcraft, historians agree that the idea took shape toward the end of the Middle Ages. [2]Peasant culture throughout the Middle Ages included belief in the possibility of sorcery. [3]In other words, most simple rural people assumed that certain unusual individuals could practice good, or "white," magic in the form of healing, divination for lost objects, and fortunetelling; or perhaps also evil, "black" magic that might, for example, call up tempests or ravage crops. [4]But only in the fifteenth century did learned authorities begin to insist on theological grounds that black magic could be practiced only as a result of pacts with the devil. [5]Naturally, once this belief became accepted, judicial officers soon found it urgent to prosecute all "witches" who practiced black magic because warfare against the devil was paramount to Christian society and "the evil one" could not be allowed to hold any sway. [6]Accordingly, in 1484 Pope Innocent VIII ordered papal inquisitors to root out alleged witchcraft with all the means at their disposal, and the pace of witch-hunts gained momentum in the following decades. [7]Nor were witch trials curtailed in areas that broke with Rome, for Protestant reformers believed in the insidious powers of Satan just as much as the Catholics did.

[8]The victims were most frequently women, no doubt in part because preachers had encouraged their flocks to believe that evil had first come into the world with Eve and in part because men in authority felt psychologically most ambivalent about members of the opposite sex. [9]Pure sadism certainly cannot have been the original motive for such proceedings, yet once trials began, horrendous sadism very often was unleashed. [10]Thus old women, young girls, and sometimes even mere children might be brutally tortured by having needles driven under their nails, fires placed at their heels, or their legs crushed under weights until marrow spurted from their bones, in order to make them confess to having had filthy orgies with demons. [11]The final death toll will never be known, but in the 1620s there was an average of one hundred burnings a year in the German cities of Würzburg and Bamberg, and around the same time it was said the town square of Wolfenbüttel "looked like a little forest, so crowded were the stakes."

_____ 1. As used in sentence 5, *paramount* means
- A. reasonable.
- B. discouraging.
- C. questionable.
- D. of greatest importance.

_____ 2. Example context clues for the word *sadism,* in sentence 9, are in sentence
   A. 8.
   B. 9.
   C. 10.
   D. 11.

_____ 3. One reason women were most often accused of witchcraft is that
   A. they were cruel more often than men.
   B. they were linked through the story of Eve to the entry of evil into the world.
   C. they could find lost objects more easily than men.
   D. their ability to care for the sick made others suspicious.

_____ 4. According to the passage, people suspected of witchcraft were
   A. driven from their homes.
   B. excluded from the church.
   C. forced to be "converted" by the church.
   D. tortured until they confessed.

_____ 5. The relationship of sentence 4 to sentence 3 is one of
   A. addition.
   B. comparison.
   C. contrast.
   D. example.

_____ 6. Sentence 6 is a statement of
   A. fact.
   B. opinion.
   C. fact and opinion.

_____ 7. It is reasonable to conclude that before the fifteenth century,
   A. the idea of "black magic" was unknown in most of Europe.
   B. people who practiced "black magic" were not thought to have made pacts with the devil.
   C. sorcery was practiced in almost all households.
   D. witch-hunts were banned by law throughout Europe.

_____ 8. Which statement best expresses the central point of the passage?
   A. Peasants throughout the Middle Ages believed in the possibility of sorcery.
   B. Educated authorities of the 1400s stated that black magic took place only as a result of pacts with the devil.
   C. A belief in black magic that began during the Middle Ages led the church to cause the hunting and torture of so-called witches.
   D. During and after the Middle Ages, people believed in magic and witches, both good and evil.

COMBINED SKILLS: Test 15

Read the passage below. Then write the letter of the best answer to each question that follows.

[1]All living cells in an animal's body require energy to power the various chemical processes going on inside them. [2]This energy is ultimately supplied by the food that animals eat. [3]These chemical processes are collectively referred to as *metabolism*, and one of the byproducts of metabolism is heat. [4]Metabolic rates vary significantly between species. [5]Warm-blooded animals (birds and mammals) have metabolic rates about five to ten times higher than those of similarly sized cold-blooded ones (reptiles, amphibians, and fishes). [6]And it is precisely because birds and mammals have such high metabolic rates that they are able to keep their bodies warm.

[7]The terms *warm-blooded* and *cold-blooded* are still in everyday use, but they are not entirely precise. [8]Anyone who has handled a snake knows this because a snake's body actually feels quite warm. [9]But very little of the snake's body heat originates internally, from its cells, most of it having been supplied from the outside, either by the sun or by a heat lamp. [10]Instead of referring to reptiles as cold-blooded, they are best described as *ectothermic*, meaning "outside heat." [11]Similarly, birds and mammals are said to be *endothermic*, meaning "inside heat."

[12]There are advantages and disadvantages to each thermal strategy. [13]Reptiles are usually sluggish first thing in the morning, their body temperatures having dropped during the cool of the night. [14]Accordingly, they have to bask in the sun to raise their body temperatures, but once they have warmed up sufficiently, they can go about their business. [15]By alternating between the sun when they are too cool, and the shade when they are too warm, many reptiles are able to maintain their body temperatures at optimum levels of about 95°F or more. [16]Endotherms, on the other hand, maintain temperatures of about 98°F all the time, so they are always ready for action.

[17]I used to keep a small crocodile. [18]He had very sharp teeth, and I had to be careful how I handled him during the daytime, when he was warm. [19]But I could do whatever I wanted at night, when he was cold, without any fear of being bitten. [20]The obvious disadvantage of being ectothermic is that the animal's activity levels are dependent upon the environment. [21]But its low metabolic rates mean that it requires far less food, which is an advantage. [22]I used to feed the crocodile a tiny piece of liver once a week, while the family cat demanded three meals every day. [23]We should therefore not think that reptiles are inferior to mammals and birds; they are just different.

_____ 1. In sentence 12, the word *thermal* means

    A. related to hunting.   C. related to mammals.

    B. inactive.   D. having to do with heat.

_____ 2. In sentence 15, the word *optimum* means
     A. most desirable.   C. always necessary.
     B. low.   D. high.

_____ 3. According to the author, the term *cold-blooded* is misleading because "cold-blooded" animals
     A. always have a high body temperature.
     B. cannot survive cold temperatures.
     C. are more affected by heat than by cold.
     D. often have a body temperature comparable to that of warm-blooded animals.

_____ 4. The main organizational patterns of the passage are cause-effect and
     A. comparison.
     B. contrast.
     C. time order.
     D. list of items.

_____ 5. The author's attitude toward reptiles seems to be
     A. fearful.
     B. appreciative.
     C. distasteful.
     D. suspicious.

_____ 6. Which of the following best expresses the unstated main idea of the last paragraph?
     A. The author enjoyed keeping exotic pets.
     B. The author's crocodile demonstrated the advantages and disadvantages of being ectothermic.
     C. Crocodiles and other reptiles are less dangerous during the night, when they are cold and inactive.
     D. An ectothermic animal is cheaper to keep than a mammal, as it eats only rarely.

_____ 7. The author implies in the last paragraph that
     A. endothermic animals are more intelligent than ectothermic ones.
     B. snakes are not actually ectothermic animals.
     C. maintaining a high metabolic rate requires a lot of fuel in the form of food.
     D. a low metabolic rate is an advantage in a cold climate.

_____ 8. Which is the most appropriate title for this selection?
     A. Endotherms and Ectotherms
     B. The Advantages of Ectothermism
     C. Common Misconceptions about Reptiles
     D. Birds and Mammals

SAMPLE ANSWER SHEET

Use the form below as a model answer sheet for the fifteen combined-skills tests on the preceding pages.

Name _____

Section _____ Date _____

SCORE: (Number correct) _____ × 12.5 = _____%

COMBINED SKILLS: Test _____

1. _____

2. _____

3. _____

4. _____

5. _____

6. _____

7. _____

8. _____

2

More about Summarizing and Outlining

This section of the book adds to what you have learned about summarizing and outlining on pages 95–100 and 103–107. It will help you take better study notes on your textbook reading assignments. Although everyone agrees that summarizing and outlining are valuable skills, they are all too seldom taught. To cite a personal example, while I was asked in high school to prepare summaries and outlines of books, stories, and articles, I was never actually taught how to do so. All of my teachers seemed to assume that someone else was responsible for helping me learn these sophisticated skills.

When I got to college, I had to do even more summarizing and outlining. For instance, many essay exam questions required summaries, that is, brief accounts of large amounts of material. I also had to summarize and outline when writing papers and giving reports, studying class lecture notes, and preparing study sheets on textbook reading assignments. Through necessity, then, I gradually learned how to summarize and outline effectively.

UNDERSTANDING SUMMARIES

All of us often summarize in everyday life. For example, in response to someone's question, we might summarize our day by saying:

"I had a good day" or "I had a bad day."

Or we might offer a slightly more specific summary:

"I had an exciting day" or "I had a depressing day" or "I had a busy day."

Or our summary might be even more detailed:

"I had a busy day. I had three classes at school this morning, spent the afternoon in the library doing homework, and then worked at my part-time job for five hours in the evening."

When we make such general statements, we are providing summaries. A **summary** can be defined as the reduction of a large amount of information to its most important points. Just as we can offer a summary of the numerous details of our day, so we can prepare summaries of the numerous details in our college course materials. Read the following two textbook passages, and then look at the summary that follows each.

Passage 1

[1]Psychologists have developed a number of suggestions for controlling anger. [2]A sense of humor can often defuse intense anger. [3]By finding something amusing in a situation, you can make tension crumble. [4]Physical exercise has also been effective in controlling anger. [5]Using the added physical strength that intense emotions produce can help to release some pressure. [6]Jogging, racquetball, hitting punching bags, and lifting weights are effective ways to use up physical energy. [7]Relaxation exercises have also been beneficial in controlling anger. [8]One type of relaxation exercise stresses tensing and relaxing muscles in various parts of your body: your arms, your legs, your feet, and even your nose and tongue. [9]Another relaxation exercise emphasizes deep breathing.

Summary of Passage 1

To control anger, psychologists suggest a sense of humor as well as physical and relaxation exercises.

Passage 2

[1]Compromise is a common and effective way of coping directly with conflict or frustration. [2]We often recognize that we cannot have everything we want and that we cannot expect others to do just what we would like them to do. [3]We then compromise, deciding on a more realistic solution or goal since an ideal solution or goal is not practical. [4]A young man who loves animals and greatly wishes to become a veterinarian may discover that he has less aptitude for biology than he had hoped and that dissecting is so distasteful to him that he could never bring himself to operate on animals. [5]By way of compromise, he may decide to become an animal technician, a person who works as an assistant to a veterinarian.

Summary of Passage 2

Compromise is a direct way of coping in which we decide on a more realistic solution or goal since an ideal solution or goal is not practical. For example, a person not good in biology or opposed to dissection may decide to be an animal technician rather than a veterinarian.

Important Points about Summarizing

1 A summary typically includes the main idea and often the major supporting details of a selection. In the summary of the first passage above, the main idea and the major details have been combined in one sentence. In the second summary, the main idea is the definition of compromise; it is followed by a brief example that helps make the definition clear. *Note that textbook summaries will often include definitions of key terms followed by condensed examples.*

2 At times a summary may be the main idea and only one or no major details; at other times, the summary may be a main idea followed by several major details. In other words, the length of a summary will depend upon your purpose. As a general guideline, though, a paragraph might be reduced to a sentence or two; an article might be reduced to a paragraph; an entire textbook chapter might be reduced to about three or so pages of notes.

3 A summary should *never* include more than one statement of the main idea. Authors—especially textbook authors—often repeat main ideas to make them as clear as possible. When summarizing, you must eliminate such restatements.

To avoid repetition, you must do the clear thinking necessary to truly understand the basic idea or ideas in a selection. You must "get inside" the material and realize fully what it says before you can reduce it to its essentials.

4 Depending on your purpose, a summary can be in the words of the author, or in your own words, or a combination of the two. If you are summarizing textbook material or a class lecture, you may be better off using the words of the author or of your teacher, especially where definitions of important terms are involved. (Notice in the second passage summarized above that the author's definition of *compromise* is used in the summary.) If you are summarizing a story or article as part of a written report, you will be expected to use your own words.

5 Your understanding of patterns of organization can often help you in summarizing material. For example, if a selection is basically a list of items, then you know your summary will also list items. If a selection is mainly a narrative (first this happened, then that happened), then your summary will briefly narrate a series of events. If a selection is mainly a series of definitions and examples, then your summary will provide both, with a focus on selecting and condensing the examples.

A Helpful Step in Summarizing: Recognizing Basic Ideas

Summarizing requires the ability to notice when an author is restating a main idea, rather than presenting another idea on the same topic. As already mentioned, textbook authors and other writers often restate ideas. By doing so, they help ensure clear communication. If the reader does not understand—or only partly understands—one wording of an idea, he or she may understand the idea when it is expressed again, in slightly different words. Effective readers and thinkers develop the ability to recognize such restatements of ideas.

Read the following passage. Then see if you can underline the two topic sentences—the sentences that express the main idea.

> [1]Our attention is selective—we focus on aspects of our environment that are most important to us or that we expect to see. [2]Thus we notice our doctor's receptionist, the office hours, and the number of people sitting ahead of us in the waiting room. [3]We may fail to see the piece of modern art that is displayed on a wall. [4]We expect our boss to give us negative feedback, so we miss hearing the nice things he or she has to say. [5]We expect a friend to be a poor cook, so we notice the parts of the meal that are poorly prepared. [6]In the process, we fail to appreciate the parts of the meal that were tasty. [7]The significant issues in our lives and our beliefs act as filters on our environment, greatly determining what will and will not get our attention.

The main idea is first presented in sentence 1; it is then restated in sentence 7. The restatement emphasizes and clarifies the main idea. Keep in mind, then, that different sentences can state pretty much the same idea. For example, the main idea above could be worded in yet another way: "What we notice and what we ignore in our environment are largely determined by what is important to us and by our expectations."

To develop your ability to distinguish a restatement of the main idea from a basically different idea on the same topic, read the following sentence:

> **One reason we don't always listen carefully is that we're often wrapped up in personal concerns that are of more immediate importance to us than the messages others are sending.**

Now decide which three of the six statements below are basically the same in meaning as the statement above and which three are basically different. Put the letter *S* (for *Same*) next to the three statements where the meaning is basically the same. After labeling each statement, read the explanation that follows.

_____ 1. Some people listen much more carefully than others.

_____ 2. One way to improve your listening skills is to look the speaker in the eye.

_____ 3. Because of personal distractions, we do not always pay close attention to a speaker.

_____4. The messages that others convey to us are sometimes very distracting.

_____5. We sometimes don't listen carefully because our minds are on personal issues.

_____6. Being preoccupied with our own concerns is one cause of our poor attention to what others are saying.

Explanation:

1. Statement 1 compares *how* people listen—some listen much more carefully than others. In contrast, the boldfaced statement is about *why* we don't always listen carefully. Although both statements are about listening carefully, they say basically different things about that topic.

2. Statement 2 is also basically different from the boldfaced statement. Rather than explaining why we do not listen carefully, it is about a way to improve one's listening.

3. Both statement 3 and the boldfaced sentence express the idea that personal distractions are one reason we don't always listen carefully. Therefore, statement 3 means basically the same as the boldfaced sentence.

4. Statement 4 is about how distracting other people's messages can be, but the boldfaced sentence is about personal distractions. The two sentences have two different meanings.

5. Like the boldfaced sentence, Statement 5 explains that personal concerns sometimes keep us from listening carefully. Thus this sentence means basically the same thing as the boldfaced sentence.

6. Statement 6 also explains that personal ("our own") concerns can keep us from listening carefully. It too is basically the same as the boldfaced sentence.

The following practice will help you develop the ability to recognize multiple statements of the main idea.

➤ Practice 1

Carefully read each opening statement (set off in **boldface**). Then decide whether each numbered statement that follows is basically the same in meaning or basically different in meaning from the opening statement. Write *S* (for *Same*) next to the three statements where the meaning is closest to the original statement.

1. **Not everything that is faced can be changed, but nothing can be changed until it is faced.**

   _____1. There's no guarantee that a bad situation will improve, but it certainly will not unless it is confronted.

_____ 2. People are generally not willing to ask for help in solving their problems.

_____ 3. If a problem is to have a chance to be solved, it must be honestly acknowledged.

_____ 4. Since many problems are impossible to solve, it's just as well to ignore them.

_____ 5. All problems can be solved if the people involved will honestly face the situation.

_____ 6. Even a problem that is solvable will not be solved unless it is faced.

2. **We may be motivated to eat by "internal cues," such as hunger pangs or low blood glucose, or "external cues," including attractive food, the time of day, or commercials for food.**

_____ 1. Overweight people are overly influenced by external cues to eat.

_____ 2. There are two types of cues that motivate us to eat: internal and external.

_____ 3. When people are not hungry, external cues to eat have no effect.

_____ 4. The motivators that cause people to eat can be categorized as either "external cues" or "internal cues."

_____ 5. External cues are even more powerful motivators to eat than internal cues are.

_____ 6. We may get the urge to eat because of inner physical conditions or from signals in our environment.

3. **Once we form an opinion of someone, we tend to hang on to it and make any conflicting information fit our image.**

_____ 1. Our first impression of another person is quickly displaced by a second, more accurate impression.

_____ 2. First impressions are very powerful. Even as we learn more about a person, we assume that our first impression was basically correct.

_____ 3. It's important not to allow ourselves to form an immediate impression of someone we've just met.

_____ 4. First impressions are difficult to change even if we learn new information that contradicts them.

_____ 5. First impressions tend to be lasting.

_____ 6. Our first impressions of people will almost invariably be proved correct by what we later learn about them.

Summarizing Short Passages

As stated earlier, many passages of paragraph length can often be reduced to the main idea and one or more major supporting details. This section will give you practice in writing passage-length summaries. It will also introduce outlining, which can be a helpful step in writing a summary.

Read the passage below. Then decide which of the five statements that follow accurately summarizes the essential information of the passage.

> [1]For some people, the need to achieve is low because they actually fear becoming successful. [2]Research by Matina Horner and others shows that this fear of success occurs in both men and women. [3]Why should someone display anxiety over getting ahead in life? [4]Several factors seem to be involved. [5]Horner implies that some individuals may fear that success will bring social rejection. [6]They fear losing their close friends or having people reject them because "now he or she is better than I am." [7]Herb Goldberg suggests that guilt is another factor. [8]People may feel guilty because they somehow "do not deserve to be better than other people." [9]This reaction is sometimes observed in children who are more successful than their parents. [10]John Sisk indicates that anxiety over losing control may also be important. [11]Successful people typically acquire a lot of money and other material goods. [12]Sisk believes that "affluence, like passion, means a loss of control." [13]As one gets more success, money, and material things, there is a risk that such things will control what we do. [14]Some people probably worry that they will lose the freedom to act independently.

_____ Write the letter of the statement that best summarizes the passage.

    A. Some men and women have a low need to achieve because they fear that success will bring social rejection, guilt, or loss of control.

    B. Some people fear that they will lose the freedom to act independently because of social rejection, guilt, and loss of control.

    C. Some people may fear that acquiring a lot of money will mean a loss of freedom to act independently.

    D. The low need to achieve is sometimes caused by the fear that success will bring social rejection.

Here is how you could have determined the best answer above—and how you can go about summarizing any passage:

1 First read the entire passage through once. Then reread it, asking yourself, "What is the topic of this passage, and what point is being made about the topic?"

2 As you reread the passage, you'll note that the topic is fear of success: the first several sentences all refer to a fear of success. You'll note also what is said about the topic: that several factors seem to be involved in this fear of success. You are now ready to put together the implied main idea: "Some people have a low need to achieve because they fear success for various reasons."

3 At almost the same time that you are asking yourself, "What is the topic?" and "What is the point being made about the topic?" you should ask, "What are the major details that support the point?" Further study of the passage reveals that it is basically a list of items—it lists the three reasons, or factors, behind people's fear of success. (Notice that two transition words in the passage—*another* and *also*—help signal that a list is being provided.) The major supporting details of the passage are the three factors: fear of social rejection, feelings of guilt, and anxiety over losing control.

You may find it very helpful while summarizing to do a mini-outline of the passage by numbering the supporting points. On scratch paper or in the textbook margin or simply in your head, you might create the following:

> *Point:*   People fear success for various reasons.
> *Support:* 1. Fear of social rejection
>   2. Feelings of guilt
>   3. Anxiety over losing control

Such an outline will help you understand the content and basic relationships in a passage. You can then proceed with summarizing the material.

4 For the passage above, you should have chosen statement A as the best summary—it is a one-sentence combination of the main idea and the three major supporting details. Statement B is incorrect because the main idea is about the fear of success, not the fear of losing the freedom to act independently. Statement C is incorrect because it covers only one minor detail. And finally, statement D is incorrect because it is about only one of the three major details.

➤ *Practice 2*

Write the letter of the statement or statements that best summarize each selection that follows. Your choice should provide the main idea; it may include one or more major supporting details as well.

_____ 1. [1]Working conditions in the nineteenth century seem barbaric today: twelve- to fourteen-hour workdays; six- and seven-day weeks; cramped, unsafe factories; marginal wages; and no legal protection. [2]Yet employers seldom had problems motivating their workers: Poverty and unemployment were so widespread that any job was welcome.
   A. Working conditions in the nineteenth century were difficult and even dangerous.
   B. Workers in the nineteenth century were more highly motivated than their twentieth-century counterparts.

    C. Widespread poverty and unemployment made nineteenth-century workers willing to put up with terrible working conditions.

    D. Legal protection and wages have improved sharply since the barbaric conditions that prevailed in the nineteenth century.

_____ 2. [1]The hallmark of representative democracy is that all citizens have the fundamental right to vote for those who will administer and make the laws. [2]Those in power have often defied this principle of democracy by minimizing, neutralizing, or even negating the voting privileges of blacks. [3]Although the Fourteenth Amendment gave blacks the right to vote after the Civil War, the white majority in the Southern states used a variety of tactics to keep them from voting. [4]Most effective was the strategy of intimidation. [5]Blacks who tried to assert their right to vote were often beaten and were sometimes lynched, or their property was destroyed.

    A. All citizens of a democracy have a right to vote for those who will administer and make laws, and nobody should try to interfere with that right.

    B. Those in power have often interfered with the constitutional voting rights of blacks through various tactics, the most effective being cruel intimidation.

    C. After the Civil War, blacks who tried to vote were often beaten.

    D. Those in power have often defied the principles of democracy in order to further their own selfish ends.

_____ 3. [1]All family systems can be roughly categorized into one of two types. [2]The *extended family* is one in which more than two generations of the same kinship line live together, either in the same house or in adjacent dwellings. [3]The head of the entire family is usually the eldest male, and all adults share responsibility for child rearing and other tasks. [4]The extended family, which is quite commonly found in traditional preindustrial societies, can be very large: sometimes it contains several adult offspring of the head of the family, together with all their spouses and children. [5]In contrast, the *nuclear family* is one in which the family group consists only of the parents and their dependent children, living apart from other relatives. [6]The nuclear family occurs in some preindustrial societies and is the usual type in virtually all modern industrialized societies. [7]In fact, the growing dominance of the nuclear family is transforming family life all over the world.

    A. There are two types of families. In the extended family, in which more than two generations of family live together, the head of the family is the eldest male and all adults share in family tasks. This type of family is common in preindustrial societies.

    B. There are various types of families. The nuclear family is the most common among modern industrialized societies. The dominance of the nuclear family is transforming family life worldwide.

    C. An extended family consists of two generations of family living together. A nuclear family consists of parents and their dependent children. It occurs in some preindustrial societies and is the usual type of family in just about all modern industrialized societies.

    D. There are two basic types of families. The extended family, which is more than two generations living together, is common in preindustrial societies. The nuclear family, made up of parents and their dependent children, is usual in modern industrialized societies.

UNDERSTANDING OUTLINES

Very often a good way to summarize something is to outline it first. An **outline** is itself a summary in which numbers and letters are often used to set off the main idea and the supporting details of a selection. For example, the passage on page 568 about controlling anger could have been outlined as follows:

Psychologists suggest several ways to control anger.
1. Sense of humor
2. Physical exercise
3. Relaxation exercises

Outlines and visual outlines, called maps, are described in this book on pages 95–102.

Important Points about Outlining

1 Both outlines and summaries are excellent thinking tools that will help you with all your reading and study assignments. Both demand that you work to identify the main idea of a selection and to understand the relationship between it and the major details that develop the idea. *The very act of outlining or summarizing will help you understand and master the material.*

2 With class lecture notes and textbook reading assignments in particular, outlines and summaries are excellent review materials. Studying an outline or a summary is easier and more productive than repeated rereading of an entire set of notes or entire text chapters. Following are tips for outlining and summarizing textbook material, with practice activities.

OUTLINING AND SUMMARIZING A TEXTBOOK CHAPTER

I will never forget two early college courses for which I had to read and study a great deal of material. For a history course and an introductory psychology course, I had teachers who lectured a great deal in class. I typically filled up ten or so notebook pages per class, leaving my head spinning and my hand cramped. I remember using up several Bic pens that semester. Besides having to know the lecture material, students were also responsible for textbook chapters not covered in class.

Several weeks into the semester, I sat down on a Saturday to study for my first psychology exam. With all the class material to cover, I knew I would have to study very efficiently, getting as much out of my time as possible. I spent most of the day reading three required textbook chapters, and that same evening I started to study the chapters. After about two hours of work I had reread and studied the material on the first four pages of the first chapter; I still had almost ninety-two pages to go. I also had a pile of lecture notes to study.

When I realized my problem, I just sat at my desk for a while, wondering what to do. It was then that my roommate, who himself faced a mountain of material to study, suggested we order a pizza. I quickly agreed. I felt like a dying man, so I figured it wouldn't hurt to have a last meal. But the pizza went down in heavy lumps. I knew my days in college were numbered unless I came up with a system for organizing and condensing all the material I had to study.

Here in a nutshell is what I learned to do with the chapters in my psychology book (I used a similar system with my extensive lecture notes):

1   I previewed and read each chapter, marking off all the definitions of key terms, along with an example in each case that made each definition clear for me. Specifically, I would put *DEF* in the margin for a definition and *EX* in the margin for an example. I also numbered *1, 2, 3* . . . major lists of items—especially lists in which a series of subheadings fit logically under a main heading.

2   Then I outlined the material, making sure that basic relationships were clear. I did this mainly by looking for relationships between main headings and subheadings within each chapter. For instance, one of the headings in the first chapter was "Methods of Psychology." I wrote down that heading and then wrote down and numbered all the subheadings that fit under it:

> *Methods of Psychology*
> *1. Naturalistic-Observation Method*
> *2. Experimental Method*
> *3. Correlational Method*

3   As part of my outline, I wrote down the definitions and examples. For example, I wrote down each method of psychology, and an example of the method. I also wrote down what seemed to be other important details about each method.

4   Then I recorded the next main heading and the subheadings under it. In cases where there were no subheadings, I tried to convert the heading into a basic question and answer the question. For example, one heading in my psychology

text chapter was "The Social Relevance of Psychology." I turned that into the question "What *is* the social relevance of psychology?" and then wrote a summary of the textbook author's answer to that question. When I was done, I had reduced thirty-two pages in the textbook chapter down to three pages of notes. I had, in effect, used a combination of outlining and summarizing to condense a large amount of information down to its most important points.

In a nutshell, then, my study method was as follows. First, I previewed and read all the material through once, marking off definitions and examples and numbering major lists of items. Then I took notes on the material by writing down definitions and examples and major lists of items. I also asked basic questions about the headings and wrote down condensed answers to those questions. Finally, I concentrated on studying my notes, testing myself on them until I could recite the material without looking at it. With my systematic preparation, I managed to score a low B on that test, and as I became better at outlining and summarizing, my scores on later tests were even better.

To get a sense of how to outline and summarize textbook material, read the following passage. Then circle the letter—A, B, or C—of the notes that most accurately reflect the content of the passage.

[1]Anxiety becomes a disorder when fears, ideas, and impulses are exaggerated or unrealistic. [2]A person suffering from *anxiety disorder* often has such physical symptoms as sweating, shaking, shortness of breath, and a fast heartbeat. [3]*Phobias,* the most common form of anxiety disorder, are continuing unrealistic fears that interfere with normal living. [4]For instance, instead of fearing only threatening animals, a phobic person may fear all animals, even those that are docile and friendly. [5]People with this phobia may panic at the sight of a harmless snake or mouse.

[6]Eating problems are another form of anxiety disorder. [7]One eating disorder, *anorexia nervosa,* generally begins when young girls grow anxious about becoming overweight. [8]Although they initially want to eat, they eventually completely lose their desire for food. [9]They diet continually, even when they are so underweight that their lives are threatened. [10]The sight of food makes them nauseated. [11]In a related disorder, *bulimia,* the person goes on eating binges and then uses laxatives or vomits to purge herself. [12]Bulimia is believed to be most common among college-age women.

[13]There are also obsessive-compulsive anxiety disorders. [14]*Obsessions* are persistent ideas or impulses that invade people's minds against their will and cannot be gotten rid of by reasoning. [15]One common obsession is an intense fear of germs. [16]Someone with this obsession refuses to shake hands or otherwise come into contact with others. [17]Obsessions often lead to *compulsions,* which are persistent behaviors. [18]Feeling they are never clean, for instance, people obsessed with fears of contamination may become compulsive about hand-washing.

A.   Anxiety disorder—an exaggerated or unrealistic fear, idea, or impulse, often with physical symptoms such as shaking or fast heartbeat.

Types:
1. Phobias—unrealistic fears that interfere with daily living, such as fear of a harmless animal
2. Eating disorders—unrealistic fear of gaining weight
    a. Anorexia nervosa—loss of desire for food
    b. Bulimia—eating binges followed by purging
3. Obsessive-compulsive disorders—exaggerated, unrealistic ideas and impulses
    a. Obsession—persistent idea, such as fear of being contaminated by germs
    b. Compulsion—persistent behavior, such as constant hand-washing

B.   Anxiety disorder—often includes physical symptoms such as sweating, shaking, shortness of breath, and a fast heartbeat

Types:
1. Phobias—fears that interfere with daily living
2. Anorexia nervosa—loss of desire for food
3. Bulimia—eating binges followed by purging
4. Obsession—persistent idea, such as fear of being contaminated by germs
5. Compulsion—persistent behavior, such as constant hand-washing

C.   Anxiety disorder—an exaggerated or unrealistic fear, idea, or impulse, often with physical symptoms such as shaking or fast heartbeat

Types:
1. Phobias
    a. Fears that interfere with daily living, such as fear of a harmless animal
    b. Anorexia nervosa—loss of desire for food
    c. Bulimia—eating binges followed by purging
2. Obsessive-compulsive disorders
    a. Obsession—persistent idea, such as fear of being contaminated by germs
    b. Compulsions—persistent behavior, such as constant hand-washing

To find the best of the three sets of notes, you must do the same thing you would do if you were outlining the passage yourself—identify the main idea and major and minor details. A careful reading of the passage reveals that the main idea of the passage is: "There are various types of anxiety disorders, which are exaggerated or unrealistic fears, ideas, and impulses that often cause such physical symptoms as sweating, shaking, shortness of breath." The major details are the three types of anxiety disorder listed: phobias, eating disorders, and obsessive-compulsive disorders. Thus the outline that best reflects the passage will define and explain *anxiety disorders* and then go on to name and explain the three types listed.

Having analyzed the passage, let's turn to the sets of notes above. Set A defines and explains *anxiety disorder* and goes on to list and explain the three types of anxiety disorder. The important minor details have been listed as well. Set A, then, is a pretty good condensation of the passage.

In contrast, set B does not account for two of the major-detail categories: eating disorders and obsessive-compulsive disorders. In set C, the category of eating disorders has been skipped, and anorexia nervosa and bulimia are incorrectly identified as phobias.

➤ Practice 3

Read each of the selections that follow. Then write the letter of the notes that best outline and summarize the material in each selection.

_____ 1. ¹Erik Erikson divided adulthood into three stages. ²In his view the central task of the first stage, young adulthood, is that of achieving *intimacy*. ³The young person who has a firm sense of identity is eager and able to fuse his or her identity with another person's in a loving relationship, without fear of competition or loss of self. ⁴A young person who avoids commitment may experience isolation. ⁵In middle age, personal and social concerns merge. ⁶Adults who feel they have contributed something of value to society and who are involved in guiding the next generation (as parents or in other roles) experience *generativity*. ⁶Those who do not experience stagnation—the sense of going nowhere, doing nothing important. ⁷Generativity lays the foundation for *integrity* in old age, a sense of a life well lived. ⁸Older people who have achieved integrity are satisfied with the choices they made and feel that had they a second life to live, they would "do it all over again." ⁹They see death as the final stop in a meaningful journey.

A. Erikson's three stages of adulthood
  1. Intimacy—a fusion with another in a loving relationship
  2. Generativity—feeling of contributing something of value
  3. Integrity—a sense of a life well lived

B. Erikson's stages of adulthood
  1. Intimacy
  2. Isolation
  3. Generativity
  4. Stagnation
  5. Integrity

C. Erikson's stages of adulthood
  1. Young adulthood
     — intimacy achieved in a loving relationship
     — avoidance of commitment may result in isolation

2. Middle age
— generativity achieved by those contributing to society and guiding the young
— stagnation experienced by those who don't contribute
3. Old age—integrity achieved through a sense of a life well lived

_____ 2. [1]Across the life span we find ourselves immersed in countless relationships. [2]Few are more important to us than those we have with our **peers**—individuals who are approximately the same age. [3]Peer groups serve a variety of functions. [4]First, they provide an arena in which children can exercise independence from adult controls. [5]Next, peer groups give children experience with relationships in which they are on an equal footing with others. [6]In the adult world, in contrast, children occupy the position of subordinates, with adults directing, guiding, and controlling their activities. [7]Third, peer groups afford a social sphere in which the position of children is not marginal. [8]In them, youngsters can acquire status and achieve an identity in which their own activities and concerns are paramount. [9]And last, peer groups are agencies for the transmission of informal knowledge, sexual information, deviant behaviors, superstitions, folklore, fads, jokes, riddles, and games. [10]Peers are as necessary to children's development as adults are; the complexity of social life requires that children be involved in networks both of adults and of peers.

A. Children need relationships with both adults and peers.
1. Peer groups provide an arena in which children exercise independence from adult controls.
2. Peer groups provide adolescents with an impetus to seek greater freedom.
3. Peer groups give children experience with relationships in which they are on an equal footing with others.
4. Adult-child relationships allow adults to direct, guide, and control children's activities.
5. Peer groups provide a social sphere in which children don't have a marginal position.
6. Peer groups transmit informal knowledge.

B. Peer groups, made up of individuals who are about the same age, serve various functions.
1. Provide an arena in which children can exercise independence from adult controls
2. Give children experience of being on an equal footing with others, allowing for experiences different from adult-child relationships
3. Provide a social sphere in which children don't have a marginal position
4. Transmit useful knowledge

C. Across the life span we find ourselves immersed in countless relationships.
  1. Peer relationships—with individuals who are approximately the same age
  2. Adolescent-adult relationships
  3. Adult-child relationships
  4. Networks of both adults and peers

_____ 3. [1]Our capacity to learn from watching as well as from doing means that the mass media have important socialization consequences for us. [2]The mass media are those organizations—television, radio, motion pictures, newspapers, and magazines—that convey information to a large segment of the public. [3]All the mass media educate. [4]The question is: What are they teaching? [5]The good news from research is that prosocial (positive and helpful) models can have prosocial effects. [6]Children who view a prosocial television diet, including such programs as *Sesame Street* and *Mister Rogers' Neighborhood*, exhibit greater levels of helping behaviors, cooperation, sharing, and self-control than children who view a neutral or violent diet. [7]Moreover, these programs have a positive effect on language development.

[8]The bad news from television research is that there is a link between the mayhem and violence in children's programs and aggressive behavior in children. [9]Although televised violence does not harm every child who watches it, many children imitate the violent attitudes and behaviors they see. [10]Prime-time programs depict about five violent acts per hour, and Saturday morning cartoons average twenty to twenty-five violent acts per hour. [11]By the time most young people leave high school, they have spent more time before a television screen than in the classroom. [12]In the process they will have witnessed some 13,000 murders. [13]Television not only provides opportunities for children and adults to learn new aggressive skills; it also weakens the inhibitions against behaving in the same way. [14]And television violence increases the toleration of aggression in real life—a "psychic numbing" effect—and reinforces the tendency to view the world as a dangerous place.

A. The mass media have important socialization consequences for us.
  1. The mass media convey information to a large segment of the public.
     a. television
     b. radio
     c. motion pictures
     d. newspapers
     e. magazines
  2. TV research reveals a link between TV violence and aggressive behavior in children.
     a. Violence on TV makes children more aggressive and violent.
     b. TV violence increases toleration of real-life aggression.
     c. TV violence reinforces the tendency to view the world as a dangerous place.

B. The mass media influence the public.
  1. Researchers have found positive influences.
     a. Prosocial models can have prosocial effects.
     b. Children's programs help language development.
  2. Researchers have found negative influences.
     a. Violence on TV makes children more aggressive and violent.
     b. TV violence increases toleration of real-life aggression.
     c. TV violence reinforces the tendency to view the world as a dangerous place.

C. The mass media influence the public.
  1. Prosocial models can have prosocial effects.
     — Programs such as *Sesame Street* and *Mister Rogers' Neighborhood* encourage helping behavior in children who watch.
  2. Children's programs help language development.
  3. Prime-time programs depict about five acts of violence an hour.
  4. TV violence increases toleration of real-life aggression.
     — By the end of high school, more young people have spent more time before a TV than in the classroom.
  5. TV violence reinforces the tendency to view the world as a dangerous place.
     — By high school, children will have witnessed some 13,000 murders on TV.

➤ *Review Test 1*

To review what you've learned in this chapter, answer the following questions.

1. Summarizing is a way to (*predict, outline, condense*) _____ material.

2. A summary will always include (*the main idea, all the major details, several minor details*) _____.

_____ 3. TRUE OR FALSE? The author's study method included reading through all the material, marking off definitions and examples and lists of items.

_____ 4. TRUE OR FALSE? One note-taking step that the author does **not** recommend is turning textbook headings into questions and summarizing in notes the answers to the questions.

_____ 5. TRUE OR FALSE? Writing an outline can be a helpful step toward writing a summary.

➤ *Review Test 2*

A. Carefully read each opening statement (set off in **boldface**). Then decide whether each numbered statement that follows is basically the same in meaning or basically different in meaning from the opening statement. Write *S* (for *Same*) next to the **two** statements where the meaning is closest to the original statement.

1–2. **Adults who were mistreated as children have a greater tendency to be violent than those who were not mistreated.**

_____ 1. Children should never be yelled at.

_____ 2. Children who are mistreated have little choice but to become violent adults.

_____ 3. Violent adults tend to be people who were mistreated as children.

_____ 4. The tendency toward violence, while powerful, can be controlled.

_____ 5. A mistreated child is more likely to become a violent adult than is a child who is not mistreated.

_____ 6. We could overcome the problem of violence in our society if only we tried harder.

3–4. **Compensation is stressing a strength in one area to hide a shortcoming in another.**

_____ 1. We need to defend ourselves against people who try to make their weaknesses less noticeable than their strengths.

_____ 2. Compensation involves having strengths and shortcomings in about equal amounts.

_____ 3. Compensation cannot turn a shortcoming into a strength.

_____ 4. In order to hide a personal flaw, we may emphasize one of our strengths; this is called compensation.

_____ 5. There are various ways in which we can conceal our weak points and emphasize our strong points.

_____ 6. We are said to be using compensation when we emphasize a strength of ours in order to hide a defect.

5–6. **Tension headache, a condition common among people who suppress their emotions (and thus build up tension in their bodies), is usually caused by a tightening of the muscles of the head and neck.**

_____ 1. Headaches of all kinds are caused by the tightening of muscles in the head and neck, a common symptom among people who suppress their emotions.

_____ 2. Learning to relax will not affect the pain of a tension headache.

_____ 3. People who suffer from tension headaches tend to have very aggressive personalities.

_____ 4. Tension headaches are usually caused by tight head and neck muscles, common among those who hold back their emotions and thus tighten their muscles.

_____ 5. When people bottle up their emotions, the stress they feel tends to tighten the muscles in their heads and necks.

_____ 6. Tension headaches usually have a physical cause—tight head and neck muscles. That muscle tightness, in turn, has a psychological cause—the restraining of emotions.

B. (7.) Circle the letter of the answer that best summarizes the selection that follows.

[1]Of all major ethnic groups in the United States, Japanese Americans are most economically successful. [2]There seem to be two major factors involved in the Japanese American "success story." [3]The first factor is educational achievement. [4]On the average, both male and female Japanese Americans complete more years of schooling than the general population. [5]For example, while 13 percent of all U.S. males complete college, 19 percent of Japanese American males do. [6]The second factor that helps explain Japanese Americans' economic success is their assimilation into the larger society. [7]Their high intermarriage rate is evidence of that assimilation. [8]About 40 percent of third-generation Japanese. Americans marry non-Japanese Americans. [9]Such merging into mainstream culture helps ensure that the doors of economic opportunity swing open for many Japanese Americans.

A. Because of their high assimilation rate, Japanese Americans are the most economically successful of all major ethnic groups in the United States. Their high intermarriage rate is evidence of their assimilation.

B. Of all major ethnic groups in the United States, Japanese Americans are the most economically successful.

C. While 13 percent of all U.S. males complete college, 19 percent of Japanese American males do.

D. Japanese Americans are the most economically successful of all major ethnic groups in the United States because of their high level of educational achievement and their high rate of assimilation into the larger society.

C. (8.) Circle the letter of the outline notes that best summarize the selection that follows.

> According to Margaret Mead, children typically pass through three stages in developing a self: an imitation stage, a play stage, and a game stage. In the first stage, children imitate other people without understanding what they are doing. They may "read" a book, but the behavior lacks meaning for them. Even so, such imitation is important because children are preparing themselves to take the stance of others and act as others do. In the play stage, children act such roles as mother, police officer, teacher, Mrs. Elliot, and so on. They take the role of only one other person at a time and "try on" the person's behavior. The model, typically a person central to the child's life, is termed by sociologists a significant other. For instance, a two-year-old child may examine a doll's pants, pretend to find them wet, and reprimand the doll. Presumably the child views the situation from the perspective of the parent and acts as the parent would act.
>
> Whereas in the play stage children take the role of only one other person at a time, in the game stage they assume many roles. Much as in a baseball game, a person must take into account the intentions and expectations of several people. For instance, if the batter bunts the ball down the third-base line, the pitcher must know what the catcher, the shortstop, and the first, second, and, third basemen will do. In the game, children must assume the roles of numerous individuals in contrast to simply the role of one other person. To do so, they must abstract a "composite" role out of the concrete roles of particular people. These notions are extended to embrace all people in similar situations—the "team." In other words, children fashion a generalized other—they come to view their behavior from the standpoint of the larger group or community.

A. Margaret Mead's stages of child self-development
   1. Imitation stage—imitating others' behavior that has no meaning for child
   2. Preparation for the mature attitude and behavior of others
   3. Play stage—acting the role of one other person at a time

4. "Trying on" the behavior of a significant other
5. Game stage—assuming and taking into account many roles
6. Viewing one's behavior from the standpoint of a larger group or community

B. How children develop
1. They prepare themselves to take the stance of others and act as others do.
2. They take the role of only one other person at a time and "try on" the person's behavior.
3. They assume many roles.

C. Margaret Mead's view of child self-development: three stages
1. Imitation stage—imitating behavior that has no meaning for child
   — Function: preparation for the mature attitude and behavior of others
   — Example: a child "reads" a book
2. Play stage—acting the role of one other person at a time
   — Function: "Trying on" the behavior of a significant other
   — Examples: Acting like mother, police officer, teacher
3. Game stage—assuming and taking into account many roles
   — Function: viewing one's behavior from the standpoint of a larger group or community
   — Example: baseball pitcher interacting with other team members

➤ Review Test 3

A. Carefully read each opening statement (set off in **boldface**). Then decide whether each numbered statement that follows is basically the same in meaning or basically different in meaning from the opening statement. Write *S* (for *Same*) next to the **two** statements where the meaning is closest to the original statement.

1–2. **People are comfortable making statements of fact and opinion, but they rarely disclose their feelings.**

_____ 1. People are less comfortable about conveying their feelings than they are about expressing facts and opinions.

_____ 2. Facts and opinions are far more reliable predictors of people's actions than feelings are.

_____ 3. As people get to know one another better, they talk less in terms of facts and opinions and more in terms of feelings.

_____ 4. It is easier for people to talk about emotions than to discuss facts and opinions.

_____ 5. People who keep their emotions bottled up tend to be very opinionated.

_____ 6. People rarely express how they feel, being much more comfortable expressing facts and opinions.

3–4. **A self-fulfilling prophecy is one that comes true because someone's expectations of an event have helped to bring it about.**

_____ 1. If a person believes strongly that a certain event is going to happen, he or she may actually influence that event to occur. Such a belief, or prediction, is known as a self-fulfilling prophecy.

_____ 2. The idea of the self-fulfilling prophecy is based upon a person's certain knowledge ahead of time of how a situation will end.

_____ 3. A situation is more likely to end well if a person gets help from others in achieving that desired end.

_____ 4. People only imagine that they have any influence over most situations.

_____ 5. When people act in ways that cause a situation to end in the manner they expect, their expectation becomes a self-fulfilling prophecy.

_____ 6. A person's expectations of an event cannot change its outcome, but they may change the person's perception of that outcome.

5–6. **If only there were evil people somewhere treacherously committing evil deeds, we could separate them from the rest of us and destroy them; but the line dividing good and evil cuts through the heart of every human being.**

_____ 1. People who appear to be good are in reality only hiding the evil that they have done.

_____ 2. Since every human being has the potential to do good and evil, we can't get rid of evil simply by getting rid of all the so-called evil people.

_____ 3. Because the world is not divided between good people and evil people, there's no way to identify and eliminate the evil ones; rather, all people are made up of both good and evil.

_____ 4. Evil people look so much like the rest of us that it is impossible to identify them.

_____ 5. Destroying the evil people in the world would make life much safer for the rest of us.

_____ 6. Some people have nothing but good in their hearts; some people are entirely evil.

B. (7.) Circle the letter of the answer that best summarizes the selection that follows.

[1]Money does not guarantee victory, but it does guarantee the *opportunity* for victory. [2]Without good financing, potential candidates do not become candidates. [3]With good financing, potential candidates can hire consultants—media experts, pollsters, direct mailing specialists, voice coaches, statisticians, speech writers, and make-up artists—to give their campaigns appeal. [4]Not only do the consultants charge a lot (perhaps $250 per hour), but the technology they employ—computers, interviews, and television—is costly. [5]Because consultants need success in order to build their reputations, they too shun underfunded candidates. [6]One student of consulting concludes that "you need $150,000 just to get in the door to see a consultant."

[7]Indeed, consultants are far more important to candidates than are political parties. [8]Not only have they usurped the role of parties in the campaign (volunteer doorbell ringers are fast becoming a relic of the past), but they also encourage candidates to de-emphasize issues and concentrate on image. [9]The "three p's"—polling, packaging, and promotion—are more important than parties, grassroots support, and the development of strong positions on the issues.

A. Political candidates require good financing for various expenses. Money buys candidates such consultants as media experts, pollsters, direct mailing specialists, voice coaches, statisticians, speech writers and make-up artists.

B. Today's political candidates require money to hire expensive consultants and the technology they use, including computers, interviews, and television. Consultants' emphasis on "polling, packaging, and promotion" has reduced the importance of parties, grassroots support, and strong positions on the issues.

C. Today's political campaigns are a fraud. They require the candidates to shun genuine grassroots support and strong positions in favor of know-nothing, high-tech media consultants and expensive surveys. The consultants themselves care more about building their reputations than they do about electing qualified candidates.

D. Political parties are far less important today than ever. Owing to the influence of consultants and the demands of media-centered campaigns, candidates de-emphasize issues and concentrate on image. "Polling, packaging, and promotion" have become more important than parties, grassroots support, and strong positions on the issues.

C. (8.) Circle the letter of the outline notes that best summarize the selection that follows.

> [1]The autonomic nervous system is composed of all the neurons that carry messages between the central nervous system and all the internal organs of the body. [2]The autonomic nervous system consists of two branches: the sympathetic and parasympathetic divisions. [3]These two divisions act in almost total opposition to each other, but both are directly involved in controlling and integrating the actions of the glands and the smooth muscles within the body.
>
> [4]The nerve fibers of the sympathetic division are busiest when you are frightened or angry. [5]They carry messages that tell the body to prepare for an emergency and to get ready to act quickly or strenuously. [6]In response to messages from the sympathetic division, your heart pounds, you breathe faster, your pupils enlarge, and digestion stops.
>
> [7]Parasympathetic nerve fibers connect to the same organs as the sympathetic nerve fibers, but they cause just the opposite effects. [8]The parasympathetic division says, in effect, "Okay, the heat's off, back to normal." [9]The heart then goes back to beating at its normal rate, the stomach muscles relax, digestion starts again, breathing slows down, and the pupils of the eyes get smaller. [10]Thus, the parasympathetic division compensates for the sympathetic division and lets the body rest after stress.

A. The body's response to emergencies: the sympathetic division and the parasympathetic division
   1. Function: prepares body for emergency when someone is frightened or angry
   2. Physical responses: pounding heart, faster breathing, enlarged pupils, halted digestion
   3. After the emergency: the parasympathetic division
      a. Function: normalizes the body after an emergency
      b. Physical responses: return to normal heart rate, relaxed stomach muscles, resumed digestion, normalized breathing, reduced pupil size

B. The autonomic nervous system: two-branched system that controls and integrates the work of the glands and smooth muscles through neurons carrying messages between the central nervous system and all the internal organs
1. Sympathetic division
a. Function: prepares body for emergency when someone is frightened or angry
b. Physical responses: pounding heart, faster breathing, enlarged pupils, halted digestion
2. Parasympathetic division
a. Function: normalizes the body after an emergency
b. Physical responses: return to normal heart rate, relaxed stomach muscles, resumed digestion, normalized breathing, reduced pupil size

C. The sympathetic division of the autonomic nervous system prepares the body for emergencies when the person is frightened or angry.
1. When someone is frightened or angry, the nerve fibers are busiest; they then carry messages.
a. This prepares the body for an emergency.
b. This prepares the body to act quickly or strenuously.
c. In response, your body changes in various ways.
1) Your heart pounds.
2) You breathe faster.
3) Your pupils enlarge.
4) Your digestion stops.
2. After the emergency, the parasympathetic division causes the body to relax.
a. Your heartbeat normalizes.
b. Your breathing slows down.
c. Your pupils get smaller.
d. The stomach muscles relax.

Check Your Performance	**SUMMARIZING AND OUTLINING**		
Activity	*Number Right*	*Points*	*Score*
Review Test 1 (5 items)	_____	× 4 =	_____
Review Test 2 (8 items)	_____	× 5 =	_____
Review Test 3 (8 items)	_____	× 5 =	_____
	TOTAL SCORE	=	_____ %

3

Five Additional Readings

The five short selections that follow come from a variety of current college texts. Using the skills you have learned in this book, see if you can take notes on the important ideas in each selection.

WHY DO MOST MOTHERS CRADLE THEIR BABIES IN THEIR LEFT ARMS?

Desmond Morris

1   One of the strangest features of motherhood is that the vast majority of mothers prefer to cradle their babies in their left arms. Why should this be? The obvious explanation is that the majority of mothers are right-handed and they wish to keep their right hands free. Unfortunately, this explanation cannot apply, because left-handed mothers also favor their left arms for holding their babies. The precise figures are: 83 percent for right-handed and 78 percent for left-handed mothers.

2   The most likely explanation is that the mother's heart is on the left side, and, by holding the baby in her left arm, she is unconsciously bringing her infant closer to the sound of the heartbeat. This is the sound which the baby heard when it was inside the mother's womb and which is therefore associated with peace, comfort, and security.

3   Tests were carried out in nurseries where some babies were played the recorded sound of a human heartbeat and, sure enough, those babies were lulled off to sleep twice as quickly as the others. We also know that the sound of the mother's heart is quite audible inside the womb and that the unborn baby has well-developed hearing. The constant dull thud of the heart, beating so close to the fetus, second by second, must become the single most intrusive message from the outside world that a fetus can experience. So it is little wonder that traces of this imprinting appear later on, in babyhood.

4   It is interesting that fathers show less of this left-side bias than mothers, suggesting that the human female is better programmed for baby-carrying than her partner. Alternatively, she may be more sensitive to the mood of her baby and unconsciously adjusts her holding behavior to make her baby feel more secure.

5   Some new observations on our closest animal relatives, the chimpanzees and gorillas, have revealed that they too show a strong bias for left-side holding of their babies. The precise figures were 84 percent for chimpanzees and 82 percent for gorillas, remarkably close to the human percentage. Significantly, these apes do not show the strong right-handedness of the human species when using implements, which confirms the fact that left-holding has nothing to do with having a dominant right hand.

6   Recently a possible additional value in cradling babies on the left side has been suggested. It has been pointed out that, because the two sides of the brain are concerned with different aspects of behavior, it is possible that the mother, in cradling the baby to her left, is showing the baby her "best side." It is claimed that emotions are more strongly expressed on the left side of the human face and that she therefore gives the baby a better chance to read her emotional mood changes, as it gazes up at her. Furthermore, the mother's left eye and ear are more tuned in to emotional changes in her baby than her right eye and ear would be. So in addition to the baby's seeing the more expressive part of its mother, there is the further advantage that the mother herself is more sensitive to the left-held baby. This may sound far-fetched, but it is just possible that it could provide a slight extra benefit for those mothers displaying the strange one-sided bias when cradling their infants.

7   How does the bias occur? Do the mothers have an instinctive preference for it, or do they learn it by trial and error, unconsciously adjusting the position of the baby until the baby is calmer? The surprising answer is that it seems to be the baby and not the mother who controls the bias. Observations of newborn infants when they were only a few hours old revealed that they come into the world with a preprogrammed tendency to turn their heads to the right. If the newborn's head is gently held in a dead central position and then released, it naturally swings to the right far more often than to the left. This happens in nearly 70 percent of babies. It means that when the mother goes to feed her infant, she finds its head more likely to turn that way, and this may well influence her decision concerning which side is best for it. If it prefers turning its head to the right it will, of course, feel more at ease when it is held in the crook of her left arm. This will bring mother and baby more "face to face." This may be only part of the explanation because the holding bias is 80 percent and not 70 percent, but it adds a further intriguing chapter to the story.

LABELING AND THE ONSET OF OLD AGE

James M. Henslin

1   You probably can remember when you thought a twelve-year-old was "old"—and anyone older beyond reckoning, just "up there" someplace. You probably were 5 or 6 at the time. Similarly, to a twelve-year-old someone 21 seems "old." At 21, 30 may mark that line, and 40 may seem "very old." And so it keeps on going, with "old" gradually receding from the self. To people who turn 40, 50 seems old; at 50, the late 60s look old (not the early 60s, for at that point in accelerating years they don't seem too far away).

2   At some point, of course, an individual must apply the label "old" to himself or herself. Often, cultural definitions of age force this label on people sooner then they are ready to accept it. In the typical case, the individual has become used to what he or she sees in the mirror. The changes have taken place very gradually, and each change, if not exactly taken in stride, has been accommodated. (Consequently, it comes as a shock, when meeting a friend one has not seen in years, to see how much that person has changed. At class reunions, each person can hardly believe how much older the others appear!)

3   If there is no single point at which people automatically cross a magical line and become "old," what, then, makes someone "old"? We can point to several factors that spur people to apply the label of old to themselves.

4   The first factor is biology. One person may experience "signs" of aging much earlier than another: wrinkles, balding, aches, difficulty in doing some things that he or she used to take for granted. Consequently, one person will feel "old" at an earlier or later age than others, and only at that time adopt the rules of an "old person," that is, begin to act in ways old people in that particular society are thought to act.

5   Personal history or biography is a second factor that influences when people consider themselves old. An accident that limits mobility may make one person feel old sooner than others. Or a woman may have given birth at 16 to a daughter, who in turn has a child at 18. When this woman is 34, she is a biological grandmother. It is more unlikely that she will begin to play any stereotypical role—spending the day in a rocking chair, for example—but knowing that she is a grandmother has an impact on her self-concept. At a minimum, she must deny that she is old.

6   A third factor in determining when people label themselves old is gender age, the relative value that a culture places on men's and women's ages. For example, around the world, compared with most women, most men are able to marry much younger spouses. Similarly, on men graying hair and even some wrinkles may be signs of "maturing," while on women those same features are likely to be interpreted as signs of "old." "Mature" and "old," of course, carry quite different meanings in Western cultures—the first is desired, while the second is shunned. Two striking examples of gender age in U.S. society are found in the mass media. Older male news anchors are likely to be retained,

while female anchors who turn the same age are more likely to be transferred to a less visible position. Similarly, in movies older men are much more likely to play romantic leads—and opposite much younger rising stars.

7 Many individuals, of course, are exceptions to these patterns. Maria, for example, may marry Bill, who is fourteen years younger than she. But in most marriages in which there is a fourteen-year age gap between husband and wife, around the world the odds greatly favor the wife's being the younger of the pair. Biology, of course, has nothing to do with this socially constructed reality.

8 The fourth factor is timetables, the signals societies use to inform their members that they are old. Since there is no automatic age at which people become "old," these timetables vary around the world. One group may choose a particular birthday, such as the sixtieth or the sixty-fifth, to signal the onset of old age. Other groups may not even have birthdays, making such numbers meaningless. Only after they moved to the reservations, for example, did Native Americans adopt the white custom of counting birthdays. For traditional Native Americans, the signal for old age is more the inability to perform productive social roles than any particular birthday. Consequently, those unable to continue in these roles tend to think of themselves as old, regardless of their age. In one survey, for instance. a Native American woman with many disabilities described herself as elderly, although she was only 37.

NONVERBAL COMMUNICATION

Michael W. Drafke and Stan Kossen

1   Nonverbal communication accounts for 55 percent of the total message we can deliver. It is so powerful that when the verbal and tonal portions conflict with the nonverbal portion, people believe the nonverbal message. This reinforces the old saying "Actions speak louder than words." The following section investigates the details of nonverbal communication.

THE BODY SPEAKS

2   Whether you realize it consciously or not, you're communicating each time you make a gesture or glance at a person. The motions people make with their body (or sometimes don't make) often communicate messages. Body language isn't always accurate or effective, but it is communication nonetheless. For example, assume that after you arrive at your job one morning, you pass a coworker in the hallway who gives you an unusual glance or at least a glance that appears to you to be strange. You might wonder for the rest of the day what that glance meant. Some employees seldom greet others that they pass in hallways or work areas. Instead, their faces seem frozen. Sometimes a person might think that a frozen stare is an indication of displeasure.

3   Once again, a word of warning: Some people are misled by body language. We already are aware that we have plenty of difficulties interpreting correctly the verbal symbols of others, even when we've had training in listening. We can also be easily misled by body language. For example, your listener's crossed arms may not necessarily mean a lack of receptivity to your message. Instead, it could merely mean that the person feels cold.

FUNCTIONS OF NONVERBAL COMMUNICATION

4   Nonverbal communication (NVC) has five basic functions. Nonverbal communication can accent, complement, contradict, regulate, or substitute for verbal communication.

5   When nonverbal communications punctuate verbal communications, the NVC is performing an **accenting** role. Poking a finger into someone's chest is an example of accenting. Punctuating a message with a sweeping motion of the hand at chest level with the palm facing out says that the conversation is over.

6   **Complementing** nonverbal communications reinforce the spoken message; complementing NVC would not convey the same message if used alone. The distance between two people is an example of complementing NVC. Standing four feet away from someone might indicate that this person is a stranger. When the person is your boss and you are four feet away and you present her with a formal salutation ("Good morning, Ms. Smith"), then the distance reinforces the message that the boss is of higher rank and the two of you have an unchallenged authority relationship.

7   Of the more interesting nonverbal communications are those that contradict the verbal message. **Contradicting** NVCs convey messages that are opposite to the

verbal messages. Often this is the way people reveal their true feelings or send the wrong or an unintended message. Even though people say that they are paying attention, if they give less eye contact than they receive (that is, if they look off into the distance rather than at the speaker), they send a contradicting nonverbal message. The message they send is that they are bored or uninterested. When verbal and nonverbal messages conflict, people believe the *nonverbal* ones.

8   A **regulating** nonverbal communication controls the course of a conversation. Raising your hand with the index finger extended indicates that you want the other person to wait a minute or to stop speaking. Tapping a coworker's shoulder twice with your index finger while she is walking away from you indicates that you want her to stop or to wait for you so you can speak to her. Touching someone's arm while he speaks also performs a regulating function by indicating to him that you wish to speak.

9   We use **substituting** nonverbal communications to replace a verbal message. This use is quite common because sometimes it is not practical or politically wise to state out loud what we are thinking. When two people are in a hurry and pass in a busy hall, they may not have the time to speak to one another, or the crowd may be too large for a spoken word to be heard unless one shouts. Instead, we often substitute an "eyebrow flash" for a spoken "How you doin', Fred?" We can't talk, but we don't want to be rude to our colleague, so we raise both eyebrows as a silent, substitute salutation. Or you may be standing behind a boss who comes down hard on a coworker for a minor transgression. It would not be politically smart to disagree verbally with this boss, but you also want to let your coworker know that you think the boss is going too far. So you shake your head back and forth in a silent "no" that is unseen by the boss.

10   Although there are just five functions of nonverbal communications, there are many types and hundreds of examples of these types. Most nonverbal messages are learned automatically, but it is still important to study them, for although many are innate, one can accidentally send an incorrect or overly revealing nonverbal message if one is not knowledgeable and careful.

IS AGGRESSION A RESPONSE TO FRUSTRATION?

David G. Myers

1   It is a warm evening. Tired and thirsty after two hours of studying, you borrow some change from a friend and head for the nearest soft-drink machine. As the machine devours the change, you can almost taste the cold, refreshing cola. But when you push the button, nothing happens. You push it again. Then you flip the coin return button. Still nothing. Again, you hit the buttons. You slam them. And finally you shake and whack the machine. You stomp back to your studies, empty-handed and short-changed. Should your roommate beware? Are you now more likely to say or do something hurtful?

2   One of the first psychological theories of aggression, the popular frustration-aggression theory, answers yes. "Frustration always leads to some form of aggression," said John Dollard and his colleagues. Frustration is anything (such as the malfunctioning of the vending machine) that blocks our attaining a goal. Frustration grows when our motivation to achieve a goal is very strong, when we expect gratification, and when the blocking is complete.

3   The aggressive energy need not explode directly against its source. We learn to inhibit direct retaliation, especially when others might disapprove or punish; instead we displace our hostilities to safer targets. Displacement occurs in the old anecdote about a man who, humiliated by his boss, berates his wife, who yells at the son, who kicks the dog, which bites the mail carrier.

FRUSTRATION-AGGRESSION THEORY REVISED

4   Laboratory tests of the frustration-aggression theory produced mixed results: Sometimes frustration increased aggressiveness, sometimes not. For example, if the frustration was understandable—if, as in one experiment, a confederate disrupted a group's problem-solving because his hearing aid malfunctioned (rather than because he just paid no attention)—then frustration led to irritation, not aggression. A justifiable frustration is still frustrating, but it triggers less aggression than a frustration we perceive as unjustified.

5   Leonard Berkowitz realized that the original theory overstated the frustration-aggression connection, so he revised it. Berkowitz theorized that frustration produces anger, an emotional readiness to aggress. Anger arises when someone who frustrates us could have chosen to act otherwise. A frustrated person is especially likely to lash out when aggressive cues pull the cork, releasing bottled-up anger. Sometimes the cork will blow without such cues. But cues associated with aggression amplify aggression.

6   Berkowitz and others have found that the sight of a weapon is such a cue, especially when the weapon is perceived as an instrument of violence rather than recreation. In one experiment, children who had just played with toy guns became more willing to knock down another child's blocks. In another experiment,

angered University of Wisconsin men gave more electric shocks to their tormenter when a rifle and a revolver (supposedly left over from a previous experiment) were nearby than when badminton racquets had been left behind. Guns prime hostile thoughts. Thus, Berkowitz is also not surprised that half of all U.S. murders are committed with handguns and that handguns in homes are far more likely to kill household members than intruders. "Guns not only permit violence," he reported, "they can stimulate it as well. The finger pulls the trigger, but the trigger may also be pulling the finger."

7   Berkowitz is also not surprised that countries that ban handguns have lower murder rates. Compared with the United States, Britain has one-fourth as many people and one-sixteenth as many murders. The United States has ten thousand handgun homicides a year; Britain has about ten. Vancouver, British Colombia, and Seattle, Washington, have similar populations, climates, economics, and rates of criminal activity and assault—except that Vancouver, which carefully restricts handgun ownership, has one fifth as many handgun murders as Seattle and thus a 40 percent lower overall murder rate. When Washington, D.C., adopted a law restricting handgun possession, the number of gun-related murders and suicides each abruptly dropped about 25 percent. No changes occurred in other methods of murder and suicide, nor did adjacent areas outside the reach of this law experience any such decline.

8   Guns not only serve as aggression cues; they also put psychological distance between aggressor and victim. As Milgram's obedience studies taught us, remoteness from the victim facilitates cruelty. A knife can kill someone, but a knife attack is more difficult than pulling a trigger from a distance.

BEFORE YOU BEGIN WRITING

Judith Nadell and Linda McMeniman

1 When you are given a writing assignment, there are several points you should attend to before you start putting words on the page. We'll discuss each point in turn.

UNDERSTAND THE BOUNDARIES OF THE ASSIGNMENT

2 You shouldn't start writing a paper until you know what's expected. First, clarify the *kind* of paper the instructor has in mind. Assume the instructor asks you to discuss the key ideas in an assigned reading. What does the instructor want you to do? Should you include a brief summary of the selection? Should you compare the author's ideas with your own view of the subject? Should you determine if the author's view is supported by valid evidence?

3 If you're not sure about an assignment, ask your instructor—not the student next to you, who may be as confused as you—to make the requirements clear. Most instructors are more than willing to provide an explanation. They would rather take a few minutes of class time to explain the assignment than spend hours reading dozens of student essays that miss the mark.

4 Second, find out *how long* the paper is expected to be. Many instructors will indicate the approximate length of the papers they assign. If no length requirements are provided, discuss with the instructor what you plan to cover and indicate how long you think your paper will be. The instructor will either give you the go-ahead or help you refine the direction and scope of your work.

DETERMINE YOUR PURPOSE, AUDIENCE, AND TONE

5 Once you understand the requirements for a writing assignment, you're ready to begin thinking about the essay. What is its *purpose?* For what *audience* will it be written? What *tone* will you use? Later on, you may modify your decisions about these issues. That's fine. But you need to understand the way these considerations influence your work in the early phases of the writing process.

6 **Purpose.** The papers you write in college are usually meant to *inform* or *explain,* to *convince* or *persuade,* and sometimes to *entertain.* In practice, writing often combines purposes. You might, for example, write an essay trying to *convince* people to support a new trash recycling program in your community. But before you win readers over, you most likely would have to *explain* something about current waste-disposal technology.

7 When purposes blend this way, the predominant one determines the essay's content, organization, emphasis, and choice of words. Assume you're writing about a political campaign. If your primary goal is to *entertain,* to take a gentle poke at two candidates, you might start with several accounts of one candidate's "foot-in-mouth" disease and then describe the attempts of the other candidate, a multi-millionaire, to portray himself as an average Joe. Your language, full of exaggeration, would reflect your objective. But if your primary purpose is to *persuade* readers that the candidates are incompetent and shouldn't be elected, you

might adopt a serious, straightforward style. Rather than poke fun at one candidate's gaffes, you would use them to illustrate her insensitivity to important issues. Similarly, the other candidate's posturing would be presented not as a foolish pretension, but as evidence of his lack of judgment.

8   **Audience.** To write effectively, you need to identify who your readers are and to take their expectations and needs into account. An essay about the artificial preservatives in the food served by the campus cafeteria would take one form if submitted to your chemistry professor and a very different one if written for the college newspaper. The chemistry paper would probably be formal and technical, complete with chemical formulations and scientific data: "Distillation revealed sodium benzoate particles suspended in a gelatinous medium." But such technical material would be inappropriate in a newspaper column intended for general readers. In this case, you might provide specific examples of cafeteria foods containing additives—"Those deliciously smoky cold cuts are loaded with nitrates and nitrites, both known to cause cancer in laboratory animals"—and suggest ways to eat more healthily—"Pass by the deli counter and fill up instead on vegetarian pizza and fruit juices."

9   Ask yourself the following questions when analyzing your audience: (1) What are my readers' age, sex, and educational levels? (2) What interests and needs motivate my audience? (3) What values do I share with my readers that will help me communicate with them?

10   **Tone.** Just as your voice may project a range of feelings, your writing can convey one or more *tones,* or emotional states: enthusiasm, anger, resignation, and so on. Tone is integral to meaning; it

permeates writing and reflects your attitude toward yourself, your purpose, your subject, and your readers. How do you project tone? You pay close attention to sentence structure and word choice.

11   *Sentence structure* refers to the way sentences are shaped. Although the two paragraphs that follow deal with exactly the same subject, note how differences in sentence structure create sharply dissimilar tones:

> *During the 1960s, many inner-city minorities considered the police an occupying force and an oppressive agent of control. As a result, violence against police grew in poorer neighborhoods, as did the number of residents killed by police.*

> *An occupying force. An agent of control. An oppressor. That's how many inner-city minorities in the '60s viewed the police. Violence against police soared. Police killings of residents mounted.*

12   Informative in its approach, the first paragraph projects a neutral, almost dispassionate tone. The sentences are fairly long, and clear transitions ("During the 1960s," "As a result") mark the progression of thought. But the second paragraph, with its dramatic, almost alarmist tone, seems intended to elicit a strong emotional response; its short sentences, fragments, and abrupt transitions reflect the turbulence of those earlier times.

13   *Word choice* also plays a role in establishing the tone of an essay. Words have *denotations,* neutral dictionary meanings, as well as *connotations,* emotional associations that go beyond the literal meaning. The word *beach,* for instance, is defined in the dictionary as "a nearly level stretch of pebbles and sand beside a body of water." This

definition, however, doesn't capture individual responses to the word. For some, *beach* suggests warmth and relaxation; for others, it calls up hospital waste and sewage washed up on a once-clean stretch of shoreline.

14   Since tone and meaning are tightly bound, you must be sensitive to the emotional nuances of words. In a respectful essay about police officers, you wouldn't refer to *cops, narcs,* or *flatfoots;* such terms convey a contempt inconsistent with the tone intended. Your words must convey tone clearly. Suppose you're writing a satirical piece criticizing a local beauty pageant. Dubbing the participants "livestock on view" leaves no question about your tone. But if you simply referred to the participants as "attractive young women," readers might be unsure of your attitude. Remember, readers can't read your mind, only your paper.

4

More about Argument: Errors in Reasoning

Learning about some common errors in reasoning—also known as **fallacies**—will help you to spot weak points in arguments.

You have already learned about two common fallacies in Chapter 10, "Argument." One of those fallacies is sometimes called **changing the subject**. In Chapter 10, this fallacy was described as irrelevant support. People who use this method of arguing try to divert the audience's attention from the true issue by presenting evidence that actually has nothing to do with the argument.

The second fallacy you worked on in Chapter 10 is sometimes called **hasty generalization**. This fallacy was referred to in that chapter as a point based on inadequate support. To be valid, a point must be based on an adequate amount of evidence. Someone who draws a conclusion on the basis of insufficient evidence is making a hasty generalization.

Below are some other common fallacies that will be explained in this chapter. Exercises throughout will give you practice in recognizing them.

Three Fallacies That Ignore the Issue

- Circular Reasoning
- Personal Attack
- Straw Man

Three Fallacies That Oversimplify the Issue

- False Cause
- False Comparison
- Either-Or

FALLACIES THAT IGNORE THE ISSUE

Circular Reasoning

Part of a point cannot reasonably be used as evidence to support it. The fallacy of including such illogical evidence is called **circular reasoning**; it is also known as **begging the question**. Here is a simple and obvious example of such reasoning: "Ms. Jenkins is a great manager because she is so wonderful at managing." The supporting reason ("she is so wonderful at managing") is really the same as the conclusion ("Ms. Jenkins is a great manager"). We still do not know why she is a great manager. No real reasons have been given—the statement has merely repeated itself.

Can you spot the circular reasoning in the following arguments?

1. Exercise is healthful, for it improves your well-being.
2. Since people under 18 are too young to drive, the driving age shouldn't be lowered below age 18.
3. Censorship is an evil practice because it is so wrong.

Now let's look more closely at these arguments:

1. The word *healthful,* which is used in the conclusion, conveys the same idea as *well-being.*
2. The author uses the idea that people under 18 are too young to drive as both the conclusion and the reason of the argument. No real reason is given for why people under 18 are too young to drive.
3. The claim that censorship is wrong is simply a restatement of the idea that it is an evil practice.

In all these cases, the reasons merely repeat an important part of the conclusion. The careful reader wants to say, "Tell me something new. You are reasoning in circles. Give me supporting evidence, not a repetition."

➤ Practice 1

Check (✓) the **one** item in each group that contains an example of circular reasoning.

Group 1

_____ 1. My wife wants to participate in the local amateur theater group, but I don't want all those actors flirting with her.

_____ 2. Sports cars continue to be popular because so many people like them.

_____ 3. Fran thinks I should break up with Randy because he gambles and drinks. But what does she know? She hasn't been able to find a boyfriend herself in three years.

Group 2

_____ 1. Mr. Casey was fined for drinking while driving and should not be allowed to teach math.

_____ 2. Barry cannot make up his mind easily because he is indecisive.

_____ 3. The candidate for mayor says she'll cut taxes, but do you really want fewer police officers protecting your city?

Group 3

_____ 1. Pearl is a poor choice for the position of salesperson—she's a lesbian.

_____ 2. The school board is considering building a swimming pool, but I don't like the idea of kids hanging out there all day and neglecting their studies.

_____ 3. The movie was boring because it became monotonous after a while.

Personal Attack

This fallacy often occurs in political debate. Here's an example:

> Our mayor's opinions about local crime are worthless. Last week, his own son was arrested for disturbing the peace.

The arrest of his son would probably have embarrassed the mayor, but it has nothing to do with the value of his opinions on local crime. **Personal attack** ignores the issue under discussion and concentrates instead on the character of the opponent.

Sometimes personal attacks take the form of accusing people of taking a stand only because it will benefit them personally. For instance, here's a personal attack on a congressman who is an outspoken member of the National Organization for Women (NOW): "He doesn't care about NOW. He supports it only in order to get more women to vote for him." This argument ignores the congressman's detailed defense of NOW as an organization that promotes equal rights for both men and women. The key to recognizing personal attack is that it always involves an opponent's personal life or character, rather than simply his or her public ideas.

➤ *Practice 2*

Check (✔) the **one** item in each group that contains an example of personal attack.

Group 1

_____ 1. My wife wants to participate in the local amateur theater group, but I don't want all those actors flirting with her.

_____ 2. Sports cars continue to be popular because so many people like them.

_____ 3. Fran thinks I should break up with Randy because he gambles and drinks. But what does she know? She hasn't been able to find a boyfriend herself in three years.

Group 2

_____ 1. Mr. Casey was fined for drinking while driving and should not be allowed to teach math.

_____ 2. Barry cannot make up his mind easily because he is indecisive.

_____ 3. The candidate for mayor says she'll cut taxes, but do you really want fewer police officers protecting your city?

Group 3

_____ 1. Pearl is a poor choice for the position of salesperson—she's a lesbian.

_____ 2. The school board is considering building a swimming pool, but I don't like the idea of kids hanging out there all day and neglecting their studies.

_____ 3. The movie was boring because it became monotonous after a while.

Straw Man

An opponent made of straw can be defeated very easily. Sometimes, if one's real opponent is putting up too good a fight, it can be tempting to build a scarecrow and battle it instead. For example, take the following passage from a debate on the death penalty.

> Ms. Collins opposes capital punishment. But letting murderers out on the street to kill again is a crazy idea. If we did that, no one would be safe.

Ms. Collins, however, never advocated "letting murderers out on the street to kill again." In fact, she wants to keep them in jail for life rather than execute them. The **straw man** fallacy suggests that the opponent favors an obviously unpopular cause—when the opponent really doesn't support anything of the kind.

➤ *Practice 3*

Check (✓) the **one** item in each group that contains an example of straw man.

Group 1

_____ 1. My wife wants to participate in the local amateur theater group, but I don't want all those actors flirting with her.

_____ 2. Sports cars continue to be popular because so many people like them.

_____ 3. Fran thinks I should break up with Randy because he gambles and drinks. But what does she know? She hasn't been able to find a boyfriend herself in three years.

Group 2

_____ 1. Mr. Casey was fined for drinking while driving and should not be allowed to teach math.

_____ 2. Barry cannot make up his mind easily because he is indecisive.

_____ 3. The candidate for mayor says she'll cut taxes, but do you really want fewer police officers protecting your city?

Group 3

_____ 1. How can Frieda Hamilton be a church choir leader? She doesn't even have a college degree.

_____ 2. The school board is considering building a swimming pool, but I don't like the idea of kids hanging out there all day and neglecting their studies.

_____ 3. The movie was boring because it became monotonous after a while.

FALLACIES THAT OVERSIMPLIFY THE ISSUE

False Cause

You have probably heard someone say as a joke, "I know it's going to rain today because I just washed the car." The idea that someone can make it rain by washing a car is funny because the two events obviously have nothing to do with each other. However, with more complicated issues, it is easy to make the mistake known as the fallacy of **false cause**. The mistake is to assume that because event B *follows* event A, event B *was caused by* event A.

Cause-and-effect situations can be difficult to analyze, and people are often tempted to oversimplify them by ignoring other possible causes. To identify an argument using a false cause, look for alternative causes. Consider this argument:

The baseball team was doing well before Paul Hamilton became manager. Clearly, he is the cause of the decline.

> (*Event A:* Paul Hamilton became manager.
> *Event B:* The baseball team is losing games.)

However, Paul Hamilton has been manager for only a year. What other possible causes could have been responsible for the team's losses? Perhaps the salary policies of the team's owner have deprived the team of some needed new talent. Perhaps several key players are now past their prime. In any case, it's easy but dangerous to assume that just because A *came before* B, A *caused* B.

➤ Practice 4

Check (✓) the **one** item in each group that contains an example of false cause.

Group 1

_____ 1. In Vermont we leave our doors unlocked all year round, so I don't think it's necessary for you New Yorkers to have three locks on your front doors.

_____ 2. The waiter went off duty early, and then the vase was discovered missing, so he must have stolen it.

_____ 3. Eat your string beans, or you won't grow up strong and healthy.

Group 2

_____ 1. A week after a new building supervisor took over, the elevator stopped working. What a lousy super he is!

_____ 2. If I don't get married by the time I'm 30, I'll never find anyone to marry.

_____ 3. All of my friends like my tattoo and pierced tongue, so I'm sure my new boss will too.

Group 3

_____ 1. If you don't choose a degree wisely, you will never be happy with your career.

_____ 2. Why can't we have a big dog in this apartment? You had a Great Dane when you were growing up on the farm.

_____ 3. John and Marie broke up right after her parents came to visit. The parents must have caused some kind of trouble.

False Comparison

When the poet Robert Burns wrote, "My love is like a red, red rose," he meant that both the woman he loved and a rose are beautiful. In other ways—such as having green leaves and thorns, for example—his love did not resemble a rose at all. Comparisons are often a good way to clarify a point. But because two things may not be alike in all respects, comparisons (sometimes called analogies) often make poor evidence for arguments. In the error in reasoning known as **false comparison**, the assumption is that two things are more alike than they really are. For example, read the following argument.

When your grandmother was your age, she was already married and had four children. So why aren't you married?

To judge whether or not this is a false comparison, consider how the two situations are alike and how they differ. They are similar in that both involve persons of the same age. But the situations are different in that the grandmother's society encouraged early marriage and that the grandmother was not working outside the home or attending college. The differences in this case are more important than the similarities, making it a false comparison.

➤ Practice 5

Check (✓) the **one** item in each group that contains an example of false comparison.

Group 1

_____ 1. In Vermont we leave our doors unlocked all year round, so I don't think it's necessary for you New Yorkers to have three locks on your front doors.

_____ 2. The waiter went off duty early, and then the vase was discovered missing, so he must have stolen it.

_____ 3. Eat your string beans, or you won't grow up strong and healthy.

Group 2

_____ 1. A week after a new building supervisor took over, the elevator stopped working. What a lousy super he is!

_____ 2. If I don't get married by the time I'm 30, I'll never find anyone to marry.

_____ 3. All of my friends like my tattoo and pierced tongue, so I'm sure my new boss will too.

Group 3

_____ 1. If you don't choose a degree wisely, you will never be happy with your career.

_____ 2. Why can't we have a big dog in this apartment? You had a Great Dane when you were growing up on the farm.

_____ 3. John and Marie broke up right after her parents came to visit. The parents must have caused some kind of trouble.

Either-Or

It is often wrong to assume that there are only two sides to a question. Offering only two choices when more actually exist is an **either-or** fallacy. For example, the statement "You are either with us or against us" assumes that there is no middle ground. Or consider the following:

People opposed to unrestricted free speech are really in favor of censorship.

This argument ignores the fact that a person could believe in free speech as well as in laws that prohibit slander or that punish someone for falsely yelling "Fire!" in a crowded theater. Some issues have only two sides (Will you pass the course, or won't you?), but most have several.

➤ Practice 6

Check (✓) the **one** item in each group that contains an example of the either-or fallacy.

Group 1

_____ 1. In Vermont we leave our doors unlocked all year round, so I don't think it's necessary for you New Yorkers to have three locks on your front doors.

_____ 2. The Via Delores restaurant isn't doing very well. People around here obviously don't like Italian food.

_____ 3. Eat your string beans, or you won't grow up strong and healthy.

Group 2

_____ 1. A week after a new building supervisor took over, the elevator stopped working. What a lousy super he is!

_____ 2. People who didn't come to my birthday party must not be my real friends.

_____ 3. All of my friends like my tattoo and pierced tongue, so I'm sure my new boss will too.

Group 3

_____ 1. If you don't choose a degree wisely, you will never be happy with your career.

_____ 2. I don't need to take art lessons. Grandma Moses never took a lesson and she became a famous painter.

_____ 3. John and Marie broke up right after her parents came to visit. The parents must have caused some kind of trouble.

➤ Review Test 1

To review what you've learned in this chapter, write the letter of the correct answer to each question.

_____ 1. A fallacy is an error in
    A. reading.
    B. reasoning.
    C. changing the subject.

_____ 2. The fallacy of straw man is
    A. calling attention to the character of the opponent.
    B. arguing against a false issue that is easy to defeat.
    C. making a hasty generalization.

_____ 3. The fallacies of circular reasoning and personal attack are specific versions of
    A. ignoring the issue.
    B. oversimplifying the issue.
    C. changing the subject.

_____ 4. Assuming that there are only two sides to a question is called the fallacy of
    A. false cause.
    B. personal attack.
    C. either-or.

_____ 5. To decide if a statement is a false comparison, you must consider how much two situations
    A. are alike.
    B. are different.
    C. both A and B.

➤ *Review Test 2*

A. In the space provided, write the letter of the fallacy contained in each argument. Choose from the three fallacies shown in the box below.

> A Circular reasoning (*a statement repeats itself rather than providing a real supporting reason to back up an argument*)
> B Personal attack (*ignores the issue under discussion and concentrates instead on the character of the opponent*)
> C Straw man (*an argument is made by claiming an opponent holds an extreme position and then opposing that extreme position*)

_____ 1. Some builders wish to build low-income homes in this area. Apparently they think we need more street crime and violence in our neighborhood.

_____ 2. Ruby is pleasant company because she is so nice to be with.

_____ 3. Helen Quinn should not be promoted to manager—she lives with an unmarried man.

_____ 4. The Secretary of Education supports sex and birth-control education in schools, but I think it's wrong that thirteen-year-olds can get abortions without their parents' permission.

_____ 5. Picasso was clearly the greatest artist of modern times, since his paintings are better than anyone else's.

B. In the space provided, write the letter of the fallacy contained in each argument. Choose from the three fallacies shown in the box below.

> A False cause (*the argument assumes that the order of events alone shows cause and effect*)
> B False comparison (*the argument assumes that two things being compared are more alike than they really are*)
> C Either-or (*the argument assumes that there are only two sides to a question*)

_____ 6. Do you own a TV, or do you like to read?

_____ 7. Earthquakes have odd effects. Last time there was one in California, I got a terrible case of food poisoning.

_____ 8. Twelve-year-olds are old enough to work, so they should be old enough to buy cigarettes, too.

_____ 9. There are only two types of voters: those who love America and those who support Erol Tindall for senator.

_____ 10. After I planted my flower garden on the first day of the month, it did extremely well; so this year, I'm going to plant on the first again.

➤ Review Test 3

A. In the space provided, write the letter of the fallacy contained in each argument. Choose from the three fallacies shown in the box below.

A Circular reasoning *(a statement repeats itself rather than providing a real supporting reason to back up an argument)* **B** Personal attack *(ignores the issue under discussion and concentrates instead on the character of the opponent)* **C** Straw man *(an argument is made by claiming an opponent holds an extreme position and then opposing that extreme position)*

_____ 1. Trashy novels are a waste of time to read because there is nothing worthwhile in them.

_____ 2. Ms. Quinn opposes hunting in public parks. Apparently, she doesn't think that people have the right to enjoy sports on public property.

_____ 3. I wouldn't use George Jackson's plumbing business. Jackson believes that UFOs are real.

_____ 4. Councilman Mandell's idea to build a teen community center is irresponsible. He wants to encourage gangs of teens to run loose through the city at all hours.

_____ 5. Students should take a word processing course in school because it's important that everyone learn word processing.

B. In the space provided, write the letter of the fallacy contained in each argument. Choose from the three fallacies shown in the box below.

> **A** False cause *(the argument assumes that the order of events alone shows cause and effect)*
>
> **B** False comparison *(the argument assumes that two things being compared are more alike than they really are)*
>
> **C** Either-or *(the argument assumes that there are only two sides to a question)*

_____ 6. Did you do your homework last night, or don't you care about school at all?

_____ 7. I wouldn't make an appointment with that new doctor if I were you—I felt perfectly fine until the day after my appointment with her.

_____ 8. "When I was your age, calling boys gave them the wrong idea," Sharon's grandmother told her. "That's not a respectable way for you to get dates."

_____ 9. Getting into a fight is no big deal. In the movies, characters are constantly walking away from huge fights with just a little cut on their chins.

_____ 10. Since Senator Nelson was elected, the world has moved steadily toward peace and democracy. What better reason can there be to re-elect him?

Check Your Performance **MORE ABOUT ARGUMENT**

Activity	Number Right	Points	Score
Review Test 1 (5 items)	_____	× 4 =	_____
Review Test 2 (10 items)	_____	× 4 =	_____
Review Test 3 (10 items)	_____	× 4 =	_____
	TOTAL SCORE	=	_____ %

5

Understanding Bias

Bias refers to a subjective view—in other words, a view that is either positive or negative. It contrasts with an objective view—one that is neutral. You have already learned about bias in two previous chapters. In "Fact and Opinion," you learned that speakers and writers often include their point of view—that is, their opinion—in what they communicate. What they say is therefore at least partly biased. That bias is sometimes revealed through value words, such as *best* and *worst* and *great* and *terrible*. In "Purpose and Tone," you learned that a selection with an objective tone is not biased and that a selection with a subjective tone is at least partly biased—it represents the writer's point of view. In this chapter, you will get more practice in recognizing biased language.

BIASED LANGUAGE

Look at the following sentences:

1. Phil spends very little money.
2. Phil is thrifty.
3. Phil is a cheapskate.

Each of these three sentences describes the same person and behavior. The first one is strictly factual. It simply tells what Phil does without making a judgment about it. The second sentence, by using the word *thrifty,* hints that Phil should be praised for his careful money management. By using the word *cheapskate,* the third sentence strongly suggests that Phil's behavior is undesirable.

Just by choosing one word rather than another, an author expresses a viewpoint. In choosing the phrase *spends very little money,* the writer of the first sentence remained *objective*—neither for nor against Phil. The writer of the second sentence expressed a bias in Phil's favor, and the writer of the third sentence expressed a bias against him. Word choices like the positive word *thrifty* and the negative word *cheapskate* are sometimes called "emotionally loaded" or simply "loaded" words. The writer uses them to express a positive or negative attitude toward a subject.

Suppose you were writing the sentence below and had to choose between the two words in parentheses. One word makes a factual statement about Cindy's work; the other expresses a bias, a positive or negative view of her work. Decide which word suggests a bias and write it in the blank.

Cindy performed her work *(faster, better)* _____ than her coworkers.

Explanation:

The biased word is *better.* The other word, *faster,* simply describes Cindy's pace. Anyone who pays attention to how fast Cindy and her coworkers work will have to agree that Cindy works faster—it's a fact. However, *better* makes a positive judgment about the quality of Cindy's work. Others may or may not agree with this opinion.

➤ Practice 1

Each sentence below can be completed in two ways, one neutral and the other biased. For each sentence, choose the biased word, and write it on the line.

1. The *(student, nerd)* _____ asked to turn his research paper in early.

2. I sat up most of the night *(remembering, regretting)* _____ my date with Linda.

3. There were hundreds of unusual *(treasures, items)* _____ for sale at the flea market.

4. Climbing stairs provides *(some, good)* _____ aerobic exercise.

5. Americans *(typically, unfortunately)* _____ eat an average of 134 pounds of sugar each year.

BIAS IN LONGER PASSAGES

Longer passages may contain a whole series of words that work together to suggest a bias in the writer's point of view. For instance, the following passage is someone's description of supermarket tabloids. After reading the passage, circle the letter of the group of words that reveals the writer's bias about the tabloids. Then write the letter of the statement that expresses the writer's point of view.

The suckers who take seriously supermarket tabloids like the *Enquirer* or the *Globe* should wise up to the fact that reporters are writing entertainment, not news. The editorial policy for these rags seems to be "anything goes." The stories are often pure fantasy, as in the article "Spirit of Elvis Haunts Widow's Microwave," or gossip reported by unreliable sources, such as plumbers of Hollywood celebrities. Read as entertainment, tabloids are good for a laugh, but nobody should base a decision on the obvious misinformation found in these publications.

_____ 1. The biased words are
- A. *supermarket, policy, stories, Hollywood.*
- B. *reporters, sources, decision, publications.*
- C. *suckers, rags, unreliable, misinformation.*

_____ 2. The author expresses a bias against
- A. Elvis Presley.
- B. Hollywood entertainment.
- C. tabloids as a source of news.

Explanation:

The words *suckers, rags, unreliable,* and *misinformation* are all "loaded" or biased words—they show that the writer is not objective about the topic of tabloids. Noticing which words are biased will help you pinpoint the nature of the writer's bias. In this case, such words as *unreliable* and *misinformation* leave us in little doubt that the writer feels supermarket tabloids are undependable sources of news. Thus the correct answer to question 2 is C.

➤ *Practice 2*

Read the passages below to see if you can detect the words that reveal each author's bias. Also, think about the direction of that bias. Then answer the questions that follow.

A.   The New Jersey Pine Barrens, 650,000 acres of wilderness, represent a vast ecological wealth of rare plants and animals, as well as a priceless reservoir of natural water. Irresponsible land developers, however, are threatening to rape parts of the Barrens and replace them with shopping malls and condominiums.

_____   1. The biased words are
  A. *Jersey, wilderness, water, malls.*
  B. *wealth, priceless, irresponsible, rape.*
  C. *acres, represent, plants, developers.*

_____   2. The author's bias is against the
  A. New Jersey Pine Barrens.
  B. land developers.
  C. rare plants and animals.

B.   The Hopi Indians of northern Arizona have admirably withstood the United States government's attempts to blend them into America's melting pot. The Hopis are rightly more concerned with seeking harmony within themselves and with their environment than they are with adopting conventional American ways. Thus their worthy culture still survives.

_____   3. The biased words are
  A. *Hopi, Arizona, environment, ways.*
  B. *admirably, rightly, worthy.*
  C. *government's, seeking, culture.*

_____   4. The author expresses a bias in favor of the
  A. United States government.
  B. melting pot.
  C. Hopis.

C. Most fiction entertains or inspires in positive ways. However, horror-fiction writers such as Stephen King and Peter Straub are guilty of influencing some people to commit acts of corruption and violence. Through their twisted imaginations, horror-fiction writers plant evil seeds in the minds of readers. On more than a few occasions, these seeds have blossomed, resulting in an individual's committing a horrifying act. Later, the individual will explain, "I got the idea from a Stephen King novel."

_____ 5. The biased words are
   A. *guilty, twisted, horrifying.*
   B. *horror-fiction, acts, readers, idea.*
   C. *writers, occasions, individual's, novel.*

_____ 6. The author expresses a bias against
   A. readers.
   B. fiction.
   C. horror-fiction writers.

D. With frequent droughts, numerous anti-watering ordinances, and a polluted environment, it's obvious that large grassy lawns are outdated. A big spread of grass may look pretty, but it has real drawbacks. In order to keep their grass green and weed-free, many homeowners use chemicals that harm the larger ecosystem. Also, keeping all that grass healthy requires a lot of water that could be put to better use. Preferable alternatives to a lawn include wide walkways, flowerbeds, vegetable beds, and the use of ground covers. Another commendable option is to use only drought-tolerant plants that thrive in a particular area. In the southwestern United States, for instance, extended patios surrounded by cactus work well. In other areas, drought-tolerant plants such as ornamental grasses, native wildflowers, "hens and chickens," and aloe can take the place of grass. Wherever they live, people can choose sensible lawn alternatives.

_____ 7. The biased words include
   A. *obvious, outdated, preferable, commendable, sensible.*
   B. *polluted, environment, ecosystem, drought-tolerant.*
   C. *chemicals, cactus, ornamental grasses, wildflowers, aloe, lawn alternatives.*

_____ 8. The author expresses a bias in favor of
   A. the southwestern U.S.
   B. alternatives to lawns.
   C. keeping lawns healthy and weed-free.

➤ Review Test 1

To review what you've learned in this chapter, answer each question with **T** or **F** or by writing the letter of the answer you choose.

_____ 1. TRUE OR FALSE? An author may express a bias in his or her choice of words.

_____ 2. TRUE OR FALSE? A biased point of view is objective.

_____ 3. A subjective statement expresses
    A. a fact.
    B. an opinion.
    C. a question.

_____ 4. A biased point of view can be
    A. negative.
    B. positive.
    C. either of the above.

_____ 5. An example of a biased word is
    A. *round.*
    B. *money.*
    C. *selfish.*
    D. *recent.*

➤ Review Test 2

Write the letter of the answer to each question that follows the passages below.

A.   Alternative education programs for disruptive students have been established in some states. While disruptive behavior in schools is a serious concern, why should taxpayers have to foot the bill for educating young delinquents? These troublemakers should either follow the rules or be expelled. If students are too rowdy to function in the traditional classroom setting, let them quit school and get a job.

_____ 1. The biased words include
    A. *alternative, bill, students.*
    B. *delinquents, troublemakers, rowdy.*
    C. *education, function, classroom, job.*

_____ 2. The author has a bias against
    A. the traditional classroom setting.
    B. special treatment for disruptive students.
    C. taxpayers.

B. A writer for *Fortune* magazine described a conversation he had after reading the autobiography of Sam Walton, founder of Wal-Mart. He told his friend how incredibly active Walton had been as a kid—"president of this, football team, newspaper boy, more, more, more." The writer's friend commented, "Nowadays they would have put him on that calming medication, Ritalin."

The scary thing is that he may be right. Chances are Sam Walton was not always an easy kid to deal with. He was brilliant, energetic, bursting with new ideas and activities. He probably drove his parents and teachers crazy at times. Can't you just picture some all-too-rigid teacher today calling his mother to say, "Mrs. Walton, Sam is rather disruptive in class. I think he has Attention Deficit Disorder. We ought to see if he responds to medication"? If that had regrettably happened and the Ritalin had "worked," would anyone know Sam Walton's name today?

_____ 3. The biased words include
   A. *conversation, autobiography, medication.*
   B. *scary, all-too-rigid, regrettably.*
   C. *active, calming, energetic.*

_____ 4. The author is biased against
   A. students who disrupt classes.
   B. teachers.
   C. medicating difficult students.

C. George Washington was not a tactician of the quality of Caesar or Robert E. Lee. His lack of genius made his achievements all the more impressive. He held his forces together in adversity, avoiding both useless slaughter and catastrophic defeat. People of all sections, from every walk of life, looked on Washington as the embodiment of American virtues. He was a man of deeds, rather than words. He was a man of substance, accustomed to luxury, yet capable of enduring great hardships stoically; a bold patriot, quick to take arms against British tyranny, yet eminently respectable. The Revolution might have been won without Washington, but it is unlikely that the free United States would have become so easily a true nation had he not been at its call.

_____ 5. The biased words are
   A. *impressive, bold patriot, eminently respectable.*
   B. *forces, substance, arms.*
   C. *Robert E. Lee, Revolution, United States.*

_____ 6. The author expresses a bias in favor of Washington's
   A. lack of genius.
   B. being accustomed to luxury.
   C. achievements during the American Revolution.

D.   The hospice movement was begun in the 1960s by two women physicians: Elisabeth Kübler-Ross and Cicely Saunders. They wanted to change medicine so that it would better meet the needs of dying patients and their families. In an ordinary hospital, death is the enemy, and doctors and nurses feel that their job is to fight death off as long as possible and by any means possible. A hospice, by contrast, does not attempt to fight or delay death, but instead simply makes the dying patient as comfortable as possible. A hospice rightly strives for death with dignity and tries to give patients as much control as possible over their final months, weeks, or days of life. When the movement first began, hospices were separate facilities, but now the emphasis is on letting dying patients stay home, with most treatment delivered by visiting nurses and physicians. As a result of Kübler-Ross's and Saunders's admirable work, other physicians have also become more aware of the special needs of dying patients, especially the relief of pain; and in-home care, including hospice care, is today one of the fastest-growing areas of medicine.

_____ 7. The biased words include
   A. *change medicine, ordinary hospital, visiting nurses and physicians.*
   B. *better, rightly, admirable.*
   C. *women physicians, special needs, fastest-growing.*

_____ 8. The author's bias is in favor of
   A. treating the dying in ordinary hospitals.
   B. hospice care for the dying.
   C. fighting off death by any means possible.

➤ Review Test 3

Write the letter of the answer to each question that follows the passages below.

A.   Alcohol-related highway deaths are the number-one killer of young people. Misguided individuals advocate counseling for teens with a drinking problem. They argue that the peer pressure teens face leads them to drink, which is sheer nonsense. With ten thousand young people dying each year from suicides, accidents, and injuries all related to alcohol, the solution is clear; get tough with spineless underaged drinkers. Throw the book at them, and we'll see that they'll suddenly be able to resist peer pressure without counseling.

_____ 1. The biased words include
   A. *highway, individuals, peer pressure.*
   B. *misguided, nonsense, spineless.*
   C. *young, problem, alcohol.*

_____ 2. The author's bias is against
  A. teen drinkers.
  B. young people.
  C. the legal system.

B. Relaxation techniques have proved remarkably effective in reducing anxiety and increasing an individual's ability to resist stress. The best-known of the relaxation techniques is transcendental meditation (TM), which can produce almost miraculous results. An overworked and out-of-shape businessman, for example, can decrease his oxygen consumption and respiratory and heart rates if he practices transcendental meditation on a regular basis. For the TM center nearest you, check your Yellow Pages.

_____ 3. The biased words include
  A. *remarkably effective, miraculous.*
  B. *anxiety, respiratory, regular.*
  C. *stress, oxygen, transcendental meditation.*

_____ 4. The author's bias is in favor of
  A. oxygen consumption.
  B. transcendental meditation.
  C. businessmen.

C. In Pittsburgh, a high-school administration has decided to take a strong stand against the flashy, expensive clothes worn by students. No longer will the students at River Heights High be allowed to show off all the latest designer clothes and accessories. This fall, a dress code was established that will limit the type and amount of jewelry worn and eliminate the overly revealing miniskirt. The new code was designed with the hope of ending the ridiculous amount of competition among students concerning clothes. This competition, administrators feel, distracts students from their class work.

_____ 5. The biased words include
  A. *flashy, overly revealing, ridiculous.*
  B. *clothes, jewelry, administrators.*
  C. *high-school administration, students, class work.*

_____ 6. The author's bias is in favor of
  A. the dress code.
  B. the miniskirt.
  C. competition among students concerning clothes.

D. During the Great Depression, President Hoover dined each night at the White House in regal splendor. He had thought about cutting back but decided it would be bad for the morale of the country. If he changed his habits one bit, it would seem a sign of lost confidence. So each evening Hoover entered the dining room in black tie, ready to consume seven full courses. Buglers in uniform heralded his arrival and departure with glittering trumpets, even when the only guest was his wife.

Such behavior earned Hoover the reputation of being insensitive, but that was not the case. He never visited a bread line or a relief shelter because he could not bear to see suffering. When the press criticized him, he withdrew, wounded and hurt. Rumors that circulated about him were as painful as they were ridiculous. It was said, for instance, that dogs instinctively disliked him; that he had masterminded the kidnapping and murder of Charles Lindbergh's infant son; that roses wilted in his hands. Hoover was doing all he could to promote recovery, more than any earlier president. Yet he was scorned. His natural sullenness turned to self-pity. "You can't expect to see calves running in the field the day after you put the bull to the cows," Calvin Coolidge reassured him. "No," said an exasperated Hoover, "but I would expect to see contented cows."

_____ 7. The biased words include
   A. *the Great Depression, his wife, recovery.*
   B. *the White House, relief shelter, calves running in the field.*
   C. *not the case, doing all he could, more than any earlier president.*

_____ 8. The author's bias is in favor of
   A. a sign of lost confidence.
   B. the critical press.
   C. Hoover.

Check Your Performance			UNDERSTANDING BIAS
Activity	*Number Right*	*Points*	*Score*
Review Test 1 (5 items)	_____	× 4 =	_____
Review Test 2 (8 items)	_____	× 5 =	_____
Review Test 3 (8 items)	_____	× 5 =	_____
		TOTAL SCORE =	_____%

6

Writing Assignments

A BRIEF GUIDE TO EFFECTIVE WRITING

Here in a nutshell is what you need to do to write effectively.

Step 1: Explore Your Topic through Informal Writing

To begin with, explore the topic that you want to write about or that you have been assigned to write about. You can examine your topic through **informal writing**, which usually means one of three things.

First, you can **freewrite** about your topic for at least ten minutes. In other words, for ten minutes write whatever comes into your head about your subject. Write without stopping and without worrying at all about spelling or grammar or the like. Simply get down on paper all the information about the topic that occurs to you.

A second thing you can do is to **make a list of ideas and details** that could go into your paper. Simply pile these items up, one after another, like a shopping list, without worrying about putting them in any special order. Try to accumulate as many details as you can think of.

A third way to explore your topic is to **write down a series of questions and answers** about it. Your questions can start with words like *what, why, how, when*, and *where*.

Getting your thoughts and ideas down on paper will help you think more about your topic. With some raw material to look at, you are now in a better position to decide on just how to proceed.

Step 2: Plan Your Paper with an Informal Outline

After exploring your topic, plan your paper using an informal outline. Do two things:

- **Decide on and write out the point of your paper.** It is often a good idea to begin your paragraph with this point, which is known as the topic sentence. If you are writing an essay of several paragraphs, you will probably want to include your main point somewhere in your first paragraph. In a paper of several paragraphs, the main point is called the central point, or thesis.

- **List the supporting reasons, examples, or other details that back up your point.** In many cases, you should have at least two or three items of support.

Step 3: Use Transitions

Once your outline is worked out, you will have a clear "road map" for writing your paper. As you write the early drafts of your paper, use **transitions** to introduce each of the separate supporting items (reasons, examples, or other details) you present to back up your point. For instance, you might introduce your first supporting item with the transitional words *first of all.* You might begin your second supporting item with words such as *another reason* or *another example.* And you might indicate your final supporting detail with such words as *last of all* or *a final reason.*

Step 4: Edit and Proofread Your Paper

After you have a solid draft, edit and proofread the paper. Ask yourself several questions to evaluate your paper:

1. Is the paper **unified**? Does all the material in the paper truly support the opening point?

2. Is the paper **well supported**? Is there plenty of specific evidence to back the opening point?

3. Is the paper **clearly organized**? Does the material proceed in a way that makes sense? Do transitions help connect ideas?

4. Is the paper **well written**? When the paper is read aloud, do the sentences flow smoothly and clearly? Has the paper been checked carefully for grammar, punctuation, and spelling mistakes?

WRITING ASSIGNMENTS FOR THE TWENTY READINGS

Note: The discussion questions accompanying the twenty readings can also make good topics for writing. Some of the writing assignments here are based on them.

"The Quiet Hour"

1. Imagine that Mayer's suggestion has been adopted and that TV broadcasting has ceased for sixty minutes every evening. Write a paragraph in which you describe the effects that such an event would have on you, your family, or the students at your school.

2. Mayer asks, "How long are we going to keep passively selling our own and our children's souls to keep Madison Avenue on Easy Street?" Do you agree or disagree with Mayer's contention that television has had a largely negative effect on our children and families? Write a paragraph in which you defend one of the following statements: "I believe TV is generally a harmful influence on children and families" or "I believe TV is not all that bad for children and families." Use specific examples to support your argument.

3. Mayer admits that it is nearly unthinkable to imagine American society without TV. Yet he believes that getting rid of TV for an hour each evening is an idea with some merit. What is another widely accepted aspect of society that you would like to see less of? Write a paper proposing the elimination of something you think is a negative influence on society. Don't worry if your proposal is impractical—let your imagination run wild as you describe how life would be improved without, for example, money, organized religion, alcohol, automobiles, or professional sports.

"How Dual-Earner Couples Cope"

1. Today, the dual-earner couple is the norm. In contrast, a generation ago it was far more common to have the man working outside the home while the woman attended to the house and children. What effects did that arrangement typically have on a marriage and family? Write a paragraph in which you explain what you believe were the good and bad points of the old pattern, in which the man was typically the only wage earner.

2. The authors describe women who experience stress because of the conflicting demands of their work (where they are expected to be aggressive and competitive) and home (where they are looked to for compassion and nurturing). Think of a time when you have felt torn by conflicting demands. Perhaps your friends expected certain behavior from you while your parents wanted something else. Or you were torn between the demands of a romantic significant other and your old crowd. Write a paragraph that describes the stress you experienced and how you handled it.

3. Papalia and Olds divide dual-earner couples into three categories: conventional, modern, and role-sharing. Based on your observation of friends with dual-income marriages (or your own marriage), what are the pros and cons of each of those three patterns? Which of the three do you think is closest to ideal? Write an essay sharing your thoughts.

"Baby Love"

1. What do you think makes a good parent? What do children need most from parents? Write a paragraph listing two or three qualities that you believe define a good parent. Provide concrete examples of how each quality might be expressed.

2. Write a paragraph for young expectant mothers that explains clearly to them what the Harlows' experiment with a terry-cloth "mother" teaches about childcare.

3. Think of two families you're acquainted with that have very different parenting styles. (It need not be one family you consider good and another you consider bad—just different.) Perhaps one family has very strict standards for its children, while the other is more relaxed. Or maybe one shows a lot of physical affection, while the other is reserved. Write an essay that compares and contrasts the two families and their children. Include some observations on how, in your opinion, the children have been affected by their parents' style.

"Personal Relationships in the Not-So-Good Old Days"

1. Most Americans today shudder at the idea of the "arranged marriage," in which families pick out "suitable" partners for their children, using such criteria as social class, shared values, and property. Today many people believe one should marry for love. But as the divorce rates show, marrying for love is hardly a guarantee of lifelong happiness. Put yourself in the place of a parent who believes in arranged marriages. Write a paragraph in which you defend the concept. Explain the ways you think an arranged marriage makes at least as much sense as a love marriage.

2. In this reading, Stark contrasts the romantic image of "the old days" as a time of warm and loving family ties with the unpleasant reality. In what other ways do you imagine the "good old days" weren't so good? Write a paragraph in which you contrast the fairy-tale image of the "good old days" with what you imagine the reality might have been. Focus on two or three specific areas. For example, you might write about what health care, personal hygiene, education, entertainment, and housing conditions would have been like in former times.

3. Whom do you know who seems to have a really good marriage? Write an essay about that couple and your observations of their relationship. In your introduction, define what you mean by a "good marriage." Then illustrate your definition by providing specific examples from the marriage you are describing.

"Julia Burney: The Power of a Woman's Dream"

1. Choose an activity that you believe is beneficial for children. It might be reading, sports, volunteering, keeping a pet, or something else. Write a paragraph in which you identify and explain three ways in which you believe this activity is good for kids.

2. Julia noticed a need in her community—a place for children to come to read—and did something about it. What is something that your community lacks that you think it really needs? Write a paragraph in which you describe the need and how it could be fulfilled.

3. Write an essay in which you identify a person who has been a positive influence in your life. Give three detailed examples, each in a separate paragraph, of how you interacted with and learned from this person. Alternatively, write an essay about three different persons who have been of value to you, devoting a paragraph apiece to detailing in specific ways the benefits you have gained from each person.

"The Influence of the Self-Fulfilling Prophecy"

1. The "Pygmalion in the Classroom" experiment suggests that a teacher's expectations of a student have a great deal to do with his or her success. Write a paragraph about a teacher who seemed to have especially high or low expectations for you. How did you perform in his or her classroom? What effect do you think the teacher's expectations had upon you?

2. Think of a person who, in your opinion, continually sabotages his or her chances for happiness or acceptance. Write a paragraph in which you give that person some advice. Explain what you see the person doing to him or herself, and suggest how he or she could change the self-sabotaging behavior.

3. Describe a time that you went into a situation expecting something bad to happen—or, at least, expecting not to enjoy yourself. Write an essay in which you compare or contrast what happened with what you believed would happen. As you consider that situation now, do you think that your attitude might have influenced what happened? Do you now feel, after reading the selection on self-fulfilling prophecies, that things might have been different if you had been more positive or less negative?

"Managing Conflicts in Relationships"

1. Think of a person you know whom you would define as one of the following: a withdrawer, a surrenderer, an aggressor, or a persuader. Write a paragraph in which you describe this person and his or her approach to dealing with conflict. Include at least one specific example of his or her behavior.

2. What advice would you give to Eduardo and Justina, the couple in the reading who are in conflict about Eduardo's smoking? What do you think Eduardo should do? What should Justina do? Write a paragraph advising the couple on how to handle their problem.

3. When have you and another person had an important conflict you needed to deal with? (To be "important," the conflict need not be earth-shattering. It is sufficient that it was a conflict you were unwilling to ignore.) Write a paper that describes the nature of the conflict, then takes the reader through the process that occurred as you and the other person dealt with it. Use transitional words such as "first," "next," and "finally" to help the reader follow the action. In the final paragraph, provide a conclusion that states how satisfied or dissatisfied you felt about the process.

"A Legendary Moment"

1. Most families tell and retell certain stories that, for some reason, have become meaningful to them. Write a paragraph in which you tell of such a memorable incident that occurred in your family. Add your own comments about why, in your opinion, the story is significant to your family.

2. Kimmel's memories of the doors in her parents' bedroom concern not only the way they looked, but also how they figured in her childhood fantasy of hiding from vampires. Write a paragraph in which you describe a feature of the house you lived in as a child. Include not only a physical description of the feature, but also how it figured into your daily life or playtime.

3. Select two people in your family (or other people you know) who have different ways of dealing with conflict. Perhaps one shouts and the other sulks, or one believes in "talking it out" while the other prefers to keep his or her thoughts private. Write an essay in which you compare and contrast those two people's styles. Illustrate your essay with examples from real life.

"How to Become a Better Listener"

1. Among your fellow students, whom do you consider an especially good public speaker? Write a paragraph in which you identify that person and describe his or her style of speaking and attitude in front of an audience. Provide details that help your reader understand what you admire about the person's speaking skills and why.

2. Write a paragraph in which you describe someone you know who is a poor listener. What does this person do that makes you define him or her as bad at listening? Describe a typical episode in which you (or someone else) is trying to talk to this person and he or she is doing a poor job of listening.

3. When you talk to other people, what behaviors in them drive you crazy? Finishing your sentences? Interrupting? Changing the subject? Chewing gum loudly? Write a paper in which you provide your own definition of a "poor listener," and illustrate it with several behaviors that really bother you. Provide vivid examples of each behavior to help your reader envision it and understand your irritation. Your paper may have a serious or a humorous tone.

"Obedience: Milgram's Controversial Studies"

1. What do you think of Milgram's experiment? Was it ethical? Do its results suggest what people would do in a "real-life" situation? Write a paragraph telling how you respond to the experiment and why.

2. Have you ever found yourself automatically obeying an order from someone in authority, then later wondering if you'd done the right thing? Write a paragraph describing what happened and how you later wished you had responded.

3. Few people would question the need for children to learn to obey. Children who do not obey their parents endanger themselves ("Don't use the hairdryer in the bathtub") and alienate their community ("Don't play ball in Ms. Mitchell's garden"). Yet this passage suggests that some people learn to obey all too well, abandoning their own morals and good sense as they follow orders. How can parents encourage their children to be appropriately obedient and still teach them to think for themselves? Write an essay in which you make suggestions to parents on how to help their children achieve a healthy balance. Include examples to illustrate what can happen when a child is raised with too much or too little emphasis on obedience.

"The Professor Is a Dropout"

1. When Lupe ran into obstacle after obstacle in her search to learn English, she nearly gave up. Write a paragraph about a time you felt extremely discouraged. What had brought you to that point? How did you proceed?

2. Write a paragraph about a class that you initially found difficult but that turned out to be not as bad as you expected. (Or write about a class you first thought would be easy but turned out to be hard.) Describe the process you went through as your perception of the class changed.

3. What are your memories of reading in your preschool days? What kind of reading did you do throughout your school years? And what kind of a reader are you today? Write a paper in which you describe your life as a reader in those three periods. You will add interest to your paper if you include titles of favorite books and memories of what particular books or stories meant to you. Alternatively, write an essay about the reasons why you have never become a regular reader.

"Taming the Anger Monster"

1. Write a paragraph in which you narrate a recent event that made you angry. Give plenty of details so that the reader can picture exactly what happened and how you reacted. Include dialogue, if appropriate. Conclude by saying how you felt about yourself after the incident.

2. Laura Houser, the woman mentioned at the beginning and end of this selection, implied that her anger had simply become a bad habit that she was able to change, once she recognized it. What is a bad habit of yours that you would like to change? What would be a healthier habit to replace it with? Write a paragraph in which you identify your bad habit, explain how it affects your life, and talk about how you might break it.

3. In this selection, the author identifies three sources of anger: time, technology, and tension. Write an essay in which you identify three things that particularly anger you. Explain typical situations in which you are likely to encounter each of these three anger-producers, why they irritate you so much, and how you respond to them.

"He Was First"

1. Pee Wee Reese used his position as a team leader to stop the anti-Robinson momentum. When have you seen an individual stand up to a group and speak up for another point of view? Write a paragraph that describes the mood of the group, the actions of the individual, and how the group responded.

2. If you had been Jackie Robinson, do you think you could have agreed to Branch Rickey's request not to fight back when you were insulted? If so, do you believe you could have honored that request in the face of what Robinson experienced? Write a paragraph in which you tell what your response to Rickey would have been and how you believe you would have handled the pressure of Robinson's experience.

3. What do you think drives people to commit the kind of vicious attacks that were directed against Jackie Robinson, as well as other "hate crimes" against racial minorities and homosexuals that we read about in the papers every day? Why do some people react to others whom they perceive as "different" with such violent hatred? Write an essay in which you discuss several possible explanations for hate crimes. An example of a central point for this paper is "I believe that people who commit hate crimes are driven by their upbringing, their fears, and their desire to impress their friends."

"Keys to College Success"

1. Studying efficiently is only one of the many challenges students face as they make the transition from high school to college. Write a paragraph that warns students about another challenge they must deal with. Two examples of topics are "how to work and take college classes at the same time" or "how to have a social life while being a working student."

2. Akers discusses headings and subheadings in detail. Read again what she has to say about them. Then write a series of headings and subheadings for one or two of the readings in this book. Choose from the following: "Baby Love," "He Was First," "Effects of the Automobile," or "The Life of the Urban Working Class."

3. "Keys to College Success" is a detailed explanation of helpful steps to take when attending classes and studying textbooks. Write a paper in which you explain a series of steps toward achieving some goal. Use time transitions to emphasize the sequence of steps. For example, you might write about steps in improving your school courses, your workplace, or your relationship with your family.

"Motivation and Needs"

1. Think of an advertisement that appeals to a person's need for approval. Write a paragraph that describes the ad in detail and that explains which human need the advertisement touches and how the ad promises to fulfill that need.

2. Quinn writes, "A peak experience is an extremely brief, momentary sense of total happiness or fulfillment." Have you ever had such a peak experience— or a time of really special happiness? Write a paragraph that describes that time. What brought it about? How did it make you feel? How long did it last?

3. Quinn writes, "There are immense differences in affiliation needs. Some people are satisfied with one or two close, deep friendships. Others crave superficial relationships with large groups. Some fluctuate between group and individual friendships." Write a paper about what satisfies your affiliation needs and how your needs have either changed or stayed the same through the years. Use specific examples of your friendships and what roles they have played at different stages of your life.

"Effects of the Automobile"

1. Clearly, the automobile has had an enormous effect on society. What is another invention that you believe has had a comparable impact on modern life? Write a paragraph about your choice. Explain some of the ways you believe it has shaped our society and influenced our lives.

2. What is the downside of the automobile and its effects on society? (Focus on societal change, not on physical problems such as air pollution or accidents.) Write a paragraph explaining the negative impact of the automobile on individuals, families, or communities.

3. Imagine that last night as you slept, automobiles everywhere disappeared. Write a paper describing how your day today would be affected by their absence. Include details from the time you woke in the morning to the time you will go to bed. How would your activities be limited? How would your world look, smell, and sound different? How would you cope?

"Rabies"

1. Before reading this selection, what did you know (or think you knew) about rabies? Were your ideas about the disease accurate? Write a paragraph in which you compare and contrast what you knew previously about rabies with what you learned from the selection. Your topic sentence could be something like this: "Before reading this selection, I had some inaccurate ideas about what rabies is and does."

2. What do children need to know in order to protect themselves against rabies? Write a paragraph in which you instruct a child how to avoid the disease. Tell about precautions to take regarding both pets and wild animals.

3. A major section of this article concerns prevention. What steps do or should you take in your life to prevent general health problems? Write an essay in which you describe in detail three major steps that you do take or could take to protect yourself from illness.

"Bad Managers"

1. When have you had a boss (or supervisor, or instructor) whom you considered incompetent? Write a paragraph in which you describe this less-than-competent person. If he or she fell into one of the categories described in the selection, name it. If not, come up with your own term for his or her particular brand of incompetence. Provide at least one example of the person's behavior that demonstrates his or her incompetence.

2. The selection refers to managers who are unable to make decisions because they believe whatever they choose will be wrong. Write a paragraph about a time you faced a difficult decision, one in which every option seemed flawed. What were the issues involved? What were the good points and bad points of each of the options you could have chosen? What did you finally decide to do?

3. Many of the types of incompetence described in this selection involve a manager's refusal to take responsibility for a problem. Instead, he or she attempts to blame someone else for the problem or passes the responsibility on to another person. Think about instances that you have observed (or heard about) of people avoiding responsibility. They could be minor, as when a child doesn't take responsibility for keeping his room clean, or major, as when young parents abandon their baby rather than care for it. Write a paper that describes several instances you've observed of people not accepting responsibility. Make clear what you believe their responsibility is and how they are avoiding it.

"Busy As a Bee? Then Who's Doing the Work?"

1. Many people today are defenders of animal rights: they strongly oppose the killing of animals for food or clothing, using them in laboratory experiments, even confining them in zoos. Write a paragraph supporting or opposing one of these positions. Should animals have the same rights and protection as humans? Why or why not?

2. Natalie Angier begins her selection by stating that laziness is "perfectly natural, perfectly sensible, and shared by nearly every other species on the planet." Think of another activity that most people would label ill-advised or unproductive, and write a paragraph that proves that this much-maligned activity is actually sensible and can have positive results. For example, you might choose to write (seriously or humorously) about the benefits of any of the following: procrastination, oversleeping, staying up at night or all night, overeating, or overshopping.

3. Think about the daily life of a pet—yours or one you're acquainted with— and the life of an animal in the wild. Write a paper that compares and contrasts those two lives in detail. Consider how the animals eat, sleep, play, interact with others of their kind, and live in sickness and in health. What kinds of things are easier for your pet? On the other hand, what has the pet lost by being tamed? Here's an example of a central point for this paper: "When compared to the life of a wild animal, the life of Jilly, my pampered house cat, has both advantages and disadvantages."

"The Life of the Urban Working Class"

1. When did you hold your first job? How old were you? What kind of job was it? How much time did it take up? Did you enjoy or dislike it? Write a paragraph that describes your first employment and what it was like.

2. The selection points out that as young people left their villages for the city, they lost their traditional family-based communities. In the cities, they attempted to create their own communities among people who worked at similar jobs or lived nearby. What would you define as your community? Is it primarily based on family ties? On ties of friendship? On neighborhood ties? Or is there another organizing factor, such as people you play sports with or work with? Write a paragraph that defines and describes your personal community.

3. Based on your observations, what classes exist in society today? How are those classes determined—by birth, occupation, education, income, or some combination of these and other factors? What are the characteristics of life in each of those classes? Write an essay that lists and describes three of the classes you identify.

APPENDIXES

Pronunciation Guide

Each word in Chapter 1, "Vocabulary in Context," is followed by information in parentheses that shows you how to pronounce the word. (There are also pronunciations for the vocabulary items that follow the readings in Parts I and II.) The guide below and on the next page explains how to use that information.

Long Vowel Sounds

ā	pay
ē	she
ī	hi
ō	go
o͞o	cool
yo͞o	use

Short Vowel Sounds

ă	hat
ĕ	ten
ĭ	sit
ŏ	lot
o͝o	look
ŭ	up
yo͝o	cure

Other Vowel Sounds

â	care
ä	card
îr	here
ô	all
oi	oil
ou	out
ûr	fur
ə	ago, item, easily, gallop, circus

Consonant Sounds

b	big
d	do
f	fall
g	dog
h	he

Consonant Sounds

j	jump
k	kiss
l	let
m	meet
n	no
p	put
r	red
s	sell
t	top
v	have
w	way
y	yes
z	zero
ch	church
sh	dish
th	then
th	thick
zh	usual

Note that each pronunciation symbol above is paired with a common word that shows the sound of the symbol. For example, the symbol ā has the sound of the *a* in the common word *pay*. The symbol ă has the sound of the *a* in the common word *hat*. The symbol ə, which looks like an upside-down *e* and is known as the schwa, has the unaccented sound in the common word *ago*. It sounds like the "uh" a speaker often says when hesitating.

Accent marks are small black marks that tell you which syllable to emphasize as you say a word. A bold accent mark (′) shows which syllable should be stressed. A lighter accent mark (′) in some words indicates a secondary stress. Syllables without an accent mark are unstressed.

Limited Answer Key

An important note: To strengthen your reading skills, you must do more than simply find out which of your answers are right and which are wrong. You also need to figure out (with the help of this book, the teacher, or other students) *why* you missed the questions you did. By using each of your wrong answers as a learning opportunity, you will strengthen your understanding of the skills. You will also prepare yourself for the review and mastery tests in Part I and the reading comprehension questions in Part II, for which answers are not given here.

ANSWERS TO THE PRACTICES IN PART I

1   Vocabulary in Context

Practice 1: Examples

1. Examples: *cutting the police force in half, reducing the pay of all city employees;* B
2. Examples: *glared at each other, refused to stay in the same room together;* C
3. Examples: *a trembling mugging victim, a crying lost child;* A
4. Examples: *twelve dollars for a pound of butter, eight dollars for a small loaf of multigrain bread, twenty-five dollars for a pound of prime steak;* A
5. Examples: *sequins, feathers, gold trim;* B
6. Examples: *a broken leg is noticeably thinner when the cast is removed, and a patient bedridden for too long will lack the lower-body strength needed to stand up;* C
7. Examples: *the cactus and the camel in the desert, the polar bear and the seal in the Arctic;* C
8. Examples: *knowledge and beliefs, rules of behavior and values, signs and language;* B
9. Examples: *the Napoleonic wars, the revolutions of 1848, the Crimean War in the 1850s, the Franco-Prussian War of 1870;* A
10. Examples: *eating tomatoes, taking a bath, letting a baby kick its legs;* B

Practice 2: Synonyms

1. reveal
2. irritating
3. serious
4. clear
5. touching
6. worst
7. quacks
8. skillful
9. cast out
10. disturbing

Practice 3: Antonyms

1. Antonym: *scarce;* C
2. Antonym: *genuine;* B
3. Antonym: *Those who agreed;* C
4. Antonym: *harsh;* A
5. Antonym: *useful;* B
6. Antonym: *Physically active;* B
7. Antonym: *whose power is limited;* C
8. Antonym: *approval;* B
9. Antonym: *sped up;* B
10. Antonym: *varied;* C

Practice 4: General Sense

1. B	6. B
2. C	7. A
3. A	8. A
4. B	9. C
5. C	10. B

2 Main Ideas

Practice 1

1. lobster: S
   seafood: G
   clams: S
   oysters: S

2. appearance: G
   handsome: S
   well-dressed: S
   shabby: S

3. heavy traffic: S
   bus not on time: S
   alarm didn't go off: S
   excuses for being late: G

4. paper cuts: S
   broken nails: S
   minor problems: G
   wrong numbers: S

5. giggling: S
   childish behavior: G
   tantrums: S
   playing peek-a-boo: S

6. poor pay: S
   undesirable job: G
   mean boss: S
   very dull work: S

7. try to be kinder: S
   eat healthier foods: S
   go to bed earlier: S
   resolutions: G

8. take stairs instead of elevator: S
   ride bike instead of driving: S
   exercise opportunities: G
   walk instead of riding bus: S

9. skip breakfast: S
   grab a donut mid-morning: S
   poor eating habits: G
   order supersize portions: S

10. different goals: S
    no common interests: S
    dislike each other's friends: S
    reasons for breaking up: G

Practice 2

Answers will vary.

Practice 3

1. S	4. P
P	S
S	S
S	S
2. S	5. S
S	S
S	S
P	P
3. S	
S	
P	
S	

Practice 4

1. S	4. P
S	S
P	S
S	S
2. S	5. S
P	P
S	S
S	S
3. S	
S	
S	
P	

Practice 5

1. S
   P
   S
   S

2. S
   S
   S
   P

3. S
   S
   P
   S

4. S
   P
   S
   S

5. S
   S
   P
   S

Practice 6

Group 1
   A. SD
   B. T
   C. MI
   D. SD

Group 2
   A. SD
   B. SD
   C. MI
   D. T

Group 3
   A. SD
   B. MI
   C. T
   D. SD

Group 4
   A. SD
   B. T
   C. SD
   D. MI

Group 5
   A. SD
   B. MI
   C. SD
   D. T

Practice 7 (Wording of topics may vary)

1. *Topic:* Blood
   Main idea: Sentence 1

2. *Topic:* The Great Wall of China
   Main idea: Sentence 1

3. *Topic:* Barbecue
   Main idea: Sentence 1

4. *Topic:* Busing
   Main idea: Sentence 3

5. *Topic:* Cardiovascular disease
   Main idea: Sentence 2

Practice 8

1. 2
2. 1
3. 3
4. 1
5. 4

3   Supporting Details

Practice 1 *(Wording of answers may vary)*

A. *Main idea:* A few important approaches will prevent illness among the poor.
   1. Focus on preventive health services.
   2. Offer more extensive prenatal care.
   3. Fight social conditions of poverty that breed disease.

B. *Main idea:* . . . four basic types of crowds.
   1. Casual crowd—people with little in common except for participating in a common event
      Minor detail: People looking through a department-store window
   2. Conventional crowd—people who have assembled for a specific purpose
      Minor detail: People attending a baseball game or concert
   3. Expressive crowd—people who have gotten together for self-stimulation and personal satisfaction
      Minor detail: People attending a religious revival or rock festival
   4. Acting crowd—an excited, explosive collection of people
      Minor detail: People engaged in rioting, looting, or other aggressive behavior

Practice 2 *(Wording of answers may vary)*

A. Higher wages
   Shortened workweek
   Unions

B. *Major detail*: Tidal
   Major detail: Shallow seas
   Major detail: Deep ocean
      Minor detail: Zone of perpetual darkness

Practice 3
1. B
2. C

Practice 4 *(Examples may vary.)*

A. Pyrrhic victory—a victory won at enormous cost
   Example—The Greek general Pyrrhus defeated a Roman army, but his own army suffered terrible losses.

2. Megalopolis—a "strip city" resulting from urban development filling in the rural spaces between metropolitan centers
   Example—The six-hundred-mile axis from southern New Hampshire to northern Virginia, including nearly one fifth of the U.S. population

4   Implied Main Ideas/Central Point

Practice 1

Paragraph 1	Paragraph 3
1. A	5. C
2. D	6. D

Paragraph 2	Paragraph 4
3. B	7. A
4. C	8. A

Practice 2

1. C	3. C
2. D	4. D

Practice 3 *(Wording of answers may vary.)*

A. *Topic:* Hurricanes and tornadoes
   Implied main idea: Hurricanes and tornadoes are quite different kinds of storms.

B. *Topic:* Broiler chickens
   Implied main idea: Broiler chickens have a hard life.

C. *Topic:* Nonverbal communication
   Implied main idea: There are various types of nonverbal communication.

D. *Topic:* The American Revolution (or: The British army vs. the American colonial army)
   Implied main idea: During the American Revolution, there were many important differences between the British army and the American colonial army.

Practice 4

Central point: Sentence 42

Practice 5

Central point: Sentence 2

5   Relationships I

Practice 1 (Answers may vary.)

1. Another
2. also
3. In addition
4. second
5. Furthermore

Practice 2 (Answers may vary.)

1. After
2. then
3. During
4. until
5. Before

Practice 3 (Wording of answers may vary.)

A. Main idea: "Regrettable comments" fall into five general categories.

1. Blunder
2. Direct attack
3. Negative group references
4. Direct and specific criticism
5. Saying too much

B. Main idea: . . . putting preventive medicine into practice.

1. Primary prevention—keep disease from occurring at all
   Example—Childhood vaccinations against polio, measles, smallpox
2. *Example*—Self-examination by women for breast cancer
3. Tertiary prevention—prevent further damage from already existing disease
   Example—Keeping diabetic on insulin; controling pneumonia so it does not lead to death

Practice 4 (Wording of answers may vary.)

Main idea: The scientific method consists of four stages.

1. Formulation of a problem
2. Observation and experiment
3. Interpretation
4. Testing the interpretation

Practice 5 (Wording of answers may vary.)

Main idea: You can take several steps to gain control of a heavy workload.

1. List quickly everything that needs to get done.
2. Divide tasks into three groups: do now, do next week, postpone till later.
3. Break each task into exact steps needed to get it done.

Practice 6

1. A
2. B
3. A
4. A
5. B
6. A
7. A
8. B
9. A
10. B

6   Relationships II

Practice 1 (Answers may vary.)

1. for instance
2. including
3. For example
4. Specifically
5. such as

Practice 2

A. *Point of purchase display*; definition—sentence 1; example 1—sentence 2; example 2—sentence 4
B. *self-handicapping strategy*; definition—sentence 1; example 1—sentence 3; example 2—sentence 5

Practice 3 (Answers may vary.)

1. like
2. in the same way
3. Just as
4. Likewise
5. Similarly

Practice 4 (Answers may vary.)

1. However
2. Although
3. Unlike
4. On the other hand
5. Nevertheless

Practice 5

A. Contrast: work and play
B. Comparison and contrast: First World War and Second World War

Practice 6 (Answers may vary.)

1. reason
2. result
3. consequence
4. cause
5. Because

Practice 7

A. *Effect:* Shoplifting
   Cause: Poverty
   Cause: Frugal customers
   Cause: Sense of excitement and fun
   Cause: Desire for social acceptance

B. *Main idea (effect):* Earth's population
   continues to rise dramatically.
   Major supporting details (causes):
   1. Technology
   2. Changing rates of deaths and births

Practice 8

1. C	6. B
2. B	7. C
3. A	8. B
4. C	9. A
5. A	10. C

7 Fact and Opinion

Practice 1

1. O	6. F
2. F	7. O
3. F	8. O
4. F	9. O
5. O	10. F

Practice 2

Answers will vary.

Practice 3

1. O	6. O
2. F	7. F
3. F+O	8. F
4. F+O	9. F
5. F	10. F+O

Practice 4

A.	B.
1. F	6. F
2. F+O	7. F+O
3. F	8. F+O
4. F+O	9. F
5. F	10. F+O

Practice 5

A.	B.
1. O	6. O
2. F	7. F+O
3. F+O	8. F
4. F	9. O
5. O	10. F

Practice 6

1. F	3. F
2. F+O	4. F+O

8 Inferences

Practice 1
1. C
2. B
3. D

Practice 2
A. 1. A
   2. B
   3. C
   4. B

C. 9. B
  10. C
  11. A
  12. A

B. 5. B
   6. A
   7. C
   8. B

Practice 3
A. 1, 4, 5
B. 2, 4, 5
C. 3, 4, 6

Practice 4
1. Simile, C
2. Simile, B
3. Metaphor, A
4. Simile, C
5. Metaphor, B

Practice 5
1. B
2. C
3. B
4. A
5. C

Practice 6
1, 3, 6

9 Purpose and Tone

Practice 1
1. I
2. E
3. P
4. I
5. P

6. E
7. I
8. P
9. I
10. E

Practice 2
1. B
2. C
3. A

Practice 3
1. E
2. A
3. D
4. B
5. C

Practice 4
A. 1. ironic, C
   2. pessimistic, A
   3. angry, E
   4. enthusiastic, D
   5. self-pitying, B

B. 6. impatient, E
   7. sarcastic, F
   8. threatening, J
   9. indignant, C
  10. apologetic, I

Practice 5
1. H
2. E
3. G

4. D
5. B

Practice 6
1. C
2. B
3. C

4. C
5. B

10 Argument

Practice 1

1. A. P
   B. S

2. A. P
   B. S

3. A. S
   B. P
   C. S

4. A. P
   B. S
   C. S
   D. S

5. A. S
   B. S
   C. P
   D. S

6. A. S
   B. S
   C. P
   D. S

7. A. S
   B. P
   C. S
   D. S

8. A. S
   B. P
   C. S
   D. S

9. A. S
   B. S
   C. S
   D. P

10. A. S
    B. P
    C. S
    D. S

Practice 2

1. C, E, F
2. C, D, F
3. B, D, E
4. A, B, C
5. B, D, E

Practice 3

1. C
2. A

Practice 4

1. B
2. B

Practice 5

1. C
2. B

Practice 6

1. C
2. D

ANSWERS TO THE PRACTICES IN PART III

2   More about Summarizing and Outlining

Practice 1

1. 1, 3, 6
2. 2, 4, 6
3. 2, 4, 5

Practice 2

1. C
2. B
3. D

Practice 3

1. C
2. B
3. B

4   More about Argument

Practice 1

Group 1. 2
Group 2. 2
Group 3. 3

Practice 2

Group 1. 3
Group 2. 1
Group 3. 1

Practice 3

Group 1. 1
Group 2. 3
Group 3. 2

Practice 4

Group 1. 2
Group 2. 1
Group 3. 3

Practice 5

Group 1. 1
Group 2. 3
Group 3. 2

Practice 6

Group 1. 3
Group 2. 2
Group 3. 1

5   Understanding Bias

Practice 1

1. nerd
2. regretting
3. treasures
4. good
5. unfortunately

Practice 2

A. 1. B
   2. B
B. 3. B
   4. C
C. 5. A
   6. C
D. 7. A
   8. B

Acknowledgments

Adler, Ronald B. "The Influence of the Self-Fulfilling Prophecy." From *Looking Out, Looking In,* 10th ed. Copyright © 2002. Reprinted by permission of Wadsworth, a division of Thomson Learning: www.thomsonrights.com. Fax 800-730-2215.

Akers, Sheila, "Keys to College Success." Reprinted by permission.

Alvarez, Julia. Selection on page 540. From *How the Garcia Girls Lost Their Accents.* Copyright © 1991 by Julia Alvarez. Published by Plume, an imprint of Dutton Signet, a division of Penguin USA and originally in hardcover by Algonquin Books of Chapel Hill.

Angier, Natalie. "Busy As a Bee? Then Who's Doing the Work?" Copyright © 1991 by The New York Times Company. Reprinted by permission.

Asimov, Isaac. "What Is Intelligence, Anyway?" Reprinted by permission of the Estate of Isaac Asimov c/o Ralph M. Vicinanza, Ltd.

Auth, Tony. Cartoon on page 303. From *The Philadelphia Inquirer Sunday Magazine,* May 31, 1992. Reprinted by permission of Tony Auth.

Baker, Russell. Selection on page 548. From *Growing Up.* Copyright © 1982 by Russell Baker. Reprinted by permission of Contemporary Books, Inc., Chicago.

Berkow, Robert, M.D., ed. "Rabies." From *The Merck Manual of Medical Information*—Home Edition. Edited by Robert Berkow. Copyright © 1997 by Merck & Co., Inc., Whitehouse Station, NJ. Reprinted by permission.

Bragg, Rick. Selection 8 on page 372. From *All Over but the Shoutin'*. Copyright © 1997 by Rick Bragg. Published by Pantheon Books, a division of Random House, Inc.

Davidson, Anne. "Taming the Anger Monster." Reprinted by permission.

Drafke, Michael W., and Stan Kossen. "Bad Managers." From *The Human Side of Organizations,* 8th ed. Copyright © 1998. Reprinted by permission of Pearson Education, Inc., Upper Saddle River, NJ.

Garland, Hamlin. Selection on page 336. From *A Son of the Middle Border* by Hamlin Garland. Copyright © 1917 by Hamlin Garland; copyright renewed 1945 by Mary I. Lord and Constance G. Williams.

Geist, Bill. Selection 2 on page 347. From *The Big Five-Oh!* Copyright © 1997 by Bill Geist. Published by William Morrow and Company.

Gergen, Mary M., et al. "Baby Love" and "Obedience: Milgram's Controversial Studies." From *Psychology: A Beginning,* 1st ed. by Gergen, © 1989. Reprinted with permission of Wadsworth, a division of Thomson Learning: www.thomsonrights.com. Fax 800-730-2215.

Kimmel, Haven. "A Legendary Moment." From *A Girl Named Zippy*. Copyright © 2001 by Haven Kimmel. Used by permission of Doubleday, a division of Random House, Inc.

Henslin, James M. "Effects of the Automobile" and "Labeling and the Onset of Old Age." From *Sociology: A Down-to-Earth Approach,* 3rd ed. Copyright © 1997 by James M. Henslin. Reprinted by permission of James M. Henslin.

Hughes, Langston. "Early Autumn." From *Short Stories* by Langston Hughes. Copyright © 1996 by Ramona Bass and Arnold Rampersad. Reprinted by permission of Hill and Wang, a division of Farrar, Straus, and Giroux, LLC.

Johnson, Beth. "The Professor Is a Dropout" and "Julia Burney: The Power of a Woman's Dream." Reprinted by permission.

Kellmayer, John. "He Was First." Reprinted by permission.

Lerner, Robert E. Selection on page 560 and "The Life of the Urban Working Class." From *Western Civilizations: Their History and Culture,* 13th ed., Volume II by Robert E. Lerner, Standish Meacham, and Edward McNall Burns. Copyright © 1998, 1993, 1988, 1984, 1980, 1973, 1968, 1963, 1958, 1954, 1949, 1947, 1941 by W. W. Norton & Company, Inc. Used by permission of W.W. Norton & Company, Inc.

Lucas, Stephen E. "How to Become a Better Listener." From *The Art of Public Speaking,* 6th ed. Copyright © 1998 by Stephen E. Lucas. Reprinted by permission of The McGraw-Hill Companies, Inc.

Mayer, Robert. "The Quiet Hour." Originally appeared as a "My Turn" in *Newsweek.* Adapted and used with permission of the author.

Morris, Desmond. "Why Do Mothers Cradle Their Babies in Their Left Arms?" From *Babywatching* by Desmond Morris, copyright © 1992 by Desmond Morris. Reprinted by permission of Crown Publishers, a division of Random House, Inc.

Myers, David G. "Is Aggression a Response to Frustration?" From *Social Psychology*, 6th ed. Copyright © 1999 by The McGraw-Hill Companies, Inc. Reprinted by permission.

Nadell, Judith, and Linda McMeniman. "Before You Start Writing." From *The Macmillan Reader.* Copyright © 1996 by Allyn & Bacon. Reprinted by permission.

National Baseball Hall of Fame Library, Cooperstown, NY. Photograph of Jackie Robinson on page 447. Reprinted by permission.

Papalia, Diane E., and Sally Wendkos Olds. "How Dual-Earner Couples Cope." From *Human Development*, 7th ed. Copyright © 1998 by The McGraw-Hill Companies, Inc. Reprinted by permission.

Quinn, Virginia. "Motivation and Needs." Adapted from *Applying Psychology*. Copyright © 1984 by McGraw-Hill, Inc. Reprinted by permission.

Stark, Rodney. "Personal Relationships in the Not-So-Good Old Days." From *Sociology*, 7th ed., by Stark. Copyright © 1998. Reprinted by permission of Wadsworth, a division of Thomson Learning: www.thomsonrights.com. Fax 800-730-2215.

Verderber, Rudolph. "Managing Conflicts in Relationships." From *Communicate!* 8th ed., by Verderber. Copyright © 1996. Reprinted by permission of Wadsworth, a division of Thomson Learning: www.thomsonrights.com. Fax 800-730-2215.

Winn, Marie. Selection on page 299. From *The Plug-In Drug: Television, Children, and Family.* Copyright © 1977 by Marie Winn. Published by Viking-Penguin, Inc.

Index